Memories on Fabric

Fat Quarter Friendly
9 Projects to Make & Display

Legacy

SUE HALE

Text © 2007 Susan Herron Hale

Artwork © 2007 C&T Publishing, Inc.

Publisher: *Amy Marson*

Editorial Director: *Gailen Runge*

Acquisitions Editor: *Jan Grigsby*

Editor: *Lynn Koolish*

Technical Editors: *Nanette S. Zeller and Gayl Gallagher*

Copyeditor/Proofreader: *Cynthia Keyes Hilton/Wordfirm Inc.*

Cover Designer: *Christina Jarumay*

Design Director/Book Designer: *Rose Sheifer*

Illustrator: *Tim Manibusan*

Production Coordinator: *Tim Manibusan*

Photography: *Luke Mulks* unless otherwise noted

Published by C&T Publishing, Inc., P.O. Box 1456, Lafayette, CA 94549

Library of Congress Cataloging-in-Publication Data

Hale, Sue.
Memories on fabric : Fat quarter friendly-10 projects to make & display / Sue Hale.
p. cm.
ISBN-13: 978-1-57120-373-1 (paper trade : alk. paper)
ISBN-10: 1-57120-373-7 (paper trade : alk. paper)
1. Photograph albums. 2. Scrapbooks. 3. Textile fabrics. I. Title.

TR501.H35 2007
746.46'041--dc22

2006020302

Printed in China
10 9 8 7 6 5 4 3 2 1

Dedication

To my three favorite men:
Bob—my hero
Bob and Matt—my wonderful sons
Thinkers, doers, and dreamers, all

Acknowledgments

I would like to thank all the members of the Herron and Hale families who made this book possible with their contributions of photos and heartwarming memories.

Special thanks to:

- My parents, Linc and Ann Herron, and to my brothers, John and Pete, for their love
- Carolyn Reese, who set me on this path, and Carol De Sousa, who gave me the inspiration for this book
- Elly Sienkiewicz, who made my path bloom with Baltimore Beauties
- My appliqué students, who made teaching so much fun and so rewarding
- My California friends, Judy, Cathy, and Marlene, and my Virginia pals, Laura, Gwen, Betty, Beth, and Nina, for believing in me
- Lori Dvir-Djerassi of Color Textiles for inkjet sheets and good advice, and Amy Barickman of The Vintage Workshop for her Sew Crafty CDs
- My editors, Lynn Koolish, Nanette Zeller, and Gayl Gallagher, for their guidance and expertise.

Contents

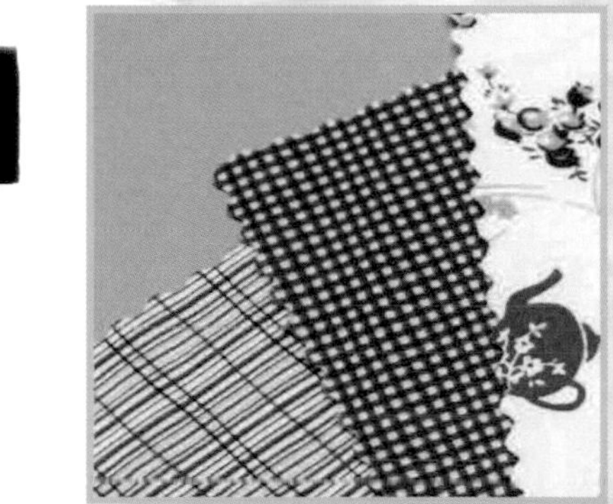

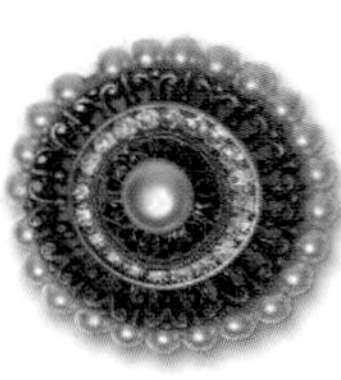

Sister Crafts

We board the train at the Clarkdale, Arizona, depot on July 31, 2005.

Dear Readers,

My experience with scrapbooking began with a phone call from Red Rooster Fabrics asking me to give a presentation on scrapbooking with fabric at Fall Quilt Market. Of course I said "Yes!" on the spot, because that meant I would be going to Quilt Market in Houston to do the presentation. After I enjoyed a ten-minute high, I experienced a reality check. I'm a quiltmaker. I had never been to a scrapbooking class. I had never been in a scrapbook store. I didn't even know anyone who scrapbooks. What had I gotten myself into? Uh-oh.

Naturally, my first stop was at a scrapbook store. Now I know how a prospective quiltmaker feels when entering a quilt store for the first time. Overwhelmed. The scrapbook store had aisles of beautiful papers, stickers, tags, fibers, beads, eyelets, magazines, books, and lots of classes. Within 20 minutes I had signed up for a class. I was hooked.

Class night arrived. I entered the classroom with my photos and the items on the supply list. The others started coming in, carrying tote bags with numerous pockets filled with things I couldn't name. Uh-oh. My supplies were not going to do. Out into the shop for more. Just like a quilt class, I thought. Some papers and wonderful fibers for a start. My classmates were friendly and helpful. They talked about their photos, cropping, matting, journaling, and embellishing. I'd been embellishing my appliqué projects for years. Scrapbooking was going to be fun! How can you beat shopping and embellishing?

As the class progressed, I realized that scrapbookers are like quiltmakers. They love what they do. Their stashes are paper pages. Their notions are embellishments, stickers, tags, and eyelets. Their resources are books, magazines, classes, and good places to shop. That's when it hit me that quiltmaking and scrapbooking are sister crafts. Here's why.

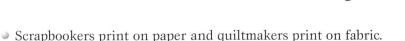

- Scrapbookers print on paper and quiltmakers print on fabric.
- Scrapbookers crop and quiltmakers trim and fussy cut.
- Scrapbookers mat and quiltmakers add borders to photos.
- Scrapbookers journal and quiltmakers write on fabric.
- And, we all love to embellish. Put just about any surface in front of us and we're ready to play!

So, let's begin. The following chapters will guide you through scrapbooking from a quiltmaker's viewpoint.

- Basic Supplies (page 6) gets you started. It tells you what you'll need and where to find it.
- Scrapbook Page Basics (page 9) explains the sewing, fusing, and gluing techniques you'll use to make scrapbook pages with fabric.
- Preparation (page 11) shows you how to choose a subject and take photos, select fabrics, and gather embellishments and memorabilia.
- Making the Pages (page 19) leads you through the process of making a fabric scrapbook page. From designing the page layout to display and finishing options, this chapter shows you how to arrange your photos and images on your page and print them on fabric, and how to dress up your page with photo trimming, fussy cutting, and image borders. You'll learn about titles, captions, and telling the story, and–the most fun of all–embellishing the page. The easy finishing techniques will get your pages out on display for everyone to see.
- The Projects section (page 40) presents nine fabric scrapbook pages. Each has ideas and instructions for making a similar project and features an embellishment technique.
- Resources (page 70) helps you find products and quotations.
- Throughout the book you'll see layout ideas and examples.

Basic Supplies

Fabric scrapbook pages are small projects that are fun to design and easy to make. Construction is simple: it requires some fusing, some gluing, and minimal sewing. Finishing is also simple, and no binding is needed. Hang the page from a wood dowel with painted and embellished wood finials or a café rod, or display it on a tabletop easel. All you'll need are some basic supplies and some embellishments for your pages.

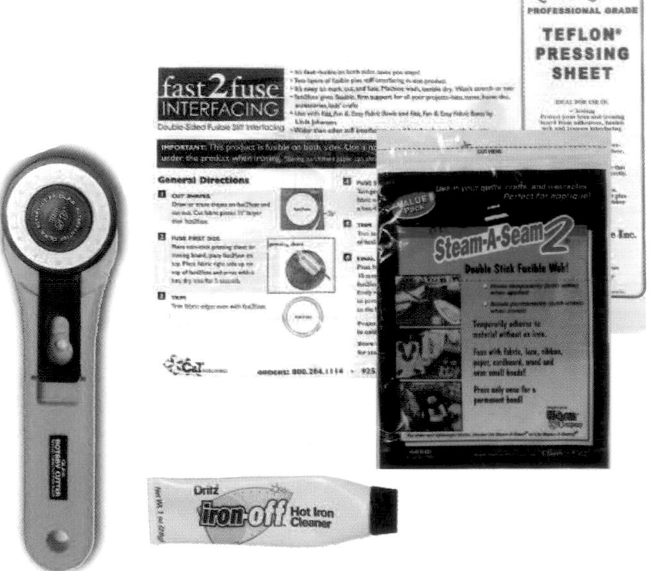

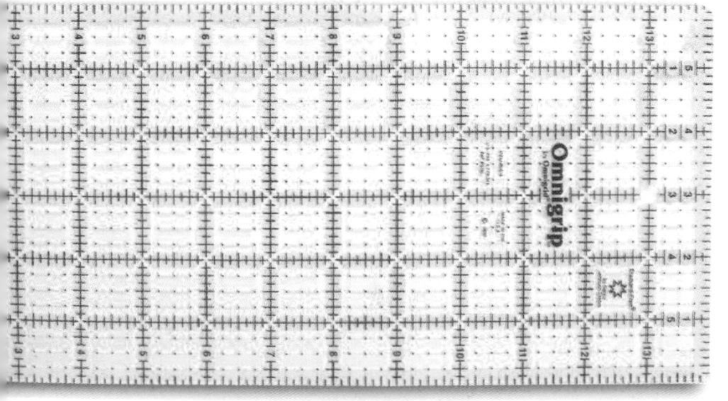

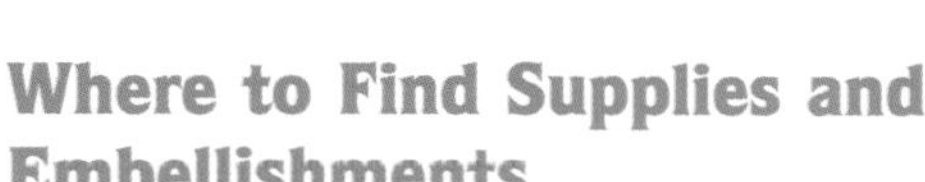

Where to Find Supplies and Embellishments

I'm a quiltmaker who loves appliqué and embellishing with silk ribbon, laces, buttons, and beads, so I love to shop at quilt shops, fabric and craft stores, and sewing machine dealers. Hobby, toy, card, gift, seasonal, and souvenir shops are favorites, too. Scrapbook stores have become a compelling destination for me. I'm a longtime fan of yard sales and flea markets, antique stores, and secondhand shops. Grocery and hardware stores yield necessities and surprising treasures. I even save the mesh bags from fruits and veggies. Not that I've actually ever used one…yet.

Add office supply, computer, and electronics stores to your list of places to shop. You'll need a camera and copier, or access to one, at a minimum. My setup at home includes a computer; a printer that copies, scans, and prints from my computer; and a digital camera. My digital camera uses a memory stick to store photos, and I can insert the memory stick into my printer and print photos directly from it. I was dragged kicking and screaming into this world of technology, but I have learned to love it.

Basic Supplies

If you're a quiltmaker, you probably already have the basics: your fabric stash, rotary-cutting tools, fusible webs and pressing sheets, threads, and some embellishments. If you're a paper scrapbooker who'd like to try working with fabric, you can use your paper and metal embellishments, vellum, fibers, stamps and inks, and acid-free pens on fabric. If you don't already have the following basics, it's time to go shopping at your quilt or fabric shop.

THE BASICS

- Fabric
- Fabric sheets for inkjet printers
- Bubble Jet Rinse
- fast2fuse double-sided stiff interfacing
- Paper-backed fusible web
- Nonstick pressing sheet
- Iron and iron cleaner
- Sewing machine and extra needles
- Needles, pins and thread
- Air-erasable marker
- Scissors
- Rotary cutter with straight blade
- Self-healing rotary mat
- Acrylic rulers: 6″ × 12″, 6″ × 24″, and 12½″ × 12½″ (These are the sizes I find helpful.)
- Point turner
- Fabri-Tac and Gem-Tac glues

OPTIONAL, BUT YOU MAY NEED THESE FOR SPECIFIC PROJECTS

- 45mm pinking or deluxe rotary cutter with pinking, wave, or scallop blade
- Mini-iron and holder
- Chenille and beading needles
- Thimble, needle threader, Needle Grabber, and Clover thread tweezers
- Beading thread
- Template plastic
- Fray Check
- Stiletto
- Tiger Tape
- Vellum and cardstock
- Acid-free Pigma pens and Gelly Roll pens
- Acid-free glue stick
- Fine sandpaper, 220 grit
- Varnish, acrylic paints, and brushes
- Eyelet setter and hammer
- Coping saw or hacksaw
- Hot glue gun

Michele and David,
12½" x 12½",
page photos by Mary Herron

What you'll need for embellishing and other supplies will depend on the fabric scrapbook page you're designing. Visit a variety of stores to see what's available and to find inspiration. For example, I was looking for specific products (satin ribbon and tulle) in the ribbon section of a craft store and came across calla lilies serendiptously on the opposite side of the aisle. The calla lilies were perfect for the wedding cake topping of *Michele and David.*

See Resources on page 70 for specific sources of supplies.

LOOK FOR EMBELLISHING SUPPLIES, TOO

- Silk, satin, grosgrain, twill, and Iron-On Ribbon
- Rickrack and decorative trims
- Perle cotton, embroidery floss, raffia, and hemp cord
- Fancy threads and fibers
- Buttons, charms, beads, eyelets, snaps, and brads
- Paper or metal tags
- Adhesive-backed dots and stickers
- Dowel rods and wooden shapes for finials: hearts, squares, and balls
- Metal rods, nuts, and washers

Asilomar or Bust,
12" x 12",
page photo by Robert R. Hale

Scrapbook Page Basics

When you're ready to construct a fabric scrapbook page, refer to this chapter for tips on machine and hand sewing, using fusible webs, and gluing soft and smooth-surfaced embellishments to your fabric scrapbook pages.

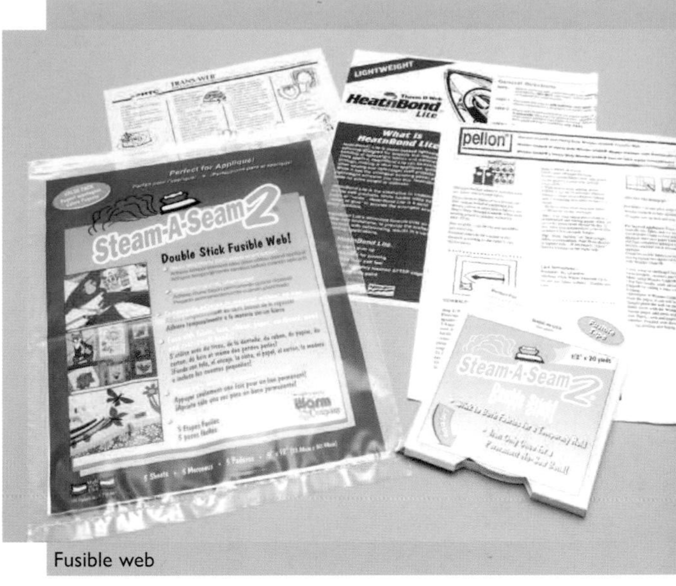

Fusible web

Sewing

Machine Sewing

Fabric scrapbook pages are easily constructed using a sewing machine, but you can sew them by hand if you prefer. You can also sew on ribbons and trims, insert rickrack in a seam or use it as an edge finish, and insert hanging tabs for your pages by machine.

It's fun to use decorative machine stitches for embellishing fabric scrapbook pages. You can couch narrow ribbons and braids with a zigzag stitch and invisible or decorative thread. Use a satin or blanket stitch to make narrow borders for photos and other images that you've printed on fabric. Or, try a scallop or leaf stitch in a contrasting color to outline the edges of the page.

Hand Sewing and Appliqué

Hand sewing is optional because you can fuse or glue most embellishments to the pages. If you like, you can hand sew soft embellishments like ribbons, laces, and trims. In particular, I hand sew vintage laces and handkerchiefs to pages because they are fragile. I like the way buttons look when they are sewn on, and I frequently choose a thread in a contrasting color.

Tip **Some buttons melt and lose color when you iron them. Test them first and sew them on last, after the page has been backed and finished.**

Fusing

You can bond most of your printed images, borders, and fabric motifs to the pages with fusible web. However, for items that are old and not replaceable, I recommend that you sew them to the pages by hand or machine in case you want to remove them at a later date.

Fusible Web

There are many good-quality fusible webs to choose from. Fusible webs are paper backed either on one side, like Wonder Under or Heat 'n' Bond Lite, or on both sides, like Steam-A-Seam 2 Double-Stick. Follow the manufacturer's directions for prewashing fabrics, iron temperature, and fusing time. Light-colored fabrics may scorch with a very hot iron or too much time pressing. Test using a small scrap of the fabric and fusible web to find out whether the iron is too hot or the recommended time is too long for the fabric you are using, and adjust accordingly. You don't want to scorch your project.

My favorite fusible web is Steam-A-Seam 2 Double-Stick. You can reposition it because it's sticky on both sides, so you can move the page elements around, and they stay in place on your design wall without pins. You can use it to fuse cottons, Ultrasuede, leather, vellum, and cardstock to your pages. Try Steam-A-Seam 2 Lite Double-Stick for fusing silk inkjet fabric sheets to your pages. It's softer and suppler than regular-weight Steam-A-Seam 2 Double-Stick.

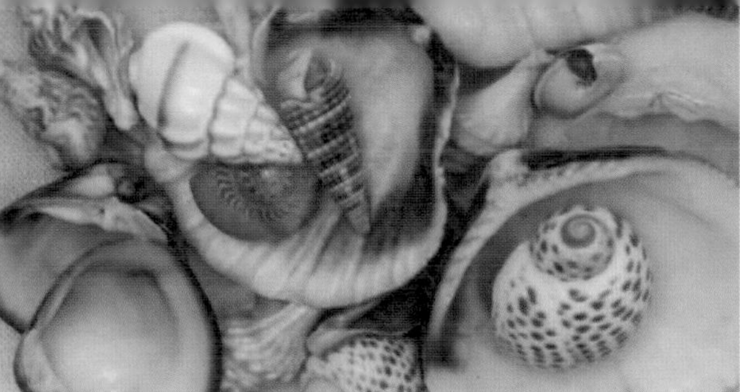
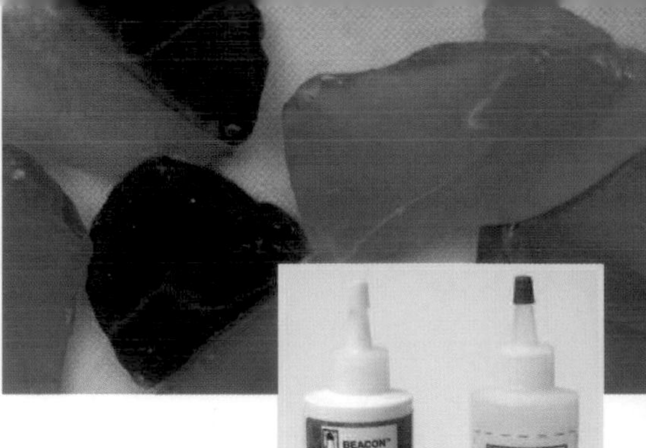

Glue soft embellishments and twigs with Fabri-Tac and smooth surfaces with Gem-Tac.

Using Steam-A-Seam 2 Double-Stick

1. Cut the fusible web a bit larger than the photo, printed image, or piece of fabric you are fusing.
2. Peel off the paper backing from 1 side of the fusible web, and place that side on the back of the fabric.
3. Sandwich this unit between a folded nonstick pressing sheet or two pieces of muslin to keep both your iron and ironing board cover clean.
4. Press for 10 to 15 seconds with a hot iron and steam. Let cool.
5. Peel off the paper backing, and trim the image or fabric to the desired size. (Removing the paper before trimming or fussy cutting will reduce dulling of your rotary cutter blade or scissors.)
6. Place trimmed pieces on the scrapbook page, cover with the pressing sheet or muslin, and fuse for 10 to 15 seconds with a hot iron and steam.

Save your scraps of fusible web in the original package or in a clear baggie, along with the directions. Use the scraps for titles, captions, tags, and small motifs.

Gluing

You can glue many embellishments to fabric scrapbook pages. My two favorite glues are Fabri-Tac and Gem-Tac. Each is formulated for a specific surface. Both glues are permanent, dry quickly, and are washable after 24 hours. Always test glues first to see how they behave and to find the best way to apply them to an embellishment or fabric.

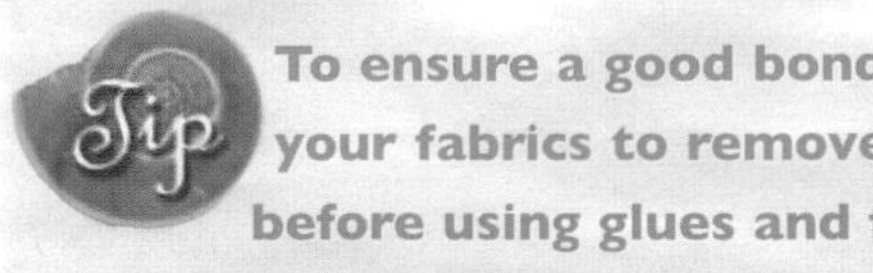

To ensure a good bond, prewash your fabrics to remove the sizing before using glues and fusible web.

Fabri-Tac

Fabri-Tac bonds soft embellishments such as ribbon, laces, trims, leather, and even wood to fabric. Lay down a fine ribbon of glue straight from the applicator tip or use a toothpick to apply small amounts of glue to the backs of embellishments. This glue goes on clear and dries clear.

Caution: The heat of an iron may cause longer lengths of glued ribbon and trim to shrink and pucker the fabric they're glued to. Puckering does not seem to occur with ribbons $\frac{5}{8}$″ wide or narrower. Test your ribbon and trims before gluing them to your page. Before applying glue, press a small piece of the trim with a hot iron to see if it will withstand the heat. Next, glue at least 6″ of the trim to a scrap of fabric and test again with the hot iron to see what happens. If puckering occurs, sew the ribbon or trim by machine or hand.

Gem-Tac

Gem-Tac bonds smooth-surfaced embellishments such as coins, washers, sea glass, charms, and buttons (with shanks removed) to porous materials like fabric and leather. For better adhesion, sand the smooth surfaces of these embellishments with 220-grit sandpaper before applying glue to them. Gem-Tac is white when you apply it but dries clear. My favorite applicator for this glue is a toothpick.

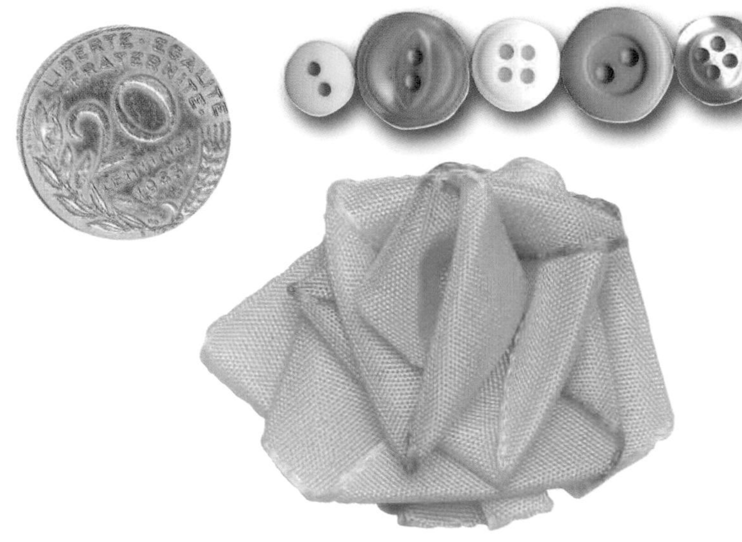

Preparation

You have the basic supplies and know the basic techniques. Now, gather your photos, fabrics, memorabilia, and embellishments, and get ready to work on your fabric scrapbook page.

Finding Subject Matter

We all use our cameras to preserve memories. In fact, just about every time you snap a photo or two, you've found a subject for fabric scrapbooking.

The Past

Look through your photos and select a few groups of photos that you especially like or that would be meaningful to someone else. Don't automatically eliminate photos that aren't perfect. Sometimes, the "just okay" photo tells the story better than the one with great lighting and composition. Ask family members if they have photos, souvenirs, or keepsakes of the same events that you can use to add to the page.

The Present

Keep your camera handy for spontaneous moments at home: a child napping, family laughing at a great joke, or a surprise visit from an old friend. Always keep the camera batteries charged, and if you don't have a digital camera, be sure the camera is always loaded with film. Take your camera with you everywhere, or keep a disposable camera in your car.

The Future

Plan ahead for special events, occasions, and accomplishments. You'll take better photos because you're already thinking about making a scrapbook page. Scribble some notes about the photos and the event. Look for just the right fabrics and embellishments before the event. Save souvenirs like ticket stubs, pins, brochures, coins, invitations, and announcements.

Great portrait shot
Photo by Heather Copenhaver

1 Zoom in for people.

You want to see faces, not shoelaces. Hold the camera at the subject's eye level so that your camera lens and the person make eye contact. Don't be afraid to fill the LCD screen or the finder completely with just one favorite face! When shooting portraits, it is better to stand a bit farther from your subject, and then zoom in. The result will be a more natural look. Zooming in also helps to minimize distracting or undesirable backgrounds, like a crowd of strangers or trees and flagpoles growing from people's heads.

2 Zoom out for landscapes.

Frame your photo when possible. A sunset photo framed by a swaying palm tree or a stately evergreen explains the setting without needing words.

3 Think in thirds.

Before you shoot, divide what you see in the viewfinder like a tic-tac-toe game. Put your subject to the left, right, above, or below the center. It's a great compositional technique. The main part of the red barn here is to the right of and below the center, and the horizon is in the lower third of the photo. This made the composition more interesting and allowed me to include the foliage on this fall day in New England.

Main subject is right of, and below center.
Photo by Sue Hale

Tip **Remember to take some supporting photos: the birthday or wedding cake, roadside signs, landmarks, historical markers, and landscapes. They add atmosphere to a scrapbook page and help tell the story, too.**

Supporting photos add atmosphere and help tell the story.
Photos by Sue Hale

4 Choose the timing.

Take photos in the early morning or the late afternoon on a sunny day. Midday sun in back of a person results in a dark silhouette. Bright light from the side casts shadows on faces and figures. Subjects facing the sun will be squinting. Dawn or dusk photos generally have a warm, orange glow and interesting shadows that add depth and texture.

5 Rotate the camera.

Take horizontal photos of groups of people and vertical photos of one or two people and tall monuments, such as this one in Richmond, Virginia.

Vertical photo of tall monument
Photo by Sue Hale

Tilt the camera for playful or interesting angles. Change your perspective. To emphasize tall items, shoot from ground level to create a unique look. This photo of the Golden Gate Bridge was taken from a cruise ship.

Likewise, if you can find a vantage point above a landscape scene or group of people, you can emphasize the overall layout and include everyone.

Interesting angles produce interesting photos.
Photo by Sue Hale

6 Use the camera s self-timer or remote control.

Take time to learn how to use these features on your camera, and invest in a tripod so that you can frame the shot *and* be in the picture! Then you won't be perching the camera on a wall or the hood of your car or trusting strangers to frame and snap the shot.

7 Plan some pictures.

Take some posed family photos every year, using the self-timer or remote control feature and your tripod. Select a background that helps tell the story: at home on the front steps or on vacation at the beach.

8 Take lots of pictures.

Invest in a digital camera so you can delete poor pictures right away and take another shot on the spot.

9 Take notes.

Who is in the photos, what is happening, why did you take it, and where and when was it? Jot down some notes and quotes to use as captions on the scrapbook page.

10 Relax.

Spontaneous, candid photos are important, too. They capture personalities, emotions, and the fun of the moment!

Fixing Old Photos

To remove distracting backgrounds, print the photos on fabric sheets, and fussy cut them as silhouettes. Use a red-eye pen from a camera shop to fix eye color. Both of these fixes can also be performed with computer software.

What about photos that are creased, scratched, torn, or stained? If the photos are treasures and the aging adds charm, use them as is. Or, enhance them digitally with image-editing software in your copier or computer at home. If you don t have the equipment or know-how, take your prints, a CD, or your memory card to a photo or copy shop and follow the simple steps on the screen on their equipment. A professional can also enhance the photos for you.

Legacy, 12" x 12"

Back of *Legacy*
Memories of my
grandmother s life

Ivory fan, lace, and *scherenschnitte* cards from late 1800s collaged and covered with crumpled fabric before being copied to fabric sheet

Gathering Memorabilia

Memorabilia are an important part of the story that you are telling. Include ticket stubs, programs, travel brochures, party invitations, announcements, and newspaper clippings. Some of these souvenirs will become keepsakes one day.

Souvenirs

Copy souvenirs onto fabric sheets (see Printing on Fabric, page 23), and collage them with photos, a title, and a caption or two. Make sure to visit souvenir shops on your travels for buttons, charms, magnets, and embroidered appliqués, which can be sewn, glued, or fused to your page. Save state coins and coins from foreign travel.

Let a collection of souvenirs, rather than photos, trigger the idea for a scrapbook page. Remember that trip to Ireland? You saved every ticket and pass, itineraries, napkins, menus, postcards, shamrocks, and even stickers.

Reduce oversized souvenirs with your copier. Experiment first on paper to make sure that you can still read the words. I reduced many souvenirs to 65% or 70% of the original size and found them readable. Reduce all the written memorabilia on a page by the same percentage.

Keepsakes

Look through your mementos, and pair them with old photos. Add a short history (see Telling the Story on page 28). Put it on the back of the page if it gets a little too long.

To collage three-dimensional items and copy them on fabric, arrange them on the copier glass, and cover them with flat or crumpled fabric. This provides some color for the background and makes the collage look like it's sitting on fabric.

Tip **When copying sharp or hard objects like coins, keys, shells, and jewelry, cover the glass with a sheet of acetate from an office supply store.**

![Tip] When using sepia-toned photos, use a small amount of that tone somewhere on the page, as in *Legacy*. The ivory lace pieces show nicely on the deep red texture. The bit of green in the border trim adds a needed third color to this page.

First try too plain

Second try too colorful and too dark

Third try just right

Selecting fabric for *Verde Cayon Railroad* and *All Aboard Tomlinsons*

Selecting Fabric for the Pages

When selecting fabrics, make sure they can take the iron's high heat. Cotton, linen, silk, denim, burlap, Aida cross-stitch fabric, Ultrasuede, Osnaburg, flannel, home-decorating fabrics, tea towels, table linens, and cotton T-shirts are good choices. I used 100% cotton quilting fabrics for most of my pages.

Let your photos and memorabilia guide you. You can use one fabric or piece several together for the page front. Fabric color, pattern, and scale work together to present the mood or theme of each page. Use pastels for a romantic theme; brights for a theme park. For men, choose geometrics, plaids, and textured solids. Audition fabrics on your design wall just as you would for a quilt project. Make copies of your photos and memorabilia on paper and pin them to the background fabrics you're considering. Don't worry about layout yet.

Color

The easiest and most logical way to start selecting your fabric is to pull colors from your photos and memorabilia. The bright red, blue, and yellow swirly textures in *Legoland* (page 40) were an easy choice. The fabrics matched the primary colors in the Lego bricks.

I struggled with choosing the right desert tones (above) in *Verde Canyon Railroad* and *All Aboard Tomlinsons.*

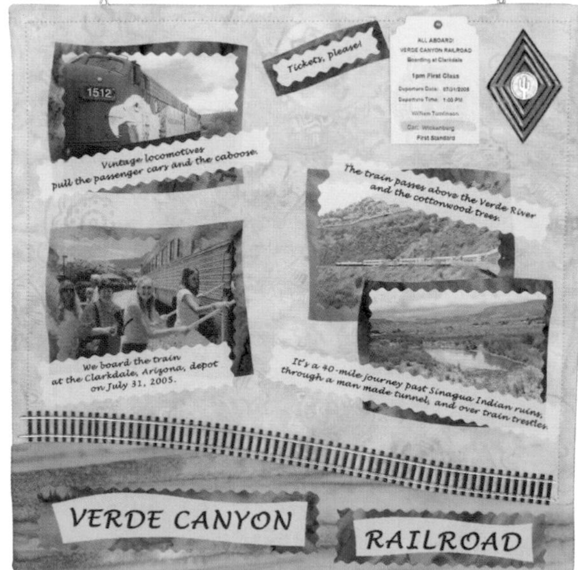

Verde Canyon Railroad, 12" x 12", page photos by Bill Tomlinson

All Aboard Tomlinsons, 12" x 12", page photos by Bill Tomlinson and Debbie Thatcher

Using patterned fabrics

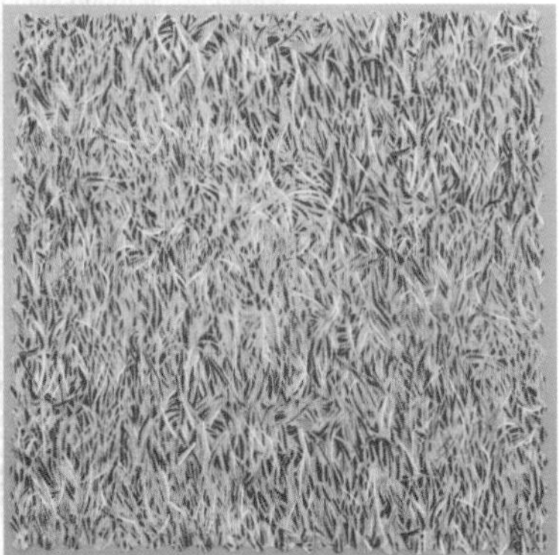

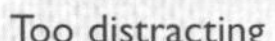

Too distracting

Nice and neutral

Small-, medium-, and large-scale prints

Pattern

The second factor to consider when selecting fabrics is pattern. Avoid very busy patterns that will distract the eye from your photos.

You can use theme fabrics with busy patterns if your layout is just right. The yellow and pink baby print in *Sweet Baby Girl* (page 49) works because the photo, letter, and birth announcement cover a lot of the busy print. Grouped together in the center, they remain the focal point. The pink dotted borders on the photo and letter provide a needed separation from the background.

Scale

Scale is the third factor to consider when selecting fabric for a scrapbook page. Look for small- and medium-scale fabrics first, keeping in mind that the interplay of color, pattern, and scale is very important.

A large-scale tone-on-tone texture will probably be fine, but once you introduce lots of color and pattern to a large-scale print, it may be overwhelming. *Serendipity*'s background is a very large-scale, multicolored floral. But the floral print and its colors are great for this page, because you only see the print in small segments along the outer edges. There's an exception to every rule!

Serendipity, 12" x 12", page photo by Sue Hale

Buying Fabric for the Pages

I like to buy fat quarters for my scrapbook pages. One fat quarter will be enough for the page front, with some leftovers for other projects. A second fat quarter is enough for the back, hanging sleeve, and image borders. You can also use long quarter-yard cuts and scraps to piece page fronts. Larger scrapbook pages will require more yardage.

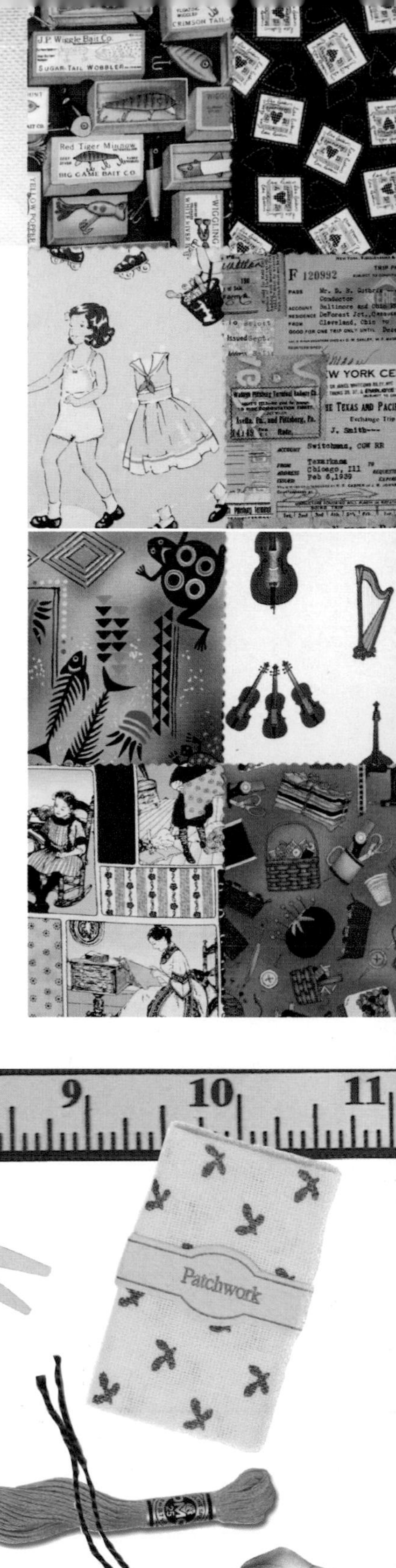

Selecting Fabric for Stickers and Tags

There are lots of theme fabrics in quilt shops. Make sure they have distinct motifs if you plan to use them as stickers on your pages. For example, I used the diamonds in the fabric to the right as stickers in back of the charms in *Verde Canyon Railroad* and *All Aboard Tomlinsons* (page 15). Remember to iron fusible web to the backs of motifs before cutting them out (see Fusing, on page 9).

Gathering Embellishments

You can buy, find, or scavenge many embellishments. Some, like dimensional flowers, rickrack, lace, and buttons, add texture to a page. Eyelets, brads, snaps, charms, and coins add shine as well as texture. You may already have snips of nice ribbon you've saved from gifts, pieces of costume jewelry you don't wear anymore, old keys, and dimensional items and small-scale tassels you've pulled off greeting cards.

Where to Buy Embellishments

Look in quilt, scrapbook, fabric, and craft stores for fancy threads and fibers for sewing buttons and beads onto your pages. Ribbon and rickrack are available in lots of colors and patterns and are easy to sew or glue to a page. Raffia in seasonal colors and hemp cord are great for hanging tags on pages. Buy small buttons and snaps for the corners of your photos, to scatter on your pages, to sew around the edges of the page as an outer border, and to glue to finials. Find charms to add a little shine to a page. Buy pearl strings to frame a page and beads to add sparkle. Look for packages of themed buttons, too. Check out scrapbook stores for metal embellishments like eyelets, snaps, brads, spirals, and metal tags. Hobby, toy, card, seasonal, and souvenir shops are treasure troves for scrapbookers. The trick is to look for small-scale stuff and figure out how to attach it to a fabric page (see Embellishing the Page, page 30).

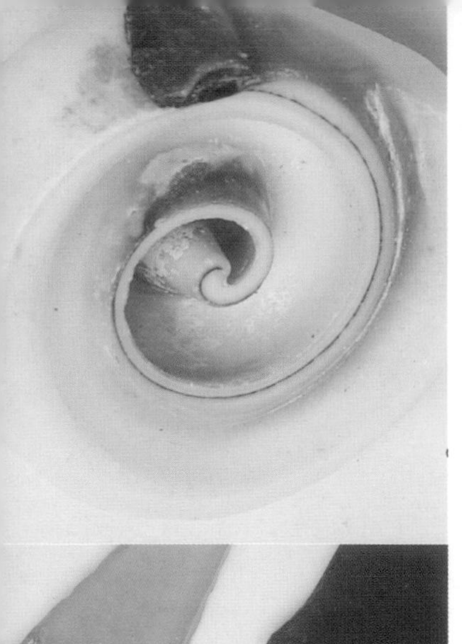

Found Embellishments

You can find elements from nature for your pages in your garden, at the beach, and in the woods. Dry some herbs, and put them in a fabric or vinyl pocket. Bundle a bouquet of dried petals in a circle of tulle, and tie it with a pretty ribbon. Pick up shells, sea glass, and small flat stones to put in clear vinyl pockets. Collect twigs, balsam needles, seed pods, bark, and berries to glue to a page or tuck in a fabric pocket.

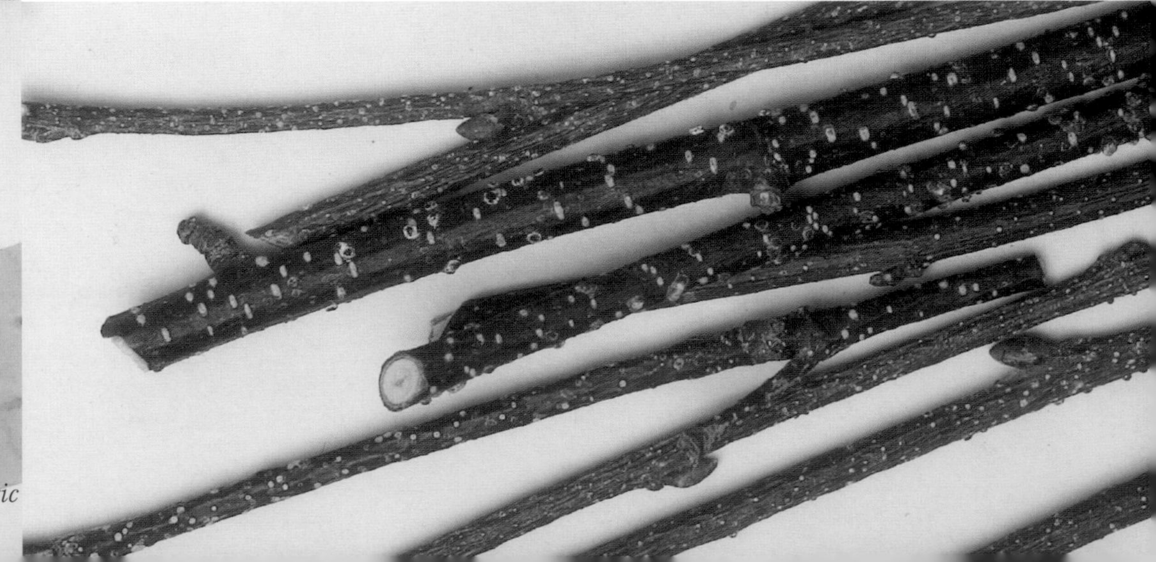

Making the Pages

Now that you have everything you need, here's how to make, finish, and display your scrapbook pages.

Designing the Page Layout

First, you'll need to make a preview window from poster board. You'll use it to frame your layout area as you design the page so you can see how much space you have for all your photos, images, words, and memorabilia.

Preview photos and other page materials.

Make a Preview Window

For 12″ × 12″ pages, start with a 15″ × 15″ square of white poster board, and cut a 12″ × 12″ square in the center. Use this window when designing all your scrapbook pages.

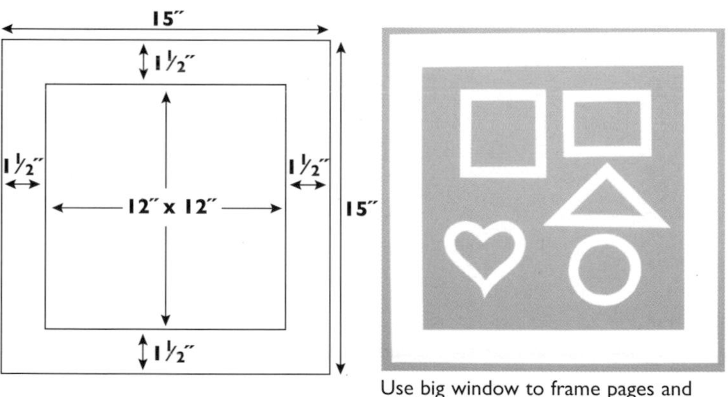

Use big window to frame pages and small windows to frame photos.

Tip **Save the 12" square from the center of the preview window, and use it to carry your page to the ironing board for fusing tasks. Use the leftover poster board to cut square, rectangular, triangular, round, and heart-shaped windows with ½" frames for viewing your photos. These frames will come in handy when you're planning your page.**

How to Start

1 Decide on the size of the page. Cut the front and back fabrics and the stiff interfacing for the middle layer at least 2″ larger than the finished size. The extra allows room for seam allowances and a little more room for your layout if you need it. For example, for a 12″ × 12″ page, cut fabric and stiff interfacing 14″ × 14″.

2 Copy or print your photos, and copy your souvenirs on plain paper first. Trim them to size or fussy cut them into silhouettes. You want to see how everything works before you print on fabric.

3 Play with different layouts (see Layout Ideas below). Place the fabric for the page front on a table. Place the preview window on top of the fabric to frame your layout area. Arrange the paper copies of photos and souvenirs within the window opening, remembering to save room for a title, captions, and maybe a story block. Reduce or enlarge the images as needed to fit the layout.

4 Decide on the final layout. You may need to walk away from the layout and let your ideas "marinate" in your head for a day or two. Sometimes small changes make the difference between a good layout and a great one. If you need room for other projects, store the page and the embellishments in a 14″ pizza box.

5 Make a final copy of your photos and souvenirs on fabric sheets (see Printing on Fabric, page 22).

Tip **Working on a table saves pinning and re-pinning everything to your design wall as you play with different layouts. Move to the design wall when you have a layout you like. Then you can stand back from it, see it as you will when it s hanging on your wall or sitting on a tabletop easel, and make needed changes.**

Layout Ideas

ONE PHOTO

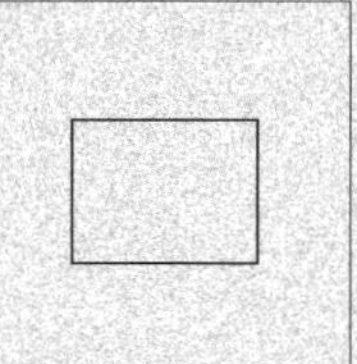
One photo centered

A single photo is the focal point of the page and is usually centered. *Madonna of the Trail* is formal and symmetrical, with its balanced story blocks. *Watson Lake* (page 53) is less formal because of the tags hanging from the ribbon on the left side of the page. Sometimes a single photo is placed to one side, as in *Asilomar or Bust*, where the photo is balanced by the three stickers opposite it and anchored by the red title bar at the bottom of the page.

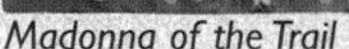
Madonna of the Trail

Asilomar or Bust

TWO PHOTOS

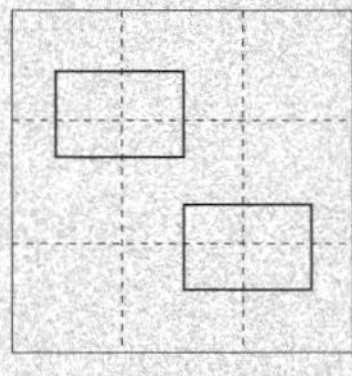
Two photos tic-tac-toe grid

A two-photo layout is the most challenging. If you place two photos side by side, enlarge one of them so it becomes a focal point. Try placing them in two of the intersections of a tic-tac-toe grid, as in *At Home*. The family photo in the lower right corner is the focal point and the little girl in the upper left is secondary.

At Home

THREE PHOTOS

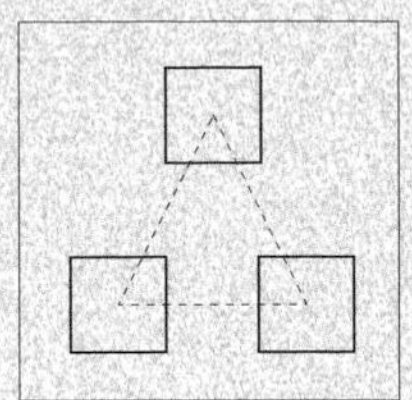

Three photos triangle

Create a triangle when using three photos. One photo can still be the focal point if you enlarge it or reduce the size of the other two. In *Letters from Matt*, the close-up photo in the lower right corner is the largest and the fringed border calls attention to it. The dark title bar grounds the composition of the page. In *Legacy*, the two oval photos and the oval pin form a triangle.

Letters from Matt

Legacy

FOUR PHOTOS

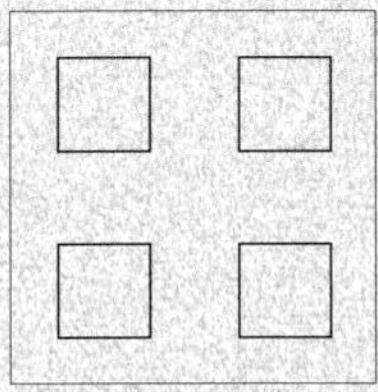

Four photos balanced

Four photos create a nicely balanced layout on a square page. In *Silhouettes*, the layout on black is crisp and formal looking. The lace in the center fills a gap without crowding the silhouettes. I used a similar layout in *Cyanotypes* by adding a story block to balance the three vintage photos on fabric.

Silhouettes

Cyanotypes

FIVE OR MORE PHOTOS

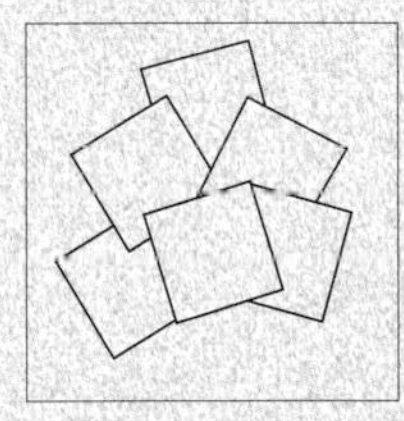

Five or more photos collaged

When you have many photos and want to use them all, you ll need to overlap or collage the photos so they fit on one 12" x 12" page. This is what I did in *Serendipity*. Another approach is to make a 12" x 12" companion page. *Verde Canyon Railroad* and *All Aboard Tomlinsons* are unified by color and by the horizontal line that the title bars and railroad tracks create. Or you can make the page bigger, as in *The Cottage at Little Lake Sunapee* (page 57).

Verde Canyon Railroad

All Aboard Tomlinsons

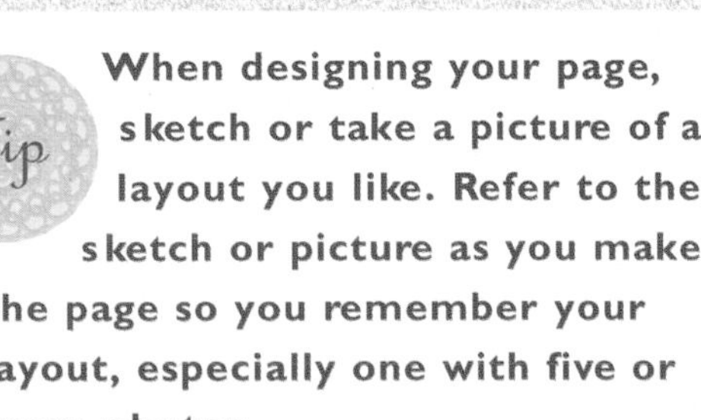

Tip When designing your page, sketch or take a picture of a layout you like. Refer to the sketch or picture as you make the page so you remember your layout, especially one with five or more photos.

Serendipity

Printing on Fabric

You can buy fabric sheets that have been pretreated to make inkjet printer and copier ink permanent and washable. You can also pretreat fabric yourself. I prefer to use pretreated sheets for their convenience. For more information about pretreating your own sheets and printing on fabric, see Resources (page 70).

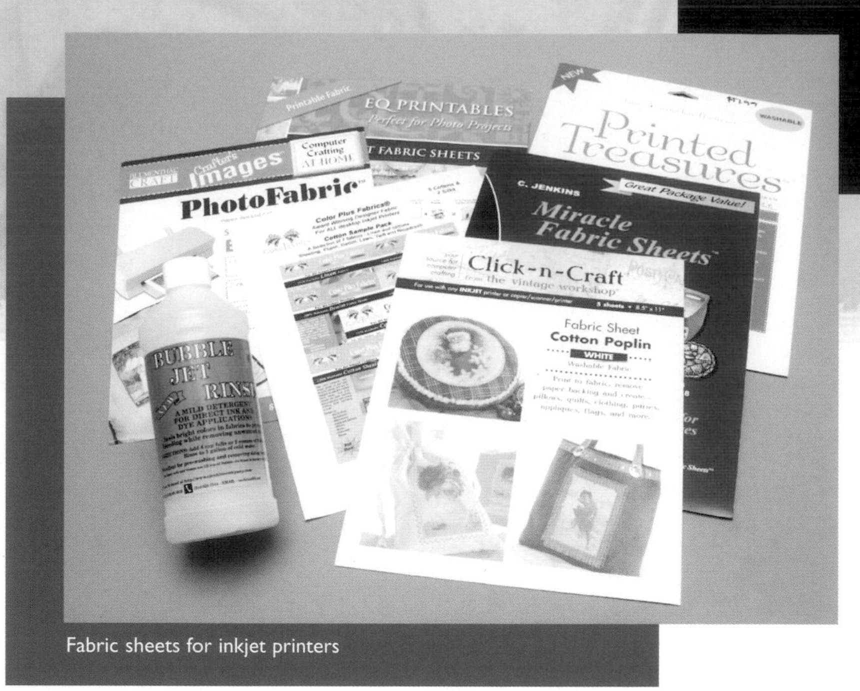

Fabric sheets for inkjet printers

Selecting Fabric Sheets

There are a number of brands of pretreated fabric sheets available in quilt, fabric, and craft shops and on the Internet. For the best results, look for cotton sheets that are at least 200 thread count.

These fabric sheets are bonded to paper so that they can feed through your inkjet printer without jamming. You'll find cotton (Pima, poplin, twill, canvas), silk, and linen. The sheets come in white, and some are available in cream or natural. White sheets will give your photos and images the truest color. Use cream or natural sheets when you want a softer look or when you are printing sepia-toned photos on fabric (*Legacy,* page 14). Experiment with the twill, silk, linen, and canvas sheets when you want a different texture to print on. Follow the directions that come with the sheets. Most manufacturers recommend rinsing the sheets in cool water or Bubble Jet Rinse to remove loose ink particles after printing.

Pretreated sheets with manufacturer-applied fusible backing are also available. These fusible sheets are harder to sew through when you are sewing on buttons and other embellishments, but they eliminate the step of ironing fusible web to the backs of fabric images. Try both to see which you prefer.

Fabric sheets are designed for use with inkjet printers and all-in-one printers/copiers. Do not use fabric sheets in a laser printer or copier.

Avoiding Copyright Infringement

A few words about copyright are needed here. Because scrapbooking is such a personal activity, you ll probably be using copies of your own photos, awards, certificates, and letters. Be sure to get written permission before you use or copy photos you have not taken yourself. And give credit to the author for quotations or poems that you use on a page.

If you use material from the Internet or design/image CD-ROMs, be sure to read the copyright restrictions and respect them.

Printing/Copying on Pretreated Fabric Sheets

All of the pretreated sheets use these basic steps, with some variations: Print, let dry, heat set, and rinse. Read and follow the manufacturer s directions for each brand you try. I recommend the following steps for printing and copying on pretreated fabric sheets:

1 Wash your hands, and clean the copier glass. Handle photos by their edges to avoid fingerprints.

2 Reduce or enlarge photos and images if needed. Always test print the photo or image on plain paper first to avoid wasting fabric sheets on mistakes. Use these test prints to lay out your page (page 19).

3 Remove lint and loose threads on the fabric sheet with a piece of tape. Trim off loose threads on the edges of the fabric sheet with a rotary cutter. Do not pull them off.

4 Determine whether the fabric sheets should be put face down or face up in the copier tray. Mark an X on one side of a sheet of paper, and place it with the X facing down in the paper tray. Print or copy something with the printer. If the printing is on the side with the X, you should place the fabric sheets fabric side **down** in the tray. If the printing is on the blank side, place the fabric sheets fabric side **up** in the tray.

5 Remove the paper from the paper tray. Place one fabric sheet in the tray in the correct print orientation (see Step 4).

6 Select Reduce/Enlarge, and choose the percentage you decided on with your test print (Step 2). Select Best for print quality and Plain for paper type. Select Black or Color, as desired. Copy.

7 Let the fabric sheet dry for at least 1 hour. Remove the paper backing.

8 Rinse the sheet according to the manufacturer's directions. I use Bubble Jet Rinse.

9 Blot the sheet with white paper towels. Lay flat to dry.

10 Press the sheet to remove creases and wrinkles when the sheet is dry, being careful not to scorch it.

11 Store unused fabric sheets flat in the package.

12 Iron fusible web to the back of the fabric sheet before trimming or fussy cutting. Omit this step if you are using fabric sheets with a manufacturer-applied fusible backing.

Make sure your fabric sheets are lint- and thread-free. Printing over lint and loose threads leaves a white image of the lint or thread on the fabric sheet, because ink does not penetrate them.

Cut 2 squares 15" × 15" of muslin and sandwich the printed fabric sheet between them before pressing. This protects the fabric sheet from any residue on your ironing board cover or iron. You can also spray both pieces of muslin with water to remove stubborn creases and wrinkles when you press the fabric sheet.

Trimming and Fussy Cutting

Now that you've printed your photos and images on fabric sheets, you're ready to trim and fussy cut them. Make sure that you have fusible web on the backs of the photos and images before proceeding. Remove the paper backing from the web just before cutting to minimize dulling of your rotary cutter or scissors blades.

Trimming

Some photos and printed images must be trimmed to a smaller size because two 4″ × 6″ photos will not comfortably fit side by side on a 12″ × 12″ page. Many images can be reduced to fit a page layout during the printing process. I choose to leave photos with people in them full size rather than reduce them to ensure that the people can be seen as clearly as possible. Then, after printing on fabric, I trim these photos to fit the layout. Trim photos and images with a straight rotary cutter blade for a formal look or with a decorative edge blade for an informal look. Or leave a 1/8″ band of the fabric sheet for an instant border, and add a second, darker border to the page for good contrast.

The Golden Mean

Photos cut to 3" × 5" are pleasing because they approximate the 8:13 ratio of the Golden Mean, a proportional formula discovered by the Greeks and still used today by artists and architects. Try using this ratio on a paper copy of your photo to see if it will work for that photo. Here s how: Multiply or divide the measurement of one side by 1.625 to find this pleasing proportion. For example, if you want the photo to be 3 on one side and longer on the other: 3" × 1.625 = 4.875", or 4 7/8". Or, if you want it to be 3 1/4" on one side and shorter on the other: 3 1/4" ÷ 1.625 = 2". Just don t get too hung up about trying to make this work. Scrapbooking is supposed to be fun, after all.

Vance, Jordan, Shelby, and Heather
At home in Amelia, Ohio
October, 2004

At Home, 12" x 12", page photos by Matt Williamson

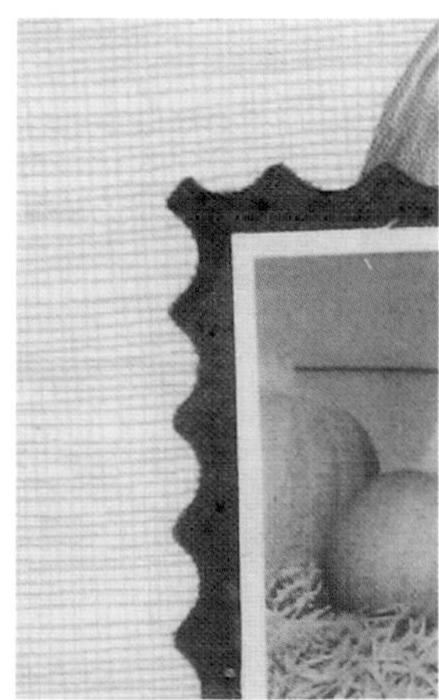

Narrow white border from fabric sheet is first border.

Madonna of the Trail, 12" x 12",
page photo by Sue Hale

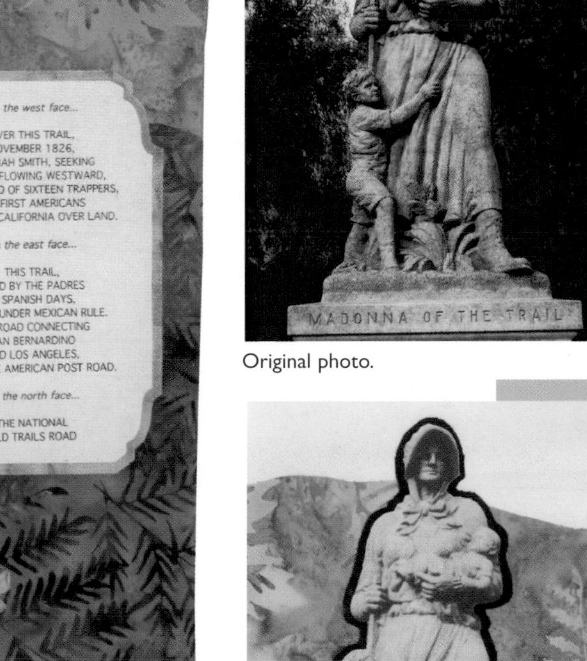

Original photo.

Fussy-cut silhouette is more effective.

Fussy Cutting

Paper scrapbookers crop photos to remove unwanted objects and undesirable elements from their photos. Fabric scrapbookers can do the same by fussy cutting fabric photos into silhouettes or other shapes. Cut silhouettes from your paper test print first to see how they look.

Create small windows with ½″ frames (see Tip on page 19) to preview how a photo looks as a circle, oval, heart, or other shape. Then draw the desired shape onto template plastic and cut it out. Iron fusible web to the back of the fabric photo and tape it, with the fusible paper side up, to a lightbox or a sunny window. Position the plastic template over the part of the photo you want for your page, and trace the shape on the paper backing. Cut the shape along the traced lines with a straight or decorative edge rotary cutter.

Tip
To cut a smooth curve, turn the photo with one hand as you move the blade along the traced curve.

Fussy cutting and silhouetting should be used with restraint. Don't overdo either. The objective is to enhance the photo to suit the mood and theme of the page. Let your eyes tell you when enough is enough.

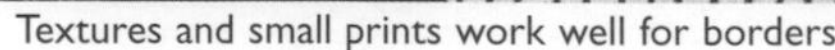
Textures and small prints work well for borders.

Adding Image Borders

The next step is to add image borders. Borders focus attention on photos, images, titles, captions, and story blocks by creating a visual separation between them and the page. Borders make these elements look more finished, and they can help to fill excess space. Made from fabric, trims, or stitchery, they can also add color and texture to the page.

Color and Pattern

Let your photos, souvenirs, and the theme of the page guide you in selecting border fabrics. Try textures or small-scale prints like tiny checks and dots in colors that contrast with the page background fabric.

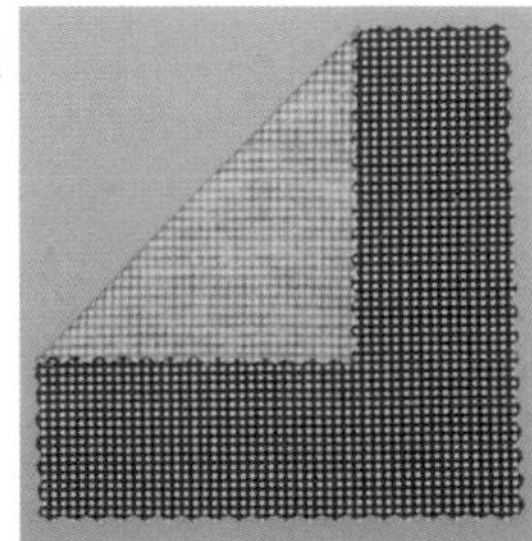
Use reverse side of prints for softer color.

Fabric Image Borders

Single and double borders work best on fabric scrapbook pages. Make your borders narrow, about 1/8″ to 3/8″ wide, so they don't overwhelm the photos and images. Cut borders with a straight or decorative edge rotary cutter, or with scissors, when you need to fussy cut or silhouette a figure. Omit borders on photos and images on collaged pages.

Tip **Fabric photo corners can be used when just a bit of contrast is needed. The red, yellow, and blue photo corners in *Legoland* (page 40) anchor the photos to the page and separate them from the bright backgrounds. Photo corners can also be used to frame story blocks. For directions on how to make photo corners, see page 42.**

Other Image Borders

There are lots of ways to border photos and images. In addition to fusing them to fabric, you can iron on or couch narrow ribbon, make your own rickrack from fabric (*Michele and David*), and sew or glue braid, lace, trims, ribbon roses, buttons, snaps, beads, and pearls. You can tear, fray, or fringe the edges of fabric, Osnaburg, or burlap to add texture (*Watson Lake*).

Michele and David

Watson Lake

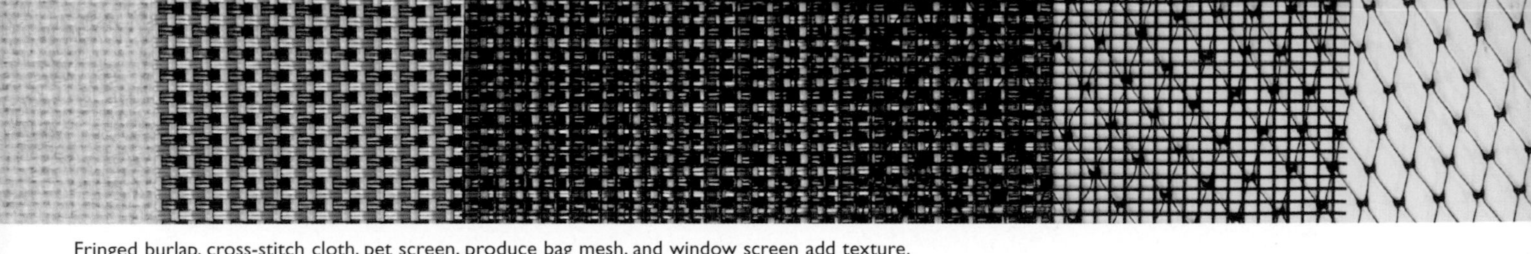

Fringed burlap, cross-stitch cloth, pet screen, produce bag mesh, and window screen add texture.

You can run a simple line of hand stitching around the perimeter of a photo with a beautiful variegated thread to call attention to it. Crazy-quilt stitches by hand might be just right around that sepia-toned photo of Great-Grandmother. You can blanket stitch the edges by hand or machine. And the possibilities with decorative machine embroidery stitches are nearly endless.

Page Borders

As quilters, we are accustomed to seeing borders on our quilts. Scrapbook pages, however, do not have much room for outer borders. You can imply borders by topstitching with a straight or decorative stitch about 1/2″ from the edges of the page. Borders are implied in *Silhouettes* with machine stitches on the outer edge and four Victorian corners, which I glued on. I fused the textured burgundy fabric in *Legacy* to a tone-on-tone floral fabric and covered the line with a pretty trim to give the appearance of a border. Often there is enough space for a narrow ribbon border, as in *Cyanotypes.* Using an edge finish like rickrack or cording (*Family Recipes*, page 60) gives the look of a border without using any space on the page. If you simply must have a border but have no room on the page for one, just add a binding in a contrasting color.

Silhouettes

Legacy

Cyanotypes

Sweet Baby Girl

Jordan Olivia Copenhaver

January 25, 2004
9:55 pm
5 pounds, 14 ounces
19 inches

Vance and Heather

Jordan s birth announcement tells the story.

Telling the Story

While you're putting the page together, think about its content, and take a few minutes to write down your thoughts. The titles, captions, and stories you write will bring your pages to life. Almost every page needs a title. It can be as simple as a name, like a baby's name spelled out in alphabet block beads (*Sweet Baby Girl*). If you can't think of a title, there are hundreds of scrapbooking magazines and books with lists suggesting titles for all kinds of topics, from daily life to celebrations and accomplishments. See Resources (page 70) for Internet sources of sayings and quotations.

Story blocks offer a spot for your memories about the moments, milestones, and history in your photos. An easy way to organize your story is to answer the five W's: Who, What, Why, Where, and When. You don't need to answer all five questions for each page. Sometimes just Who, When, and Where is enough. For example, a birth announcement tells the story pretty succinctly; you may only need to add the title.

Use captions to fill in details missing in the photos. Add them to photos of activities that need some explanation.

Caption tells date and place of train trip.

Writing by Hand

Handwriting is much more personal than computer lettering. It becomes part of the legacy of the page and exudes a warmth and personality that computer lettering does not provide. Copy handwritten letters and recipes, signatures from guest books and certificates, and pages from journals or baby albums onto fabric sheets to personalize your pages. Write some of the titles, captions, and stories in your own hand.

Before writing on fabric, iron freezer paper to the back of the fabric to stabilize it. If you write the title and caption below your photo on a pretreated fabric sheet, do so before removing the paper backing to eliminate the need for freezer paper. Practice writing your title, captions, and stories on paper first. When you're satisfied with your words, tape them to a lightbox, and trace the words on the paper-backed fabric. If you don't have a lightbox, write on your fabric with an air-erasable pen, and trace the letters with your pen. Or just go for it, and write directly on your fabric.

I like writing on fabric with Pigma Micron and Gelly Roll acid-free pens by Sakura. With the .05 nibs, I don't have to trace over my letters a second time to make them clear. If you ask others to write on fabric for a page, offer them the Gelly Roll pens, because they roll very easily on fabric.

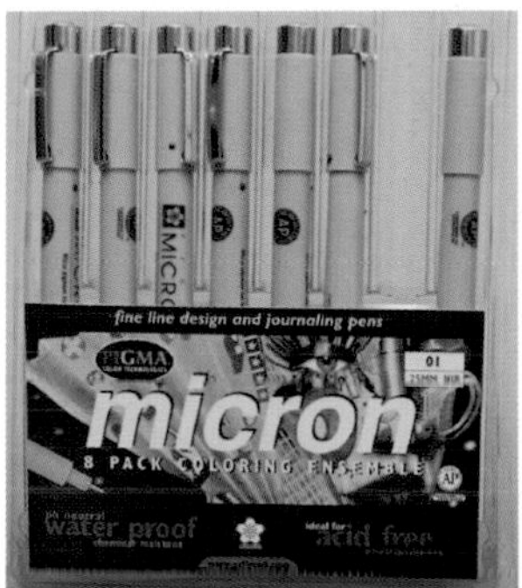

Writing on the Computer

Computer programs have dozens of fonts, sizes, colors, and special effects to choose from. Try your titles, captions, and stories in different fonts, and print them on paper first to see whether they suit the theme of the page and whether they fit. Use fonts that are easy to read, and adjust the size of the letters as needed. Read and revise your words until you are happy with them. Check your spelling. Remember, your computer will not be able to proof all names for you. Printing in colors adds a nice, informal touch, but there may be some loss of color when you rinse the fabric sheet.

MAKING A LABEL FOR THE BACK

Don't forget to make a label for the back of the scrapbook page. Write your name, the date, and a line or two about why you made this page. If it's a gift, put "to" and "from," the date, and why you made it. In 50 years, someone will be glad to know the origin of and the reason for this scrapbook page.

Embellishing the Page

Embellishments (page 17) are the frosting on the cake for fabric scrapbook pages. For me, this is the most fun. You can make just about anything you can imagine from scraps of fabric, bits of ribbon, and a little ingenuity. Look through the Projects (pages 40–69) for instructions on making embellishments for your pages.

Two Rules for Embellishing a Fabric Scrapbook Page

1 Embellishments, whether you make, buy, find, or scavenge them, should be relevant to the theme of the page. Don't embellish just to fill space.

2 Embellishments should enhance but not overwhelm the photos, words, and memorabilia on the page. It can be tempting to fill the page with all that good stuff you've been gathering, but sometimes less is better. Once it's glued to the page, you can't change your mind, so step back and think about when to stop.

Tip

Embellishments that can be crushed or melted, like dimensional flowers or items made of plastic, should be attached after the page is finished and ready for display. Also avoid placing hard three-dimensional items, like coins or brads, within or near the seam allowance. It s best to keep them at least 1/2" away from the page edges.

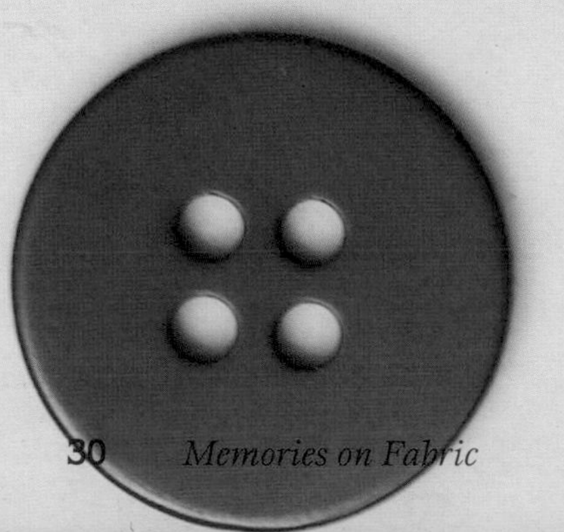

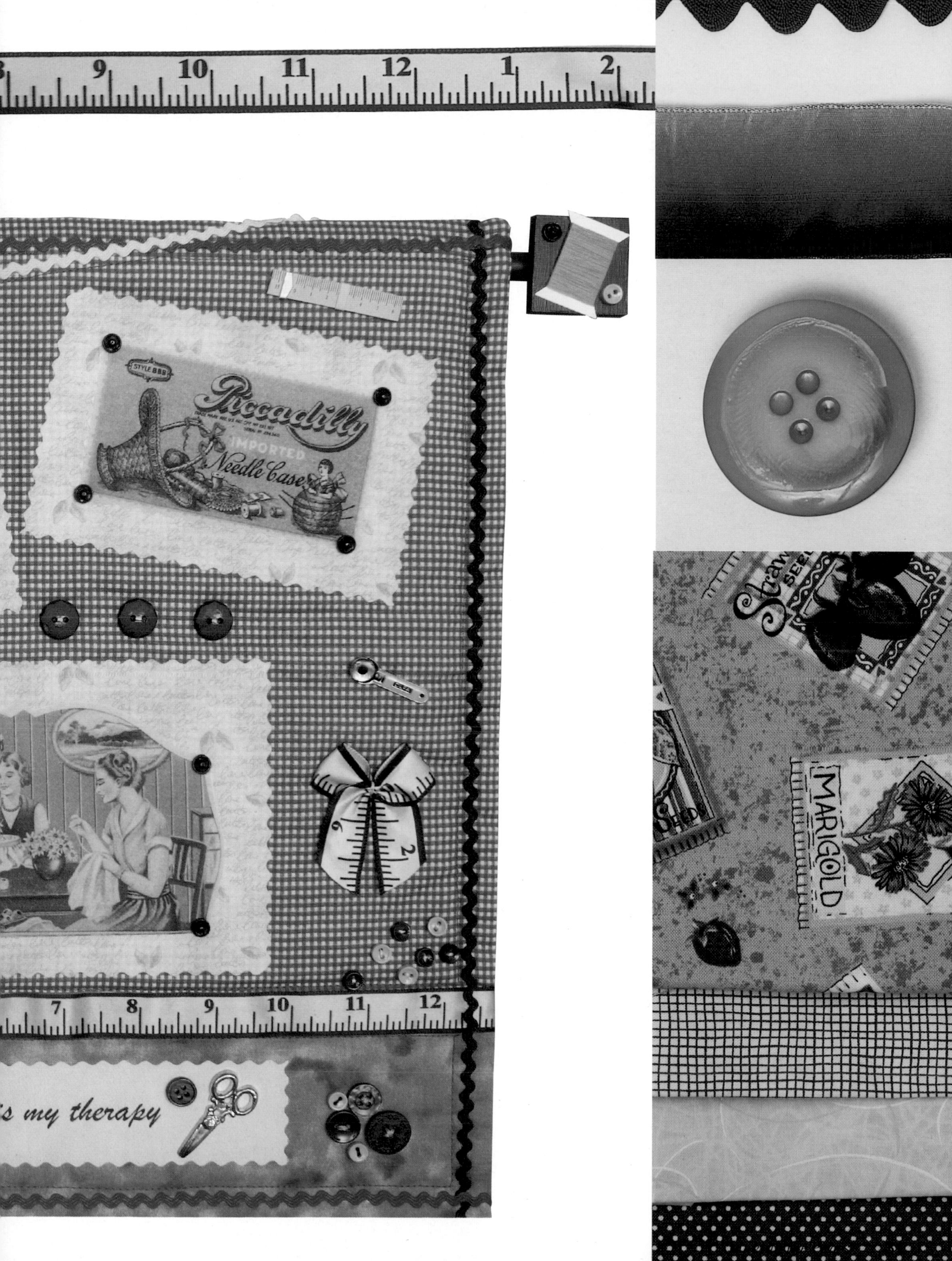

STYLE 888
Piccadilly
IMPORTED
Needle Case
's my therapy
MARIGOLD
SEEDS

Wood easels for 12 square pages

Display Options

TABLETOP EASELS

Tabletop easels are a great way to display your fabric scrapbook pages, especially if they have stories or other information on the back. Just follow the Finishing Instructions below and display the page on an easel. Easels are available at craft stores in acrylic, wood, plastic, porcelain, and brass. See Resources (page 70) for more on where to find easels.

DECORATIVE HANGING RODS

Many of my pages hang from wood hanging rods with finials that I made and embellished. For this option, you'll need to sew on a hanging sleeve or insert ribbon tab hangers *before* the page is completed. See Finishing the Page with a Hanging Sleeve (page 35) or with Ribbon Tab Hangers (page 35) for full instructions. You will also find instructions for making Bow Tab Hangers (page 36), which are glued on *after* the page is completed. For step-by-step instructions for making and embellishing wood hanging rods and finials, refer to Making Decorative Hanging Rods (page 37).

Other decorative rods, like railroad tracks, threaded rods, and branches, are connected to the pages *after* the finishing steps. For more detail, see Other Hanging Options (page 38).

Displaying and Finishing

I've taken lots of photos over the years and framed some of my favorites, but if you're like me, most are filed in boxes. By making fabric scrapbook pages, you can put more of these photos on display. But before you can finish your fabric scrapbook page, you'll need to decide how to display it (see Display Options, right) and whether to add an edge treatment (page 34), such as rickrack. I display my pages on a tabletop easel, or I hang them from a decorative rod. Look through the Projects (pages 40–69) to see the different display options. The way you display your fabric scrapbook page will determine how you finish it.

Finishing Instructions

The finishing steps for fabric scrapbook pages are simple. I use fast2fuse double-sided stiff interfacing as the middle layer for most of my pages. It's a stiff interfacing that is fusible on both sides. It provides good support for embellishments as well as needed stability to display the page on a tabletop easel. If you have embellishments that are unusually heavy, such as large coins, breakable items, or costume jewelry, try fast2fuse heavyweight for added support. Once the page front and back are fused to this interfacing, you won't need to do any machine quilting. If you use batting instead of fusible interfacing, you'll need to machine or hand quilt the page to hold the layers together.

WHAT YOU'LL NEED

Because most of my finished fabric scrapbook pages measure 12″ × 12″, the instructions below provide detail for this size. For larger fabric scrapbook pages, remember to add 2″ to the length and width of the finished size of your page.

- Embellished fabric scrapbook page front, 14″ × 14″
- fast2fuse double-sided stiff interfacing, 14″ × 14″
- Page back, 14″ × 14″
- Air-erasable pen
- Nonstick pressing sheet or muslin
- Point turner
- Matching thread
- Rotary cutter, ruler, and mat
- Scissors (fabric and paper)

ASSEMBLING THE PAGE

1. Trim the page front and page back to 12½″ × 12½″, or ¼″ larger on each side than the finished page size.
2. Trim the stiff interfacing to 12″ × 12″, or the same size as the finished page.

Tip Sometimes your page design may extend beyond the planned 12" × 12" page size thats why I start with 14" × 14" fabric and fast2fuse stiff interfacing. Its okay if your page is bigger. Just trim it square, and adjust the size of the page back and fast2fuse as needed.

Note: If you are adding an edge treatment (see page 34) or finishing your page with Ribbon Tab Hangers (page 35) or a hanging sleeve (page 35), refer to those pages before proceeding with the page assembly.

3. Center the stiff interfacing on the wrong side of the page front, leaving a ¼″ seam allowance on all sides. Trace around the interfacing with an air-erasable pen. This is your stitching line for sewing the front and back together.
4. Align the page front on the page back, right sides together. Pin. Sew around the edges on the marked stitching line, leaving an 8″ opening on one side for turning. For sharper points, take a diagonal stitch or two at each corner.

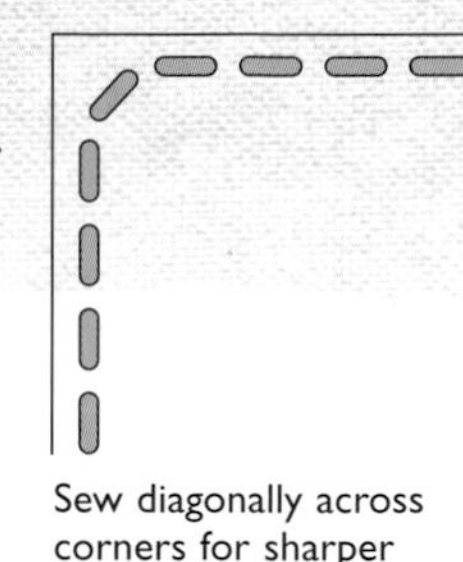

Sew diagonally across corners for sharper points.

5. Trim the corner seam allowances at an angle, and press the seams open.
6. Turn the page right side out, and *carefully* push out the corners with a point turner. Press flat.
7. Place the stitched page on top of the stiff interfacing. If the interfacing is larger than the page, mark and trim the interfacing so that it is ⅛″ smaller than the page.
8. Roll the stiff interfacing in half, and insert it through the 8″ opening. Work it into two corners first, open it flat, and then work it into the other two corners.

Insert stiff interfacing through opening.

9. Fold in the seam allowances of the side opening, and press.
10. Cover the page with a nonstick pressing sheet or muslin. Press for 10 seconds on each side of the page with a hot iron and steam to permanently fuse it to the stiff interfacing.
11. Whipstitch the side opening closed.
12. Sew or glue on finishing touches such as three-dimensional objects, plastic embellishments, and vellum envelopes. Do this last to avoid crushing or melting them with the iron.

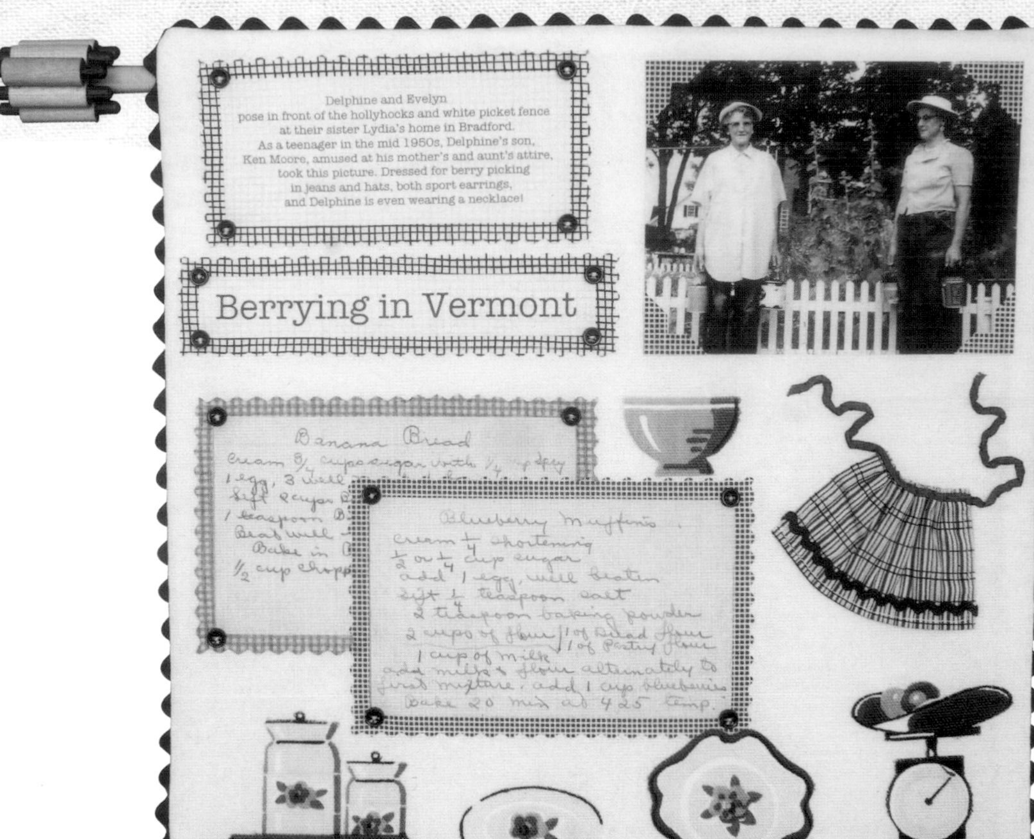

Delphine and Evelyn
pose in front of the hollyhocks and white picket fence
at their sister Lydia's home in Bradford.
As a teenager in the mid 1950s, Delphine's son,
Ken Moore, amused at his mother's and aunt's attire,
took this picture. Dressed for berry picking
in jeans and hats, both sport earrings,
and Delphine is even wearing a necklace!
Berrying in Vermont

Berrying in Vermont

Rickrack edge treatment

Adding an Edge Treatment

Edge treatments, like rickrack, piping, some laces, and other trims, must be inserted within the seam allowance *before* the page front is sewn to the back.

1. Follow Steps 1–3 of Assembling the Page on page 33. Repeat Step 3 on the right side of the page front. This is your stitching line for applying rickrack.
2. Cut a $1\frac{1}{2}$-yard length of medium-width rickrack, piping, lace, or other trim. Start at the center of the bottom edge, and pin the rickrack to the stitching line. Sew down the center of the rickrack, being careful when turning the corners.

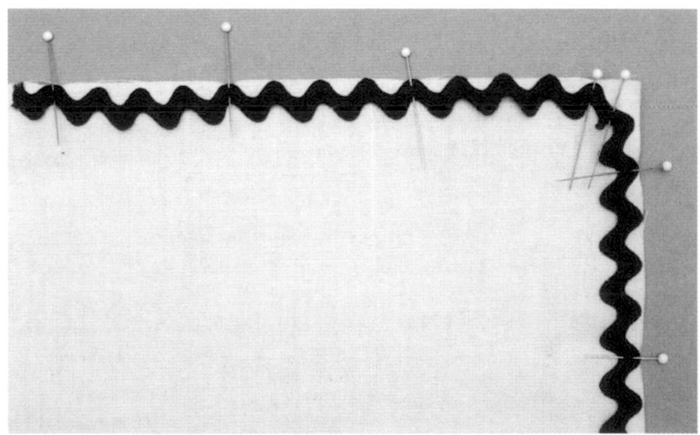

Pin rickrack on marked line, and sew.

3. Complete Steps 4–12 of Assembling the Page.

Tip To determine edge treatment yardage for pages larger than 12" × 12", total the measurements for each of the 4 sides and add 6".

Finishing the Page with a Hanging Sleeve

Sleeve directions are for a 3/8″ dowel or other small-diameter rod.

1. Cut a 4″ × 12″ rectangle of fabric.

Be sure to measure your page before cutting the sleeve, and adjust the length if needed. Cut your sleeve the same length as the finished width.

2. Fold over the edge 1/4″ on each short side, sew them down, and press.
3. Fold the strip in half lengthwise, right sides together.
4. Sew raw edges together on the long side with a 1/4″ seam allowance. Press the seam allowance open.

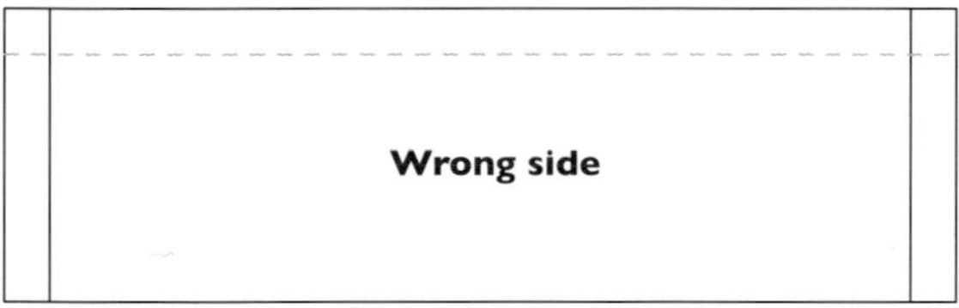

Fold sleeve right sides together; sew raw edges together.

5. Turn the sleeve right side out. Press so that the seam is centered on the back of the sleeve.
6. Trim the page front and back 1/2″ larger than the finished page size, or 12 1/2″ × 12 1/2″.
7. Center the sleeve on the right side of the page back, and 3/4″ below the top raw edge. Pin and sew the two long sides of the sleeve to the page back.
8. Complete Steps 3–12 of Assembling the Page (page 33).

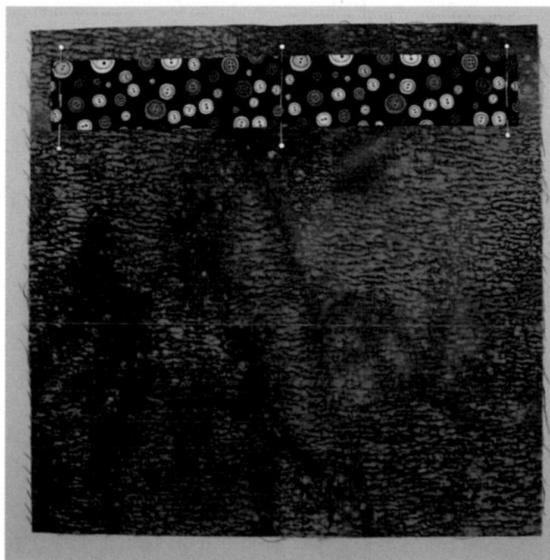

Pin and sew sleeve near top edge.

If you use a heavier fabric like a tea towel for a sleeve, cut a 2" × 12" strip. Press 1/4" under on all 4 edges. Hem the 2 short edges, and sew the long edges to the page back.

Finishing the Page with Ribbon Tab Hangers

Additional supplies:
1/4 yard of 1 1/2″-wide ribbon

1. Follow Steps 1 and 2 of Assembling the Page (page 33).
2. Cut 2 lengths 3 1/2″ long of 1 1/2″-wide ribbon.
3. Fold each length of ribbon in half widthwise, wrong sides together. Pin the ribbon to the top edge of the page back, 2 1/4″ in from each side and matching raw edges.

Pin ribbon tabs to page back.

4. Complete Steps 3–12 of Assembling the Page (page 33).

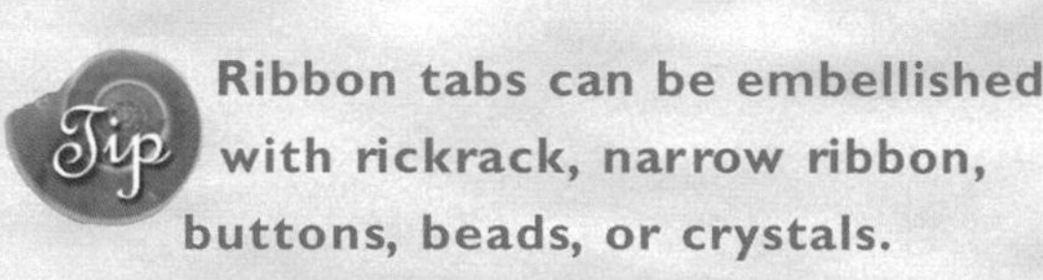

Ribbon tabs can be embellished with rickrack, narrow ribbon, buttons, beads, or crystals.

Finishing the Page with Bow Tab Hangers

Additional supplies (makes 2 Bow Tabs):

- *1 yard 1″-wide grosgrain ribbon*
- *Fray Check*
- *Fabri-Tac glue*

Cut notch.

1. Cut 2 lengths 5″ long, 2 lengths 6½″ long, and 2 lengths 2½″ long of the 1″-wide grosgrain ribbon.
2. Cut a V-shaped notch at one end of each 5″ ribbon. Apply Fray Check to all cut ends on *all* ribbon lengths.

Fold ribbon to form loop.

3. Take 1 notched 5″ ribbon, and fold the top (un-notched) end to the back so the ribbon forms a loop and measures 3¼″. Glue the loop with Fabri-Tac to secure in place.

Make circle.

4. Make a circle with 1 length of ribbon 6½″ long, overlapping ends about ¼″, so that when flattened it will create a bow about 3″ wide. Glue the overlapped ends to secure in place.

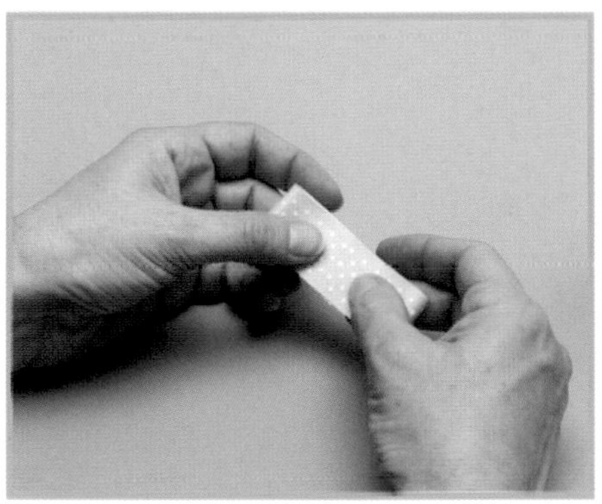

Flatten and glue to form bow.

5. Flatten the ribbon circle to create a bow, and glue the center to secure in place.

Wrap bow.

6. Wrap the bow with 1 length of ribbon 2½″ long, and glue the center to secure in place.

Glue to loop.

7. Glue the wrapped bow to the loop from Step 3, leaving a scant 1″ above the bow for the hanger loop.
8. Repeat Steps 3–7 to form a second bow tab hanger.
9. Complete Steps 1–12 of Assembling the Page (page 33).
10. Glue the bow tab hangers to the completed page with Fabri-Tac, 1″ in from each side.

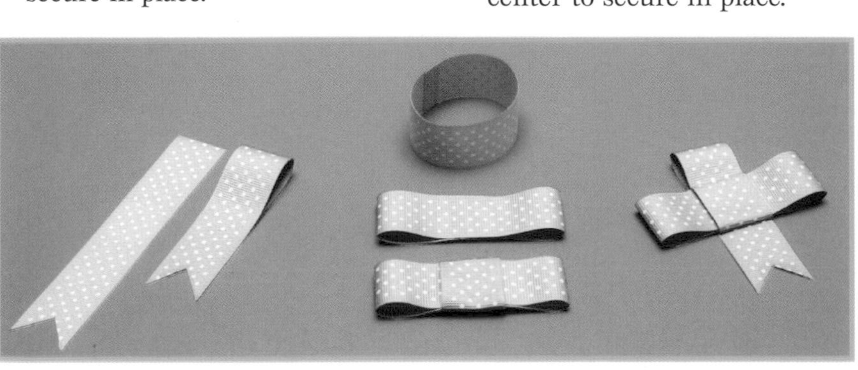

Making Decorative Hanging Rods

You can make hanging rods with wood dowels and finials from the craft store that you paint and embellish to complement the theme of your page. I like 3/8″ dowels for these small fabric scrapbook pages. For finials, look for flat wood shapes such, as hearts, spools, rolling pins, squares, trees, leaves, and cactus which can be decorated with coins, metal spirals, buttons, bows, beads, or other embellishments to match those on your page.

If you prefer, hang your page from a purchased café curtain rod. You will probably need to shorten it for a 12″ × 12″ page. To do so, simply remove the finials from the café rod, and mark the rod 2″ wider than the finished page. Cut on the mark carefully with a hacksaw or jeweler's saw.

EMBELLISHING WOOD HANGING RODS AND FINIALS

What You'll Need

- 36″ long 3/8″ dowel
- Dowel caps or wood shapes for finials
- Coping saw
- Fine sandpaper, 220 grit
- Acrylic paints
- Foam brushes
- Small synthetic brush for detail work (optional)
- Matte or gloss interior varnish
- Embellishments
- Fabri-Tac and Gem-Tac glues

Prepare and Paint Dowel and Finials

1. Cut the dowel to 14″ with a coping saw (or 2″ longer than the finished width of the page).
2. Sand the dowel and wood pieces with sandpaper to remove rough areas. Wipe with a damp (not wet) paper towel and let dry.
3. Cover your work surface with paper or plastic.
4. Paint the dowel and dowel caps. You will need two (maybe three) coats of paint for complete coverage. Let the paint dry between coats.

> **Tip** Between coats of paint and varnish, wash the brush and squeeze it dry. Cover your paint with plastic wrap. Acrylic paint dries very quickly.

5. Apply 1 coat of matte or gloss varnish. Let it dry.
6. Add three-dimensional embellishments last. Use Fabri-Tac to adhere soft items like thread-wrapped spools (page 69), ribbon flowers, and twigs. Use Gem-Tac to adhere smooth items like coins, charms, and washers.

Judy, Sue, and Cathy - packed for Empty Spools

Asilomar or Bust
Metal spiral is glued to finial.

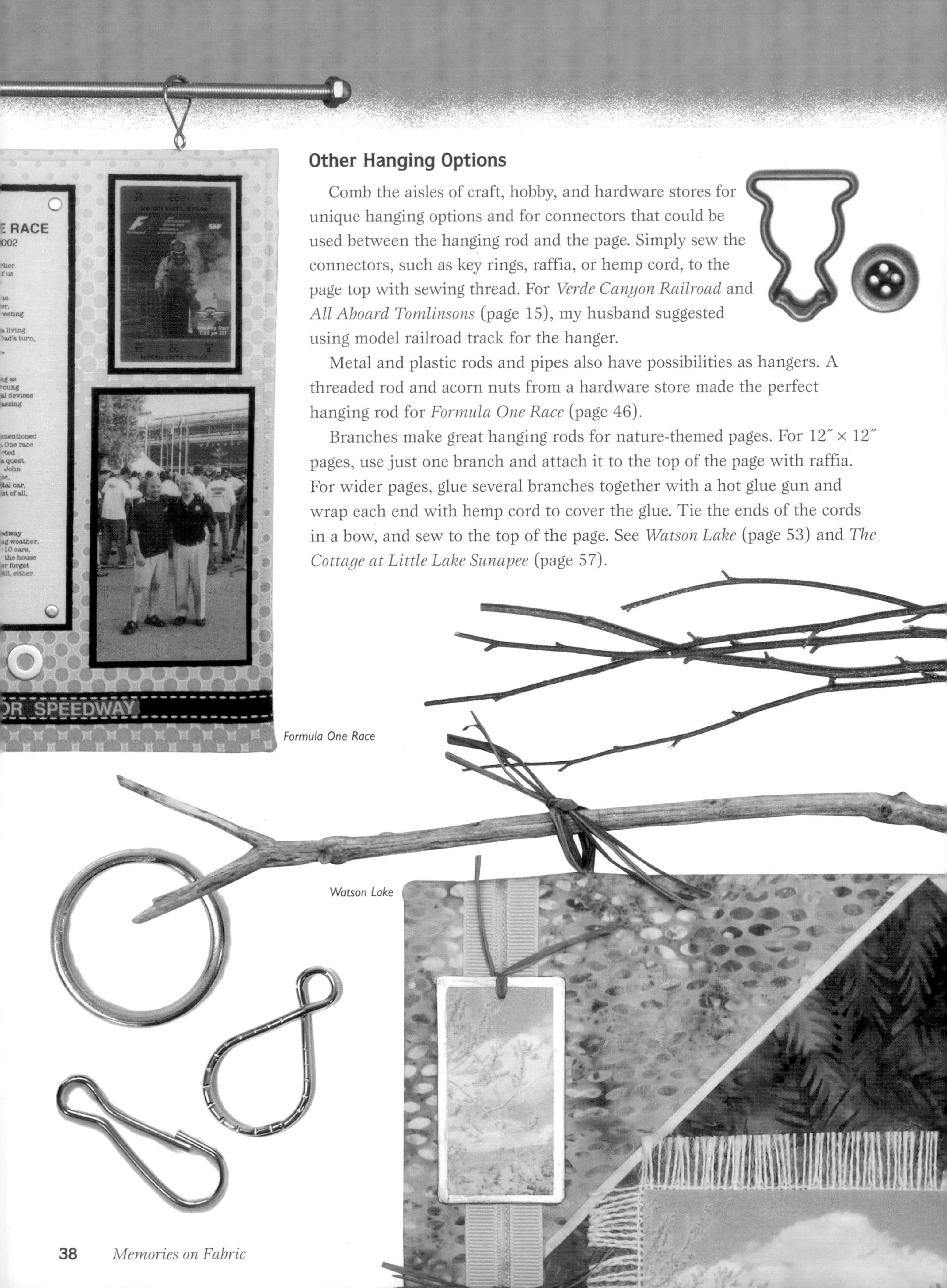

Other Hanging Options

Comb the aisles of craft, hobby, and hardware stores for unique hanging options and for connectors that could be used between the hanging rod and the page. Simply sew the connectors, such as key rings, raffia, or hemp cord, to the page top with sewing thread. For *Verde Canyon Railroad* and *All Aboard Tomlinsons* (page 15), my husband suggested using model railroad track for the hanger.

Metal and plastic rods and pipes also have possibilities as hangers. A threaded rod and acorn nuts from a hardware store made the perfect hanging rod for *Formula One Race* (page 46).

Branches make great hanging rods for nature-themed pages. For 12″ × 12″ pages, use just one branch and attach it to the top of the page with raffia. For wider pages, glue several branches together with a hot glue gun and wrap each end with hemp cord to cover the glue. Tie the ends of the cords in a bow, and sew to the top of the page. See *Watson Lake* (page 53) and *The Cottage at Little Lake Sunapee* (page 57).

Formula One Race

Watson Lake

Projects

Liquitex
ACRYLIC
ARTIST COLOR
NAPHTHOL CRIMSON
59 mL e 2 U.S. fl. oz.
Thread Heaven
Thread Conditioner

A Day at the Theme Park

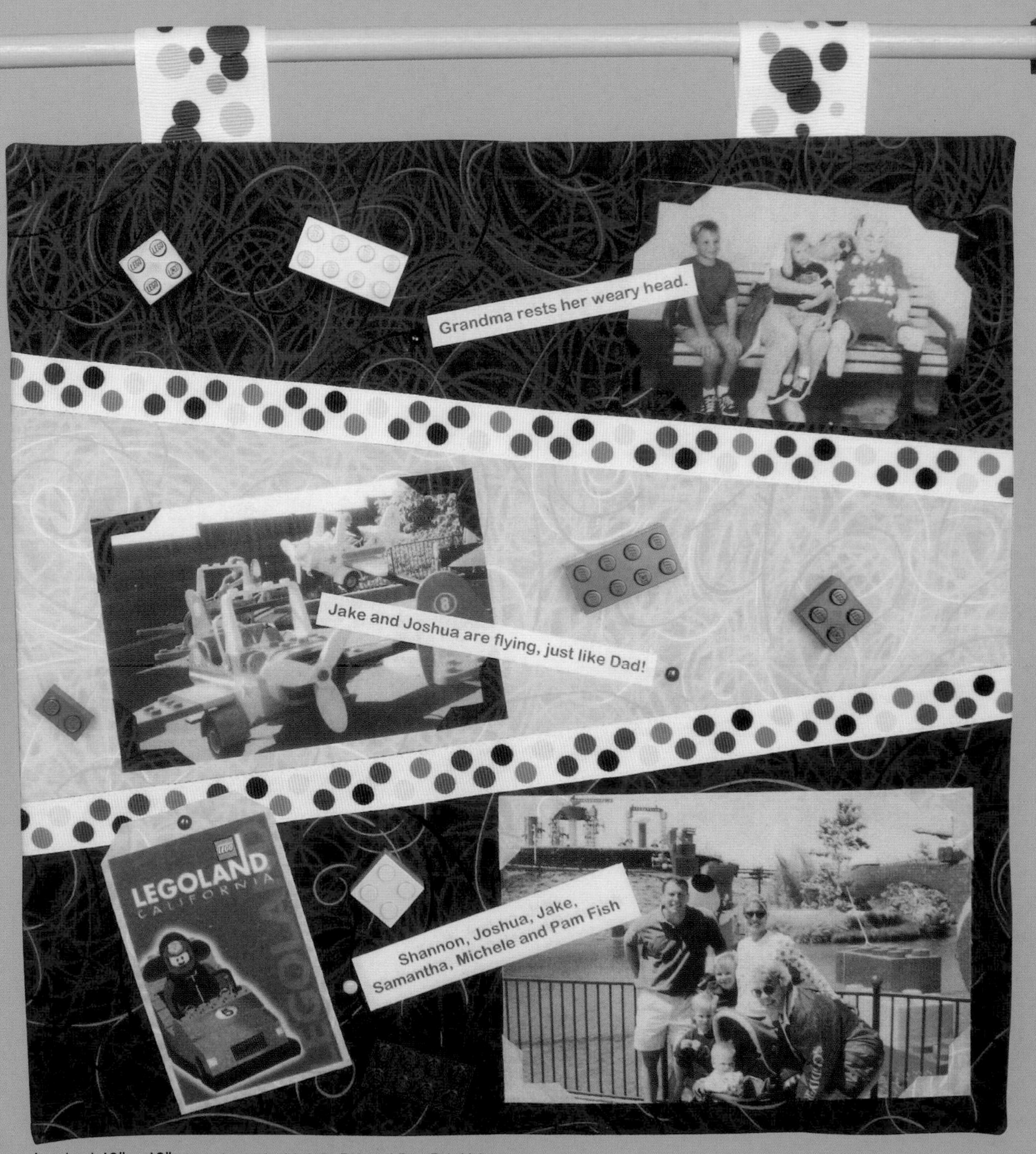

Grandma rests her weary head.
Jake and Joshua are flying, just like Dad!
LEGOLAND
CALIFORNIA
Shannon, Joshua, Jake,
Samantha, Michele and Pam Fish

Legoland, 12" × 12", page photos by Michele Fish and Pam Fish Hale

Oh, to be a kid again and spend a day or two at a theme park! Happy theme park visits are great subjects for scrapbook pages. Snap a picture of the whole family and of the park's sign to use as your title. Or use your ticket as the title, as I did here. Select bright background fabrics and fuse your photos and captions at different angles to give the page energy. Visit theme park souvenir shops for charms, buttons, magnets, embroidered appliqués, and party decorations to attach to the page. Didn't do it when you were there? Visit their souvenir shops on the Internet. Try craft and scrapbook stores for novelty buttons and packages of summer-themed embellishments. Ask friends and family with young kids and lots of little toys for help. That's how I got the Lego bricks! Leave room for captions or a short story about the day so you won't forget how special it was.

What You'll Need

For Basic Supplies, refer to pages 6–8.

- 3 photos, 1 ticket, captions, and theme park souvenirs
- 1 fat quarter of bright fabric for the page front center, fabric tag, and photo corners
- 2 fat quarters of bright fabric for the page front top and bottom and the photo corners
- 1 fat quarter for the page back
- 2 white inkjet fabric sheets
- 2 sheets of Steam-A-Seam 2 Double-Stick fusible web, 9″ × 12″
- 1 yard of 5/8″ coordinating ribbon for accent trim
- 4 brads
- 1/4 yard of 1 1/2″ coordinating ribbon for hanging tabs
- 14″ × 14″ square of fast2fuse double-sided stiff interfacing
- 3/8″ dowel, cut 14″ long
- Fine sandpaper, 220 grit
- Acrylic paint and brush
- Wood shapes or souvenirs for finials
- Gloss varnish and brush
- Hot glue gun for wood shapes or Gem-Tac glue for smooth surfaces (such as Lego bricks)

Making the Page

Refer to Scrapbook Page Basics, pages 9–10 and Preparation, pages 11–18.

Make the Page Front and Back

1. Cut 1 square 14″ × 14″ of fabric for the page front. Cut 1 rectangle 7″ × 14″ of fabric for the page front top and 1 rectangle 7″ × 14″ of fabric for the bottom.
2. Place the 14″ × 14″ square on your ironing board. Place the top rectangle on the square, right side up, aligning the top and side edges. Place the bottom rectangle on the square, right side up; align the bottom and side edges.
3. Use the *Legoland* photo as a guide. Fold under the inside long edges of each rectangle at a gentle angle so that a photo can be positioned in each wedge at least 1″ from the outer edges. Press the fold lines, and pin the rectangles in place.
4. Topstitch a scant 1/8″ along the folded edges of the rectangles. Trim the excess fabric from behind the top and bottom wedges.
5. Cut 2 lengths 18″ long of the 5/8″ ribbon. Center the cut ribbon over each seam, and sew the ribbon, along both edges, with matching thread. Trim the extra ribbon length even with the side edges.
6. Cut 1 square 14″ × 14″ of fabric for the page back.

Design and Print

Refer to Designing the Page Layout, pages 20–21 and Printing on Fabric, pages 22–23.

1. Copy or print the photos, the ticket (or other souvenirs), and captions on paper.

2. Use the preview window (page 19) and the paper copies to design your layout. Adjust copy sizes as needed to fit.
3. Make a final copy of the photos, ticket (or other souvenirs), and captions on the fabric sheets. Remove the paper backing.
4. Rinse the fabric sheets according to the manufacturer's directions, and let dry.

Put It Together

1. Frame the layout area with the preview window.
2. Iron fusible web to the back of the dry fabric sheets.
3. Remove the fusible paper backing. Trim the images and captions as needed to fit the page.
4. Arrange and fuse all printed items to the page, except the ticket.
5. Pierce the fabric with a stiletto, and attach a brad next to each caption.
6. Use the ticket to make the fabric tag (see Special Techniques, below), and attach it to the page with a brad.
7. Make the photo corners (see Special Techniques, below), and fuse them to the photos.
8. Finish the page with 1½″-wide ribbon tab hangers (see Finishing the Page with Ribbon Tab Hangers, page 35).
9. Glue or sew three-dimensional souvenirs to the page.
10. Sand, paint, and varnish the dowel and wood finials (see page 37). Insert the dowel through the hanging tabs. Glue the finials to the dowel with a hot glue gun or Gem-Tac.

Special Techniques

Make a Fabric Tag

1. Cut 2 rectangles ½″ wider than the ticket (or other item) on all sides.
2. Iron fusible web to the back of 1 rectangle. Align and fuse the rectangles together, wrong sides facing. Fuse the fabric ticket to the rectangle.
3. Fussy cut into a tag shape.
4. Attach the tag to the page front with a brad.

Make Photo Corners

Makes 4 photo corners.

1. Iron a 1½″ × 2½″ piece of fusible web to a strip of fabric similar in size. Note: The fusible web is larger than needed to ensure proper coverage on finished photo corners.

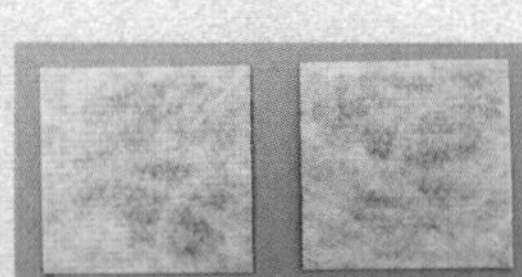
Cut into squares.

2. With the paper side facing up, cut the strip into 2 squares ⅞″ × ⅞″.
3. Cut each square in half diagonally to form 4 triangles.

Cut on diagonal.

4. Draw a line through the center of the triangle from the long edge to the opposite point. Mark a dot on the center line ¼″ above the long edge and a dot ¼″ from each side of the center line on the long edge. Connect the dots with a ruler to draw a small inner triangle.

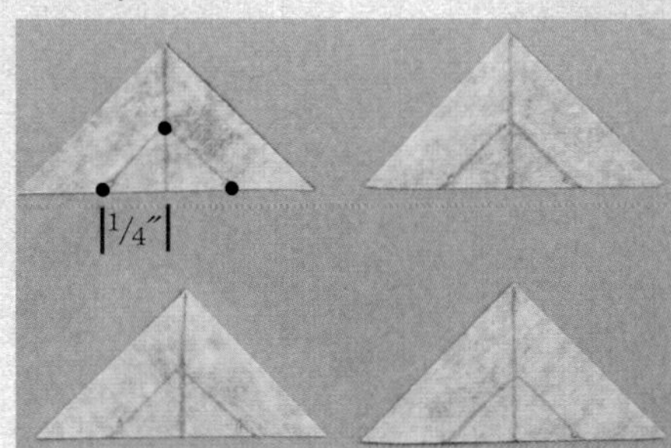

Mark for cutting notches.

Tip Tape the tip of the triangle to your table to keep it from wiggling around while you are marking the cutting lines for the notch.

5. Cut out the inner triangle to form a notch. Use 4 corners for each photo.

Cut notches.

Letters Home

Letters from Matt, 12" × 12", page photos by Steve Zeman

My younger son spent his junior year in Germany in the early 1990s. I saved Matt's letters and envelopes, and he kept his souvenirs and coins. I printed a page from one of his letters for part of the page background. The pinked and fringed edges of the main photo's border simulate the torn edges used in paper scrapbooking. Iron-On Ribbon applied with a mini-iron frames the photos on the left. The twill tape with Journey printed on it and the blue dots were scrapbook store finds. You'll find plenty of travel theme embellishments there, even tiny passports and suitcases! Since the story of his year abroad is printed on a T-shirt on the back of the page, this page is displayed on a tabletop easel I found in a craft store.

What You'll Need

For Basic Supplies, refer to pages 6–8.

- 1 letter 8½″ × 11″, photos, title, souvenirs, and coins
- 1 fat quarter of fabric for the side strip and page back
- 1 fat quarter of fabric or scraps for the title bar and torn-edge photo border
- 4 white inkjet fabric sheets
- 3 sheets of Steam-A-Seam 2 Double-Stick fusible web, 9″ × 12″
- 1 package of narrow Iron-On Ribbon for photo borders
- Mini-iron (optional for Iron-On Ribbon)
- Printed twill tape
- 4 blue plastic adhesive-backed dots
- 6″ of 6-strand embroidery floss for the tag
- Rotary cutter with pinking blade
- 14″ × 14″ square of fast2fuse double-sided stiff interfacing
- Fabri-Tac and Gem-Tac glues
- Tabletop easel

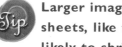

Select border fabric with good contrast to the background fabric so the torn edges will show.

Making the Page

Refer to Scrapbook Page Basics, pages 9–10 and Preparation, pages 11–18.

Make the Page Front and Back

I printed the letter, full size, on an 8½" × 11" pretreated fabric sheet. I made the page front 12½" × 12½" instead of the usual 14" × 14" to avoid cutting into the letter during the finishing steps.

1. Print the letter on a fabric sheet, and remove the paper backing. Rinse according to the manufacturer's directions, and let dry.

Larger images printed on fabric sheets, like this letter, are more likely to shrink and dry distorted. Wait until the images are dry, and then square them up before sewing or fusing web to them.

2. Square up the fabric letter and press it. Measure the height and width.
3. Subtract the height of the letter from 13″. Cut your title bar fabric to measure this calculated height by the width of the letter.
4. Subtract the width of the letter from 13″. Cut your fabric to create a side strip that measures this calculated width by 12½″ tall.
5. Make the 12½″ × 12½″ page front by sewing the title bar to the bottom of the letter using a ¼″ seam allowance. Press the seam allowances open. Then, sew the side strip to the left side of the letter. Press the seam allowances open.
6. Cut 1 square 12½″ × 12½″ of fabric for the page back.

Design and Print

Refer to Designing the Page Layout, pages 20–21 and Printing on Fabric, pages 22–23.

1. Copy or print the photos, souvenirs, and title on paper.
2. Use the paper copies to design your layout. Adjust copy sizes as needed to fit. You will not need a preview window for this page. Just remember to leave enough room for 1/4″ seam allowances on all sides.
3. Make a final copy of the photos, souvenirs, and title on the fabric sheets. Remove the paper backing.
4. Rinse the fabric sheets according to the manufacturer's directions, and let dry.

Put It Together

1. Iron fusible web to the back of the dry fabric sheets.
2. Remove the fusible paper backing. Trim the photos, souvenirs, and title as needed to fit the page.
3. Make a torn-edge border (see Special Technique, right) for the main photo. Fuse the photo to the border.
4. Arrange and fuse all the printed items, except the souvenir tag, to the page.
5. Fussy cut the souvenir tag. Tie a knot in the embroidery floss, and glue the floss to the souvenir tag with Fabri-Tac. Fuse the tag to the page.
6. Glue the twill tape onto the page with Fabri-Tac.
7. Cut the Iron-On Ribbon in lengths sufficient to border the edges of the remaining photos. Follow the ribbon manufacturer's directions for pressing time and temperature, and fuse in place.
8. Finish the page for a tabletop easel display, omitting Step 1 of Assembling the Page (page 33) because the page is already trimmed to size.
9. Polish the coins and glue them onto the page with Gem-Tac. Glue the adhesive-backed dots to the page.

Make tag and fuse to page.

Special Technique

Make the Torn-Edge Image Border

1. Measure the fabric photo. Cut a piece of border fabric 1/2″ wider than the photo on all sides.
2. Cut a piece of fusible web the same size as your photo. Center and iron it to the back of the border.
3. Staystitch around the edges of the fusible web with matching thread.
4. With the fusible web paper side facing up, cut wavy edges around the fabric with a pinking blade.

Cut wavy edges.

5. Leave the paper backing on the fusible web. First, use a pin to pick out the small threads to fringe the hills made by the pinking blade. Next, pick out the longer threads along each side, one at a time, to minimize tangling. Stop fringing at the staystitching line.

Fray edges.

6. Place the border on a pressing sheet, paper side down. Place the photo, fusible side down, on the border, and fuse in place. Remove the paper backing from the bordered image, and fuse to the page.

Guys' Day Out

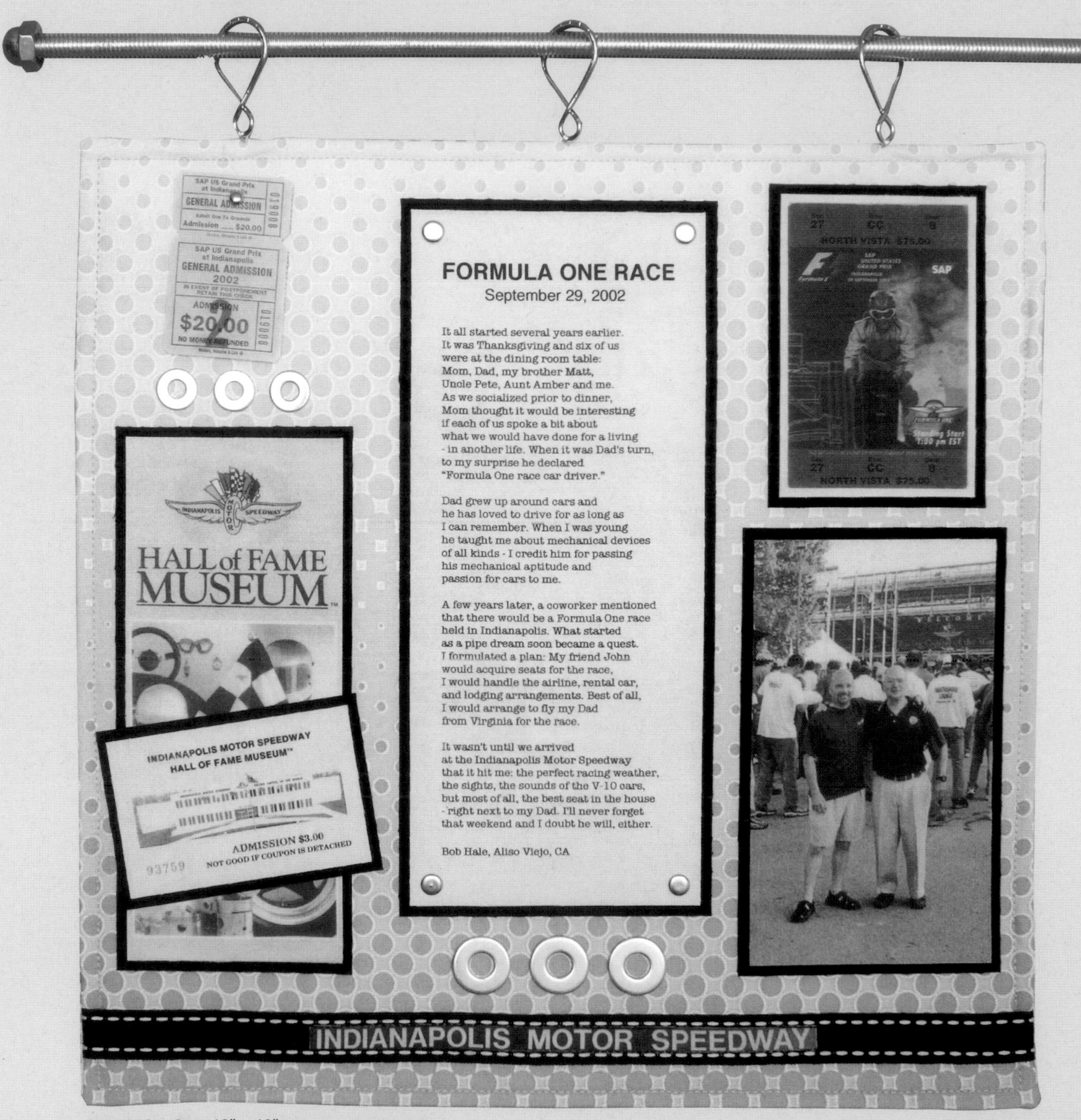

SAP US Grand Prix at Indianapolis
GENERAL ADMISSION
Admission $20.00
SAP US Grand Prix at Indianapolis
GENERAL ADMISSION
2002
ADMISSION
$20.00
NO MONEY REFUNDED
FORMULA ONE RACE
September 29, 2002
It all started several years earlier.
It was Thanksgiving and six of us
were at the dining room table:
Mom, Dad, my brother Matt,
Uncle Pete, Aunt Amber and me.
As we socialized prior to dinner,
Mom thought it would be interesting
if each of us spoke a bit about
what we would have done for a living
- in another life. When it was Dad's turn,
to my surprise he declared
"Formula One race car driver."
Dad grew up around cars and
he has loved to drive for as long as
I can remember. When I was young
he taught me about mechanical devices
of all kinds - I credit him for passing
his mechanical aptitude and
passion for cars to me.
A few years later, a coworker mentioned
that there would be a Formula One race
held in Indianapolis. What started
as a pipe dream soon became a quest.
I formulated a plan: My friend John
would acquire seats for the race,
I would handle the airline, rental car,
and lodging arrangements. Best of all,
I would arrange to fly my Dad
from Virginia for the race.
It wasn't until we arrived
at the Indianapolis Motor Speedway
that it hit me: the perfect racing weather,
the sights, the sounds of the V-10 cars,
but most of all, the best seat in the house
- right next to my Dad. I'll never forget
that weekend and I doubt he will, either.
Bob Hale, Aliso Viejo, CA
NORTH VISTA $75.00
SAP
HALL of FAME
MUSEUM
INDIANAPOLIS MOTOR SPEEDWAY
HALL OF FAME MUSEUM™
ADMISSION $3.00
NOT GOOD IF COUPON IS DETACHED
93759
INDIANAPOLIS MOTOR SPEEDWAY

Formula One Race, 12" × 12", page photo by Alan Peltier

An engaging dinner-table conversation led to this weekend of fun at the races for my husband and son. I redesigned this layout several times until I realized that the story block belonged in the center because the story itself is the star of this page! For other masculine themes, think NASCAR races, car meets, sports events, fishing trips, home-improvement projects, and bachelor parties. Find metal snaps, eyelets, brads, and all sorts of ribbons at scrapbook and craft stores. Look for the shiny figure-8 key rings to connect the page to the hanging rod in snap and ring assortment packs at a craft store. Visit your hardware or home-improvement store for washers and threaded rods for the hanger and acorn nuts for finials.

To make the title for the page, I enlarged a 4" × 6" photo to 8$^1/_2$" × 11" so the lettering on the sign was large enough to use as the title on the bottom of the page.

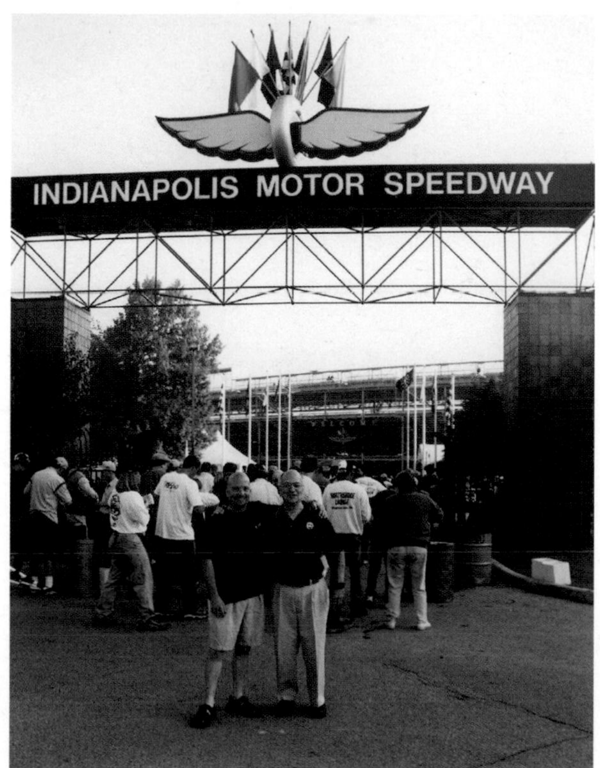

Enlarge photos with signs to use as page titles.

What You'll Need

For Basic Supplies refer to pages 6–8.

- 1 enlarged photo 8$^1/_2$″ × 11″ with a sign for the page title
- Souvenirs, ticket, and story block
- 2 fat quarters of fabric for page front and back
- 1 fat quarter of fabric for photo borders
- Scrap of fabric for back of ticket
- 3 white inkjet fabric sheets
- 3 sheets of Steam-A-Seam 2 Double-Stick fusible web, 9″ × 12″
- $^1/_2$ yard $^5/_8$″ ribbon
- 4 metal snaps
- Eyelet setter and hammer
- 1 metal brad
- 14″ × 14″ square of fast2fuse double-sided stiff interfacing
- 6 washers in 2 sizes (3 each)
- 3 figure-8 key rings
- $^5/_{16}$″ diameter threaded rod, cut 14″ long
- 2 metal acorn nuts ($^5/_{16}$″) for finials
- Gem-Tac glue

Making the Page

Refer to Scrapbook Page Basics, pages 9–10 and Preparation, pages 11–18.

Make the Page Front and Back

1. Cut 2 squares of fabric 14″ × 14″ for the page front and back.

Design and Print

Refer to Designing the Page Layout, pages 20–21 and Printing on Fabric, pages 22–23

1. Copy or print the $8^{1}/_{2}$″ × 11″ photo, souvenirs, ticket, and story block on paper.
2. Use the preview window (page 19) and the paper copies to design your layout. Adjust copy sizes as needed to fit.
3. Make a final copy of the $8^{1}/_{2}$″ × 11″ photo, souvenirs, ticket, and story block on the fabric sheets. Remove the paper backing.
4. Rinse the fabric sheets according to the manufacturer's directions, and let dry.

Put It Together

1. Frame the layout area with the preview window.
2. Iron fusible web to the back of the dry fabric sheets and border fabric.
3. Cut a 14″ length of the $^{5}/_{8}$″ ribbon, and sew it $1^{1}/_{4}$″ above the bottom of the page.
4. Remove the fusible paper backing from the fabric sheets. Trim the sign from the photo for the page title. Trim the other images as needed to fit the page.
5. Fuse the photo, souvenirs, and story block to the border fabric.
6. Set the 4 snaps on the story block (see Special Technique, right).
7. Remove the fusible paper backing from the border fabric. Fuse the story block to the center of the page. Arrange and fuse the photo and souvenirs to the page. Fuse the title to the ribbon.
8. Fuse the ticket to the wrong side of a fabric scrap and fussy cut. Attach it to the page with a brad.
9. Finish the page (see Finishing Instructions, pages 32–33).
10. Glue the washers to the page with Gem-Tac.
11. Sew 3 figure-8 key rings to the top of the page, 4″ apart. Insert the metal rod through the rings, and screw on the acorn nuts.

Special Technique

Set the Snaps

1. Mark a dot for the snap in each corner of the bordered story block, $^{1}/_{4}$″ to $^{3}/_{8}$″ in from each edge.
2. Remove the fusible paper backing. Clip a small hole at each mark for the snap.

Clip small hole at each mark.

3. Insert a snap through the hole from the front, and flip the story block face down on a board or telephone book.

Set your snaps and eyelets on an old kitchen cutting board.

4. Insert the eyelet setter in the snap, and pound the flange flat with a hammer to secure it. Repeat for each corner.

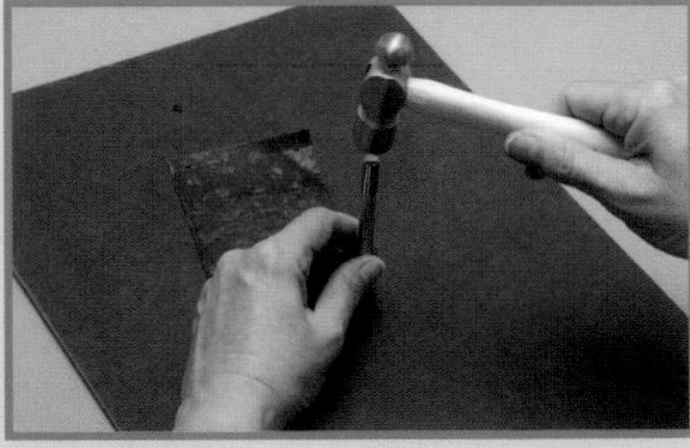

Pound flange flat.

Make the holes and set the snaps or eyelets before fusing the fabric image to the page front. You ll have fewer layers to cut through.

Bundle of Joy

Sweet Baby Girl, 12" × 12", page photo by Vance Copenhaver

A newborn's first photo, birth announcement in a vellum envelope, and a handwritten letter from the happy new mom make a neat gift page for Grandma. Check your quilt shop for a cute baby print and the craft store for pink or blue ribbon and jumbo rickrack. While you're there, check the cake-decorating section for little baby-shower embellishments. Visit the scrapbook section for alphabet block beads, twill tape or satin ribbon printed with "It's a girl" or "It's a boy," packages of tiny buttons and safety pins, cardstock, and vellum. Hang the page with grosgrain bow tabs for a girl or ribbon tabs for a boy.

What You'll Need

For Basic Supplies, refer to pages 6–8.

- Photo, letter, and announcement
- 1 fat quarter of a baby print fabric, tiny check, or dot for the page front
- 1 fat quarter for the photo borders and page back
- 3″ square of fabric for the heart
- 1 white inkjet fabric sheet
- 1 sheet of white cardstock
- 2 sheets of Steam-A-Seam 2 Double-Stick fusible web, 9″ × 12″
- Rotary cutter with pinking blade
- 1″ grosgrain ribbon: *Girl:* 1½ yards; *Boy:* ¼ yard
- 1 package of Jumbo Rickrack
- 3″ × 3″ square of template plastic
- Alphabet block beads
- Small buttons and safety pins
- 1 yard of ⅛″ satin ribbon
- 14″ × 14″ square of fast2fuse double-sided stiff interfacing
- 1 sheet of vellum 8½″ × 11″
- Acid-free glue stick
- ⅜″ dowel, cut 14″ long
- Fine sandpaper, 220 grit
- Acrylic paint and brush
- 2 acorn dowel caps, ⅜″ (Lara's Crafts, see Resources, page 70)
- Gloss varnish and brush
- Fabri-Tac glue
- Hot glue gun

Making the Page

Refer to Scrapbook Page Basics, pages 9–10 and Preparation, pages 11–18.

Make the Page Front and Back

1. Cut 2 squares 14″ × 14″ of fabric for the page front and back.

Design and Print

Refer to Designing the Page Layout, pages 20–21 and Printing on Fabric, pages 22–23.

1. Copy or print the photo and letter on paper.
2. Use the preview window (page 19) and the paper copies to design your layout. Adjust copy sizes as needed to fit.
3. Copy the announcement card on cardstock.
4. Print a final copy of the photo and letter on the fabric sheet. Remove the paper backing.
5. Rinse the fabric sheet according to the manufacturer's directions, and let it dry.

Put It Together

1. Frame the layout area with the preview window.
2. Iron fusible web to the back of the dry fabric sheets, the border fabric, and the heart fabric.
3. Remove the fusible paper backing from the fabric sheets. Trim the photo and letter with the pinking blade. Fuse them to the border fabric. Then, trim the borders with the pinking blade.
4. Remove the fusible paper backing from the border fabric. Arrange and fuse the photo and letter to the page.

5. Sew the 1″ grosgrain ribbon $1\frac{5}{8}$″ above the lower edge of the page.
6. Glue the rickrack along the lower edge of the ribbon with Fabri-Tac.
7. Trace the heart shape onto template plastic, and cut it out. Place the template on the back of the fusible-backed heart fabric, and trace. Cut out the heart, remove the paper backing, and fuse the heart above the ribbon.

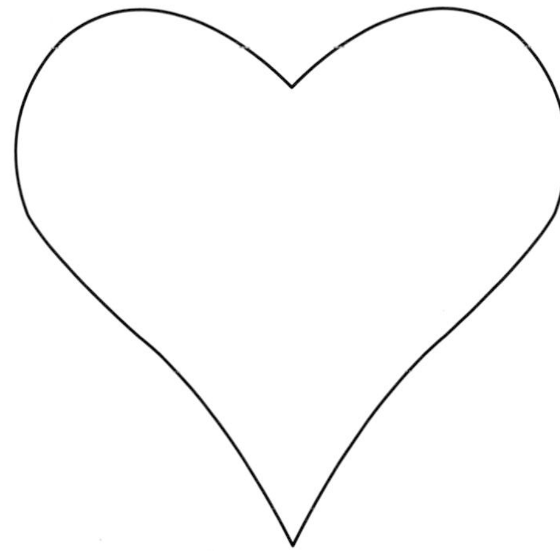

Trace heart on template plastic.

8. Sew the alphabet block beads on the grosgrain ribbon, forming the baby's name. Sew buttons and safety pins on the page.
9. Cut 5 lengths 6″ long of $\frac{1}{8}$″ satin ribbon, and tie each into tiny bows. Glue 4 bows on the page, reserving 1 for the vellum envelope.
10. Finish the page with bow tab hangers for a girl or ribbon tab hangers for a boy (pages 35–36).
11. Make a vellum envelope (see Special Technique, below). Glue the envelope to the page with Fabri-Tac. Glue the last $\frac{1}{8}$″ bow to the flap.
12. Sand, paint, and varnish the dowel and the dowel caps. Insert the dowel through the ribbon tabs, and glue the dowel caps to the dowel with a hot glue gun.

Special Technique

Make a Vellum Envelope

1. Cut a square of vellum at least $1\frac{3}{4}$″ wider than the longest side of the card. Place the vellum on-point on your rotary mat.
2. Center the announcement card on the vellum, using the rotary mat lines as a guide. With a sharp pencil, draw a light line around all sides of the card.

Tip Always make a sample envelope with plain paper first to check for fit.

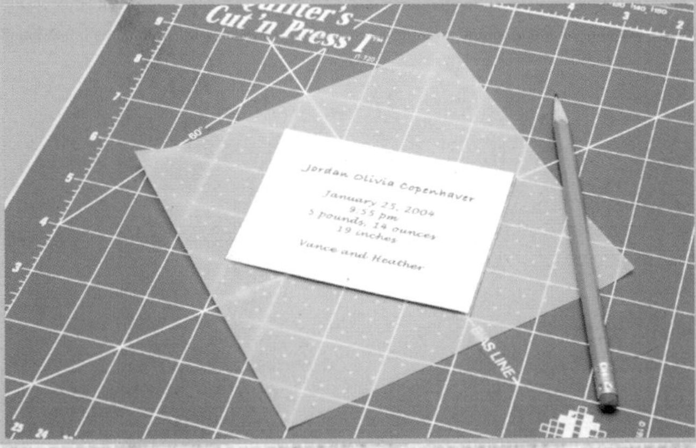

Draw light lines around card.

3. Create 4 flaps by folding the vellum just *outside* the drawn lines, providing room for the card to fit when the envelope is complete. Use template plastic for folding the vellum. The rigid plastic will aid in obtaining crisp, straight fold lines. Erase the lines.

Fold just outside line.

4. Unfold the vellum, and trim all 4 sides with a pinking blade, keeping a scant 1/4″ away from the fold line intersections.

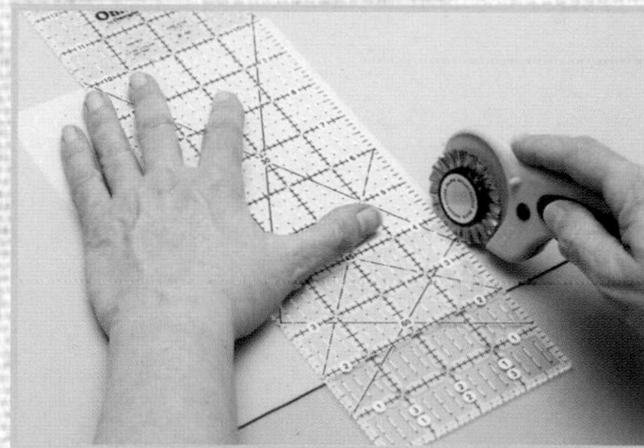

Trim edges.

5. Cut notches where the fold lines intersect.

Cut 4 notches.

6. Place the card on the envelope, and refold the side and bottom flaps. Mark a horizontal trimming line on the bottom flap. Unfold the envelope, remove the card, and trim on the line with a pinking blade.

Mark horizontal line, and trim.

7. Glue the bottom flap to the side flaps with a touch of glue stick. Insert the card.

Glue bottom flap to side flaps.

To avoid creasing the paper during the finishing steps, attach vellum envelopes after the scrapbook page is assembled and ready for display.

Nature's Beauty

Watson Lake, 12" × 12", page photo by Sue Hale

I took this picture on a perfect spring day. The lake was still, and the reflection was beautiful. Unfortunately, I had the camera's date and time stamp turned on, and it printed in bright orange in the bottom right corner. It was even more noticeable when I enlarged the photo. That's what embellishments are for! At the scrapbook store, I found a package of little metal signs. Nature's Beauty was just the right size to conceal the stamp. I also found the metal-edged tags there. I colored the sign and the edges of the tags with a marker to coordinate with the fabric and ribbon. You'll also find tags to embellish in all sizes and shapes in office-supply stores. Add some texture to the photo with a fringed burlap border. There are lots of great subjects from nature: mountain scenes, waterfalls, beaches, fields of wildflowers, and autumn foliage are just a few. Don't forget to scavenge a fallen branch if you can; it makes a neat hanger.

What You'll Need

For Basic Supplies, refer to pages 6–8.

- 1 photo 5″ × 7″ and title
- 1 fat quarter of dark fabric for the center block
- 1/2 yard of a medium fabric for the page front and back
- 1 white inkjet fabric sheet
- 1 cream or natural inkjet fabric sheet
- 3 sheets of Steam-A-Seam 2 Double-Stick fusible web, 9″ × 12″
- Rotary cutter with pinking blade
- 1/3 yard of burlap
- 1 1/2 yards of 1/8″ satin ribbon
- 1 yard of 3/8″ grosgrain ribbon
- Tiger Tape or white correction tape (optional)
- 14″ × 14″ square of fast2fuse double-sided stiff interfacing
- 1 small metal sign
- 3 small tags with metal edges, approx. 1 1/4″ × 2 1/2″
- COPIC marker, E15, Dark Suntan
- 2 1/4 yards of raffia
- Branch, cut about 17″ long
- Fabri-Tac glue

Making the Page

Refer to Scrapbook Page Basics, pages 9–10 and Preparation, pages 11–18.

Make the Page Front and Back

1. Cut 2 squares 14″ × 14″ from the medium fabric for the page front and back.
2. Cut 1 square 9 1/2″ × 9 1/2″ from the dark fabric. Iron fusible web to the back and trim to 8 1/2″ × 8 1/2″ square.
3. Center the dark square, set on-point, on the page front. Fuse it in place.

Design and Print

Refer to Designing the Page Layout, pages 20–21 and Printing on Fabric, pages 22–23.

1. Print 2 copies of the 5″ × 7″ photo and 1 copy of the title on paper.
2. Use the preview window (page 19) and the paper copies to design your layout. Adjust copy sizes as needed to fit.
3. Make 2 copies of the photo on the white fabric sheet (see Tip at the top of page 69). Make a final copy of the title on a cream or natural fabric sheet. Remove the paper backing.
4. Rinse the fabric sheets according to the manufacturer's directions, and let dry.

If you can t find cream or natural fabric sheets, mix a little brown acrylic paint into white paint thinned with water, and apply it to a white fabric sheet with a sponge or foam brush after printing.

Put It Together

1. Frame the layout area with the preview window.
2. Iron fusible web to the back of the dry fabric sheets.
3. Remove the fusible paper backing from the title and 1 of the 5″ × 7″ photos. Trim the photo with a straight edge rotary cutter blade and the title with a pinking blade. Set the second photo aside for making the tags.
4. Cut 4 lengths of the 1/8″ ribbon 9″ long. Glue them along the edges of the 8 1/2″ square with Fabri-Tac, trimming as needed.
5. Cut an 8″ x 10″ rectangle of burlap. Spray it with water, and square it. Press it, and trim to 7″ x 9″. Cut a 5″ x 7″ rectangle of fusible web. Center the web on the burlap, lining up the edges of the web with the strands of the burlap. Fuse in place, and staystitch around the fusible web with matching thread.

Center fusible web on burlap.

6. Pull the jute strands out of the burlap, one at a time, until you reach the stitching lines. Fringe all sides.
7. Center the trimmed photo on the burlap, fusible side facing down, and fuse. Remove the fusible paper backing from the burlap, center it on the dark square, and fuse.
8. Cut a 14″ length of the 1/8″ ribbon. To keep the ribbon straight, adhere a strip of Tiger Tape or white correction tape 1 1/8″ from the left side of the page. Place the ribbon along the right side of the tape, and glue it to the page with Fabri-Tac. Remove the tape.

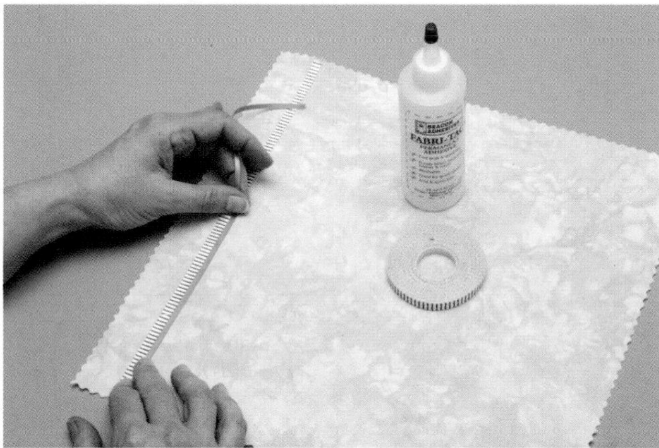

Glue ribbon next to tape.

9. Cut 2 lengths 14″ long of the 3/8″ grosgrain ribbon. Glue or sew a length of the 3/8″ ribbon on each side of the 1/8″ ribbon.
10. Finish the page (see Finishing Instructions, pages 32–33).
11. Make the tags (see Special Technique, page 56).
12. Cut 2 lengths (3 or 4 strands) 12″ long of raffia. Tie the raffia to the branch, leaving a loop below the knot. Sew the loop to the top of the page about 2″ in from each edge. Secure each raffia knot with a dot of Fabri-Tac.

Special Technique

Make the Metal Tags

1. Color the metal edges on both sides of the tag with the marker, and let dry. Repeat for a darker finish.
2. Remove the fusible paper backing from the second 5″ × 7″ fabric photo. Select 3 areas for the tag fronts and 3 areas for the tag backs, each approximately 1¼″ × 2½″. Trim the selected areas to fit the tags.
3. Fuse the tag fronts to the metal tags and let cool. Repeat for the tag backs.
4. Cut 9 lengths 6″ long of raffia. Thread 3 lengths through the hole on each tag, and tie it in a knot. Trim. Sew the tags to the page along the ⅛″ ribbon.

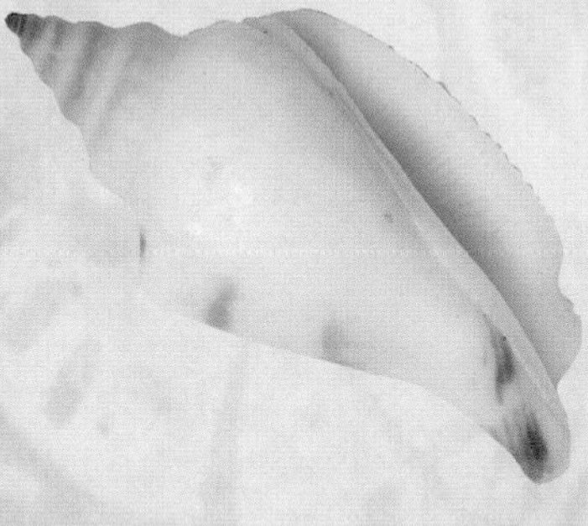

Tags add texture and movement to scrapbook pages. To make a fabric tag, simply fuse 2 pieces of fabric together, cut a tag shape, embellish, and attach to the page with a brad.

You can also buy tags, with or without metal frames, to embellish.

Choose from paper, plastic, and fabric in circles, squares, and rectangles. Fuse fabric motifs or embellish them with fabric, tiny shells, ribbon, fancy fibers, buttons, and paper stickers.

Summer Vacation

The Cottage at Little Lake Sunapee, 14" × 21 1/2", page photos by Robert R. Hale, David B. Hale, and Sue Hale

This cottage was the setting for many happy family gatherings over the years. I fused a collage of photos to a landscape of sky, mountains, and lake and glued on some natural elements I'd collected there. You can scrapbook your own favorite vacation spot on a panoramic page like this. If your favorite destination is the beach, fuse a landscape of sky, sand, and sea. You'll have room for lots of photos if you leave them borderless. Add a clear vinyl pocket or two, and fill it with shells and sea glass you've collected or purchased from a craft store. Scrapbook stores have lots of beach-themed embellishments to doll up your page. Look for little bikinis, sunglasses, flip-flops, and swim fins! Add a sleeve, and glue some shells to the ends of a dowel to complete the theme.

What You'll Need

For Basic Supplies, refer to pages 6–8.

- Photos, drawing (or an enlarged photo), and captions
- 4″ × 22″ rectangle of fabric for sky
- 4½″ × 22″ rectangle of fabric for lake
- 6½″ × 22″ rectangle of fabric for mountains
- ½ yard of muslin for the foundation
- ⅔ yard of fabric for outer border and page back
- 3 white inkjet fabric sheets
- 1 natural inkjet fabric sheet
- Scrap of Osnaburg fabric or clear vinyl (see Resources page 70), for pocket
- 6 sheets of Steam-A-Seam 2 Double-Stick fusible web, 9″ × 12″
- Rotary cutter with a pinking blade
- 16″ × 24″ rectangle of fast2fuse double-sided stiff interfacing
- Natural elements for pocket
- Wood and novelty buttons, brads, and state coin
- Stiletto
- Index card
- 6 to 8 birch twigs and birch bark
- Spray starch
- 5 small branches for hanging rod
- 3 yards hemp or cotton lacing cord
- Fabri-Tac and Gem-Tac glues

Making the Page

Refer to Scrapbook Page Basics, pages 9–10 and Preparation, pages 11–18.

Make the Page Front

1. Cut a muslin foundation 14″ × 22″.
2. Align the 4″ × 22″ sky fabric with the top edge of the muslin. Pin in place.
3. Align the 4½″ × 22″ lake fabric with the bottom edge of the muslin. Pin in place.
4. Sew along the outer edges with a scant ¼″ seam allowance.
5. Cut 2 rectangles 6½″ × 11″ from the fusible web, and press them to the back of the 6½″ × 22″ mountain fabric. Trim the top edge of the fabric to look like mountains and the bottom edge straight for the shoreline. Place the mountain fabric on the layered muslin, aligning the outer edges and overlapping the sky and lake fabrics. Fuse in place.

Design and Print

Refer to Designing the Page Layout, pages 20–21 and Printing on Fabric, pages 22–23.

1. Copy or print the photos, drawing (or enlarged photo), and captions on paper.
2. Make a 15½″ × 23″ preview window (page 19) with a 12½″ × 20″ opening (optional). Use the preview window and the paper copies to design your layout. Adjust copy sizes as needed to fit.
3. Make a final copy of the photos on the white fabric sheets and a final copy of the captions on the natural fabric sheet. Remove the paper backing.
4. Rinse the fabric sheets according to the manufacturer's directions, and let dry.

Put It Together

1. Frame the layout area with the preview window.
2. Iron fusible web to the back of the dry fabric sheets.
3. Remove the fusible paper backing. Trim the photos and captions with a straight edge rotary blade, allowing room for a brad on each caption. Trim the drawing (or an enlarged photo) with a pinking blade.
4. Arrange the photos and fuse to the page. Sew the drawing (or fuse an enlarged photo) to the center of the page.
5. Fuse the captions to the photos. Pierce a hole with a stiletto, insert the brads, and fasten.
6. Trim the page front to 12½″ × 20″.
7. Cut 2 strips of fabric 1½″ × 12½″ for the side borders, and sew them on with a ¼″ seam allowance. Cut 2 strips of fabric 1½″ × 22″ for the top and bottom borders, and sew them on.
8. Cut a 14½″ × 22″ page back.

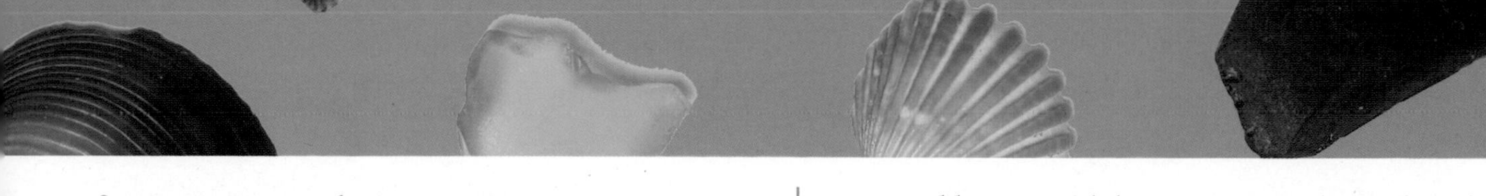

9. Finish the page (see Finishing Instructions, pages 32–33).
10. Make the memorabilia or clear vinyl pocket (see Special Techniques, below).
11. Glue the birch twigs together with Fabri-Tac to make a small bundle. Glue the natural elements, like the birch bark, memorabilia pocket, and birch twig bundle, to the page with Fabri-Tac. Sew on a wood button with heavy cotton or linen thread. Glue the smooth-surfaced embellishments, such as the novelty buttons, coin, and arrowheads, with Gem-Tac.
12. To make the branch hanging rod, wrap and tie the branches with hemp cord or cotton lacing, and sew the ends to the top of the page.

Special Techniques

Make a Memorabilia Pocket

Pull threads to fringe.

1. Cut a 3½" × 5½" rectangle of Osnaburg, and apply spray starch. Staystitch both long sides ¼" in from the edge with matching or coordinating thread.
2. Pull threads, one at a time, and fringe the long sides up to the stitching.

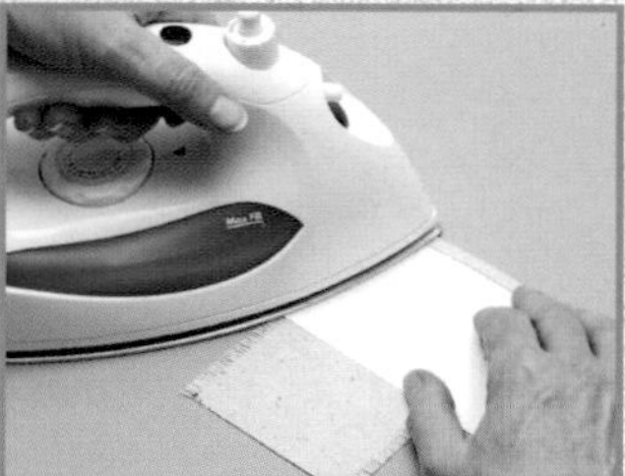
Fold and press short side.

3. Fold a short side under ¼", and press. Use an index card to keep the hem straight.

Glue the overlap.

4. Fold the pressed hem over to the opposite short side, overlapping the edges ¼". Flatten the pocket, with the hem centered on the front, and finger-press. Apply Fabri-Tac to the pressed hem, and glue the overlap in place.

Fill pocket with balsam needles.

5. Sew one fringed end closed. Fuse the caption to the pocket. Pierce a hole in the caption with a stiletto, insert the brad, and fasten. Glue the twig closure to the pocket with Gem-Tac. Fill the pocket with balsam needles. Sew the other fringed end closed. If you squeeze the pocket, you can smell the fragrant balsam. It s my own squeeze and sniff page!

Make a Clear Vinyl Pocket

1. Cut a square or rectangle of clear vinyl large enough to accommodate your souvenirs.
2. Machine stitch the vinyl to the finished scrapbook page along 3 sides, using matching or invisible thread. Do this after the page is finished and fused to the fast2fuse stiff interfacing so you won t melt the vinyl when finishing the page.

Fill vinyl pockets with your treasures.

Tip Vinyl likes to wiggle around on your cutting mat when cutting and on your fabric when sewing. Cure the problem by taping the vinyl to your mat along an edge you are not cutting and taping it to the fabric along the top edge before you sew it.

Family Recipes

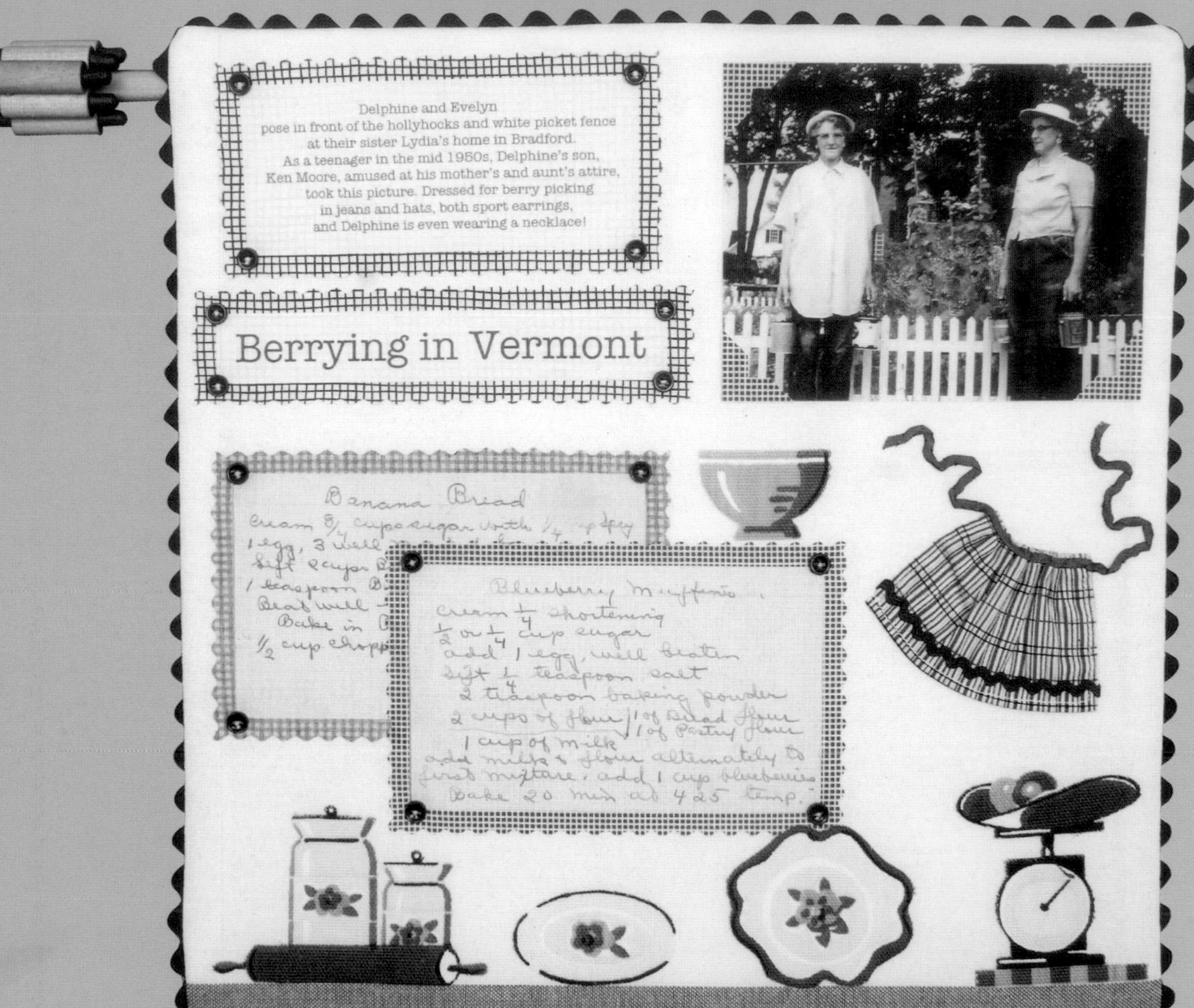

Delphine and Evelyn
pose in front of the hollyhocks and white picket fence
at their sister Lydia's home in Bradford.
As a teenager in the mid 1950s, Delphine's son,
Ken Moore, amused at his mother's and aunt's attire,
took this picture. Dressed for berry picking
in jeans and hats, both sport earrings,
and Delphine is even wearing a necklace!
Berrying in Vermont
Banana Bread
Blueberry Muffins

Berrying in Vermont, 12" × 12", page photo by Kenneth E. Moore

Handwritten recipes are wonderful reminders of home and family. For this project, I used a kitchen towel with a blue stripe as the background for family recipes so I'd have a shelf for the kitchen motifs to sit on. If you can't find a towel like this, make your own shelf by sewing a striped or checked fabric or ribbon to a square of muslin. Look for fabrics with teacups and fruits and veggies for motifs to adorn your page. You'll find lots of colorful buttons and iron-on appliqués in fabric stores to embellish your recipe page. Check out scrapbook stores for packages of kitchen-themed stickers. Find tiny baking ornaments in seasonal stores and dollhouse miniatures in hobby shops. Try your grocery and cooking stores for little cookie cutters and fragrant spices that you can glue to a page or fill a pocket with. Don't forget to visit your craft store for miniature wooden rolling pins.

What You'll Need

For Basic Supplies, refer to pages 6–8.

- Photo, recipes, title, and story block
- 1 kitchen towel (see Resources, page 70) or a fat quarter of fabric for page front
- 1/2 yard of kitchen-motif fabric for stickers, page back, and sleeve
- Fabric scraps for recipe, title, and story borders, photo corners, and apron
- 2 white inkjet fabric sheets
- 4 sheets of Steam-A-Seam 2 Double-Stick fusible web, 9″ × 12″
- Rotary cutter with pinking blade
- Small buttons
- 10″ of 1/8″ satin ribbon for apron strings
- 4″ of baby rickrack for apron
- 1 1/4 yards of medium rickrack for edge finish
- 14″ × 14″ square of fast2fuse double-sided stiff interfacing
- 3/8″ dowel, cut 14″ long
- Fine sandpaper, 220 grit
- 10 craft wood rolling pins (Lara's Crafts; see Resources, page 70)
- Acrylic paint and small brush
- Light stain for the dowel and rolling pins
- Hot glue gun
- Fray Check
- Fabri-Tac and Gem-Tac glues

Making the Page

Refer to Scrapbook Page Basics, pages 9–10 and Preparation, pages 11–18.

Make the Page Front and Back

1. Cut 1 square 14″ × 14″ from the towel with at least 3/4″ of the stripe showing on the bottom edge for the page front. Or cut a 14″ × 14″ square of fabric.
2. Cut 1 square 14″ × 14″ of fabric for the page back.

Design and Print

Refer to Designing the Page Layout, pages 20–21 and Printing on Fabric, pages 22–23.

1. Copy or print the photo, recipes, title, and story block on paper.
2. Place the preview window (page 19) on the kitchen towel so that 1/2″ of the stripe shows at the bottom. Use the preview window and the paper copies to design your layout. Adjust copy sizes as needed to fit.
3. Make final copies of the photo, recipes, title, and story block on the fabric sheets. Remove the paper backing.
4. Rinse the sheets according to the manufacturer's directions, and let dry.

Put It Together

1. Frame the layout area with the preview window.
2. Iron fusible web to the back of the dry fabric sheets, the border fabrics, and the photo corner fabric.
3. Remove the fusible paper backing from the fabric sheets. Trim the photo, recipes, title, and story block as needed to fit.
4. Fuse the photo to the page. Fuse the recipes, title, and story block to the border fabrics.
5. Remove the fusible paper backing from the border fabrics. Trim the borders with a pinking blade. Arrange the recipes, title, and story block and fuse to the towel.

Embellishments for recipe pages are easy to find.

6. Iron small pieces of fusible web to the back of individual kitchen fabric motifs, and fussy cut for stickers. Fuse the fabric stickers to the shelf and top of a recipe.
7. Make and fuse photo corners (page 42) to the photo.
8. Sew buttons on the corners of the recipes, title, and story block with contrasting thread.
9. Make the apron (see Special Technique, below), and glue with Fabri-Tac or stitch with matching thread to the page.
10. Finish the page using the medium rickrack. (See Finishing Instructions starting on page 32. Be sure to follow the special instructions for Adding an Edge Treatment on page 34, and Finishing the Page with a Hanging Sleeve on page 35.)
11. Sand and stain the dowel and the rolling pins. Sand and paint the rolling pin handles.
12. Stack and glue 5 rolling pins to 1 end of the dowel with a hot glue gun. Insert the dowel through the sleeve. Stack and glue 5 rolling pins to the other end of the dowel.

Special Technique

Make the Apron

1. Cut a $3^3/_4'' \times 2^1/_2''$ rectangle from apron fabric. Cut 4″ of baby rickrack and 10″ of $^1/_8''$ satin ribbon.
2. Turn edges under a scant $^1/_4''$ on all 4 sides of the apron rectangle. Press. Hem all sides with a short machine stitch.

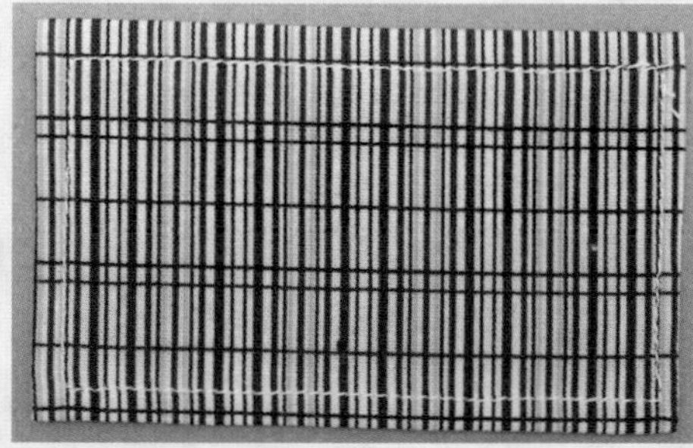

Hem apron.

3. Glue the baby rickrack with Fabri-Tac near the lower edge of the apron rectangle, and glue the ends to the back of the apron.

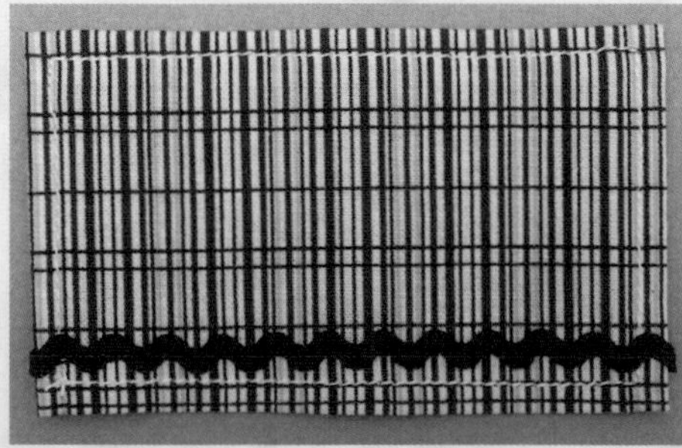

Add rickrack to apron.

4. Sew 2 rows of basting stitches, about $^1/_8''$ apart, near the top edge. Pull these gathering threads until the top edge measures $1^1/_4''$ wide. Tie off the threads at both ends. Put a dot of Fray Check on each knot to secure it.

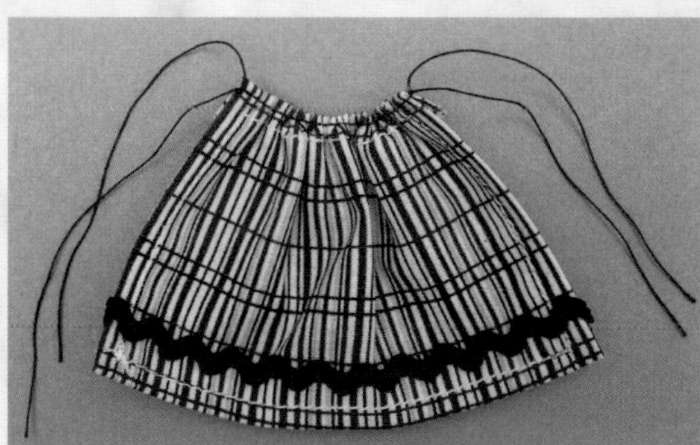

Gather top edge of apron.

5. Glue the $^1/_8''$ ribbon to the gathered edge with Fabri-Tac, making sure the ties on each side are equal in length.

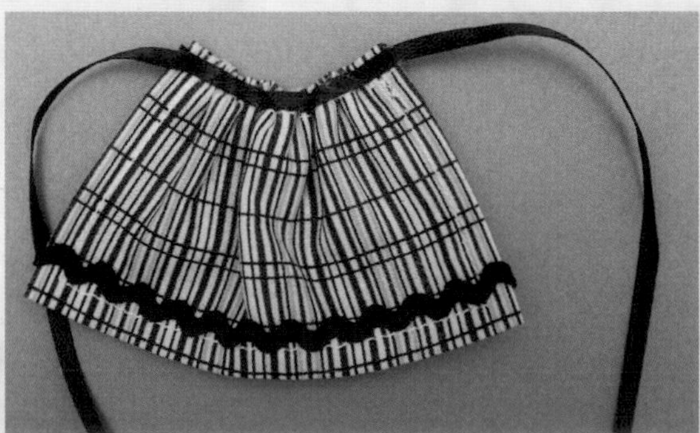

Glue ribbon ties to apron.

Garden Flowers

Roses in the Garden, 12" × 12", page photos by Sue Hale

I've always loved flowers and gardens, but my first gardening experience was a failure. In weeding my mother's garden as a child, I pulled up all her fledgling primroses! Now, wherever I travel, I take pictures of gardens, both formal and informal. The hollyhocks were at Williamsburg, Virginia; the black-eyed Susans were next to a vegetable stand in New Hampshire; the beach roses were at Cape Cod. Select a trio of your favorite flower-garden photos and embroider easy silk-ribbon roses and leaves near them. Use Steam-a-Seam 2 Lite and a thimble to push the blunt chenille needle through the fabric. A Needle Grabber will help you pull the needle through to the back if you are embroidering with ribbon on fused layers. You'll find these notions and silk ribbons at quilt and fabric stores.

What You'll Need

For Basic Supplies, refer to pages 6–8.

- Photos of gardens and title
- 2 fat quarters of fabric for the page front, page back, and sleeve
- 1 fat quarter of fabric for the photo borders and edge trim
- 2 inkjet fabric sheets
- 4 sheets of Steam-A-Seam 2 Lite Double-Stick fusible web, 9″ × 12″
- Rotary cutter with wave edge blade
- 1 package each of 4mm silk ribbon in rose and green
- Thread to match rose and green ribbon
- Size 26 chenille needles
- Needle Grabbers and thimble for embroidery
- 14″ × 14″ square of fast2fuse double-sided stiff interfacing
- 3/8″ dowel, cut 14″ long
- Fine sandpaper, 220 grit
- 1 package of 1″ split balls (Lara's Crafts; see Resources, page 70)
- Acrylic paint and brush
- Gloss varnish
- Hot glue gun

Making the Page

Refer to Scrapbook Page Basics, pages 9–10 and Preparation, pages 11–18.

Make the Page Front and Back

1. Cut 2 squares 14″ × 14″ of fabric for the page front and back.

Design and Print

Refer to Designing the Page Layout, pages 20–21 and Printing on Fabric, pages 22–23.

1. Copy or print the photos and title on paper.
2. Use the preview window (page 19) and the paper copies to design your layout. Adjust copy sizes as needed to fit.
3. Make final copies of the photos and title on the fabric sheets. Remove the paper backing.
4. Rinse the fabric sheets according to the manufacturer's directions, and let dry.

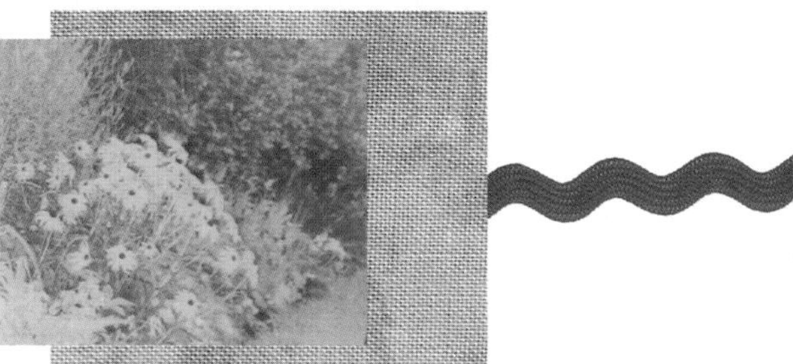

Put It Together

1. Frame the layout area with the preview window.
2. Iron fusible web to the back of the dry fabric sheets. Iron 1 sheet of fusible web to the border fabric. Trim and set aside the excess border fabric for making the edge trim.
3. Remove the fusible paper backing from the fabric sheets. Trim the photos and the title as needed to fit the page.
4. Fuse the photos and title to the border fabric. Remove the fusible paper backing, and trim the borders with a wave edge blade.
5. Arrange and fuse the photos and title to the page.
6. Embroider the spider-web roses and leaves (see Special Techniques, below) on the photo and around the title.
7. Finish the page with a hanging sleeve (see Finishing the Page with a Hanging Sleeve, page 35).
8. Cut 1 rectangle 4″ × 13″ from the remaining border fabric. Cut a 3″ × 12″ piece of fusible web and fuse it to the wrong side of the rectangle. Cut the rectangle with a wave edge blade to create 4 wavy strips.
9. Remove the fusible paper backing, and fuse the edge trim strips to the page as shown, trimming as needed.
10. Sand, paint, and varnish the dowel and split balls. Glue a split ball to 1 end of the dowel with a hot glue gun. Insert the dowel through the sleeve, and glue the second ball to the dowel.

Special Techniques

Tips for Working with Silk Ribbon

1. Use a greaseless hand cream before you start.
2. Work with 18" lengths of ribbon to minimize wear on the ribbon.
3. Keep your stitches loose to preserve the soft look of the ribbon.

Embroider the Roses and Leaves

MAKE THE NEEDLE EYE LOCK

1. Cut an 18″ length of 4mm silk ribbon.
2. Cut 1 end of the ribbon diagonally, and pull it about 2″ through the eye of a chenille needle.
3. Pierce the ribbon with the needle about 1/4″ from the diagonal cut, and pull on the tail so that the pierced end slides down and locks at the needle's eye.

Lock ribbon at eye of needle.

KNOT THE TAIL

1. Cut the tail of the ribbon diagonally.
2. Take a short running stitch at the tail, hold the ribbon near the tail, and pull it down over the eye of the needle, all the way down the length of the ribbon. This makes a *very* small, soft knot.

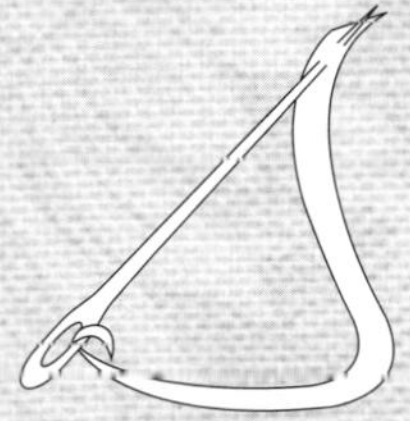
Knot ribbon tail.

MAKE THE SPIDER-WEB ROSES

1. Use thread that matches the ribbon, and sew 5 evenly spaced 1/4″-long spokes for the rose base. Repeat until you have enough bases for all the roses.

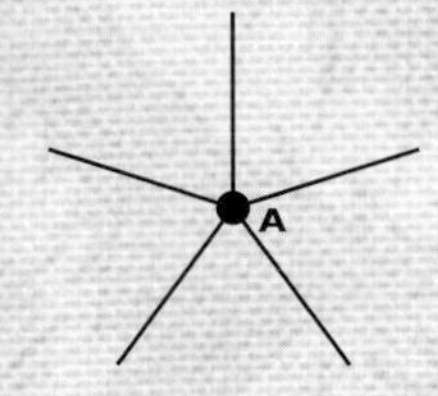

Sew 5 evenly spaced spokes.

2. Thread the chenille needle with 18″ of 4mm rose silk ribbon. Lock the ribbon at the eye of the needle, and knot the tail.
3. Bring the needle up from the back at A.
4. Use the needle to weave the ribbon over the first spoke, under the second spoke, over the third spoke, and under the fourth spoke. Repeat this over/under pattern until the spokes are completely covered by the ribbon.

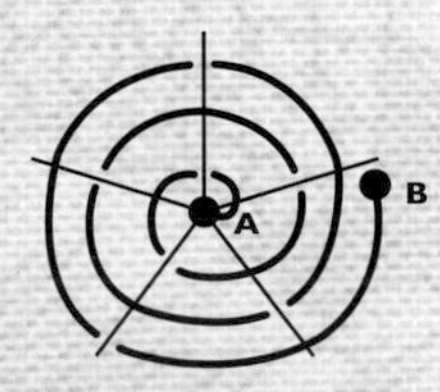

Weave needle over and under spokes. Right-handed stitchers will travel counter-clockwise and left-handed stitchers will travel clockwise.

Let the ribbon twist and turn all it wants. This is what makes the roses so pretty.

5. Pull the needle through to the back at B. Loosely carry the ribbon to the next base, and repeat Steps 3–5.
6. To finish, pull the ribbon through to the back, cut it, and sew it to the back with matching thread.

18" of 4mm ribbon will make 2—3 roses, depending on the length of the spokes.

Finished spider-web roses

MAKE THE LEAVES

The leaves are made with the Japanese ribbon stitch.

1. Thread a chenille needle with 18″ of 4mm green silk ribbon. Lock the ribbon at the eye of the needle, and knot the tail.
2. Bring the needle up from the back at A, near a finished rose. Lay the ribbon flat, and hold it in place with your thumb about 1″ away from A.
3. Pierce the ribbon with the needle at B about 3/8″ from A. Gently pull the ribbon over your thumb and through to the back of your page. Do not let the ribbon twist. Gently pull on the ribbon to complete the leaf. The finished leaf will curl softly in at the tip.
4. Repeat Steps 2 and 3, adding 2 to 4 leaves per rose and loosely carrying the ribbon between each leaf.
5. To finish, pull the ribbon through to the back, cut it, and sew it to the back with matching thread.

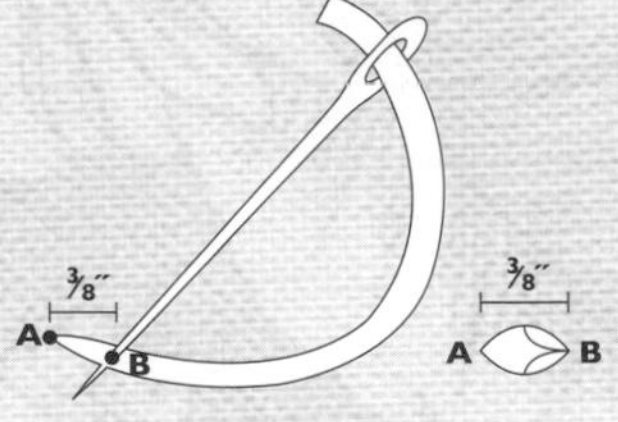

Come up at A, and go back down at B.

Sewing Is My Therapy

Sewing Is My Therapy, 12½" × 13", images from the Click-n-Craft Sew Crafty I CD from The Vintage Workshop

Images of needle cases from a CD-ROM inspired this page. To make this project just like I did, you'll need a computer, a printer, and the Click-n-Craft Sew Crafty CD from The Vintage Workshop. Just follow the tutorial on the CD, and remember to test print on paper first. Or you can take some photos of your own quilts, your quilting room, quilting friends, and a quilting class and put together a similar page.

Check out your stash for sewing notions, buttons, and bits of leftover ribbon and trim. I found the buttons, black snaps, and rickrack in mine. Find packages of miniature sewing and quilting notions and tiny buttons at a craft or scrapbook store. Look for measuring tape ribbon by the yard, baby rickrack, more buttons, snaps, and little sewing machines and spools of thread on cards at a fabric store. The little rotary cutter pin had been in my stash for more than 10 years, just waiting for a good home. What a great gift this would make for a sewing or quilting friend!

What You'll Need

For Basic Supplies, refer to pages 6–8.

- Click-n-Craft Sew Crafty CD from The Vintage Workshop (see Resources on page 70) or photos, and title
- 1 fat quarter of fabric for the page front
- 1 fat quarter of fabric for the title bar, page back, and hanging sleeve
- Scraps of fabric for image borders
- 3 white inkjet fabric sheets
- 2 sheets of Steam-A-Seam 2 Double-Stick fusible web, 9″ × 12″
- Steam-A-Seam 2 Double-Stick fusible tape, 1/2″- wide roll (optional)
- 1/2 yard of measuring tape ribbon
- Rotary cutter with pinking blade
- 1 yard each of 3 colors of baby rickrack
- 1 package of miniature sewing notions
- Assorted buttons
- Sew-on black snaps, Size/No. 4/0
- 14″ × 14″ square of fast2fuse double-sided stiff interfacing
- 3/8″ dowel, cut 15 1/2″ long
- Fine sandpaper, 220 grit
- Acrylic paint and brush
- 1 package of 1 1/4″ wood squares (Lara's Crafts; see Resources, page 70)
- Matte varnish and brush
- 1 sheet of white cardstock
- Fabri-Tac and Gem-Tac glues
- Hot glue gun

Making the Page

Refer to Scrapbook Page Basics, pages 9–10 and Preparation, pages 11–18.

Make the Page Front and Back

1. Cut 1 rectangle 11 1/2″ × 15″ of fabric for the page front and 1 rectangle 3 1/2″ × 15″ of fabric for the title bar.
2. Sew the title bar to the bottom of the page front with a 1/4″ seam allowance.
3. Sew the measuring tape ribbon over the title bar seam with matching thread, or fuse with 1/2″-wide fusible tape.
4. Cut 1 rectangle 14 1/2″ × 15″ of fabric for the page back.

Design and Print

Refer to Designing the Page Layout, pages 20–21 and Printing on Fabric, pages 22–23.

1. Print the images from the CD-ROM (or use your own photos) and the title on paper.
2. Make a 15 1/2″ × 16″ preview window (page 19) with a 12 1/2″ × 13″ opening (optional). Use the preview window and the paper copies to design your layout. Adjust copy sizes as needed to fit.
3. Make final copies of the images and the title on the fabric sheets. Remove the paper backing.

To print multiple images on a fabric sheet, print one image, turn the fabric sheet around, and place it in the copier tray again. Print the second image on the same sheet.

4. Rinse the fabric sheets according to the manufacturer's directions, and let dry.

Put It Together

1. Frame the layout area with the preview window.
2. Iron fusible web to the back of the dry fabric sheets and border fabrics.
3. Remove the fusible paper backing from the fabric sheets. Trim the images and title with the pinking blade, or fussy cut with scissors.
4. Fuse the fabric images to the border fabric. Remove the fusible paper backing, and trim the borders with a pinking blade.
5. Arrange and fuse the images and the title to the page.
6. Trim the page to 13″ × 13½″.
7. Pin and sew the rickrack ⅞″ in from the edges of the page with matching thread.

Gluing baby rickrack is challenging! Try sewing it on with a tiny zigzag stitch.

8. Sew the buttons on the page with contrasting thread. Glue on the snaps and other smooth embellishments with Gem-Tac. Keep hard or three-dimensional embellishments at least ½″ from the seam allowance.
9. Finish the page with a hanging sleeve (see Finishing the Page with a Hanging Sleeve, page 35).
10. Sand, paint, and varnish the dowel and the wood squares. Embellish the wood squares with spools (see Special Technique, right), and tiny buttons and snaps. Glue a wood square to 1 end of the dowel with a hot glue gun. Insert the dowel through the sleeve, and glue the second square to the dowel.

Special Technique

Make Spool Embellishments

1. Draw 2 rectangles ⅞″ × 1¼″, with a pencil, on the back of white cardstock.
2. Draw an X on each rectangle from corner to corner.
3. Draw a vertical line a scant ⅛″ in from each long side, stopping the line before crossing the X.
4. Cut out the rectangles, and trim away the ⅛″ area to make 2 spool shapes.

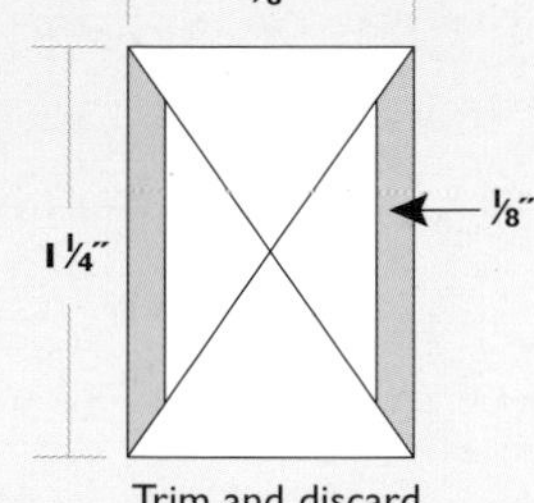

Trim and discard shaded area.

5. Glue 1 end of the thread to the back of each spool with Fabri-Tac. Let the glue dry.
6. Wrap the thread around the spool, keeping the thread as straight and flat as possible.

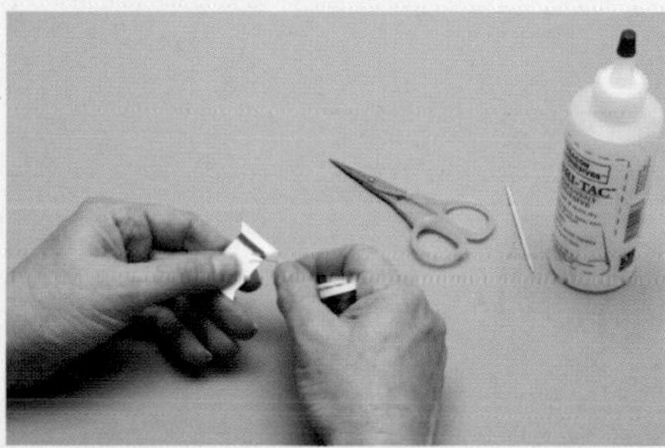
Keep wrapped thread straight and flat.

7. When the thread area is completely covered, turn the spool to the back and cut the thread, leaving a ½″ tail. Apply a tiny dot of Fabri-Tac to the thread tail, and tuck it under the wrapped thread with a toothpick.

Don t wrap the thread too tightly over the edges of the cardstock. It will cause the cardstock to buckle.

Create spools of many colors.

Resources

CD-ROMS

www.thevintageworkshop.com

CD-ROMs, printables and downloadable artwork, fabrics, and papers

EASELS AND HANGERS

www.easels.com

Tabletop easels in wood, brass, plastic, acrylic

www.easelsbyamron.com

Tabletop easels in acrylic, wood, brass, copper, pewter, bronze

EMBELLISHMENTS

www.fabricartshop.com

Paints, threads, yarns, Angelina fibers, crystals

www.homesew.com

Novelty trims, ribbons, specialty threads, buttons, pressed flowers

www.hotribbon.com

1/8″ fusible ribbon in 20 colors plus silver and gold metallic

www.jcarolinecreative.com

Cute appliqués, novelty buttons, wonderful ribbon

www.kreinik.com

Iron-On Ribbon, thread, braid

www.quiltingarts.com

Threads, yarns, ribbon, fibers, trims, beads, charms, images on fabric

www.ultrastyledesigns.com

Ultrasuede pieces and by the yard

TEA TOWELS

www.quilterstudio.com

Plaid, check, ticking, striped, and flour-sack towels

PRETREATED INKJET FABRIC SHEETS

www.colortextiles.com

www.printedtreasures.com

www.thevintageworkshop.com

www.cjenkinscompany.com

www.electricquilt.com

QUOTATIONS, POEMS, PHRASES, TITLES

www.quoteland.com

www.quotegarden.com

www.wisdomquotes.com

www.scrapbook.com

WOOD CRAFTS AND CUTOUTS

www.larascrafts.com

Dowel caps, wood shapes, painted wood stickers, alphabet tiles

MAKING FABRIC SHEETS AND PRINTING ON FABRIC

www.bryerpatch.com, *Photo Fun,* or *More Photo Fun* (see Books below)

BOOKS

Fast Fun & Easy Scrapbook Quilts: Create a Keepsake for Every Memory, Sue Astroth, C&T Publishing, 2004.

Quilt Savvy: Fallert's Guide to Images on Fabric, Caryl Bryer Fallert, American Quilter's Society, 2004.

Photo Fun: Print Your Own Fabric for Quilts & Crafts, The Hewlett-Packard Company, Edited by Cyndy Lyle Rymer, C&T Publishing, 2004.

More Photo Fun: Exciting New Ideas for Printing on Fabric for Quilts & Crafts, The Hewlett-Packard Company, with Cyndy Lyle Rymer & Lynn Koolish, C&T Publishing, 2005.

Blending Photos with Fabric, Mary Ellen Kranz, The Electric Quilt Company, 2004.

The Art of Fabric Books: Innovative Ways to Use Fabric in Scrapbooks, Altered Books & More, Jan Bode Smiley, C&T Publishing, 2005.

Beading Basics: 30 Embellishing Techniques for Quilters, Mary Stori, C&T Publishing, 2004.

CLEAR QUILTER'S VINYL

Look for Quilter's Vinyl at your local quilt shop or order online from www.ctpub.com

FOR MORE INFORMATION

Ask for a free catalog:
C&T Publishing, Inc.
P.O. Box 1456
Lafayette, CA 94549
800-284-1114
email: ctinfo@ctpub.com
website: www.ctpub.com

QUILTING SUPPLIES

Cotton Patch Mail Order
3404 Hall Lane
Dept. CTB
Lafayette, CA 94549
800-835-4418; 925-283-7883
email: quiltusa@yahoo.com
website: www.quiltusa.com

NOTE: Fabrics used in the pages shown may not be currently available; fabric manufacturers keep most fabrics in print for only a short time.

About the Author

Born during World War II in New England, Sue Hale began making quilts 18 years ago when she lived in Southern California. Soon, she was working at The Fabric Patch and teaching appliqué classes there and at other area shops. Sue has also taught her original designs at the Road to California Quilter's Conference and on a cruise to Alaska. Her appliqué work has appeared in *Quilter's Newsletter Magazine*, two volumes of Elly Sienkiewicz's Baltimore Beauties series, and *Elm Creek Quilts: Return to Elm Creek* by Jennifer Chiaverini.

Sue has worked as a consultant and editor for Benartex. She is currently the marketing director for Red Rooster Fabrics. She is active in Mountain Top Quilters, the Arizona Quilters Guild, The Appliqué Society, and several mini groups. She has two 30-something sons in California and lives in Prescott Valley, Arizona, with her husband.

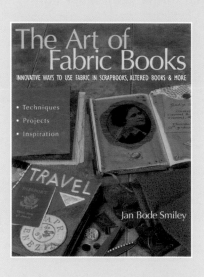

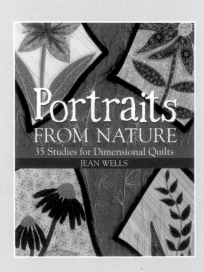

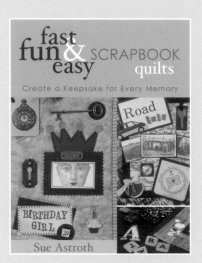

Council for Standards in Human Service Education (CSHSE) Standards Covered in This Text

The Council for Standards in Human Service Education (CSHSE) developed ten national standards that guide Human Services departments and help students understand the knowledge, values, and skills of developing human service practitioners. These guidelines reflect the interdisciplinary nature of human services.

STANDARD	CHAPTER
Professional History	
Understanding and Mastery...	
Historical roots of human services	4
Creation of human services profession	
Historical and current legislation affecting services delivery	
How public and private attitudes influence legislation and the interpretation of policies related to human services	
Differences between systems of governance and economics	4, 5
Exposure to a spectrum of political ideologies	12, 13
Skills to analyze and interpret historical data application in advocacy and social changes	
Human Systems	
Understanding and Mastery...	
Theories of human development	
How small groups are utilized, theories of group dynamics, and group facilitation skills	3, 6, 13
Changing family structures and roles	
Organizational structures of communities	1, 2, 4, 11, 12, 15
An understanding of capacities, limitations, and resiliency of human systems	2, 6, 14
Emphasis on context and the role of diversity in determining and meeting human needs	1, 2
Processes to effect social change through advocacy (e.g., community development, community and grassroots organizing, local and global activism)	4, 8, 11, 12, 14
Processes to analyze, interpret, and effect policies and laws at local, state, and national levels	2, 12
Human Services Delivery Systems	
Understanding and Mastery...	
Range and characteristics of human services delivery systems and organizations	10
Range of populations served and needs addressed by human services	
Major models used to conceptualize and integrate prevention, maintenance, intervention, rehabilitation, and healthy functioning	
Economic and social class systems including systemic causes of poverty	13, 15
Political and ideological aspects of human services	12
International and global influences on services delivery	15
Skills to effect and influence social policy	11, 12

Adapted from the October 2010 Revised CSHSE National Standards

Council for Standards in Human Service Education (CSHSE) Standards Covered in This Text

STANDARD	CHAPTER
Information Management	
Understanding and Mastery...	
Obtain information through interviewing, active listening, consultation with others, library or other research, and the observation of clients and systems	7
Recording, organizing, and assessing the relevance, adequacy, accuracy, and validity of information provided by others	
Compiling, synthesizing, and categorizing information	7, 9
Disseminating routine and critical information to clients, colleagues, or other members of the related services system that is provided in written or oral form and in a timely manner	9
Maintaining client confidentiality and appropriate use of client data	
Using technology for word processing, sending e-mail, and locating and evaluating information	7, 9
Performing elementary community needs assessment	1, 7
Conducting basic program evaluation	
Utilizing research findings and other information for community education and public relations and using technology to create and manage spreadsheets and databases	
Planning and Evaluating	
Understanding and Mastery...	
Analysis and assessment of the needs of clients or client groups	1, 5
Skills to develop goals and design and implement a plan of action	8
Skills to evaluate the outcomes of the plan and the impact on the client or client group	
Program design, implementation, and evaluation	5–10
Interventions and Direct Services	
Understanding and Mastery...	
Theory and knowledge bases of prevention, intervention, and maintenance strategies to achieve maximum autonomy and functioning	
Skills to facilitate appropriate direct services and interventions related to specific client or client group goals	
Knowledge and skill development in case management, intake interviewing, individual counseling, group facilitation and counseling, location and use of appropriate resources and referrals, and use of consultation	
Interpersonal Communication	
Understanding and Mastery...	
Clarifying expectations	
Dealing effectively with conflict	
Establishing rapport with clients	
Developing and sustaining behaviors that are congruent with the values and ethics of the profession	10, 13

Council for Standards in Human Service Education (CSHSE) Standards Covered in This Text

STANDARD	CHAPTER
Administration	
Understanding and Mastery...	
Managing organizations through leadership and strategic planning	5, 9
Supervision and human resource management	
Planning and evaluating programs, services, and operational functions	8, 9
Developing budgets and monitoring expenditures	10
Grant and contract negotiation	
Legal and regulatory issues and risk management	10, 12
Managing professional development of staff	
Recruiting and managing volunteers	6, 15
Constituency building and other advocacy techniques such as lobbying, grassroots movements, and community development and organizing	4, 6, 14
Client-related Values and Attitudes	
Understanding and Mastery...	
The least intrusive intervention in the least restrictive environment	
Client self-determination	4
Confidentiality of information	
The worth and uniqueness of individuals including ethnicity, culture, gender, sexual orientation, and other expressions of diversity	3, 13
Belief that individuals, services systems, and society change	
Interdisciplinary team approaches to problem solving	8
Appropriate professional boundaries	
Integration of the ethical standards outlined by the National Organization for Human Services and Council for Standards in Human Service Education	13, 15
Self-Development	
Understanding and Mastery...	
Conscious use of self	3, 11, 13
Clarification of personal and professional values	13
Awareness of diversity	
Strategies for self-care	
Reflection on professional self (e.g., journaling, development of a portfolio, project demonstrating competency)	3

STANDARDS FOR EXCELLENCE SERIES

Designed to help students advance their knowledge, values, and skills, the Standards for Excellence Series assists students in associating the Council for Standards in Human Service Education (CSHSE) National Standards to all levels of human services practice.

FEATURES INCLUDE

- **Standards for Excellence grid**—highlighting chapters where various standards are addressed.
- **Standards for Excellence critical thinking questions**—challenges students to think critically about the standards in relation to chapter content.
- **Multimedia links**—correlates content to multimedia assets throughout the text, including video, additional readings, and more.
- **Self-study quizzes**—found throughout the text, self-study quizzes test student knowledge and comprehension of key chapter topics.
- **Chapter review**—links to a scenario-based chapter review including short-answer discussion questions.

Community Organizing

Theory and Practice

Joyce S. McKnight
Empire State College, State University of New York

Joanna McKnight Plummer

Boston Columbus Indianapolis New York San Francisco Upper Saddle River
Amsterdam Cape Town Dubai London Madrid Milan Munich Paris Montréal Toronto
Delhi Mexico City São Paulo Sydney Hong Kong Seoul Singapore Taipei Tokyo

Editor in Chief: Ashley Dodge
Editorial Assistant: Amandria Guadalupe
Managing Editor: Denise Forlow
Program Manager: Carly Czech
Project Manager: Doug Bell, PreMediaGlobal, Inc.
Executive Marketing Manager: Kelly May
Marketing Coordinator: Jessica Warren
Procurement Manager: Mary Fisher
Procurement Specialist: Eileen Collaro
Art Director: Jayne Conte
Cover Designer: Karen Noferi
Interior Designer: Joyce Weston Design
Manager, Visual Research: Ben Ferrini
Photo Researcher: Carolyn Arcabascio, PreMediaGlobal, Inc.
Manager, Rights and Permissions: Paul Sarkis
Image Permission Coordinator: Martha Shethar
Cover Art: Shutterstock, JDS
Media Director: Brian Hyland
Digital Media Project Manager: Tina Gagliostro
Full-Service Project Management: Sudip Sinha, PreMediaGlobal, Inc.
Printer/Binder: RRD/STP Crawfordsville
Cover Printer: RRD/STP Crawfordsville

Credits and acknowledgments borrowed from other sources and reproduced, with permission, in this textbook appear on appropriate page within text.

Library of Congress Cataloging-in-Publication Data
McKnight, Joyce S.
Community organizing : theory and practice / Joyce S. McKnight, Empire State College, State University of New York, Joanna McKnight Plummer.
pages cm.
Includes bibliographical references and index.
ISBN-13: 978-0-205-51681-0
ISBN-10: 0-205-51681-5
1. Community organization. 2. Community development. I. Title.
HM766.M43 2013
307.1'4—dc23 2013035553

18 2022

ISBN 10: 0-205-51681-5
ISBN 13: 978-0-205-51681-0

Contents

12. Navigating the Political Labyrinth 209

13. Value Systems and Ethics 237

Preface

Never doubt that a small group of thoughtful, committed citizens can change the world. Indeed, it's the only thing that ever has.

—Margaret Mead

This text was designed to be a textbook and "how to" reference guide for thoughtful, dedicated citizens who are determined to change their world (or at least part of it) through their commitment and loyalty to one another and their dedication to fostering "common unity."

This text provides a unique approach to community organizing for the human services and social work profession by providing practical tips, templates, and in-text and online resources that give future community organizers a road map to navigate a number of best practices in the field. While the main theories that support community organizing are illustrated through an urban and rural community case study approach, the book illustrates how these theories inform and can help direct the type of organizing that will work best for a specific community based on its personality, needs, and resources.

This text and its accompanying resources were developed with the following premises:

1. People know what they need and can work together to achieve it when given effective intellectual tools and analytical frameworks.
2. Everyone can and should be included in community building.
3. Local action is often the most effective action.

Chapter Themes

- **Chapter 1** provides detailed cases studies based on urban and rural communities, and compares and contrasts the complexities of these communities and community organizing.
- **Chapter 2** introduces community organizing thinking, including systems thinking, focal systems, and community formation.
- **Chapter 3** introduces the ever-changing kaleidoscopic community and how disciplines like cognitive psychology, sociology, and social psychology aid in understanding community life.
- **Chapter 4** explores varieties of grassroots community organizing including place-based relational organizing, social entrepreneurship and innovation, mutual economic aid, self-help, community-based advocacy, social movements, and collaboration among organizations.
- **Chapter 5** provides an overview of the community organizing cycle by outlining the development and function of the leadership team, a participatory approach to community research, and participatory approaches to planning, implementation, management, and evaluation.

- **Chapter 6** explores how to create and sustain a diverse leadership team to help you understand and thrive within these interpersonal dynamics and provides you with concrete tools to lead, manage conflict, and successfully navigate challenges.
- **Chapter 7** provides guidance on how to address inadequate information and an inadequate understanding of community assets, weaknesses, and service gaps. (An expanded discussion of research strategies appears in Appendix A.)
- **Chapter 8** examines the planning and implementation phases of the community organizing cycle, including defining the mission, setting measurable outcomes and evaluation criteria, and deciding on the major processes and action steps to begin work.
- **Chapter 9** explores ongoing management and evaluation issues such as choosing a management approach or approaches and creating a management information system.
- **Chapter 10** addresses practical organizational questions including the best ways to structure your continuing effort, issues involved with budget development and management, fund-raising concerns, financial accountability, and ethical standards for financial management and marketing. (An expanded discussion of budgeting and fund-raising appears in Appendix B.)
- **Chapter 11** focuses on power and helps you analyze power relationships within your focal community, learn to identify and use different kinds of power, and focus on ways your organizing team can generate "people power" to gain and maintain control of your destinies.
- **Chapter 12** explores policies, politics, laws, and regulations through the analogy of a football game to guide you through the political maze of multiple levels of policy, the challenges of the legislative process, and the morass of regulation.
- **Chapter 13** focuses on the belief that we can create and sustain healthful, attractive geographic communities and emotionally satisfying non-geographically based communities by working together locally and networking globally, and it guides you through a wide variety of ethical frameworks that undergird effective organizing.
- **Chapter 14** provides many practical suggestions for making optimal use of Web resources for community organizing and community building and explores the many possibilities of online communities and networks.
- **Chapter 15** explores organizations that support community organizing.

Online Features

There are many features of this text to enhance your experience; however, they are only as useful as you make them. By engaging with this text and its resources, you'll gain a variety of community organizing skills through:

- **Web resources**, including links to important Web resources for community organizers
- **Online handbooks** addressing topics such as place-based and relational organizing, social entrepreneurship and social innovation, economic mutual aid, self-help, community-based advocacy, social movements, and interagency collaboration.

Learning Outcomes

Students will be able to achieve a variety of learning outcomes by using this text and its resources, including:

- **Community Organizing skills**—students can develop skills involving leadership, planning, and implementation.
- **Oral communication skills**—students can develop their oral communication skills by engaging with others in and out of class to discuss their comprehension of the chapter based on the chapter's learning objectives.
- **Research skills**—students can develop research skills and techniques, including how to collect the needed data and assemble the information they will need to create a clear, complete picture of the assets, needs, and service gaps of the focal community
- **Assessment and writing skills**—students can develop their assessment and writing skills in preparation for future licensing exams by completing topic-based and chapter review assessments for each chapter.
- **CSHSE national standards**—students can develop their understanding and mastery of CSHSE's national standards by discussing the critical thinking questions presented in the Standards boxes.

We hope you enjoy using this book and the resources we have prepared as you work with other thoughtful, committed people to change the world for the better.

Acknowledgments

This book is dedicated to Hugh F. McKnight for his unflagging support, to all of those students and community members whose lives and struggles are reflected in the pages, and to all those who will use its insights to improve the quality of life for us all.

Many thanks to those who made this book possible: Dr. Drew Hyman, professor emeritus at the Pennsylvania State University, for the initial concepts and inspiration; Hugh McKnight, husband, father, attorney, pastor, professor, behind-the-scenes editor, and extraordinary human being; Jimmy R. Plummer, husband to Joanna McKnight Plummer for all of his support and technological knowledge; Dean Thomas Mackey of the Center for Distance Learning of the SUNY/Empire State College for his patience with the "endless book"; all of the upper-level and graduate students who vetted earlier editions; and Barbara Smith-Decker, Doug Bell, and Carly Czech, the editors who helped turn an academic tome into a comprehensive guide.

Joyce S. McKnight
Joanna McKnight Plummer

CHAPTER 1

A Look at Communities

Pete Ryan/National Geographic Image Collection/Alamy

What is a community? The word *community* can be divided into two parts: "common" and "unity." Communities are comprised of people who share common bonds, often feel responsible for the well-being of one another, and work together for the betterment of life for all. There are several types of communities including geographic, partial, dispersed, interest, and virtual, but most community organizing is done in geographic communities.

Geographic communities are places where people live in proximity to one another and share the experiences of daily life. Geographic community organizing involves shared efforts, often over many years, by people committed to improving the quality of life for everyone living in a particular geographic locale. Places chosen for community organizing frequently have a sense of history. They have names, recognized boundaries and enough services to enable residents to live comfortably without having to leave the area. For instance, many places that are suitable for geographic community organizing have elementary schools, churches and other places of worship, doctors' offices, service organizations, fire and police protection, municipal governments, grocery stores, and community

Information Management

Understanding and Mastery: Performing elementary community-needs assessment

Critical Thinking Question: Choose a place with which you are already familiar. Drive or walk through it, carefully observing its sights, sounds, and smells. What are your overall impressions of the community's assets and needs? What led to these impressions? What immediately jumps out at you as likely to need attention?

Chapter Outline

parks. Some examples of geographic places that you might choose as the focus of community organizing include:

- City neighborhoods consisting of several blocks, often with historical names like "Little Italy," "Chinatown," "the French Quarter," or "Chelsea."
- Incorporated towns and villages of less than 25,000 people (larger cities seem to work better when organized as neighborhoods).
- Rural school districts encompassing a large geographic area but a relatively small population.

Case Study 1: The Smithville Neighborhood

Imagine that you are walking on a major street in a medium-sized city in the Northeastern United States. You are in the downtown area around 6 p.m. on a warm June evening and head west on the way to a friend's house, passing through a section of city that has been gentrified with many bustling small shops, upscale restaurants, and sidewalk cafes. A number of well-dressed people chat in front of the gilded entrance of a live theater company. There are comfortable benches and flower gardens. Street lights start to come on and white lights twinkle from the trees. At the border of the shopping district, renovated brownstones look like upscale single family residences. A uniformed police officer says "good evening" as you pass.

As you head further west, you enter Smithville, a so-called inner city neighborhood where you note that the ambience is changing. You notice more ethnic groceries, pawn shops, and second-hand stores. Most are closed for the evening with steel folding gates covering their doors and windows. The curbs and sidewalks are broken; there are no trash receptacles, and food wrappers and other small items tumble in the wind. A few nearby houses are boarded up. You see several social service agencies, including a local homeless shelter, a soup kitchen, a drug rehab center, and a group home for the developmentally disabled. Gang graffiti is painted on the corner of a building you pass. Although it's getting dark, many school-aged children are still outside shouting and laughing while small groups of young men and women hang out on the street corners. An occasional ambulance or police car siren can be heard, along with the sound of firecrackers or perhaps gunfire a few streets away. Several people sitting on their front steps loudly play the guitar or radio, and gospel music comes from a storefront church.

As you reach the corner, you see a colorful mural depicting smiling people of all races. On the next block, you pass a community garden and a small "pick-up" basketball game on a litter-strewn city playground. Several mothers with their babies chat as they carry clothes into the local laundromat. A family skitters across the street without the safety of a crosswalk because there are none in the area. At the end of the street, an elderly woman waters a flower box on her porch.

Turning onto a side street toward your friend's house, you notice that some of the houses are well cared for with small, neat front yards while others are boarded up and in dire need of repair. Several empty lots are covered with sharp gravel. Next to these single-family homes are multi-story apartment complexes in the flat-roofed "modern" style that now looks outdated. At the first complex, children play in the parking lot next to a swing set with no swings while gray-haired folks sit in lawn chairs in front of the second complex. Teenage boys and girls walk by hand in hand. Everyone seems to be enjoying the evening.

Your friend's house is tucked away on a small lot toward the end of a one-way street. She has invited you over for a cup of coffee and is an active member of the Smithville Neighborhood Association. She asks you about your impressions of the neighborhood and shares her own, emphasizing its strengths, weaknesses, hopes, and dreams.

She shares some of the history of Smithville and the Neighborhood Organization. "Smithville" is a portion of the city named for John Smith who, in the mid-nineteenth century, chose the ten-block-by-fifteen-block area as the site of the first iron furnace and its company housing because it was close to a navigable river on the east, a railroad line on the west, the city center on the south, and a coach and carriage route on the north. The land was empty when Smith chose it, but the Smithville valley was soon identified as a city neighborhood. For decades the predominately wooden frame houses were filled with Scots-Irish iron and steel workers, later with Eastern Europeans and then Italians. During World War II, these white Europeans were joined by a few African Americans from the Deep South who found good jobs for the war effort. The 1950s into the late 1970s were prosperous for everyone. The steel mills began to fail in the 1980s as production was moved overseas. The neighborhood declined precipitously after the loss of the steel industry. Many people moved from the neighborhood, abandoning their properties. Those who stayed were unable to find good jobs and were unable to maintain their former standard of living. The neighborhood population dropped from 25,000 in the 1960 census to just 15,000 in the 1980 census, while the real median household income dropped $10,000 in the same period. In the mid-1990s, a group of concerned residents formed the Smithville Neighborhood Organization. Although things are far from perfect as you noticed in your walking tour, things improved somewhat after the turn of the twenty-first century. Air and water quality have improved. New jobs have been created in medicine, the arts, and clean energy. Recently, immigrants from Guyana and the Caribbean have been added to the diverse mix and are known for the improvements they have made in once-abandoned properties. The various races and ethnicities get along reasonably well. While there are still numerous problems in Smithville, those who are involved with the Neighborhood Organization are feeling hopeful. Your friend invites you to join their efforts by becoming a paid intern through the AmeriCorps and even offers you a place to live in the neighborhood.

When you get home, you take notes on what you have experienced, emphasizing the positive aspects of the neighborhood, noting some of the likely challenges, and finally considering some of the places where there may be conflict among people or their goals. You have made a good start toward an analysis of an urban neighborhood.

Case Study 2: The Town of Middle View

Some time after your visit to the urban Smithville neighborhood, you decide that you would like to explore a rural village to compare and contrast urban and rural communities. You choose to visit the Town of Middle View because you have an older friend who has recently retired there. Middle View is located in upstate New York. It has 4,500 full-time residents with a weekend summer population approaching 20,000. It is comprised of the central Village of Middle View and several smaller hamlets. It shares a single consolidated school district with three other rural towns. You arrive by car at the town limits on a crisp clear autumn morning, driving along a two-lane state highway that follows a sparkling river. As you drive along, you pass different kinds of rural housing including a few prosperous farms with large barns, well-cared-for farm houses and large herds of dairy cattle, suburban-style houses set on moderate-size lots, and two mobile home parks. The first such park is attractive with mature trees and landscaped flower beds. Its mobile homes are set on permanent foundations with large lots. There are outdoor and indoor play areas for the children and a small grocery store for staples. The second is far more rundown and fits the stereotype of a "trailer park." The lots are small, the lanes are muddy and narrow, and the trailers are set on cement blocks without permanent foundations. There has been at least one recent house fire, and some of the remains still stand. As you drive near the river, there are advertisements for campgrounds and rental cabins. These signs of human habitation are interspersed with long stretches of a colorful mixed hardwood forest and dark green pines. You pass through a hamlet with a convenience store/gasoline station, a community church, a small restaurant, and a cluster of wooden houses.

At last you arrive in the Village of Middle View, an incorporated settlement surrounded by the Town of Middle View. There are about 900 full-time village residents. From mid-June to Labor Day, the number of Middle View Village residents swells to about 4,000 on weekends and 2,500 during the week. The full-time village residents are divided into three major groups: "native" families, some of whom have lived in area since before the American Revolution; a group of solid citizens; and business people who originally moved to the area from Major City and its suburbs twenty-five to thirty years ago—although most still speak of themselves as being "from the city." In addition, there is a growing group of upper middle class people who are recent retirees and have chosen to live in their now winterized "summer" homes. Members of the latter two groups see themselves as community leaders and often serve on the town board, the village board, and/or the school board, while the "natives" often live back in the mountains and live by doing odd jobs. They rarely, if ever, participate directly in civic concerns but are often at the heart of informal community caring: holding fund-raising spaghetti dinners to raise money to pay for others' medical bills, participating as volunteer firemen and emergency medical technicians (EMTs), swapping services such as car repairs, checking on the elderly, and dozens of other acts of kindness.

The village boasts five Protestant churches, a Roman Catholic church, a bank, two or three small manufacturing plants, the consolidated school, a modest-sized supermarket, several small town parks, a library, a consolidated fire district, the Town Hall, a senior citizens' center, an outreach medical center, two professional offices, two motels, and three restaurants. All are strung along the main street that has one traffic light.

Most houses are on side streets. Many are small and rather close together with tidy lawns. They are mostly of wood-frame construction and are about one hundred years old. Well-cared-for homes are interspersed with dilapidated ones. One subdivision with ranch style homes on the outskirts of the village resembles a suburb. At one end of Main Street are a few large, restored Victorian homes; two have been converted into bed and breakfasts. There is a medium-sized lake connected to a scenic river. Both are suitable for fishing and small boats and are surrounded with summer homes and a growing number of winterized year-round residences. The village provides two public beaches, tennis and basketball courts, and two medium-sized parks with picnic pavilions. There are community-wide celebrations scattered throughout the year.

When you reach your friend's house, she takes you to the local diner for a mid-afternoon slice of pie and tells you that, although the area seems pristine and beautiful, problems lurk literally under the surface. Although there is a village water system, the water mains are nearly a century old and periodically break during the harsh winters. The whole area depends on antiquated individual septic systems which were not much of a problem when the permanent population was small, but greater numbers of year-round residents have put increasing stress on the rocky soil which cannot absorb the increased sewage. The water table as well as the lake and river system are threatened. Water and sewer needs are aggravated by the bedrock that is located very close to the surface and by antiquated state laws and regulations that preclude new approaches to processing human waste, such as self-composting toilets.

For many years, lumbering in the forests and paper production in nearby mills provided a decent income for working class area residents. Most of the paper mills have now closed, and much of the lumbering has gone to the Scandinavian countries. Locals now make a hand-to-mouth living doing a variety of odd jobs for the summer residents and retired people. Businesses have been slowly closing. Most of the campgrounds, motels, and rental cottages are owned by older couples who are struggling to make a living as fewer city families can afford long vacations. Winters with little or no snow have ruined businesses that depend on snowmobiling and other winter sports, so seasonal businesses that thrive in the summer and early fall struggle to remain open during the winter. There are a few economic bright spots, such as an active, informal coalition that has been working to increase tourism. Recent reactivation of passenger train and freight service after a seventy-year hiatus has increased both summer and winter visitors. On balance, the local economy seems to be bobbing up and down as businesses open and close without apparent reason.

On the school front, shrinking class sizes and budget limitations make it difficult to maintain high quality educational services. Two years ago, because of a proposed 12% property tax hike, the school district budget failed in the largest voter turnout in school district history! As a result, heightening tension now exists between the residents and school district, which has trouble getting budgetary support because incomes of young families are low and most older homeowners are on fixed incomes with no grandchildren in the schools. The gap between the property owners and the schools is exacerbated by the fact that most of the public school teachers live outside of the district and are seen as burdens on the shrinking tax base.

There is also a split along economic lines regarding the present and future prospects facing teens and young adults of the school district. For many years, a relatively small number of talented young adults have participated in school events, have gotten good grades, have gone to college, and later have obtained good jobs outside of the area. In contrast, students from economically poorer homes have "faded" from school in ninth grade, have dropped out as sophomores or juniors, and soon have had children outside of committed relationships—thus creating a subgroup of rootless "twenty-somethings" and their young children without much hope for the future. Some of these teens and young adults have turned to delinquent behaviors. There is a surprising amount of alcohol abuse, depression, and vandalism among teens and young adults throughout the Town and Village. On a positive note, however, the Middle School has recently initiated an after-school program targeted toward at-risk youngsters. Participants in this grant-based program have shown improvement in their school work.

Unlike Smithville, Middle View does not have a formal community organization. A relatively small group of committed citizens are active in local politics, the local churches, the Chamber of Commerce, and the local service club. These people know one another and are often responsible for new positive initiatives aimed at improving the area.

You stay with your friend for a few days. You tell her that you are tiring of your life in Industrial City and are thinking of moving to Middle View. During your visit, the two of you attend a Town Council meeting, eat in several of the local restaurants, chat with her neighbors, and kayak on the river. You drive back to your home two hours away in Industrial City and think about life in Middle View. Once home, you write notes on the strengths and weaknesses of the Town and Village of Middle View, pose additional questions, and think about some possible changes that could improve the lives of its people.

Planning and Evaluating

Understanding and Mastery: Analysis and assessment of the needs of clients or client groups

Critical Thinking Question: Observe a place where people live and/or work together in close proximity over an extended period of time and consider the following questions: How does the physical environment impact the sense of mutuality or "common-unity"? Who participates, what do they do, and why do they do it? What are some written rules and regulations that govern interactions? What "unwritten rules" seem to apply? Would you like to live or work there? What specific factors led you to your conclusion?

Variations on the Theme

The urban and rural geographic case studies described above provide rich descriptive illustrations of the many concepts covered in this book. However, many of the same principles and practices can be applied to partial communities, dispersed communities, communities of interest, and virtual communities. A brief description of each of these communities follows.

Although community organizing frequently focuses on "complete communities" (places like neighborhoods and villages that offer most of the goods and services residents need), partial communities (i.e., smaller residential areas and social institutions) may also benefit from organizing efforts. Occasionally their residents may want to use community organizing techniques to address concerns such as poor maintenance, noise, drug abuse, pets, pest control, rent increases, unfair enforcement of rules and regulations, or interpersonal and intergroup conflict. On a more positive note, they may want to increase neighborliness, improve the appearance of the facility, support one another in time of need, or share celebrative events. Suitable locations for this kind of partial or limited geographically based organizing include:

- Apartment complexes
- Mobile home parks
- Rural hamlets
- Subdivisions
- City blocks
- "Complete institutions" (e.g., prisons, college campuses, schools, nursing homes, military installations)

Explore more about the importance of migrant hometown associations. Consider how immigrant hometown associations might be helpful to people in the home countries as well as migrants dispersed throughout the world.

Dispersed communities (or diasporas) are groups of people who share a common sense of purpose, history, and a sense of duty to one another, although they may be scattered across the world. Many ethnic and religious groups—such as Mennonites, Jews, Muslims, North American First Peoples, Roma, Africans, Haitians, and Chinese—primarily identify themselves by their shared heritage, commitment to one another, and sometimes their homeland rather than their current geographic locations. Immigrant communities have always been characterized by a sense of common culture, continuing allegiance to a homeland, and caring networks. Today improved communication tools and transportation have made it easier for people to retain close ties with their homelands and have made travel between countries much easier than formerly.

The possibility of continuing close ties has, in turn, led to new ways of solidifying the sense of community. Foremost among these are hometown associations, membership organizations that enable people to connect their new homes (i.e., their "communities of residence") with their old homes (i.e., their "communities of origin"). Hometown associations have sprung up all over the world. They connect migrants with one another, provide them with mutual support in their new homes, and provide a vehicle to send monetary support back to their hometowns. Members quite often think of themselves as belonging to a single community that exists in several places: a hometown in their country of origin, an ethnic neighborhood in their country of residence, and a community of others from their hometown that are living in similar ethnic neighborhoods. Hometown associations are examples of ways migrants organize themselves to maintain their culture identity across the miles.

Human Systems

Understanding and Mastery: Emphasis on context and the role of diversity in determining and meeting human needs.

Critical Thinking Question: Explore the experiences of a migrant population that interests you. What are the strengths for immigrants of maintaining strong ties among people from the same hometown? What are the advantages for the hometowns? What problems, if any, might arise from maintaining strong ties to one's country of origin rather than focusing on one's new community?

Communities of interest are primarily organized around people with shared concerns or interests that are important components of their individual identities but are not geographically or culturally bound. Common interests range from recreation and the arts to medical problems and social ills. These communities often begin as quasi-groups of people who do not know one another but share common characteristics, interests, or concerns. For example, the Harley Davidson motorcycle community has "members" all over the world. As individuals, these people simply share a common interest, but they become a true community when they begin to communicate on a regular basis and develop social tics based on their shared interest in Harley Davidson motorcycles. Communities of interest may become formal organizations or remain loosely tied. Members of communities of interest often find ways to meet face to face through conventions, conferences, and other means—although face-to-face interaction is not absolutely necessary.

Human Systems

Understanding and Mastery: Organizational structures of communities

Critical Thinking Question: What differentiates a community of interest from an aggregation of people who just happen to purchase the same product or attend the same sporting event? What specific processes turn a loosely structured group of strangers into a cohesive whole with a sense of their common-unity?

Explore a community of interest by choosing a personal interest or passion and using a combination of personal inquiries and Web-based research to identify any organizations that are related to it. Pay special attention to the factors that led people to develop this community of interest, ways the community is structured locally and beyond, activities that create a sense of "common-unity" among members, the processes and methods that are used to promote communication and community building, and how well (or poorly) the various levels and elements of the community of interest seem to work with one another. Consider what this exploration has taught you about the nature of communities of interest.

Engage in social networking communities such as Facebook, LinkedIn, Second Life or a specialized network devoted to an area of interest. Consider ways in which social networks are similar to face-to-face communities as well as ways they may differ.

Virtual communities are a new and constantly evolving phenomenon that exists online and shares some characteristics of all communities, such as formal and informal rules of interaction, role expectations, primary relationships, subsystems to handle various issues, thematic boundaries, and stability across time. Virtual communities do not require face-to-face interaction but can fill many of the functions once reserved for these personal interactions. For instance, you may find that Facebook and other social utilities can fulfill part of your individual need for emotional support and friendship.

As virtual communities bring together people with shared interests who may live miles apart, participants don't always have to play their day-to-day social roles but may rather reinvent themselves or create an avatar (visual representation of themselves) that participates with other avatars in a virtual world. However, virtual communities are relatively new, and so insights into how they operate are still emerging.

Assess your comprehension of Community Types by completing this quiz.

Summary

In this introductory chapter, you were first introduced to the concept of community and then took a virtual tour of two very different fictitious geographic communities: Smithville, a city neighborhood, and the rural Town and Village of Middle View. This virtual tour is intended to help you imagine what it might feel like to live in these very different kinds of communities and begin to think about the kinds of organizing efforts that might be needed to improve their quality of life. They will be used as examples and illustrations throughout this book. (Please note Smithville and Middle View are based on many real geographic communities, but they *are* fictitious so do not attempt to connect them to specific communities, organizations, or people.) The chapter emphasized complete *geographic communities* because they are the most common targets of community organizing, although some time was spent on other kinds of communities that can also benefit from the ideas and skills you will learn here, including *partial geographic communities* (e.g., blocks, apartment complexes, schools, and institutions), *dispersed communities* (comprised of people who may be scattered throughout the world but who identify with a common "home"), *communities of interest* (such as hobbyists, co-religionists, scholars, and others who experience a sense of common-unity and belonging through shared commitments and experiences), and *virtual communities* that have emerged with the advent of social networking. In the chapters that follow, you will journey through analytical frameworks and practical ideas that will enable you to be an active participant in community organizing activities wherever you find yourself.

Assess your analysis and evaluation of this chapter's contents by completing the Chapter Review.

CHAPTER 2

Systems Thinking and the Kaleidoscopic Community

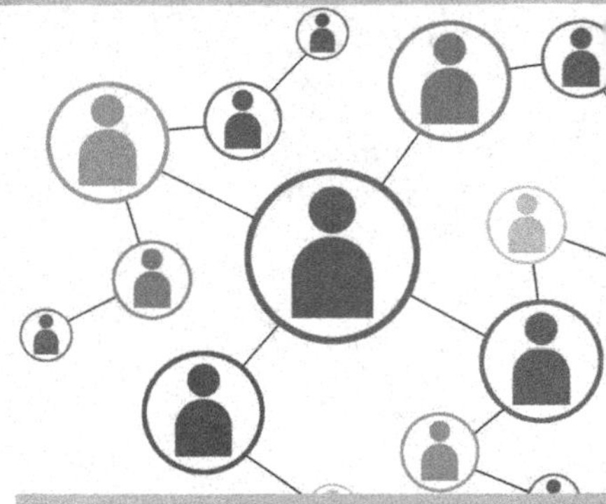

Mathias Rosenthal/Shutterstock

Chapter Outline

In Chapter 1, you read two comprehensive community case studies, one urban and one rural, and experienced a bit of what it feels like to live in each. This chapter introduces systems thinking and the kaleidoscope metaphor as useful analytical tools for community organizing. Smithville and Middle View will be used as case examples here and throughout this text.

Systems Thinking

Systems thinking is an analytical approach that allows us to perceive relationships and processes among the parts of a whole. It can be and has been used as a tool for understanding everything from the interrelationships among the subatomic particles within an atom to the motion of galaxies. Here, systems thinking will be introduced as an approach you can employ to understand relationships and processes within and beyond the **focal community system** (the community you have identified as in need of an organizing effort). You will learn to discern the **micro-systems** (smaller systems) that make up the focal community as well as the **mezzo-systems** (systems just beyond the focal community), the **macro-systems** (the systems that encompass the other two layers), and the **meta** or overlapping **systems**, (the "neighbors" of your focal community system). We begin by using a microscope as a metaphor for the **analytical skills** (mental activities) you will need to master systems thinking.

In some ways, your mind can work a little like a standard microscope—such as the one in Figure 2.1—by the way it focuses in and zooms

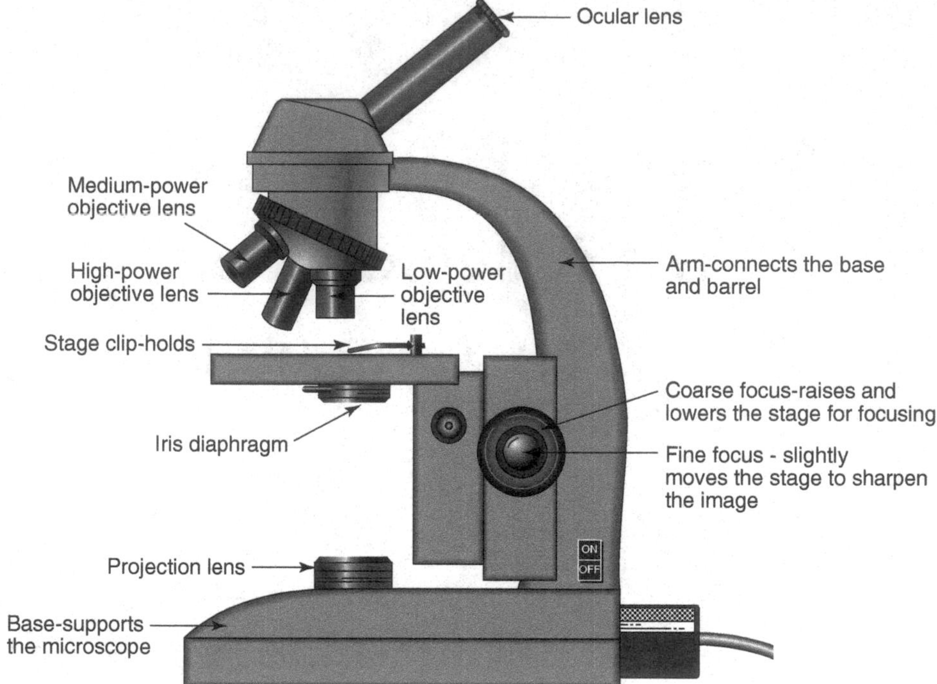

FIGURE 2.1 Microscope Metaphor for Relationships among Systems Like using a microscope, your mind can zoom in and out to look at something in more or less detail.

out. Picture yourself examining a slide of pond water under a standard microscope. The microscope has several levels (or powers) of magnification. As you look at your slide of pond water through the microscope, the low-power ocular lens gives you a blurry image of the whole drop of water. This is comparable to the **macro-system** in systems thinking. In community organizing, the macro-system is the big picture surrounding your focal community. In both the Smithville and Middle View examples, the macro-system level includes the natural, social, cultural, and economic environments of the United States in the early twenty-first century. These factors impact both communities, but their exact impact is ever-changing and vague.

If you want to know a bit more about the pond water, you would click the revolving nosepiece until you reached a second level of magnification, which clarifies a portion of the sample a bit more. You then could begin to discern animals, plants, air bubbles, and specks of dirt that had been invisible before. In community organizing, this is the **mezzo-system** (or middle level). Like the change in the microscope, the change from thinking about the focal community's macro-system to thinking about its mezzo-system feels like a mental "click" that brings a deeper level of detail into focus. For Smithville and Middle View, the mezzo-system contains many policies, organizations, and authorities that differ for each of them and, therefore, impact them differently. The mezzo-system includes, laws, governmental structures, non-profit organizations, religious denominations, and businesses, all of which are largely designed outside of either focal community but nonetheless impact them.

If you wanted to know still more about the pond water, you would increase the magnification to the third level by "clicking" again. The larger bits of matter would fade into the background and you would see a whole "community" of very small organisms going about their short lives interacting with one another. You might watch in fascination as a group of cells clumps together in one corner or as a paramecium swims along with its multiple "oars." If you were a biologist, you would have some idea of each kind or colony of creature and their interrelationships with one another. You have reached the **focal system**: life in a focal area of the sample. Community organizers do the same: they study human organisms in relationship to one another. For example, the Smithville neighborhood and the Town of Middle View are each likely choices for geographically based community organizing efforts with the goal of improving the quality of life for everyone in a delimited geographic area. Throughout the text, this level will be referred to as the focal community system or sometimes just the focal system. Most of your efforts will be concentrated at this level.

If you were actually a biologist looking at the pond water slide, it is likely you would "click" again to an even sharper but smaller section of the slide. There you would reach the micro-system level where even more little "creepy crawlies" could be seen in detail. The clump of cells would differentiate into its individual components. The paramecium would become a complex organism with recognizable body parts. In community organizing, the micro-system level includes a closer view of the separate people, organizations, and associations that make up your focal community system as they interact with one another. In both Smithville and Middle View, the micro-systems include: various ages, genders, socio-economic groups, clubs, educational institutions, local churches, sports clubs, and many other small groupings common to all geographic communities in the United States. In Smithville, these generic micro-systems are joined by diverse ethnic groups and races. In Middle View, they include the "old-timers" who have lived there for generations, the newcomers who live there all year, and the summer residents and the tourists who come occasionally.

The microscope metaphor is useful because you and your **organizing team**—the group of community members that shares responsibility for the organizing venture—can learn to literally focus and refocus your attention on the various levels to determine their impact on one another and, especially, on your goals for the focal system. Just as the microscope helps a biologist understand the ecological complexities in a smear of pond water, periodically moving mentally up and down through the focal, micro-, mezzo-, meta-, and macro-systems of a community will help you understand its ever-changing dynamics.

Explore systems thinking by accessing the SlideShare video Introduction to Systems Thinking by educational consultant Patrick Woessner. What are some of the ways systems thinking might be used to analyze complex processes?

Analyzing Community Systems

Focal community systems are composed of smaller micro-systems, cooperate and compete with meta-systems, and relate to various larger mezzo-systems, and all of these system levels exist within macro-systems.

Your key task in community organizing is the identification of a focal community system that will be the main place you intend to work and the starting point for your analysis. Systems thinking enables you to thoroughly understand your focal community system and its interrelationships with other systems.

The best choice for a focal community system is a **complete community** that should have most of the following characteristics:

- Exist over a reasonable period of time (i.e., longer than a few hours).
- Have established roles through which people interact in predictable, ongoing patterns.

- Show evidence of established customs (behaviors) and laws (policies).
- Be comprised of micro-systems (i.e., smaller divisions) that meet specific needs or represent specific populations and interests.
- Have an equilibrium (or balance of power) that is relatively stable over time.
- Have discernible boundaries that may be geographic, ideological—limited to adherents of a particular belief system, based on social issues (e.g., the rights of particular minority groups, instances of injustice, etc.), and/or legally defined (such as a political district).

Focal community system boundaries may be well defined or somewhat fuzzy. Usually, some functions—that is, activities necessary for community life—are performed within its boundaries, some are performed outside its boundaries, and some are performed both inside and outside. For example, the Smithville neighborhood has a few small stores, an elementary school, a health clinic, and multiple religious groups. But residents must go outside of the neighborhood's boundaries to buy large quantities of groceries, make substantial purchases such as cars or furniture, see a movie, have major medical tests, or attend high school or college. Most jobs require commuting, and all of the major services, such as street repairs, are the responsibility of the city. The Town of Middle View, on the other hand, is more self-contained. It has a branch of Walmart, a small hospital, a consolidated school system serving pre-K to grade 12, various recreation venues, two banks, several churches, and effective municipal services. As a basis for further investigation and application of systems thinking, choose a complete community that you know well and begin to mentally (or physically) explore it. Jot down some of your observations.

Assess your comprehension of Complete Community Systems by completing this quiz.

Micro-systems

Micro-systems are the major internal components or parts of a focal system. Micro-systems are the first "click" of the organizer's mental microscope below the focal community system. The micro-systems are where community life is lived.

Micro-systems of geographic focal systems such as Smithville and Middle View can be broken down into smaller bits, each of which has a life of its own. Many of the micro-systems in Smithville are defined by physical proximity, so we will look first at some of its geographic micro-systems (e.g., blocks and block clusters). Smithville is a neighborhood of Industrial City and is divided by streets, avenues, and alleys. Streets run north/south, avenues run east/west, and both have two-way traffic. Alleys are smaller passageways that were once used for coal delivery and are now often used for garbage collection. A city block includes all the buildings located between two streets and two intersecting avenues; Smithville encompasses approximately 150 city blocks. Some blocks have their own unique characteristics and can be considered separate micro-systems. Other blocks share many characteristics with nearby blocks and are best viewed together as "block clusters."

Remember as you walked through Smithville, you noticed that some blocks and block clusters had multi-story apartment buildings only a few feet away from large older homes with multiple apartments. Some buildings were commercial with only a few small apartments over the businesses, but most were single-family homes and duplexes with small front yards and back patios. The buildings on some blocks were well kept; other blocks were a mixture of well-maintained homes and dilapidated ones; and still other blocks were mostly empty, gravel-filled lots with a few run-down buildings.

On some blocks and block clusters, you saw people of different skin colors speaking many languages and seeming to get along well. Other blocks felt tense, and you saw gang symbols, swastikas, and Klan markings on the walls. A few other blocks appeared to be culturally homogenous.

A resident with whom you stopped to talk said that Smithville's blocks and block clusters also vary by the general age of the people living there. He noted that a block that once rang with children's laughter may have become quiet and sedate as its residents grew older and then once again filled with baby strollers as homes were sold or rented to younger people.

While many of the micro-systems in Smithville are based on geographic proximity, some are related to other shared characteristics such as stage of life. For instance, families with children may have concerns regarding the quality of their children's education, street safety, safe play spaces, and access to affordable, family-pleasing food in family-size packaging. Older children and teens may want recreational areas—such as: basketball courts, swimming pools, and indoor gyms—within a safe walking distance. Working people may desire reliable public transportation and high-quality, flexible child care. Older folks may want a senior activities center, nearby shopping and physicians' offices, convenience stores that sell small portions of food and beverages, and shady places to sit and talk. Members of various ethnic and religious groups may want to have places for worship and celebrations.

Sometimes, a community's micro-systems may have similar purposes but differ in organizational membership and location. For instance, some but not all blocks and block clusters in Smithville have "block clubs" that periodically hold block parties and gatherings, represent the interests of their blocks or block clusters to the Smithville Neighborhood Organization, or have their own Crime Watch organizations to guard one another's properties. Each block club has connections to all of the others and to the Smithville Neighborhood Organization but also maintains its independent identity.

Micro-systems are often strengthened by networking, so they may cooperate with one another to benefit the whole neighborhood. For instance, the Smithville Neighborhood Organization—composed of block clubs, businesses, non-profit organizations, and individuals—in order to stabilize rents recently petitioned the city to stop neighborhood gentrification. The Neighborhood Organization holds yearly meetings that generate petitions from the neighborhood to the municipal government, city schools, and organizations beyond the neighborhood level. In another example of networking across micro-systems, a group of Middle View parents created a town-wide Youth Baseball League that enables young people from the village, hamlets, and incorporated parts to the countryside to compete with one another during the summer months.

While Smithville's geographic micro-systems usually cooperate with one another in helpful ways, they sometimes compete for limited resources. For instance, two block clusters may compete with one another for city funding for a new playground, or block clubs may even compete with one another over who can give the best block party! In the Town of Middle View, the village and hamlets may compete for state-level funding for water and sewage projects or for which area of town receives the first high-speed Internet service.

A geographic community's micro-systems also include specific sectors of community life so that it is possible to focus on any local organization as a separate micro-system. For example, the parents of Smithville elementary school children recently focused on the elementary school micro-system and advocated for afterschool programs that would be located on both sides of a busy street.

Now that you have considered the Smithville and Middle View examples, continue to apply what you are learning by once again focusing on a complete community you know well. Focus your attention on its component parts (i.e., micro-systems). Identify the smaller systems that comprise your focal system. Look for things like differences among residential areas and components of the built environment. Identify sub-communities by looking for variations in age, socio-economic class, ethnicity, length of residency, home ownership, employment patterns, religion, extended family relationships, and any other characteristics that seem to differentiate among groups. Pay special attention to potential conflicts as well as places where most people are likely to be in agreement. Draw a picture or chart of these micro-systems and their relationships with one another. You should find that a mental picture is emerging that is leading you to a clearer understanding of your focal community system.

Human Systems

Understanding and Mastery: Emphasis on context and the role of diversity in determining and meeting human needs

Critical Thinking Question: How can community members embrace and celebrate the community's diverse micro-systems rather than allow differences to become a cause of conflict?

Cooperation and Conflict among Meta-systems

Meta-systems are other communities that are similar to the focal community, with which it must both cooperate and compete as shown in Figure 2.2.

Figure 2.2 represents three systems that are similar to one another and that sometimes cooperate (shown by their overlapping areas) and sometimes compete (shown by the areas with no overlap). Let's use Smithville as an example to demonstrate how this works. Smithville borders two other similar urban neighborhoods: Fair Hills and Riverview. All three neighborhoods have similar populations, problems, and strengths. Sometimes all three neighborhoods cooperate. For instance, leaders of their community organizations all participate on the city-wide Association of Neighborhoods and cooperatively advocate with city government officials and politicians for the needs of all inner-city neighborhoods for better city services, adequate policing, and improved neighborhood schools. On the other hand, these same neighborhoods often compete for limited resources, such as special funding initiatives for improved housing, a new business such as a grocery store, or rehabilitated playgrounds. While community leaders (organizers) are often expected to take part in such cooperative ventures, they are also expected to make focal community interests a priority.

FIGURE 2.2
Meta-systems
Source: Copyright © by Pearson Education, Upper Saddle River, NJ.

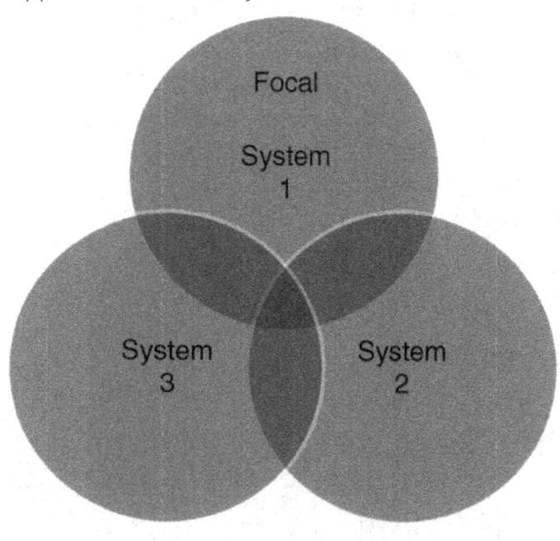

Now consider the community system you have been exploring. Identify other systems that are similar to your focal community system. Look for the ways these communities are similar to your focal system and the ways they differ, especially in terms of history, economics, socio-economic and cultural patterns, housing stock, environmental quality, and relative power. Identify ways your focal community system might cooperate with these meta-systems as well as ways they compete with you for limited resources. Pay special attention to potential conflicts as well as places where most people are likely to be in agreement. Draw a picture or chart of these meta-systems and their relationships. Save all of your material as it will prove useful later.

The Impact of Mezzo-systems

Mezzo-systems are the political, economic, and cultural systems that surround and support your focal community system and have a direct or indirect impact on the success of your community organizing efforts. Representatives of focal community systems often must reach beyond the focal system to broader mezzo- systems, especially to various levels of government. Because Smithville is a neighborhood in Industrial City, the Neighborhood Organization leaders must go to the city government and its offices for intervention in such areas as street cleaning and maintenance, housing code enforcement, garbage collection, policing, parks, and transportation. Smithville is also part of county government so it had to petition county decision makers to prevent the County Department of Social Services from locating too many group homes in the neighborhood. On the other hand, the Town of Middle View has a town supervisor and four elected council members called the Town Board. Representatives of the village and local hamlets recently petitioned the Town Board for an ordinance preventing hydro-fracking for natural gas within the bounds of the town. Like Smithville, Middle View is also impacted by the county government so its citizens recently formed an ad hoc committee to ensure that the town is included in the county's comprehensive recreation plan. Both focal communities have school districts that handle public education issues. Thus, community organizing efforts often address issues in the school district mezzo-system. For instance, the Smithville Neighborhood Organization recently petitioned the city-wide school board to require students to wear uniforms because organization members believe that this would cut down on bullying over clothing and lessen opportunities to display gang symbols.

Human Systems

Understanding and Mastery: Processes to analyze, interpret, and effect policies and laws at local, state, and national levels

Critical Thinking Question: Under what circumstances is it appropriate for similar communities to be allies in the political process? When, if ever, is competition among similar communities appropriate? What practical and ethical considerations would you use in making such decisions?

Beyond these local governments, both Smithville and Middle View are affected at the mezzo-system level by state and national laws, policies, and policy makers. For example, the Community Block Grant Program historically has been the way for the national government to redistribute tax dollars to cities and, eventually, to distressed areas. A reduction of these resources at the national level had profound effects on Smithville as the city's promised repairs to sidewalks, curbs, and storm drains were deferred when expected Community Block Grant money became unavailable. Meanwhile, Middle View's proposal for a new sewer system—based on the latest in environmentally sustainable technology—was refused by the State Department of Environmental Conservation because the new technology was not yet covered under old agency regulations. On a more positive side, Smithville received some infrastructure improvements through the President's job plan which was implemented after the 2008 economic crisis. Middle View has benefited from state financing of a comprehensive planning effort that will eventually lead to state funding for a new water system.

In addition to including different levels of government, mezzo systems can sometimes incorporate networks of government, not-for-profit, and private institutions that focus on particular aspects of life and are frequently spoken of as systems. Your organizing team may find yourselves encountering such mezzo-systems as the education system, the health care system, the transportation system, and the disaster relief system. For example, when Middle View was struck by a "300-year" flood, the focal community system leaders rallied town government, local churches, public schools, the fire department, and willing individuals while simultaneously seeking help from the disaster relief mezzo-system, which was comprised of a network of organizations that included local, county, and state emergency management resources; the American Red Cross; the utility companies; and a variety of denominational and service organizations. Each partner in the mezzo-system did its part to restore order and link everyone in town to needed services. The process was frustrating because each outside organization had its own **jurisdiction** (i.e., policies, procedures, and personnel that affected the emergency response), but in the end everyone managed to work together to ensure recovery.

Now that you have some idea of how mezzo systems impacted Smithville and Middle View, identify the various levels of government that most directly affect life in your focal community system. Pay special attention to the roles of government officials, regulatory agencies, enforcement, the judiciary, and the media. Explore government websites, and read documents such as comprehensive plans and zoning maps. Attend a local government meeting and observe the political process in action. Talk with at least one elected official (or staff member) who represents your focal community system. Begin to compare the goals and objectives of government officials and agencies with those expressed by community members. Continually ask yourself what you are learning about the way things "really" work in your focal community.

Human Systems

Understanding and Mastery: Processes to analyze, interpret, and effect policies and laws at local, state, and national levels

Critical Thinking Question: What are the major challenges facing local governments today? How might these challenges impact the likely success or failure of your community organizing efforts?

Macro-systems: Broad Natural, Economic, Social, and Cultural Environments

So far, we have moved from the micro-systems that make up a focal system to the meta-systems that parallel it, and outward to the mezzo-systems, such as municipal government, local economics, and service networks, that most directly affect its quality of life. We will now focus on macro-systems—the natural, social, and cultural environments which surround the focal system and its micro- and mezzo-systems.

The **natural environment** includes: the air, surface water (rivers, lakes, and streams), ground water, forests, soils, minerals, and geologic stability of the focal system, the region, the nation, and the world. The natural environment of Smithville and its surrounding region is somewhat degraded because of its history as an industrial and commercial neighborhood and its location in a medium-sized "rust belt" city, surrounded by other rust belt cities and former mining operations. This environmental degradation has serious implications for neighborhood goals. For instance, the Smithville Neighborhood Organization found that its goal of turning an empty corner lot into a mini-playground for toddlers and preschoolers was impossible because the lot is polluted with used motor oil from its previous use as a car-repair center. Other currently vacant lots are polluted with heavy metals that precipitated from the air over years of heavy manufacturing. These so-called brown fields are useless for new development without extensive restoration. The local rivers are polluted with mine acid, and although the fish population is returning, it has been deemed unfit for human consumption. A combination of toxins—including lead paint in the pre-1950s housing stock, heavy metals, and continuing air and water pollution—has been implicated in a higher-than-expected incidence of childhood cancers, miscarriages, and developmental disabilities in Smithville and throughout the region.

Middle View, on the other hand, has a rather pristine natural environment that is being threatened by recreational development and increased year-round residences that have taxed the carrying capacity of the soil and have depleted the ground water. Global climate change has adversely affected Middle View. As recent winters have clearly become warmer, winter sports such as skiing, snowmobiling, and ice fishing—sources of tourist income second only to summer activities—have decreased. Even summer activities have been adversely affected by climate change as changing weather patterns have caused a shift toward more dramatic weather patterns, including high straight-line winds and extended periods of dry weather, interspersed with devastating flooding.

The **economic environment** (e.g., the meta-system through which the goods and services needed for life are obtained) is mostly managed on a global scale. This globalization has led to the centralization of economic power, as well as the globalization of distribution and supply, which has sometimes resulted in the loss of local neighborhoods' economic strength, especially in rural areas and inner cities. Both Smithville and Middle View have been adversely affected by these trends. For instance, in the 1960s, Smithville was a bustling working class neighborhood. Most men worked as laborers in the major industry which, in its heyday, employed over 10,000 workers. Those who did not work for this major employer worked for the manufacturers and services that supported it. Most women were stay-at-home moms who kept immaculate homes and voluntarily coordinated most community events. Even then the neighborhood was somewhat diverse and supported many local businesses and organizations, from ethnic clubs, such as the Polish-American Club, to ethnic churches, such as various Orthodox denominations. There were many small stores that provided everything from fresh produce to shoes, furniture, and jewelry. Few people owned cars, and those who ventured outside of the neighborhood used either trolleys or trains. In the prosperous 1950s and 1960s, the city's major industry valued its skilled workforce and wanted to keep peace with the strong labor unions and so provided some luxuries, such as community swimming pools and lavish annual picnics and Christmas parties. Because the major employer provided everything from parks to medical facilities, there was no need for major community projects. This employer also provided many opportunities for specialization beyond high school, so there was no need for people to seek higher education. The neighborhood and the surrounding city were economically self-sustaining and even a little smug: World War II was over and the United States was on a roll! This continued until the early 1980s when the major industry decided that U.S. labor was too expensive and moved production overseas. In the decade between the 1980 and 1990 census, the median household income in the city dropped $10,000. In Smithville, it dropped $15,000. Many longtime residents left Smithville, and its population dropped 20% in those ten years. Homeowners could no longer afford to pay their property taxes. Homes were sold at a loss or were simply boarded up and left to the city government for tax sale. City government officials attempted to recruit new residents primarily from the Caribbean and the newly opened Eastern European countries and Russia. These new arrivals added to the cultural diversity of Smithville, but their recruitment and (especially) the financial incentives given them by the city government bred resentment among the "natives." These economic earthquakes deeply affected the Smithville focal system. Where once the neighborhood had been lively and economically self-sustaining with many small but prosperous businesses and well-maintained properties, it became a peripheral community filled mostly with hopelessness. Community organizing efforts like the Smithville Neighborhood Organization are struggling now to bring new life, but it often seems like a "two steps forward, one step back" proposition. The future is unclear. On the one hand, if the conservative agenda of globalization and the centralization of the world's wealth in a relatively few individuals and institutions continues unchecked, it is likely that Smithville will continue to decline or barely "bob along" in its current patterns. On the other hand, the liberal agenda may encourage too much dependence on government programs with miles of bureaucratic red tape—which may likely result in strangling local creativity. A third way which emphasizes (1) sustainability, (2) local or regionalized economics, (3) alternatives for mutual economic support, and (4) citizen engagement will be difficult, but it may return power to the community and result in a higher quality of life. Community organizers are bound to be in the thick of the debate over these alternatives.

Globalization and the centralization of economic power have adversely affected Middle View as well. In the 1950s and 1960s, Middle View was very different from what it is today. It had four primary economic bases: farming, lumbering, tourism (especially that of summer residents), and "main street" businesses. The family farms of yesterday—along with farm-based economic efforts such as feed mills, cheese factories, and local dairies—are largely in the past. Because Middle View is located in rolling wooded terrain with many wet patches between the hills, it is not suitable for large industrial farms or even large herds of dairy cattle. Farms are few and far between, although new trends emphasizing localized food purchasing along with "right to farm" legislation have begun to help increase their numbers. Although the forests surrounding Middle View are verdant, very little lumbering takes place, especially because the once-thriving paper-making industries are now nearly non-existent. Paper making has almost entirely been moved first to Norway, Sweden, and Finland—and more recently to northern Russia and even China and South America—as multi-national companies have searched for inexpensive labor and, in some cases, fewer environmental regulations. The loss of paper and lumbering has had an impact on Middle View comparable to the loss of Smithville's manufacturing capacity. Reasonably well-paid workers have either moved from the area or have been forced to replace their full-time, year-round jobs with odd jobs and seasonal labor. The loss of stable jobs, in turn, has affected local retail businesses, professional practices such as dentistry and law, restaurants and bars, churches, and the local school district. The local food pantry has experienced more visits and fewer donations.

Historically, Middle View has depended on an influx of summer families. Women and children stayed the whole summer while men commuted to the city and returned to "the cottage" on weekends. This reliable summer population is now almost non-existent. Macro-economic changes—especially the decrease in real earned income, increased demands for constant productivity at all levels, and the need for women to enter the workforce not by choice but by necessity—have changed the pattern of summer residence so that now summer home owners consider themselves fortunate to spend a few stolen weekends at camp and, even then, bring their computers. Tourists who once spent two weeks or more renting rooms and cottages in the many private motels that dot the countryside now usually spend two or three days there at most. These changes have further reduced the viability of local stores and services. The central village now lacks a reasonably sized grocery store, a hardware outlet, or a jewelry store. More and more family-owned motels and rental cottages close each summer.

Where Middle View was once economically semi-autonomous and most money earned in the community stayed in the community, globalization has impacted the retail business. Now the proliferation of so-called **Big Box** stores, such as Walmart and Home Depot, with relatively low prices, has added more nails to the coffin of **Main Street** (locally owned) businesses. In spite of a growing counter-trend toward supporting local businesses and increasing numbers of small niche retailers such as Dollar General, locally owned Main Street retailers continue to struggle. The loss of community-minded businesses and professional people, in turn, has adversely affected the voluntary sector—such as service clubs that have traditionally supported many charitable, educational, and recreational activities.

The **social environment** refers to the overall patterns of community life shared by everyone in the nation and is formally defined by laws, regulations, courts, and foundational documents, such as the U.S. Constitution. Informally it is defined by patterns of settlement among different ethnic groups and economic classes. In the United States, for example, everyone shares a federal form of government that includes: municipal, county, state, and national components. We participate in a representative democracy where individuals are elected to speak on our behalf and represent our interests. We have freedoms of the press, assembly, and religion and a two-party political system. Despite regional differences, most of us can move freely from neighborhood to neighborhood, or from state to state, without having to declare our whereabouts to the police. We can worship freely or choose not to worship at all. But with these rights come responsibilities. We have the responsibility to pay taxes, obey the law, and vote. Young men must register for the draft. Parents have responsibility for assuring that their children are educated until at least age 16, and so forth.

The **cultural environment**, though similar to the social environment, usually refers to ways of thinking, acting, believing, and behaving that are transmitted through families and religious affiliations over broad geographic areas. In many ways culture and cultural change are contradictory. On the one hand, many cultures change very slowly and are tenacious across time and space as we observed in Chapter 1 in our discussion of diasporic communities and can be seen in ancient conflicts in regions of the world like the Middle East. On the other hand, at least the superficial aspects of culture such as fashions, music, art forms, religious practices, and **memes** (ideas, behaviors, styles, and images that spread rapidly from person to person) change quickly, especially since the advent of the Internet.

Human Systems

Understanding and Mastery: An understanding of capacities, limitations, and resiliency of human systems

Critical Thinking Question: How will the massive changes occurring in natural, economic, social, and cultural macro-systems in our time be likely to affect our daily lives and local communities?

The United States as a whole is culturally diverse and is becoming more so, but cultural diversity varies widely across geographic regions, as well as among different community types. Some cultural environments are **monocultures**, where almost everyone shares similar belief systems and practices, while other cultures are very diverse. Middle View is located in a mostly rural region of the United States that historically has been monocultural. Most residents, not only in Middle View itself but across the region, are white, and many have lived in or near their "home territories" for generations. They share the same cultural Christianity and have many of the same expectations for themselves and their children. Smithville, on the other hand, is like many city neighborhoods: it is **culturally diverse** and becoming more so. It is a mixture of long-term working class white residents, equally long-term African Americans, and newer Hispanics, Caribbean peoples, and Russians. While there is some tension among the various ethnic groups and generations, most everyone gets along well and seems to enjoy sharing one another's cuisines, recreation, and viewpoints. These diverse people are likely to organize around common concerns such as garbage pick-up, policing, and shared pleasures like block parties where everyone brings samples of ethnic foods, dancing, and music.

Now that you have explored ways macro-systems impact Smithville and Middle View, turn your thoughts to your focal community. Identify key strengths and weaknesses of the natural environment that impact or may impact your focal community system in the future. Consider geographic features, weather patterns, and air and water quality. What effects is climate change likely to have? Identify global economic factors that affect the well-being of members of your focal community. How do factors such as globalization affect people on a day-to-day basis? Identify key political policies at the national and international level that affect the quality of life in your target community. What opportunities and threats do they represent? *Culture* in the broadest sense refers to values and the practices, policies, objects, and materials that support them. Identify major national and global values, beliefs, practices, and communication patterns that impact your focal community or its major micro-systems. How do these macro-level cultural changes affect values and behaviors at the local level? Continue thinking about these issues, and be sure to share your concerns with others in your focal community.

Assess your comprehension of Micro-, Mezzo-, Meta-, and Macro Systems by completing this quiz.

Kaleidoscopic Community Systems

Although the art and science of community systems analysis including the ability to mentally move among the various levels is extremely important, you will spend most of your time working to perfect your understanding of the focal community system. The image of a kaleidoscope—which creates new colored patterns whenever the tube is moved or shaken—captures the continual shifts in the roles and relationships of community members that characterize community decision making and action.[1]

Just as the beauty and fascination of a kaleidoscope depends on its varied pieces, their relation to one another, and the light shown on the whole process, a focal community system can best be understood through (1) identifying its various people, groups, associations, and formal organizations; (2) observing their interactions at different times and in various circumstances; and (3) shining the light of both analytical reason and creativity on the whole process. Let's turn first to the human components of this metaphor.

Individuals are the building blocks of community. They vary in age, socioeconomic status, gender, occupation, level of education, ethnicity, personal preferences, and hundreds of other ways that make each person different from another. Individuals are very often focused on the challenges and joys of daily life, including their personal physical and mental health, care for family members, work obligations, varying schedules, and many other distractions that isolate them from others and from full engagement in community life. Additionally, the individualistic nature of U.S. society makes it easy for individuals to feel lonely, isolated, and despairing of the efficacy of collective efforts, or, conversely, leads them to competition and conflict in the struggle to "make it." Although sometimes they seem buried in the everydayness of life, everyone in every focal community system has unique talents, perspectives, and traits that add richness, variety, and beauty to the quality of community life. Some have amazing talents. For example, Smithville is home to several renowned jazz musicians, a legendary movie star, an expert on African-American history, a visual artist known for her murals, and the inventor of several patented electrical products. Middle View is home to an expert on wildflowers and edible plants, a celebrated sculptor, the author of several classic books for children, and a once notorious bank robber turned bar owner. These individuals, as well as the hundreds of people with more ordinary talents, make each community a fascinating place to live—and many of them want to contribute to the place they call home.

Quasi-groups (or "almost" groups) are composed of members who share common characteristics, have an emerging awareness of shared interests, and may eventually decide to act together—especially if brought together by a community organizer. In Smithville, for instance, parents of small children are a quasi-group because they share common interests and challenges. But until they recognize common interests and concerns, they will remain a very loosely connected collection of individuals. However, when common concerns emerge—such as the need for an easily accessible, clean mini-park—and the need for the mini-park begins to be addressed, then group formation will begin. As group formation continues, other shared needs and possible solutions may emerge and multi-faceted friendships (primary group relationships) may develop. Additional projects may be initiated and, eventually, a formal organization may emerge. A similar movement from quasi-group to formal organization took place in Middle View among individuals who enjoyed snowmobiling. At first, these intrepid winter sports enthusiasts met casually on the trails and in their favorite local hang-outs. As they became better acquainted, they realized that they shared many concerns such as maintaining positive relationships with private property owners, keeping bridges and trails in reasonable repair, and ensuring everyone's safety. As these shared goals became apparent and their friendships grew, their quasi-group became a formal club that has now existed for many years.

Primary groups (e.g., extended families and friendship circles) are characterized by close emotional ties. They give meaning to life and define our sense of personal worth. Primary groups are durable and dedicated, but they can be closed, which makes it difficult for newcomers to gain entrance or influence the group. Primary groups are extremely important in all community organizing efforts because loving relationships provide the motivation and stamina to continue even difficult or threatening ventures, as well as the trust which is at the heart of all successful ventures. The importance of primary groups and relationships can be seen by comparing two attempts at developing a community center in Middle View. In the first attempt, the town supervisor formed a high-level collaboration with the County Human Services administrator, the director of the County Community Action Agency, and the superintendent of the school department to obtain state and federal funding to develop a school-based community center. The County Community Action Agency took the lead in the project and hired an outside director to manage it. Even though the initial effort had significant grant funding from the county, state, and local levels—and the director had a masters' degree in human services management—the center's first year was a disaster and its first director left. The center was about to close but, in a last, almost half-hearted attempt,

Community Action hired a new director whose position was supplemented by two local Americorps workers. The two Americorps workers already had primary connections in Middle View. The older of the two was a 52-year-old mother (and now a grandmother) who had lived in Middle View all of her life. The younger worker was a recent graduate of Middle View High. Both women had dozens of long-term friends and family members in both the Town and Village of Middle View. They knew the focal community (and most of its micro-systems), respected one another, and had the trust of the new director. Within a few short months, the community center blossomed with activities for all ages and economic levels. These activities greatly enhanced the quality of life for everyone in Middle View. Residents of Middle View have since embraced the center and have formed the Friends of Middle View Community Center to ensure its continuation even after the grant funding runs out. As an added bonus, the center's success has so impressed the original funders and other outside resources that it is likely that the center will have a long, healthy, and useful life.

In Smithville, primary groups are often women-centered and are held together by a network of blood-related extended family members (aunts, mothers, grandmothers, sisters, nieces, etc.), as well as "honorary" extended family members who are usually given family-like titles of aunt, grandmother, or sister and slightly more formal relationships such as the women that African-American churches often identify as "mothers of the church." Although such women are often identified with African-American culture, they also exist among working class white families, the Hispanic and Caribbean communities, and other ethnic groups. Often the matriarchs of different ethnicities know one another and work together well for community betterment. (In fact, the only place they do not exist is among the upper middle class of mostly white people who have been buying condominiums and gentrifying the neighborhood.) These community-based women's networks have done amazing things in Smithville. They have cleaned up a neighborhood park once given over to the drug trade, prostitution, and gang connections and have stormed City Hall and forced the city to repair curbs and storm drains and add crosswalks at dangerous intersections. Although they feel great compassion for people, they also have joined together to prevent the neighborhood from becoming the city's only location for various group homes and halfway houses. Individually and together, they have linked hundreds of young families to needed food, clothing, medical care, and educational opportunities. Their relationships with one another—as well as their connections throughout the community—make them a force to be reckoned with. Gang leaders, police officers, and mayors have been known to tremble when these women confront them. The women have backbone, courage, and hope. Working with and through them is absolutely vital to successful inner-city organizing.

Associations have relatively informal organizational structures and are focused on specific and rather limited shared interests. Focal communities are alive with such associations—just listen to cancellations on a snowy day anywhere in the northern or midwestern United States! Smithville brims with associations, including the Thursday Night Cooking Club, the Community Gardening Group, the Wednesday Night Prayer Circle at the African Methodist Episcopal Church, the salsa group at the Polish Club, the Guyanese Cricket Club, the "Bar-b-quers" who meet monthly at one another's homes for ribs and beer, and the Teen Hip-Hop Ensemble. More threatening associations include three local gangs and at least one petty theft ring. The list could go on and on. Middle View has a local Mothers of Preschoolers (MOPS) chapter, the Middle View

Community Choir, an Alzheimer's Support Group, a boating club, a Lakefront Homeowners Association, two bowling leagues, a mountain bikers association, the Middle View Blue Bells (a women's singing group), a local garden club, and is rumored to have a loose association of drug dealers, a clique of spouse swappers, and an ongoing network of teens and young adults who meet weekly on a deserted beach for beer, bonfires, and sex. Associations are somewhat hard for outsiders or newcomers to find because they usually lack formal listings in the telephone book or on the Internet. The lists above are a sample of associations that are fairly typical of focal communities. If you want to locate one, ask a local person whom you trust (and who trusts you) to find leads to it.

Formal organizations have clear legal structures and exist for limited purposes. Generally, participants only interact with each other within the context of the group or organization. They are formally organized, usually hierarchically structured, and focused on a particular mission, goal, or function. A formal organization is usually characterized by an organizational charter, a proprietor or a board of directors, an executive director, and, often, paid staff members. Formal organizations are often the most visible part of a focal community system. Smithville and Middle View are a study in contrasts. Smithville's organizations include, but are not limited to, education-related organizations from preschools and child-care programs to a branch office of the community college and medical care offered in places as varied as a free clinic housed in the local YMCA to private offices where practitioners offer everything from traditional medicine and conventional medical care to holistic alternatives. Places of worship include Christian churches that vary in size, theology, and architecture—from small storefronts to imposing old edifices, a small synagogue, a mosque, and a Hindu temple. Human service needs are met through branches and central offices of a wide variety of non-profit, for benefit, and public human services organizations. Shopping opportunities and financial service needs are addressed by individual entrepreneurs, thrift shops, pawn shops, branches of downtown banks, local credit unions, several currency exchanges, and ATM machines that are everywhere. In short, these formal organizations and more make it possible to live a full life without ever leaving the neighborhood.

While Smithville sometimes feels overcrowded with formal organizations, life in Middle View sometimes feels as if formal organizations are few and far between and that many are missing. Primary medical care is offered at a small local clinic in Middle View village, but most medical services require at least a thirty-minute trip to the local regional hospital or to its surrounding specialists. There are few child-care programs or preschools. Most child care is provided by family members and friends. The consolidated school district covers many miles of forested land. It is not unusual for children to have two-hour bus rides each way. The nearest vocational school and community college is thirty minutes away, just like the regional hospital. While Department of Social Service representatives come to Middle View Village once a month, most human services must be accessed in the same larger town that's thirty minutes (and three to five gallons of gas) away. There is only limited public transportation. Only Christian worship is formally available. There are four mainline Protestant churches, three independent congregations (two of which are located on back roads), and a small Roman Catholic Church. There is a local funeral home, one general store, two convenience stores, six restaurants, and five bars. The local post office has been threatened with closure but so far has avoided that fate.

Assess your comprehension of the Components of Kaleidoscopic Community Systems by completing this quiz.

Now that you have taken a look at the different people and groups who interact in the kaleidoscopic focal community, you can begin to trace some typical interactions among them. Table 2.1 provides a brief view of these interactions.

Each of these individuals and groups can potentially impact the quality of life in your focal community as they live their daily lives and communicate with one another.

Table 2.1 Interactions among Community Members

	Individuals	Quasi-groups	Primary Groups	Associations	Formal Organizations
Individuals	Initiate informal discussions of community needs.	Talk with others and learns of common concerns and the possibility of mutual action.	Make family and friends aware of an issue, encourages them to "do something."	Look for like-minded people who are already beginning to address the individual's interests and concerns.	Form a new organization to accomplish desired goals.
Quasi-groups	People with common concerns find one another and begin to talk and organize.	Members of two or more informal groups recognize concerns that link them.	Members begin to share their concerns with close family and friends who may join the effort.	Begin to look for existing informal associations that may want to join forces or give guidance in forming an association.	Emerging group expresses its concerns to an existing organization and solicits its help or challenges it for an appropriate response.
Primary groups	Face an issue that adversely affects one of their members and recruit individuals to help.	Reach beyond their immediate support networks to others who are facing similar concerns and draw them into the circle of friendship	Seek other primary groups within the community for mutual aid, such as when a whole community raises funds for a family in distress.	Learn from existing associations how to move to the next level without sacrificing love and caring.	Provide moral support to representatives or go as a group to solicit help from existing organizations or challenge them for an appropriate response.
Associations	Recruit like-minded people to support the emerging cause and seek their unique contributions.	Identify quasi-groups that share the association's interests for recruitment and networking	Add personal contacts to those related to association work, such as shared meals, long talks on matters with deep personal meaning, share hugs, smiles and other tokens of friendship.	Join with other associations in shared efforts for the good of the focal community. Strategically oppose associations who oppose their goals.	Join with formal organizations in shared efforts for the community good. Engage in social action efforts as in opposing threats from powerful formal organizations.
Formal organizations	Recruit individuals to contribute their goods or services and to volunteer.	Target segments of the population for advertising/ marketing efforts.	Make primary groups aware of goods and services.	Solicit assistance from associations that may further their organizational missions.	Collaborate with other formal organizations on broad initiatives.

Source: Copyright © by Pearson Education, Upper Saddle River, NJ.

Let's use Smithville and Middle View to show how various community members and groups can connect with specific neighborhood efforts which fit their interests and talents, thus adding to the individual's sense of engagement, self-worth, self-esteem, and self-actualization. Linking individuals with neighborhood needs provides an inexpensive solution and creates a win–win situation for both the community and individual. Here's a helpful tip: once an individual volunteer is drafted, engage that person right away because no one likes to offer his or her services and then be ignored.

Now let's look at some examples of engagement in the Smithville neighborhood and the Town of Middle View, based on the categories in Table 2.1.

Individuals to Other Groups and Organizations

Mary Smith is a middle-aged woman who lives in a neatly kept apartment in the heart of Smithville. She has lived there for many years and has raised five children as a single parent after her husband died of a stroke at age forty. Three of her adult children still live in the neighborhood. She is considered one of the mothers of her church. People often seek out her assistance because of her innate wisdom and inspirational faith. Mary owns a small second-hand store where she sells her own baked goods and handcrafts. Mary has contacts at all of the various levels shown in Table 2.1. She has befriended many people—from the children who drop by her store for a cookie and a hug to her senior citizen neighbor to whom she daily takes supper. Even local gang members know that they can count on "Mother Mary" for a smile, a meal, and good advice. Mary is especially friendly with other women who share her concerns about the quality of life for neighborhood children. Recently, the women have been talking about how dangerous the local park has become and what action they might take on this issue. They are a quasi-group that is about to become a more formal organization composed of Mary's women friends and her family members. She has been elected president of the new organization. The quasi-group has identified various organizations in the focal community and its mezzo-systems with decision-making power, so Mary visits their leaders and makes her case.

Quasi-groups to Other Individuals, Groups, and Organizations

In Middle View, a quasi-group of local parents is concerned that there are few, if any, safe and inexpensive after-school activities for their teens. Several mothers who have been talking for some time about their younger teens have formed an organization that they tentatively call the Teen Connection. They have recruited members of their immediate and extended families, including some of the teens, and have taken steps toward becoming a not-for-profit organization. They have recently identified a group of parents and grandparents of older teens and young adults who are interested in some of the same issues. The two quasi-groups have decided to remain separate but to work together on issues of common interest. The Teen Connection has identified several formal organizations in Middle View and has spoken with the YMCA, the community youth group, and the local schools about creating and posting a common calendar of teen events on Facebook. Members also have been exploring financial and planning resources available from the county, state, and national governments and international service clubs. Progress is slow but members of the original quasi-organization are pleased with the results thus far.

Primary Groups to Individuals, Groups, and Organizations

On a cold December evening, a Smithville mother and her seven children, ages thirteen months to thirteen years, were attempting to cross a major street dividing the neighborhood, which had no traffic light and no crosswalk for six blocks in either direction. A speeding pick-up truck came screeching around the corner and hit the mother and four of the children, permanently disabling a ten-year-old girl. Immediately, a quasi-group formed to collect money for the family (who had no health insurance) and to provide Christmas presents and holiday food. Members of a local church visited the family, regularly drove the mother to the regional medical center, and provided child care for the younger children. Formal organizations, such as the Salvation Army, provided other assistance, and the local Neighborhood Watch built a ramp so the little girl could return home in her wheelchair. Once the immediate emergency had passed, the family petitioned the Neighborhood Organization to confront the city government with the dangers of the crosswalk situation. The Neighborhood Organization discovered several similar incidents had occurred over the years and contacted members of these extended families who were willing to tell their own stories to the press and city government. The efforts of these multiple families (aided by the Neighborhood Organization) resulted in the creation of at least one new crosswalk.

Associations to Individuals, Quasi-groups, Primary Groups, and Formal Organizations

In Smithville, the Wednesday Night Prayer Group at the African Methodist Episcopal Church began to share their concerns about their adult children and their adult children's friends. Several ladies asked for prayer for young women who were single parents with limited incomes who seemed to be alternating between moderate stability and homelessness and desperation. Several of these young women were involved in abusive relationships; they often struggled to put nutritious food on the table or clothing on their children's backs. Several prayer group members decided to put their prayers into action. Each prayer group member agreed to contact several of these young women (who were a quasi-group because they shared many characteristics in common, but they were not yet particularly bonded together) to join them at a potluck dinner that would include home-style cooking and child care. Periodically, the prayer group women would invite these young ladies (many of whom were directly or indirectly related to prayer group members who considered all of them "family") to join with the older women periodically for such potluck dinners. The members thought that these initial potlucks might lead to an ongoing informal association which could link young women with older ones. It was hoped that the older women would help with child care, listen to relationship concerns, and mentor the young women in practical skills, such as homemaking. The younger women would, in turn, provide the older women with friendship, respect, and at times assistance with the struggles of growing older. Everyone would be encouraged to support one another physically, practically, emotionally, and spiritually. The idea was a success, and the informal association went on for some time. Friendships deepened among all the women. They toyed with the idea of continuing as an informal association under the church's charter but decided to become a formal non-profit organization that would provide mentoring and various kinds of support services to Smithville women of all ages. They formed a steering committee, recruited a preliminary Board of Directors, created by-laws, found a skilled attorney willing to offer *probono* (free) services, and incorporated as a non-profit corporation under state and national law. They still meet weekly for prayer and have very close personal ties with one another, but now their formal organization annually serves hundreds of Smithville women, as well as many who live elsewhere in Industrial City.

Formal Organizations to Individuals, Groups, and Organizations

At the time of the May 2011 "Three-Hundred-Year flood" in the Town of Middle View, employees and volunteers from several formal organizations saw the need to contact and help affected residents. Various organizations jointly prepared a flyer that described available services, contact information, and face-to-face meeting sites. Members mailed the flyers to all residents; dropped them off at local convenience stores, laundromats, bars and restaurants; and distributed them through the local service clubs, schools, and churches. Individuals told their families and close friends. Quasi-groups of volunteers and associations—such as the volunteer fire company and snowmobile club—spread the word about available services. When the crisis was over, the county emergency management authority held an open meeting for individuals, extended families and friends, quasi-groups, and formal organizations to provide feedback on the emergency response to help improve services. This information was added to a national and international emergency response database to use for planning and training purposes worldwide.

Although Table 2.1 depicts a somewhat linear world with logical connections among the various parts, the kaleidoscope metaphor and vignettes above remind us that these interactions are non-linear, occur simultaneously, and may impact other constituencies in surprising ways.

As you have seen in these examples, the "kaleidoscopic community" is comprised of interactions among individuals, quasi-groups, primary groups, associations, and formal organizations. Reflect on your exploration of your focal community system. Create a table listing key components of each category, the strengths or threats each brings to the overall quality of community life, and questions you would like to ask about each of them. (Note: This list will grow constantly as you continue your exploration and will become an important resource for further research.)

Human Systems

Understanding and Mastery: Organizational structures of communities

Critical Thinking Question: What tools and techniques might be needed to enable community organizing teams to keep track of the important components of their kaleidoscopic community and facilitate networking among them?

Assess your comprehension of the Interactions Among Community Components by completing this quiz.

Bringing People Together

One of a community organizer's most important roles is to weave various participants of the community into interactional patterns that result in concrete improvements in the quality of life and create a sense of contentment and belonging. **Weaving** is a non-linear process that eventually becomes part of your thinking and behavior as a community organizer. Although difficult, this process involves keeping a "mental filing system" of the participants you encounter and making connections between people who help one another or share common interests, as well as among associations and institutions. This process is more art than science because you can't predict the outcome of the links you'll make or where such important links will be made. Therefore, you may need to introduce people through formal and informal meetings, make individual and conference telephone calls, host social or educational events, and use **listservs** (computerized mailing services) and various social networking sites.

Ultimately, your mental filing system will provide opportunities for linking participants and promoting listening and summative reflections. After that, step back and see what happens. These interactions may lead to wonderful connections or go nowhere. In the long run, a focus on positives rather than negatives—and on ways people can work together rather than on conflicts—can make a major difference in their quality of life.

Kaleidoscopic, Non-geographic Communities

While most of this chapter has focused on geographic communities—which are the most frequent targets of community organization efforts—many of the organizing principles can be applied to the dispersed communities, communities of interest, and virtual communities that were mentioned in Chapter 1.

Many immigrant groups and refugees are spread across the world in dispersed communities. These **diasporas** occur for a variety of economic and social reasons, but all are characterized by geographic dispersion coupled with cultural unity. Not too many years ago, dispersion meant that clusters of displaced people would settle in ethnic neighborhoods where they would keep the "old" ways and traditions but would be forever isolated from their original homelands. Rapid communication and global travel have changed this reality so that clusters of people who share a similar culture now live in diverse communities all over the world.

Many individuals and families in Smithville participate in ethnic-based micro-, focal-, mezzo-, and macro-systems simultaneously. For example, Freya Jones (not a real name) is twenty-four years old and the daughter of Jamaican immigrants who moved to New York City when Freya was two years old. Her family settled in a Jamaican area of the Borough of Queens. Her parents found it hard to buy a home in New York City, so when some of their friends and extended family members found that inexpensive homes were available in Smithville, they took a chance and moved there when Freya was ten. At first Freya's family stayed with her aunt until they were able to obtain first-time homeowners' loans from the city. Freya and her parents have lived in Smithville for fourteen years. While they mostly socialize with other Jamaicans in Smithville and other city neighborhoods, they also actively participate with their diverse Smithville neighbors and feel at home there. In spite of their feeling of comfort in Smithville, they miss Jamaica, Jamaican culture, and widespread friends and family. As a result, they frequently visit other Jamaicans in New York City, Toronto, London, and Jamaica itself and are in constant touch on Facebook and via telephone. For several summers, Freya was sent to her grandparents in Jamaica and even today she says that she feels she has a Jamaican self and a U.S. self. Freya's parents, Freya, and indeed almost every Jamaican in Smithville is concerned about the way Caribbean immigrants are treated in the United States, Canada, and Europe and about ongoing struggles in Jamaica itself. Many send money to relatives when they can and support projects there. Freya, especially, feels strongly that all of the Caribbean peoples suffer from historical trauma that originated in slavery, and she has been working for social justice for the people of the region whether they live in Jamaica or are scattered across the world. She celebrates her unity with cultural Jamaicans everywhere by wearing her hair in dreadlocks, listening to Jamaican music, and practicing Rastafarianism. She dreams of going to Ethiopia one day because she believes her real roots are in Africa. Members of every ethnic group in Smithville have similar stories and connections.

Communities of Interest

Communities of interest share many of the characteristics of geographic and dispersed communities but are bound together by shared concerns, beliefs, and values rather than geographic proximity or cultural origin. Communities of interest often develop over many years through writing, discussion, and connected knowledge that provides a broad consensus about what it means to be part of that community, especially in relationship to other communities with differing values. For some, membership in a community of interest is an important part of how they define themselves personally and socially. It can even become their **master status**, meaning that almost everything they say or do is done in association with their community-of-interest identity. Other members may participate in several different communities of interest and may not be very attached to any of them. Despite individual variations in the centrality of their commitment, all members within a community of interest are characterized by their acknowledgement of participation and their investment in their community through time, money, energy, and care for other members.

Communities of interest depend on "safe spaces" where people with common interests meet comfortably, become acquainted, and develop strong ties that are characteristic of true communities. Such a community of interest was developed in Middle View several years ago when two lesbians moved into the area and found that they were lonely and ostracized for their life-style. Quietly, they learned of other lesbians in the area and, in informal conversations, learned that these women were also very lonely and felt a need for a place to gather in safety. They decided to turn a few rooms of their rambling farmhouse into a bookstore and tea room. They furnished it with comfortable sofas and chairs, made both tea and coffee available for nominal sums, and stocked their shelves with lesbian-related books and other items. They did not advertise publicly, but the word soon spread that their home/bookstore was a safe place to gather. Newcomers to the area and women exploring their sexual preferences often came to the bookstore—nervously at first—but most made it their "second home," a place to be comfortably themselves. As the years have gone by, some women no longer frequent the store as much as they did earlier in their lives, but when interviewed by an outside researcher, all expressed their appreciation for the role of the bookstore at crucial times in their lives.[2]

Virtual Communities

Virtual communities are an emerging phenomenon, and there has been much debate over whether communities can really exist without face-to-face contact. Although many people associate virtual communities with social networks such as Facebook, MySpace,

Table 2.2 Comparison of Virtual and Real Communities

	Real	Virtual
System Dynamics	Characterized by four levels: micro, focal, mezzo, and macro.	Also true of virtual communities.
Components	Individuals, quasi-groups, primary groups, associations, and formal organizations but with relatively finite space boundaries and numbers of participants.	Also true of virtual communities but special boundaries are enlarged and numbers of participants and potential participants may number in the millions.
Kaleidoscopic Attributes	The above components interact in ever-changing, creative ways.	Also true of virtual communities, but the process is faster and possibly less predictable.
Intents or Purposes	Betterment of a geographic area, friendship, professional connections, shared interests, social action/advocacy, linking those of common ethnic/racial or religious origin, helping people with physical, emotional or relationship issues.	Also true of virtual communities.
Communication Structures	Face-to-face encounters, formal meetings, committees, telephone trees, community forums.	There are now at least partial electronic means for all of these purposes.
Leadership	Usually a small core group which may be formally constituted with officers or a steering committee. Leaders are facilitators who ensure that goals are accomplished in a civil manner and take care of details.	Virtual communities often have similar structures. Moderators often ensure goal accomplishment, encourage civil communications, and care for administrative details.
Inclusiveness	Usually attempt to be inclusive but can be blocked by a variety of tangential issues, related to economic status, such as time, place and expense of meetings.	Same is true but inclusiveness may be globally hampered by an ongoing digital divide between rich and poor.
Level of Individual Engagement and Sense of Belonging	Varies from having a central position to being relatively unimportant.	Also true of virtual communities.

Source: Copyright © by Pearson Education, Upper Saddle River, NJ.

Twitter, and LinkedIn; dating sites such as eHarmony and Match.com; and forums or blogs, these only begin to scratch the surface of virtual communities. In fact, all of the systems and kaleidoscopic attributes that affect geographic focal communities can and do affect virtual communities. Table 2.2 compares virtual and real communities on several dimensions.

Assess your comprehension of the Similarities and Differences between Real and Virtual Communities by completing this quiz.

Much to many people's surprise, there are very few important differences between real communities and virtual ones—and a few distinct advantages that include low impact on the environment and increased diversity of participation.

Summary

Over the course of your professional and personal life, you will participate in many geographic communities and communities of interest. Communities are ever-changing, which makes community organizing both challenging and engaging.

In this chapter, we explored the individual and interrelationships within communities. The focus on systems thinking and the microscope metaphor laid the groundwork for community analysis. By identifying a focal system and understanding its related micro-, mezzo-, and macro-systems, we were able to take a closer look at the Smithville and Middle View focal community systems and begin to discern how their interrelationships are kaleidoscopic (or constantly changing). As we carried the kaleidoscope metaphor forward, we defined several levels of social reality which include individuals, quasi-groups, primary groups, associations, and formal organizations. We then explored the interrelationships among these groups through illustrations from the Smithville and Middle View cases.

We examined dispersed communities and communities of interest and compared real and virtual communities. This chapter focused on the question "What is a community?" and responded by providing a systemic view and frameworks to aid in your understanding of community and community organizing, as well as to lay the groundwork for the chapters to follow.

Assess your analysis and evaluation of this chapter's content by completing the Chapter Review.

CHAPTER 3

Frances M. Roberts/Alamy

Living and Working in Communities

Chapter Outline

There is nothing quite as practical as a good theory. This chapter, "Living and Working in Communities," continues this focal system approach and the kaleidoscope metaphor, while briefly introducing useful theoretical frameworks—drawn from cognitive psychology, community psychology, symbolic interactionism, and role theory—to use as analytical tools for community organizing.

Building Your Internal Picture of the Focal Community

In this chapter, you will see that we human beings have many ways of defining—and in some ways creating—our own social reality in a process that's both internal and external, both psychological and sociological. Everyone inside and outside of a focal community system creates **cognitive-emotional constructs** or **schemas** (more or less clear ideas, mental images, and emotions) about it. Everyone involved—including you as the community organizer—is continually building and rebuilding these personal schemas of the focal community system* that are based on experiences, perceptions, and judgments about communities in general. These judgments may be about specific kinds of communities (i.e.,

**Focal community system*, *focal community*, and *focal system* are used interchangeably to keep your focus on both the "community" and "system" aspects of this level of community life.

rural, suburban, poor, working class, ethnic, affluent) and about the focal community system in particular. One of your key tasks is to help participants articulate these various viewpoints and meld them into a common understanding of the focal community system, its assets, and what is needed to make life better for everyone.

Self-Development

Understanding and Mastery: Conscious use of self

Critical Thinking Question: Our views of community life are largely based on cognitive–emotional schemas that have often developed over many years. Consider your impressions of your chosen focal community system, then think back over ways past life experiences might have influenced your current views. In what ways might these experiences and impressions influence your view of the focal community? What can you do to make sure that they do not adversely affect your organizing efforts?

For example, in your imaginary journey through the Town of Middle View, you probably arrived with certain stereotypes about rural community life. While visiting, you met many different people and observed them at work and play. You found that each had opinions about everything from the local economy and the needs of teens and young adults to environmental concerns and the basic honesty of town government. As a newcomer, you listened carefully and tried to create your own picture of life in Middle View. If you were attentive to your own thinking processes, you realized that your initial perceptions and judgments changed as your impressions of Middle View shifted from its being a *typical* rural place to being a *specific* place with unique people, assets, and problems. You realized subconsciously that Middle View has characteristics that are shared by all communities, that are common to some communities, and that are uniquely its own. If you had stayed longer, you would have noticed an increased understanding and a change in your mental picture as new encounters and observations provided more pieces to your perceptual puzzle.

To understand how internal constructions of community develop, we must explore some concepts from developmental and cognitive psychology. In *The Equilibration of Cognitive Structures*, the famous developmental psychologist Jean Piaget used the terms **assimilation** (fitting an experience into your established mental pathways), **accommodation** (creating new or altered pathways for accepting dramatically new information and experiences into your thinking), and **equilibration** (putting things back in balance). He believed that learning is **iterative**—that new information is shaped to fit with existing knowledge and existing knowledge is modified to accommodate new information. You will use all these mental processes as you examine new community systems or explore familiar ones.

For most community organizers, assimilation and accommodation of new ideas and experiences is ongoing as you compare current experiences with prior constructions of community reality. Sometimes your current experiences will fit well with your previous ideas; at other times, new information or experiences will cause you to change your views in significant ways. This is natural, normal, and an important part of truly focusing on a community system.[2]

Client-Related Values and Attitudes

Understanding and Mastery: The worth and uniqueness of individuals including: ethnicity, culture, gender, sexual orientation, and other expressions of diversity

Critical Thinking Question: Use your human service skills to learn how people sharing similar life experiences can have different viewpoints. Identify three approachable, yet different people in your focal community. Where did they agree? In what ways did their perceptions of community life differ from one another and from your own perceptions? How was your own schema (i.e., impression) of your focal community changed as a result of these conversations? How might understanding individual cognitive schemas help you in your organizing effort?

Basic thinking processes have several implications for community organizers because the same community can seem very different depending on the perspective you choose. Think back to your imagined tour of the Smithville neighborhood in Chapter 1. If you have been taught a deficit vision of such neighborhoods and, therefore, defined them as "cultures of poverty," you probably went to Smithville expecting gun shots and evidence of drug deals on every corner—and you could find it. On the other hand, if you expected to find people doing their best to live peaceful, satisfying lives under difficult circumstances, you would have noticed the laughter, people doing favors for one another, and flower boxes on almost every porch. The best community organizers are realistic about deficits, but they are able to see and harness community assets as well.[3]

Explore Social Cognition and Cognitive Schema. Consider how differing cognitive schemas might impact individuals' views of their community.

The nature and tenacity of mental schemas help explain why it can be so hard to change people's minds and their negative perceptions of a community, neighborhood, situation, group, or individual because everyone you meet will have a different cognitive–emotional schema of the focal community. Often community organizers are frustrated when old images of community realities linger after statistics show that significant improvements have been made. Cognitive–emotional theory assures us that such distorted perceptions are not surprising: they are based on established schemata, which, by definition, are hard to change.

Cognitive psychology provides analytical tools to help you understand how people often develop opposing views about the same set of circumstances and also gives clues about how change takes place over time. If you point out positive steps that have been taken, share success stories, and celebrate the good things, people become more hopeful. Over time, hope builds internal peace that drives individuals to bring about lasting change.[4]

Assess your comprehension of the Cognitive Schemas in Understanding Communities by completing this quiz.

Getting Acquainted with the Focal System

In addition to understanding yourself and coping with your own emotions and values, it's necessary to understand the sociological and cultural context of the focal community. Use what you know as a social scientist to explore the community. Extract quantitative data from such sources as the census and planning agencies to get a numerical picture of the area. Then, compare this data to systematic observations of the community, informal discussions with the people you meet, and examination of such artifacts as local newspapers, community bulletin boards, and public places. Walk or drive around to get the feel of the place. Check websites that focus on your focal community. Continually **triangulate** (compare) your data so that you get a clear picture of social and cultural reality:

- Be aware of making premature judgments or closure based on personal experiences or stereotypes. *Remember: there are ways in which every community is unique, every community is like a number of other communities, and every community is like all other communities.*

- Use a systems approach to analyze the community; choose a focal system and then identify its micro-, meta-, mezzo-, and macro-systems.
- Determine the strength (permeability) of the boundaries between and among the various systems and how they affect one another.
- Constantly evaluate and re-evaluate power relationships among individuals and groups.
- Discern the history of the community through printed information and by listening to stories of days gone by.
- Keep a journal or ongoing research diary of your observations, changing perceptions, and organizational, associational, and personal links, as well as reflections on your experiences.
- Identify the local norms (unwritten rules), including appropriate dress and expected public behaviors, and, if possible, conform without compromising your own sense of identity.
- Spend the majority of your time observing and listen more than you speak.

Learning the "Rules"

While you are learning all that you can about your focal community system, you will also be learning how to fit in as an accepted and respected part of community life. Communities vary in their response to newcomers: some are completely closed, others have a cultural history of "welcoming the stranger," and still others are composed of individuals who have no sense of community. The process of getting acquainted varies among each and helps you to discern group boundaries within your focal community system.

A **group boundary** is the more or less demarcated line between focal community members and the outside world. There are two types of boundaries: symbolic and social. **Symbolic boundaries** generally reflect members' internal cognitive–emotional schemas about the characteristics of community members and non-members. These symbolic boundaries then translate into **social boundaries** that are defined in more visible ways through choice of housing, religious practices, dress, and patterns of interaction.[5] Figure 3.1 shows several types of community boundaries.

Closed communities have no port of entry for newcomers, often because they treasure their exclusive status or want to protect their safety and privacy. In practice, members of closed community systems pay attention only to each other, ignore or actively exclude newcomers, and are generally difficult for newcomers to influence. The Town of Middle View is an example of a rather closed community. Newcomers often complain that they would have to live there thirty years or more to become accepted participants in community decisions.

Communities with **permeable boundaries** have implicit or explicit membership criteria but have many open doors. They typically have a **core group** who relate well to one another and may ignore newcomers, others who act as **gatekeepers** so that only those people who seem similar to the core group are made welcome, and still others who are **boundary spanners** who go out of their way to welcome diverse new members. As time has gone on, Middle View has become more and more permeable as people from the cities have retired there and old-timers realize that more openness is needed for survival. **Open communities** may run the gamut from those whose members have

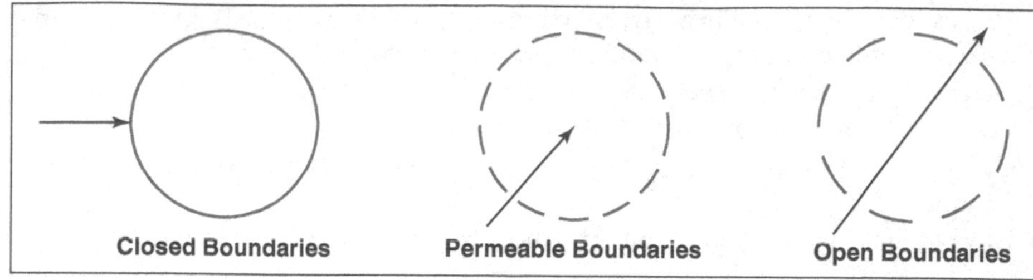

FIGURE 3.1 Community Boundaries
Source: Copyright © by Pearson Education, Upper Saddle River, NJ.

at least some common characteristics, values, and shared relationships to those that are so open that they may not be true communities at all. For instance, some geographic communities—such as new developments, mobile home parks, and apartment houses—may lack any sense of "we-ness" and function as collectives or quasi-groups rather than true communities.

Smithville has some characteristics of an open community. It has become known as "the place people settle when they first come to town," "the place people come when they lose almost everything," and the "place people leave as soon as they can." Completely closed and wide-open communities can each pose difficulties. Closed communities may be impossible to join whereas extremely open communities have few ways for people to connect. Open communities with bad reputations, such as Smithville, may have a high turnover of engaged residents, which means that community organizations have to continually rebuild.

Focal communities consciously or unconsciously develop a shared consensus about what it means to belong. This **collective identity** is largely unconscious and incorporates individual members' understanding of the place the community holds in the broader world, the values and emotional significance individuals attach to membership, and the socially meaningful categories that outsiders apply to the community.[6] **Norms** (cultural repertoires), **traditions**, and **narratives** (stories) are all important parts of collective identity or sense of we-ness.[7] For example, most citizens of Middle View see the town as a prime example of rural America, with the small-town values of mutual support and kindness and the positive characteristics of fresh air, sunshine, and safety. Many Smithville folks see the neighborhood as "tough but lively" and sadly neglected by those with power in the city. They enjoy many connections among friends, family, local establishments, and places of worship. These residents see themselves as hard-working people struggling to get along. However, there are two other major competing identities within Smithville itself. A few people have adopted deviant roles as prostitutes, drug dealers, or gang members while a few see themselves as upwardly mobile professionals who are privileged to live in what is becoming the "cool" part of the city. All of these perspectives are part of the collective identity of Smithville. Members of the overall community focal system and its micro-systems often take these **folkways** and **mores** (unwritten rules) for granted, but they are often opaque

> **Human Systems**
>
> *Understanding and Mastery: How small groups are utilized, theories of group dynamics, and group facilitation skills*
>
> **Critical Thinking Question:** Identify three or four organizations or communities with which you are familiar. Think about each in turn. Were the same group of people involved over a long period of time, did the membership change rapidly, or was it somewhere in between? Did the group welcome new members, or was it hard to become part of things? Were some people more welcome than others? How would a potential member know whether she or he was welcome? Questions such as these will help you determine whether your focal community system is closed, permeable, or completely open. In what ways was the degree of openness helpful for the organization? In what ways was it negative?

to the newcomer. You can discern the components of collective identity by careful listening, observing, asking questions of those who actively welcome you, and inviting a wide variety of group members to tell their stories and those of the group, an activity most people enjoy.

Assess your comprehension of Group Boundaries and Collective Identities by completing this quiz.

"Fitting In" to Community Life

As you strive to become an accepted part of your focal community system, it's likely that you will move from being an outsider to being accepted as part of the "scene." Like so many elements in community organizing, developing this **collective identity** is a reciprocal process in which you begin to add "community member" to the unconscious list of your statuses and roles—and those you encounter begin to treat you as "one of us." Table 3.1 gives you a list of questions to periodically ask yourself about the relationship between your membership in the community and your **self-identity** (how you experience yourself as a person).

Similarly, Figure 3.2 illustrates fitting into community life as a process of identifying with the community, having the community accept you, and having those outside of the community identify you as a community member.

Your integration into an existing focal community will require accommodation on the part of everyone. You must move toward adopting important aspects of the collective

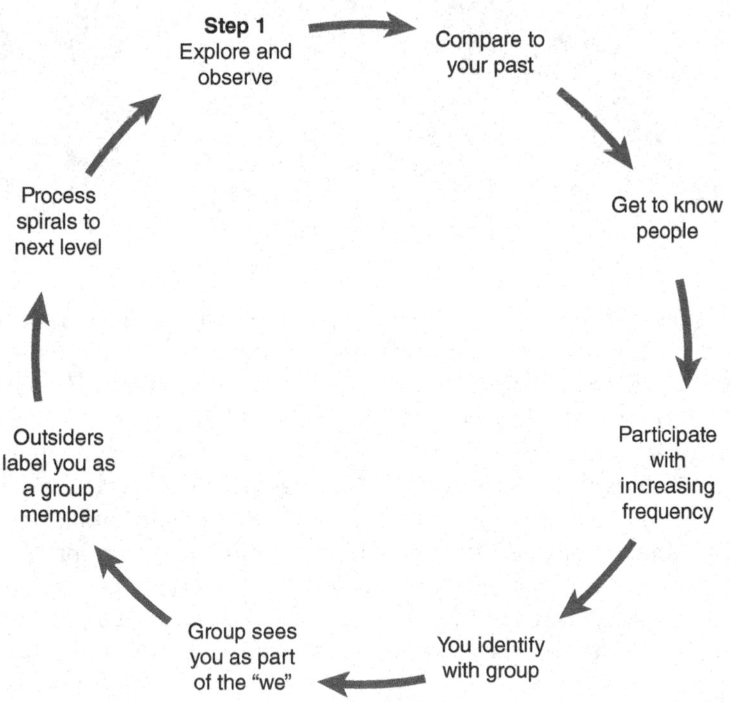

FIGURE 3.2 Fitting into Community Life
Source: Copyright © by Pearson Education, Upper Saddle River, NJ.

Table 3.1 Relationship between Community Membership and Self-Identity

Element of Self-Identity	Reflective Question
Identification with the community	Do I identify myself as a member of this community?
"Fit"	In what ways do I perceive myself as being like other members of the community? In what ways am I different from them?
Accuracy of perception	How certain am I of the accuracy of my perceptions? What has led to this evaluation?
Evaluation	In general is it a good thing for someone to be identified with this community? Why?
Self-evaluation	Do I feel good about being identified with this group? Why or why not?
Outsiders' evaluation	How do I feel about how outsiders view my membership in the focal community? How important are their feelings to me?
Subjective importance to me	How important is membership in this community compared to my involvement with other people and communities in my life?
Investment of time and energy	What does the amount of time and energy I spend on this say about its relative importance?
Attachment	How emotionally involved am I with the fate of the community and with relationships with other members?
Mutual fate	How much of my own fate seems to be tied to that of the community and its mission?
Interconnection between self and community	How much of my identity and self-esteem is merged with being a community member?
Social engagement	How much time do I spend with people from this community?
Behavioral involvement	How much of what I do on a daily basis is done in my community member role?
Congruence of personal and community ideology	How many of my own core beliefs agree with those espoused by community members?
Narrative (story)	What would I say to someone who asked me to tell the story of the group and my involvement in it?

identity into your individual identity. Conversely, the collective identity must change a bit to include you.[8] This may not be easy. Many poor and minority communities have had negative experiences with community organizers who claimed to want to help them but who were really furthering their own agendas. Members of such communities suspect that every new organizer is an **imposter** or a voyeur. Minority communities, poor neighborhoods, and isolated rural villages often rightly feel that such imposters damage their group cohesiveness, their ability to act in solidarity, and their credibility in the larger world—which has implications for you as the community organizer and for the prospects of your organizing effort.[9] As a community organizer, you must carefully examine your motives and make necessary adjustments, if needed. Although it may be tempting to use community organizing and other volunteer work to further your own career, this should be avoided.

Self-Development

Understanding and Mastery: Reflection on professional self (e.g., journaling, development of a portfolio, project demonstrating competency)

Critical Thinking Question: Think about a time you moved to a new home, began a new job, or joined a new organization and eventually felt that you were an accepted part of the community. What did you do to become acquainted? What early experiences told you whether you were likely to be accepted or have trouble fitting in? Was there anyone who "broke the ice" for you? What specifically did he or she do to help you feel comfortable? What did you do to increase your level of acceptance? What specific events occurred that let you know that you finally "fit in"?

Such temptations can be subtle. For instance, it is unethical to use community organizing to further a personal research or teaching agenda unless you have received permission from your institution's Institutional Review Board for the Protection of Human Subjects and the participants are informed of your intent and have given you permission to use what you have learned in publications beyond the community. (That's why the Town of Middle View and Smithville are fictitious: they were created to protect human subjects.) It can also be tempting to consciously or unconsciously use your organizing efforts as a sign of superiority, which almost always communicates itself to other members of the organizing task force as condescension. No one wants to be anyone's "pet project." If you cannot respectfully involve everyone you meet in the organizing process, you probably should withdraw from the effort.

Assess your comprehension of Social Integration by completing this quiz.

Using Symbolic Interaction Theories

As you move through the community organizing process, not only will you begin to internally define your identity within the focal community system, but other community members will begin to define their expectations of you as well. In turn, these evolving expectations will determine your behavior and the behavior of those you meet. In sociology this reciprocal process of developing expectations is called symbolic a interactionism. There were two main bodies of symbolic interactional thought.

Charles Horton Cooley, George Herbert Mead and Herbert Blumer the major theorists of the **Chicago School** combined psychological and sociological concepts and developed a micro theory of social psychology which asserted that we create the social world through the decisions we make in our encounters with one another. The results of these encounters are defined by how you interpret and respond to me and how I interpret and respond to you. Negative results can be changed if our interpretations are changed. Thus, people of good will can learn to get along together if they listen carefully and are willing to look for areas of common understanding. The Chicago School provides hope that people with vastly different views can nevertheless learn to work together for the common good. The sociologists of the Iowa School had a slightly different approach. They insisted that interactions are not only based on individual decisions about how to act in social settings but also on unwritten (yet nevertheless real) "rules for behavior" that have solidified over time. In their view, we begin each encounter with an individual or a group with predetermined expectations of one another rather than starting from a completely clean slate. Let's look at the implications of each of these viewpoints for community organizing.[10] Iowa School theorists emphasize that social positions or social statuses are the building blocks of a community. Everyone is a bundle of identities or social statuses, each of which has greater or lesser salience depending on the social context, and each of which has social expectations attached. As you enter a focal community system, you bring an established set of identities—including **ascribed statuses** such as age, gender, physical characteristics, and ethnicity—together with **achieved statuses** such as education, profession, and membership in organizations, groups, and other communities. It is quite natural to define yourself in terms of positions that form the heart of your self-identity because your definitions usually help you fit into new situations. Situations in which your self-definition and community expectations are congruent are the easiest in which to fit in. To be blunt: if you are a white, middle-class Methodist with a mid-western accent, you'll probably fit fairly well into Middle View but may seem out of place in Smithville.

From the Iowa School perspective the process of "fitting in" first involves understanding how members of the focal community are likely to view your unique set of social characteristics (i.e., statuses) and conversely how you view the social characteristics of community members. Secondly, "fitting in" involves a process of bringing these perspectives into congruence so that you become a part of the focal community system's collective identity. In other words you reach a point where you feel that you belong and other members of the community agree. A collective identity has several components, including an internal component consisting of a sense of belonging and emotional bonding with one another, coupled with indifference or even antipathy to outsiders,[11] and an external component composed of outsiders' views. Collective or communal identity involves the interplay of processes of internal definition (how members experience themselves) and external definition (how others perceive them).[12] Through their behaviors, opinions, language, and appearance, group members define expectations and characteristics that differentiate them from others. In fact, members often rate the social attractiveness of other group members not by their personalities but by whether they act and think like good group members.[13]

Explore structure-functionalism as a sociological perspective at The Iowa School. What are the strengths and weaknesses of the Iowa School version of symbolic interactionism as a way of understanding communities?

The Iowa School sociologists also assert that communities consciously or unconsciously define the statuses (positions) that people need to play for the community to remain cohesive. Sometimes these statuses are defined by law and sometimes by custom. For instance, the Town of Middle View is a legal entity. By law, it is led by a town supervisor and four members of the Town Council who are elected by residents. It has a town clerk who manages the daily routine and several legally required offices such as tax collector, dog enforcement officer, and road supervisor. Over the years, many different individuals have filled these offices, but their duties and expected behaviors have remained essentially the same, and life in Middle View has remained stable. The Town of Middle View also has customs (unwritten laws) that help define who will do what. For instance, for many years there was an unwritten rule that the town supervisor would be a prosperous, white, male, late middle-aged, Republican member of an "old" family, so when a white woman who had "only" lived in Middle View for twenty years was elected supervisor on an independent party ticket that had resulted from community organizing activities, many feared that things would fall part within the community but they did not. The structural school teaches you to be aware of ways your **ascribed statuses** (age, sex, skin color, family connections, etc.) and your **achieved statuses** (education, employment, memberships, etc.) are likely to fit into community life.[14] It will also help you identify laws and customs that define various positions as well as the kinds of people who are likely to hold them.

Assess your comprehension of The Iowa School of Symbolic Interactionism by completing this quiz.

While the Iowa School shows us how communities define relationships and act cohesively in spite of changes in who holds particular positions, the "Chicago School" of **symbolic interactionism** focuses on the process of interaction and how our social identities are built through day-to-day encounters. Charles Horton Cooley, one of the founders of the Chicago School of social psychology, asserted that you create your **sense of self** (how you judge your position in life and your worth) through the **"looking glass self"** (the judgments you see mirrored in the eyes of others). If you see approval and love, you experience pride and self-confidence. If you see disapproval and animosity, you experience embarrassment and shame.[15] George Herbert Mead,[16] a student of Cooley, and Mead's follower Herbert Blumer[17] further elaborated on Cooley's ideas by adding the concepts of **role making** and **role taking** to the process of identity development.

The role-taking and role-making process can best be illustrated by an example. Imagine that you are a member of the leadership team of the Smithville Neighborhood Organization (SNO). A significant number of your neighbors want the SNO leaders to speak with Industrial City's director of public works about the terrible condition of the neighborhood storm drains. The leadership team selects you to be their spokesperson with the director. You prepare carefully for the meeting, choosing just the right clothes and the right information to take and rehearsing what you are going to say and how you are going to say it. You are engaging in **role making**. The meeting day arrives, and you are ushered into the director's office. You present your case to him. At this point you are **role taking**. Meanwhile, before and during the meeting, the director has been doing his own **role making**. He has a large corner office with an administrative assistant outside and a large mahogany desk that is facing the door. He has a large, comfortable desk chair with a much harder, smaller chair for visitors like you. He is dressed formally in a business suit and has prepared maps and charts that show his areas of responsibility.

You feel intimidated. His **role taking** begins when you enter the room. He offers you a seat across the desk from him. He offers to have his assistant bring coffee. He seems to listen carefully to your request and carefully frames his reply, which emphasizes how many projects he is responsible for, how little money is available, and how all of them are more important than your request, but that he will try to do what he can. As you listen to him, a part of you is deciding what to do next (role making). Once it is your turn, you decide what to say (role taking), and so forth. Role making and role taking will continue even after you both leave the meeting. You will continue to think about what he has said and what to do next—and so will the director. Mead and Blumer asserted that what we call society is created by such daily encounters. As you talked with the director, you were helping to create the role of community organizer—not only for yourself but for other community organizers. As the director responded, he also was creating what it means to be a public official in a small U.S. city.

Assess your comprehension of Symbolic Interactionism Theories by completing this quiz.

Symbolic interactional processes in community organizing can be easily demonstrated in your own life. Think about times when you have entered a new group, organization, or place. Chances are that you watched how others acted. Implicitly or explicitly you asked:

- "What is going on here?"
- "What does it mean?"

- "How does this experience link to other experiences in my life?"
- "Who are these other people?"
- "What is expected of them?"
- "Are some of them more important than others?"
- "What does each of them expect of me?"
- "Are there existing conflicts among them that I should avoid?"
- "Who can I trust to guide me?"
- "How shall I behave?"

If you are wise when you enter a new situation, you probably spend the first few days, weeks, or months orienting yourself to the situation. You do a lot of listening. You watch people talk with one another and go about their daily lives while comparing your observations to other experiences in your life and to probable interpretations you have encountered through self-directed learning or formal schooling. You note how some things are similar to past experiences and how some others are different. Sometimes you cautiously venture an opinion or asked a direct question. If your opinions or questions are well received, you venture further. If they meet with laughter, a stony silence, or angry glares, you probably retreat to discover what went wrong. You mentally consider different approaches and try to anticipate their results. After mentally "trying on" different possible scenarios, you probably participate in real life situations.

When you imagined what others expected of you, you were role taking. Each time you actually said or did something, you were role making. This involved the words you chose, your tone of voice, your facial expressions, your body language, and even your dress. As you participated in the life of the group, you paid attention to the reactions of others. In other words, you received feedback. You may have chosen someone you trusted to give you explicit feedback, or you may have simply mulled over your experiences. You probably found that your perceptions changed as you became more and more acclimated to the new social situation. You learned what to say and what not to say. You learned about formal and informal communications and power differences, and how to dress appropriately. You developed a sense of belonging, made friends, and may have even made some enemies, but you felt at home. As you look back, you may smile at assumptions you brought to the new situation and may be a bit embarrassed by things you said or did before you knew how to behave. You may even be able to point to specific instances when you stopped being a stranger and became part of things.

Explore the history of symbolic interactionism and its major theorists at "Symbolic Interactionism: Mead". Where would you probably find the symbolic-interactionist approach useful in community organizing?

If you relive your entry experiences in several life situations, you find that some approaches worked well while others did not. Those that worked well in a variety of situations can be thought of as your social learning style. As a community organizer, awareness of your own social learning style helps you to effectively enter into community processes. Knowing how to enter a community and gain acceptance is especially important when gaining access to new communities.

Integration into Community Life

Integration into community life is like Chinese checkers or other games where each player starts from a different position. You must understand your position in relation to the target community or group. There are three major positions: "insider," "outsider," and "insider-outsider." Most community organizers find themselves in all three positions at points during their lifetime.

Insiders have an established place by reason of longevity and reputation. Sometimes you become an insider through your own efforts or by your family heritage. Insider status varies by location and tradition. In some communities such as Middle View and tightly knit neighborhoods like parts of Smithville, it's impossible to be considered an insider until your family has lived in the area for three generations. In other communities, especially more recently developed ones, you become an insider simply by living or participating in the area for a few weeks or months. All communities, even the poorest, have insiders and outsiders. The advantage of being an insider is that people feel they know and can trust you. If you come from a "good, local family" or have "made good for yourself," you'll probably have automatic credibility and feel "at home." Because you grew up in the community, you'll probably find that you have a priceless advantage: a **tacit** (unconscious, "gut-level") understanding of the community's history and how to get things done.

However, insider status can have disadvantages as well. Because people feel that they know you, they may hardly believe that *you* would have anything to offer! You may also be handicapped by your ascribed status. If you are young, for example, you may have to struggle with being thought of as a child by those who have known you all your life. If you have been a quiet homemaker, people may be surprised when you loudly speak up at a community organizing event. If you are a member of an unpopular ethnic group or if your extended family has a bad reputation, you may have little chance of being heard by those traditionally in power. If you have made mistakes in the past, you may be shunned. You may experience internal struggles as well, such as reluctance to hurt other people's feelings even when obvious mistakes have been made. In spite of these pitfalls, insider status will often give you an advantage over newcomers.

Outsiders are organizers who do not belong or who don't intend to belong to the community. If you come into a focal community as an outsider, you may come with an agenda or may have been invited to help, but neither you nor group members regard you as a permanent part of the focal community system. As an outsider, you are most effective when you're aware of your status as a stranger and willingly provide information and guidance without imposing an agenda. Likewise, the community groups who best use the wisdom of outsiders are those who take information and structural suggestions and then use their own wisdom to adapt this input to their unique situation. It is flattering to be thought of a person with all of the answers, but the wise outside community organizer turns the decision-making process over to members of the target community, making sure that the process itself is inclusive and fair.

Insider-outsider is a term for those who live or work in the focal community, have expertise in community organizing, and want to contribute but are recognized neither as outside experts nor as "real" leaders of the community. Insider-outsiders may be newcomers, returning wanderers who grew up in the community, or long-time residents who are stepping out of their expected roles and bringing new ideas. All face the problem of permeating the boundaries of the community to offer their knowledge and skill—without being rejected as know-it-alls or discounted because "someone who has chosen to live among *us* couldn't possibly know anything."

Often an insider-outsider is initially known only by visible activities: the heavy lady in line at the grocery store, the Little League coach, or the "Smith boy" who grew up across the street. Because they are not quite insiders, no one really knows their areas of expertise or quite trusts their motivations. The insider-outsider must engage in a journey from stranger to respected community member—a process that takes time and patience.

Overcoming Reticence

Whether you are an insider, outsider, or insider-outsider, there are times when you may experience internal or psychological barriers to effective organizing. Overcoming what ordinary people call **reticence or shyness**—or what symbolic interactionists call **embarrassment** or **shame**—can be one such psychological barrier.[18] Reticence describes the anxiety and tension you feel when engaging in a new situation, which is related to the need for belonging and the fear of rejection. While everyone needs to belong to someone or something, fitting in or feeling comfortable comes more easily to some people than others. If you need suggestions for overcoming shyness or fear, here are a few tips:

- Remember that different groups and communities take different amounts of time to accept a newcomer, so give them and yourself plenty of time.
- People vary in their interest in others, their attention to people outside of their immediate circle, and in their basic friendliness. Some people will welcome you, some will ignore you, and a few may be hostile, but these reactions reflect *their* state of mind rather than anything about you.
- There will be days when you feel lonely and isolated, so keep in touch with old friends and keep some material reminders around you of who you have been and are.
- Pay attention to your physical health by eating properly, exercising, and getting enough rest.
- Remember that acceptance or rejection does not have anything to do with your intrinsic worth as a human being.
- Listen carefully to those you encounter and find ways of reaching out to them in practical ways. Nothing eases shyness and self-doubt like turning your attention to the needs of others.

The journey of creating yourself in a new situation begins with what sociologist Erving Goffman called the **presentation of self.**[19] In practical terms, this means dressing the way most people your age and gender dress, keeping your home and office neat and not extravagantly decorated, buying locally, receiving your mail locally, participating in community organizations and associations, and sharing the challenges and joys of living in a particular location.

Discerning Expected Behaviors

Once you overcome your reticence, the second stage of entering or re-entering a community involves quiet observation, noting how insiders relate to one another, and learning the unwritten rules of community life. The best way to do this is to "hang out" unobtrusively and observe people going about their daily lives. Most neighborhoods or communities have "common places" (or "nodes") where people naturally gather and informally socialize. These can include convenience stores, playgrounds and parks, cafés, local post offices, beauty parlors or barbershops, and neighborhood bars, as well as recognized community events such as youth sports, parades, and festivals. All are good places to observe patterns of interaction. It may seem simplistic, but communities have personalities. Some seem grim and cold, where residents attend to their tasks without speaking or smiling, store clerks do their jobs perfunctorily or resentfully, drivers are aggressive, and children are surly. Other places feel warm and welcoming, where people have pleasant smiles and ask about each other's families and pets. In some places, people of various classes, races, and ethnic groups seem to share their common space warmly or at least cordially. In other places, there are frequent shouts of anger, name calling, and animosity among neighbors and between different blocks. Some places change personalities with the seasons. In Middle View, for example, behavior varies between the "high season" and the "rest of the year." During the majority of the year, everyone knows one another by sight, if not by name. Interactions are warm and friendly; the pace is slow. In the summer, the pace quickens and Middle View becomes a "little piece of the city." The "summer people" and tourists seem to bring their "city ways" with them. Their driving is a bit more aggressive and they become frustrated when grocery store clerks chat with "regulars," but their presence seems to "wake up" the sleepy village. There are concerts on the green, the beaches are immaculate and crowded, and the local arts community thrives. When Labor Day arrives, the village goes back to sleep.

Community ambience seems to have little to do with prosperity, lack of prosperity, or with the individuals who make up the community system. It is important to observe typical interactions and adjust behavior to fit unobtrusively.

Trying New Roles

The third stage of fitting in is practicing interactions with people and trying on new roles (behaviors). Engaging people in initial conversations can be scary, but it is often these small gestures that pay the biggest dividends. The process involves action and reflection. It often works best to introduce yourself to a single approachable person and make a neutral remark about the shared context. If he or she responds in a friendly way, the next step may be to ask them about themselves, listen carefully to what they say, and mention points of commonality while keeping the spotlight on them. As you converse, it is important to learn things about that person and his or her position in the focal community. People enjoy meeting someone who takes the time to learn about them, including their names, their interests, and a little bit about their past history. They usually like to learn about points of common interest. Topics vary with the social context, but common ones are children, careers, geographic connections (i.e., "Where are you from?"), and shared acquaintances. Such conversations begin the process of discerning **weak ties** (people, places, and affiliations you may have in common, no matter how tenuous) and identifying shared and overlapping **social networks** (webs of interrelated people).[20]

After each encounter, think about your new acquaintance, mentally rehearse his or her name and relationship to the rest of the community, reflect upon how he or she responded to your overture, and think about what all of this means to your evolving picture of the community and your place in it. Make sure you talk with all kinds of people, including children (with the consent of their parents), teens, the elderly, and others who are likely to be on the margins. The more you engage people with different perspectives the clearer the picture you get of the community or group and the more acceptance you gain for yourself. This getting-acquainted stage may occur quickly, especially in the case of such time-limited encounters as conferences or other short-term events, or it may take decades in the case of extremely closed communities. It is generally wise not to move too quickly.

Becoming Part of Things

The next stage is becoming **assimilated** (becoming an accepted part of community life). If the community has permeable boundaries, chances are that it will have members who self-consciously see themselves as "bringers," folks who welcome newcomers. It is very important to allow yourself to be "brought." Accept invitations to public and private events and reciprocate by inviting others to your home. Show up for group events, take part, and volunteer for basic tasks such as set up and clean up. Contribute financially to community events if you can. Keep meeting people and reflecting on what you learn from each of them. Even though it is natural to give more credence to first encounters than later ones, be careful not to just get acquainted with a few people and assume that their perspective is the only perspective. Reciprocity is very important in the assimilation phase. You should be ready to receive help and encouragement as well as to give them.

Sometimes it may take months or even years of just "showing up," and proving yourself reliable and caring—but eventually you will become respected and will be thought of as trustworthy and wise. The length of this process depends on your initial position in the community, your strategies for entry, the nature of the community itself, and your personal characteristics, such as kindness, approachability, and humility. Some newcomers—such as pastors, teachers, and social workers—have the advantage of an already established social position waiting for them. If their predecessors have gained credibility and respect, it is likely that they will already be granted a modicum of credibility and respect. However, initial respect can be strengthened or quickly undermined by your own actions. Some stumbling blocks to acceptance include coming off as an expert without learning what is already being done, appearing to brag about your knowledge and skills, and being obtuse about the impact that your social positions—such as gender, age, appearance, ethnicity, or profession—may have on others' perceptions and responses. The process of gaining and retaining acceptance is difficult, but given time you will create a recognized **personal trajectory** (recognizable direction for your involvement). You begin creating your personal trajectories the moment you enter a community or decide to engage in an issue. Therefore, it is important to understand how you fit into ongoing patterns and learn to adapt your behavior appropriately.

Self-Development

Understanding and Mastery: Reflection on professional self (e.g., journaling, development of a portfolio, project demonstrating competency)

Critical Thinking Question: Reflect on your focal community system. Are you an insider who has lived there for years and has an established place in the community, an outsider who is completely new and has either chosen to become involved or been asked to come in as an advisor or consultant, or an insider-outsider who has been around awhile but is not yet recognized for your organizing abilities? How is your position likely to affect the ways your approach the organizing task? How will you gain trust and credibility?

Assess your comprehension of How to Fit into Community Life by completing this quiz.

Summary

In this chapter, you were first introduced to the idea that your understanding of a focal community system is dependent on an evolving **cognitive-emotional** process that involves both mind and heart and that is based on your past experiences, information you have gleaned about similar communities, and your ongoing reflection on your perceptions and feelings.

You then learned that the social world is not something static that has always been here and always will be here, but rather that it is created and re-created by human actions. There is no written rule book "out there" waiting to be found, nor is there one and only one way of doing things. We human beings create the social order by the cumulative effect of our specific behaviors. Here a few examples: If you attend a council meeting in your home town, the participants and you create what it means to have a local government. As I write this textbook and you read it, we are creating what it means to be "author" and "reader," even though we are separated by both time and distance. As you go through life, and if you listen carefully, you will hear people say things like, "*They* won't let that happen. The *system* just isn't set up that way,"—forgetting that "they" are "we," real people who can make new decisions and, thus, change the world for better or worse. The final sections focus on you as a participant in the community organizing process and provide tools for analyzing your own position in community life and appropriate strategies for your participation in community organizing efforts. After reading Chapter 1 (which introduced the concept of community), Chapter 2 (which gave you practice in systems thinking), and this chapter (which has focused on the psycho-social aspects of life in community), you are ready to learn about different kinds of community and to focus on the community organizing cycle itself.

Assess your analysis and evaluation of the chapter's contents by completing the Chapter Review.

CHAPTER 4

Jeff Greenberg/Alamy

Varieties of Community Organizing

Chapter Outline

At this point, you have become familiar with the dynamics of Middle View and Smithville, the geographically based communities that are the primary examples for this text. You have learned to use systems theory in community organizing and have explored the psychological and social–psychological aspects of communities. In this chapter, you will explore seven different varieties of community organizing that can be applied in various focal communities. Each is somewhat different from the others, although two or more can be mixed and matched as needed.

This chapter gives an overview of these approaches so that you can choose those best suited to your circumstances, explore them more deeply, and apply them. While there are several ways community organizing efforts can be categorized, the following relate well to terms used in the field:

1. Place-based relational organizing
2. Social entrepreneurship or social innovation
3. Economic mutual aid
4. Self-help
5. Community advocacy
6. Democratic social movements
7. Collaboration

Note that Table 4.1 briefly lists each strategy and when it is usually used:

Table 4.1 Varieties of Community Organizing

Approach	Purpose	Key Participants
Place-based/relational initiatives	To improve the overall quality of life in a relatively small geographic area over many years.	Dedicated citizens who feel called to care for their immediate neighbors through a variety of activities.
Social entrepreneurship/ social Innovation	To meet a specific targeted need.	Individual founders or small groups concerned about innocent suffering.
Mutual economic aid	To improve the economic status of participants through cooperative efforts.	Individuals, families, micro-business owners, farmers, and others who share their time and resources to ensure that everyone has enough.
Self-help	To cope with emotionally or physically draining issues.	Those who have experience or who are experiencing the target issue.
Community advocacy	To assure fair treatment and justice for those living in a geographic focal community.	Those whose lives or livelihoods are affected by injustice.
Social movements	To demand fair treatment and justice primarily for those who are comparatively powerless.	Those whose lives are affected and those who support the justice of their cause.
Collaboration	To enable established social institutions and organizations to work together toward the common good.	Representatives of various agencies and organizations.

Source: Copyright © by Pearson Education, Upper Saddle River, NJ.

Place-based Relational Organizing

Place-based organizing improves the quality of life for all of the people residing in a relatively small geographic area and generally consists of a variety of shared events, projects, programs, and celebrations, each of which may seem unimportant but when taken together make the focal community an enjoyable place to live. When you think of place-based relational organizing, picture the people you have met who always seem to be doing something formally or informally to make life better for everybody. Many seem to be everywhere at once—working with the parent–teacher association (PTA) to raise money for a new playground, organizing book sales so that the library can purchase new computers, planting bulbs in the local park, providing leadership in various groups, and—not incidentally—welcoming those in need into their homes. Most do not think of themselves as community organizers. If you ask, they'll tell you that they just want to be good citizens and make life better for their friends, family, and neighbors. They want a community where everyone is safe, productive, and happy, and they are willing to work toward that goal in many different ways. Perhaps because such people are everywhere, it is relatively easy to overlook their work or take it for granted.[1] Although some writers in the community organizing field refer to this as "women centered" or "feminist" organizing, here it is referred to as **place-based relational organizing** because it is not really gender specific but rather comes from an ethic of care.[2] Place-based relational organizing is based on the tendencies of caring people to value interpersonal relationships, initiate organizing efforts based on the needs of those they love, elicit the help of those they already know well, and share ideas freely and creatively. This type of organizing is often somewhat informal and builds on existing personal, family, and neighborhood networking. Place-based relational organizing was first described by feminist scholars as they explored the ways women make a difference in their communities.[3] Although it is not exclusive to women, place-based relational organizing does often depend on women's wisdom and engagement and works best in communities where women are taken seriously within their homes, extended families, and immediate neighborhood.[4]

Human Systems

Understanding and Mastery: Organizational structures of communities

Critical Thinking Question: Place-based organizers are often at the heart of community events. Think of a place you call home or you once called home and the events that happen regularly year after year that make life more fun for your friends and family (e.g., Easter egg hunts, Fourth of July fireworks, summer festivals, Halloween parades, and breakfasts with Santa). Identify the people that regularly volunteer at these events, determine the number of times the same names or organizations have been associated with these events over the years, and make a list of names that seem to reoccur time after time. These people will often be the core of place-based, relational organizing.

Place-based relational initiatives are often a partnership between **catalysts**, caring professionals who live or work in the focal community system, and **natural leaders**, who have local credibility because of their long-term family, relational ties, and reputation for giving good advice and practical aid in time of trouble. Together, catalysts and natural leaders provide a bridge between resources outside the community and assets within the community.

Place-based organizing is an organic process that evolves, sometimes over decades, and is frequently comprised of many small projects and events which improve the overall quality of life for everyone. While particular projects may involve a changing cast of characters, over the years place-based relational organizing often depends on a few dedicated people who deeply identify themselves with the community and the well-being of all residents. Place-based relational organizing works best in neighborhoods and small rural communities, such as Middle View, where there is a solid core of dedicated people who have generational ties to the locality, are open to caring newcomers, and understand that creating and maintaining a high quality of life—for those in that particular place—is a lifetime task. This type of organizing is more difficult in places like Smithville, where few people have long-term roots or where everyone is focused on individual concerns so that no one feels responsible for shared well-being.

To improve the quality of life in well-defined, relatively small places such as neighborhoods, villages, rural towns, housing developments, and mobile home parks, explore place-based/relational strategies and tactics. Under what circumstances would you be likely to use a place-based or relational approach to community organizing?

Assess your comprehension of Place-based Relational Community Organizing by completing this quiz.

Social Entrepreneurship and Social Innovation

Social entrepreneurship and social innovation organizing initiatives are generally focused on helping those who are unable to help themselves including needy people, marginalized groups, or even animals, plants, and natural environments.[5] The main difference between social entrepreneurship and social innovation is that social entrepreneurship projects are principally the brainchild of a single individual while social innovation efforts are most often team based. Do you have a burning desire to serve a particular target group, have some ideas about how you would like to accomplish your goals, and want to lead a new organization to provide this needed service? If yes, then you're probably a social entrepreneur. On the other hand, if you and several others have been talking about an unmet need and have been exploring possible alternatives together, you're all social innovators.

Social entrepreneurship, as used here, refers to altruistic efforts that are begun by a **founder** (a highly committed individual) and that depend almost entirely on his or her vision, energy, and commitment. **Social innovation**, as used here, refers to efforts that are begun and maintained by a core group of committed people who share the work. Some efforts are almost completely founder centered, others have a strong founder with hand-picked supporters, and still others have various levels of shared power.

Social entrepreneurship is generally triggered by a life-changing encounter with others' suffering through a single event or an evolving process that founders characterize as "hearing a call" or "discovering my passion," which ignites a fiery desire to make a difference for those in need. Successful social entrepreneurs are charismatic, driven, and single-minded. They have a vision of what needs to be accomplished and the ability to communicate their vision to others. Successful social entrepreneurs have keen organizational skills, an ability to clearly define project needs, determination, and a willingness to endure personal sacrifices for their cause. Some have well-established connections and a solid personal resource base. Others have only their strong wills and winning ways. Many are willing to begin with few resources, except for the strength of their vision and, often, their faith in a higher power.[6]

Founders tend to fall on a continuum between those who are primarily activists and those who are more business oriented.[7] Similar to entrepreneurs in the private sector, founders often have trouble transitioning from visionary to manager, and then have trouble letting go when it is time to retire.[8] Many of the world's oldest and most dynamic organizations were founded by social entrepreneurs (think Clara Barton and the American Red Cross). Social entrepreneurs often capture the public's imagination because they embody the American belief that success is based on individual initiative and personal drive. However, long-term efforts that survive and thrive de-emphasize this cult of personality and spotlight the work of the organization.[9]

Let's now look at an example of social entrepreneurship in Smithville, where its youth have all of the stereotypical problems associated with inner-city young people, not limited to drugs, petty crime, vandalism, gangs and quasi-gangs, early pregnancy, high drop-out rates, and prevailing hopelessness. About fifteen years ago, Mary, a dedicated artist and musician from a prosperous nearby community, felt compelled to go to Smithville to create an innovative arts center—a safe zone where young people could interact, learn arts-based skills, and eat an evening meal during the school year and both lunch and dinner during the summer. This philanthropic musician and artist used her own money and donations from friends to begin her outreach project. She located free space for her project, recruited a hand-picked volunteer Board of Directors as well as adult artisans, and began "doing business." Young people loved her, and her project quickly became known among them as a safe, enjoyable place to be. However, she became known as an unorthodox rebel among the established youth-serving agency providers and was ultimately seen as a threat to their funding because this 60-year-old whirlwind was surprisingly successful. The local United Fund provided her with a small grant and insisted that she keep records of outcomes. Almost everyone was astounded at the significant reduction in teen pregnancy and increase in high school graduation rates that could be directly attributed to her program. Moreover, she was able to show a significant decline in drug use and vandalism in the project's focal neighborhood when compared to other neighborhoods served by the more traditional agencies with much larger staffs, more impressive facilities, and much larger budgets. Her young participants told United Fund evaluators that her program had helped them change their attitudes about life and their decisions about their behaviors. All of those interviewed praised her personally for the intensity of her care and willingness to go more than the extra mile for them. Many of them not only turned their own lives around but became mentors for younger people. Now age seventy-five, Mary's energy is flagging, and board members are aging, too. The transition from her leadership promises to be difficult.

Social innovation, on the other hand, is characterized by the work of a small, dedicated group using democratic processes to meet a well-defined need. These efforts may take place within a geographic focal community system, or they may represent a community of interest that exists across geographical systems. Many social innovation efforts begin with an encounter with a particular individual, family, or small group. The call to action often begins with a simple statement, "Somebody *ought* to do something about. . . ." until the realization strikes that there is no one "out there" to do it except themselves! Social innovation efforts typically move slowly, with false starts and setbacks, but are highly effective because they rely on shared insights, complementary abilities, mutual support, and multiple bonds. They are likely to be stronger and more resilient than efforts that depend on a single individual, and their use of democratic principles—and inclusion of a variety of people, including potential beneficiaries—strengthens the participants' abilities to engage in other democratic processes.[10] Participation in social innovation efforts requires consensus building, which can be time consuming and frustrating. Even efforts that seem simple and straightforward usually take much more time and energy than expected and often meet opposition. Social innovation requires significant dedication from core members or a steering committee, and many efforts fail because the individuals are unwilling or unable to invest the time and energy needed for success. Social innovation may not work if time is critical or if only one or two people believe in the project while others are lukewarm.[11]

Now let's flash back to Middle View in the mid-1970s when the high school guidance counselor found that a significant number of her students were running away from home to join the "hippies" and street people in San Francisco and New York City, where their rural innocence put them in danger. She mentioned her concerns to the pastor of a local church known for both international and local missions. The pastor, in turn, brought it before the congregation at their annual mission conference, and seed money was raised. The initial concept was to provide a temporary group home where young adults could live and continue to go to school while working things out with their families. The pastor and counselor recruited a small group of interested people who became an association and then a non-profit organization with a formal board of directors. These social innovators persevered for four years of missteps and frustration but eventually created a social agency that

Professional History

Understanding and Mastery: Historical roots of human service

Critical Thinking Question: Choose a historical person who was known for his or her commitment to those in need. Briefly describe their characteristics and the skills they used in making the dream a reality. How did they gain support for their efforts? What challenges did they face? What was their legacy?

still provides temporary shelter, family mediation, counseling, and long-term shelter to teenage runaways, potential runaways, and "throw-aways" (teens unwanted by their parents). It is now an integral part of Middle View's service system.

Table 4.2 provides a comparison of social entrepreneurship and social innovation to use when deciding which strategy is best for your own personality and for project goals.

Table 4.2 Comparison of Social Entrepreneurship and Social Innovation

	Social Entrepreneurship	Social Innovation
Your personal characteristics	Imagination, drive, intrinsic motivation (self-starting), charisma, and stamina. Enjoy both positive and negative attention. Like to get credit for your efforts, but willing to take blame.	Shy, uncertain, and have to be extrinsically motivated (pushed into action). Think and work best when bouncing ideas off others.
Your convictions about direction	Deeply convinced of the rightness of your cause and methods.	Willing to work with others to discern appropriate directions. Willing to listen and adapt others' ideas to your own and vice versa.
Your desired outcomes	Focus on getting the job done. Pay little or no attention to the process of getting there or inclusion of others, except as a means to an end.	Focus on the process with an emphasis on involving others, including intended recipients, as an end in itself.
Your time commitment	Willing to do whatever it takes to get the job done.	Dedicated, but project is one of many personal, work, and community commitments.
Your patience	Anxious to accomplish as much as possible, as quickly as possible.	Willing to take the time necessary to build consensus and agreement.
Level of group commitment	You are excited about the project. Everyone else is involved because you asked them to be.	Several people are equally committed. Each is willing to invest a reasonable amount of time to make the project happen and to contribute ideas for planning and implementation.
Strengths of the strategy	Founder's skills and business sense includes a solid business plan.	Synergy, stability, and mutual support of core group.
Weaknesses of the strategy	Over-dependence on founder; "founder syndrome" where effort fails when founder leaves (or fails to leave).	Depends greatly on seriousness of core group. Often fails if few devote necessary time, energy, and decision-making skills.
Supportive resources	Social entrepreneurship is new business category with many available resources.	Collaborative tools for groups and participatory research techniques available to help groups work together smoothly.

Source: Copyright © by Pearson Education, Upper Saddle River, NJ.

Social entrepreneurship and social innovation each have strengths and weaknesses. Most founders are willing to devote free labor, their own financial resources, and the determination to keep going through good times and bad, which is invaluable to the start-up phase of any enterprise.

Explore social entrepreneurship or social innovation approaches for community organizing efforts. Compare and contrast social entrepreneurship with social innovation. Under what circumstances would each be appropriate?

The main strength of the social innovation model is its synergy and stability. Small groups have more networking resources than do single founders, as each group member brings his or her own connections, links to outside resources, and potential to recruit new participants.

Assess your comprehension of Social Entrepreneurship and Social Innovation by completing this quiz.

Economic Mutual Aid

Economic mutual aid (sometimes called the **informal economy**) parallels the formal economic system and enables people to have a reasonable level of prosperity through sharing what they have in more or less systematic ways. Most economic mutual aid is taken for granted as is illustrated by the following story from Middle View.

Since the demise of the lumbering, mining, and paper industries, many people in Middle View are sustained through an informal economy that is primarily self-supporting. The following story illustrates Middle View's informal economy.

Jenny Jones is a single parent with two school-aged children and a baby. Jenny has some hairstyling skills, owns an old but adequate car, and loves children. She works part-time in the local convenience store and receives some child support from the children's fathers. She has many friends her own age who have children of various ages. Jenny's neighbor, Susan Scott, is a widow in her late seventies who has become an honorary grandmother to Jenny's children. Jenny checks on her every day, helps her with her housework, and shares an occasional meal. Mrs. Scott bakes cookies for the children and occasionally watches them while Jenny runs errands. Bob Baker, who lives a mile down the road, is a fifty-year-old retired veteran who hasn't found steady work since the local paper mill closed ten years ago. Bob has carpentry, plumbing, and electrical skills. Many people from all walks of life call on him for minor repairs and occasional major projects. He drives a truck that is more rust than metal. Although everyone knows they are "supposed" to pay Bob by check, for income tax purposes, no one refuses when he asks for payment in cash. Bob charges well below the commercial rate for his services, is always available on the spur of the moment, and has a large network of friends who also provide snow removal and leaf-raking services "under the table." Mrs. Scott often says that she could not stay in her home without the help of good neighbors like Bob and Jenny. Harriet Huffman, a retired school teacher, a multi-generational summer resident who now lives full-time in Middle View with her retired banker husband, is another player in this mini-drama. Harriet volunteers weekly in the local food pantry and thrift shop. Let's follow these folks on their journeys through the informal economy.

It is a fine Saturday morning in late August. Because it is nearly time for school to start, Jenny has been sorting through her children's clothes from last year. She has discovered many wearable clothes that they've outgrown, but they'll still need many things for the new school year. She wants to get them each two or three completely new outfits and to fill in the rest of their wardrobes as inexpensively but nicely as possible. She looks at her pile of usable but outgrown children's clothing and sets some aside for her friends' children. She then boxes up the other usable clothing to donate to the local thrift shop. She grabs some canned goods that she wants to donate to the food pantry, which is adjacent to the thrift shop, asks Mrs. Scott to keep an eye on the kids, and heads out for her errands. At the thrift shop, Jenny gives Mrs. Huffman her items to sort. Coincidentally, Mrs. Huffman herself has just donated several boxes of her grandchildren's slightly worn, brand-name clothes and has just finished putting them on the display shelves in the "back-to-school" section. Some are still in their packages, and all have been marked far below their original prices. Jenny is able to find several nice outfits for her children. Mrs. Huffman herself is not above shopping at the Thrift Store. In fact, she notices some very cute baby things in Jenny's donation box and buys them for her newest grandchild. Both Jenny and Mrs. Huffman know that all of the thrift store proceeds are put into an account that helps people pay for emergency heating fuel, gasoline, car and home repairs, and household necessities.

Meanwhile, Mrs. Scott has discovered that one of her electric light fixtures is sparking and sizzling. She's afraid of fire and immediately calls Bob Baker. Bob's truck won't start so he walks the mile to her house. When Bob inspects the light, he realizes that he will need some parts. Mrs. Scott does not own a car, but, by this time, Jenny has returned from her errands and can take Bob to the local hardware store. Bob buys the parts, returns to Mrs. Scott's house, and fixes the electrical problem. Mrs. Scott pays him $30 in cash (well below what she would have paid for an electrician). Jenny drives him home, where he discovers that his truck needs a new engine. So, the next morning (Sunday), he walks to what is known in Middle View as the thrift shop church and talks to the pastor about his plight. Because the thrift shop is a ministry of the church, the pastor calls an emergency meeting of its board. Bob is known and respected throughout the community for his hard work and kindness; many church members want to help him. A mechanic who is a member of the congregation volunteers to put in the engine if one can be found. The thrift shop board members agree that the shop will pay for a rebuilt engine for the truck if Bob can locate one. The next morning, Bob and the mechanic locate a suitable rebuilt engine and the thrift shop board president and treasurer co-sign a check payable to the junkyard dealer. The mechanic tows Bob's truck to his repair shop and installs the engine in between serving his paying customers. Within a few days, Bob can resume his handyman business, including helping the mechanic put in a new deck. And Middle View's informal economy spins on.

Economic mutual aid has been going on in tightly knit communities like Middle View for millennia. Recently, attempts have been made to systematize mutual economic aid and define principles and practices that can support it.[12] Economic mutual aid strategies turn usual ways of thinking about economic development upside down because they are focused locally and regionally, rather than globally; often offer micro-credit loans to poor women who traditionally are considered to be poor credit risks; use such strategies as Local Economic Exchange Systems (LETSs)[13], time banks[14], and local currency systems that are outside of national and international monetary systems[15]; and encourage Membership-Based Organizations of the Poor (MBOP) that are managed by poor people themselves[16]. All of these strategies formalizing mutual economic aid are based on broadly democratic principles and practices, and many are based loosely on Gandhian economic principles.[17]

Explore information on implementation of economic mutual aid strategies. Consider economic mutual aid strategies that might be useful in your focal community system.

Characteristics of successful groups include an emphasis on saving as well as lending money, involvement of people who already know and trust one another, slow and steady effort, and organizational structures and policies that encourage equal participation among everyone involved. Mutual economic aid approaches enable even very poor people to aspire to economic self-sufficiency. By allowing poor families to increase their income, they increase access to basic material goods, such as healthy food, clean water, adequate clothing, and shelter. They help improve the overall health and strength of whole populations while retaining the economic strength of isolated (peripheral) communities, such as inner cities and rural villages. Many celebrate the often unacknowledged economic contributions of women and enable them to gain some economic independence.[18] This results in a better balance of power between the genders within families and communities, the release of women's creative energy, better education and nutrition for children, and reduction in domestic abuse and sexual trafficking.

Professional History

Understanding and Mastery: Differences between systems of governance and economics

Critical Thinking Question: What changes in national and international social policies are needed to support locally based mutual economic aid efforts? What could be done to encourage these policy changes?

Although many of these formal and semi-formal mutual economic aid efforts are generated from the top down by development agencies, they are also organized at the grassroots level. Recently in Smithville, there has been a groundswell by a loosely networked group of place-based, relational community activists to intentionally introduce some mutual economic aid strategies. Figure 4.1 shows some of the emerging economic mutual aid activities in Smithville.

While many mutual economic aid efforts depend on outside seed money, the Smithville effort began among its place-based, relational network, whose members frequently lamented how Smithville had become something of a "food desert." There was no reasonably priced food market, and fresh local fruits and vegetables were impossible to find, even in season. One "catalyst" learned that farmers a few hours away were frustrated because they were forced to throw away produce that could not be easily picked mechanically and was not worth hauling to the closest really major city. She asked a few farmers if she could buy these leftovers at a bit above cost and haul them to Smithville. The farmers agreed because some money was better than none. Others in the relational network borrowed pickup trucks, and volunteer drivers went to get the excess vegetables, which were taken to Smithville and sold inexpensively at a weekly ad hoc farmers market in a church parking lot. Soon, members of the Smithville community garden associations asked if they could sell their vegetables at the weekly markets and were welcomed. During the summer and early fall, there was too much fresh produce to use, so it was informally decided to preserve the bounty. After each market day, the leftover vegetables were taken into the church's fully appointed kitchen, where a group of women and a few men met every week to share recipes and learn to preserve food, with the older women teaching the younger chefs. Eventually, this Thursday Night Cooking Club filled its own winter larders and those of everyone they knew, but there were still leftovers. So, they added

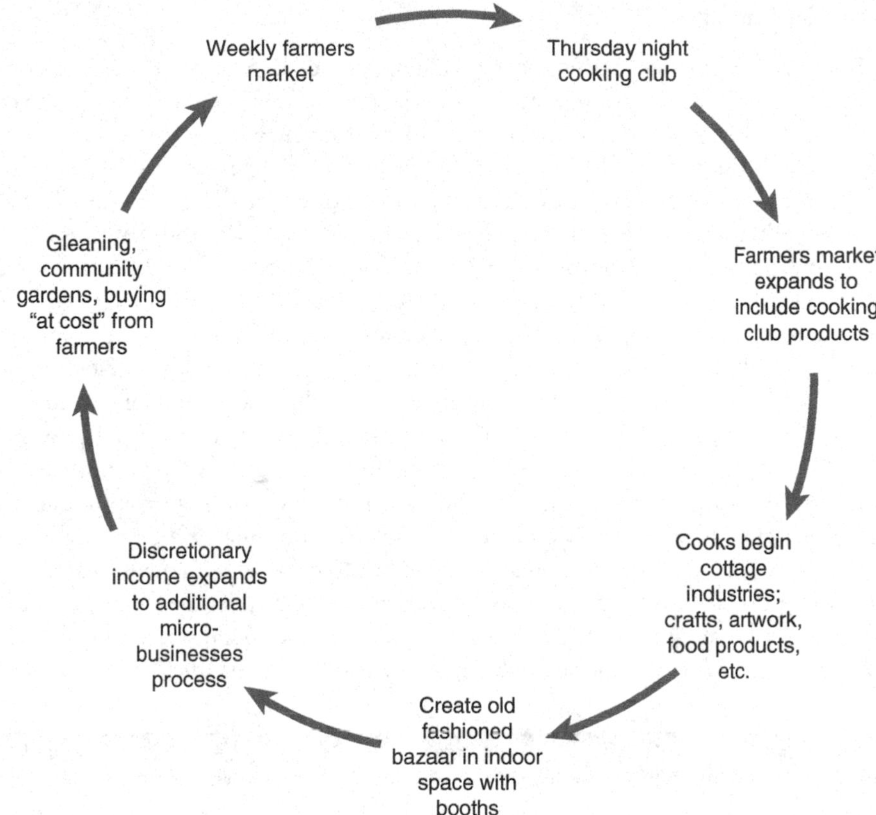
Weekly farmers market
Thursday night cooking club
Farmers market expands to include cooking club products
Cooks begin cottage industries; crafts, artwork, food products, etc.
Create old fashioned bazaar in indoor space with booths
Discretionary income expands to additional micro-businesses process
Gleaning, community gardens, buying "at cost" from farmers

FIGURE 4.1 Emerging Economic Mutual Aid Activities in Smithville
Source: Copyright © by Pearson Education, Upper Saddle River, NJ.

their preserves and other canned goods to the farmers market offerings, with proceeds going to the cooks themselves. As they earned money from the food products, several purchased craft supplies to turn hobbies into small cottage industries. At first, these products were added to the outdoor market, but soon it became clear that indoor space was needed. Participants pooled their own money (along with some small grants from private foundations and interested individual donors) and leased space in an abandoned local store. They created a kind of bazaar or micro-business incubator. As their micro-businesses grew, they sought help from experts and learned how to develop micro-credit groups to loan one another money at no or very low interest, and backed members' micro-loan applications. The loan payback rate was close to 100%. Several of the micro-businesses expanded until they each employed a few people at well above minimum wage. The prosperity of families has increased with very little outside financial input, there is greater food security, and a spirit of mutual reliance and support has blossomed.

Review Yes! Magazine for ideas that would encourage development of sustainable economic structures for your community. Consider how and where sustainability concerns fit into your organizing efforts.

Economic mutual aid strategies offer a sound alternative to the forces of globalization that have nearly destroyed rural and inner-city economies, widened the worldwide gap between the rich and poor, and threatened environmental sustainability. Economic mutual aid strategies are useful alone or as part of an overall place-based relational strategy for community economic development.

Assess your comprehension of Economic Mutual Aid by completing this quiz.

Self-help Groups

Self-help groups are associations that enable people to share experiences and coping strategies to meet specific physical and emotional needs.[19] Self-help groups vary in content, such as those that enable participants to control self-destructive behavior such as alcoholism and other addictive behaviors. Some assist people in coping with a wide variety of physical and emotional challenges; others focus on relationship issues. Still others enable people to cope with the struggles of loved ones, such as groups for parents of autistic children or for families of the addicted. There are hundreds of self-help groups throughout the United States, and more are created daily in both face-to-face and online venues.

Explore available mental health self-help groups or other self-help groups. Why are self-help groups so popular particularly in the United States?

Although the terms are sometimes used interchangeably, self-help groups can be differentiated from support groups, which are sponsored and led by professionals. Support groups may further an institutional agenda or give power and control to professionals rather than participants. In contrast, self-help groups cost little or nothing to organize and are not dependent on outside funding or approval. They provide participants with positive role models, supply emotional and practical support, ease loneliness, facilitate sharing, enable individuals to cope with changes in status, and offer a way to serve others.[20] Their collaborative nature builds democracy and often provides emotional support and advocacy. In fact, major social movements, such as those focused on the rights of the disabled, began as self-help efforts.[21]

Client-related Values and Attitudes

Understanding and Mastery: Client self-determination

Critical Thinking Question: In what ways would client-initiated self-help groups be more likely to support client self-determination than support groups organized and led by human service professions or members of other helping professions?

Like anything managed by humans, self-help groups can fall prey to such weaknesses as over-dependence on a few leaders who are not open to change or who gripe about perceived injustice, wallow in self-pity, and fail to stimulate hope and positive coping. Others are overwhelmed by a few strong personalities or split by interpersonal conflicts and rivalries.[22] Most issues, however, can be avoided by applying basic communication rules; making participants aware of dangers and possible pitfalls; setting clear, mutually agreed upon rules for communication, including inclusivity; and regularly spending group time evaluating the group's effectiveness.

Read the self-help handbook for[24] ideas for development of self-help groups. Consider the advantages and disadvantages of a face-to-face self-help group versus an online self-help group.

The choice of in-person or online settings depends on the needs of participants, as both venues share more commonalities than differences.[23] Each offers a safe space surrounded by people who understand the participants' struggles, have useful suggestions to offer, and pledge to help them. Everyone receives and gives. Each depends on the willingness of participants to honestly and compassionately share intimate personal experiences with those who are initially strangers. Each depends on group members to learn about the situation and mutually evaluate approaches to managing it. Each venue has millions of participants. However, there are some differences. Table 4.3 compares face-to-face self-help with online groups.

Table 4.3 Comparison of Face-to-Face and Online Groups

Face-to-Face Groups	Online Groups
Appeal to women	Appeal to men
Appeal to those who are lonely and desire opportunities to meet outside of the group context	Appeal to those who prefer to remain anonymous and separate their need for support from their daily lives
Appeal to those who share socially acceptable struggles	Appeal to those who feel that their situation is shameful or embarrassing (such as one that involves a stigma)
Work best for those who have time and logistical support to attend meetings	Work best for those with little time or who keep odd hours, are homebound, or must keep their activities secret
Work best for conditions shared by many people in a geographic area	Work best for rare conditions
Work well in populous areas with good transportation	Work well for people in isolated areas with poor or expensive transportation
Often link newcomers with sponsors who are available for crises and day-to-day support	Are available twenty-four hours a day, seven days a week, especially late at night when a sponsor may be unavailable
Work well for people who lack technological savvy, have poor computer access, or are uncomfortable with computers	Work well for those who are comfortable with computers and have good access
Provide immediate emergency help	Difficult to manage emergency help
Logistics such as meeting place, meeting times, recruitment, transportation, and so on may be difficult	Are easy to set up using social networking tools
Provide personal and emotional safety, as most sessions are closed to those who do not share the focal concern	Cannot guarantee personal and emotional safety, as it is difficult to ban participants who might be abusive or scornful

Source: Copyright © by Pearson Education, Upper Saddle River, NJ.

Self-help groups should be undertaken only by those who share the challenge being faced and can devote the time and energy needed to maintain momentum.

Assess your comprehension of Self-help Groups by completing this quiz.

Community-based Advocacy

The Smithville Neighborhood Organization you have heard about in other examples was formed because a group of Smithville neighbors was fed up. Industrial City had spent millions of dollars renovating the downtown, but the Smithville neighborhood lacked sidewalks, safe street crossings, adequate storm drains, and regular garbage pick-up. A large local park was inaccessible and dangerous. The group became a leadership team, formed a community organization, developed resolutions to take to the mayor and city council, and applied pressure until their demands were met. Later on, tenants in a large housing complex in Smithville were frustrated by their landlord who would not fix leaking toilets or broken playground equipment. Although quiet hours were posted, some tenants partied all hours, and drug dealers haunted the public areas. One brave woman held a meeting at her apartment to address these concerns. Six or seven people showed up and decided to form a tenants' association which confronted the building owners with their demands. Both of these Smithville groups were engaged in community-based advocacy.

Administration

Understanding and Mastery: Constituency building and other advocacy techniques such as lobbying, grassroots movements, and community development and organizing

Critical Thinking Question: What factors do you think community organizing teams should consider when choosing a community advocacy strategy? What ethical considerations, if any, are important?

All community advocacy efforts are social processes that involve interaction among those who are suffering injustice, governments or powerful interests that are directly or indirectly responsible for the injustice, media representatives who are largely responsible for interpreting the situation, and the general public who can be influenced to support or reject the cause.[25] Advocates use a variety of tactics to gain broad public support for their cause and pressure their adversaries into making desirable changes.

There are three major approaches to community-based advocacy: Alinsky-style organizations, radical membership-based organizations, and unaffiliated groups of individuals and organizations that arise spontaneously in response to community issues. Table 4.4 compares and contrasts these three types.

Alinsky-style organizing is named after Saul Alinsky, who was one of the first people to be identified professionally as a community organizer. Alinsky began his work in the 1940s in the sprawling Chicago slum called the Back of the Yards, a neighborhood comprised mostly of poor European immigrants from diverse cultural backgrounds who shared their poverty and lack of voice in city affairs. Alinsky's breakthrough insight was that the Back-of-the-Yards residents needed to be rationally organized—with clear demands and an effective structure that demonstrated their power in numbers, clarity of goals, and determination to force the all-pervasive Chicago political regime to listen to them. He chose to work through existing neighborhood organizations—especially churches, unions, and ethnically based social clubs—and used community meetings to develop a list of specific, agreed-upon demands to present to city decision makers. Alinsky chose churches as primary sites for organizing not because he was religious but because churches were practically the only institutions in the Back of the Yards that could easily reach the numbers of committed people.[27]

Alinsky-style advocacy emphasizes organizing *organizations* rather than *individuals* and is based on the mutual self-interest of its participants. Common strategies include the identification of community issues, creation of resolutions through a general community assembly, presentation of these resolutions to appropriate policy makers, and follow-through to sure that the resolutions result in action, which may be accomplished by neighbors working together or may require outside intervention (usually from local government).

At this writing Alinsky-style organizing is perhaps best represented by faith-based organizations including the Gamaliel Foundation, People Improving Communities through Organizing (PICO) and the Industrial Areas Foundation (IAF), the inheritors of Alinsky's original efforts. Local Alinsky-style efforts are primarily managed by volunteers chosen by member organizations, which include churches, synagogues, and mosques; neighborhood associations; and interdenominational organizations. Although a few chapters employ professional organizers supplied by their network, many are locally led. Support for the work comes from dues paid by participating organizations, foundation funding, fund-raising, and thousands of volunteer hours. While the

Table 4.4 Comparison of Types of Community Advocacy Groups[26]

Characteristic	Alinsky-style	Secular–Radical	Spontaneous
Primary purpose	Provide a focal community system with a consistent, insistent voice for justice.	Force authorities or adversaries to change specific conditions; often identified at a regional or national rather than local level.	Gain response from authorities on a specific local issue of grave concern, such as increased criminal activity or dangerous infrastructures.
Formation	Congregations, religious organizations, and other altruistic groups commit to improving the quality of life in the focal community.	Membership organizations made up of people from targeted neighborhoods recruited door-to-door and in public rallies.	Quasi-groups that quickly become organizations in response to a perceived threat to community well-being or arise more slowly from a multitude of small injustices.
Membership	Congregations and other altruistic locally based organizations.	Dues-paying members.	Loosely structured—anyone who wants to can support the cause.
Financing	Organizational dues, some financing from foundations, denominations, etc.	Members' dues, support from "radical" foundations, fund-raising.	Donations and fund-raising.
Management	Local or regional; shared by representatives of congregational core groups and representatives of other member organizations.	Often centralized in well-educated leaders at the national level; little substantial local decision making.	Grassroots participants organize their own approach to decision making; often consensus-based
Approach to authority	Polite, reasonable, forgiving, loving, expect the best.	Confrontational and dramatic	Combination; often form two related groups: one emphasizing peaceful communication and the other confrontation.
Tactics	Candlelight vigils; respectful discussions with officials; well-organized, peaceful meetings.	Disruptive, "in-your-face" confrontations often geared to generate publicity and public embarrassment.	Begin quietly and respectfully but become progressively more abrasive if demands are not met.
Use of violence	Never use violence or political actions likely to result in violence.	Sometimes use violence or threat of violence as a last resort.	Use Gandhian non-violence which may result in arrest or violence perpetrated on them by authorities; work hard to control violent urges among members.

Source: Copyright © by Pearson Education, Upper Saddle River, NJ.

original Alinsky model emphasized the development of a unified local voice to confront political authorities, most affiliates today use a combination of mildly confrontational political strategies blended with asset-based community building at the street or block level.[28] For example, a local chapter may simultaneously urge city government to pave a street, provide community policing, and organize neighborhood clean-ups, informal block parties, and community kitchens. The Alinsky model may sound somewhat familiar to you because the Smithville Neighborhood Organization has relied heavily on its affiliation with one of the faith-based organizing networks for many years.

Alinsky-style organizing works best when the target place has strong neighborhood congregations, an existing neighborhood improvement association supported by organized street or block clubs, and established businesses—the building blocks for an "organization of organizations." It does not work very well where congregations are regional rather than locally based, small and inwardly focused, or believe that social justice efforts are unnecessary or where religious faith has no relevance to the vast majority of people. In addition, Alinsky-style organizing does not work well where there are few local businesses or organizations or where the population is mostly comprised of transient renters without neighborhood roots.

Secular–radical community advocacy was born in the social movements of the late 1960s and early 1970s, often spurred by young, white students and graduates of elite private colleges and universities. The Association of Community Organizations for Reform Now (ACORN) and its surviving affiliates are the prototype of secular–radical organizing.[29] While Alinsky-style initiatives are primarily organizations of organizations, secular–radical advocacy is membership-based. Professional organizers enter a focal community system at the invitation of residents or because their national office has identified the neighborhood as ready for organizing. These professionals mount door-to-door campaigns to recruit dues-paying members by promising that the new organization will do something about community concerns and by giving examples of successful campaigns in other focal communities. The dues are usually reasonable and are intended to symbolize members' personal commitment to the organizing effort rather than its major source of income. A membership meeting is called when the organizer and his or her regional or national superiors determine that there are enough local members for dramatic social actions, such as protests and sit-ins. Generally these meetings are tightly controlled by the professional organizers who define the action campaigns and assign members to specific tasks. There is usually little place for local leadership or for non-confrontational actions, such as mutual economic aid efforts, local clean-ups, community gardens, and the like.[30]

The major weakness of secular–radical movements is that too much power rests in a small elite group of liberal intellectuals from outside of the focal community rather than with neighborhood leaders. Most secular–radical organizers are young, idealistic, and incredibly naïve. Few are people of color or members of oppressed minorities, and almost none have lived in poverty. Many have a "know-it-all" attitude that leads to ill-considered social action tactics, alienates allies and enemies alike, leads to rapid burn-out among the young organizers, fails to bring about real change, and causes deep disappointment for the dues-paying membership.[31] The major strength of the secular–radical organizing is the individual membership model, especially when coupled with local leadership. Unlike Alinsky-style organizations that are dependent on ongoing institutional support and only indirectly represent neighborhood residents, membership-based organizations are largely independent of outside funding, develop pride of ownership within their members, and encourage the development of indigenous leaders.[32]

Spontaneous Community-based Advocacy arises when focal system residents feel threatened by outsiders from mezzo- or macro-systems or by powerful forces within the community focal system itself. Middle View has been experiencing such a battle between a relatively powerless community-based advocacy group and powerful economic interests for the hearts, minds, and votes of ordinary people and political decision makers. Here is the story of the hydrofracking battle of 2012. Hydrofracking is a process in which thousands of gallons of chemically treated water are forced at high pressure into the shale rock hundreds of feet below the earth's surface. The high-pressure water–chemical combination fractures the shale to release natural gas, which can then be brought to the surface. Throughout the world, the natural gas industry and some politicians have celebrated hydrofracking as a quick solution to the world's energy woes and assumed that it would be immediately and readily embraced everywhere. But some people, including numerous Middle View residents, fear that hydrofracking may permanently ruin the water table, pollute lakes and streams, and even destabilize the geological base—thus causing earthquakes.[33]

Because the Town of Middle View sits on one of the richest gas shale deposits in the United States, it's a prime target for hydrofracking, which has become a very controversial local issue. Some owners of fallow farms look forward to promised leased agreements, some unemployed construction workers look forward to at least temporary jobs, and powerful organizations such as the Chamber of Commerce and the County Farm Bureau have embraced the economic development potential of hydrofracking. Middle View residents oppose it because they depend on wells for their water and fear permanent pollution of the water table and the lake, which supports the local economy as a major source of recreation and tourism. These opponents organized a local advocacy group that was loosely connected to similar groups at the regional, state, and national levels and began to use social action tactics to engage the powerful economic interests that support hydrofracking. These anti-fracking advocates won the first round of what has become an escalating local controversy with state and national implications. Through a variety of social action tactics, the community advocacy group convinced the Middle View Town Council to put in place a local ordinance banning hydrofracking in the town. The powerful energy companies, in turn, filed a lawsuit against the town—asserting that hydrofracking is under the jurisdiction of the State Department of Environmental Conservation (DEC) and local zoning laws have no authority to regulate it. They also recruited local allies in the economic development community, such as the Chamber of Commerce and the County Farm Bureau, with financial support from the energy companies. These groups created a coalition in support of hydrofracking, which spent thousands of dollars in media campaigns that extolled its economic benefits and reassured the public of its safety. The community advocacy group responded with rallies, marathon telephone and e-mail campaigns, and one-on-one discussions with their neighbors and politicians to spread their views. The battle raged on several fronts.

In social systems terms, anti-fracking advocacy groups are fighting the hydrofracking battle at (1) the *macro-level* through worldwide anti-fracking movements; (2) the *mezzo-level* through actions to delay implementation of permissive DEC guidelines and counter-lawsuits to the one filed against the Town of Middle View;

and (3) the *focal system level*, through efforts geared at educating Middle View citizens and decision makers about the dangers of hydrofracking by raising money to fight the lawsuit, placing yard signs around town, encouraging people to call the governor's office, busing residents to protests at the state capital, and conducting their own media campaigns mostly through Facebook and other social media. So far, these tactics have delayed DEC implementation of hydrofracking in the state. But as soon as the community advocates gain some ground, the powerful counter-forces invest more money and effort into touting hydrofracking's economic benefits and providing reassurance about its ecological impact. The battle struggles on and is likely to continue for years. (4) The impact of differences of opinion over hydrofracking at the *micro-level* among neighbors, friends, and family members has led to at least one divorce.[34]

While the hydrofracking controversy in Middle View is an example of spontaneous community advocacy linked intimately with worldwide protests, spontaneous community advocacy can take place in micro-systems as well. For instance, Smithville has a high-rise housing project that dates back to the early 1960s that fits the public stereotype of life in "the projects." It's filled with gangs, drug sales, prostitution, and senseless violence. Police refuse to answer calls there, claiming that it's too dangerous due to several officers having been hurt there over the years. Although the buildings are owned by the city housing authority, everything seems broken—from the elevators to the drains. Finally, a group of long-term residents became angry. They formed a tenants' association that used a combination of confrontation and negotiation to bring about needed changes, especially in the housing authority and police–tenant relationships. They created a "mini-neighborhood watch" to maintain order and insisted on a reasonable level of discipline from children, teens, and young adults. The association is run by street-wise, compassionate community matriarchs who support one another and to whom, when they speak, everyone listens.[35] From the outside, spontaneous community advocacy sometimes seems make-shift, but it is often the difference between a livable community and chaos.

Review more information on theories related to community advocacy. Consider the forms of community advocacy that are needed in your focal community and the strategies you will use to actualize them.

Community advocacy is needed where a local community has been ignored by those in power and allowed to disintegrate or when those in power threaten to reduce the quality of community life. Effective community advocacy groups are democratic, provide opportunities for residents to set agendas, decide on strategies, provide both symbolic and actual leadership, follow through with tactics, and maintain momentum. Your role is to be the servant-leader who makes sure that logistics are handled. Try your hand at these skills: (1) identify a multi-faceted issue that has a potentially negative effect on your focal community system; (2) read and listen to everything you can find out about it in your local media; (3) talk with members of your target community representing both sides of the issue; (4) make mental note of the arguments, strategies, and tactics each side is using; (5) analyze how well these approaches are working in terms of building public support and in bringing about the change their constituents desire; and (6) determine what you would recommend if you were leading this advocacy effort.

Assess your comprehension of Community-based Advocacy by completing this quiz.

Social Movements

While community advocacy efforts are geographically based, social movements are broader and can be more accurately defined as communities of interest whose members are committed to social change across wide geographic areas. In fact, the word *movement* itself implies a wave of change that "moves" quickly across land and sea in a multitude of directions and often seems to arise spontaneously in many different places. Just reflect for a minute and you can probably think of several contemporary and historic social movements: the various "Occupy" efforts of 2011–2012, disability rights, gay rights, various historical waves toward women's rights, environmental conservation, demands for civil rights from many different minority groups, the pre–Civil War abolition movement, the labor movement, and more. Probably few of the great leaders of social movements past and present set out to be spokespeople at the forefront of profound social change. Instead, they found themselves at the right place, at the right time in history, and chose to accept the challenge.[36]

The late political theorist and historian Charles Tilly asserted that social movements of the disenfranchised first emerged around 1768. In Tilly's model, social movements have several important components: political objectives; a repertoire of actions and symbols for making political decision makers and the public aware of these objectives and the necessity of favorable action; and WUNC, which is an ability to demonstrate **w**orthiness, **u**nity, **n**umbers, and **c**ommitment that convinces decision makers that the movement will not go away. The goal of movement organizing is to constantly increase its WUNC.[37]

In 1966, anthropologist David Aberle conceived a four-part model of social movements based on their focus and intent that is still used today (Figure 4.2).[38]

You can use the four-quadrant Aberle model to determine whether (1) a social movement is primarily focused on individual or societal change; (2) its goals involve minor shifts in behavior, viewpoints, and ideologies; or (3) major (radical) shifts are envisioned.

- **Alternative social movements** are individually focused and require limited change. Recycling would be an example.
- **Redemptive social movements**, such as Alcoholics Anonymous, are individually focused and require radical changes in individual beliefs and behaviors.

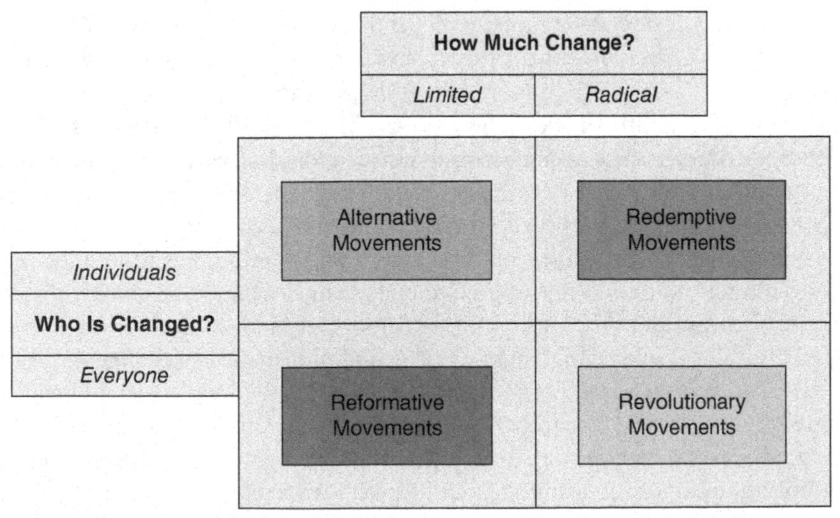

FIGURE 4.2
The Aberle Model
Source: Aberle, David. "A Classification of Social Movements" in The Peyote Religion among the Navajo. Norman, OK: The University of Oklahoma Press, 1966.

- **Reformative social movements**, such as the disabilities awareness movement, focus on all of society but have limited objectives.
- **Revolutionary social movements**, such as the sustainability movement, seek to fundamentally change social structures and the premises upon which societies are based.

In addition to the Aberle model, there are other classifications of social movements based on the source of their core values. **Religiously or culturally based movements** are exemplified by the Indian freedom movement under Gandhi, the American Civil Rights movement under Martin Luther King Jr., and the anti-apartheid movement in South Africa under Nelson Mandela and Episcopal Bishop Desmond Tutu.[39] **"New social movements"** based in rationality and self-interest focus on (1) identity politics, such as gender, physical conditions, race, and ethnicity; or (2) global issues, such as climate change or animal rights that have little to do with class conflict, religion and values, or economic issues.[40] **Radical–secular social** movements insist that the world is divided between a few powerful oppressors and the majority of us who comprise an exploited oppressed. For them, life is a **zero-sum game** with definite winners and losers. The community organizer's or community educator's role is to awaken the oppressed, alert them to their mistreatment (a process called **conscientization**), partner with them, and together use a repertoire of social action tactics to cause revolutionary social change.[41] The various Occupy movements of 2011–2012 are a fairly recent example of such radical–secular movements.

There is an implicit assumption in the social movement literature that social movements always bring desirable change, but that is not always the case. **Counter-revolutionary movements** meet Tilly's criteria but aim at preserving the social status quo, convincing people to act against their own best interests or pulling society back to the values of an earlier time.[42] These counter-revolutionary or reactionary movements are generated by fear of loss of power or loss of the familiar. Counter-revolutionary movements are similar to revolutionary movements in that they are conflict-oriented and view life as a zero-sum game with winners and losers—with participants afraid to be on the losing side.

We live in a time of proliferating social movements. From the mid-nineteenth to the late twentieth century, meta-networks gained speed and momentum through inventions such as the telegraph, telephone, radio, and television. The late twentieth and early twenty-first centuries have seen the invention of the internet and instantaneous, world-wide interactive communication, and the ability of such sites as YouTube to record live instances of injustice.

The Web has made both a quantitative and a qualitative difference in social movements. From the quantitative perspective, technology has made it possible to reach millions of people quickly and easily, adding speed and immediacy to the social change process. However, remember that technology is fundamentally ethically and morally neutral. It can be used to include or to exclude, to quickly disseminate the truth or embroider lies. Vast sources of information available through search engines can be false or even dangerous. The speed of information exchange can leave little time for reflection or wise decision making. The so-called digital divide can further separate the "haves" who can access technology from the "have nots." Therefore, critical thinking, discernment, clear personal ethical standards, and open access to technology are important factors in assuring that the Web serves society.

Human Systems

Understanding and Mastery: Processes to effect social change through advocacy (e.g., community development, community and grassroots organizing, local and global activism)

Critical Thinking Question: The late Charles Tilly hypothesized that successful social movements need to demonstrate WUNC: that they are worthy, unified, numerically strong, and that their members are committed for the long haul. Choose a successful social movement that interests you, read about it in several different sources, and identify its WUNC and the factors that led to its success.

Read more about democratic social movements and social movements and adult education. Consider the various kinds of social movements and their relationship to local community organizing efforts.

This text concentrates on democratic social movements that are based (1) internally on clear communication and direct involvement of participants and (2) externally, using a non-violent repertoire of strategies and tactics to gain 67 public attention for changing political policies or immoral cultural values (such as increasing gaps between wealth and poverty) and practices (such as charging usurious credit rates or outsourcing jobs to countries that lack labor or environmental laws).

Assess your comprehension of Social Movements by completing this quiz.

Collaborations

Collaborations are comprised of representatives of formal organizations (hospitals, mental health organizations, etc.) and associations (service groups, professional groups, church agencies, etc.) who are assigned by their employers to work together to avoid duplication of services, fill service gaps, and stretch limited resources.[43] Figure 4.3 is a "Collaboration Pyramid" developed by community collaboration expert

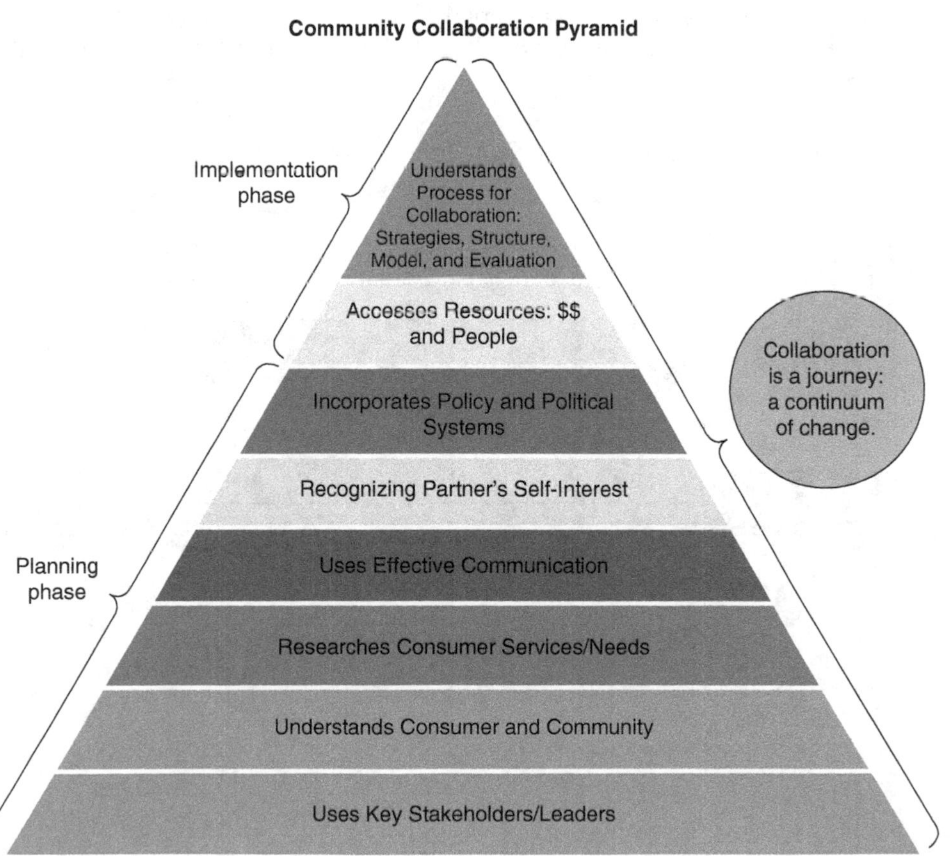

FIGURE 4.3 Collaboration Pyramid
Source: Bacheldor, Laura. Developing Tools for Measuring Collaborative Effectiveness: Two Case Studies" . Saratoga Springs, NY: SUNY/Empire State College unpublished master's thesis, 2007.

Laura Bacheldor for her master's degree in social policy. The pyramid helps define the skills needed for successful collaborations and moves upward from initial planning to implementation.[44]

Collaborations have four dimensions as illustrated by Figure 4.4. On the horizontal axis, they vary from involuntary to voluntary, and on the vertical axis they vary from service level to management level. Each quadrant represents different reasons and results of collaboration.

On the horizontal axis, **involuntary collaboration** occurs when funders push for organizations to work together to save money through reducing overhead, eliminating redundant services, and curtailing new program creation. In fact, some funders order their grantees to "collaborate or else." Needless to say, such involuntary or forced collaboration leads to tension and resentment. **Voluntary collaboration**, on the other hand, is freely chosen, allows for creative expansion of resources, enhances connected learning, and builds trust.

The vertical axis indicates where collaboration occurs. The top indicates collaboration among policy makers, such as chief executive officers and board members. The bottom indicates cooperation among direct service providers.

The intersection of the two axes results in four quadrants, each with different properties:

- **Quadrant 1: Consolidation** occurs when separate agencies are forced to combine services usually to save money. For example, consolidation of health care services occurred in Industrial City over a period of about ten years as three medium-sized hospitals were merged into one large facility with attendant loss of jobs and services.

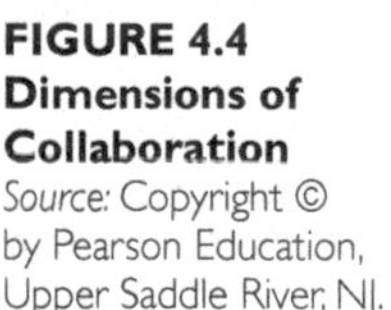

FIGURE 4.4 Dimensions of Collaboration
Source: Copyright © by Pearson Education, Upper Saddle River, NJ.

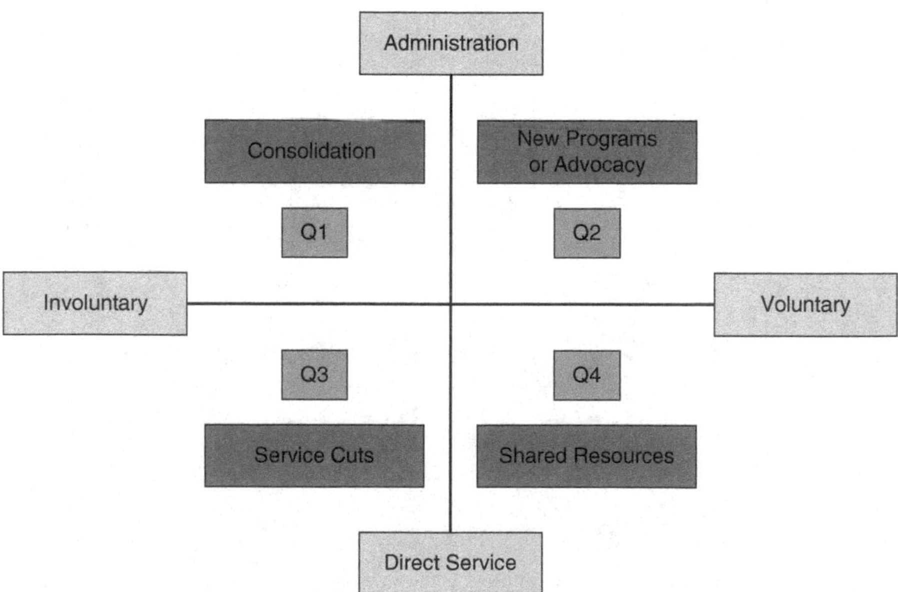

- **Quadrant 2:** The upper right quadrant represents voluntary collaborations among agency administrators for the purpose of providing **new programs** or **advocacy** and is often used to accomplish tasks each collaborator would normally be forced to do separately, such as demographic and other forms of social science research, advocacy for a whole service sector, or creation of new programs and projects that no single existing organization is equipped to do alone. For example, in Industrial City (the home of Smithville), all the youth-serving agencies joined together to sponsor a yearly summer recreation program. Each agency took a week and provided planned activities for inner-city youth that provided a ten-week program that no single agency could have done alone. Elsewhere in Industrial City, executives from several residential programs serving the infirm elderly joined together to advocate for fair reimbursement for their services and livable regulations.
- **Quadrant 3:** The left lower quadrant symbolizes involuntary collaboration at the direct service level that occurs when **service cuts** make it impossible to really help people and everyone must share limited resources.
- **Quadrant 4:** In the lower right quadrant, **shared resources** allow workers in various agencies to easily refer clients to one another. This ensures that clients' needs are met no matter where they enter the service system and that no one "beats the system" by getting duplicated services. This works well in Middle View. For many years needy people had to go from place to place to get help, but now they are given comprehensive aid at the combined food pantry and thrift shop. This not only helps those who are truly in need but also prevents smart "scam artists" from making money by going from church to church with the same sob story and receiving aid from everyone.

Effective collaborations are difficult to sustain. They require a broad and inclusive vision, mutual trust, participants who are authorized to act, and sufficient time for negotiation. All are often in short supply. For instance, most organizations operate in a continuous growth mode. Executives are rewarded for their ability to increase revenues, develop new programs, and effectively market existing programs rather than for their willingness to save costs—especially if such savings come through collaboration with competitors or through consolidating services. Second, in our highly competitive society, successful people are raised to believe that the world is composed of winners and losers and that it is dangerous to trust anyone, especially one's competitors. Third, because participants in collaborative efforts represent organizational rather than personal interests, few are free to commit organizational time, effort, or resources without going through an extensive approval process. Finally, the demands of day-to-day operations often leave little time for the concentrated thought needed to make wise, collaborative decisions or for the many telephone calls, e-mails, and written reports that collaborations seem to inevitably entail. Often, collaborative responsibilities seem to sink to the bottom of everyone's "to do" lists.

At some time in your career, your employer will probably require you to participate in a collaborative effort, your community organizing team will decide that inter-organizational collaboration is the best way to meet community needs, or you may want to work with others for the common good. Here are a few things you should know about the collaborative process:

- Collaborations have limited life spans, have distinct phases of group development, need clear rules of communicative engagement, frequently experience conflict and power struggles, and often fail to live up to their early promise.[45]
- It is not your fault if collaborations fail or move along slowly. In fact, any collaborative effort is better than isolation and chaos.
- Collaborations have life spans: some begin with a definite goal and disband once the goal is reached. Other collaborations reach limited objectives, take pride in solid accomplishments, and leave the doors open for future efforts. More frequently, collaborations are amorphous and idealistic with missions such as "building a better tomorrow together," which make it hard to measure success or ascertain when the work is done. Such collaborations may begin with great enthusiasm, creativity, and funding but (1) evolve into bureaucracies which add another layer to the target system, (2) break into spin-offs, or (3) are integrated into existing organizations.[46]
- Some collaborations experience so much competition and antipathy among member organizations that future collaborations are nearly impossible and the focal community system is in much worse shape than before.[47]

Collaborations also need clear rules for positive engagement that vary according to whether they are forced or voluntary, as well as whether they occur at the service or executive level:

- Members of forced collaborations communicate best when rational discourse is used, including parliamentary procedure, clear minutes, and firm direction. Voluntary collaborations succeed when participants respect one another, use connected learning, listen carefully to each another, and build freely on one another's ideas.
- Consensus and exchange power can quickly devolve into conflict, tension, and even threats. Such rapid changes of group mood are disconcerting but very common.

Administration

Understanding and Mastery: Constituency building and other advocacy techniques such as lobbying, grassroots movements, and community development and organizing

Critical Thinking Question: Why is the idea of collaboration among organizations so compelling even though it is difficult to sustain and rarely works well?

Read more about collaboration theory and practice to find suggestions for implementation. Consider the strategies you would use to encourage successful collaboration.

A thorough understanding of various dichotomies discussed throughout this book—especially rational discourse/connected knowing, consensus/conflict, power/empowerment, and clarity on small group dynamics—will provide the intellectual tools and emotional distance needed to keep things on an even keel while progressing toward shared goals that benefit the focal community system.

At their best, collaborations meet the goals of the collaborators and strengthen the quality of life in focal community systems. They enable communities and service organizations to do more with less by (1) sharing resources, (2) developing creative but relatively inexpensive solutions to longstanding problems, and (3) building networks for solving future issues. At their worst, collaborative failures result in feuds, massive wastes of time and taxpayer or donor money, and longstanding resentments that make further collaboration impossible.

While all of the other varieties of community organizing are primarily dependent on people who represent their own interests, needs, and concerns, collaborative efforts are usually composed of representatives of formal agencies and organizations who are expected to put organizational interests above their personal preferences and the needs of the collaborative effort. If you look around your focal community, you will probably find that there are many attempts at collaboration going on simultaneously. Take some time to explore one of them. Observe or participate in a meeting of agency representatives in a real-life venue such as a local government or school board planning workshop, an interagency council meeting, or a recorded planning session from a source such as C-Span or your local public access station. Pay attention to interactional patterns such as who speaks and for how long, evidences of changes in emotional tone or content, areas where you sense agreement, and areas where you sense conflict. Reflect on places where there was explicit or implicit agreement and where there seemed to be conflicts of interest and how each affected the meeting's outcome. If you were involved, what role would you play? How would you reconcile your loyalty to your employer with your loyalty to the community? As a participant, how would you lead the group toward consensus rather than conflict?

Assess your comprehension of Collaborations by completing this quiz.

Mixing and Matching

Successful community organizing depends on using appropriate strategies and tactics. The following **typology** (comparison of the varieties of community organizing) can help your team determine which approach best fits your needs, but these strategies are not mutually exclusive. Tables 4.5 and 4.6 illustrate ways in which the various strategies can cross-fertilize one another. Table 4.5 uses housing in the Smithville neighborhood as an example of a multifaceted issue facing a geographic community. Table 4.6 uses the

Table 4.5 Primarily Place-based: Overall Improvement of Housing in Smithville

Place-based	Innovation	Economic mutual aid	Self-help	Advocacy	Social movement	Collaboration
Neighborhood consensus to increase home ownership.	Non-profit formed to rehabilitate properties and build new ones.	Club formed with members taking turns assisting one another in raising down payments.	Potential homeowners share skills, teach each other how to do necessary repairs, etc.	Community association advocates with city for access to state and federal funds.	Community delegates join national movement to access fair mortgages and home ownership.	Association identifies several housing-related agencies and forms a collaborative team.

Source: Copyright © by Pearson Education, Upper Saddle River, NJ.

Table 4.6 **Primarily Self-Help: Provide Services for Persons with Asperger's Syndrome and Their Families in the Middle View Region**

Self-Help	Collaboration	Advocacy	Social Movement(s)	Social Innovation
Provides contact among affected individuals and families who desire to help one another; offers conversation and support both face to face and online.	Members contact agencies and school districts for assistance. Collaborative meetings held with success.	Members realize that agency and educational supports are limited. Advocates with school district(s), private agencies, and state government for appropriate services.	Links to broader nationwide movement, including those focused on autism, Asperger's syndrome, and broader issues of neurodiversity.	Develops a warm welcoming center providing services, counseling, and coaching.

Source: Copyright © by Pearson Education, Upper Saddle River, NJ.

challenges facing individuals with Asperger's syndrome and their families who live near Middle View to illustrate overlapping types.

Summary

Community organizing takes a variety of forms and occurs in many different places under many different circumstances. This chapter provides descriptions and a basic analysis of the strengths and weaknesses of seven different types of community organizing: (1) place-based relational, (2) social entrepreneurship and social innovation, (3) mutual economic aid, (4) self-help, (5) community advocacy, (6) collaboration, and (7) democratic social justice movements. All share the belief that democratic processes are foundational to a high quality of life and should be practiced in every community organizing venue. The chapter is linked to seven online handbooks that explore each type of organizing in further detail. Together, the chapter and handbooks can be used as a framework for specific community organizing efforts. Although both are meant to provide a rational framework for most community organizing tasks, many specific projects either (1) fit into a primary category and one or several related categories or (2) begin in one category and move to another, such as when a self-help group becomes a new social movement. In such cases, you will find it useful to explore the handbooks for all categories that seem to fit their circumstances in order to choose strategies and tactics that fit their needs. Community organizing is a wonderful adventure—enjoy your participation in it!

Assess your analysis and evaluation of the chapter's content by completing the Chapter Review.

CHAPTER 5

The Community Organizing Cycle

Gines Valera Marin/Shutterstock

Chapter Outline

Welcome to the Community Organizing Cycle—a framework that will used in the next few chapters to examine the interrelated processes of leadership (Chapter 6), research and learning (Chapter 7), planning and implementation (Chapter 8), and management and evaluation (Chapter 9).

To put it simply, community organizing is a non-linear process. It begins with the emergence of **a leadership team** (a small group of committed people that takes responsibility for the organizing effort). The leadership team guides the organizing effort through a cyclical process that includes:

- **Research:** developing a thorough understanding of the focal community's demographics, assets, needs, and probable approaches to solutions
- **Planning:** agreement on a mission, desired outcomes, processes that will lead to desired outcomes, and evaluation measures
- **Implementation:** collecting resources, trying out ideas, and beginning to actually do what has been planned
- **Management and monitoring:** keeping an established effort going at a high level, making adjustments as needed
- **Evaluation:** comparison of actual results with desired results defined in the planning process

Figure 5.1A is an overview of this process. The arrows generally flow from research to planning to implementation to evaluation and back to the leadership team to begin the cycle again. However, planning

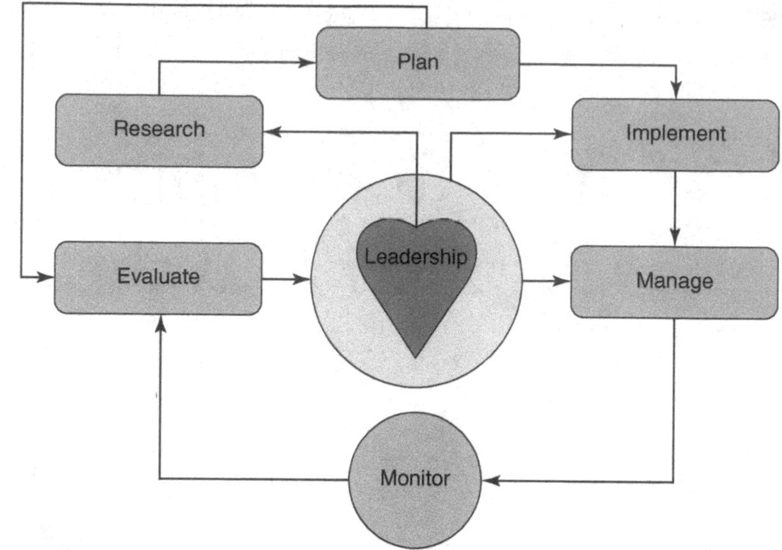

FIGURE 5.1A The Community Organizing Cycle
Source: Copyright © by Pearson Education, Upper Saddle River, NJ.

Administration

Understanding and Mastery: Managing organizations through leadership and strategic planning

Critical Thinking Question: What are the advantages and disadvantages of following an organizing cycle rather than just letting things happen spontaneously?

and evaluation are linked because, to be useful, evaluation must be linked to an assessment of whether the mission has been accomplished and outcome goals have been achieved. The leadership team is the "engine" of the whole process and provides guidance to those responsible for each stage. Members are ultimately responsible for the success of the whole enterprise, as well as each of the stages.

This model can be applied to any organization.

Let's apply the organizing cycle to a typical family with the mother as its leader. Imagine it's Saturday in a moderate income, single-parent household composed of a mom and her two children, John (age 11) and Susan (age 13). Mom's job is to get everyone through the day and safely into bed at a reasonable hour each night. Over the longer run, it's her responsibility to keep her household housed, healthy, fed, clothed, doing well at school or work, and as happy as possible. With some input from the children, she has already done some long-range planning and has set some policies. She has made household rules that (1) allow each child have two major outside commitments (sports, music, art, scouting, etc.) per school semester, (2) expect each child to take care of his or her room, and (3) give each child one major household chore that rotates every four months. The family has a sit-down evening meal once a week, followed by a family meeting, and all three do something fun (and moderately expensive) twice a year. On this weekend morning, the **plan** is for John to tackle the weekly inside housework while Susan mows the lawn and Mom runs errands. In the afternoon, John has a Little League game and afterwards will go out with his team for ice cream. Susan has a sleepover with three of her closest friends at 7 P.M. Mom hopes that everyone, including the three young guests, will get up and out the door for church in the morning. **Implementation** begins when both children and Mom sit down to breakfast and discuss the day. There are many details to be added to each person's tasks for the day to go well. Mom has to pick up snacks for the girls, prepare something quick for supper, deposit her paycheck, get gas in the car, and wash and dry John's uniform. John has to vacuum the carpet; dust; get down some sheets, blankets and pillows for his sister's party; and locate his baseball glove. Susan has to mow the lawn, feed the pets, check if any of her girlfriends need rides, and weed the family garden. Mom promises to bring home fast food for lunch, when they'll check their progress. Each leaves to begin morning chores. Although the **management** of the assigned tasks does get done, it is not all smooth going. Mom gets behind schedule when she is caught in line at the gas station. The soda she planned to buy for the girls' party is no longer on sale. John spends most of the morning hunting for his baseball glove, has to hurry through the chores, and breaks Mom's good vase. Susan calls her friends before starting her chores, talks most of the morning on her cell phone, and is only half done mowing the lawn when Mom comes home with lunch. The **program monitoring** phase is when the three sit down with burgers and fries to discuss the morning. Mom is a bit irritated by how little has been accomplished at home but reminds herself that, since her ultimate goal is to have them learn responsibility, she will use this for formative evaluation as a **teachable moment**. Mom first talks with John about how the broken vase was important to her because it belonged to her grandmother. Mom's leadership task now becomes enforcement of **program compliance** as they discuss the situation and agree that John and she will try to repair the vase with crazy glue and, if that doesn't work, Mom will buy a replacement vase and John will have $1 taken out of his weekly allowance until it is paid off. Mom will try to find him additional paid chores so he can pay it off more quickly. Mom and Susan then make a **program modification**. Even though Susan has been counting on using the afternoon to prepare for her party, they agree that party preparations will be set aside until Susan finishes mowing the lawn. There are a few "Aw Moms" from both kids, but they ultimately do as asked. Mom takes John to his game. Susan mows the lawn and then prepares for her party. Mom is pleased and a little surprised when she gets home. Susan has completed the lawn, has things ready for the party, and has even made iced tea and sandwiches for supper! Although we only have followed the family for a single day, the threesome also organize longer periods of time as well as special events. For example, the family has **summative evaluation** sessions at weekly family meetings where they review the past week and plan for the next. At the next weekly meeting, Mom asks the children what they remember from the past week and what they have learned about living together as a family. Susan mentions that she learned to do the hard things first, then the easier ones. John mentions the need to put his sports equipment where he can easily find it and to be more careful around breakables. They talk about the week ahead and make plans to mesh their schedules. They cycle back to **program planning** as they talk a little bit about possible changes in rules, and so it goes. Admittedly, this is an idealized version of family life, but it shows that the organizing cycle can be applied anywhere.

Assess your comprehension of Generic Organizing Cycles by completing this quiz.

Focus on Leadership

Leadership is the heart and soul of all human endeavors. In community organizing, leadership emerges almost immediately when there is a movement from quasi-group to association status (see Chapter 2). Six common leadership approaches include (1) single leadership, (2) power elites, (3) representative democracies, (4) self-selecting teams, (5) cells, and (6) connectivities.[1] Let's examine each in turn, so you and your emerging leadership team can begin thinking about the advantages and disadvantages of each approach.

FIGURE 5.1B Leadership: The Heart of the Organizing Cycle
Source: Copyright © by Pearson Education, Upper Saddle River, NJ..

The **single leader** model occurs when one strong person rises to power. In nations, this frequently occurs in times of chaos and confusion, and usually through a combination of an individual's intelligence, ability to consolidate power, charisma, compelling ideology, and economic or military might. In community organizing, single leaders often emerge when someone has a deep—almost compulsive—commitment to a social goal (as is the case with social entrepreneurs) or a situation arises where decisions must be made quickly and a strong authority is needed (as in the case of emergency or disaster response). The single leader model can be effective when the leader is compassionate, puts the needs of his or her people first, and is willing to listen to them. The single leader model, though, often falls into tyranny and dictatorship when the leader puts his or her own needs first.

Rule by an elite few is very common. A relatively mild form occurs in community organizing whenever a group of "old families," the "educated elite," or "experienced leaders" provide resources tied to their right to make decisions for everyone else. For example, Middle View's resident aristocrats include Mrs. Jonathan Snodgrass, the widow of the founder of a major local industry, and her closest friends who represent the only "old money" in the area. Mrs. Snodgrass established the Snodgrass Foundation to "provide for the needs of children and youth in the Middle View community." Her friends are on the foundation board and inevitably support what she wants. Mrs. Snodgrass has definite ideas about what is worthy of Snodgrass Foundation support and often dictates the details of its grants. For instance, the Middle View Park Association had an opportunity to refurbish an antique carousel that its members felt would be a tourist attraction and provide local children hours of summertime pleasure. It was to be free of charge, open daily to the public during the summer, and carefully secured against inclement weather from mid-October to mid-May. The Snodgrass Foundation was approached for funding its restoration and ongoing maintenance. Mrs. Snodgrass agreed to fund the project but only on condition that the carousel would be kept completely glass enclosed, carefully locked, and only available on rare occasions. Mrs. Snodgrass's reasoning was that "this area is filled with rough people who don't care about nice things. If the carousel is open and in frequent use, 'those people' would ruin it." It didn't matter to her that a glass-enclosed carousel isn't as much fun as one open to the sights and sounds of summer, or that other nearby communities had open-air summer attractions with little or no vandalism. Rather than fight with Mrs. Snodgrass, however, the Park Association agreed to her conditions, and as a result riding the carousel is a lot like riding inside a glass aquarium!

Mrs. Snodgrass and her friends are examples of local "**aristocrats**," who believe that they are meant to make decisions for the "lower classes," an attitude sometimes referred to as **noblesse oblige**. However, ruling elites in the form of **oligarchies** or **hegemonies** can have a darker side, that is, trading favors with one another while exploiting the relatively powerless.[2] For example, Smithville has recently been experiencing a process called **gentrification** where several fine old homes in the neighborhood have been converted from small, low-income apartments into spacious condominiums and then sold to middle or upper-middle class families, which has displaced many lower income people. When the Smithville Neighborhood Organization (SNO) investigated the situation, they found that a network of bankers, realtors, contractors, planning consultants, university business professors, and politicians had used Industrial City's long-range comprehensive plan processes to push for such gentrification. Each of these stakeholders had gained some benefit, as shown in Figure 5.2, to the detriment of existing residents—many of whom had been displaced and all of whom had seen their rents rise.

For several hundred years now, **democracy** (rule by the majority of citizens directly or through their elected representatives) has been seen as a major bulwark against the excesses of dictators and oligarchies. In the United States, we are taught that democracy is intrinsically good; that all other forms of leadership are intrinsically bad; and that community organizers, social workers, and educators should do everything in their power to involve people in democracy and democratic processes. While generally true, democracy can have undesirable results unless it is governed by rules and safeguards to prevent mob rule and protect minority rights. The Bill of Rights in the Constitution is in part designed to prevent the majority from abusing democratic power. Community leaders can open the decision-making process and mitigate tendencies toward oligarchy and hegemony through orderly debate, well-defined rules of order, formal voting, and clear record keeping. In most social systems democracy is the best form of leadership. However, remember that democracy can become mob rule if it does not make provision for the rights of minorities or if it is based on fear and frenzy aroused by those with hate-filled agendas, an important reminder of why the Bill of Rights was inserted into our Constitution. Some of the world's greatest atrocities have originated from democracy

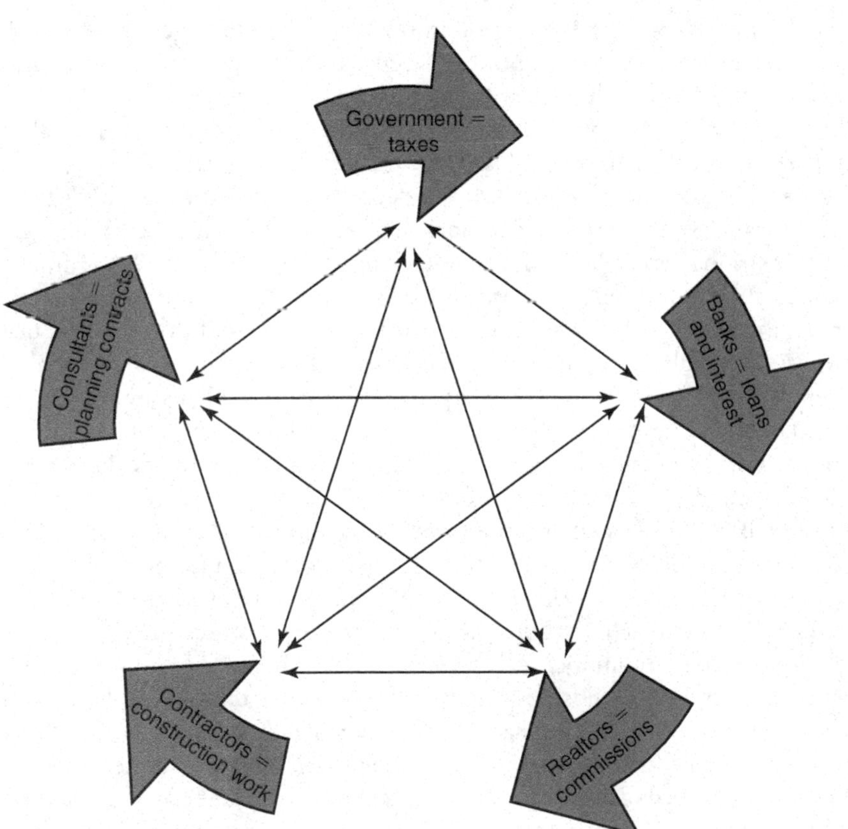

FIGURE 5.2 Smithville Gentrification: Who Is Missing? The current residents of Smithville are absent from this illustration because no one consulted them. The entire gentrification project has benefited those already in power, while it has excluded many of Smithville's voiceless and powerless citizens. *Source:* Copyright © by Pearson Education, Upper Saddle River, NJ.

run amok.[3] While we generally think of such countries as Rwanda and Nazi Germany in this context, it can happen in local community systems as well. For example, in the 1950s and 1960s, at the height of Industrial City's economic boom, Smithville was a primarily white ethnic, working class neighborhood comprised of skilled laborers who were mostly homeowners. When the industrial-based economy crashed in the 1980s, some Smithville residents slid into poverty while others left the area. From 1990 to 2000, many formerly owner-occupied homes were divided into inexpensive rental units that housed small contingents of immigrants from the Caribbean and Guyana. Although most were Pentecostal Christians, some were Hindus, Rastafarians, and Muslims—many were not yet U.S. citizens. Although there were no facts to indicate that the quality of neighborhood life was deteriorating, a number of the original homeowners began to worry aloud about crime, drugs, gangs, and loss of property values. Industrial City's newspaper and television stations began to report on criminal incidents and arrests in Smithville that would have escaped notice or been buried on the back pages had they occurred in more prosperous parts of the city. This reported "crime wave" caused the mostly white, retired homeowners to create their own association (outside of the SNO) to demand more policing. The police, in turn, were pressured to make more arrests, which increased the local perception of a crime wave. Association members formed vigilante committees and a branch of the Ku Klux Klan began to persecute the new residents. The local police did nothing until the FBI was called in. City government turned its back on the injustice being perpetrated on the newcomers because the immigrants could not or did not vote. Majority rule turned into majority tyranny.

Cell-based leadership is common in revolutionary and reactionary social movements where secrecy is important. It is based on an ideology rather than a hierarchy. Cells are small outposts, hidden within a broader social context, united by a common vision and ideology, but only tenuously connected to one another structurally. Often, members of separate cells do not know one another, so enemies cannot trace one small cell group to others. Because each cell is independent of any central authority, cells can operate locally even if the central authority collapses. Al-Qaeda, the terrorist group responsible for the September 11, 2001, attack on the World Trade Center in New York City, is a cell-based organization, as was the French resistance movement during World War II.[4] By nature, cell organizations are nearly invisible, but they do exist nearly everywhere, especially among members of stigmatized social groups in potentially hostile environments. For instance, the majority of Middle View residents are conservative heterosexuals who do not approve of homosexuality. When Mary Smith and her partner Patricia Newton bought a home in the Middle View area, they made discrete inquiries about lesbian, gay, bi-, and transgendered (LGBT) connections and were put in touch with a small group in a neighboring town. Mary and Patricia quietly identified other LGBT folks in Middle View, invited them to their home, and formed a mutual support and advocacy group. They were very discrete, quietly developed local friendships, and linked to other small LGBT groups throughout the conservative rural region. Everyone in the local LGBT community feels safer because of these connections and enjoys life more because of these friendships. On the other hand, clandestine, cell-based groups are not always benign. Middle View has a number of violently anti-gay people who also link to one another quietly, meet in homes, and are in touch with other secret anti-gay groups in communities throughout the region. Rumor says that they have planned and have conducted overt and covert acts of violence against the gay community, including the suspected arson of a known gay bar. No one has been able to stop them because notice of meetings is by word of mouth, planning sessions move from place to place, and it is said that the lack of reprisal for violent incidents stems from the involvement of some highly connected people in police, religious, and government circles. The majority of Middle View citizens are unaware of the activities of either group or prefer to ignore them.

Team leadership, the type most often used in successful participatory community organizing (and the focus of Chapters 6, 7, 8, and 9) has emerged since the World War II and is broadly based on the Total Quality Management movement in industry.[5] Team leadership is often project- or problem-centered, and involves members who each bring important perspectives, communication skills, and expertise to the endeavor. In team leadership, people—not positions—are important. Leadership teams select their own **conveners** (leaders) based on the latter's knowledge of the situation and their ability to facilitate effective communication. So, in a community setting, it's quite possible for a team that includes the mayor to be led by an unemployed, impoverished homemaker.

Leadership teams have a broad mission which they clarify jointly. The best team members share expertise generously, build on one another's ideas, share responsibility for failures, and are open to outside input. Leadership passes from person to person, depending on the skills needed by the group. Ideally, there is little jealousy or competition. However, team leadership can devolve into destructive factions if one or more members see the team as a means to power and control.

Leadership teams can be made up of volunteers or representatives of existing agencies and organizations. The SNO is an all-volunteer model composed of local residents who participate as interested individuals sharing leadership with other interested individuals. There is no hierarchy, neighborhood voting, or formal appointment process. Membership is open: if you show up, the team will put your talents to work. The Middle View Health and Welfare Council, on the other hand, is an example of a team-led organization that is closed to the general public. For many years, Middle View has had a Health and Welfare Council composed of appointed representatives from local churches, private human service agencies, county government, the schools, and health care providers. The council meets monthly, sponsors joint events such as family health fairs, and makes recommendations to various levels of government about the health and welfare needs of the Middle View area. All members have equal voice in decision making, and leadership roles rotate among them. People without clear organizational affiliations are not eligible to participate.

Connectivism is the tendency of individual entities (whether neurons, ants, deer herds, or humans) to naturally align in beneficial ways despite the lack of a discernible leader.[6] The term comes from biological studies and is emerging as a new way of looking at organizational development and shared learning. Connectivism in community organizing appears to be especially evident in Web-based social movements in which activities are largely devoid of formal bureaucratic structures. Interest groups and task forces form and re-form as needs arise and change, in an organic self-organizing process that behaves much like plant rhizomes or neural connections in the human brain. Emerging groups are loosely and somewhat chaotically tied through face-to-face conversations, telephone contacts, and social networking sites, such as Facebook, YouTube, and Twitter. The amazing thing about connectivism—whether in nature or in human societies—is how often these "leaderless" activities develop just what is needed in a given situation. Connectivism allows people in focal communities to easily find good ideas and adapt them to their circumstances, while simultaneously sharing their own innovations with others and strengthening all. Connectivism's weakness is that it can easily descend into anarchy, be overtaken by tyrannical manipulation, or simply fade away for lack of interest.

To those comfortable with clear hierarchies, connective leadership feels chaotic. For instance, in Middle View there is small but persistent pressure toward sustainable economic practices. Although some individuals and groups are identified with parts of this emerging effort, no one seems specifically responsible for central policy and management. A few people have founded a local "folk school" to help artisans market their products and teach traditional arts and music; others are working on a community garden and encouraging residents to buy locally produced food; and still others have focused on sustainable recreation such has hiking and kayaking rather than activities requiring gasoline-powered vehicles. Many have added extensive recycling to their home routines. Some people are aware of the global sustainability movement and incorporate its ideas, while others are very locally focused. Some efforts have been successful while others have faded away, but the trend has been toward locally based economic sustainability, less waste, a cleaner environment, and a sense that Middle View is part of the larger world.

Explore Harold Jarche's slide share on connected leadership for an in-depth understanding. What practical steps could be taken to ensure that your community organizing effort benefits from connected leadership?

This section introduced you to several different approaches to leadership in various times, places, and social systems across history and around the world. To make sure you understand the key concepts, identify an example of each type, briefly summarize its history, evaluate its strengths and weaknesses, and discuss how positive social change might have been accomplished under the circumstances. Consider the implications of what you have learned for you as a leader of a participatory community organizing effort.

Professional History

Understanding and Mastery: Differences between systems of governance and economics

Critical Thinking Question: What forms of leadership are most likely to work well in community organizing settings and why?

Leadership in community organizing emerges through a kind of resonance among the personalities, values and preferences of participants, internal group dynamics, and demands of the external situation. Emergencies or situations that require rapid decision making, specific knowledge, and well-developed skills often respond well to individual leadership. Executive-level collaborations often resemble aristocracies. A few are threatened by outside opposition and function best as cells. Very limited initiatives may work well as pure democracies. However, by far the majority of organizing efforts evolve team leadership composed of volunteers who organize to improve the quality of life in their focal community system. The most successful of all seem to combine the structure of team-based leadership with openness and opportunities for connectivity. For the remainder of this chapter, you will explore how the community organizing cycle works under the guidance of leadership teams that encourage participation and connectivity.

Assess your comprehension of Historic Forms of Leadership by completing this quiz.

Focus on Participatory Research

Let's visit Figure 5.1 once again, this time concentrating on how the leadership team ensures that community research is done in a participatory manner that involves those directly affected by the organizing effort (see Figure 5.1C).

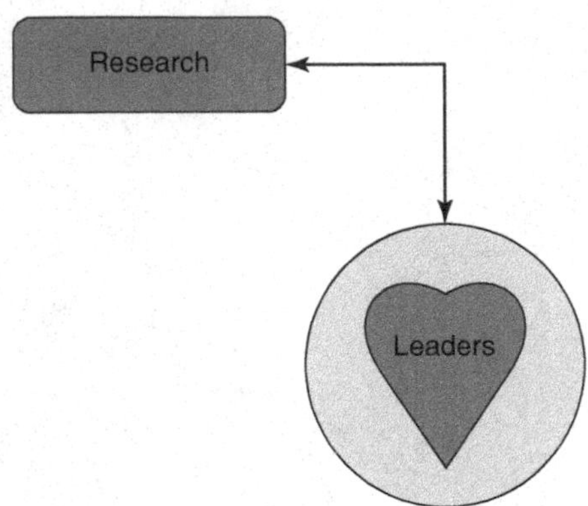

FIGURE 5.1C Participatory Research Section
Source: Copyright © by Pearson Education, Upper Saddle River, NJ.

Imagine that you have been talking to friends and acquaintances and have discovered that many of you have shared concerns and all of you feel that something must be done. You decide to hold an initial meeting to discuss the situation in a more formal way, and at the initial meeting you are part of a small group that volunteers to lead the organizing effort. This initial small group is the core of the community leadership team. Soon after the team begins meeting, you will probably be tempted to "jump to solutions" by quickly deciding what is to be done and starting to do it. However, you will soon learn that you cannot accomplish very much without information about the nature and extent of the problem, what is already being done, and some possible approaches that might be taken. In social science terms, you must undertake the **research** component of the organizing cycle. Your goal in the research component is to gather **data** (i.e., facts and figures) and consolidate them into **information** (i.e., understandable terms) that you can use in the planning and implementation phases. Although leadership teams sometimes decide to have the research task conducted by outside professionals, there are several good reasons to do your own investigation through a process called **participatory research**. That process saves money, enables you to define your goals, guarantees that you own the information, enables you to develop skills that can be used both in the current organizing effort and in future efforts, and provides resulting information that is generally more valid than that gathered by relative strangers because it can be checked against your life experiences. Well-organized participatory research increases your team's **knowledge power** which, in turn, increases your leadership team's credibility with community members, government decision makers, and the media, a process called **empowerment**. You may decide that just a few people (**designated learners**) will do the research and report back to the leadership team or that everyone on the team will participate.

Participatory research is not conducted once for all time. It is a two-way process between **designated learners** (those conducting the research) and the leadership team, which enables your team to constantly reflect on the meaning of what is learned and how it can be applied to your organizing task. The best participatory research carefully follows accepted quantitative and qualitative social science research models so that it is hard to dismiss as untrue. Because community research requires sophisticated research skills, it will be examined in depth in Chapter 7 and augmented by Appendix A at the conclusion of the text.

Focus on Planning

As can be seen in Figure 5.1D, once the leadership team has completed a thorough analysis of the information uncovered through research, the focus of the community organizing cycle moves to planning.

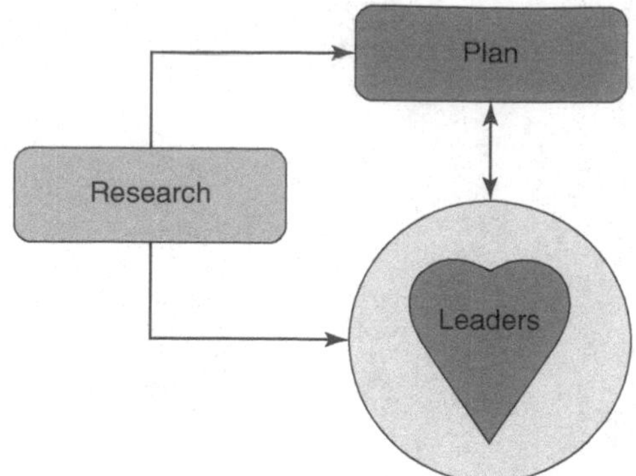

FIGURE 5.1D Planning
Source: Copyright © by Pearson Education, Upper Saddle River, NJ.

Long-range planning begins after the leadership team consolidates the findings of participatory research and reflects on its meaning. The goals of long-range planning are to define the community organizing effort's **mission** (overall purpose), set specific **measurable outcome goals** that can be used to determine success or failure, and begin to define the **strategies** (overall approaches) and **tactics** (specific actions) it will take to accomplish these goals. Long-range planning is one of the primary tasks of your community leadership team.

Planning can be either rational or haphazard as described in Table 5.1.

Rational–deductive or **root planning** involves visualizing desired outcomes, setting measurable goals, collecting needed data on current needs and resources, converting

Table 5.1 Approaches to the Planning Task[7]

Rational–Deductive (Root Planning)	Limited Successive Approximations or Muddling Through (Branch Planning)
Investigate theories of why the problem exists.	Explicitly or implicitly assume that you know the nature of the problem.
List values (goals) of the focal system determined by asking its members to list all possible outcomes, rate each on desirability, and then identify and prioritize all options.	Outline all of the options you can think of in no particular order. Don't worry about values; they really don't matter too much.
Build from fundamental theory, empirically tested if possible.	Build from current situation in small degrees.
Empirically evaluate the costs and benefits of each option based on carefully chosen theories.	Compare options based on past controversies, experiences of others, your own experience, and any theory that seems relevant.
Base plans on options that maximize community values and desirability of outcomes.	Choose action(s) that move in small steps, shifting and adjusting as experience dictates.
Ends–means analysis. Select desired ends, then means.	Experiential "seat of the pants" analysis; pursuit of individual or group interests.
Make long-range calculations.	Consider only the short range.
Define the "community good" as whatever maximizes the cost–benefit ratio. There is one "best" plan.	Define "good" is whatever the planning team can agree on that meets their needs.
Conduct a comprehensive analysis. Consider every important factor.	Use an incremental model responding to various interest groups and stakeholders.

data into useful information, developing action plans, implementing these plans, evaluating results, and providing feedback for ongoing efforts. **Limited successive approximations** or **branch planning** ("muddling through") are more common than rational deduction. In reality, most community groups muddle through: they identify a problem, speculate about its probable causes, conduct little if any systematic research, talk some more about possible solutions, jump into a likely project, and make course corrections as needed. Sometimes very valuable projects are born this way. More often, this lack of systematic planning causes endless headaches.

Planning and evaluating can be rational and carried out in a step-by-step way (referred to as root planning), very disorganized with many false starts, failed attempts, backtracking, and intuitive leaps (referred to as branch planning), or a combination of both. Choose a completed organizing project with which you are familiar. Study Table 5.1 which compares root and branch planning. In what ways did your chosen project use root planning? In what ways was branch planning used? In what ways was the route taken successful? In what ways could it have been improved? Think back to the varieties of community organizing discussed in Chapter 4. Which are more likely to benefit from root planning? Which are likely to thrive on the seemingly disorganized branch planning approach?

Planning and Evaluating

Understanding and Mastery: Analysis and assessment of the needs of clients or client groups

Critical Thinking Question: While most professionals would probably agree that some form of rational–deductive or root planning probably may be best, many informal community groups tend to muddle through. How can you as a professional encourage rational planning while still empowering inexperienced local leaders?

Planning refers to the formulation of ideas and actions into a scheme designed to accomplish some goal or objective. Planning is **proactive** because it considers anticipated future actions. It is **directive** in setting out a proposed course of action, and it is a **process** that leads to strategies, action steps, and tactics designed to implement policy outcomes. Planning begins with the selection of a **focal system** and proceeds to investigation of its micro-, mezzo- and macro-levels and **research** on its demographics, as well as perceptions and measurements of its assets and needs. This research guides the selection of **an organizing strategy,** development of a **mission**, and definition of measurable **outcome goals** that can be straightforwardly evaluated. The outcome goals are then implemented through **tactics** or **action steps**. The planning process is a cumulative spiral in that **evaluation** is done periodically to assess and reassess the effectiveness of strategies and tactics to produce **desired outcomes.**

While planning seems linear, it usually involves many drafts as input is received and integrated from **stakeholders**, a term which describes a variety of people including consumers, funding sources, government regulatory bodies, the general public, and opponents. Stakeholder input leads to modifications as new ideas and information come to light. Most plans go through several **iterations** (versions) before being put into final form, and even then the best plans remain open to reasonable change. Community **buy-in** (acceptance) is very important so any major changes should be considered by all the stakeholders before becoming part of a formal document. Although this can be time consuming, many otherwise excellent efforts have been delayed or destroyed because key stakeholders felt that they had somehow been left out of decisions on crucial issues. Timing is critical in the planning phase. If dialogue is cut off too quickly, important considerations may be overlooked or important constituencies may be slighted. If the process is too lengthy, the delay may stifle growth, anger those responsible for monitoring the planning process (such as regulatory or funding agencies), or cause you to miss important deadlines.

By the end of the planning phase, your leadership team should have a well-defined mission, clear outcome goals that define how your focal community will be better because of your efforts, a fairly clear idea of the strategy or strategies that will be likely to lead the desired outcomes, and some thoughts about specific **action steps** (tactics) that will be needed. Once that is achieved, you will be ready to begin the implementation phase.

Planning and Evaluating

Understanding and Mastery: Program design, implementation, and evaluation

Critical Thinking Question: What steps can you take to make sure that your leadership team identifies desired outcomes and explores different ways of achieving them, rather than jumping to solutions?

A word of warning, though: inexperienced community organizing groups often fall into the trap of jumping to solutions. In other words, they begin with a product or action (for example, founding a teen center or offering counseling services) rather than beginning with identifying desirable results. To discern the difference between these two approaches, think about your own life goals. What do you want for your family or yourself? Many folks would say "I want a well-paying job with material security." But is that *really* what you want? If you think about it, you will probably realize that you want a life where you have the basic things you need, positive relationships with people who care about you, and a sense of personal meaning and satisfaction. Ask youself, "Is a well-paying job the only way to get these things?" Think of other means to the same end. For instance, you could start a small business and work for yourself; pool your resources with some other people so that each of you only have to bring in a little income for all of you to prosper; grow, build, or make almost everything you need; live frugally so that you can live more with less; work intensely for a short period of your life, save money, and then move to somewhere inexpensive; and so on. As you think about it, you will soon realize that there are probably dozens of satisfying ways to meet your basic needs outside of a traditional job. Practice this "ends to means thinking" the next time you consider an issue in your focal community system. It will open many possibilities—some of which will be more exciting than anything you could imagine if you start out with a preconceived solution.

Explore more about planning issues. Consider the steps needed to ensure successful participatory planning.

Assess your comprehension of the Planning Portion of the Community Organizing Cycle by completing this quiz.

Focus on Implementation

Now let's look again at Figure 5.1, specifically at the processes on the right sides and bottom of the figure that show the flow from program planning to program implementation and the movement into the operational phase.

Once you solidify a plan or vision that includes values, mission, outcome goals, and probable actions, movement toward implementation begins. Figure 5.1E is a simplified version of a complex process. The transition from planning to implementation is often an awkward and somewhat scary time as you experiment with different **tactics** (specific

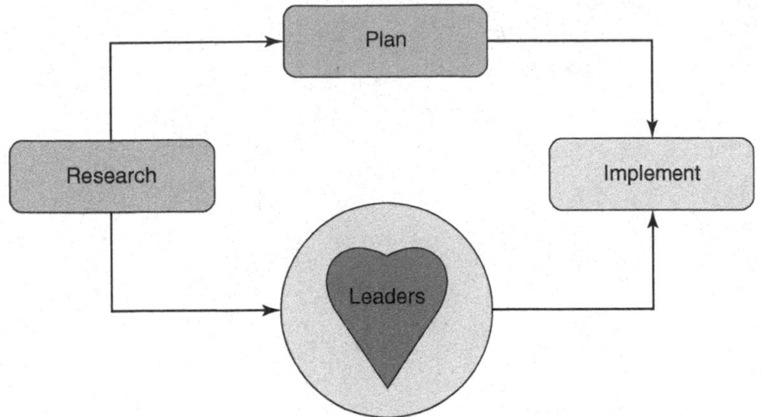

FIGURE 5.1E From Planning to Implementation
Source: Copyright © by Pearson Education, Upper Saddle River, NJ.

approaches), make necessary changes, and respond to crises all while maintaining organizing momentum. Experimentation often includes **pilot projects** (preliminary or practice efforts) before full implementation.

Your leadership team will undoubtedly examine many different strategies and tactics during the implementation process. Some will involve building **consensus** or agreement among all the people, associations, and formal organizations that are affected by your organizing effort. Others may involve **conflict** and the use of **social action** strategies that combat injustice. Because they are so complex, the specifics of these approaches are addressed more completely in Chapter 8.

Eventually your leadership team will settle on the major strategies and tactics you plan to use, divide the implementation effort into different components, and move forward with them. Since components are typically implemented at different speeds, there may be confusion. Your leadership team must make sure that everyone understands what is expected; that they receive regular updates; that perceptions from everyone—including program beneficiaries—are included throughout the implementation process; and that everyone receives necessary training in what is expected. Implementation can take anywhere from a few weeks to several years depending on the organizing task. It is typically characterized by frequent changes as the organizing team strives to get things "just right." Eventually, though, things will settle down and steady day-by-day direction will displace constant change.

Focus on Management

Now let's turn to the management of community organizing efforts. In the community organizing cycle, implementation, management, and leadership are interrelated as can be seen in yet another visit to Figure 5.1. (See Figure 5.1F.)

Leadership involves defining and maintaining an overall mission, but **management,** a term which originally came from the French word *ménage* or "household," refers to accomplishing the daily "housekeeping" work of community organizing often through directing the work of others. Management of community organizing efforts is particularly challenging because managers are often simultaneously responsible for the many meetings and events that compose a community change process, as well as day-to-day business operations and troubleshooting. There is always something or someone vying for the manager's attention.

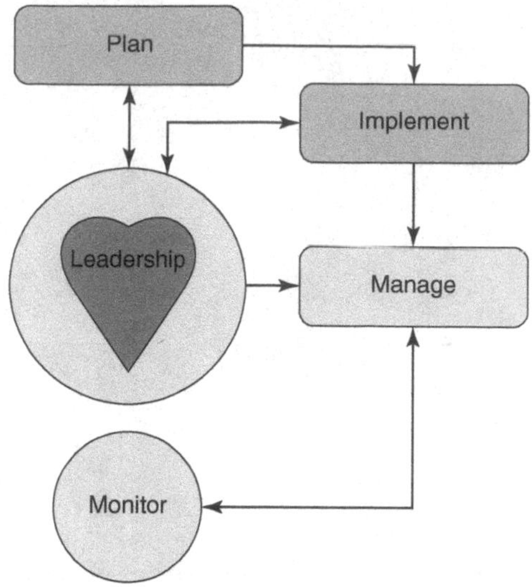

FIGURE 5.1F From Implementation to Management and Monitoring
Source: Copyright © by Pearson Education, Upper Saddle River, NJ.

Management science has evolved many different theories and models, each of which uses its own labels for similar processes. Four that seem particularly relevant to community organizing are **bureaucratic management** based on rational goals and standardized processes; **relationship-based management** based on team cohesion and high morale; **distributed management** based on the open systems model emphasizing creative, rapid responses to an ever-changing environment; and **contingency-based management** which uses the competing values model. Each form of management is discussed briefly here and more fully in Chapter 9.

Although bureaucratic management is usually associated with established organizations rather than new associations, some attention should be given to the strengths and weaknesses of bureaucratic management because it is often seen as the way things should be done. Bureaucratic management (sometimes called **Theory x**) is the familiar

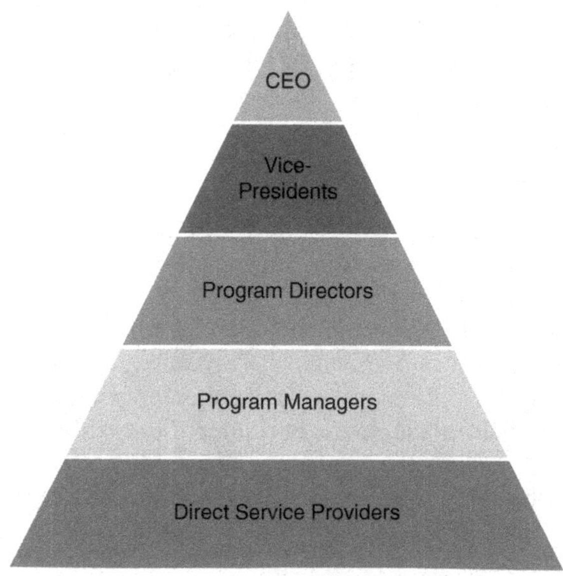

FIGURE 5.3 Bureaucratic Management
Source: Copyright © by Pearson Education, Upper Saddle River, NJ.

pyramid shown in Figure 5.3, with a chief executive officer at the top and various levels of authority beneath.

Social entrepreneurship and collaborations are based on a traditional business model and so often use bureaucratic management from their inception. The other varieties of organizing usually begin with a blend of relationship-based, distributed, and contingency management but then become more and more bureaucratic as they move from quasi-groups to associations to formal organizations (see Chapter 2). There are many historical examples of the bureaucratization of community organizing efforts. For example, the American Red Cross began with a dream Clara Barton and her friends brought back to the United States from Switzerland and has evolved into a huge bureaucracy with several major national programs and thousands of local chapters. The main strength of bureaucratic management is that everyone knows what is expected. Day-to-day operations run smoothly because there are rules and policies that cover almost any possible situation. The main weaknesses of bureaucratic management are its inability to respond quickly and creatively to emerging needs and a tendency to put organizational needs about the needs of its constituents.

Relationship-Based Management (sometimes called **Theory y**) was developed in the 1950s and 1960s as a reaction to the tendency of bureaucracies to create paralyzing layers of rules and regulations that stifle employee creativity, satisfaction, and flexibility. It is based on the humanistic psychology of Carl Rogers and Abraham Maslow[8] and emphasizes the responsibility of managers to allow workers to engage in personally rewarding tasks to meet their needs for belonging, self-esteem, and self-actualization to maximize job satisfaction and productivity. While relationship-based management may have improved worker satisfaction, it deemphasized accountability, which sometimes resulted in lack of discipline and productivity. Relationship-based management works best in community organizing efforts that emphasize the rewards of voluntarism, the opportunity to develop friendships, and the pleasure of joining with other people to support a good cause. Place-based and relational organizing and many self-help groups are likely to use relationship-based management.

Distributed management literally means that responsibilities for decision making are spread among many different people who understand the basic values, mission, and desired outcomes of the organization and have broad authority to act independently.

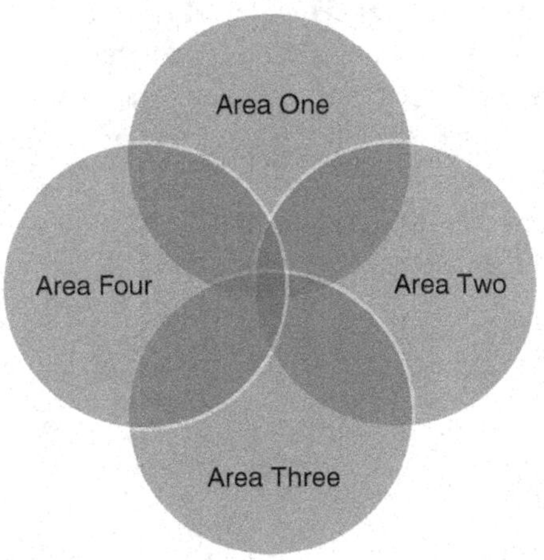

FIGURE 5.4 Distributed Management

Source: Copyright © by Pearson Education, Upper Saddle River, NJ.

Distributed managers come together at regular intervals to share ideas and make sure that there is cohesion among the parts but do not answer to a single authority figure. There is no hierarchy. The elements of distributed management overlap and are illustrated by Figure 5.4.

Distributed management works well when participants are spread across wide geographic areas, in situations where decisions must be made quickly with little fuss, and where there are significant variations from place to place or program to program.

Contingency-Based Management is the practical side of team leadership and so fits well with the basic participatory strategy recommended here. While team leadership involves joint decision making about broad issues such as mission, values, outcomes, strategies, and major actions, contingency management means using whatever models and techniques are appropriate for particular situations. The SNO is a good example of contingency management. Its leadership team is well respected and admired for taking primary responsibility for setting organizational priorities and being the visible "face" of the neighborhood. Its members are acknowledged publicly as "movers and shakers," and several have been appointed to city-wide commissions. They have earned the right to be called leaders. On the other hand, since SNO is an all-volunteer group, these same highly respected leaders must take responsibility for some very practical tasks. For instance, before each monthly meeting, they walk through the neighborhood handing out flyers, listening to people, and inviting them to attend. They divide meeting-day tasks among themselves, making sure that the building and meeting room are unlocked, snacks are available, everyone who attends receives both a smile and an agenda, some trustworthy person is available to provide child care, and anyone who needs a ride to the meeting gets one. Between meetings they make sure that minutes are completed and distributed to the membership and other interested people, new attendees are contacted, and volunteers follow through on their commitments. Throughout the year they make sure that detailed financial records are kept, bills are paid, and any required reports are filed. Many community organizing efforts mix and match the four kinds of management to maximize flexibility and participation.

Review more about managing not-profit organizations. Consider what management issues might be unique to community organizing efforts.

Monitoring supports management and involves keeping track of activities through direct supervision and accurate record keeping. It is both a managerial duty and a way of ensuring managerial accountability. Accurate monitoring is especially important for initiatives that are dependent on financial support from international, government, or private foundations and have to comply with myriad external standards. Externally, you may need to comply with various regulations of local, county, state, and federal agencies or funding sources. Internally, there may be a variety of committees and teams which are responsible for short- and mid-term decision making that needs accurate and up-to-date information. Balancing these requirements is challenging. More specifics and common questions about management are addressed in Chapter 9.

Assess your comprehension of Types of Management by completing this quiz.

Focus on Evaluation

Monitoring is closely related to evaluation, so let's now revisit Figure 5.1 and examine the evaluation process. (See Figure 5.1G.)

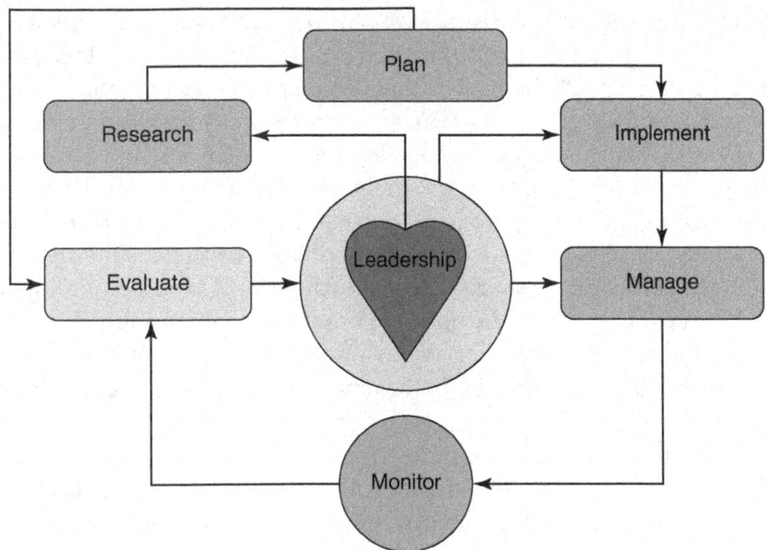

FIGURE 5.1G
Evaluation
Source: Copyright © by Pearson Education, Upper Saddle River, NJ.

Evaluation should be a constant process that allows the leadership team to monitor events in the focal, micro-, mezzo- and macro-systems that may impact the organizing mission, make changes as needed, and then reflect on the results of those changes (a circular process of action–reflection–renewed action that is called **praxis**). There are two levels of evaluation. On a day-to-day basis, evaluation is a reflection on how well reality measured up against hoped-for results. At its most basic, this means asking programmatic questions like "What went well?" "What went poorly?" "Was there praise?" and "Were there complaints?" It also means asking such logistical questions as "Did we have enough food?" "Were there enough restroom facilities?" or "Did the audio system work well?" In the long run, however, big questions like "Have we identified the real needs of the focal system?" "Are we empowering the community?" "Are our mission and goals appropriate?" "Are our key strategies and tactics appropriate and ethical?" "Should we be doing something different?" "What are the next steps?" and "How will we know when we have succeeded?" are far more important and link success to mission and purpose. These big questions cannot be answered accurately unless they are clearly linked to the planning process, and thus Figure 5.1G directly connects evaluation with planning and monitoring. Planners must identify measurable outcome goals—and evaluators must use them to measure results and report back to the leadership team—so that needed changes can be made.

In the planning and evaluation literature, the terms *formative evaluation* and *summative evaluation* are used for two separate but related processes. **Formative evaluation** connotes judgments used to make changes in an ongoing process. In many ways, community organizing efforts resemble improvisational productions, and so **formative evaluation** can be seen as an artistic process that allows the leadership team to mold and design its approach to meet changing conditions. Because it enables leaders to judge how well strategies, tactics, policies, and procedures are working, formative evaluation should be conducted frequently in the early days of an organizing project and in times of rapid change, and then less frequently during periods of relative stability.

Summative evaluation (summing up of accomplishments) resembles a critical review at the end of a production that sums up its good points and bad points. Summative evaluation is primarily a way of holding the leadership team accountable. Summative evaluation involves measurements that are linked to outcomes goals, reported in written form. In new organizing efforts, summative reflection should be done at least quarterly and at least on a yearly basis thereafter. Regular summative evaluation enables the leadership team to develop and maintain adequate records to satisfy internal stakeholders as well as outside funders and legal requirements. In initiatives that receive outside financing, funders generally send evaluation teams or expect regular reports documenting progress. Accurate, easily available records are critical to program management and to the continued existence of programs. Unclear financial records or sloppy case reporting can lead to defunding or even legal action. Even when the initiative is not externally accountable, good record keeping and outcomes measurement often uncover unmet needs or desirable changes. These discoveries, in turn, may necessitate another planning cycle as shown in Figure 5.1.

Review more about evaluating not-profit organizations. Consider what evaluation issues might be unique to community organizing efforts.

The organizing cycle is a tool to help you make rational sense of an irrational process. When followed in a step-by-step way, the cycle can help your leadership team remain on track toward fulfilling its mission, but please remember that life does not always move smoothly in a step-by-step manner. For example, impatience may drive the effort directly from idea to action without careful planning and development (skipping from research to implementation); a plan may prove unworkable during the program development and implementation stages, requiring a shunt back to the planning stage; or a formative evaluation during implementation may call outcome goals into question, thereby leading to new policy research.

Assess your comprehension of Evaluation by completing this quiz.

Summary

The community organizing cycle pulls together all the tasks of research, planning, implementing, managing, and evaluating a community organizing effort into one diagram that illustrates the dynamic nature of the process and gives you an overview of what needs to occur.

The community organizing cycle is just that—a cycle that organizations go through time after time in their life spans. Organizations that do not pay attention to periodic renewal die or “hibernate” to rise again. Organizational death takes different forms. Some organizing efforts die when violence or the threat of violence becomes too frightening, as was largely the case with the anti–Vietnam War movement after student protesters were killed at Kent State University in May 1970. Others lose support because of unwise actions or interpersonal conflicts. Still others complete their missions. Many go through periods of intense activity, followed by something akin to hibernation. For instance, Myles Horton, founder of the Highlander Folk School, said that social movements and social change seem to move in waves where a period of intense activity will be followed by a period of rest and consolidation. Intense activity and growth can be exciting but is difficult to manage. Wise organizers use consolidation or rest periods to ensure that the gains made in periods of activity become institutionalized as an accepted part of the community or culture.

Figure 5.1 described in this chapter is intended to be a "map" that your leadership team can use as you work together to ensure the success of your chosen venture. Chapters 6, 7, 8, and 9 further elaborate important portions of the process.

Assess your analysis and evaluation of the chapter's contents by completing the Chapter Review.

CHAPTER 6

Hill Street Studios/Eric Raptosh/Blend Images/Alamy

Building an Effective Leadership Team

Chapter Outline

In Chapter 6 you will apply systems thinking to your leadership team and explore typical communication issues and group processes you are likely to find within it. Let's look again at the Community Organizing Cycle from Chapter 5, with a focus on development of the leadership team (see Figure 6.1).

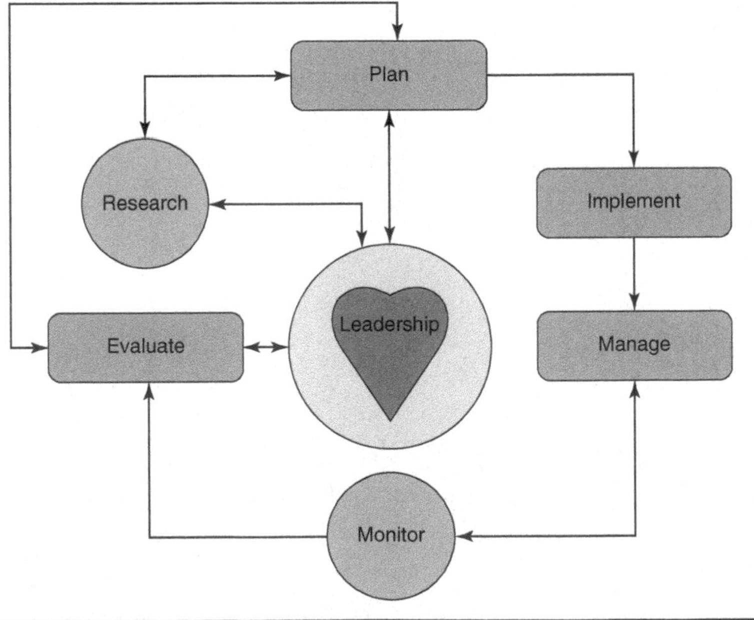

FIGURE 6.1
The Leadership Team: At the Heart of the Community Organizing Cycle
Source: Copyright © by Pearson Education, Upper Saddle River, NJ.

The focus of this book is on **participatory research**, also known as *educación popular* or, in English, "popular education": community organizing efforts that arise spontaneously from within focal community systems rather than being imposed from outside. Almost all such efforts begin with a few committed leaders who make sure that community members' involvement remains high. The initial reasons for these efforts varies, as discussed in Chapter 4, and is shown here in Table 6.1.

Table 6.1 Leadership Development for Each Variety of Community Organizing

Variety	Who?	How?	What?
Place-based/ Relational	Natural nurturers and catalysts who care deeply for all of the people in a specific geographic focal system.	Multiple ties with one another through family, friendship groups, places of worship and shared acquaintances.	Long-term commitment to target system and to one another. Meet both formally and informally. Open group boundaries.
Social Innovation	Usually an individual or small group who are concerned about the needs of a powerless target group.	Identify one another through mutual contacts, workshops, information sessions, personal connections to people in the target group.	Often begin as quasi-groups, move to associations, and eventually become more formalized as Board members of formal organizations.
Mutual Economic Aid	Often a group of friends or family members who help each other economically through the informal economy, micro-loans, barter, etc.	Identify one another informally and link their efforts to outside resources, such as micro-credit and other sustainability initiatives.	Depending on the nature of the endeavor, can be formal and specific (such as micro-credit circles, time banks) or more informal (such as friends handing down baby clothes or sharing garden vegetables).
Self-help	Folks who share the same physical, emotional or relationship challenges.	Identify one another through personal contacts, referrals from care givers, or advertisements in various media.	Online or face-to-face meetings facilitated by people who share the issue.
Community Advocacy	Residents of a geographic community brought together by a shared need or threat.	Brought together through word of mouth or a mass organizing event.	Develop a steering committee to guide social action decisions and/or create a formal advocacy group
Social Movements	Large numbers of people across wide geographic areas who share similar social concerns.	Brought together through media and increasingly through the internet.	Often use cell group structures and/or a few people who coordinate activities through the Web.
Collaborations	Representatives of agencies and other formal organizations.	Self-organized to support their sector or industry or forced to collaborate by funders.	Often create complex committee structures supported by traditional planners.

Source: Copyright © by Pearson Education, Upper Saddle River, NJ.

Recruiting a Leadership Team

Assume that you have decided that something good needs to happen in your chosen focal system. You know that your concern is worth the time and effort, but you're also fairly sure that you cannot do much alone. You decide that your first tasks are to (1) locate people who share your concerns, (2) raise their awareness of your common interests, (3) introduce them to one another, (4) build some trust through friendly interaction, (5) begin to work with them to research the problem, and (6) initiate action. There are two primary strategies you might use to locate initial team members and build organizational momentum. **Large-scale strategies** often begin when a few interested, relatively powerful people organize an initial organizing meeting or rally. These have the triple intent of introducing key stakeholders and the general public to the issues, building momentum and resources, and recruiting an ongoing leadership team. **Organic strategies** begin with a small core group that grows slowly through personal invitations and involvement of members' social networks. Each strategy will be explored in turn.

Large-Scale Strategies for Leadership Recruitment

Large-scale strategies are often used in social innovation, community advocacy, social movements, and collaboration. Figure 6.2 is a flow chart for initiating such actions.

Large meetings can be advertised as **rallies** (where those attending will focus on issues and concerns, often in an atmosphere of celebration and/or confrontation); **workshops** (where those attending will meet in small groups and work toward possible solutions to a pre-defined issue); **information gathering** (in which the main task will be to bring together people from many walks of life to learn more about an issue or concern); or **community conversations** (where participants will be asked to share their perceptions of the issue so everyone can gain greater clarity). Whichever method is chosen, it should be organized to allow maximum input from as many people as possible; should include a way to collect and collate the data; and should provide a feedback mechanism so participants will know that their ideas have been heard and will be implemented, if possible. You will find it helpful to have each participant sign in with name, address, and telephone number so you can use this information to create a mailing or e-mail list to facilitate this feedback. As soon as possible after the meeting, send each participant a written message thanking them for their participation, summarizing the proceedings, and briefly discussing next steps.

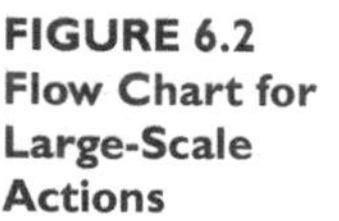

FIGURE 6.2 Flow Chart for Large-Scale Actions

Source: Copyright © by Pearson Education, Upper Saddle River, NJ.

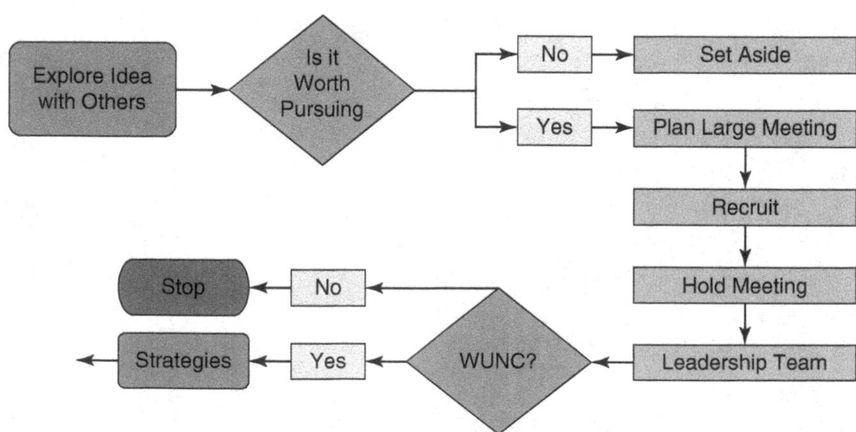

Continuously share information with everyone who has shown concern about the effort, including those who may have expressed an interest but are unable to initially participate. Such communication lets people know that they are important and are connected to the emerging organization. E-mail is particularly efficient for communication and also allows for immediate feedback from recipients, but it is equally important to use more traditional ways of communicating, including telephone calls, announcements at religious services and other public gatherings, notices on public bulletin boards, door-to-door visits, and newer technologies, such as text messaging and blogging. Such communication efforts are time consuming but are very important steps that cannot be easily delegated early in the group formation process.

The following example from Industrial City (home of the Smithville neighborhood) illustrates the large-group method for initiating an organizing effort. Since the mid-1980s when a major industry employing 10,000 workers moved its major manufacturing operations overseas, Industrial City has been having economic difficulties. Not only have thousands of the core industry's workers lost their jobs, but an equal number of jobs were lost in peripheral industries and related support services. It has been a very difficult time for everyone in Industrial City, but it was especially hard on the newly displaced workers. The most difficult time occurred within the first five years after the crisis. Many of the newly unemployed were family men in their forties who had worked all of their lives for the core industry. Although most were high school graduates, all of their vocational skills were industry specific and non-transferable. Many were too young to have earned vested pensions and too old for entry-level service positions. For the most part, they felt frustrated, lonely, depressed, and despairing. Even when they hunted long and hard for work, there were no longer any jobs that paid enough to support established families with mortgages, teenage children, and consumer debt.

In the face of the collapsed economy, powerful business interests, elected officials, agency representatives, educators, and even a few union officers banded together in a loose collaboration aimed at reindustrialization and other new investment in the area. Most of their strategies were designed to protect the investment community, support the property tax base, provide incentives for peripheral industries and the service sector, and preserve the few high-paying industrial jobs. But there was no "place at the table" for the displaced workers who not only had lost their jobs but their union status as well. As a result of this lack of representation, economic development efforts often made the already well-off more prosperous and the displaced workers more desperate.

Ironically, no one thought about involving the displaced workers in the city-wide effort to revitalize the economy. Although there are many reasons for this, one major one was that many displaced workers believed that their unemployment was a personal failure. Like most of us, they had been taught from birth that anyone who lives in the United States, works hard, and is loyal to his or her employer will inevitably eventually succeed—so they suffered in lonely silence. Suicide, alcoholism, and divorce rates rose. Employment professionals despaired as well, because job placement rates were low in spite of resume-writing clinics, job-hunting clubs, skilled career counseling, and many short-term training programs. Eventually, as highly qualified, hard-working people continued to be without living-wage jobs, a few displaced workers and their advocates began to realize that the "new version" of unemployment was a systemic issue and not an individual one. A quasi-group began to form that brainstormed about how to create a community advocacy effort for the unemployed. Their rallying cry became: "Wage base, not just tax base!" Their representatives gained support from the branch campus of a major university, the Catholic diocese, and the local newspaper. A large-scale community conversation was held, which generated significant interest and greater understanding of the systemic issues. The initial rally generated a smaller meeting that evolved into a community organizing effort that combined mutual economic aid and community advocacy.

Such large-scale tactics have advantages and disadvantages. They can make a significant number of people aware of shared concerns, promote media attention, and jump-start action on an issue, but they can also create problems if people come to simply vent their anger, push their own agendas, or expect immediate solutions. These large-scale tactics tend to blossom quickly and fade just as rapidly, so immediate follow-up and specific action strategies are very important.

To more fully understand the large-scale approach to community organizing, attend a large-scale community meeting or rally or, alternatively, go to YouTube and search under "community rallies." Choose four or five clips that show people taking on different issues that interest you. What was the purpose of each of the rallies? What characteristics do they have in common? Why did their organizers choose a large community meeting or rally instead of other means of organizing?

Administration

Understanding and Mastery: Constituency building and other advocacy techniques such as lobbying, grassroots movements, and community development and organizing

Critical Thinking Question: Review the varieties of community organizing discussed in Chapter 4. Which are would be best served by large-scale organizing strategies and why?

Leadership Arising from "Organic" Initiatives

While some community initiatives begin with large-scale gatherings, many others grow more organically, the way wildflowers grow from scattered seeds or irises grow from rhizomes. **Organic initiatives** begin with a single individual or a small group who share mutual concerns and build their organizing efforts slowly by word of mouth, adding a few people at a time. For this type of initiative, the transitional step from informally talking about a concern to actually doing something about it involves a move toward formal, focused meetings and the beginnings of a leadership team.

Organic initiatives often begin with people who know each other well in other contexts. The strengths of the organic growth model are its stability and deep commitment within its core group. Unlike large-scale efforts that attempt to create cohesive organizing efforts from quasi-groups whose members barely know one another, the initial members of organic groups usually have **multiple ties** (a sociological term that indicates people who simultaneously relate to one another in different social contexts, such as family, work, recreation, and worship). Multiple ties make initial team cohesion easier. On the other hand, that very cohesion may make it difficult for new members to join and for new ideas to be shared. Because such leadership teams depend so heavily on interpersonal relationships, they are somewhat more likely to break down if personal animosity develops between members. In addition, many organic initiatives are begun by well-intentioned but inexperienced leaders who "just want to do something" about a mutual concern. Sometimes, this inexperience is helpful because it enables such groups to tackle problems that other "wiser" people might find too daunting. On the other hand, inexperience can lead to breakdown in the leadership process and the organizing cycle.

Administration

Understanding and Mastery: Recruiting and managing volunteers

Critical Thinking Question: Both large-scale and organic community organizing rely heavily on continually recruiting committed volunteers. What strategies and tactics work best for volunteer recruitment and retention? In what ways might these vary among various types of community organizing?

Many organizing initiatives start slowly, like a plant growing from a tiny seed. To experience an organic initiative choose a relatively short-range project that you feel would help improve the quality of life in your focal system. Talk with some other people who share your concerns, and determine if they are interested in working with you on the project. Hold an initial meeting with at least three people. Afterwards, reflect on probable next steps. If there is interest, follow through with the organizing effort. If there is little or no interest, set it aside for another time. Reflect on what this experience taught you about organic community organizing.

Assess your comprehension of Leadership Team Recruitment by completing this quiz.

The Evolving Leadership Team: The Form, Storm, Norm, Perform, and Adjourn Cycle

Whether your community organizing leadership team emerges from a large public rally or from incremental organic development, you will undoubtedly move through a typical developmental cycle often described as form, storm, norm, perform, and adjourn.[1]

In the **form period**, participants begin to build positive relationships and mutual trust. When people first meet, they are generally polite and tend to try to find common ground in mutual friends, common experiences, and common interests. The following practical arrangements can make the formation process easier for your leadership team:

- Have a specific time, meeting place, stated purpose, and preliminary agenda.
- Personally invite all of those who have expressed an interest.
- Provide a comfortable meeting room or provision for simultaneous telephone or Internet connections that allow people to communicate easily.
- Provide a way of publicly recording and organizing the conversation such as a flip chart, whiteboard, the whiteboard attachment in conferencing software, or use of the recording function in online conferencing.
- Set ground rules for communication (such as listening, taking turns, and encouraging shy people).[2]
- Use round robin introductions that give everyone an opportunity to give their name and express their hopes and dreams for the organization.
- Conduct a semi-structured workshop for generating ideas and setting priorities that gives everyone an equal opportunity to speak, encourages active listening, and discourages nastiness.
- Allow plenty of time "around the edges" of the formal meeting for people to get acquainted, share mutual connections, and begin to feel comfortable with one another.
- Provide food, beverages, and other physical comforts, such as good lighting and easily accessible restrooms.
- Choose someone to facilitate the conversation and to periodically summarize the conversation.
- Appoint someone else to take notes and turn them into meeting minutes so that good ideas are retained.
- Ensure timely sharing of meeting minutes with those present and with those who may have expressed an interest but were unable to attend.

Leadership teams spend varying amounts of time in the formation phase. Some with rather simple tasks and homogenous membership move through formation and the rest of the cycle very quickly. Others with complex tasks, competing objectives, and diverse membership may spend many weeks in the formation phase. However, all follow the general group formation cycle, even when the members know each other very well in other settings.

Even when members know each other well, agree on their mission, and have enthusiasm for the venture, tensions will begin to emerge as participants realize that they have different viewpoints, different ways of approaching the problem, personality quirks, and different levels of commitment and energy. These tensions inevitably create a **storm period**. Many leadership teams falter during the storm period because their leaders become discouraged or give way to panic, disagreements pull the group apart, or participants feel so uncomfortable with disagreement that they leave entirely. Your challenge is to reassure everyone that such storms are to be expected and can be weathered if faced honestly and hopefully. In most cases, deep active listening and careful use of group process techniques will strengthen group bonding and the ability to weather future difficulties.[3]

The storm period can be emotionally taxing for everyone. Although there is a tendency in our individualistic society to blame storms on personality clashes, they are really a struggle to define interactional patterns and mutual expectations. Brewing storms have definite cues. Attendance at meetings may decrease. A few people may dominate the conversations. There may be sub-groups of rebels meeting outside of regularly set times. Everyone may become quiet when the leader enters the room. Participants may sit with arms folded, leaning back in their chairs with scowls on their faces. Meetings that were once full of laughter may become silent and perfunctory. People may begin spending precious meeting time arguing about seemingly minor details while ignoring major differences of opinion over mission, purpose, and desired outcomes. All these are cues of a brewing storm.[4]

Everyone on the leadership team will be tempted to just ignore the gathering clouds and pretend that everything is fine. This is almost always a mistake. It is usually best to recognize that conflicts are brewing and to bring them up to the surface with the whole group as calmly and as objectively as possible. One way to do this is to state the concerns as you see them and then ask that the group set mutual **rules of engagement** to ensure that everyone has an opportunity to both speak and listen. You can then function as a mediator, actively looking for points of common ground and for the validity in even seemingly destructive ideas.[5] While most leadership teams manage their storm periods reasonably well, it may be necessary to bring in an outside mediator if a significant number of people feel that the team is getting nowhere.

In stormy meetings, it is usually best if each participant speaks in turn and is given a chance to speak without interruption. Before speaking, everyone should be asked to first restate the last speakers' comments and receive confirmation from that person that his or her viewpoint has been understood. It is surprising how many times people who think that they vehemently disagree with one another are simply voicing the same concerns or solutions in different terms! Emotions should be treated as valid and relevant. Active listening should be used to discern both the objective content of what is being said and the feelings behind it. Even in shared leadership teams, it is often helpful to appoint a facilitator to summarize individual comments clearly and concisely, to the individual's satisfaction, as well as to summarize general areas of conflict and consensus.[6]

Storm periods can be aggravated or prolonged by individual behaviors so your own self-awareness and self-control are very important. For instance, it is almost never a good idea to ignore a brewing storm in hopes that it will go away. Even though it may be tempting to share your worries and irritation with trusted fellow group members, it is never helpful to gossip about others, mull over the brewing storm aloud, or complain about one group member to another. Such behaviors may feel good at the time, but they inevitably lead to mistrust and animosity. Although sometimes it can be helpful to bring individual "combatants" together outside of the group setting to work out their differences in private, this should be done carefully because it can create the appearance that there is an "in crowd" who "really" make the decisions and that other participants are unnecessary. Storms must be faced courageously, and their resolution should involve everyone.

It is not uncommon for storms to last for days, weeks, or even months, but if everyone remains as calm as possible, remembers the mission and desired outcomes, and carefully and clearly states areas of emerging agreement, it is likely that a new consensus will emerge and the leadership team will become stronger because you have demonstrated that you can disagree without disintegrating. Ironically, some of the strongest community organizing efforts have survived the worst storms.

Most worthwhile organizing efforts can weather storms and emerge stronger if everyone involved shows patience and courage. A few projects may perish, but they usually are the ones that:

- Are weak to begin with.
- Have several destructive members pursuing their own agendas.
- Refuse to face their storm or ignore it until it is too late.
- Do not have a structured, compassionate way of incorporating different points of view into group goals.

Although it is painful, storming is one major way your emerging leadership team goes about defining how you will work together, the unwritten (and perhaps written) rules that will govern teamwork, the roles members will play, and power relationships among participants. Such **norming** is an ongoing process throughout the life of the group, but most is done during and shortly after the storming phase. As these **group norms** (unwritten rules) are created and rehearsed, a sense of unity, group identification, and "we-ness" is built. Group norms typically cover everything from the simple to the complex and may include such things as whether:

- Refreshments are served before, after or during the meeting or not at all.
- Participants dress in business clothes or casual clothes.
- Children are allowed and how they are cared for.
- Laughter is permitted and encouraged, or everyone is expected to be serious.
- Decision making is formally structured, using formal procedures such as *Roberts' Rules of Order*, or if it operates by consensus.
- Time frames are strictly adhered to or meetings are allowed to go over time.
- Most decisions are made in committees, in behind-the-scenes negotiations, or by the group as a whole.
- An elected leader or executive committee is allowed to make decisions on the group's behalf, or even minor decisions are made by everyone.

- There are status differences by social position, race, ethnicity, class, or gender, or everyone has an equal say.
- New members are welcome and, if so, how they are brought into full participation.

These are just a few areas where leadership teams develop norms or expected ways of behaving.

Leadership teams in the **perform** stage have weathered their storms, have developed effective norms, and have become working units that are able to accomplish their goals fairly smoothly. But keep the following in mind: the form, storm, norm, and perform cycle is not "once for all time." The various stages may be revisited when major internal or external changes occur. For instance, a smoothly performing leadership team may revert to the form or storm stages if (1) new members are added; (2) the mission changes radically; (3) important participants leave; (4) major changes occur in the market or client base; or (5) the micro-, focal, mezzo-, and macro-systems undergo major shifts. However, subsequent changes that occur after the initial cycle are usually easy to accommodate.[7]

When community organizing efforts end, they face an **adjourn** phase. There are several reasons for such endings: a clear conclusion when a problem is solved, a law is enacted, or an agency is founded; or the effort withers because there is no real need for it, "premature death" occurs because of an inability to handle internal or external conflict, or it falls prey to a kind of "fading away" found in organizations that operate decade after decade, long after the initial impetus for action has ended. Others are like the mythical phoenix that dies and then rises from its own ashes. One of your leadership team's many challenges is to discern when the time has come to end an effort or change direction and enable participants to move on.

Human Systems

Understanding and Mastery: How small groups are utilized, theories of group dynamics, and group facilitation skills

Critical Thinking Question: From childhood on you have probably been involved in a variety of small groups. Take a mental journey back to some of these experiences and briefly relive them from start to finish, then compare and contrast them. What evidence do you see of the form, storm, norm, perform and adjourn process? What factors enabled some groups to survive to the "perform" stage? What factors caused others to fail? What do your experiences tell you about the process of small group development?

Remember, the group phases are neither good nor bad; they just happen. The storm periods of group dynamics are often painful and stressful. At such times, it is best to remember that they are also inevitable. The norm periods can be very creative, and the perform periods can be very satisfying. Returns to the storm phase can be frustrating and endings can be sad, but if communication patterns are kept open, the group will thrive and accomplish its desired outcomes—not just in spite of its troubles, but often because of them. If your group adjourns, you should help the group celebrate its past and look to the future with hope.

Assess your comprehension of the Form, Storm, Norm, Perform and Adjourn Phases of Group Development by completing this quiz.

Leadership Teams as Living Systems

In many ways, leadership teams act as living systems that are greater than the sum of their parts. It is, therefore, possible to speak of them metaphorically as if they had conscious intent without necessarily engaging in **reification** (i.e., giving a nonliving entity a human personality). Leadership teams can act, learn, and decide.[8]

Internally, systemic communication is dependent on several factors:

- The situational context (i.e., the time, place, and reason given for the group interaction).
- The communicator(s): their personal credibility and status in the group and in the focal community, as well as personal characteristics such as the ability to clearly state ideas
- The message
- The receiver(s): their ability to "hear" the message as it is filtered through their personal viewpoints and experiences
- The interactional patterns that emerge as you communicate with one another over time

A change in any dimension tends to result in changes throughout the system. Understanding communication within leadership teams requires a grasp of the communicators' attitudes, values, and beliefs; the context of the organizing effort; the cultural and linguistic orientation of members; and a range of psychological factors. Communication in leadership teams is both complex and dynamic. It's complex because various systemic dimensions operate simultaneously and their influence changes as interaction occurs. It's dynamic because it changes over time.

Leadership teams tend to be either open or closed systems. Most community organizing efforts are open systems whose membership varies over time as people come and go. Closed systems, on the other hand, have a relatively static membership, do not welcome newcomers, or have a reason for limited membership. In community organizing, open leadership teams have life and vitality but may have little sense of the ongoing existence of the effort or the need for long-term commitment to its mission and goals. Because attendance in open systems varies from week to week, it can seem as if the leadership has to be reinvented every time it meets and that it never moves from talk to action. On the other hand, closed leadership teams can become very ingrown and ineffective, especially if they depend too much on a few people. New people can easily feel rejected and isolated so that if the "select few" lose interest, the whole organizing effort may be lost.

Leadership team members should make sure that they are open to newcomers but that the team has enough form so that its mission and purpose are clear to participants and outsiders alike. Having a systematic way of welcoming and involving newcomers in the ongoing life of the leadership team is one way to ensure that there is a good balance between openness to new people and ideas while maintaining your ongoing mission.

Human Systems

Understanding and Mastery: An understanding of capacities, limitations, and resiliency of human systems

Critical Thinking Question: Small groups, including leadership teams, tend to exist on a continuum between completely closed and completely open. Think about some small groups where you have been a participant or an observor, and rate each on a continuum of completely open to completely closed. What were the characteristics of the closed groups versus the open ones? In each case, was its level of openness appropriate to its desired outcomes? If not, what tactics could the group leader have used to ensure an appropriate level of openness? What could "ordinary" members have done to increase group openness?

Communication Patterns

Leadership teams develop typical patterns of communication, which include the wheel, overlapping, and all-channel types.[9] Figure 6.3 shows these typical patterns.

In **wheel-type communication**, members communicate through a single leader, much as the spokes of a wheel depend upon its hub. Wheel-type communication

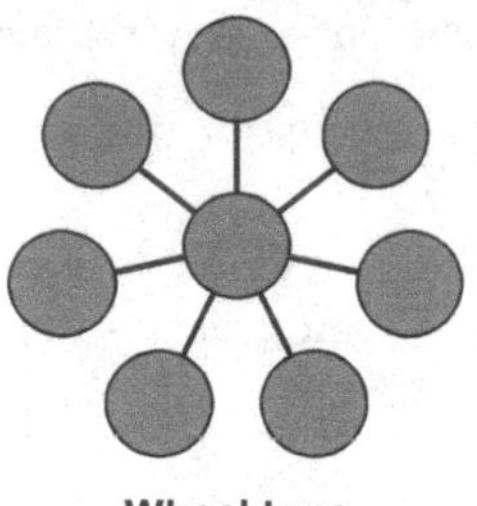

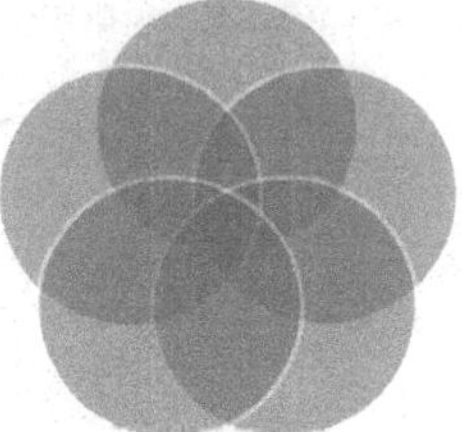

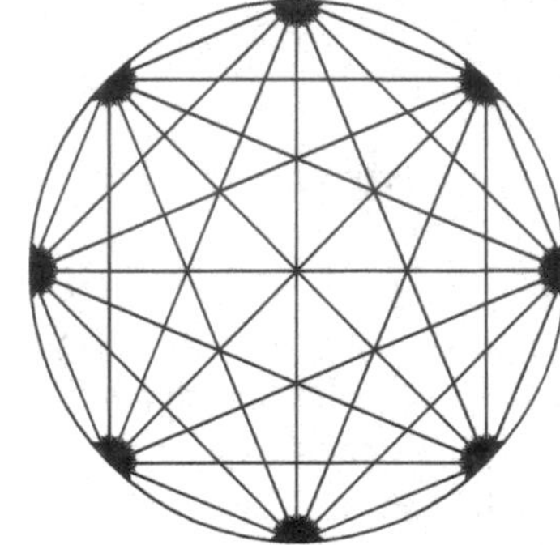

FIGURE 6.3 Communication Patterns in Leadership Teams: Wheel, Overlapping, and All-Channel Types

Source: Copyright © by Pearson Education, Upper Saddle River, NJ.

occurs in leadership teams that are dependent on a single strong, charismatic leader. In the **overlapping** type, group members communicate mostly with those closest to them either physically or emotionally, although there is some overlap. Overlapping communication tends to give team members who participate in many different systems advantages over those who are only engaged in a few. Overlapping messages are often incomplete or garbled, can make people feel left out, and result in poor decision making—so leadership teams with overlapping communication patterns must spend time and energy to keep everyone "on the same page." In the **all-channel** team, everyone communicates on an even footing and has an equal chance to be heard. All-channel groups are usually the most effective but are also the hardest to maintain because everyone must make an effort to speak and must ensure that everyone else is heard. Moreover, in community groups, all-channel communication must be maintained during meetings and between meetings. All channel groups are often dynamic but can be chaotic. In situations where anyone can speak for the group, it often seems that no one really speaks for the group, causing it to appear fragmented and ineffectual.

The most effective leadership teams seem to be a combination of the wheel, overlapping, and the all-channel modes where members take turns functioning as "transfer stations" and make sure everybody knows what others are thinking and that those with common interests and concerns are linked appropriately. This connecting function is both enjoyable and challenging. In practice, it means that everyone must be constantly aware of

Human Systems

Understanding and Mastery: How small groups are utilized, theories of group dynamics, and group facilitation skills

Critical Thinking Question: It is not uncommon for all three of the communication patterns we have explored to occur in the same event! Observe a meeting or event you normally attend. Pay close attention to communication patterns. What were the predominant forms of communication? When were they used? In what ways were the forms of communication appropriate and helpful in furthering the group's purpose? Where did they get in the way? What might have been done to improve the clarity and effectiveness of communication?

creative ways people might be brought together to share mutual interests and build on each other's ideas. In practical terms, this means that each member of the leadership group must be willing to take the time and effort to introduce people with mutual interests to one another; share resources you find with those you know who might be interested; and generally become known as a helpful, supportive, and essentially unselfish. Often it means discerning connections that are not immediately obvious, bringing them to light, and catalyzing whole new approaches to tired old problems.

Assess your comprehension of Communication in Leadership Teams by completing this quiz.

Team-Directed Learning

Like individuals, leadership teams have preferred styles of learning and working together. Understanding your leadership team's preferred learning style can help it be more effective and avoid some common pitfalls. Adult educator J. A. Dickenson in an unpublished doctoral dissertation[10] compared group learning to the individual learning styles defined by experiential learning theorist David A. Kolb.[11] Joyce McKnight, the author of this text,[12] then expanded it to community organizing. Figure 6.4 shows how Kolb's model can be applied to community organizing leadership teams.

Kolb concentrated on four dimensions of learning based on individuals' preferred styles of thinking and acting. The thinking dimensions are **abstract conceptualization** (i.e., grasping the "big picture") versus **concrete experience** (i.e., orientation to a specific detail). The behavioral dimensions are **reflective observation** (i.e., thinking about the meaning of events before acting) versus **active experimentation** (i.e., learning by doing, without much forethought). Kolb combined these dimensions into four learning styles: **convergent** (abstract conceptualization/active experimentation); **divergent** (concrete experience/reflective observation); **assimilator** (abstract conceptualization/reflective observation); and **accommodator** (concrete experience/active experimentation). McKnight built on Kolb's discussion of individual learning styles to adapt it to learning within community organizing teams and identified four major learning team types, as shown in Table 6.2.

McKnight found that the most effective leadership teams have a balance of all four learning styles. They begin with the conceptualization of the problem (the big picture).

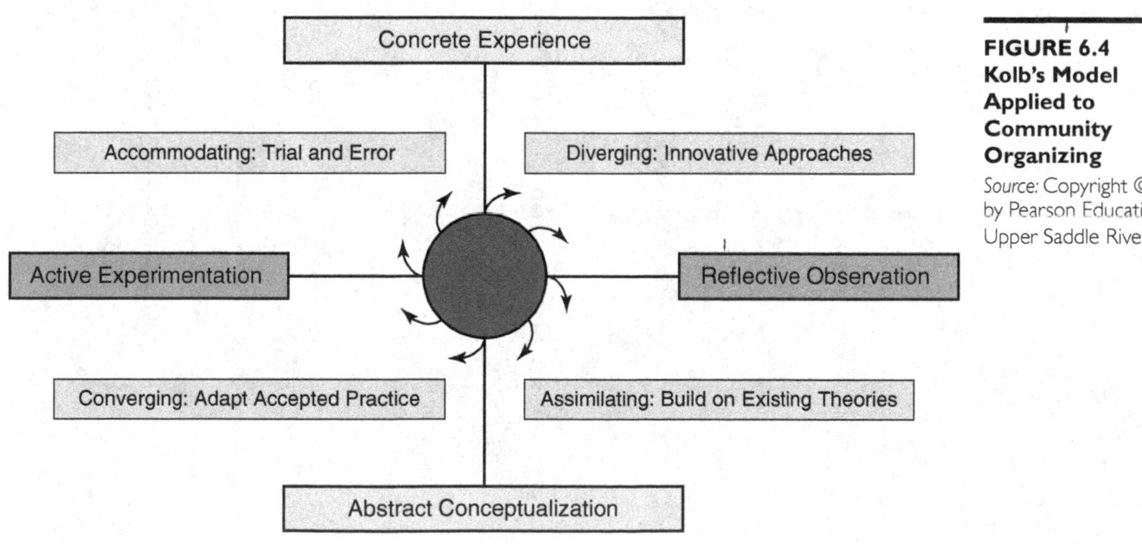

FIGURE 6.4 Kolb's Model Applied to Community Organizing
Source: Copyright © by Pearson Education, Upper Saddle River, NJ.

They then move to a consideration of the details (the specific resources needed to make the plan a success), which includes (1) reflective observation on the best approaches and continual judgments about what works and what does not; (2) active experimentation to bring the group's goals into reality, then (3) returning to the big picture and repeating the steps to refine the process. Your leadership team must be constantly aware of any imbalances in its approach to learning and intentionally incorporate all four styles.

Assess your comprehension of Team Learning Styles by completing this quiz.

Facilitating Effective Community Leadership Teams

Facilitation is a term frequently used in the helping professions in conjunction with small group dynamics that can be applied to community leadership teams. Facilitation consists of specific behaviors such as reflective listening, open questions, reflective summation, and reframing inflammatory issues that enable a group process to move smoothly and effectively. Although the facilitator or facilitators in group work are usually highly skilled professionals who are well versed in both individual and group dynamics, facilitation can also be a shared process. Let's now explore facilitation skills needed by leadership team members.

Team leadership requires that everyone assume responsibility for decision making, and so communication positions may change within the course of a single meeting. At times you will step forward to assume the position of facilitator; at other times you will step back to allow someone else to guide the group. Whatever their position at any given moment, group members must speak frankly and honestly, listen carefully and thoroughly, mediate disputes compassionately, and sort through seemingly contradictory elements carefully to make wise decisions. This can be a daunting task, especially for those who may not have had prior experience with team-based leadership. Tables 6.3, 6.4, and 6.5 provide you with very specific ways to

Table 6.2 Learning Styles Used by Community Leadership Teams

Type	Preferred Kolb Styles	Concentrate On	Strengths	Weaknesses	Examples of Success
Convergent	Abstract conceptual-ization and active experimentation	Technical tasks and problems	Practical solutions and coalition building	Overly hasty decisions; "jumping to solutions"	Building physical structures.
Divergent	Concrete experience and reflective observation	Incorporation of diverse viewpoints	Creative solutions using collaborative techniques	Creative solutions may be impossible to implement.	Maximum use of minimum resources; conflict turned into cooperative action.
Assimilator	Abstract conceptualization and reflective observation	Development of ideologies and theoretical frameworks	Thoughtful consideration of important values and policies	Much talk and little (or inappropriate) action	Creative policy formation and broad-based values change.
Accommodator	Experience and active experimentation	Immediate action	Getting things done quickly; risk taking	Failure to provide for long-term follow through, unintended but negative results	Quick results in emergencies

Table 6.3 Facilitation of Effective Leadership Team Communication

Participation during Meetings	Desired Outcome	Evidence	Qualities Required of Participants	Qualities Required of Facilitators
Talking	Participants feel their contributions are important to the group.	Everyone contributes at least once during the course of the meeting. Conversation is active and flowing, though thoughtful silences and times of contemplation are accepted and welcome.	Ability to think about proposed issues together with a willingness to express own ideas. Ability to be quiet and listen if one is talkative or has lots of ideas. Ability to speak up if one has thoughts to share if individual is a quiet person. Ability to come to the meeting, focus on its agenda, and be "present," even if there is lots to do outside the meeting	Ability to set context of communication expectations. Ability to listen and summarize points of consensus. Ability to observe group interactions and effectively use techniques to "draw out" reticent participants. Ability to encourage the more active participants to listen without dampening their enthusiasm.
Asking questions	Participants feel their presence and contributions are respected and appreciated by all group members.	The questions that everyone is thinking are asked!	Ability to think critically about the various aspects of the work. Willingness to risk comfortable relations to ask the questions that get to the heart of issues. Ability to frame questions respectfully.	Ability to clarify questions so that everyone understands the issues being addressed. Ability to encourage everyone to feel comfortable asking questions. Ability to calm emotional outbursts. Ability to make respectful responses to all questions.
Acknowledging and resolving conflicts	Participants are able to put the highest good of the group and its common goals above individual or agency agendas.	Issues that are unacknowledged publicly but known to all team members are acknowledged and talked about by the whole team. There are no outside meetings where "real issues" are being discussed.	Ability to separate personal and agency agendas from those of the whole group. Ability to state inconsistencies without blame. Ability to change one's mind and to accept responsibility for one's own issues or mistakes.	Ability to mediate conflicts. Ability to remind participants of the need to stay focused on objectives. Ability to calmly acknowledge and deal with controversies.

Source: Copyright © by Pearson Education, Upper Saddle River, NJ.

Table 6.4 Facilitation of Effective Leadership Team Decision Making

Decision Making	Desired Outcome	Evidence	Qualities Required of Participants	Qualities Required of Leaders
Clear decision making processes	Everyone understands how decisions will be made.	Commitment to participate in the decision-making process and to support the decision once it is made.	Ability to compare and contrast voting versus consensus as means of decision making and decide which is appropriate to the task at hand.	Ability to articulate the decision-making process to be used. Ability to highlight points of agreement and areas of disagreement. Ability to state the consensus and to restate it if necessary. Ability to balance time constraints with the need to act.
Making decisions	Participants know when talk has ended and a decision has been made.	Everyone knows the next steps agreed upon and what is expected of each person present or each organization represented.	Alert attentiveness during key moments of the meeting. Ability to have presence of mind and clarity on one's perspective. Ability to balance one's own perspective and the needs of the group. Ability to truly hear an opposing view, see a concept or idea in a new light or perspective, and change one's mind.	Ability to create an agenda and modify it if necessary. Ability to "read" people to determine if there is confusion or underlying disagreements that need to be voiced. Ability to come to agreement on next steps and to summarize decisions orally and in writing.
Volunteering for tasks	Participants readily step forward when volunteers are needed.	There are seldom, if any, silences when the facilitator asks who will do what.	An understanding of personal strengths, interests, and resources as well as those of one's organization. Honesty about the time one is likely to be able to commit.	An understanding of the likely personal and organizational interests of participants. Ability to link participants with tasks they are likely to enjoy and where they will feel successful. A willingness to revisit the proposal if volunteers are not forthcoming. A willingness to follow up with volunteers.
Bringing information to the group	Participants have the skills needed to collect and integrate needed information and report back to the group in a timely manner.	The leadership team is able to generate the information needed to make good decisions without paying outsiders.	Ability and willingness to do the research one has volunteered for in a timely manner.	Willingness to check on volunteers without "babysitting" them. Ability to re-delegate assignments without insulting the original volunteer or slowing the group process unnecessarily. Willingness to train or assist volunteers in the information gathering task.

Table 6.5 Practical Considerations

Practical Considerations	Desired Outcome	Evidence	Qualities Required of Participants	Qualities Required of Leaders
Accountability to each other and the group	Trust in one another leading to accomplishing agreed-upon tasks.	There are no unscheduled meetings about people or the work. The work is getting done. Members are comfortable with the timeframes and with the manner in which the work is getting done.	Ability to address concerns with a fellow team member (one on one or at a group level) when someone has said one thing and done another, regardless of an individual's status or authority. Ability to identify and address discrepancies in verbal and written communications and in one's work.	Ability to calmly address concerns with all team members, regardless of status, both separately with individuals and with the group as a whole. Practice non-blameful problem solving with team members whose assignments are not being completed.
Equalizing Power	Everyone, no matter what their status, is able to speak and be respectfully heard.	Everyone, including non-English speakers, participates at about the same level. Those with little position power are heard while those who have obvious position power listen carefully to others and do not dominate.	Ability to THINK (i.e., make sure that what one says is **t**rue, **h**elpful, **i**nspiring, **n**ecessary, and **k**ind). Accomplish this by addressing concerns of fellow team members, understanding one's own strengths and weaknesses as a communicator, monitoring and moderating poor communication habits, and showing willingness to put the good of the project or the greater good of community ahead of self or agency interests.	Make sure that everyone has a chance to speak. Work ahead of time and in between sessions with those in obvious power positions to encourage active listening and coach those with little power in communication skills. Actively solicit input from relatively powerless people. Encourage persons with extensive experience to mentor those with less experience. Paraphrase contributions of shy people carefully and courteously.
Note taking/ written communications	All team members are kept clearly and fully apprised of decisions and activities.	Participants have in hand a clear, well-written, and accurate record of group's work to date, including key decisions and any other pertinent information.	Ability to take accurate notes, write clearly and succinctly, and distribute agenda and minutes in timely ways that reach everyone.	Work closely with note taker (and translator if necessary) to ensure that notes are clear and accurate. Make sure that notes are disseminated to everyone. Use notes in creation of next agenda.

Source: Copyright © by Pearson Education, Upper Saddle River, NJ.

facilitate leadership team processes. Remember that although the tables refer to "participants" and "leaders," you will find yourself occupying each position. You will find it helpful to refer to these tables frequently whenever you are part of a community organizing leadership team.

Explore tips on group facilitation skills. Consider your strengths and weaknesses as a group facilitator and what you might do to improve your facilitation skills.

Assess your comprehension of Leadership Team Facilitation by completing this quiz.

Interactional Processes

Let's now turn from facilitation skills to an examination of group processes and power relationships. Exchange, cooperation, competition, and conflict are four principle aspects of interaction in every system. Here we will look at how they operate within organizing teams.[13]

Exchange relationships occur when participants exchange goods or services (including information) and are guided by the **norm of reciprocity**, an unwritten social rule that if I help you, you will help me sometime and vice versa. In leadership teams, knowledge or information may be treated as a medium of exchange. Members share information to develop closer ties as individuals; to gain advantages for themselves or their organizations; or, more benevolently, to add to the group's store of shared knowledge. Information is a powerful currency. When information and other resources are shared freely, trust is built and the organizing effort is likely to be strengthened. Effective leadership teams share information freely, generously, and gratefully with one another, the organizing effort's constituents, and potential allies.

Cooperation occurs when people work together to achieve common goals. Synonyms for cooperation include teamwork,[14] collaboration,[15] and connected learning.[16] Cooperation is very important in leadership teams. In practical terms, cooperation can be facilitated by (1) assigning people with complementary interests to shared tasks, (2) formally and informally assigning new members to mentors who help them learn the group history and welcome them into the effort, and (3) publicly and privately thanking people who make contributions and work well with others. Simply using the pronoun "we" often, rather than "I" or "you," can encourage cooperation and a sense of mutuality.

Competition is "a struggle over scarce resources regulated by shared values."[17] Competition implies "winners" and "losers." It is a very common American value and, therefore, manifests itself in community organizing teams of all kinds. It is especially evident where members represent organizational interests in addition to their own. Not infrequently, members compete both individually and as organizational representatives for status within the group, recognition for their contributions, and authority. Competition is a two-edged sword. Some competition keeps people interested and involved. Too much competition can destroy the team's bonds and derail its mission. You should recognize that while competition is inevitable it is usually at least mildly destructive. It can often be mitigated by simply acknowledging that members have competitive agendas, freely talking about them, intentionally finding points of mutual agreement, and sometimes "agreeing to disagree" on minor points to move forward on major ones.

While mild competition can lead to creativity, **conflict** and **coercion** are almost always negative. They occur because many people believe that there are inevitably winners and losers in life and that must they fight hard to be winners. While in leadership teams competition is often mitigated by written or unwritten **norms** and **policies**, those who use conflict and coercion ignore such rules. Their goal is to succeed no matter what. Conflict and its related tactic, coercion, can be (1) blatant, such as threatening to remove financial or other resources from the mutual effort, or (2) underhanded, characterized by the formation of competitive sub-groups, gossip, whining, and spreading general dissension.

Exchange, cooperation, competition, and conflict or coercion can all occur in the course of a single meeting. It is also possible for a single group to be high on some dimensions or low on several others.[18] For example, leaders in Industrial City (the home of Smithville) once tried to create a collaborative effort aimed at increasing everyone's health and well-being. Participants represented almost all of the major stakeholders in Industrial City's health and welfare community, including representatives of two major hospitals who were locked in a kind of corporate warfare. In meeting after meeting, this collaboration moved from polite exchanges of mutually useful information to enthusiastic plans for mutual collaboration to thinly veiled competition and conflict, usually over access to power, authority, and funding. These coercive activities were usually between representatives of the two hospitals and occurred while everyone else watched uncomfortably. The whole process resembled a hard-fought sporting event. It might even have been enjoyable if it had not paralyzed the collaboration, which led to its eventual demise. On the other hand, a proposed teen center in Middle View failed to gain momentum because no one cared enough to maintain the effort.

Assess your comprehension of Interactional Processes by completing this quiz.

Power in Leadership Teams

One definition of power is the energy to get things done. Here we will be looking at how power dynamics work in leadership teams. You will first examine the positive role power can have in leadership teams and will later examine some negative forms of power, especially those that are endemic in small groups.

Benign or positive forms include resource power, position power, expert power, and personal power or charisma. Each is briefly defined here in Table 6.6.

While the forms of power described above have both positive and negative sides, **passive aggression** and **manipulation** are purely negative. Passive aggression is the power to keep things from happening—usually by not doing what is expected or by doing an assignment in a halfhearted way. Passive aggression usually appears in times of low morale, stress, or frustration. Manipulation occurs when an individual or a subgroup deviously puts its own needs above the common good. Ironically, manipulation requires an empathetic understanding of others' motivations. It is empathy without a heart.[19] Your challenge is not to deny that power and power imbalances exist in community leadership teams but to channel them in ways that will enable desirable outcomes for your focal community.

Table 6.6 Power in Leadership Teams

Type	Definition	Functions	Possible Dysfunctions
Resource Power	Ability to provide or withhold needed resources.	Provide resources, including people, money, and ideas.	May exercise inordinate control over group decisions.
External Position Power	Based on social position within broader systems.	Provide links to and credibility with important people, social networks, professions, and established organizations.	May use their connections to coerce team to comply with their ideas.
Internal Position Power	Based on formal and informal roles within the leadership team.	Determine how meetings are conducted and what information is shared, and ensure that everyone is heard.	May control communication flow to accomplish personal rather than group goals.
Expert Power	Based on possession of scarce knowledge or skills.	Supply hard-to-obtain information and technical services.	May withhold needed information, give self-serving advice, charge high fees, or try to impose "one size fits all" solutions.
Personal Power (Charisma)	Energy, commitment, and contagious enthusiasm.	Provide inspiration that keeps everyone enthusiastic and feeling that the effort is worthwhile.	May overpower others, keep them from making optimum contributions, and prevent the leadership team from developing an adequate plan for succession.

Source: Copyright © by Pearson Education, Upper Saddle River, NJ.

Roles Team Members Play

Community leadership teams operate very much like sports teams. Think about a basketball team. Players first learn basic skills, such as dribbling, passing, making lay-ups, shooting free-throws, and guarding against the other team's players. Then they are expected to practice putting these separate skills together to ensure a smooth performance. In addition to developing particular skills, they are expected to know when to use them during actual games when the team needs to work together. Although many basketball teams have "stars," many star-based teams do not win titles. Most championship teams seem to be the ones that work together, whose stars are willing to pass the ball to others, and whose players know their basic skills and use them. Similar to players' positions on a sports team, community organizers have positions and roles in the community organizing "game," as defined in Table 6.7.

Assess your comprehension of the <u>Roles Team Members Play</u> by completing this quiz.

No single person can effectively hold all of these positions or effectively play all of these roles, but they are not formally assigned or static. They move from person to person, sometimes within the same meeting and certainly over the course of an organizing effort. Those with special talents for one or more of these positions should be encouraged to develop them because a good balance among them can ensure success.

Unfortunately, there are several unhelpful positions and associated behaviors (roles) commonly found in community groups. In fact, some of the

Table 6.7 Helpful Positions and Roles

Position (Status)	Behavior (Roles)	Positive Results
Catalyst	Recognizing need for action, bringing people together.	Ignites activity.
Expressive Leader	Befriending (finding out the cares and concerns of participants), active listening, mediating, recognizing contributions, celebrating group successes.	Participants feel needed and enjoy being together.
Instrumental Leader	Keeping group on task, setting agendas, keeping discussions on track and focused, making sure records are kept and disseminated. Representing group to the general public.	Tasks are accomplished efficiently and effectively.
Strong Fighter	Stands up for his or her opinions but once convinced can be counted on to strongly support the mission with courage and determination in spite of difficulties.	Consistent stubborn commitment pushes through difficulties and leads to eventual success.
Quiet listener	Quietly pays attention to what everyone is saying and then often says just the right thing to unite people or keep them on target.	Promotes unity by articulating the common sense of purpose.
Conceptualizer	Is able to articulate a broad vision.	Clarifies the mission and keeps core values in front of participants and the public.
Detail Person	Makes lists, clarifies assignments, follows up on people's promises, solves problems, and generally keeps events flowing smoothly and on time.	The complement to the conceptualizer. Makes sure that "devilish details" do not ruin group efforts.
Mediator	Finds common ground in opposing viewpoints, reframes issues, articulates hidden concerns.	Weaves and splices seemingly unrelated or contradictory ideas into viable and creative plans and actions.
Devil's Advocate	Intentionally brings up opposing viewpoints and identifies places where the organization will probably face opposition.	Enables the group to examine potential weaknesses before they are uncovered in public venues.
Information Bringer/Inside Educator	Conducts participatory research and presents findings to group in understandable ways.	Provides well-organized information to support decision making and action.
Bridge Builder	Has many contacts inside and outside the organization.	Links diverse individuals and groups, strengthening the mission.

Source: Copyright © by Pearson Education, Upper Saddle River, NJ.

traits that lead to positive results in some contexts can lead to problems if they occur at the wrong time or in the wrong way.

- **Enthusiastic dominators** have a high need to participate and often use the group time poorly. Even though dominators may have useful contributions to make, their constant need to speak can be intimidating to quieter people and aggravating to others who have important points to make, and can cause the group to lose its momentum.

- **Aggressive dominators** interrupt others, fail to listen, put others down, and refuse to consider other viewpoints. While enthusiastic dominators genuinely embrace the team's mission and see themselves as helpful participants, aggressive dominators truly believe that their ideas are better than anyone else's.
- **Passive aggressives** say they will do something and then either don't do as promised or do it poorly.
- **Freeloaders** depend on others to do the work while they take the credit, claim an identity as part of the group, and benefit from others' efforts.
- **Cynics** (also called "yes-but-ers" because they like to preface remarks with "Yes, but . . .") find something wrong with everything that is suggested and cast a pall of hopelessness.
- **Clowns** can play a useful part in reducing tension, but they can also distract the group from important tasks.
- **Disruptors** steal the meeting agenda. They are often loud, disorganized in their thinking, stuck on minor points, or take the conversation totally away from the point at hand to something unrelated and confusing. While many disruptors are simply self-centered, others may be legitimately mentally ill.
- **Personalizers** bring their personal issues with other group members into the group context and are unable to work with them objectively.
- **Manipulators** are sociopaths who sometimes have well-defined personal or organizational hidden agendas but, just as often, simply like to see if they can make others do what they want by tricking participants into playing various emotional games.[20]
- **"Rabbit chasers"** may be very creative individuals who tend to pursue tangents that are not related to the task at hand. They tend to draw others with them and can cause a massive waste of time and energy.

Each of these negative behaviors can be disruptive and difficult. But if they are allowed to dominate, other group members are likely to feel frustrated and unneeded. Likewise, if the facilitator calls attention to them in the group setting, others may fear that they too will be "put down" in public.

Participants in community organizing efforts typically act and speak in ways that others come to identify as typical of them. Some of these behaviors are helpful and lead to successful outcomes and pleasant shared experiences while others are unpleasant and disruptive. Explore your own communication patterns. Ask someone you trust about their perceptions of your typical approach to group participation. Ask them what you do right and ways you might improve. Think about what they have said and compare their feedback with your own perceptions. In what ways are your typical behaviors helpful? In what ways can they be problematic? Experiment with your group roles until you feel that you have the right balance.

Human Systems

Understanding and Mastery: How small groups are utilized, theories of group dynamics, and group facilitation skills

Critical Thinking Question: What insights about team member roles would be most useful in your community organizing practice?

Explore the Team Building skills section of the online Free Management Library to learn more.

Summary

This chapter gives you and other members of the leadership team a framework that you can apply throughout your community organizing efforts and to which you can return as needed. It is based on the premise that community organizing is not primarily an individual venture but depends on teamwork and mutual responsibility—starting with isolated individuals who become a quasi-group and then take on the characteristics of a leadership team.

Assess your analysis and evaluation of the chapter's content by completing the Chapter Review.

VLADGRIN/Shutterstock

Participatory Research

Chapter Outline

The community organizing cycle (first discussed in Chapter 5) is your guide through the organizing process. In Chapter 6 you learned how to build and maintain an effective leadership team. In this chapter, you will focus on the research phase of the community organizing cycle. Figure 7.1 is presented here to remind you where research and learning fit into this cycle.

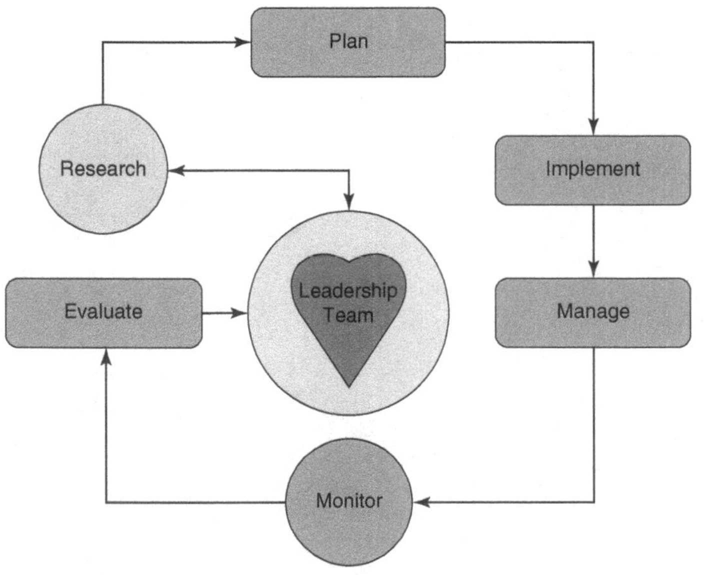

FIGURE 7.1
Research and Learning as a Component of the Community Organizing Cycle
Source: Copyright © by Pearson Education, Upper Saddle River, NJ.

You and your leadership team will learn to use a process called **participatory research** in which the research task (asking and answering key questions about the focal community and what needs to be done) lies with you rather than a professional organizer or other outside expert. You will learn how to use connected knowing processes, accepted social science research techniques, analytical frameworks used by professionals, and instrumental (applied) learning to help members of your leadership team generate the information you all will need to make good decisions.

Connected Knowing: The "Engine" of Participatory Research

Throughout the community organizing cycle and particularly in the research (and learning) phase, the leadership team or its **designated learners** (those who have volunteered or have been appointed to execute certain research and learning tasks)[1] engage together in making sense of complex issues and intricate systems by constantly asking, "What do we need to know?" "What does this all mean?" and, especially, "What are its implications for action?" In participatory research, you make sense of your findings, build on each other's insights, and decide what to do and how to do it through an ongoing process of **connected knowing.**[2]

The best way to illustrate connected knowing is through an example. Let's follow the progress of a group of Smithville women who became a sophisticated leadership team from their humble start as casual acquaintances who used the same coin laundry. Imagine two or three young moms casually chatting as their families' clothes tumble in the dryers and their toddlers play in the steamy laundromat. As they fold clothes and corral children, they talk about how it is impossible for their kids to play in the local park because it has been taken over by gangs, it is filled with used condoms and syringes, and the swings and slide are broken. Someone says sadly that she doesn't dare take her kids to the park anymore because her toddler was badly cut on the knife-like edge of the metal slide and had to have stitches. As they talk, they feel angrier and angrier. At first, they simply tell additional horror stories and build on one another's complaints until finally someone says, "Let's try to do *something*." This simple remark changes their focus, and they begin talking about how to involve others in cleaning up the park and how they might push the City Park Department into continuing to keep it clean.

Although many such conversations might have been dropped at this point, these moms followed through. They kept meeting at the laundry and then at one another's homes. They built on each other's ideas. Soon they gathered their friends for a "park clean-up and fix-up day." After the initial clean-up, they recruited some other mothers, grandmothers, concerned dads, and granddads and divided everyone into two-person teams who took turns cleaning up the mess. The organizing mothers took up a collection to buy lidded garbage cans.

Although they were engaging local residents as much as possible, the organizers realized that they needed strategic information and tactics to involve the city and other mezzo-systems (although no one knew that term). Each took responsibility for learning as much as possible about how other communities had gotten attention. Together they learned some of the data gathering and presentation techniques that will be discussed later in this chapter and invented some of their own. They used the information they gathered to create a written report about the dangers of the park that included stories about children who had been hurt, data on the number of such incidents, and pictures of the broken slides, trash, and empty syringes. In addition to the written report, they videotaped interviews of children talking about how much they wanted a safe place to play and included photos of a mural the children had created that showed their ideal playground. Once the organizers consolidated this information, they tried to follow protocol by taking their report to the City Parks Commissioner in his office. He promised to look into their complaints. After waiting several months for his promised visit and promised changes, they took their report, photographs, and videos to the local media. Soon their effort (and the city's lack of response) was on the nightly news and was featured in the newspaper. Local celebrities joined their cause, and there was even a small article in the national media. Not surprisingly, the City Parks Department responded within a few days after the news reports, and major repairs were finally made amid much media fanfare and a neighborhood-wide celebration at the newly refurbished park. Now several years later, no one can say exactly who started the initial playground conversation or how it evolved so quickly into effective action, but everyone knows that some organizing mothers built off one another's ideas with a positive result, and, perhaps just as important, everyone believes they could do it (or something like it) again if need be. This **connected knowing** process, based on mutual respect and caring, is the energy that enables creative leadership teams to accomplish amazing feats with few material resources; it is the essence of the participatory research process discussed here.

While connected knowing in community organizing sometimes emerges spontaneously, as in the preceding example, it more often takes someone with courage and vision to "jump start" the process—someone like you. Even with a few volunteers, you and your leadership team can use connected learning to build on each other's ideas. Your goals for the group process will be to (1) enable the team to cooperatively discern and prioritize outcomes; (2) gather and consolidate information; (3) create compelling documentation of the needs and viability of proposed solutions; (4) identify key decision makers; (5) present the case appropriately to the proper decision makers using the kind of information they expect and can understand; and (6) if necessary, use mildly confrontational tactics to get attention and action.

The connected learning process used in participatory research can be time consuming and requires that you give up your individual control, but it teaches inexperienced community leadership team members research and presentation skills that can be generalized to other situations; often leads to creative, cost-effective solutions; and is impressive, especially to political decision makers who are aware that community leaders are not only voters but also influence other voters.

Commitment to connected learning is necessary but not sufficient to guarantee success. Team members need to learn to use accepted social science research processes to gather data, produce coherent documentation, and develop strategies to improve the quality of life in their focal community system.[3] Participatory research and learning differs from traditional academic research not so much in technique but in its emphasis on *community* ownership of research findings. Emphasis is *not* on ownership by an academic researcher or outside sponsoring organization.

Assess your comprehension of Connected Learning by completing this quiz.

There are several types of learning that occur in community organizing milieus, including data gathering and consolidation of information among other types. Let's now explore these two turn.

Data Gathering and Consolidation of Information

Data gathering and **consolidation of information** is what most people think of when they hear the words *learning* or *research*. It involves gathering **data** (facts and statistics), consolidating this information in understandable terms, and then making sense of the information in light of community needs and goals. Common ways of gathering needed data include reading, listening to experts, and conducting research using accepted social science techniques. Most grassroots community organizing efforts do the data gathering and consolidation work themselves. Collaborations of established organizations, government agencies, and research universities occasionally have the financial backing to hire professionals. The following discussion focuses on how members of your leadership team can gather, consolidate, and interpret the data needed to make good decisions. Those who guide the emerging effort are referred to as the community leadership team, while those who do most of the data gathering and information consolidation on their behalf will be referred to as **designated learners** (i.e., people who have volunteered, have been appointed, or have been hired to learn on behalf of the emerging community organizing effort).[4]

While it is beyond the scope of this book to give you an in-depth description of social science research, designated learners need to become familiar with major techniques and specific approaches. The chapter gives an overview. Appendix A* will help you with specifics.

Because a focal community system is always comprised of micro-systems and is embedded in mezzo- and macro-systems, your leadership team's research task involves exploring and organizing relevant data from relatively narrow local concerns to mezzo-systems and broad macro-systems. The most effective research consists of comparing and contrasting your findings at different levels of the system, a process that happens naturally in the creative thinking that was compared to "clicking through" the various levels of a microscope in Chapter 2. In this process, the researchers must be alert for relevant information wherever it may be found and actively search for connections among seemingly unrelated data and information.*

Information Management

Understanding and Mastery: Compiling, synthesizing, and categorizing information

Critical Thinking Question: What information will you need to collect in order to gain a thorough understanding of your community? How will you organize it?

Web-based research is a good place to begin exploring. You will find that Web research in community organizing feels like entering an unknown territory and being assigned to map landmarks, resources, and dangers. It feels daunting, confusing, scary, and exciting all at the same time. But rather than charging into the wilderness, it is best to begin with a broad outline. Divide up the territory, clarify exploration strategies and records to be kept, keep in touch periodically during the

---

*Concepts in this chapter that are expanded in Appendix A are marked with an asterisk (*).

exploration process, and meet frequently at "base camp" to pull information together and make sense of it.

In addition to helping you map the territory, there are several other ways Web searches can be useful. For instance, your team may have an idea for a specific approach or have ideas for a specific project. In such cases, you should use key words in your search engine that are likely to lead you to organizations with purposes similar to yours (e.g., teen centers, community gardens, self-help groups, or mutual aid). Your search will most likely lead you to websites for particular projects and programs. You can use these websites for ideas about program design, funding, and organizational structure and compare them to your own focal community. If you find an interesting organization, you may want to call and ask questions. Some people will be very friendly, others will not, but telephones can be powerful tools for sharing ideas and making connections.

It is a good idea to use an academic search engine, such as EBSCOHost (available through most college or university libraries), if you want to understand how others have approached similar situations and whether they have been successful. An academic search for journal articles on your topic will give you good ideas for possible approaches, criteria for success, and additional search terms to help you explore the topic. Librarians are generally quite willing to help because libraries have a community service mission.

If you want assistance with funding, you can use your search engine and type in "funding for . . ." although you'll have to be very careful that the sites you find are legitimate. Beware of any site that charges money for its services. If you want to find self-help or advocacy groups, try various combinations of "help for . . ." or ". . . advocacy" or ". . . rights." Any site you find should be evaluated carefully.

Your specific data gathering strategy will depend on the topic. You will often find it helpful to begin with government sites to see what is officially available on your focal community or issue. The following list includes some of the most useful sites that provide raw data for community organizing: the U.S. Census Bureau; national government sites; USA.gov: "US Government Made Easy"; state sites; and county, town, village, tribal, and city sites. Government websites are helpful in finding factual data about a geographic target area, and government agencies may help you with particular projects.

Once oriented to government resources, you may want to explore other organizations with missions similar to yours. One way to do this is to use your search engine to review examples of similar projects and programs. As is wise in all Web research, carefully judge the quality of the information you discover.

Information Management

Understanding and Mastery: Using technology for word processing, sending e-mail, and locating and evaluating information

Critical Thinking Question: The Web has greatly simplified initial community research by putting thousands of pieces of data at your fingertips.* Practice the Web-search techniques by exploring your focal community, tentative outcome goals, and possible programatic approaches. Save anything you may find useful. As you conduct your search try various techniques for locating information, note what worked well or poorly. What did your exploration teach you about Web-based research?

Assess your comprehension about Web-based Research by completing this quiz.

Eventually, work on the Web will yield decreasing data, so you will want to enhance computer research with primary information from the community members themselves. Most people think of surveys first when considering ways of collecting community information.*

Unfortunately, surveys are much harder to design, deliver, collect, and interpret than they seem. However, if properly designed, they can provide valid and reliable information from large numbers of people. There are two main criteria for surveys and other types of quantitative research: (1) **validity** refers to whether the research measures what it is intended to measure and (2) **reliability** refers to whether the research findings are likely to be easily replicated if other researchers follow the same protocols. Many surveys are reliable in that they can produce similar results when replicated with similar population samples, but their validity (the "truth" of their findings) may be easily compromised by design problems, such as **leading questions** (questions that are worded so that every available response supports the researchers' biases), **poor sampling** (choice of distribution methods or people to survey), **low rate of return, biased self-selection of respondents**, and **respondents' bias** (the desire to look good). For example, in a notoriously embarrassing case based on poor sampling, the *Chicago Tribune* boldly printed a "Dewey Beats Truman" headline before the 1948 election results were in. Truman, of course, defeated Dewey. The erroneous headline happened because a telephone poll showed that Dewey would win by a landslide. He would have, if all the voters had had telephones! Working class and poor people did not usually have them, but they did vote—for Truman!

In spite of its faults, carefully executed survey research can answer important questions quickly and easily and can provide a basis of comparison with other sources of information. Table 7.1 lists some of the strengths and weaknesses of survey research.

Table 7.1 Strengths and Weaknesses of Survey Research

Strengths	Weaknesses
Relatively inexpensive (especially if self-administered)	Questions minimally applicable to fit a large population because they are too general to be useful.
Useful in describing the characteristics of a large population	Very general questions are likely to miss important specifics.
Can be administered from remote locations using mail, e-mail, or telephone.	Inflexible; once designed, it cannot be changed.
Very large samples are possible, increasing statistical significance.	Wording is extremely important. Bias easily creeps into questions.
Large sample sizes allow for multi-variable analysis.	It is impossible to know the reasons why people respond.
Many questions can be asked, thus adding flexibility.	Generating a high rate of return is often problematic.
There is flexibility in the design and implementation phases, which allows you to choose the questions, mode of delivery, and return mechanisms that fit your needs and budget.	It is sometimes difficult to track duplicate responses.
There are now many free or inexpensive survey-generating websites.	Respondents vary widely on knowledge of topic.
	Even in anonymous surveys, people usually choose to make socially acceptable responses.
	Choice of method is critical to response rate and validity.

Source: Copyright © by Pearson Education, Upper Saddle River, NJ.

Carefully designed survey research can be very helpful but it must be designed ethically. Your designated learners should answer the following questions before implementing survey research:

- What questions do we need to answer that can only be answered through a survey?
- How shall we design the questions?
- How shall the questions be worded?
- How can we include those who actually know the extent of the need we have identified?
- Whom should we ask? (Choosing the sample)
- How shall we distribute the survey?
- How can we be sure to reach our main target group (those who are most affected by our concerns)?
- How will we ensure confidentiality?
- How much will this cost? How much can we afford to spend?
- How can we maximize the rate of return?

Review how survey questions can affect results. Consider how the wording of questions of surveys you've conducted, what questions could lead to potential biases?

Assess your comprehension of Survey Research by completing this quiz.

It is impossible to cover all the nuances of survey research here; entire books, university courses, and businesses focus on it. However, the hints and suggestions in Appendix A will give you an idea of what is involved when someone innocently suggests, "Let's do a survey!"

While quantitative research—such as Web searches, use of census data, and surveys—give you a broad idea about community perceptions, **qualitative research** (listening to people and taking an in-depth look at specific examples) helps you identify and explain complex structures and interactions within your focal system and its related systems.

Qualitative research, like other forms of systematic inquiry, is judged on both validity and reliability—but a third factor, **generalizability** (the judgment of the readers about its relevance), is added to the mix. To be generalizable, your team's research reports must written clearly, honestly, and with **narrative detail** (telling the complete story) so that your readers can determine whether the findings are relevant and believable and whether they have relevance to their own needs and interests.

Despite many conflicts in the sciences and social sciences about the merits of quantitative and qualitative research, both are important and useful in community organizing. Quantitative techniques tend to be reliable (in that they can be repeated relatively easily with similar results) but depend greatly on their research design (that is, asking the right questions in the right way) for their validity. Qualitative studies tend to be valid because they rely on in-depth exploration and feedback from participants but may be less reliable because every situation is different and kaleidoscopic community processes lead to constant change. Qualitative studies also tend to be more useful to readers because their stories, examples, and honesty about possible researcher biases make it easier to place information in a matrix of understanding.

Typically, researchers combine several qualitative research methodologies to provide more valid results. **Triangulation of methods** (also called multiple methods), in which three or more methodologies are used and the results compared against each other, is common and provides a more complete understanding of a focal system. Observation, in-depth interviews, use of artifacts and written materials, focus groups, narratives, and arts-based techniques—such as producing local theater or music, creating community murals, and the like—are qualitative methods commonly triangulated in community organizing.

Observation begins with your commitment to fully experiencing the world around you in a four-step process that can be remembered with the acronym EDIT: **e**xperience, **d**escribe, **i**nterpret, and **t**ransfer. That is, the observer describes what has been noted, interprets its meaning, and then transfers (applies) what has been learned. The EDIT process is based on inductive reasoning as it builds from specific details to hypotheses about what is occurring, rather than beginning with preconceived notions and working down to an experimental proof.

Interviewing involves systematically talking with people and recording what you learn. There are several forms of interviewing that are relevant to community research, ranging from questions you ask in a chance encounter with someone to those using formal samples and interview protocols. Most interviews fall in between. Specialized forms of interviewing include focus groups, narratives or story telling, and structured reflections on drama, dance, and the visual arts.

Artifacts are anything that is produced from human activity. Important artifacts for your participatory research effort will include (1) private documents such as diaries, journals, correspondence, and e-mails; (2) semi-public written documents such as meeting minutes and written organizational policies and procedures; and (3) public documents such as published newspaper accounts, statutes, and regulations. It is interesting to compare the "public story" to the "private story" to determine congruencies and discrepancies. In addition to written documents, artifacts may include visible evidence of human activity. For instance, in rural areas, one can determine where residents do most of their business dealings by observing which side of an intersection or driveway has the most gravel—data that can be useful in differentiating community boundaries.

Information Management

Understanding and Mastery: Obtain information through interviewing, active listening, consultation with others, library or other research, and the observation of clients and systems

Critical Thinking Question: How will you combine the Web-based, quantitative, and qualitative information you gather in order to gain a clear picture of your target community? How will you share what you have learned with the designated learners and the leadership team?

Triangulation is the last stage of qualitative data gathering in which you comb through all the notes and recordings you've made, looking for patterns that make sense of what is happening and helping you understand how others view the situation. Triangulation has been compared to walking around a statue or viewing a scene from various perspectives. It is the mental and emotional process of looking carefully at each piece of information, combining them into a whole, and then holding the parts and the whole in creative tension. This step takes practice and wisdom.

Qualitative research involves the triangulation of information from many different sources. To gain some experience using qualitative techniques, read the material on qualitative research. Create a qualitative research plan for exploration of the assets and needs of your community focal system.

Assess your comprehension of Qualitative Research by completing this quiz.

Some people find the very word *research* terrifying because of its association with the mysteries of statistics, but it is simply a way of systematically asking and answering questions. This chapter and Appendix A are a primer on the major social science research techniques used by community organizers so that designated learners can be comfortable in gathering, consolidating, and using research materials. Further, you will be able to present information to decision makers in the conventional ways they expect.

The next step in participatory research is to consolidate information into written reports and tables. Consolidation of information serves both internal and external functions. Internally, it enables the organizing team to understand system dynamics and make wise decisions. Externally, it provides material to tell the story of the emerging effort to potential supporters, ease the fears of potential enemies, and clarify the effort to potential stakeholders and the general public. The best reports integrate stories gained from qualitative exploration with the numerical facts gained from quantitative methods. Stories speak to the heart; numbers speak to the head.

Analytical Frameworks

By the completion of the data gathering and consolidation phases, your leadership team should have a clear picture of the focal system and its components—it will have the beginnings of an intuitive understanding of what is needed. **Analytical frameworks** are intellectual tools that enable you to further understand and evaluate what is happening in your focal community system.

Community organizing is a field of applied social science whose intellectual leaders are mostly professionals from the fields of social work, public affairs, sociology, rural sociology, and community education. These scholars, many of whom work for colleges and universities, have developed comprehensive approaches to community research and its applications, which are part of their institutions' service mission and are intended to be used by emerging community groups. This section explores several of the best:

- The **asset-based approach** of John Kretzman and John McKnight of Northwestern University[5]
- A **problem-centered approach** developed by Drew Hyman from the Pennsylvania State University and author Joyce McKnight from SUNY/Empire State College[6]
- The **Gap Analysis Technique** invented by Betty Reid Mandell and Barbara Schram[7]
- **Sustainability indicators** being developed by the world-wide sustainability movement[8]

The Asset-based Approach

The **Asset-based** or **Community Building** approach is most useful in geographic focal systems, such as Smithville and Middle View. Its premise is that communities should concentrate on building their strengths instead of focusing on community weaknesses or on bringing in outside resources. The Asset-Based Community Development (ABCD) approach to neighborhoods and communities aims at identifying strengths and assets rather than liabilities. Let's now look at the steps involved in the asset-based approach:

- **Step 1:** Identify the geographic target community (the focal system).
- **Step 2:** Identify the formal organizations within the target geographic area, prioritize those that are most important either to your community or to your mission, and talk with their leadership. Identify their missions, their view of their role in the neighborhood, their plans for the future, key people who are involved, and what needs they may have for volunteers or paid employees. Note how they may be linked to each other and to broader social systems. Be sure to keep good notes.
- **Step 3:** Identify semi-formal organizations or associations that may provide positive resources and add to the positive quality of life in your focal community system.
- **Step 4:** Identify the primary groups, such as families and friendship networks, with special attention to the core people who hold these networks together.
- **Step 5:** Search for individuals with talent, strength, and integrity.
- **Step 6:** Keep good notes and contact information on everyone you encounter in a place where all designated learners and the planning team can easily access it.
- **Step 7:** Look creatively at the information you have gathered. What institutions, agencies, and individuals could you link to one another to improve life in the community?
- **Step 8:** Pick a project that is an "easy win" and begin. Look at your list of assets and contact the representatives of organizations and associations, as well as talented individuals who are most likely to help you with it. Link them into a formal or informal project team. As you link people together, they will find more things in common. Often your community will literally blossom with community gardens or clean-ups and later with larger, more challenging projects and advocacy efforts.

Explore ABCD Institute to learn more about the asset-based approach to community development. Consider how you might apply the asset-based approach to community development to your organizing effort.

Do something. Evaluate it. Do something else. Remember that some people will be interested in the whole community and the long haul, while others may only want to be involved in one project. Don't worry if the group concerned with the needs of the whole community is a small one because their main task is to discern possible links among organizations, associations, families, and friendship groups and individuals. Bring them together, encourage them to think creatively, encourage them as needed, and watch as the focal community blossoms.

For several years now, Middle View community leaders have been more or less intentionally using the asset-based approach for economic and cultural development. They have identified government resources, business organizations such as the Chamber of Commerce, business owners, the local summer music camp, practicing artists, and many others who have joined together in creative ways to enhance the summer tourist offerings. For example, the music camp has joined with a local gourmet restaurant to offer a reasonably priced combined dining–concert experience. The town government, local folk school, historical society, public library, and individual artists and musicians have created a summer arts series that draws people to the "downtown" area. Middle View Village is buzzing and blossoming as new ideas constantly emerge. Indeed, it seems as if many different people have more or less unconsciously developed the knack of making such positive connections so the core leadership team has to do very little to catalyze new ideas—the "garden" is growing on its own.

Assess your comprehension about Asset-based Community Development by completing this quiz.

The Problem-centered Approach

The **problem-centered approach** is probably the mostly commonly used by those who have identified a specific burning issue or concern that they want to address. Let's look at some examples from Middle View and Smithville, based on an amalgam of real cases. Middle View is isolated from the nearest medium-sized city by narrow, winding roads and fierce winter storms that make winter transportation difficult. For many years its small hospital lacked a kidney dialysis program. Dialysis patients frequently had to go for six-hour treatments two or three times per week coupled with two hours of travel. Many were exhausted and discouraged, but then a transplant recipient, who had been a dialysis patient herself, decided that something needed to be done. She organized the patients who were well enough to participate, their families, and some of the local medical personnel. They collected data on the number of patients in the area, their treatment needs, particularly poignant stories, and the figures showing that a locally available dialysis unit could actually save money in reduced infections and inpatient hospitalizations. They presented the data to state-level politicians, to the local hospital board, the Kidney Foundation, and an insurance company–run private provider agency. Steady advocacy, solid financial information, local fund-raising, and some help from the state representative on regulatory and licensing issues eventually led to a small but effective locally based dialysis clinic. The problem was solved. Local advocacy groups often begin with specific issues or problems, too. For example, several years ago in Smithville, the only direct bridge from downtown to the neighborhood was scheduled to be closed for up to two years, thus threatening to shut down bus routes and increasing a five-minute commute by car to forty-five minutes over back streets. The bridge issue galvanized the neighborhood, and a community advocacy effort forced the city to build a temporary by-pass. This successful effort became one of the catalysts for the current neighborhood organization.

While such efforts can be awe-inspiring, they must be based on careful participatory research. The following is a list of questions participatory researchers should ask:

- What are the important aspects of the problem?
- What outcomes do we really want?
- Who are the important players or stakeholders?
- Who are potential audiences for our advocacy efforts?
- Are there pay-offs from our advocacy project for various players, including both friends and enemies? How can we use these pay-offs to bring at least some of our opponents to our way of thinking?
- Who has the power in the situation and what is its nature?
- What other social problems may be taking precedence over this issue, especially in the mezzo- and macro-level systems that impact it? How can we move it closer to the top? In other words, what are the politics involved?

The development of systematic answers to these questions, and others that your group may generate, will help you implement approaches that (1) acknowledge conflicting views and interests but (2) still make consensus building possible.

Gap Analysis

The **Gap Analysis** is a third useful analytical process and combines the research process discussed here with the planning and implementation processes discussed in Chapter 8. The gap analysis technique can be used in most community efforts, but it is especially useful when focused on specific issues, either as stand-alone concerns or as part of a broader community mission. Figure 7.2 is a flow chart of the first phase of the Gap Analysis process, that is, identifying the Gap.*

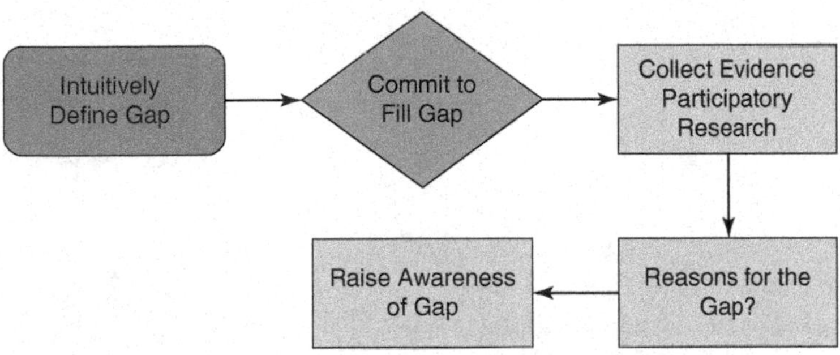

FIGURE 7.2 Gap Analysis Process, Phase 1: Identifying the Gap
Leadership team members intuitively recognize a need in the target system, resolve to do something about it, use participatory research techniques to measure it, and begin to make others aware of it.
Source: Copyright © by Pearson Education, Upper Saddle River, NJ.

- Phase 1: Identifying the Gap
  - **Step 1:** Identifying the gap intuitively
  - **Step 2:** Committing to filling the gap
  - **Step 3:** Collecting evidence about the "size and shape" of the gap
  - **Step 4:** Figuring out reasons for the gap by analyzing information
  - **Step 5:** Raising consciousness about the gap

The next step is illustrated in Figure 7.3, which is a flow chart of phase 2 in which the gap is magnified by looking at it in a larger context.

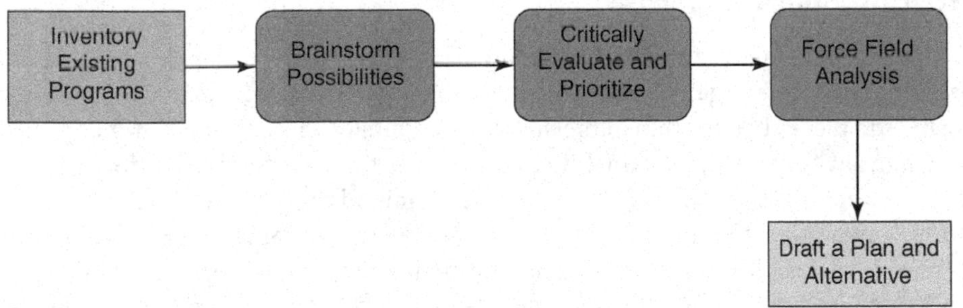

FIGURE 7.3 Magnifying the Gap
The leadership team moves its focus from the gap to the "landscape" around it. By looking at existing resources, creative possibilities, and various forces affecting the situation, the team begins drafting an initial plan as a beginning point for discussion.
Source: Copyright © by Pearson Education, Upper Saddle River, NJ.

- Phase 2: Magnifying the Gap within a larger context
  - **Step 1:** Inventorying other programs
  - **Step 2:** Brainstorming ideas
  - **Step 3:** Critically evaluating suggestions and ranking them
  - **Step 4:** Doing a force field analysis which determines factors in favor of the project and those against it
  - **Step 5:** Drafting a plan and an alternative

The next phase, which focuses on identifying which action steps are needed, is illustrated in Figure 7.4.

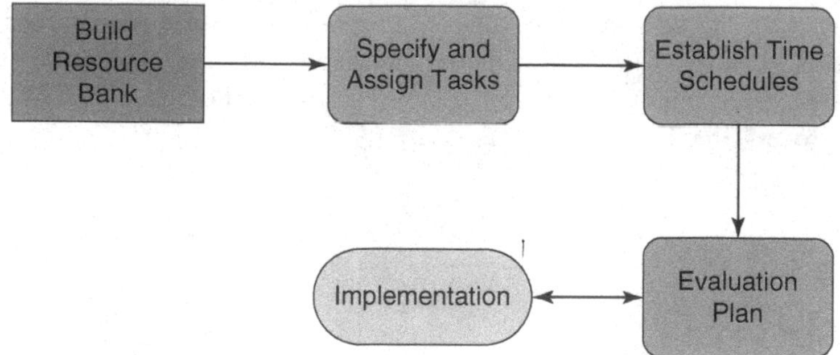

FIGURE 7.4 Microscoping (Action Steps) The leadership team decides on a specific implementation plan and moves forward. *Source:* Copyright © by Pearson Education, Upper Saddle River, NJ.

- Phase 3: Microscoping to identify the action Steps*
  - **Step 1:** Building a resource bank
  - **Step 2:** Specifying and assigning tasks to be done
  - **Step 3:** Establishing time schedules
  - **Step 4:** Evaluating the plan and following up

The Gap process is a concise summary of the steps used in all good planning and is often applied in existing human service organizations and formal collaborations where it is generally very straightforward. On the other hand, new community organizing efforts tend to be more formless, move more slowly, have more variance in participation, and are harder to keep on track. They are also great fun, can lead to lifelong friendships, and elicit creative ways of meeting important human needs.

Assess your comprehension about Gap Analysis Technique by completing this quiz.

Sustainability Analysis

The concept of **sustainability** has become a world-wide movement often characterized by grassroots organizations that combine the word *sustainable* with the name of a specific place. The movement began with Sustainable Seattle and now has branches throughout the world. Sustainability asserts that the paradigm of unlimited growth that characterizes global society cannot be sustained and will eventually deplete the world's resources. Community organizing efforts that embrace sustainability look at the ways current behaviors are strengthening the viability and sustainability of a focal system, ways such behaviors are threatening it, strategies for increasing the likelihood of sustainability, and ways of measuring whether these tactics are working. The sustainability model described here can be applied to any geographic system, but it is most commonly used in geographic regions that share environmental resources such as watersheds.

The sustainability movement predicates a **paradigm shift** (a major shift in the way people view reality). Figures 7.5 and 7.6 illustrate the change from exploitation of the environment to long-term sustainability.

The goal of the "old paradigm" is constant economic growth. Constant economic growth is sustained by all other social institutions. All social institutions such as

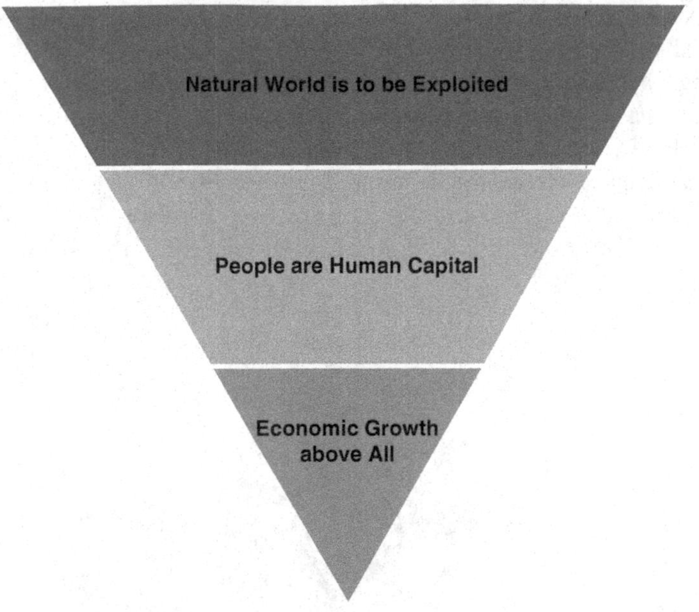
Natural World is to be Exploited
People are Human Capital
Economic Growth above All

FIGURE 7.5 The Old Paradigm In the old paradigm, everything serves continuing economic growth. *Source:* Copyright © by Pearson Education, Upper Saddle River, NJ.

education, religion, health care, criminal justice, and government are called industries and are organized in ways that support the economy. The value of human beings is based on their position in the economy and is called human capital. The natural world is to be exploited to increase production and economic growth.

The "sustainability paradigm" turns the old paradigm upside down. It asserts that all life on earth depends on the natural order—on finite supplies of air, fresh water, and minerals and on temperature balance—and that unlimited exploitation of natural resources cannot be maintained. It also asserts that well-being does not come from

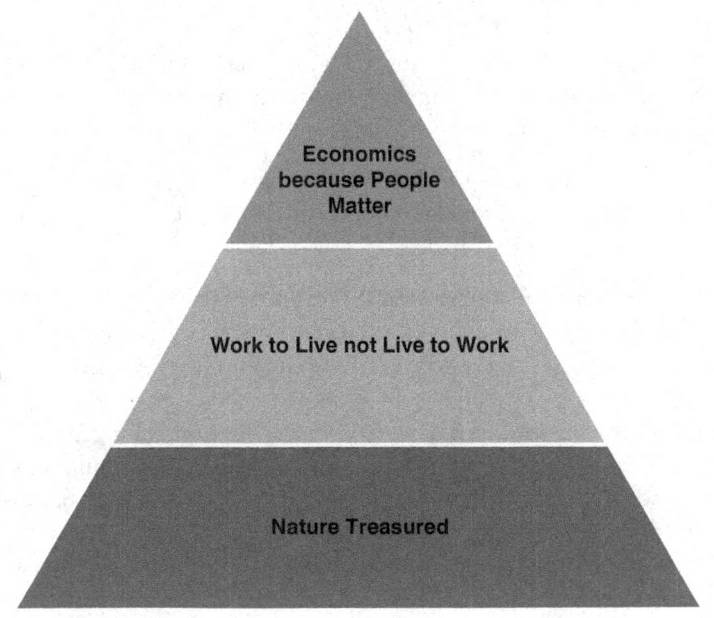
Economics because People Matter
Work to Live not Live to Work
Nature Treasured

FIGURE 7.6 Sustainability Paradigm In the sustainability paradigm, the economy serves the people, not vice versa. *Source:* Copyright © by Pearson Education, Upper Saddle River, NJ.

amassing consumer goods but from clean air, sufficiency of healthful food and fresh water, decent shelter, health care and wellness practices, loving relationships, opportunities for learning, and inner peace. The goal of social and economic institutions is to ensure that everyone has enough. Finally, it asserts that economics is not the master of human beings but should be our servant.

Organizing efforts based on sustainability often use the compass points as their framework for analyzing the health of a community or region. Your leadership team must consider all points of the compass for the development of a healthy focal system (see Figure 7.7).

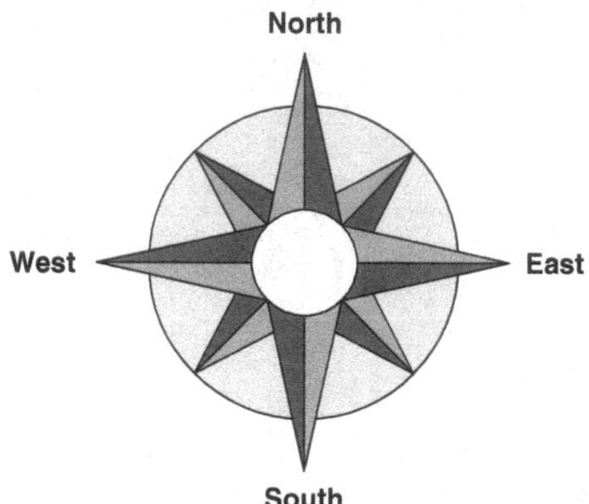

FIGURE 7.7
The Sustainability Compass
All four compass points must be in balance for a high-quality life:
N = Nature. Our environmental heritage, our use of resources, and our impact on the earth
E = Economy. Our livelihoods, our wages, and our capacity to keep even the poorest out of absolute poverty
S = Society. Our collective social institutions such as government, religion, family, education, health care, human services, and justice that together comprise and gauge the health of our culture and democracy
W = Well-being. The ability of individuals and families to sustain health, happiness, and the capacity to learn and take advantage of all life has to offer
Source: Copyright © by Pearson Education, Upper Saddle River, NJ.

If you choose to use the sustainability research model, divide your emerging task force into subgroups charged with assessing focal system needs for each of the four compass points. While each focal community will be unique, some typical sustainability goals might be to:

- Provide more transportation choices.
- Promote equitable, affordable housing.
- Enhance economic competitiveness.
- Support existing micro-systems within the focal community.
- Coordinate and leverage government policies and investment.
- Value and build on diversity.

Once each of the four teams is satisfied that they have identified suitable goals, the teams should define **indicators** to measure the current situation and to evaluate changes over time.

Good indicators are hard to create, but they have:

- Validity (the indicator measures what it is supposed to).
- Lack of ambiguity (everyone knows what exactly is being measured).
- Availability (it does not take a great deal of time to find, measure, and organize the findings).
- Timeliness (it can be measured quickly if rapid decision making is needed).
- Relative stability over time (comparisons are important in sustainability research; therefore, indicators must be consistent so that accurate comparisons are possible).
- Accuracy and reliability of measurement.
- Understandability (it should be easily understood by anyone with average mental abilities).

- Relevance to policy (it should provide information needed for wise policy formation).
- Low cost and relative ease of collection.
- Creativity.
- Ability to sustain the measurement effort.

All of the indicators taken together should result in clarity about all four compass points and should show how economic and social indicators support well-being and the health of the environment. Creating indicators can be interesting and even fun. For instance, one of the water quality indicators that Sustainable Pittsburgh[9] participants chose was the number of ducks present at the confluence of the Allegheny, Monongahela, and Ohio Rivers on a certain day every year. Because ducks only go where there are healthy water plants, the more ducks, the higher the water quality! Other communities have used the number of flower boxes and small gardens in the neighborhood as indicators of intangible qualities like hopefulness.

Once valid reliable indicators are selected, reasonable targets and target dates for evaluation purposes are set. Follow-up is extremely important because indicators are often created and measured for only a year or two until funding resources are depleted. To be useful, indicators must be measured consistently over time so that comparisons can be made.

Explore sustainability and sustainability research at Learning for Sustainability Network. Consider how you can make sustainability an important component of your community organizing approach.

Assess your comprehension about Sustainability Framework by completing this quiz.

Information Management

Understanding and Mastery: Performing elementary community-needs assessment.

Critical Thinking Question: Which analytical framework or frameworks seem likely to be most useful to your leadership team and why?

The asset-based approach, the problem-based approach, Gap Analysis, and sustainability indicators are all tools that your participatory research group can use to define desirable outcomes and processes. Because all are legitimate forms of social science research, they give your group credibility with decision makers and are useful for your planning purposes.

Summary

In this chapter, you learned the basics of participatory research, including how to enable a community leadership team to use connected knowing processes, apply social science research techniques, and use analytical frameworks to clarify and make use of the information you collect to attain your community organizing goals.

Assess your analysis and evaluation of this chapter's contents by completing the Chapter Review.

CHAPTER 8

Kayte Deioma/PhotoEdit

Planning and Implementation

Chapter Outline

At this point in the community organizing cycle your leadership team will have thoroughly researched the assets and needs of your chosen focal community system and will be ready to move from information gathering to action. This chapter continues the journey as you concentrate on planning—which involves clearly defining your vision, mission, outcomes, and major actions—and implementation, which makes your vision a reality. We will begin by examining the planning phase by revisiting the planning cycle illustrated here in Figure 8.1.

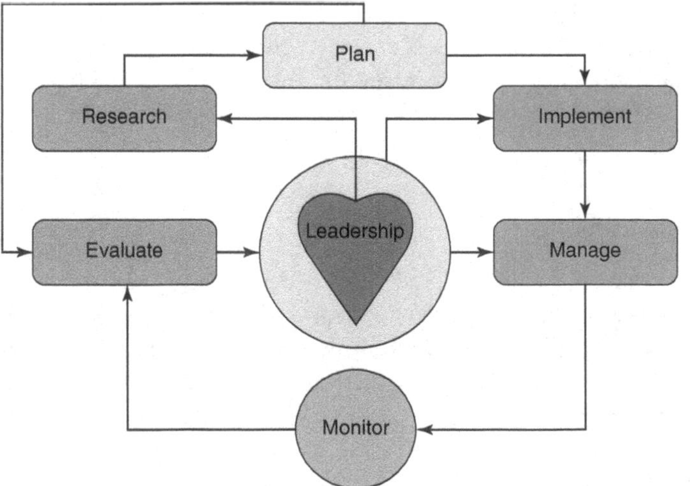

FIGURE 8.1
The Planning Phase
Source: Copyright © by Pearson Education, Upper Saddle River, NJ.

Community organizing plans are a design for change based on what your leadership team has discovered in the research and analysis phase of the organizing cycle. Your approach to planning should be based on (1) the variety of community organizing you have chosen (see Chapter 4) and (2) the "ideal type" of planning that works best in circumstances like yours. To help you make good decisions and make the process run more smoothly, you should begin your planning process by identifying the variety (or varieties) of organizing discussed in Chapter 4. Table 8.1 can be used as a reference.

Table 8.1 Long-Range Planning across Different Types of Community Organizing

	Place-based Relational Organizing	Social Entrepreneurs	Social Innovation	Economic Mutual Aid	Self-help	Advocacy and Social Movements
Type of Planning	Relational Planning	Traditional Planning	Participatory Planning	Participatory Planning	Relational Planning and Advocacy Planning	Advocacy Planning or Participatory Planning
Distinguishing characteristics	An organic process where one helpful idea leads to another, guided by a vision of a high quality of life	Long-range planning is done by the entrepreneur using traditional planning techniques, similar to those required in creating formal business plans	Planning is seen as an informal but connected activity. Research and writing tasks are often assigned to designated learners who report to an organizing team.	The most effective approach is participatory planning to determine people's own needs and adapt ideas to local circumstances. Less successful efforts use top-down traditional planning.	Self-help organizations have an internal support function based on relational planning that then evolves an advocacy function.	Planning is usually linked to specific action campaigns and a long-range vision of justice.

Source:

Four Types of Planning

Once your leadership team has gathered information and has made at least a tentative decision about the variety of community organizing you are using, you will be ready to select the type of planning that is likely to be most useful. The planning literature defines four **ideal types** of planning: **traditional**, **relational**, **advocacy** (or **equity**), and **participatory**. The four ideal types are defined in Table 8.2.*

*Note: In social science, an "ideal type" is one that perfectly fits a mental model. For instance, you probably have a mental model of a bird as something that has feathers, wings, can fly, can sing, eats seeds and insects, and so on. This is your ideal type that you use to categorize a creature as a bird. Of course, you can imagine a creature that would not fit your ideal bird type completely but would still be a bird: penguins, ostriches, and crows, for example. The same thing is true of the ideal types discussed here. Most planning efforts will not completely meet the criteria for any of the ideal types.

You will find that, from their beginning, some projects are a mixture of these ideal types while others may begin with one ideal type and move to another as organizing continues, as seen in Figure 8.2.

Table 8.2 **Comparison of Four Ideal Types of Planning**

	Relational Planning	Traditional Planning	Advocacy/Equity Planning	Participatory Research and Planning
Task and Process Goals	To increase quality of life through increased trust and caring.	To address broad community problems and issues, often government mandated.	To ensure that powerless groups have a voice in long-range planning.	To solve targeted problems through the active engagement of those most deeply affected.
Assumptions about community structure and problem conditions	Strong, caring relationships build strong communities.	Traditional structures, such as government, are best suited to identify and solve problems.	Advocates have to fight on behalf of the powerless to ensure that their needs are addressed.	The best solutions come from a participatory process led by those directly involved.
Focal system	People united by geographic proximity, relational ties, common concerns, or all of the above.	Focal system often a legal entity, viewed as an object for examination.	Often defined by outside advocates who believe a target group is being treated unjustly.	Focal system defined by participants who are immersed in the system and want an improved quality of life.
Basic change strategy	Working together to improve the quality of life makes life better in both the present and the future.	Long-range planning and policy implementation by government or other external bureaucratic systems.	Equalizing power relationships through social action tactics.	Participants control the process. They develop, implement, and manage strategies and tactics for themselves.
Approach to research/ planning	Guided by intuition and "heart knowledge."	Information gathered by professionals who make recommendations to decision makers.	Research and educational strategies demonstrate power imbalances and needed political action.	Information gathered, consolidated, and interpreted by participants.
Characteristic tactics and techniques	"Talking through" what is needed, then doing it.	Rational, technical presentation of recommendations with implementation by established organizations.	Data presented in a way that demonstrates injustice and promotes outrage.	Participants share analysis of results from strategies and tactics they determined.
Assumptions about focal systems and sub-systems	Ever-changing patterns of relationships; clear, caring, and respectful communication is key.	Focal systems and sub-systems need to be managed by experts.	Professional organizing among the powerless is needed to raise awareness of false consciousness.	Focal system and sub-systems should be managed by those who live in them.
Typical practitioner roles	Warm, caring person with relationship-building skills.	Employee of sponsoring agency who provides technical expertise.	Expert volunteer wishing to help a disenfranchised community or group.	Equal participant offering community planning as needed; occasionally an outside consultant.
Orientation toward authorities/ power structure	Largely irrelevant.	Subordinate.	Equal.	Participatory group is its own center of power.
Types of power	"Soul" relationship.	Knowledge.	Political/threat.	Productive (ability to accomplish desired tasks).

Source: Copyright © by Pearson Education, Upper Saddle River, NJ.

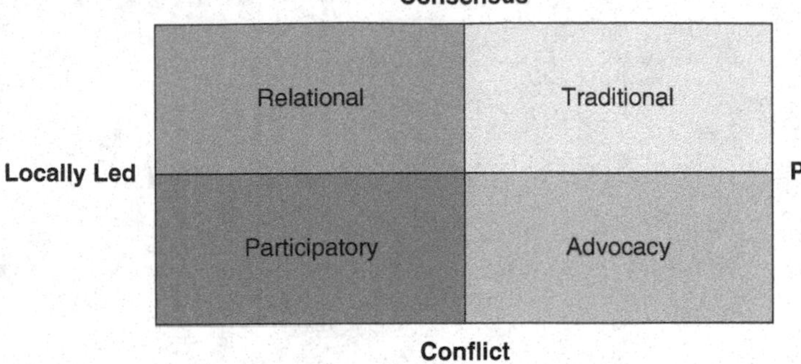

FIGURE 8.2 Mixing and Matching Types of Planning

Source: Copyright © by Pearson Education, Upper Saddle River, NJ.

Any particular planning effort can be divided along two dimensions. The horizontal dimension has to do with leadership of the process and is a continuum between local control and control by professional planners. The vertical dimension is a continuum between consensus-based approaches, which emphasize collaboration with existing bureaucracies, and conflict or advocacy approaches, which emphasize giving powerless people a voice in the planning process. Using this model, planning processes can move from block to block. For example, if the professional planner strongly believes in justice and inclusion, traditional planning may take on aspects of participatory and advocacy planning. Relational planning may become advocacy planning when participants realize that many of their friends and neighbors are experiencing injustice. At times, relational planning becomes traditional planning if participants decide to bring in a consultant to facilitate the process. Frequently, relational planning becomes participatory planning when members of the focal community decide that "something has to be done and we are the people to do it."

Planning and Evaluating

Understanding and Mastery: Skills to develop goals, and design and implement a plan of action

Critical Thinking Question: Consider the variety of community organizing your leadership team is likely to use, and ask yourself which type you will probably use. What factors support your choice?

Explore the Participatory Process Planning Guide. What are the advantages of planning *with* community people rather than planning *for* them? Are there any potential disadvantages? If so, what might they be?

Assess your comprehension of the Four Major Types of Planning by completing this quiz.

The Planning Questions

Once you have decided on suitable type(s) of planning, you will need to address key planning questions. Note that these move from very broad to quite narrow and lead to specific actions needed for implementation. Table 8.3 addresses these planning questions and some important considerations for each step. A Middle View example then follows to give you an idea of how the process worked in real life.

When Middle View was planning its runaway prevention project (a social innovation effort), the leadership team developed a series of questions, which they then answered. The questions were:

- What is our overall **mission** (purpose)? Another way of asking this is, "In general, how will the focal community be better when we succeed?" For example, the

Table 8.3 Things to Consider during Planning

Stage	What It Entails	Considerations
Vision	Informal process of asking "What do we need to do to improve this situation?"	At this phase you should be listening carefully to everyone, especially those who will be directly affected by your effort. Beware of premature closure or letting your own preconceived notions or biases get in the way of effective consensus building.
Mission statement	Consensual creation of a short (one or two paragraphs maximum), clear statement of what you intend to accomplish.	Take the time to create a mission statement that is clear, concise, and actually defines what you intend to do. Avoid broad statements and excessive claims. Research suggestions on how to create mission statements and follow them.
Define outcome objective(s)	Statements of the measurable results you hope to achieve for your target population or, better yet, what this population wants to achieve for itself.	Do not mix outcomes with processes. For example, if you want to prevent suicide in a designated target population, your outcome goal would **not** be to provide *x* number of hours of individual counseling time; it would be to reduce the suicide rate by *y* percent or in *z* absolute numbers.
Define evaluation measures	Clear definitions of how you will know that you have achieved your desired outcomes.	These are very hard to create. They must be valid in that they really measure outcomes, are easy to collect and monitor, and are easy to collect for the evaluation phase of the organizing cycle. Be sure that you can actually collect and maintain the data needed before you commit to a particular outcome measure.
Define processes	What you are actually going to do to achieve your desired outcomes.	Avoid the temptation to start with processes. They should flow naturally from your mission and outcome goals and should be simple, relatively inexpensive, accessible to your target population, and as open to their input as possible.
Build appropriate organizational structures	How your effort is going to be organized in the long run.	You will need to decide the kind of organizational structure that will best help you fulfill your mission. Different options are discussed in Chapter 10.
Resource development and budgeting	The financial, human, and other resources you will need to meet your outcome objectives.	Financial plans should flow from your mission and outcome objectives, not from resources that may be available. Chapter 10 and its Appendix define the budgeting process in great detail.
Action steps	What needs to be done, when, and by whom to make your dreams real.	Define this as carefully as possible and give yourselves adequate time. Everything takes longer than you think, so keep working away at your plan even if you run into barricades.

Source: Copyright © by Pearson Education, Upper Saddle River, NJ.

mission of Middle View's runaway prevention project was "to enable at-risk teens to grow into successful adults by providing an anchor in Christ and community."

- What are our **outcome goals**? Outcome goals focus on specific measurable ways life will be better in the focal community because of your activities. In the runaway prevention program, the focal community was teenagers within the Middle View Schools, particularly the micro-system of those at risk of running away from home. The leadership team identified the desired outcomes as an *increase in family* *stability* as measured by fewer incidences of running away and teen homelessness, an *increase in knowledge and skill development* as evidenced by higher school retention and graduation rates, *improved decision making among youth* as evidenced by reduced incidence of status offenses (such as running way, incorrigibility, and truancy), and *ongoing stability in adulthood* as measured by completion of education or military service beyond high school, stable adult employment, successful marriages, and successful parenting.

- What **processes** will we use to reach these outcomes? Processes are the specific things that will be done to bring about the desired outcomes. The processes chosen for runaway prevention included family crisis intervention, mediation and problem solving between parents and teens, an overnight "cooling off" shelter while crises were being handled, longer term group home care if indicated, and ongoing follow-up with families and youth.
- How will we **evaluate** our progress as we go along (**formative evaluation**)? The formative evaluation of the whole program was done at monthly board meetings in a standard format that included reports from the executive director and all of the committees, followed by discussion of old and new business. Once the program was running, measurement of client outcomes was done at weekly treatment planning meetings focused on the needs of clients and their families and tracked the outcome goals, not just the services rendered.
- How will we know when we have succeeded (**summative evaluation**)? Although summative evaluation comes later in the community organizing cycle after implementation and management, it must nevertheless be designed into the planning phase. Summative evaluation is always linked to outcome goals. In the runaway prevention case, incidence of running away, truancy rates, referrals to Child Protective Services for status offenses, and graduation rates all provided quantitative data on the success of the program. Qualitative data included the results from interviews with adult family members, youth, school personnel, and agency representatives who shared their perceptions of program success.
- What **organizational structures** are best? Several different ways of structuring community organizing efforts are discussed in Chapter 10. The leaders of the runaway prevention project explored options like becoming a program of the county children's services department or remaining a local church mission. But in the end they decided to incorporate under the broad name of Middle View Concerned for Youth, with the runaway project as a sponsored program. The thought was that the Concerned for Youth corporation might eventually want to sponsor other youth-oriented projects, but in the end the runaway project remained its only effort.
- What **resources** will we need to accomplish our outcome goals? What do we have available now? What will we have to generate? What is our **expense budget**? What is our **revenue budget**? In the runaway prevention example, generating answers to these questions was an ongoing process. The first few years were the hardest as there were many false starts due to trial-and-error approaches. The project began with just a little over $1,000 from a church mission project, a few hundred dollars more from contributions, and a small grant from the local United Way. Money for a down payment on an old house was raised through a donation letter and local fund-raisers. A small grant was obtained. The project opened for business on a shoe string. At first, the leadership team decided that a house should be purchased to

provide a homelike atmosphere. Care would be provided by live-in house parents working largely for room and board; and administrative guidance and professional counseling would be provided by a full-time executive director working first as a volunteer and later for a minimum salary. There would be some non-personnel expenses, such as food and utilities, and some one-time expenses for building repairs, re-modeling, and code enforcement. They further decided to keep costs as low as possible by relying heavily on volunteers and community contributions. The original budget was $20,000 in 1978 dollars. In some ways this austerity strategy worked, as they were able to successfully operate for a year or so, demonstrate that there was a need for the services, and leverage that success into a much more reasonable and stable budget. But the stress and strain caused many tensions among the staff, which led to "burn out" of the house parents and the director—all of whom had no relief from being on 24-hour call to the police and the rest of the community. Upon reflection, former members of the leadership team believe that the project was very worthwhile but that if more time had been spent on the research and broad planning phases of the organizing cycle, the first years would have been far less painful.

What **action steps** should be taken, by whom, and in what order? The runaway prevention project's leadership team formed committees to divide their tasks. There was a building committee, a budget committee, a program committee, a fund-raising committee, and a by-laws/administrative committee, all guided by a fifteen-member board of directors (the uneven number was intended to avoid tie votes, although it was probably a bit too large to be truly effective). Each of the committees was assigned well-defined tasks that included what was to be done, who was to do it, when it was to be completed, and how it would be evaluated. The completion deadlines were put on a timeline and first monitored by the board of directors and later overseen by the board and the executive director.

Assessing the Situation

After answering the above questions, your leadership team will have a well-defined mission, clear outcomes, an idea of which processes will likely to lead to success, preliminary revenue, expense and budgets, a workable business structure, and a preliminary evaluation plan. But, you will still face the challenge of making your vision a reality. So your team can use one or more approaches to analyze the situation: the Gap Analysis method discussed in Chapter 7, the balancing method shown in Figure 8.3 that follows, or a SWOT (**s**trengths, **w**eaknesses, **o**pportunities, **t**hreats) analysis.

FIGURE 8.3
Factors Affecting Program Success

Source: Copyright © by Pearson Education, Upper Saddle River, NJ.

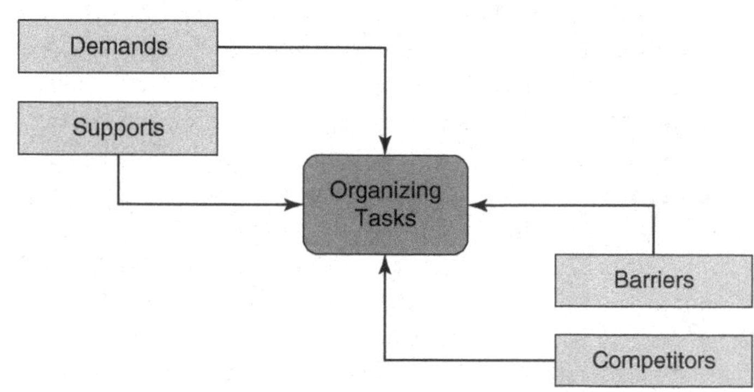

Much of your chance for success will depend on the balance among a number of factors. Here Figure 8.3 shows a simple system depicting some of the factors that can be used as a framework for brainstorming.

Imagine that Figure 8.3 is a sort of seesaw with organizing tasks as the fulcrum. **Demands** include all of the people who want the effort to succeed. In the case of Middle View, these people included counselors, teachers, and other school officials who wanted young people to have stable living situations so they could learn, parents who were at wits' end in dealing with incorrigible teens and wanted help to be available locally, the police who wanted an alternative to the juvenile justice system, and some teens themselves who wanted to be able to successfully navigate adolescent challenges. **Supports** include those people and organizations that are willing to provide human, material, and financial resources. In Middle View, this included several local churches, the local United Way, some high school teachers and guidance counselors, other leadership team members who later became the board of directors, a volunteer attorney, and the County Juvenile Court judge. **Barriers** are anything that blocks the way. Some barriers are comprised of people and organizations that are in direct opposition to the organizing effort, while others are simply part of the mezzo- and macro-systems whose bureaucratic responsibilities can block progress. There were few local barriers to the runaway prevention program except for some people who were concerned about the location of the shelter near their homes. Major barriers came from the mezzo-system: lack of available outside funding, bureaucratic rules and regulations especially regarding health and safety requirements, as well as program requirements from the state department of social services. **Competition** often comes from existing organizations with similar missions, as well as from dissimilar organizations that nevertheless draw from the same resources. For instance, the runaway prevention program competed directly with several other group homes within the county, as well as with county agencies like Child Protective Services (which had a shelter program of its own, forty miles distant). It competed indirectly with other municipal, county, and state services such as highways, bridges, public health, mental health, public welfare, state parks, and many other interest groups. The equation is simple: demands and supports for the organizing effort must outweigh barriers and competition. The leadership team's task is to find specific things that can lead to surmounting these obstacles.

Planning and Evaluating

Understanding and Mastery: Skills to develop goals and to design and implement a plan of action

Critical Thinking Question: Analyze your focal system and potential directions using Gap and balancing methods discussed. Compare and contrast your analyses. In what ways are such systematic approaches helpful in maintaining direction and momentum?

You can couple a SWOT analysis process with the seesaw approach to help the leadership team identify specific next steps. In a SWOT analysis, the leadership team asks:

- *What are the* ***strengths*** *of our effort as it currently exists?*
  In the Middle View runaway prevention effort, strengths included the commitment of the leadership team; the respected positions they held; their knowledge and skills in the areas of psychology and adolescent development; and the initial support of a committed church, the high school staff, the wife of the president of a major industry, the county juvenile judge, and the local United Way. The leadership team decided to build on community support by creating a letter which told the poignant

stories of some of the young people who had been left homeless or had been hurt while on the run, backed up with statistics about the problem and a description of the proposed solution(s). This letter was sent to many community leaders and to the local newspaper that printed several stories emphasizing the local need and the local effort. Additional community leaders were recruited to the board of directors and were encouraged to talk with their personal contacts within the county and state mezzo-systems to ask for their support.

- *What are our **weaknesses?***
  The weaknesses were a lack of support from critical components of the mezzo-system, including the directors of county Child Protective Services and the county Office of Juvenile Justice, whose directors thought that support should go to existing programs and who expressed concern about the qualifications of the project leaders. The leadership team (which had become a formal board of directors) decided to work to win over these leaders. The board president joined a collaborative effort among directors of youth-serving agencies and gained their respect by contributing time and energy to their joint work. Other board members visited agency leaders, shared the descriptive letter, talked with them about the credentials of the board (which included an MSW (Master of Social Work), two masters-level counselors, an accountant, and an attorney), listened to their concerns, and most important of all, gained their buy-in by incorporating some of the agency leaders' good ideas into the ongoing planning process. These activities built credibility. Internal weaknesses included a lack of expertise on the business side of program development including revenue and expense budgeting; a lack of political savvy in dealing with municipal, county and state politics; lack of knowledge of the mezzo- and macro-systems focused on the needs of youth; and a lack of specific research, planning, and organizing skills that sometimes led to inaccurate information and unnecessary initiatives. To overcome these weaknesses, the board carefully recruited additional volunteers with appropriate expertise.
- *What are our **opportunities?***
  Somewhat ironically, the strategies used to address weaknesses led to new opportunities which included assistance from the county judge for referrals; ability to match local funding with state funding at a 10%/90% rate, which greatly enhanced the overall budget; assistance from existing private youth-serving programs whose directors graciously provided assistance; volunteer help from local professionals in procuring property; attainment of non-profit status; design and maintenance of the accounting system; and repair of the property once procured.
- *What are some possible **threats?***
  Threats included competition for limited funding from other public and private agencies; delay of needed health, safety, and program approvals by state level agencies; and the volatile nature of client situations with the ever-present possibility of disastrous publicity. Participation in collaborative activities with other agencies somewhat mitigated the competition for funding as other agencies were reassured that the new effort would add to the service system rather than deplete it. Unfortunately, problems with regulatory agencies were ongoing despite an increase in support from both the local community and the county mezzo-system. These were mitigated somewhat by support from such political leaders as town council

members, the juvenile court judge, and even the U.S. congressperson. A major threat arose when the director of a rival agency worked his way onto leadership of a review panel and manipulated its evaluation, leading to denial of second-year funding. Thankfully, the runaway prevention project's leadership team then learned that the matching money which would have been used for the second year of the grant could instead be used for a much larger and longer lasting funding source. Good came from a potential disaster. Most threats seem to come out of nowhere. During the runaway prevention agency's first pilot year a young man and his sister came to the shelter after a falling out with their natural parents and failure in foster home placement. Soon after their arrival the young man was accused of a brutal rape. The local police (who were important stakeholders in the runaway project) took him into custody for questioning. The agency director and the agency's attorney insisted on being present during the interrogation, which angered the police and led to deterioration of police–agency relations. Eventually, after much anguish on everyone's part, the young man was proved innocent through DNA evidence, but it took over a year to restore a positive relationship between the agency and local police.

Explore the web for more about how to use SWOT analysis. Consider how you might use a SWOT analysis in understanding issues faced by your community organizing effort.

Your organizing effort will, of course, have its own SWOT list. In addition to carefully brainstorming your SWOT, your leadership team should identify areas that are unknown and therefore need additional research and investigation. This is a really important step. For instance, you may want to know if there are other organizations or programs with similar missions emerging that may be a threat to your efforts. You may want to explore the mezzo-system—especially municipal, county, state, and national policy making—to determine if there are any proposed laws or budget recommendations that will affect your efforts. You may want to determine if there is any local gossip about your efforts or hidden opposition from apparent friends. The leadership team should be encouraged to bring lingering questions or doubts to the surface so they can be investigated. As you saw in Chapter 5, some organizing groups address these planning questions in very formal ways, others "muddle through," and most probably do a bit of both—but all must answer these questions and continually revisit them.

Assess your comprehension of Situation Analysis by completing this quiz.

Implementation: Defining the Next Steps

Plans are only a design for change; change itself is brought about through conviction and action. Implementation puts legs under your plans. Since organizing is a cycle, there is no clear-cut demarcation between planning and implementation, but Figure 8.4 shows the general movement.

There are four ideal types of implementation described in the community organizing literature: (1) relational development, (2) community/locality development, (3) social action, and (4) popular education or participatory development. **Relational development** is based on friendship, family, and other personal ties. **Community** or **locality development** refers to top-down approaches that are imposed on communities by those in authority and usually emphasizes economic strategies. **Social action**

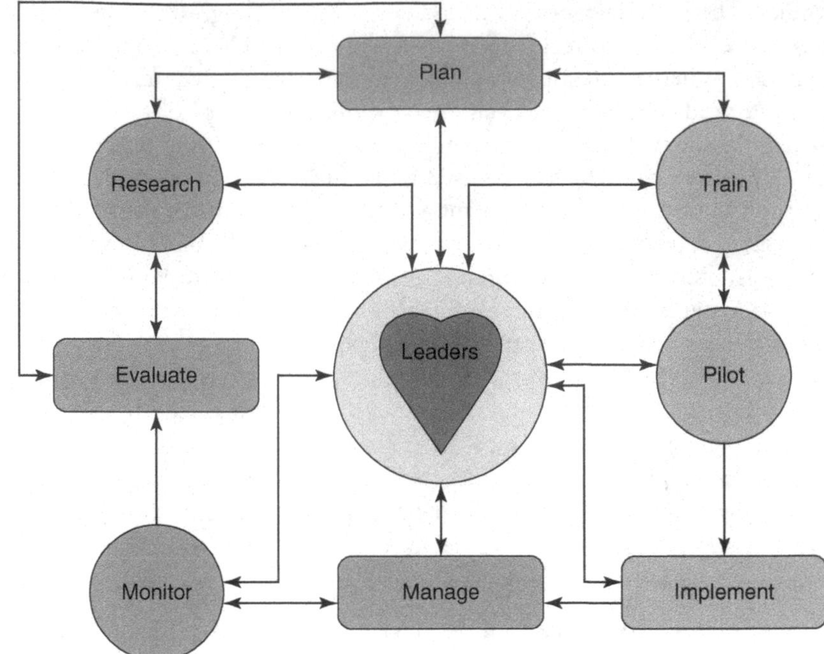

FIGURE 8.4 The Implementation Process
Note that this version of the organizing cycle adds training and piloting between planning and implementation. The former two processes are not used in every organizing venture, but they are discussed here because they are often needed.
Source: Copyright © by Pearson Education, Upper Saddle River, NJ.

approaches are also imposed but are based on the conflict model of society that pits relatively powerless action groups against powerful target groups. **Popular education** or **participatory development** refers to implementation that is accomplished by members of the target system. In practice, these four types of implementation are not mutually exclusive, but they are separated here for clarity.

Table 8.4 outlines the characteristics of these four implementation approaches and maps them to the varieties of community organizing discussed in Chapter 4.

Relational Implementation

In **relational implementation**, communities are viewed primarily as networks of relationships so the leadership team seeks to link people at the institutional, associational, primary group, family, and individual levels in an ongoing network of mutual care. Relational efforts focus on the family, friendship circles, other primary groups, and neighborhoods. They are rooted in home and family rather than the public arena. Relational implementation often begins slowly in places where people meet frequently and talk openly about issues that affect the quality of their lives. Many relational efforts are quite ordinary and, therefore, easily overlooked. Many informal helping efforts, social innovations, and community advocacy efforts over the years have been spawned and perfected over coffee at the diner, conversations in line at the post office, and beauty shop gossip.

Implementation in relational organizing is a person-centered, organic process. It grows from the perception that individual hurts may have community-based causes and community-based solutions. Projects grow organically with the slow application of ideas and insights to community problems, often with no written plan. Instead, there's a sense of an overall direction that grows from an implied consensus. Those using this model see power and politics quite differently from those operating from other implementation models. In relational organizing, power arises in the private sphere of relationships and is conceptualized as limitless and collective.

Table 8.4 **Implementation in Practice**

Variables in Actual Practice	Relationship-based Efforts	Community or Locality Development	Social Action	Popular Education
Organizing varieties	Place-based Relational, social entrepreneurship and innovation, mutual economic aid, and self-help	Collaboration	Community advocacy, social movements	Place-based Relational, Mutual economic aid, and self-help community advocacy
Task goals	Projects, programs, events, and resources that continually improve the quality of life in a focal community system	Major institutional and infrastructure changes, usually related to economic issues	Guarantee that an exploited group has needed rights and services and that those who exploit them are brought to justice	Ongoing community education process that enables exploited people to meet their own goals and protect their interests
Process goals	To assure that community institutions, associations, family and friendship networks, and individuals are linked to creatively strengthen the quality of life	To implement decisions of a comprehensive planning process or to disseminate research findings from university to locales	To bring about social justice for the powerless through policy change, legislation, or judicial means	To bring about outcomes developed through participatory research and popular education processes
Assumptions about community structure and problems	Problems can be solved best by helping one another	Problems can best be solved by experts	There are "haves" who are in control and fight to keep it; and "have nots" who need to be empowered	Problems can best be solved by the people affected
Focal system	Defined in terms of networks of relationships	Defined by outside authority	Defined by activists who may be inside or outside focal system	Defined by the participants
Basic change strategy	Asset-based approach	Locality development	Social action	Mutual aid supported by social action
Characteristic tactics and techniques	Linking people, associations, and institutions with a common interest in improving the quality of life	Meetings, hearings, workshops led by experts	Protests, boycotts, use of the legal system, bargaining, etc.	Internal trust and consensus building through decision-making meetings; consensus, and social action tactics as appropriate
Assumptions about interests of focal system and sub-systems	Relationships are at the heart of all systems and subsystems	Experts know best	Ordinary people are powerless victims who can learn to fight	Given the chance, people can help themselves by implementing creative solutions
Practitioner roles	Friend	Expert, "teacher"	Rabble rouser	Equal participant
Orientation toward authorities and power structures	Desire to be left alone to work things out	Obedience	Disobedience, suspicion	Self-advocacy; finding a voice
Typical types of Power	"Soul Power," relationship power	Knowledge Power, political Power	Threat Power, coercion	Productive Power, relationship Power

Source: © 2009 Joyce S. McKnight with thanks to Rothman (1974, 2001), Hyman, (1990, 2001), and John Kretzman and John McKnight (1993).

Those engaged in relational organizing are not naïve. Because they actually live in a targeted community, many have experienced powerlessness first hand. Relational organizers don't compete with established powers but develop their own power to solve problems in their own way through a process of connected learning. Relational implementation moves in fits and starts as plans and action steps are vague, general, and rarely written down unless required for outside funding.

Relational organizing is based on creating and maintaining warm interpersonal relationships that improve the emotional, interpersonal, and practical aspects of life in a focal community system. Discerning, befriending, connecting, weaving, clarifying, bridging, interpreting, strengthening, splicing, and serving are all **roles** (behaviors) that strengthen relational organizing and should be cultivated among everyone:

- **Discerning** neighborhood assets is a complex activity that usually begins with informal discussions in homes and community free spaces. When a consensus emerges that something must be done about a particular concern or issue, such discernment leads to action.
- **Befriending** involves becoming a valued member of the community by helping others in practical ways, such as giving a ride to the hospital or babysitting. Those who offer friendship are quickly accepted as part of the community and are often thought of as natural leaders.
- **Connecting** or **linking** involves informally bringing together people with similar interests to focus on common goals for the good of the whole community.
- **Weaving** is a complex process that emerges from linking and involves ensuring that existing and emerging social ties form emotionally sustaining patterns and effective networks.
- **Clarifying** is a continual process of figuring out what is going on and determining how different people perceive ongoing processes and their roles in those processes. It involves empathy and listening skills.
- **Bridging** involves finding ways to unite different interest groups and individuals so that everyone benefits.
- **Interpreting** is a form of mediation and relates to bridging. It involves a thorough understanding of various positions and relaying accurate, unbiased information to all participants.
- **Strengthening** is subtle and involves helping participants continue their efforts when the going gets rough by listening, taking an interest in each other's personal and family struggles, and providing practical, concrete help as needed.
- **Splicing** involves healing strained or broken relationships among participants.
- **Serving** is the practical role that holds the relational process together. Serving means that participants find no task too small, too dirty, or too menial if it is necessary to ensure that essential work is completed.

Because those engaged in relationship-based efforts believe that friends, families, and neighbors have a responsibility to care for one another in good times and bad, their efforts are a natural outgrowth of caring. They don't wait for government permission or funding to act. They depend on each other far more than on government or other outside resources. Many relationship-based efforts in both Middle View and Smithville are so ubiquitous that they go unnoticed. For instance, when a young boy from a working class Middle View family was diagnosed with a serious form of leukemia, the whole community sprang into action. As medical costs mounted, a local church started a bank account for the family; the boy's middle school class, the local Lions Club, the volunteer firefighters, and a local bar held fund-raisers; and dozens of individuals donated funds, gasoline, and food to support the family's needs. Thousands of dollars were raised. No government structures were involved at all.

In Smithville, members of the Smithville Neighborhood Organization (SNO) were upset by littering near a local convenience store. Three elderly ladies decided to approach the owner. When he told them that he was too tired and busy to pick up the litter on his lot (which had grown to monstrous proportions), they volunteered to pick it up and have it carted away if he would agree to keep the area clean. An informal agreement was struck, the ladies and some of their friends picked up the litter, and the store owner has kept up his end of the bargain. No code enforcement or other unpleasantness was needed.

Client-related Values and Attitudes

Understanding and Mastery: Interdisciplinary team approaches to problem solving

Critical Thinking Question: Relational organizing is based on the cultivation of mental and emotional habits and positive behaviors that enable you to make positive contributions and enjoy yourself while you are doing it. What are your relational strengths as well as areas where you feel you could use more work? How might you improve your relational skills?

Assess your comprehension of the Roles Involved in Relational Organizing by completing this quiz.

Locality Development

The terms **locality development** and **community development** are often used interchangeably and refer to the processes and products used to implement formal economic development activities and large community projects, such as schools, libraries, parks, and infrastructure. Locality development is both a process and a product. The process goals are to (1) facilitate negotiation among key stakeholders, (2) gain public support for large public projects, and (3) facilitate problem solving by engaging pre-identified stakeholders with one another and with those at the mezzo- and macro-system levels who have determined that a given project is needed. The intent is to negotiate details so that key stakeholders will agree to cooperate and will be satisfied with the results. The outcome goals of locality development are public projects that meet the needs of major stakeholders.

Locality development processes use workshops, meetings, and public hearings as venues to disseminate information, solve problems, and develop consensus. These events are generally organized by government officials, agency representatives, or paid consultants. Although many working groups incorporate citizens' insights into problem solving and implementation, others are primarily informational or perfunctory with communication flowing from experts to the community. Locality development presumes the basic goodwill of everyone involved.

Locality development is a product (or products) that enhances the economy of a focal system. Common locality development projects include roads and bridges, sewage and water, railroads and other means of transportation, public schools and libraries, loans and tax breaks for businesses, and changes in zoning laws. Key participants usually represent important economic interests. Although some provision is usually made for input from "ordinary citizens," processes are usually designed to accommodate key economic and political players.

The comprehensive planning process in Middle View exemplifies locality development. The Town of Middle View is mandated by the state to engage in comprehensive planning efforts on a regular basis (usually every five to ten years). These comprehensive plans are then used to define needed economic development, infrastructure requirements, and zoning. Municipalities use the data and conclusions as a basis for funding requests to state and federal agencies and as tools for setting their own outcome objectives. Such comprehensive plans are very important because they guide decision making at the local and mezzo levels over many years. Originally, comprehensive planning (and related implementation) was mandated by states as an antidote to unplanned growth, "sweetheart deals" among powerful people, and the exclusion of citizens from having input into important community decisions.

Openness and community engagement are still major process goals. However, over the years, the comprehensive planning process has become a closed system with technical planners and expert consultants frequently moving between public service and private practice. Intelligent town officials know that it's wise to hire established consultants to guide the process—not only because they have technical expertise in a field that is full of jargon and nuance but because established relationships can smooth the process. Middle View town officials hired a seasoned consulting firm to implement their comprehensive planning process and to do the technical work of consolidating the information gathered and writing the plan. The consultants' process alternated private meetings of the committee with public meetings linked by written reports that were produced by the firm. The strength of the process was in the professionalism of the planners, their knowledge of the mezzo-system, and the quality of the final plan. The plan and its follow-up will meet some important economic development goals. One portion addresses the need for a well-designed sewage disposal plant that will protect the fragile mountain soil from overuse by antiquated septic systems. Another provides for replacement of leaking water pipes and ensures the safety of town wells. Still other provisions protect the purity of the lake and river areas, provide for green spaces, and encourage creative recreational and economic uses of a formerly abandoned railroad. Because the plan has been carefully written to comply with the state specifications and specific funding streams, it is likely that important local projects will be implemented with little or no impact on local taxes. The main weaknesses were in the process, which occurs in comprehensive planning efforts everywhere. Those who had the loudest voices were those with powerful interests, who were somewhat sophisticated in government operations, who were aware of the importance of comprehensive planning, and who had time to invest in it. Middle and working class people, young adults and youth, and some neighborhoods were noticeably absent from the deliberations or were not aware of important provisions until it was too late to change them. There were many reasons for these weaknesses, including practical issues such as the time and place of scheduled meetings and inadequate publicity, but other reasons involved the lack of general awareness of the importance of comprehensive planning. Many people are either unaware of its impact or think of it as an empty exercise. On balance, though, the contents of the final plan were largely in everyone's best interests. Middle View is better off because there is a comprehensive plan to direct development. Middle View's experience of both the positive and negative aspects of locality development strategies seems to echo in many localities around the world.

Locality development usually occurs in formal settings such as comprehensive planning efforts. To see locality development in action, attend a public meeting such as a local planning or zoning board, a long-range planning meeting for the school district, or a comprehensive planning workshop. Use the observational skills discussed in Chapter 7 to learn as much as you can about the locality development process and then reflect on it. In what ways was the meeting you observed inclusive? What groups or constituencies were conspicuous by their absence? What groups or constituencies seemed most likely to benefit from the meeting's results? In what ways were the results likely to benefit the focal community system? In what ways might the results be harmful?

Administration

Understanding and Mastery: Planning and evaluating programs, services, and operational functions

Critical Thinking Question: Both Human Services and Social Work emphasize clients' involvement in decisions affecting them. Over your career you will probably participate in many community development efforts as leader, professional representative, or community participant. What can you do to make sure that those who are directly affected by planning decisions have a real voice in the process?

Social Action

Social action efforts are based primarily on the conflict model of society and have an overt goal of improving the lot of those exploited by powerful economic and social interests. This is accomplished through strategies designed to (1) create social movements, (2) gather sympathy from decision makers and the general public, and (3) persuade the target group to stop their exploitative practices. Social action efforts involve imbalanced power relationships that must be changed; a change agenda (mission); specific measurable outcomes, strategies, and tactics to bring about change; a group of onlookers to influence; and a target group defined as adversaries. The outcome goals are changes in policies and practices that will benefit the exploited group. This is accomplished through swaying the weight of public opinion toward the desired change while simultaneously coercing the adversaries into making desired changes or capitulating.

The political historian Charles Tilly[1] asserted that social action and social movements are distinguished from other political actions by (1) a **campaign**, which he defined as "a sustained, organized public effort making collective claims on target authorities"; (2) a **social movement repertoire** of potential actions, including the "creation of special purpose associations, public meetings, solemn processions, vigils, rallies, petition drives, statements to and in the public media; and pamphleteering"; and (3) **WUNC.** or "participants' concerted representations of . . . **w**orthiness, **u**nity, **n**umbers, and **c**ommitment on the part of themselves and their constituents." WUNC causes target authorities and the general public to take the effort seriously.

WUNC is demonstrated by the following behaviors:

- *Worthiness* is often demonstrated by sober demeanor, neat clothing, and the presence of clergy, dignitaries, and mothers with children. It is also demonstrated by touching stories of unfair treatment of innocent people such as children, the elderly, hard-working families, and the like, as well as stories that cause potential supporters to identify themselves as possible victims.
- *Unity* is demonstrated through matching badges, banners, or costumes; marching in ranks; and singing or chanting.

- *Numbers* include headcounts at demonstrations, names on petitions, messages from constituents, filling streets or venues, and so on.
- *Commitment* includes braving bad weather, visible participation of the old and handicapped, resistance to repression (being beaten), ostentatious sacrifice (being imprisoned), and substantial contributions of time, money, reputation, and personal relationships.

Two main social action strategies include (1) using the adversarial nature of established political and judicial processes to bring about change and (2) using demonstrations, speeches, sit-ins, and public marches to raise awareness of injustice. Social activists generally prefer one of these broad strategies over the other. Differences in these two main strategies sometimes lead to conflict within social action organizations, but both have a place.

Campaign tactics support social action strategies and are chosen for their likelihood of changing the behavior of the target system, increasing public support for the social action group's agenda, or both.[2] Often several different tactics are used in a single place, or similar tactics may be used simultaneously in different venues. Your leadership team should choose the campaign tactics that are most likely to work in your focal community and its surrounding mezzo-systems.

Our focus is exclusively on social action tactics that include the use of legitimate third parties, bargaining and mediation, *ahimsa* or non-violent resistance, and non-violent coercion. A significant number of social activists have advocated violence, but for ethical and moral reasons it is not included here. Table 8.5 examines typical social action tactics.

Social action strategies and tactics are successful when the target group makes the changes demanded.

For a case in point, let's look at Smithville, where social action tactics have been used with some success. Smithville has a faith-based social action organization—an "organization of organizations"—and a secular membership-based organization. The SNO—made up of churches, community-based organizations, and a few individual members—works politely but firmly with government through yearly neighborhood forums that formulate and present various resolutions to city officials. The SNO's policy is to use the least coercive tactics possible to get desired results, and they've found that presenting a reasonable resolution to the appropriate official or agency usually works. At other times, leaders schedule private meetings with key officials and allow the officials to set time and place. In quiet, pragmatic sessions, activists use mediation tactics and listening skills to enable reasonable compromises. Sometimes bargaining occurs in which local activists agree to support city officials' broader agendas at the county, state, and national levels in return for official attention to neighborhood needs and concerns.

Negotiations around Community Development Block Grants[3] are a good example of this kind of bargaining and consensus building. Community block grants were originally designed to ensure that local municipalities rather than national agencies have the final say in where some federal tax dollars are spent. The process is rather convoluted, but in essence it is a redistribution program. Some of your federal taxes collected by the IRS are given back to the states, which then pass the money back to municipalities, who must file yearly applications justifying their needs and accounting for how the funds will be used. The law and regulations stipulate that neighborhood leaders must be engaged in the planning and proposal process. In struggling municipalities like Industrial City, block grants provide a much needed supplement to local tax dollars, so neighborhood leaders are called upon periodically by municipal authorities to participate in planning for the distribution of funds and to advocate with their congressional representatives for adequate program funding.

Table 8.5 Social Action Tactics

Tactic	Definition	When Used	Strengths	Weaknesses	Challenges
Legislative action	Works with legitimate authorities at appropriate levels of government for legislation or regulatory change.	When action group has access to and the support of relatively powerful decision makers.	Develops ongoing relationships with legitimate authorities; enables group to have credibility as "reasonable" people.	The social action group may be asked to compromise important principles for short-term gains.	Requires time, political savvy, and well-developed connections.
Dispute resolution: mediation or arbitration	Uses trained neutral parties to facilitate communication (**mediation**) or come to a binding agreement (**arbitration**).	When clear rules of engagement are in place and all parties agree to honor whatever decisions are made.	Often results in well-defined agreements and sometimes in improved mutual understanding.	Requires relative equality of power between the disputants.	Expensive for the social action group. Formal legal counsel is usually needed.
Collective bargaining	Representatives of two groups negotiate on behalf of their constituents. In **consensual bargaining**, each side plans to give up something. **Conflict bargaining** involves a "winner take all" approach.	Used to develop formal written contractual agreements. Results are taken back to constituencies for approval or rejection.	Works well when negotiators have equal power, the right to speak and act for a well-defined constituency, and influence with their constituencies once an agreement is reached.	Team members can put their own needs above those of their constituents. One or both partners can break the negotiated agreement.	The results of months of good-faith bargaining can be rejected by negative votes from the constituents.
***Ahimsa* (ahimsā; non-violent resistance)**	Non-violent tactics used primarily by Gandhi and Martin Luther King Jr.	Involves non-cooperation with oppressors and allowing oneself to be mistreated without fighting back.	Non-violence involves moral or soul power and succeeds when people are attuned to their moral consciences. It is especially effective when the abused non-cooperators are perceived to be innocent.	Violence used against non-violent protesters can be dramatic and lethal. Requires friendly media coverage and solid societal values that reject innocent suffering.	Remaining non-violent in the face of violence.
Coercive tactics	Tactics designed to force compliance by disrupting the normal flow of activities.	Used when peaceful approaches have failed and drama is needed.	Can force an immediate, conciliatory response.	Requires constant maintenance of effort. Conciliatory response short-lived.	Preventing escalation to violence on either side.

Source: Copyright © by Pearson Education, Upper Saddle River, NJ.

On the other hand, when officials become intransigent over particular issues, organizers initiate such tactics as letter writing campaigns, polite attendance at city council or school board meetings, and quiet gatherings (such as candlelight vigils) to call attention to the situation. While participants aren't afraid to make their voices heard, most are pragmatic enough to know that because they will need to negotiate with officials at other times, it's best to keep lines of communication open. Moreover, most participants find violence and confrontation morally repugnant; they are simply more comfortable using mediation and compromise than confrontation. A major strength of the SNO is that participants have learned to encourage residents to meet their own needs so that confronting government has become less necessary. Longtime members of the Smithville community say that SNO has made slow but sure progress on some issues identified in neighborhood meetings, such as rehabilitation of housing in a substantial sector of the neighborhood, but progress in other areas has been stymied by other city priorities and entrenched power. Promises have often been broken, such as improvements to storm drains and side streets. The SNO has had its ups and downs, such as maintaining momentum through personnel changes at the participating churches and withdrawal of key leaders due to illness, family, work, threats of reprisals, or discouragement. At other times, new people have taken up the effort and pushed forward in a wave-like movement.

In contrast to SNO, Smithville's secular membership-based organization (a local affiliate of the now defunct ACORN network) is based on a more confrontational approach. For instance, members stormed one city council meeting to demand block grant funding for the local community arts center (which had never received such funding in the past). They came late, talked loudly, cursed, wore dirty clothes, and insisted on breaking into the established agenda, ignoring protocol. Their leader, a paid outside organizer, had clearly prepped them to create a dramatic event. Although they were given an opportunity to present their case during the public portion of the meeting, they instead chanted their demands, then rose and left. Their attitude affronted city council members and the mayor, who simply shook their heads at the interruption, picked up their agenda, and continued. Although that particular campaign tactic did not work, some of the coercive tactics of the ACORN affiliate—such as marches, sit-ins, and disruption of public meetings—received rapid attention and led to the refurbishment of a desolate urban park, more protective lighting in dangerous areas, and swift punishment of abusive police officers. The choice of tactics depends on your leadership team's objectives. The consensus-based approach favored by organizations like SNO is appropriate if your organization wants to gain a respected voice at the table over the long haul, and if those in power are fairly likely to respond reasonably and humanely. More coercive tactics, like those of the ACORN affiliate, may be necessary when your goals are immediate, the situation is threatening to innocent people, or those in power are cruel or intransigent. Often a balance is needed. In fact, many successful social action efforts have two separate components: one composed of negotiators who are willing to compromise and another that specializes in the use of more coercive tactics.

Human Systems

Understanding and Mastery: Processes to effect social change through advocacy (e.g., community development, community and grassroots organizing, local and global activism)

Critical Thinking Question: What activities help an organization develop its WUNC (worthiness, unity, numbers, and commitment)? Why is WUNC so important in facilitating social change?

Assess your comprehension of Social Action Tactics by completing this quiz.

Popular Education: Implementation of Participatory Research

You will recognize many of the ideas in this section because popular education is the implementation phase of the participatory research model advocated in this text. The term is based on the phrase *educación popular*, commonly used in Latin America to refer to processes, demands, and results emerging from the efforts of oppressed and exploited people themselves.[4] Popular education as used here blends social action and relational organizing. On the social action side, such efforts are initiated by those who realize that they and their neighbors are victims of **oppression** (compliance in their own mistreatment) and feel called to awaken others. This awakening from **false consciousness** (the implicit belief that existing power relationships are inevitable or deserved) is called **consciousness raising**. The goal of consciousness raising is twofold. It makes people aware that the way things are is not a result of fate or a punishment for their individual faults and failings but is caused by social structures that keep the rich rich and the poor poor. A second goal is to encourage those who are newly awakened to stand up for themselves. This often means engaging in social action while at the same time engaging in mutual economic aid and other forms of self-help.

The locus of control in popular education begins and remains with the people who must live with its results. The community organizing cycle is controlled by a leadership team whose members are directly impacted. Popular education has characteristics of relational organizing and social action efforts, and sometimes even uses locality development techniques. However, it differs from these three approaches in that it is totally controlled by members of the focal system themselves. The term "popular" in "popular education" means "from the people" and refers to actions by ordinary people on their own behalf. Popular education efforts use consensus methods internally but often use social action tactics with those who exercise unjust power. Popular education as a systematic approach to community organizing is a reaction to (1) the top-down, condescending approaches of locality development; and (2) the tendency of some social activists to impose their own ideologies on target populations.

Human Systems

Understanding and Mastery: Processes to effect social change through advocacy (e.g., community development, community and grassroots organizing, local and global activism)

Critical Thinking Question: The core ideas of popular education are that relatively powerless people can overcome their belief that the "way things *are*" is the "way that things are *supposed* to be", thereby gaining the courage to actively create their own destinies. This is an important part of community organizing, but history frequently shows that in practice this simply means exchanging one form of tyranny for another. How can you play a role in such transformative learning without forcing your own political agenda on people?

Implementation of popular education approaches has both internal and external dimensions. As your leadership team uses the popular education approach, you will learn by doing and have a sense of "feeling the way" semi-blindly through the community organizing cycle.[5] One challenge will be learning how to use the natural gifts, acquired knowledge, and skills of participants in empowering and respectful ways. You may be surprised to find that you already have members with the knowledge and skills needed to implement action or can easily recruit them from within your focal system. Second, you will find that it's possible to use self-directed and connected learning processes to gain needed information to make wise decisions. Third, you will learn that there are few, if any, irreparable mistakes and that a conscientious process of action, reflection, and renewed action (**praxis**) can be very effective in overcoming seemingly impossible difficulties. Successful popular education initiatives are based on mutual trust, connected learning, and faith in the ultimate rightness of your mission.

Assess your comprehension of the Popular Education Ideology and Techniques by completing this quiz.

Mixing and Phasing the Implementation Strategies

Relational development, locality development, social action, and popular education are ideal implementation types that rarely succeed alone in a community milieu. In real life, they are often mixed and phased. For example, locality development organizations used to accept the old model of persuading people to adopt new technologies, which subsequently led to resentment, occasional misuse of land, and long-term loss of productivity. Locality development specialists today are more likely to engage local people from the beginning and respect local customs and local wisdom. While this is an improvement, there is still a tendency for development agencies to adopt a top-down approach, engage only established leaders, and fail to develop ongoing models of community engagement.

Although radical social movements exist and some have become more violent and have evolved into terrorism, the overall trend is for communities to initiate their own responses to human need and injustice through the process of participatory action and grassroots initiatives (popular education). These local efforts judiciously use both locality development and social action techniques to control the quality of life in their own communities.

Relationships are so ubiquitous that they are frequently overlooked, yet they are at the heart of effective communities and the basis of high quality of life. Relational development uses techniques developed over years of community organizing, the wisdom of feminist scholars, and an ethics of caring as a firm foundation for community change.

The challenge for community organizers is to use each implementation strategy appropriately within the context of mutual respect. The time has passed for community organizers to play the messiah role for other people. Connection, collaboration, and active participation of all involved are the keys to effective community change.

Planning and Evaluating

Understanding and Mastery: Skills to develop goals, and design and implement a plan of action

Critical Thinking Question: Review the decisions your leadership team has made about the variety of community organizing to be used, your mission, desired outcomes, programs and processes, and evaluation criteria, and then review the four types of implementation. Which type will your group probably use? What factors influenced your choice?

Training and Pilot Projects

Training prepares participants for action and may be formal or informal. In relational organizing, training is generally informal, specific, and done on an as-needed basis. For instance, some of those concerned about the ongoing well-being of Middle View are members of a local service club that is frequently asked to help with various community events. One such fund-raiser is a bicycle race along country roads sponsored by the local Chamber of Commerce that attracts cyclists and their families to the town. The service club is paid a fee to provide volunteers to direct the cyclists along the route and provide assistance, if needed. These volunteers are briefly trained on safety precautions and procedures by race organizers on the day of the race. Such brief training is built into almost every local event. In Smithville, the Neighborhood Watch has recruited responsible adults to watch for unusual or potentially criminal activity. These volunteers have been formally trained by the local police on strict protocols about what they can and cannot do. Training is usually infused in locality development processes. For instance, in the Middle View comprehensive planning process, the consultants taught participants to use connected learning methods through the way they organized small groups and facilitated their sessions. No one ever said, "We are going to teach you a process that will enable you to work together smoothly" but that is what happened. Social action efforts often engage in three kinds of training: (1) consciousness-raising about the implications of the issue, (2) training about personal safety and conduct during non-violent actions, and (3) specific tasks related to other tactics. Training is especially important in popular education because its strategies depend on an awareness of injustice on the one hand and the possibility of effective engagement on the other. Training efforts should include consciousness-raising within your focal community about injustice, provide insights into possible causes, and move toward possible responses. These reflective activities can be done through community meetings, workshops, theater and other arts, or any other techniques that enable people to share their life experiences and to begin to realize that what they thought were individual faults and personal troubles often have their roots in injustice. Members of your leadership team should participate as equals rather than as experts, share what you have learned and some hopeful approaches to action, but leave plenty of room for insights from others. The goal of training in popular education is to break through fear and hopelessness and to develop shared confidence, mutual trust, tools for taking action, and a willingness to risk.[6] **Pilot projects** are used to determine whether a strategy, tactic, or program process is likely to have the desired result. Such programs combine experimentation and training. Pilot projects are often used to (1) determine whether academic theories will work in practice, (2) test whether particular programs or processes will produce the desired outcomes, (3) compare two processes to one another on a variety of criteria, and (4) identify potential pitfalls. Pilot projects are commonly used in efforts where public money will be used and where successes are likely to be replicated in several locations. Pilot projects are not very common in relationship-based efforts, social action, or popular education because such undertakings tend to grow organically by trial and error rather than using a formal experimental method, usually lack funds for experimentation, often have participants who are convinced that their course of action is the right one and so do not see the need for a trial period, and are under time constraints to grow quickly.

Although radical social movements exist and some have become more violent and have evolved into terrorism, the overall trend is for communities to initiate their own responses to human need and injustice through the process of participatory action and grassroots initiatives (popular education). These local efforts judiciously use both locality development and social action techniques to control the quality of life in their own communities.

Relationships are so ubiquitous that they are frequently overlooked, yet they are at the heart of effective communities and the basis of high quality of life. Relational development uses techniques developed over years of community organizing, the wisdom of feminist scholars, and an ethics of caring as a firm foundation for community change.

The challenge for community organizers is to use each implementation strategy appropriately within the context of mutual respect. The time has passed for community organizers to play the messiah role for other people. Connection, collaboration, and active participation of all involved are the keys to effective community change.

Assess your comprehension of the Four Approaches to Implementation by completing this quiz.

Summary

In this chapter, you have continued to move through the community organizing cycle and have examined (1) four ideal types of planning, (2) how they apply to the varieties of community organizing approaches, and (3) examples of their application that your leadership team can generalize to its own situation. You then moved to the implementation phase, examined the four ideal types of implementation, explored the strategies used by each, and were challenged to determine the appropriate uses of each. The next chapter will complete the community organizing cycle by examining management and evaluation.

Assess your analysis and evaluation of this chapter's content by completing the Chapter Review.

Management and Evaluation

Jim West/Alamy

Chapter 9 is the conclusion of your journey through one circle of the community organizing cycle. Here you will examine some approaches to managing an emerging organization, monitoring its progress, periodically evaluating that progress, and summarizing its impact. Your passage through these final phases is highlighted in Figure 9.1, a reprise of Figure 5.1.

Chapter Outline

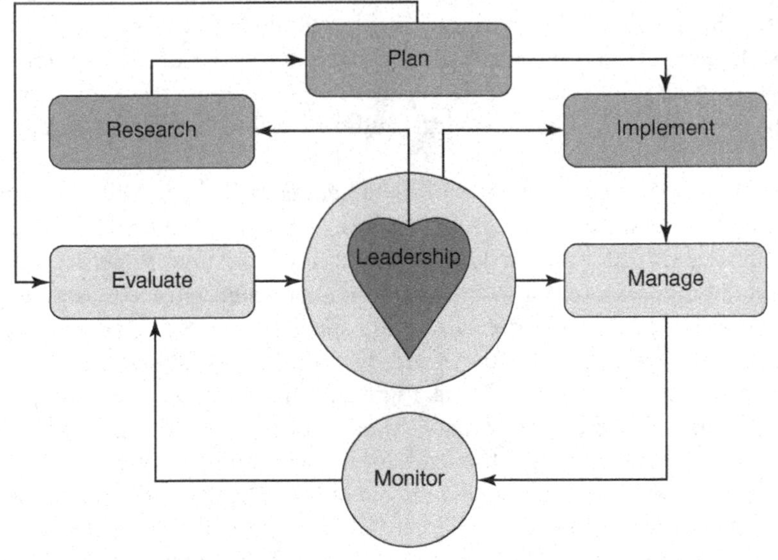

FIGURE 9.1
Management in the Community Organizing Cycle
Source: Copyright © by Pearson Education, Upper Saddle River, NJ.

Five Types of Management

As your effort moves from dream to reality you will find that there are more and more concrete daily tasks that must be addressed or things will become "messy." The term *management* is derived from the French word for "housekeeping," so a manager is someone who organizes and conducts the hourly and daily affairs of an organizational "household." Management involves deciding what needs to be done; getting it done in the best, most effective and efficient manner; and constantly evaluating results. While leadership involves broadly defining the vision and mission and guiding the whole community organizing cycle, management assures that tasks are accomplished properly and in good order. Not all leaders are good managers. Not all managers are good leaders. Each has its own role set of knowledge, skills, values, and behaviors. Effective management depends on the interaction of four major factors: the mission, the organizational structure, the tasks to be managed, and the strengths of the individual manager.

Table 9.1 compares five broad types of management found in the management literature and will enable you to compare and contrast their uses in community organizing.

Most of us are familiar with **bureaucratic management**, which has a pyramid-type organizational structure with a chief executive officer at the top who carries out the policies of the governing body within its day-to-day operations. Bureaucratic organizations usually are formally incorporated with boards of directors, by-laws, and clear operating procedures. The organization itself has legal status as a **fictitious person** and is treated as an autonomous actor for social and legal purposes. While the board of directors has ultimate authority for policy formation, the executive director and his or her management team are responsible for setting the direction of the organization and seeing that its organizational mission is accomplished. Work is highly structured. Communication is almost entirely top-down through non-interactive means, such as work orders, memos, and informational meetings. Collaborative decision making, if it exists, is only among top executives. The assumption is that upper management knows best and that other staff members, volunteers, and clients have little to offer. The manager is clearly the boss. Bureaucratic managers are generally very respectful of legal authority, try hard to please funding sources and regulatory agencies, resist innovation, and worry about the impact of change. They depend on legal authority, knowledge power, and productive power.

In community organizing, bureaucratic management is most frequently found in economic development–based efforts such as long-range planning where administrative authority often begins with an elected or appointed chief executive officer who initiates, manages, and monitors a formal planning and implementation process. In many instances, policies, procedures, and expectations are spelled out by law or regulation. The underlying assumption is that only those with technical expertise and established power are fit to manage day-to-day operations. Rigid administrative practices and procedures make it difficult for bureaucratic organizations to flexibly adapt, which explains why community organizers may have difficulty working with representatives of established bureaucracies—even when individual employees try to be helpful. Bureaucratic management works in organizations with career ladders where people work for pay and prestige. This management approach doesn't work well in voluntary organizations where people work to improve the quality of life for themselves or others, for personal satisfaction, or in service of God or others.

The characteristics of **relationship-based management** are presented in the second column. In community organizing, relationship-based management is frequently found in place-based organizing, self-help groups, and social innovation efforts. It was first

Table 9.1 Types of Management

Practice Variables	Bureaucratic Management	Relationship-based Management	Distributed Management	Participatory Management	Contingency Management
Variety of organizing	Entrepreneurship, collaboration	Place-based, relational, self-help, social innovation	Social movements	Community advocacy, mutual economic aid, social innovation	All
Task and process goals	To accomplish tasks within the guidelines of formal policies and procedures	To be a "learning organization" that uses the talents of everyone to benefit the target system	To be able to move quickly as opportunities present themselves	To be a self-directing organization that succeeds with little outside interference	To use management skills that best fit each situation
Assumptions about community structure and problems	Efforts must have clear hierarchies, written policies, clear procedures, and structures for accountability.	Mutual trust supersedes formal rules and hierarchies. Many good things are accomplished informally.	Existing organizations and methods support power imbalances and need to be supplanted.	The people who actually live or work in a community know best.	There are many ways to approach challenges, but usually one or two are best.
Focal management system	Formal corporation	Networks of relationships	Flexible, moving target: "cells"	Defined by the participants	Matched to the situation
Basic change strategy	Top-down imposition of new structures	Positive human relations that incorporate everyone's good ideas	Ideological purity	Internal consensus; team management	Whatever works best for desired outcomes
Characteristic tactics and techniques	Clear chain of command, memos, informational meetings, written orders	Consensus approaches with attention to smooth, personal relationships; celebrations; and emphasis on strengths	Informal discussions; individual decisions within an ideological frame	Team meetings, frequent communication, open discussion, and finalizing through consensus	Vary by situation
Assumptions about interests of focal system and subsystems	Upper management knows best	Caring is the basis of good decisions	Power must meet power	Teamwork improves the quality of life	Alert responses are best
Tasks to be managed	Ongoing services	Multiple community events	Campaigns	Linked efforts	All of these
Practitioner roles	Producer, coordinator, director, monitor	Facilitator, mentor, broker, cultural manager	Innovator, visionary, coordinator	All roles as appropriate	All roles as appropriate
Orientation toward authorities and power structures	Authorities are legally constituted. Managers ensure their rules are followed.	Authority must be earned by servant leaders.	Power structures are inevitably evil and must be changed.	Power and authority is democratically shared.	Ideally, power is shared, but sometimes managers must make decisions.
Typical types of power	Legal authority, Knowledge Power, and Productive Power	"Soul Power," relationship power	Charismatic, threat power or coercion, charisma	Productive power, relationship power, knowledge power	Whatever is appropriate to the task

Source: Copyright © by Pearson Education, Upper Saddle River, NJ.

presented in the business literature by Douglas McGregor in 1957, primarily as an alternative to the coercive "scientific management" of Frederick Taylor, which was used in twentieth-century manufacturing. McGregor outlined contrasting views of management he called Theory X and Theory Y.[1] McGregor's premise was that most managers have an intrinsic view of human beings that they use as a basis for their management style. Theory X managers view people as basically lazy, or even evil and believe that they must be forced to work. Theory Y managers believe that most people want to spend their time in worthwhile endeavors and find engaging work intrinsically rewarding. Relationship-based management evolved from Theory Y, which derived from the ground-breaking work of humanistic psychologists Carl Rogers[2] and Abraham Maslow.[3] Maslow's Hierarchy of Needs—with its emphasis on belonging, self-esteem, and self-actualization—is still a classic of relationship-based management.

Relationship-based management is based on mutual loyalty and trust. As much as possible, managers ensure that people's basic needs and needs for safety are met and that the organizational culture provides a sense of belonging. This, in turn, provides emotional space for everyone to attain self-esteem and self-actualization. Maslow's hierarchy and McGregor's Theory Y were largely based on the individualistic paradigm characteristic of the modern era (mid-twentieth-century America). Theory Y emphasized a warm, almost parent–child relationship between manager and subordinates. More recently, the paradigm has shifted toward the idea that satisfaction in work and life is based on networks of relationships, so today's relationship-based management emphasizes mutually supportive relationships among equals. Its core is the belief that trust, mutual respect, and friendship can overcome most external obstacles. Managers in relationship-based management resemble person-centered counselors. They cultivate an awareness of the needs and interests of individual participants and an understanding of the affective dimension of formal and informal subgroups, and they work to build a warm, fulfilling organizational culture. They also understand that organizations are more than their products and that everyone thrives in a climate of warmth and mutual understanding. They work in large and small ways to build such a climate and see themselves as servants of the focal system and of their colleagues. Relational management styles are most effective in voluntary organizations where participants' primary motivation is satisfaction, derived from interacting with compatible people while making a useful contribution to society.

Distributed management is based on systems thinking and spreads decision-making power, information, and authority for daily operations across the organization so that decision making occurs at the level most appropriate for rapid, appropriate action. This type of management has become more common in all kinds of organizations due to the growth of the Internet and effective long-distance conferencing tools. It has also been spurred by the need for rapid innovative decisions and the growth of the continuous quality improvement (CQI) movement in services and total quality management (TQM) movement in manufacturing.

A weakness of distributed management is that cohesion may be lost and "mission creep" may occur as local managers interpret broad organizational goals in different ways. Confusion can be a problem for active participants and outsiders, such as the media, and for target populations as well, because one manager may say one thing and another may say something else. Internal competition may occur as various managers assert their views and recruit followers. Solving these difficulties involves establishing clear lines of communication among managers with comparable duties and honest vertical communication among levels of management. Managers in distributed organizations must remember that clear communication is the heart of effective practice and not peripheral to it. Exchange relationships, information power, trust, and willingness to participate actively are extremely important. Distributed management is useful in community organizing efforts that have a wide geographic spread and varying local conditions. It gives local leaders opportunities to act quickly without waiting for orders from above that may be neither applicable nor effective.

Participatory management is associated with popular education.[4] It is the community organizing equivalent of TQM or CQI and the "learning organization" in the business world.[5] Participatory management is based on teamwork and a flattened chain of command. Important management functions are delegated to work groups, task forces, or teams composed of volunteers who have appropriate interests, knowledge, or skills that can be applied to a specific task. Unlike bureaucratic organizations that are stratified by job titles and privilege, team members are considered equals. Team leaders are democratically selected by team members for their skills in facilitating group interaction and their wisdom regarding the task (rather than by job title, status, or seniority). Unlike bureaucratic departments that tend to become permanent fixtures, teams are formed and disbanded according to organizational needs. Participatory management models are heavily outcome-oriented, their budgeting tends to be project-based rather than static, and reward structures are based more on teamwork than individual performance. Participatory management works best in new or growing organizations that begin with persons who embrace collaboration and connected learning—which is ideal for popular education initiatives. For those who enjoy working with others to actualize a common dream, participatory management is very empowering, makes good use of everyone's talents, and can be personally rewarding. On the other hand, participatory management does not work very well when imposed on an existing bureaucracy or in competitive organizational cultures that rely heavily on rewards for individual initiative, and it sometimes becomes unwieldy as organizations grow larger.

Members of participatory management teams must to be willing to both lead and follow and should have a thorough understanding of both the instrumental and expressive nature of group leadership. Members should be willing and able to assist others to discover their own talents and skills and to allow others (or the group as a whole) to take credit for their contributions. Relationship and productive power are particularly important in participatory management. Participatory management works best in popular education efforts. Although many locality development efforts and social action endeavors claim to embrace participatory management, this is an illusion because most are bureaucratically managed with power centered in a few individuals. If your effort is bureaucratic in nature, your leadership should be transparent about it. It is unwise to hide bureaucratic management with the trappings of participatory management because it leads to resentment. If an effort is bureaucratic (top-down) in nature, it should be honestly so.

Read the TQM blog to learn more about participatory management and total quality management. Consider how the principles of TQM used in business settings might be modified for use in a voluntary community organizing effort.

Contingency management theory developed because management scholars observed that each of the other theories worked sometimes and failed at other times. It asserts that appropriate management methods depend a great deal on the situation at hand, organizational goals, and the match between management approaches and the rest of the cycle.[6] Figure 9.2A is a simplified model of the Competing Values Framework, one of the most common models of contingency management.

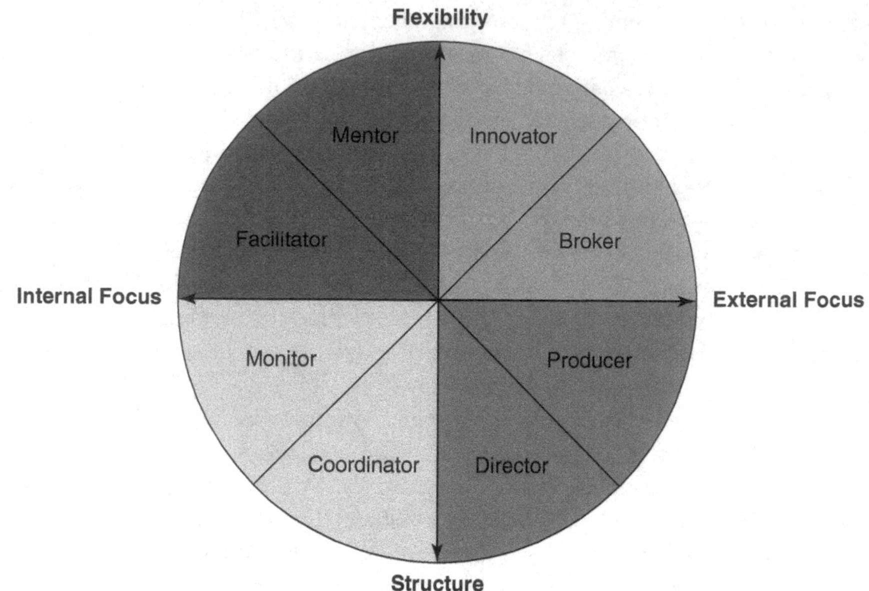

FIGURE 9.2 Characteristics of the Competing Values Framework
Source: Copyright © by Pearson Education, Upper Saddle River, NJ.

In Figure 9.2[7] The circle has a vertical continuum (Flexibility ←→ Structure), and a horizontal continuum (Internal Focus ←→ External Focus), which divide management tasks into four quadrants. The shading varies as it moves from right to left.

The **innovator** and **broker** tasks in the upper right-hand quadrant require flexibility and innovation, skills that are especially useful early in organizational life. The innovator role involves dealing with change and especially with adapting creative ideas and practices, while the broker role involves procuring human, financial, and material resources at a reasonable cost and in a timely manner. For example, in its infancy, the juvenile runaway prevention program in Middle View required the ability to quickly respond to changes, the ability to adapt existing models to the Middle View situation, and skill in cooperating with stakeholders.

The **producer** and **director** tasks in the lower right-hand quadrant involve providing excellent services and marketing them on a consistent basis. **Producers** make sure that external undertakings are accomplished. The specifics vary among the varieties of community organizing. For instance, in Smithville, several members of the Smithfield Neighborhood Organization (SNO) provided the hot dogs, buns, chips, and charcoal; arranged for grills; obtained permission from homeowners and landlords; and held a series of mini-block parties to strengthen friendships among neighbors. Another SNO member worked on community advocacy goals by coordinating recruitment and transportation for ten community members who attended a City Council meeting to request that attention be given to neighborhood storm drains.

Directors make sure that participants know what is expected of them. For instance, SNO oversees the community crime watch. One of SNO's members has been given the task of crime watch manager. His task is to make sure that every crime watch volunteer obtains the proper legal clearances and knows how and where to perform his or her duties.

The two quadrants on the left (the internal foci) support the external mission by stabilizing internal activities. The **coordinator** and **monitor** roles in lower left-hand quadrant emphasize the ability to make sure that routine processes run smoothly and efficiently and that records are accurate and easily accessible. The lower left-hand quadrant focuses on the flow of activities and accurate record keeping. **Coordinators** balance time, people, and material resources to make sure that work gets done. For instance, Middle View has an annual local history day that celebrates the past, bringing together several history-related organizations such as storytellers, re-enactors, folk musicians, and artisans for an all-day event attracting tourists from throughout the region. The coordinator is responsible for identifying and registering participants, assigning them locations and time slots, arranging for public restrooms and rest areas, assigning the set-up and take-down crews, making sure attendance records are kept, and handling any emergencies that may occur. **Monitors** can be very important in newly funded programs that are being assessed by regulatory agencies and evaluated by outside funding sources and auditors. Monitors use record keeping tools to measure activities and to ensure that performance is within desired quality standards. Monitors must pay close attention to details. They handle routine data, compile statistical information, interpret the meaning of evaluative research, compile periodic reports, and make sure that these reports are filed promptly and properly. Poor monitoring and reporting can have serious consequences. Many years ago now members of the Board of Directors of the Industrial City Community Action Agency were accused of malfeasance not because any funds had actually been embezzled but because two funding streams were improperly blended.

The **facilitator** and **mentor** roles in the upper left-hand corner focus on supervisory tasks including the maintenance of discipline, morale, and professionalism. The **facilitator** makes sure that people work together well with a minimum of conflict and a maximum of mutual respect, is often responsible for guiding meetings and building consensus, and is crucial in participatory research and popular education efforts. **Mentors** provide guidance to volunteers and employees, provide feedback on performance, and demonstrate expected behaviors by direct teaching and by example.

Contingency theory reminds us that all of these roles are necessary in smooth-running organizations and that the "art" of management is in discerning the proper balance among them.

Administration

Understanding and Mastery: Managing organizations through leadership and strategic planning

Critical Thinking Question: Contingency management theory is based on the idea that effective management is a product of several factors. Think about your focal community system, your leadership team, the management milieu, and the sort of situations you are likely to encounter. Review the competing values framework. How are each of the roles likely to "play out" in your organizing effort?

Assess your comprehension of the Competing Values Framework by completing this quiz.

Planning, implementation, and management approaches often seem to be matched on important dimensions Figure 9.3 shows some likely relationships among these functions.

Other variables that will impact your management choices include the following:

- **The length of time your organization has been in existence.** Older organizations tend to have established policies and procedures, so a top-down bureaucratic approach is appropriate both internally and externally. This is also true of

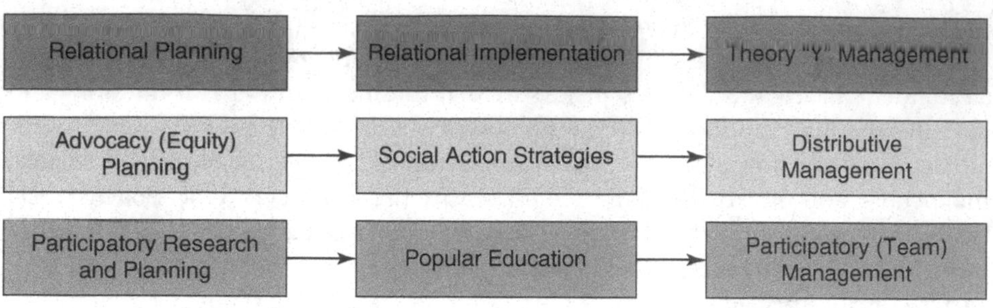

FIGURE 9.3 Relationships among Planning, Implementation, and Management Functions

Source: Copyright © by Pearson Education, Upper Saddle River, NJ.

organizations, such as local governments, that have legally defined purposes, policies, and procedures. Newer organizations that must collaborate with established organizations or are subject to bureaucratic regulations may need to adopt bureaucratic management styles to manage required record keeping and interface with bureaucratic sponsoring organizations.

- **Its mission, purpose, and context.** Participatory and relational management are more appropriate when issues are complex, many viewpoints are needed, and no single individual or small group is likely to have true expertise. Bureaucratic or authoritarian management is appropriate in emergency situations when it's important to act quickly without much debate. Distributed management is suitable when portions of the organization are isolated from one another, conditions vary across geography or among focal issues, or the organization is vulnerable to dismemberment from hostile forces. Contingency management is a process rather than a philosophy and frees you to do whatever is needed.
- **Expectations of participants.** Some participants find it easy to take responsibility for their own work and enjoy working with others to create something. Others are used to being told what to do, find it hard to believe in their own freedom, and fear or resent being required to take responsibility for the venture. A helpful rule of thumb in management is that often it's easier to change organizational structures than to change people's personalities and behavioral preferences.
- **The personal style and philosophy of the manager.** Some managers believe the Theory X position that most people are lazy and need direction. Such people are often authoritarian in nature and are uncomfortable if they are not clearly in charge. They feel hypocritical or hostile when expected to adopt participatory or relationship-based management styles and frequently communicate these underlying attitudes to those who work with them. Such attitudes are common in established bureaucracies, government offices, large agencies, founder-type social entrepreneurship, and volunteer efforts that are based on a military-style hierarchy such as volunteer fire departments and neighborhood watch groups. In such cases, everyone will probably be more comfortable if managers can exercise clear authority. Other managers truly enjoy collaboration and teamwork, and both their colleagues and they thrive in participatory or relationship-centered management.

Administration

Understanding and Mastery: Managing organizations through leadership and strategic planning

Critical Thinking Question: Five ideal types of management used in community organizing were discussed. Which type will your group probably use? What factors led to your choice?

There is no "correct" management style, only a correct approach in particular situations. Management decisions must be based on what is needed given the talents, skills, and motivations of the people available. You are now on the cusp of completing a single revolution of the community organizing cycle. By now you have probably realized that the cycle is rarely, if ever, completed once and for all—it is a continuing process.

Assess your comprehension of the Five Types of Management by completing this quiz.

Evaluation

Most people think of evaluation as something that occurs at the end of a process, like a final exam. Others think of evaluation as a "hoop you have to jump through" to obtain or retain the resources necessary to justify continuing your work. Still others think of evaluation as an accounting process in which practitioners record the number of services rendered, with little or no measurement of whether these activities had positive results. Although evaluation does fill these functions in community organizing, its major purpose is to ensure (1) that your effort remains on track with its mission and values and (2) that you accomplish desirable outcomes for the focal community system.

When you examine Figure 9.1 closely you will note that evaluation is linked directly to both management and planning. This is because effective evaluation allows you to determine whether you have done what you set out to do. This is based on the logical premise that once your mission, values, and outcomes are clear, then *every single activity should be chosen in light of its ability to ensure that the desirable outcomes are being implemented and managed with them in mind.* Thus, your program planning efforts should include an evaluation plan (note the double arrow between evaluation and planning in Figure 9.1). Evaluation requires the development of **formative evaluation plans**, implementation of **continuous quality improvement processes** that ensure stakeholder satisfaction, and creation of a **management information system** (record keeping system) that ensures that the information collected (1) accurately measures progress toward the desired outcomes and (2) provides easily retrieved and replicable information for reporting purposes and a procedure for **summative evaluations** for external stakeholders. Let's look at each in turn.

Creation of **formative evaluation plans** is part of the planning phase of the organizing cycle (which is why planning is linked to evaluation in Figure 9.1) and is linked directly to the selection of outcome goals that measure positive changes in the quality of life for those within your focal system. Outcome goals were discussed thoroughly in the planning section of Chapter 8 so here we will concentrate on how you use these goals and measurable objectives in the evaluation phase of the organizing cycle. Evaluation begins early in the implementation phase through intentional periodic reviews called **formative evaluation** that your leadership team should conduct periodically to determine if your effort is on track—based on its organizing mission, its values and outcome goals, and whether the processes being used are the best available. As a general rule, formative evaluation should be frequent during the early weeks and months of an endeavor and done less often as the effort stabilizes. Formative evaluation is done by the whole leadership team or by their designees and should be based primarily on accurate quantitative data coupled with observation, informal interviews, and focus groups. Key questions include the following:

- What is our status in achieving the outcome goals? Will they be achieved on time?
- If so, what can we do to make sure this trajectory continues?

- If not achieved on time, were they the right goals to begin with?
- If so, what is needed to get them back on track? What additional resources do we need?
- If not the right goals, is there something we missed in the initial assessment, or have conditions changed in some way?
- Should we revisit the planning process and re-think the mission, outcome goals, or priorities? (Note: Such a radical decision should be made very carefully. Many organizing efforts fail because the leadership team gives up too easily or too often completely re-thinks its mission and outcome goals.)
- If the mission and outcomes are still desirable, are the current processes working well enough? If so, they probably should be left alone. If not, you should briefly return to the research, planning, and implementation stages of the cycle to identify issues and make necessary changes.

Each formative analysis with recommendations should be presented to the leadership team. Don't assume that consensus by your leadership team will automatically spread to all of your stakeholders. If changes are made, they should be introduced carefully to both internal and external stakeholders so there is "buy-in." Remember that some people respond well to change while others resist it. Because community organizing efforts depend heavily on the good will of volunteers and the general public, plenty of time and energy should be given to getting all constituents on the same page if major changes are made.

In many ways evaluation in all varieties of community organizing is a process of continuously discerning and meeting the needs of your focal community system. In this section you will explore how concepts from **total quality management** (TQM) and **continuous quality improvement** (CQI) can be applied to evaluation. TQM was originally developed after World War II by W. Edward Deming and Joseph Juran, who assisted the Japanese in rebuilding their shattered manufacturing sector.[8] Their ideas worked so well that they were adopted by manufacturing operations around the world, becoming especially popular in the 1990s. These ideas continue in various forms. Because they were originally designed for manufacturing, TQM concepts and particularly their emphasis on statistically based quality control do not quite fit service organizations, and so beginning in the 1980s, leaders in human services, education, and government began adapting TQM concepts to their work and changed the name to CQI. Both TQM and CQI share several common characteristics including an emphasis on pleasing internal and external customers; continually measuring outcomes; employee, volunteer, and customer involvement in the process; a flattened decision-making hierarchy; and responsive changes based on feedback. These characteristics make the quality movement very compatible with the participatory processes used in the community organizing cycle.

CQI emphasizes "**customer** delight and satisfaction." Although the very term "customer" with its connotation of buying and selling seems far from the intent of most community organizing efforts, it really means those who benefit from your efforts. Like other organizations, community organizing efforts have both external and internal customers. Your **external customers** depend on the variety of community organizing you have chosen and include those within your focal community system who will directly benefit from your efforts; external funders; the micro-, mezzo-, and macro-systems that are enhanced or challenged by your actions; and the general public, which benefits from an improved quality of life for some or all of its members. Your most important **internal customers** are your volunteers who gain personal satisfaction and empowerment from their participation. Staff members are considered internal customers; regulators are considered external customers. CQI begins with the identification of both external and internal customers and their needs, a process you pursued during the research and planning phases of the community organizing cycle. Providing readily available, accurate data for immediate decision making and more formal periodic evaluation is accomplished by the development of a usable **management information system** (MIS). Involvement of the leadership team, volunteers, supporters, and especially members of the focal community system is at the heart of the community organizing cycle you have been studying, and this involvement can be powered by the techniques used for the implementation of CQI. CQI emphasizes flattened management, meaning that it emphasizes participatory, distributed, and contingency management over bureaucracy. Finally, CQI emphasizes the careful but prompt implementation of suggested changes derived from feedback and the continuous nature of the evaluation process. All of these factors make CQI very compatible with community organizing processes.

Over many years, organizations that have used TQM and CQI have learned when and how it works best as well as factors that cause it to fail. Effective CQI begins with the leadership team who must clearly understand its principles and philosophy and explicitly agree to support it. Many CQI efforts have failed because upper management (in your case the leadership team) has insisted on overruling the findings of CQI teams. Your leadership team must be willing to trust the process. Here are some suggestions for successful implementation.

- Quality improvement efforts sometimes fail when they are imposed on ongoing, established organizations, so be sure that their principles and practices are built into your community organizing effort from its beginning.
- Make sure that everyone on your leadership team understands the philosophy and processes that you will be using. Use these processes from the very beginning of your efforts so that they become an intrinsic part of your organizational culture.
- The leadership team is responsible for identifying issues that need attention and developing them. Make sure you do not form overlapping teams whose decisions could contradict one another.
- Choose teams carefully with an eye to having a mixture of skills and approaches. Make sure that participants understand and buy into the concept and have the communication skills needed to work together well. Encourage teams to select their own leadership based on participants' skills and interests rather than on job titles or social status. Encourage them to rotate leadership depending on which approach to a particular goal is needed.
- Provide training in group dynamics and in the technical knowledge and skills needed for the specific tasks.
- Enable participants to identify their own skill sets, emphasize the equality and importance of everyone's efforts, and analyze the quality and quantity of their contributions. Some supervisors feel threatened by this equality, and their fears must be recognized and acknowledged.
- Trust your teams. Once you have carefully built the teams and trained them, let them do their work with as little interference from the top as possible. Provide them with sensitive information if it is needed for good decision making.
- Implement your teams' suggestions or explain why their suggestions are not feasible or why they may have to be delayed. Many organizations delegate tasks to teams, accept their reports, and then fail to implement their suggestions without telling

team members why—which causes frustration and demotivation for those directly involved and for those reluctant to waste their time.

- Give credit. Always give credit to individuals and teams who contribute good ideas. This is especially important in community organizing because it depends so heavily on personal satisfaction rather than remuneration. Likewise, leaders should never claim credit for something that has actually been generated by team effort.
- Measure effectiveness. Teams should be encouraged to develop benchmarks or key performance indicators connected to their suggestions so that once the suggestions are implemented, their effectiveness can be easily monitored and adjusted as needed.
- Enjoy the process. CQI can enhance community organizing efforts as it builds camaraderie and empowers individuals, teams, and the whole organizing effort.

Evaluation is related most directly to long range planning and begins with the creation of an MIS that will enable your leadership team to guide the organizing effort, make adjustments as needed, and measure your progress toward your desired outcomes. The term *management information system* may conjure up visions of complex computer programs, endless data, and complex analytical tasks, but it actually means the way you collect, store, retrieve, and collate data to measure progress toward carefully chosen outcomes. Community organizing efforts typically have little money and less time, so your management information system should follow the KISS (keep it simple, stupid) principle and should be designed for both ease and accuracy. The following set of questions will help the leadership team (or a sub-group charged with the creation of the MIS) with its design.

Administration

Understanding and Mastery: Planning and evaluating programs, services, and operational functions

Critical Thinking Question: Continuous quality improvement requires that managers constantly take the desires of internal and external "customers" into consideration. Identify your project's internal and external customers. What factors will your leadership team need to monitor in order to ensure their ongoing satisfaction?

- What are the outcome goals from our comprehensive plan? What criteria have we set for measuring success?
- What are the specific activities we will use to bring about the desired outcomes?
- What information will we need to gather on each of these activities to determine what is being done and how well we are doing it?
- Which audience(s) will need the information? What information will each audience need? (Note: The audience will not only include your leadership team but also your focal community, volunteers, mezzo-systems that regulate your activities, and funding sources. Be sure to note the specific information each of these audiences requires.)
- When (at what intervals) will we need the information?
- What human, technological, and financial resources will we need to facilitate data collection?
- How will we collect the data? (Note: See Chapter 7 and Appendix A for full coverage of research techniques.)
- How will we store, retrieve, and collate the information?
- Who will manage the process? To whom will they be accountable?
- How and to whom will the information be released?

Explore the Free Management Library to learn more about management information systems and other management and evaluation tasks. Consider what kind of simple but adequate management information system might be needed by a voluntary community organizing group.

The answers to these questions should be used to create a written document that will include flow charts and other visual tools and that covers the entire MIS. This should be presented to the leadership team (the governing body) for approval, an implementation timeline developed, and responsibilities assigned.

Since community organizing leaders tend to be visionaries and innovators rather than "detail people," those responsible for the MIS will have to be carefully recruited for systems thinking skills, attention to detail, and commitment to organizational goals. Ideally, they should also have some skills in facilitation and mentoring so that they can explain the record keeping process clearly to non-technical people. Those responsible for the MIS implementation phase are charged with creation of specific processes and procedures of data gathering, recording, storage, and retrieval and should have the ability to analyze and simplify systems, identify needed information, create forms, and work with computers and databases (or create manual systems that can be easily computerized).

Pilot projects should be used before training on full implementation of your MIS to work out any glitches in the record keeping system. Because many community organizing volunteers and paid staff members are action oriented, find record keeping odious, and have a tendency to skimp on paperwork, training is a *very* important part of MIS implementation. Experience shows that you can increase buy-in and reduce time and frustration by thoroughly training staff and volunteers to: (1) understand the importance of record keeping, (2) see how everyone fits into the process, and (3) handle the record keeping details through supervised practice. Give people the opportunity to formulate questions and present them to you ahead of time so that you can be sure that the content of the training session meets their needs.[9] If at all possible, training should be tailored to individual learning styles. Some people learn technical skills best if they can participate in a highly structured, time-limited format where they follow an instructor who demonstrates the process, gives time for practice, allows time for shadowing an experienced person, and then gives opportunities for more and more complicated scenarios. Learners who learn technical processes slowly or become anxious under perceived time pressure may prefer to be shown a process and then given time to practice it on their own. Technical training usually works best for everyone when learners can immediately apply what they have learned before the details get lost. Once the MIS is implemented, changes should be made infrequently because constantly changing forms and processes frustrates volunteers and staff and complicates the data retrieval process.

Management of an MIS is a daily challenge for most organizations and requires a delicate balance of skills. MIS managers must have skills in coordinating and monitoring and make these functions a priority without allowing them to impede the organizing mission. MIS managers must be well organized and able to retrieve needed data quickly and organize it coherently to use in various kinds of formative and summative evaluations.

Information Management

Understanding and Mastery: Compiling, synthesizing, and categorizing information; disseminating routine and critical information to clients, colleagues or other members of the related services system that is provided in written or oral form and in a timely manner; using technology for locating and evaluating information; using technology to create and manage spreadsheets and databases.

Critical Thinking Question: Review your organizational mission and outcomes. Develop measures of success. Outline the major components of a management information system that will measure your progress. What challenges did you face in completing this task?

Assess your comprehension of Formative Evaluation Techniques and Practices by completing this quiz.

Summative evaluations are the external face of your organization and are commonly created to satisfy demands for accountability from stakeholders such as funding sources, government officials, regulatory agencies, and members of the general public. Although each of these audiences requires accurate information, each may need and want to know different things about your efforts. You will find that evaluation is a painful chore if you have to create separate evaluations for each of these stakeholders from scratch each time you have a request for results, so the wisest course is to create a master template and database that can be used whenever an evaluation is requested. Some of major recommendations for evaluation are as follows:

- Develop an evaluation plan or template that can be used for nearly every required evaluation and provide it to major funders or bankers.
- Carefully document the information found in your plan so that it can be easily retrieved as needed.
- Record enough information in a clear form so that someone outside the organization could easily use it to complete a similar evaluation and obtain the same results. (Note: This is the principle of reliability in social science research that was discussed in Chapter 7.)

Many organizations find it helpful to prepare a standard evaluation format with some of the information (sometimes referred to as "boiler plate") already filled in. Such a format can be easily and quickly modified for specific reports.

1. Title page (name of the organization, date)
2. Table of Contents
3. Executive summary (one-page, concise overview of findings and recommendations)
4. Purpose of the report
5. Background of your organization
    a. Organization description and history
    b. Product, service, or program description
        i. Description of the community need that is being met
        ii. Mission, vision, and values (based on your strategic plan)
        iii. Outcomes and performance measures (based on your strategic plan)
        iv. General description of how the product, service, or program works (based on your implementation model)
        v. Staffing (based on your implementation and management models)
6. Questions that will be answered through the evaluation process
7. Methodology
    a. Types of data and information collected
    b. How data and information was collected.
    c. How data and information were analyzed
    d. Cautions about limitations of the findings or conclusions and their use
8. Interpretations and conclusions
9. Recommendations

Appendices: content of the appendices depends on the goals of the evaluation report, such as:

a. Instruments used to collect data and information
b. Data (presented in tabular or other format)
c. Testimonials, or comments made by users of the product, service, or program
d. Case studies of users of the product, service, or program
e. Any related literature such as brochures, research studies, internal reports, and external evaluation statements

So far, you have examined general evaluation principles and practices that can be modified to apply to any community organizing process. Table 9.2 provides a brief view of the role evaluation plays in each of the organizing strategies.

Table 9.2 Evaluation for Each Organizing Strategy

Strategy	Leadership Team	Mission	Desired Outcomes	MIS	Quality Indicators	Summative Evaluation
Place-based Relational	Open group of committed people who embrace the focal community.	Improved quality of life in a delimited geographic area.	Residents have their basic life needs, safety requirements, belonging, and life satisfaction needs met over the long haul.	Statistics on income, housing, educational levels, etc.; life satisfaction measures; family stability; intangibles.	Building on existing assets and new opportunities; practical caring for one another.	No real summation; the process of community caring is continual and lifelong.
Social Innovation	Individual or small group committed to a particular issue or concern; sometimes becomes a formal board of directors.	Improve aspects of life for a specific target group (other than themselves).	Members of the target group have their lives improved in specific, measurable ways.	Successes are measured on achievement of consumer-based outcomes; both quantitative and qualitative measures.	Program changes geared to improvement of statistical results; incorporation of improved standards of practice learned from similar efforts.	Yearly cumulative reports or final report at the end of a funding cycle.
Mutual Economic Aid	Circles of people committed to helping one another achieve economic self-sufficiency.	Improved economic well-being.	Measurable economic improvement for all participants.	Increased income, better nutrition, increased capital assets, savings.	Pay back rates for loans, mutual accountability for use of funds, accurate accounting.	Usually summarized on at least a yearly basis, but generally ongoing from year to year.
Self-help	Individual or team who recruit others with similar needs.	Support, understanding, and advocacy for one another in difficult times.	Peace of mind during times of crisis; satisfaction of helping others.	Formal records not usually kept, but stories are prized.	Not usually done; one major weakness of this approach.	Often not done; many self-help groups disintegrate.
Community Advocacy	Leadership team comprised of organizational representatives or individuals who are selected (or self-selected) to represent focal system concerns.	Obtain needed resources; fight exploitation by powerful interests; demand local voice.	Resources so focal community system thrives.	Measures of increased resources or improved quality of life; prevention of community exploitation.	Flexible choices of action tactics; changes as needed.	At end of a specific "campaign."
Collaboration	Agency representatives.	Join together to increase client services or share resources.	Enough resources for client needs and agency survival.	New programs; agency funding levels; regime support for service sector.	Willingness to work together, minimum of competition and in-fighting.	Often required by funders on a yearly basis.

Source: Copyright © by Pearson Education, Upper Saddle River, NJ.

Assess your comprehension of Evaluation Processes in Various Types of Community Organizing by completing this quiz.

Remember that success in community organizing of any kind is not really possible without intentional evaluation that others can measure. In today's atmosphere of accountability, if something has not been written in measurable terms, most policy makers do not believe it has actually been done. The evaluation process enables participants to assess the past to build the future. It is crucial in effective organizing, and so it is ironic how many organizing efforts fail to effectively evaluate their programs.

Administration

Understanding and Mastery: Managing organizations through leadership and strategic planning

Critical Thinking Question: In this section techniques for formative and summative evaluation were discussed in some detail. What challenges will your organization face in implementing a systematic yet doable evaluation process?

Summary

This chapter completes your study of the community organizing cycle that began with an emphasis on management approaches and management skills that you will find useful in the day-to-day work of community organizing. The cycle then ends with evaluation techniques that you will find useful for continuing quality improvement and for accountability to your organization's stakeholders. Remember the cycle is just that—a cycle that you can and should revisit frequently as you engage in particular community organizing endeavors and especially as you begin new efforts throughout your professional life.

Explore more information on evaluation and evaluation techniques. Consider how you will link your desired outcomes to accepted evaluation techniques.

Assess your analysis and evaluation of this chapter's contents by completing the Chapter Review.

Organizational Structures, Budgeting, and Funding

hkeita/Shutterstock

This chapter will help your team to decide which organizational structure is right for your purposes, make responsible budget decisions, and raise needed funds.

Chapter Outline

Organizational Structures

Sometimes the best strategy is to insist that existing institutions do their jobs or obey legal and moral laws through **advocacy or social action**. In such cases, you should create a community advocacy effort or small social movement designed to last only as long as it takes to accomplish your goals. For instance, when many Smithville residents became aware of an up-tick of criminal activity, police corruption, and racial profiling, their first response was to go to a Smithville Neighborhood Association (SNO) meeting to complain. The SNO, in turn, appointed some of the most vocal protesters to a task force charged with addressing these issues. The task force identified a significant number of residents with similar concerns, did research on the nature and extent of the problem, decided that the police department should be held accountable, and developed some social action tactics to force the department to listen and act responsibly. These tactics included neighborhood rallies, media awareness campaigns, meetings with the mayor and police commissioner, and insistence on a state-level investigation of the police department. They campaigned to the mayor and city council for a change of top police leadership and kept up these demands over a period of months. In a more consensual vein, they sought out police officers who were known to be honest and helpful and included them in brainstorming sessions about how to improve the neighborhood. They contacted their state and national legislators for help with funds for community policing. Slowly, with pressure from the community, the media, and honest political leaders—as well as some outside resources—things began to change for the better. When the advocacy group was no longer needed, a police–community relations board made up of citizen-activists was created to address specific issues as they arise. While far from perfect, the Industrial City police force is much improved, and inner-city neighborhoods, such as Smithville, are significantly safer places to live.

Some initiatives are best served by **quasi-groups** (people who are not really sure they are a group) or associations (loosely tied, very open organizations of like-minded people; to refresh your memory, see Chapter 2 for definitions). Middle View, for instance, has a loosely knit group of community leaders (i.e., catalysts) that individually, in small groups, and occasionally in **ad hoc committees** (committees that exist only for a short time and for a limited purpose), keep watch over Middle View and donate time and energy to whatever is needed to make it an enjoyable, safe, and pleasant place to live. Without these people, Middle View would have no flowers in its public gardens, no docents for its historical museum, no seasonal festivals, and no tourist train. These catalysts generally know one another or know of one another. They communicate face to face, on the telephone, and on Facebook. They use connected learning to build on good ideas. Although they individually participate in various formal organizations, they have no interest in becoming an organization themselves. Such informal leadership networks exist in every cohesive focal community. Their very lack of formal structure has the advantage of freedom and flexibility, enabling caring people to do what is needed without worrying unduly about mediating internal conflicts, getting permission from government or other authorities, being bound by unreasonable regulations, or being hampered by the need to pay staff. The disadvantage of informal associations is that they are like the wind: you can see the results of their efforts but they have no discernable form, substance, or clear lines of authority and accountability. Since they do not exist in a legal sense, they cannot handle money, own property, hire staff, or perform other business functions on their own. When they become involved in an organizing effort that requires purchase of property, loans, grants, capitalization, paid staff members, or the other accoutrements of formal organizations, they have to choose between adoption by a pre-existing organization or else becoming an independent legal entity. We will discuss these options next.

If your leadership team is committed to addressing a particular social need, you may want to consider contacting an existing organization with a comparable mission, sharing your ideas, and asking them to adopt your initiative as one of their own programs. Adoption can be especially useful if there is community endorsement for your initiative but you lack the time, energy, money, or support base needed to create a whole new organization. Adoption can save time, energy, and costs, as well as provide an already established support base and reputation, central management, and accounting structures. Adoption has the advantage of circumventing the arduous, complex, and somewhat expensive incorporation process and can provide access to existing infrastructure such as websites and links, facilities, and insurance protection. It can also avoid duplication of effort and unnecessary competition. Almost any organization can be a suitable adoptive partner as long as your missions are compatible. In appropriate circumstances faith-based organizations, existing non-profits, public agencies, for-profit businesses, or collaborations among several different existing organizations can all be suitable adoptive partners.

While on first glance adoption can seem like a good choice, it can lead to **cooption** or loss of control over your organizational mission. Cooption occurs when the goals and mission of your initiative are taken over by the adopting organization for its own purposes, so that your original mission is mutated beyond recognition to match an existing program or becomes lost in a maze of other priorities. Cooption nearly occurred with the runaway prevention program in Middle View. Because the County Child Protective Services (CPS) was charged with the care of runaways and other status offenders, the community catalysts approached them for help with their proposal to provide community-based emergency housing, crisis intervention, and mediation within Middle View itself. They invited the CPS director to a community meeting to get his help with their plans. Instead of listening to their perception of community needs, he discouraged them from initiating their own program, reassured them that his agency was already effectively handling the problem, and urged them to invest the money they had already raised into the CPS's runaway shelter (which was located 40 miles away and provided none of the desired intervention and follow-up services) and to put their energy into finding more local foster parents. Those attending were very disappointed. They had no interest in supporting the existing shelter since it did not meet their goal of enabling teens to remain in their own hometown and school, it separated them from their families, and it had no comprehensive plan for follow-up. After the "adoption" meeting community interest in the whole project waned, but the catalysts were determined. They met again privately, coalesced into a leadership team, and decided to develop their own locally based nonprofit organization which has successfully served teens and their families for nearly four decades.

The balance between accepting much-needed support and giving in to cooption is particularly tricky for self-help and support groups. For instance, care providers can sometimes be very important allies and sponsors while at other times they can disguise selfish corporate interests. For example, Industrial City (home to the Smithville neighborhood) has a very active local National Alliance on Mental Illness (NAMI) group that provides a drop-in center, advocacy, informal case management, and support services for dozens of mentally ill individuals and their families throughout the city. Each year in October, the Industrial City NAMI (IC-NAMI) sponsors a mental health awareness week with public events, screenings, candlelight vigils, and workshops. Because IC-NAMI is an all-volunteer group, it has very little money and must depend on sponsors for its programs and projects like Mental Health Awareness Week. Over the years, the week's sponsors have included the local hospital that has inpatient and partial hospitalization units, a large non-profit mental health agency with many county and social security contracts, and several pharmaceutical companies that manufacture psychotropic medications. On the one hand, IC-NAMI has been grateful for their financial support and has valued its collaborative relationships. On the other hand, over the same time period, many IC-NAMI members have been rightly concerned about the low quality of care given by the hospital and the mental health agency, problems with transitions between inpatient and outpatient care, general lack of follow-up, overreliance on medications with serious side effects, and the use of warehouse-type group home care rather than independent living arrangements. These conflicts with the mental health providers and sponsors eventually caused the IC-NAMI Board to decide that it was untenable to advocate for better mental health care while accepting support from the very agencies they opposed. Faced with this ethical quandary, the IC-NAMI Board decided to pull away from its corporate sponsors, even though this meant sacrificing financial support and caused even more tension between IC-NAMI and the mental health providers.

Adoptions take time, mutual respect, have false starts, and may fail at the last minute—but they *can* be effective given patience and wisdom. The following example from Middle View illustrates this process. A number of years ago, catalysts in Middle View and its surrounding towns held a community meeting to address economic decline. Participants decided that residents needed to have locally available higher education and training opportunities in order to compete effectively in the global workplace. They formed a local leadership team which, in turn, contacted the local state senator, who enthusiastically agreed to help. He arranged for the leadership team to engage a professor of higher education from the State University to design a "cooperative college." The professor's model was to have involved twelve different institutions, each of which was to offer some courses locally and accept courses taken from the partner institutions as components of its degree programs. "Mating eleven dinosaurs" proved impossible for structural, philosophical, and financial reasons, but the local leadership team kept trying to find ways of offer local access to higher education. Eventually, a nearby community college (located in another state) adopted the project, negotiated the problems of cross-border public higher education, and created a small branch campus that awards associate degrees. In addition, a few of the original partners agreed to offer bachelors' level courses and access to their degree programs.

If neither short-term advocacy nor adoption by an existing organization works, your team may conclude that the only way to accomplish your mission, honor your values, and attain your desired outcomes is to become a separate, formal organization. Formal organizations come in several forms. In the United States, formal organizations are defined by their ownership and tax status. **Public agencies** are created through legislation and funded directly by local, state, or federal taxes. This option will not be discussed because it is unlikely that your organizing effort will be able to initiate a new public agency in today's political climate. **For-profit** organizations are privately owned and may be sole proprietorships, partnerships, limited corporations, or corporations and exist mainly to make **profits** (i.e., returns on investment over and above the cost of doing business) for their owners and investors who, in turn, pay taxes on their profits. **For-benefit** organizations make profits for their owners who pay taxes on them but balance profit making with a service mission. **Nonprofit corporations** are discussed in the next section.[1]

One of your first organizational choices will be whether or not to formally incorporate. Sole proprietorships, partnerships, and the various forms of limited corporations are all fairly simple to initiate and are often the best choice if your organizing effort has limited goals, a small budget, and is likely to have a limited life span. On the other hand, formal incorporation can be a challenge and may require substantial legal consultation, but there are advantages to formal incorporation, including limits to the liability of the incorporators. You should consider incorporation if your effort has long-term outcome goals, intends to own property, will need major funding, or may be exposed to liability. (Note: When the time comes to choose an organizational structure, you should be sure to recruit an accountant and attorney to your leadership team, as laws and accounting requirements change constantly. Violations or perceived violations of the tax laws governing non-profit organizations can cause endless problems.)

All corporations, whether non-profit or profit-making, must be chartered by a state government and must negotiate for operating privileges in other states. Profit-making corporations produce a wide variety of goods and services, but their main mission is to make a profit for their investors. For benefit, B-corporations, or L3C corporations couple profit making with altruism and in a few states are given special tax consideration. In addition to earning profits for their investors, B-corporations must have one or more altruistic missions. They must (1) create a positive environmental impact, (2) strengthen the communities in which they are located, (3) provide employee welfare, or (4) provide a public service. They are not eligible for government or private grant funding but can receive government and foundation contracts. As of August 2011, several states had enacted legislation creating B-corporations.[2] B-corporations have the advantage of having fewer operational constraints than private non-profit corporations but are sometimes seen as opportunistic because of the profit-making designation.

Many community organizing efforts decide to become non-profit corporations. **Non-profit corporations** (aka **non-profits**) are a uniquely American invention. They pay no local, state, or federal taxes because they are presumed to serve the common good. They have no owners. Governing board members serve for free so there is no profit incentive. Any **revenues** (i.e., monies) received must be used for the organizational mission. Because dishonest people can be tempted to claim non-profit status for their organization as a way of avoiding taxes, state and federal laws make it very difficult to obtain a non-profit designation, but your team may find it worth the effort because non-profit status is often required for various forms of funding.

Many people are unaware that the Internal Revenue Service (IRS) applies the term *non-profit* to a wide variety of organizational types, each of which contributes to society. We will look at several of them, beginning with **501c-3 organizations** because they are the most common. As your leadership teams becomes familiar with its organizational options, you will hear people talking about something called a "501c 3," which refers to a section of the U.S. tax code that defines "public good" organizations that are exempt from federal taxes and are able to offer tax deductions for contributions. Numerous community organizing efforts eventually evolve into 501c-3 organizations. Many people are surprised to learn that 501c-3 non-profit organizations can vary from tiny efforts, like the runaway prevention center in Middle View, to huge organizations, such as major hospitals with large budgets, multiple campuses, well-paid employees, and positive balance sheets. People wonder how such huge enterprises could ever be considered non-profit. They fail to realize that there are major differences among **revenues** (the money that is brought into an organization), **expenditures** (the money that is paid out for goods, services, and salaries), and **profits** (the money that is paid to the owners of the enterprise). Non-profit organizations have no owners or stockholders. They generate revenues and have expenditures but do not generate profits for anyone. Members of their Boards of Directors do not receive profit from their participation and, in fact, these Boards are highly regulated. Contributions to 501c-3 (public good non-profit) organizations are tax deductible because there is a presumption that donors to organizations with this designation are supporting good works that would otherwise be neglected or would have to be paid for through public funds. Donations to them, therefore, simply leave out the government as a third party. The 501c-3 designation requires a rigorous application process at both the state and national levels designed to assure the government that the organization truly serves the public interest and is structured so that it is likely to survive and accomplish its goals. All nonprofit organizations are exempt from federal and state taxes, but only donations to 501c-3 designees are tax deductible for donors. To provide grants, direct funding, or *per diems* (daily fees for service), most foundations, private funders such as the United Way, major donors, and government grantors require your organization to have 501c-3 status.

Although many community organizing efforts in the United States seek 501-c3 private non-profit status, this move should be considered carefully. The tax-exempt 501-c3 status has many advantages: it provides legal protection to individual members of the board of directors, makes the organization eligible for a wide variety of private and public grants, secures legitimacy in the eyes of the government and the general public, guarantees freedom of decision making within the constraints of its established by-laws, and provides the stability of a board of directors so that no single individual can take the organization too far off track. On the other hand, gaining and maintaining the 501c-3 designation brings challenges. Increasingly, non-profit organizations have to compete for funding in a highly competitive and somewhat cut-throat milieu. In recent years, 501c-3 organizations have been required to provide ever more detailed reports to the IRS. The difficulty of attaining 501-c3 status varies from state to state, from decade to decade, and in how political various regimes interpret corporation law and enforce regulation. For instance, when the runaway prevention program in Middle View was incorporated in the mid-1970s, it was relatively easy to apply for and attain both state and federal non-profit status. In contrast, the SNO applied for non-profit status for a similar program in 2011 and found it nearly impossible to attain state-level permissions. Finally, and probably somewhat ironically, 501-c3 organizations are difficult to disband, so you should be reasonably sure that your organization will have a reasonable life span.

In general, 501-c3 status is desirable if

- You determine that your effort is likely to continue over a relatively long period of time.
- It meets a unique need in the service system that requires a new approach.
- It has potential board members who are well respected and who have the time needed to commit to the venture.
- It is likely to meet initial IRS and state-level criteria for evaluation and record keeping.

Non-profit ventures depend greatly on the attention, sophistication, and reputation of their board members. If you decide to apply for 501-c3 status, you should be prepared to spend time developing an extensive set of by-laws and be willing to invest in an attorney who is well versed in the laws of the state where you want to incorporate.

Faith-based community organizing efforts may opt to be designated **churches or integrated auxiliaries** rather than 501C-3 organizations. The word "church" as used in the tax code does not encompass just Christian places of worship. It is used as a designation for any organization that meets all or most of a long list of criteria for faith-based organizations. It includes all of the major world religions, many sects and cults, and even some individual entrepreneurial ventures. Many worthwhile community organizing efforts (especially social innovations) begin within organizations that are

Administration

Understanding and Mastery: Legal and regulatory issues and risk management

Critical Thinking Question: Search for "[your state] State's requirements for nonprofit incorporation" and explore the rules and regulations for non-profit incorporation. What would be required to incorporate your proposed community organization? What advantages would there be to 501C-3 status? What difficulties would you face? Would you recommend that your leadership team incorporate its efforts? Why or why not?

legally defined as churches or integrated auxiliaries and fall initially under the tax laws, insurance codes, and regulations that affect the church itself. Churches are permitted to offer a variety of human service programs and community activities as part of their missions under a special category called an integrated auxiliary. Organizations that qualify as churches are not required to apply for a tax designation, and, in fact, the IRS urges them to refrain from doing so. Churches and integrated auxiliaries are exempt from the challenges of 501c-3 organizations, including Form 990 reporting requirements, which means a great savings of time and energy. Contributions to churches and integrated auxiliaries are tax exempt, but historically they have not been eligible for state or federal funding and are not always eligible for foundation funding either.

Church sponsorship has many of the same plusses and minuses as any kind of adoption by a larger, established agency. On the one hand, you will have the protection of a larger, recognized organization. Conversely, your efforts will be supervised by its governing body, which will have the right to define your policies and practices and override the decisions of your leadership team. Your clientele may feel threatened by your close association with a particular church, and your financial and volunteer resources may be limited by the size of the sponsoring congregation because many people are reluctant to volunteer anywhere but their own place of worship. Your leadership team and a lawyer should look at these criteria to determine if you qualify for church status and, indeed, if you *want* to quality for it.

A dilemma over whether to become a 501c-3 organization or remain a church-related auxiliary occurred with the Middle View food pantry. The food pantry was originally a mission of an established Christian congregation with deep historical roots. For some years it was housed in the church building, and then the church decided that the food pantry needed a building of its own. They built a small building to house both the food pantry and an associated thrift shop. Times grew tougher in Middle View, and the need for food pantry services increased greatly. Members of the food pantry board (a committee of the church's governing body) felt that they could no longer handle the growing demand. They approached a local service club and the Town Board for help in constructing a larger food pantry and supplying it with commercial refrigerators and other needed equipment. As a result of their initiative, the food pantry became a major community organizing effort that involved hundreds of people in large and small ways. As the project grew, the question of legal structure arose. It was clear that the food pantry was no longer simply the mission project of a single congregation but belonged to everyone in the community. The food pantry committee, the church's governing board, members of the service club, and a variety of other interested people decided that since the food pantry now belonged to everyone it should become a separate 501c-3 organization with its own board of directors. Once it became a secular organization, the food pantry was able to use its independent status to gain support from government and human service mezzo-systems that would not have been available had it remained directly church affiliated. The founding congregation still provides most of the volunteers and many of the contributions, but the new structure is a better fit.

Explore the Internal Revenue Service (IRS) for tools to assist non-profit organizations. Consider the IRS definition of "churches" in comparison with your community organizing initiative. What are the legal pros and cons of becoming an integrated auxillary of an existing church, becoming a church in your own right, or opting to become a 501C-3 organization?

While the majority of long-term organizing efforts eventually become adopted components of existing public or private organizations, free-standing 501c3 organizations, or church-related auxiliaries, the IRS does allow for several other tax-exempt categories you may want to consider. While such organizations do not make a profit for owners or stockholders and are, therefore, not taxed, nevertheless because they exist for the benefit of their members rather than for the public good (as determined by the IRS), donations to them are not tax deductible. Americans love to create associations. The list of organizations and associations that are eligible for tax-exempt status certainly supports this notion. Here are some types of tax-exempt organizations taken from a recent IRS publication.[3] Each of the legal definitions is quite specific and subject to change, so they will not be elaborated on here.

Civic leagues and social welfare organizations include:

- Labor, agricultural, and horticultural associations
- Business leagues and similar organizations
- Social and recreational clubs
- Fraternal beneficiary societies and domestic fraternal societies
- Employee associations
- Local benevolent life insurance associations, mutual irrigation, telephone companies, and similar associations
- Cemetery companies
- Credit unions and other mutual financial associations
- Veterans' organizations
- Black lung benefit trusts
- Title-holding companies for single parents
- State-sponsored high risk health coverage organizations
- State-sponsored workers' compensation re-insurance companies

A few of these categories such as membership-based organizations may be interesting to your organizing effort. For instance, in Middle View several senior citizens have decided to form a membership-based organization called Aging in Place, which will provide a form of mutual economic aid broadly based on the concept of time banking. Members agree to offer volunteer services to one another so that they can remain in their own homes as long as possible. They will pay an annual fee to cover insurance for folks providing transportation to appointments and for incidental organizational expenses. Membership will be open to anyone within the Middle View community who considers himself or herself to be a senior citizen, is willing to pay the modest membership fee, and provides at least two letters of reference attesting to their trustworthiness. Aging in Place is an example of a locally based tax-exempt membership organization whose fees are not tax deductible. Meanwhile, in Smithville, a group of community advocates have decided to form a membership-based organization to advocate for improved city services. This, too, is an example of a tax-exempt, membership-based organization with non-deductible fees. The main advantage of membership-type organizations over 501c-3s is that members have nearly complete control over their mission, policies, procedures, and activities. Their main disadvantage is that they must be self-supporting as they are not eligible for public or private grants or tax-deductible contributions.

Sometimes the best thing for community organizers to do is to provide the funding others need to accomplish their goals. **Foundations** and **giving circles** are two forms of non-profit organization that exist primarily to provide financial support to community initiatives. Foundations are charitable trusts or non-profit corporations whose principle purpose is to make grants to organizations, institutions, or individuals for scientific, educational, cultural, religious, or other charitable purposes. There are two broad types: **private foundations** and **public foundations** (i.e., **grantmaking public charities**). Private foundations are a way for individuals, families, or corporations to structure their charitable giving. Public foundations are umbrella organizations that derive their support from individuals, private foundations, and government sources. They often provide administrative services for small foundations and charitable trusts, especially those serving local community interests.[4]

While foundations have historically "belonged" to wealthy individuals, families, or corporations, **giving circles** allow people with limited funds to join forces to invest in causes they support. There are three types of giving circles. The most common are formed by **small groups** of friends with similar social concerns who meet regularly to pool their resources, develop criteria for donations, and give grants to worthy individuals and organizations. Members find them to be a pleasant social outlet as well as a way of increasing the impact of their giving. **Informal networks** are loosely connected groups of people with similar interests who respond financially when they are alerted to pressing needs. They have few if any rules for dispersal of funds and often directly support needy individuals or the good work of a single individual. **Formal organizations** are a cross between the informality of the giving networks and small groups and the bureaucratic structures of foundations. They tend to be larger than the other two types, require more initial investment, and adhere to stricter grant-making standards.[5] Your leadership team may want to consider whether you want to include some kind of funding structure in your plans.

Explore the Giving Circle movement. In what ways might the giving circle concept be useful in your work?

Political organizations are non-profit but non-tax-exempt entities created primarily to influence public policy issues, support specific legislative initiatives, and represent their members' viewpoints to political bodies or regulatory agencies. They are required to seek 527 status. This status is primarily used by the IRS to exclude donors to such organizations from the benefits of tax deduction since their contributions are presumed to further their own passions and concerns rather than serving the general public good. Examples of 527 organizations cross the political spectrum and include such recognized organizations as the Sierra Club, MoveOn.org, the American Association of Retired Persons (AARP), the Christian Coalition, the National Rifle Association, political action committees (PACs), and political parties of all stripes. Social Movement Organizations (SMOs) generally must register as 527 organizations. Tax-exempt statuses are sometimes mixed and matched. Some organizations have a 501c-3 branch for charitable activities and a separate 527 organization for political activism.

Assess your comprehension about the Considerations in Your Choice of Organizational Structures by completing this quiz.

Organizing Internationally: Non-governmental Organizations (NGOs)

Although this book is primarily geared toward community organizing efforts in the United States, some of you may be interested in organizing efforts in other countries or in efforts that stretch across borders. If this describes your effort, you will need to become familiar with the world of non-governmental organizations or NGOs. The term *non-governmental organization* was coined at about the same time as the founding of the United Nations in 1947 and accurately describes their function. NGOs are private organizations that provide social, humanitarian, and educational services independent of governments or international government organizations (IGOs) such the United Nations, its affiliates such as UNICEF (originally the United Nations International Children's Emergency Fund) and UNESCO (United Nations Educational, Scientific and Cultural Organization), as well as a wide variety of international bodies that are formed by international treaties between governments. NGOs vary in size from huge efforts such as the International Red Cross to small, local projects. Each nation and international government organization has its own laws, rules, and regulations regarding the structure, rights, and responsibilities of NGOs that you will have to explore if you plan to work outside the United States.

Human Services Delivery Systems

Understanding and Mastery: Range and characteristics of human services delivery systems and organizations

Critical Thinking Question: You have read about the various ways community organizing efforts can be structured. Make a list of the pros and cons of each for your community organizing effort. Choose the one you think would be best and write a rationale for your choice.

Budgeting Basics

No matter which organizational structure you choose, your organization will need a **budget process**, a way of organizing and managing your finances. Budgeting is an ongoing activity that occurs before, during, and after decision making about organizational structures and before the acquisition of funding. Budgeting is a crucial part of community organizing, but many grassroots organizers have very little or no experience with it. This section and parts of Appendix B* focus on what your leadership team will need to know about budgeting.

You will find that the following rules are basic for budgeting:

1. A budget is a plan for spending money to reach specific goals by a certain time.
2. Any budget is only as good as the time, effort, and information people put into it.
3. No budget is perfect because none of us can totally predict the future.
4. To reach your goals, all budgets and plans must be monitored and adjusted as time goes on.
5. Budgeting is a thoughtful and deliberate process which is closely tied to the planning component of the community organizing cycle.
6. Budgeting is inclusive and should bring together the perspectives and interests of your stakeholders.
7. Budgeting is an ongoing process that requires ongoing monitoring, data gathering, analysis, revised projections and assumptions, and consideration of alternatives needed.

Explore the web for examples of budgets. Compare and contrast these budgets. Consider challenges you'll face in developing budgets.

There are several kinds of budgets:

- The organizational or **operating budget** is used to manage all activities and is composed of the budgets of all projects and programs under the umbrella of the entire organization.*

*Ideas that are expanded upon in Appendix B are indicated by an asterisk (*).

- **Specific budgets** are for individual programs, units, or activities.*
- **Capital budgets** are tools used to help plan and manage **capital projects**, which are those requiring relatively large, one-time expenditures. Examples include buying or constructing a building or acquiring expensive equipment.*
- **Cash flow budgets** show when your organization can expect major revenues and expenditures. They are used to help you make financial plans that will allow your operation to run smoothly so you can pay the bills without panic.*

Good budgeting practices are difficult even in organizations that have highly qualified paid staff who have established connections with funding streams and the time for negotiations, attention to detail, and rapidly changing circumstances that are common in financing community efforts. Good practices are even harder for initiatives that are dependent on the limited time and sometimes the limited skills of volunteers. However, even in organizations operating on very limited resources, the money and time spent on the budgeting and budget management processes is well worth it. In fact, given a choice between hiring a paid director and hiring a paid bookkeeper or accountant, you should choose the accountant.

Guiding the Budgeting Process

The leadership team is responsible for the budgeting process, which is a subset of planning and based directly on your mission and outcome goals. Budget-related tasks of the leadership team include:

- Establishing general budget policies.
- Formally reviewing and approving the budget.
- Regularly reviewing financial and narrative reports.
- Comparing your budget history with similar organizations if the data is available.
- Developing long-range financial forecasts and operating plans.
- Establishing draft budget guidelines by setting expense and income targets.
- Establishing guidelines or formats for the budget document itself.
- Holding budget information sessions for members, clients, staff, or contributors (or for government funding sources such as the federal, state, or county legislature or city council).

Often budget preparation itself is delegated to a finance team or finance committee that develops an expenditure budget and an income budget, which must be equal. The finance committee then makes recommendations to the full leadership team (board of directors and the like).

Expenditure Budgeting

Whether expenditure budgeting is done by your full leadership team or is delegated to a finance team or committee, the leadership team must choose among approaches: budgeting by a central authority, participatory budgeting, or distributed budgeting.

- **Budgeting by a central authority** is particularly common in collaborations and comprehensive planning efforts that are closely tied to public sector funding and to social entrepreneurship efforts that have a single founder. Under this budget development strategy, a central operating authority sets expense and income targets for the coming year for the whole organization and then for each individual unit. In this way, the units know in advance the income that is available and are better able to estimate any income they may have to generate themselves. They are forced to work within the framework they are given.

- **Participatory budgeting** is the preferred mode for most varieties of community organizing and parallels other parts of the community organizing cycle. Participatory budgeting begins during the research phase as you investigate program options and their costs and then accelerates once outcome goals and performance measures are set. The actual work of budgeting may be done by a committee of the whole, designated individuals, or a small group. Participation is the key word in participatory budgeting, followed by **openness** (availability of budget information), **transparency** (clarity for everyone on how the budget is created and managed), and **accountability** (budget processes that are set up so that embezzlement or misappropriation of funds is impossible). Those in charge of the process should make sure that all of those who have major interests in the effort have an equal voice in the various iterations of the process. Teams should be given authority to design and manage their own budgets. If budget cuts are needed, the teams should be given the reasons for them. Budgeting and budget management should be honest and boring; there should be no unpleasant surprises for anyone involved.*
- **Distributed budgeting** parallels distributed management. It is a dialogue between the central leadership team and its micro-systems and is similar to participatory budgeting. In distributed budgeting, the leadership team has the broad financial view while the dispersed leaders know their own programs, geographic locales, financial needs, and potential resources. The leadership team collects current information and estimates on future ventures and expenditures from each of its far-flung spin-offs and, in turn, gives their managers information on funding that is likely to be available and advises them on future program directions. Budgeting information flows back and forth between various micro-systems and the leadership team but is rarely, or never, shared among the various ventures.*

Zero-based Budgeting

Budgeting by a central authority, participatory budgeting, and distributed budgeting all begin each year with a past budget history of income and expenditures that is used to build the following year's budget plan. ***Zero-based budgeting*** (ZBB) changes that premise by beginning afresh each year. ZBB is not really a budget process but a method of re-examining the reasons behind budget items. It should be used when your organization shows signs of needing reinvention; when efforts that have been running for a while lose their momentum, clarity, or purpose; or when you contemplate major changes or you find that the balance of funding for different sub-systems no longer reflects external demands. ZBB was quite radical when it was first created in the 1960s as an alternative to budgeting practices that simply added additional funds to existing budgets, year after year, to cover inflation. Zero-based budgeting has no built-in assumptions or automatically included items. It challenges you to answer the questions: "If this product (activity or unit) were not here today, would we start it? If so, how can we strengthen it? If not, should we eliminate it? If so, how can we eliminate it?"*

Your choice of budgeting strategy depends on the organization, its stage of development, and the type of organization. Most new participatory organizations will benefit from a participatory budgeting strategy, while community collaborations may benefit from a top-down approach. Distributed organizations may benefit from a participatory approach that is delegated to teams at the various units or sites, whereas organizations that have existed for a while—and which may be flagging in their effectiveness—may respond best to ZBB.

Review the Free Management Library's tips for budgeting and financial management in non-profit organizations. What tips will you find most useful as you face the challenges of budgeting and financial management?

Assess your comprehension of Budgeting Basics by completing this quiz.

Income Budgeting and Funding

Many organizations start with funding opportunities and work backward to program development. In participatory organizing, you begin with the needs of your focal community system and simultaneously keep your eyes and ears open for funding. If you follow any of the budgeting processes just described here or in Appendix B in good faith you will be able to develop a reasonable expenditure budget. Once you know what you need, you will be ready to search for resources. Here are some tried-and-true tips:

- Never, **ever** start with available funding and work backwards to a need. Start with a real community need and only then look for funding. (You would probably be shocked at the number of human services organizations that start with available funding and then try to demonstrate a need. Such practices are unethical and ultimately lead to failure because they cannot be sustained.)
- Remember that resources need not always to be in the form of cash. They can be in the form of volunteer hours, material donations, space, or transportation. Not only can many of these in-kind resources be used to provide direct services, but many can be matched with cash from other funding sources to increase your total budget.
- Be sure to investigate local as well as regional and national resources. (Hint: many sources of funding can be found with an Internet search.)
- Be sure to target funding sources that support your project's mission (i.e., do not be tempted by funding that does not fit your mission because it is generally not worth pursuing).
- Pursue funding sources that you realistically can attain given available human resources. In general, this means that you should avoid applying for small grants with complicated application procedures, grants or contracts that have historically gone to already established organization, or grants that known to be highly competitive.
- Prioritize funding sources that promise long-term stability.
- Create a diversified funding base that does not depend too much on a single source of funds.

- Divide the total project need among the various types of funding available, taking into account the type of organization you are developing (i.e., for-benefit or traditional non-profit), the resources available for the type of organization, and which aspects of the program are likely to be funded for each need. (For instance, foundations and major donors often like to fund "brick and mortar" projects that last for many years but steer away from funding operating expenses. Most grants and contracts can be used for direct services but often provide little for administrative expenses. Annual giving campaigns may be the most useful for funding administrative and similar expenses.)
- Set realistic targets for funds from each major source.

Administration

Understanding and Mastery: Developing budgets and monitoring expenditures

Critical Thinking Question: Foundations can be helpful sources of capital funding, particularly for social entrepreneurship and social innovations. What role might foundations play in funding your organization?

Once the information on needs and potential resources has been gathered and digested by those in charge of income generation, a balanced income budget can be created and submitted to decision makers.

Income budgeting is a continuous process because funding is a constant concern, especially for new initiatives. It is likely that income budgets will be revised frequently depending on the availability (or loss) of income sources.

Income budgeting can be tricky. It is often tempting to seek funding just because it is available, but you should be sure that funding source requirements (1) match desired outcomes, (2) do not compromise the mission of your organization (i.e., do not come with too many strings attached), and (3) are not more administrative trouble than they are worth. Organizations that chase after a different kind of grant every time their old grant runs out find that their mission becomes diffused and they are losing their identity—which results in the loss of interest by volunteers, staff, donors, and funders. The overall goal of income budgeting should be organizational stability—even if that means somewhat limited growth.[†]

Explore more about non-profit fundraising. What fund-raising strategies will you probably find most useful? What fund-raising challenges do you expect to encounter?

The following are rules of thumb gained from decades of successes and failures:

- Cultivate multiple funding sources so that your initiative is not vulnerable to the many dangers inherent in support from a single funding source—anything from complete cooption to disintegration.
- Develop long-range support for the central mission and work constantly on developing networks.

[†]Appendix B covers the following funding sources and gives the pros, cons, and eligibility requirements for each: public grants, contracts, block grant allocations, foundation grants, benefactors, dues and memberships, mutual economic aid, in-kind contributions, fees for service, fund-raising events and campaigns, and partnerships with businesses.

- Understand the role government at all levels plays in your funding and in the regulation of your activities as well.
- Collaborate with other similar agencies in professional organizations and in community efforts, but don't let them co-opt your mission.
- Cooperate with others when necessary, but be aware that competition, especially for funds, can be vicious. Be assertive and clear with your stakeholders, collaborators, funders, and yourselves about how your initiative fills its own unique niche.
- Make sure that potential and past supporters know about your successes and give credit to those who made them possible.
- Choose your funding sources wisely.
- Be constantly on the lookout for new funding opportunities.
- Be constantly wary of potential threats to existing funding.
- Make sure that you are not spending more money than you are gaining from a particular funding source. This is especially true of competitive grants where the staff time expended may not be worth the unlikely chance of receiving the funds.

Assess your comprehension on Revenue Budgeting and Fundraising by completing this quiz.

Budget Management throughout the Year

Once the yearly expense and income budgets are approved, they become tools used by decision makers at all organizational levels. Each of these levels has its own role in budget monitoring and feedback. A budget is similar to a map: it is a guide through the projected weekly, monthly, quarterly, and yearly financial ups and downs of an organization. Just as a pre-prepared road map may not be able to predict all of the conditions that will be encountered on a road trip, a budget cannot predict everything your organization will encounter on its journey.

The leadership team (board or other governing body) has ultimate responsibility for fiscal management of the organization and in some cases may be held personally liable for mismanagement. So, before every decision-making meeting, provide your leadership team with accurate monthly, or at least quarterly, budget reports that compare past, projected, and actual budget expenditures. Everyone should take budget monitoring responsibilities seriously, be trained to read budget reports, and feel comfortable about asking hard questions. Even in very small organizations where the same people have to serve on several different teams (or committees), you should have a budget team (committee) dedicated to budget management that should work closely with other teams, such as fund-raising and marketing, long-range planning, regulatory compliance, and capital projects. Such teams do much of the real work of your organization. Meeting times and places should be flexible, scheduled to include as many people as possible and, if necessary, include electronic media (such as conference calls, video conferencing, community cable television, and so forth) blended with face-to-face meetings to maximize participation. Team meetings are the place to work out specific plans and suggestions. You should use the leadership team meeting to pull these plans together into a coherent whole and to formally approve actions that require changes of direction, expenditure of significant funds, or applications for new funding. Day-to-day, routine budget management is the responsibility of unit and financial managers.

Accountability and Audits

Unfortunately, it is all too easy for those opposing a community initiative (especially one that is engaged in social action) to accuse an organization of financial irregularities. Credible, carefully audited accounting practices can save you many headaches, up to and including litigation. Even in small organizations you should have someone who is well trained in accounting handle the "books"—including documentation of all revenues and expenditures. You should arrange for both internal and external audits by reputable individuals or firms. Your budgeting team, under the auspices of the leadership team, should keep financial records in good order and in accepted formats that are ready for inspection by auditors, the leadership team, and any interested stakeholder. Because embezzlement can and does happen, you should be sure that your accounting system is as embezzlement-proof as possible.*

Review more about nonprofit financial management and accountability. What financial management and accountability issues are you likely to find most challenging?

Assess your comprehension of Financial Accountability by completing this quiz.

Cash Flow Problems

Cash flow refers to whether or not your organization has the money directly on hand to pay its bills. Problems with cash flow are probably the greatest cause of anxiety among financial managers. Interrupted or reduced cash flow—caused by unexpected loss of income, unexpected costs, and other situations—can cause innumerable problems.

Unexpected loss of income occurs fairly frequently in community organizing, especially those initiatives dependent on government funding. Government funding is based on a three-step process: (1) "**enabling legislation**" (government jargon for giving permission) authorizes a program, (2) monies are allocated through the budgeting process, and (3) disbursement regulations are developed by the executive agency in charge of oversight. Cash flow can be interrupted if the enabling legislation fails to obtain funding at the budget level (so-called unfunded mandates fall into this category), if the regulatory agency fails to create or modify disbursal regulations and procedures in a timely manner, through mechanical failures (such as computer breakdown), or even through a personal emergency or vacation of the individual responsible for "cutting the check."

Government funding can also be significantly reduced if a chief executive—such as the president, governor, county executive, or mayor—refuses to release or "sign off" on funds allocated by the legislative branch. In addition, enabling legislation, especially at the federal level, may be affected by "signing statements" made at the time a bill is signed into law, in which the president asserts the authority to refuse to abide by the legislation. (There is considerable controversy regarding whether the executive branch actually has authority under the Constitution to refuse to release duly allocated funds, but constitutionality matters little if you are waiting for badly needed funding.)

If pledges are lower than anticipated, funding from such organizations as United Way or a State Employee Funding Agency (SEFA) can be reduced. In such cases, funding is usually reduced on a prorated basis across participating organizations unless donations specifically designated to your agency have been received.

Individual decisions may also adversely affect agency cash flow: direct donors may fail to honor pledges, fee-for-service clients may fail to pay their bills, expected payments from *per diem* referrals may not occur, or members may not pay their dues. Your budget system should be flexible enough to handle these contingencies.

You may encounter unexpected costs as well, related to emergencies—such as the increase in posttraumatic stress disorders following disasters such as an earthquake, hurricane, terrorism, or the spread of disease; legal requirements for higher quality; different or expanded services due to a lawsuit or changing expectations of regulatory agencies; legal costs above or beyond the scope of the organization's liability insurance; and unexpected costs caused by extensive damage to buildings or other property. Such events can literally come from nowhere, such as when the Middle View Thrift Shop and its associated church faced a $20,000 expense for bat eradication!

Other unexpected costs are personnel related. Typical sources of unexpected personnel costs include increases in government levies such as Social Security, unemployment, or workers' compensation; increases in the cost of employer-provided benefits such as health insurance; negotiated increases in salaries or benefits, especially in unionized organizations or where salary expectations are defined by funding contracts.

Unexpected costs that arise in non-personnel expenditures also hurt. Some typical rising or unexpected non-personnel costs include transportation costs due to increased gasoline prices; higher heating, cooling, and other utility costs; increased cost of building maintenance and repair due to increased cost of materials; increased food costs in residential or day programs; changes or renovation of buildings due to changes in government health and safety regulations; and increased cost of liability insurance and increases in property and other taxes in the case of for-benefit organizations. These are not comprehensive lists, of course. The very nature of unexpected costs is that they are—well—unexpected.

Contingency plans are one way you can survive budget managers' nightmares. Funding emergencies have four phases:*

1. A preliminary phase in which you become aware that possible funding problems are on the horizon
2. An intermediate phase where plans must be made and quickly implemented
3. A crisis phase
4. An evaluation phase in which you must redo the budget(s) to reflect the new situation

Assess your comprehension of Cash Flow Problems and Contingency Planning by completing this quiz.

Ethical Budget Management

It is tempting in an ethics section to simply make a list of prohibited behaviors, but ethics is a decision-making process that can be facilitated by intentional organizational structures.

Two of the world's great religions, Christianity and Confucianism, developed similar "golden rules" for ethical behavior. The Christian version, in King James English, states, "Do unto others as you would have them do unto you." The Confucian version is somewhat more pragmatic: "Do *not* do anything to others which you would *not* want them to do to you." Both versions of the rule are relevant to ethical budgeting practices.

Imagine yourself as a donor, either directly from your personal funds or indirectly through your tax dollars. How would you want your money to be used? Where would you want it to go? Where do you *not* want it to go? What information do you expect in return for your contributions? Basic ethical budget practices lie in the answers to these simple questions. Here are some possible answers to which your leadership team can add others. Donors want to:

- *See that their money goes where they think it is going.* Oddly enough, this is not always done, especially by disaster-related organizations. Donations have been used for administrative costs or to develop contingency funds for the next disaster rather than being used for the situation at hand.
- *Know that direct services are maximized.* Donors want you to use their money to do the published mission of the organization. They do not begrudge you a decent salary (although they do not want it to be many times their own), nor do they begrudge their dollars funding the administrative staff, marketing budget, or equipment necessary to maintain support for your effort. However, if your administrative costs exceed 30% of your total expenditures, they will feel cheated and may report you to the Better Business Bureau or other watchdog groups that monitor charitable organizations. Also, if your administrative/service delivery ratio is too high—for example if 80% of your expenditures are administrative rather than service oriented—you may lose your 501c-3 status.
- *Make sure that education is really education, not propaganda.* Donors usually do not mind real educational efforts that provide the public with necessary information that enables them to be protected from potential danger or to unite in a worthy cause, but they do not want you to pretend that the money they have donated is going to educational purposes when it is actually going to market your organization.
- *Hire competent, hard-working staff and pay them decently but not exorbitantly.* In general, donors do not mind if you pay yourself a decent wage or hire your daughter as a program manager, as long as each of you is well qualified to do the job and is working hard. They do mind "sweetheart" deals in which unqualified owners, board members, administrators, direct service providers, or their close friends and relatives are given preference over more highly qualified candidates.
- *Respect donors' privacy.* Most donors do not want you to share their names with others, even other charitable organizations representing similar causes, without their permission. They also do not want to be cited as a donor in your marketing campaigns unless they give you explicit permission to do so.
- *Be who you seem to be.* Donors expect you to have a unique organizational identity. They resent being fooled because your organization uses a name that is similar to another's. Don't steal another agency's hard-earned reputation.
- *Keep accurate, honest, "transparent" records.* Donors expect you to keep records that are easy to follow, conform to government regulations, are readily available, and clearly show that your organization is operating legitimately.

Remember that contributions represent your donors' belief in your cause. Their donations come from their own life work. Respect that.

In a world where it seems that truly ethical practices are rare, it is important to be ethical and to demonstrate ethical practice. Therefore, financial management practices should be transparent to all constituents and should provide convincing evidence of the integrity of your organization. Here some ways you can do this:

- *Have a respected and respectable leadership team.* Members of your leadership team should have impeccable reputations for honesty and hard work. Moreover, they should not have personal political agendas and should *never* receive direct or indirect financial gain from their participation. You should publish their names and affiliations on your written materials and on your website.

- *Have clear accounting structures.* This was mentioned earlier, but it bears repeating. Accounting structures should be clear, up to date, and follow accepted practices. Multiple accounts should be managed according to contractual or regulatory requirements and should also be cross-referenced for easy tracking. Mandatory reports, such as the Federal Form 990, should be clear, detailed, and honest.
- *Have internal checks and balances.* There should be no temptation or opportunity for anyone to misappropriate funds. Therefore, no single person should be given complete responsibility for financial processes. For instance, two people should account for money raised even for something as simple as a bake sale. Receipts should be required for all purchases reimbursed by the organization. Receipts should be given for all donations (whether cash or in-kind), as well as for money received as fees for service. Whenever possible, payments and donations should be by check or credit card, not cash. Only a few persons should be approved to accept cash payments. All cash received should be immediately placed in a locked area until it can be safely deposited. Periodic internal audits should be conducted and available to the governing board and regulatory agencies. Use redundancy and checks and balances.
- *Ensure external accountability.* You should have annual or biannual external audits conducted. Budget reporting requirements of funding agencies should be followed scrupulously. A yearly budget report should be published and made generally available.

Ethics in budget management is a matter of the practical application of the Golden Rule and transparent record keeping. Do no evil. Keep good records so that others do not suspect evil where none exists.

Interpersonal Communication

Understanding and Mastery: Developing and sustaining behaviors that are congruent with the values and ethics of the profession

Critical Thinking Question: Think about the ethics of personal and organizational money management. What does the ethical management of financial resources entail? What is your ethical responsibility for finances as a member of a community organizing leadership team? How would you respond to an ethically questionable financial decision advocated by fellow team members?

Test your understanding of ethical budget management by taking this short Quiz.

Summary

Chapter 10 and Appendix B provide you with specific, detailed guidance on organizational structures, budgeting processes, funding, contingency planning, and ethical financial practices, as well as giving you the needed tools to form an organization that will fulfill its mission, honor its values, and achieve its outcome goals.

Assess your analysis and evaluation of this chapter's contents by completing the Chapter Review.

CHAPTER 11

Jim West/ImageBroker/Glow Images

Power and Empowerment

Chapter Outline

Community organizing efforts often are composed of relatively powerless people who must face powerful individuals and organizations but may lack the confidence to do what needs to be done. In this chapter, you will learn how power operates and how to **empower** (increase the power of) everyone involved in your organizing effort—including members of the focal community, volunteers, and yourself. Its intent is to enable you and those you serve to understand and use power ethically and effectively. You will explore power as a general concept and learn how to convert your understanding of power into empowerment of individuals, organizations, and communities.

Two Ways of Discerning Power

There are two major views of power: power as an **attribute** or **capability** and power as a **result of interaction.**[1] Let's first look at power as an attribute and move from individuals, to groups, to organizations within your focal system, and finally to power within mezzo- and macro-systems.

Power as an Individual Attribute

In the view of power as an individual attribute, power is something an individual can possess and accumulate. From this perspective, power is like money: you can earn it, have it given to you, give it away, or save it. When you spend it or give it away, you have less of it; when you hoard it or steal it, you have more.

An **attribute** is a combination of personality traits reinforced by behaviors and social position that eventually becomes a recognized component of your identity. There are many characteristics that can become attributes. For example, if you can count on Mary to willingly, respectfully, and unselfishly share what she has with others, chances are you will say, "Mary is kind" and attribute kindness to Mary as a part of who she is. Likewise, if Mary can consistently make things happen (or keep things from happening), you will say "Mary is powerful" and attribute power to her.

People use attribution as a shorthand for knowing what to expect of people. In our Mary example, over time you have come to expect certain behavior from Mary so while changes may surprise you, you probably won't change your overall opinion of her. We make such attributions all the time, but if you are trying to discern who has attributed power in a community, you must intentionally listen for some key words such as *is* and sometimes *must* or *have to* (e.g., "Mr. Jones **is** powerful"; "If you want to get anything done around here, you **have to have** Bob Jones in your corner"). If you hear such phrases over and over in reference to someone, make a mental note because that person has attributed power, and you will have to reckon with him or her.

Human Service Delivery Systems

Understanding and Mastery: Skills to effect and influence social policy

Critical Thinking Question: Power is sometimes viewed as an individual attribute. Identify someone who is seen as powerful. List some of the personal attributes, behaviors, and social connections that have led people to this conclusion. Evaluate your own level of attributed power. What characteristics have led you to this assessment? What might you do to increase your level of attributed power?

Power as an Attribute of Certain Classes or Categories of People

Power can be analyzed as a shared attribute of groups, organizations, and focal communities as well as being viewed as an individual characteristic. For instance, in the 1950s and 1960s, political scientists argued over the nature of power as an attribute of political systems and divided themselves into the **elitist school** and the **pluralist school**. Although the two have melded over the years, you will find that applying these broad theoretical frameworks at the micro-, focal-, mezzo-, and macro-levels helps you analyze power relationships at every level. (See Chapter 2 to review systems theory.)

Elitism

Elitists believe that in every social system there are a few individuals who *really* make the decisions and control what happens. This view of society was first articulated in C. Wright Mills' book *The Power Elite*, published in 1956.[2]

There are several different models that have been suggested for the elitist perspective:

- In a **power elite** power flows only one way, from those who hold power to everyone else in the community.[3]
- In a **democratic elite** a small group holds most of the power but there is a way for the people (constituents) to provide feedback through voting or through the organization of social movements and activities (such as massive campaigns that may include e-mails, telephone calls, letter writing, media contacts, and promises to give or withhold financial support). It is likely that the United States is a democratic elite based on its history.[4]
- In a **segmented elite** different sectors or segments of society are believed to be controlled by their own small groups and are relatively *equal* in power. For example, there is a military elite, a sports elite, a religious elite, an economic elite, and so

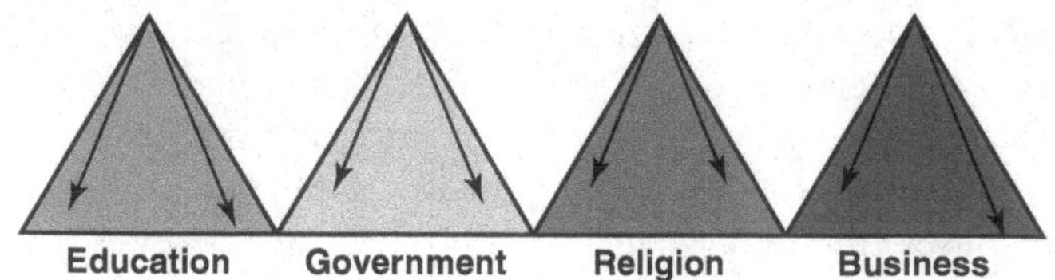

FIGURE 11.1 Segmented Elites Model

Source: Copyright © by Pearson Education, Upper Saddle River, NJ.

forth.[5] Empirical studies in real communities have shown that different people tend to be involved in different issues with little overlap among them.[6] Figure 11.1 illustrates the segmented elites model.

- In the **strategic elites** model, however, there is a hierarchy of elites. For instance, in any given time and place there may be a political elite, a military elite, an educational elite, a business elite, a recreational elite, a religious elite, a media elite, and so on, but these elites will *vary* in importance.[7]

The community of Middle View shows some evidence of segmented elites. Its political elite is composed of those who hold elected office and key appointments on town commissions. They are generally middle-aged, white, male businessmen, or prosperous retirees. Most have lived in Middle View for several decades or have been long-term summer residents. There is another group composed of old, local families. While most of them are not economically rich, they have multiple inter-generational connections and tend to vote and act in unison, which gives them power in numbers as well as the advantage of knowing everyone's personal stories for generations. Third are the "summer people" who have their own powerful association and keep in regular touch over the winter months via newsletter. They are a force to be reckoned with, especially regarding taxes and any economic development that threatens the ambience of the community. There are other elites as well: a "church goers elite" counterbalanced somewhat by the "bar regulars"; a "sports elite" that controls the Little League and other community teams; a "senior citizen elite" that makes sure that multiple services are provided to people over age 60; and a "small business elite" that runs the local Chamber of Commerce and coordinates many community promotional events. There is even a "snowmobile elite" that controls local trails, rules of the snowmobile road, and competitions. Mixing among the elites occurs because some individuals participate in several systems and because many families have representatives in several systems as well. There are many examples, but let's look at two in particular. For example, an industrialist who has retired to Middle View is a member of the Town Council, an elder in his local church, president of the Chamber of Commerce, past president of the local service organization, "trail coordinator" of the snowmobile club, and has a weekly golf match with the school superintendent. Another relatively young woman traces her local ancestry to before the American Revolution, comes from a family that has always held political office, and is president of the Parent Teacher Organization. Her mother has been Town Clerk for thirty years, her father is a successful local businessman, and her brother is the elementary school principal. If you asked a random sample of Middle View residents, "Who runs Middle View?" most would name these two individuals and a dozen others. So, you could easily map their connections and decide where they "fit" into your organizing efforts.

Remember that at the focal community level in the United States, elites and segmented elites do not sit in smoke-filled rooms and make decisions for the rest of us. They talk with each other on the golf course, at dinner parties, in fellowship hours after church, and around the edges of service club meetings. But note that when it comes to community organizing efforts, they hardly ever talk with those who are not part of their social circle. Their limited interactions result in a shared view of the world that may not resemble the way non-elite people experience life. Remember, too, that elite members of your focal community might not be considered elite anywhere else (the "big fish in a small pond" syndrome) so you have to determine where members of your focal community's elites fit into the bigger picture of mezzo- and macro-systems.

Human Systems

Understanding and Mastery: Organizational structures of communities

Critical Thinking Question: Examine a focal community system of your choice. What evidence do you see of the existence of a power elite? How is it likely to affect your work? What evidence do you see of democratic elites? What strategies might your group use to influence them? Identify the segmented elites. Which of them are most likely to be important in your organizing effort? How will you influence them?

Pluralism

The pluralistic view of power means that pockets of power can exist simultaneously for many different people and organizations, and that there are no such things as "power elites" (or if they do exist, they are constantly changing).[8] This view makes sense in light of real life communities because experience shows that communities *do* have individuals, families, informal associations, and formal organizations that have an inordinate "say" in what happens. But while these powerful people know one another and often agree, they rarely speak with one voice or literally control what happens.

Elitism and Pluralism: A Dynamic Balance

From today's perspective, the elitism-versus-pluralism argument seems abstract and irrelevant. Most scholars who hold the elitist model admit that there is no monolithic "power elite" but rather there are "segmented elites." Those holding the pluralist model have modified their views to include **stratified pluralism**, which means that some groups and quasi-groups have more power than others. After years of argument, almost everyone who studies power in political systems and communities believes that communities are neither manipulated by the few (the elitist model) nor are they pure democracies (the pluralist model). Rather, they are an amalgam of the two. To identify your focal community's unique balance of power, look for elites, segmented elites, strategic elites, and evidence of pluralism (i.e., "pockets" of influential people, groups, and organizations). Then look for ways that your focal community system has openings for democratic dialogue. You can mentally move back and forth between the two extremes to understand what is *really* going on in a focal community through the use of systematic analytical techniques such as power mapping.

Review the power mapping slide share. Consider the pockets of power in your own project. Create a power map based on the sample found from this site.

Assess your comprehension of Power as an Attribute by completing this quiz.

Power as a Product of Interaction

While many political scientists view power as attribute and define it as a commodity that can be gained, lost, and traded, interactional sociologists and social psychologists view power as a by-product of interaction. (See Chapter 3 to review symbolic interactionism, especially role taking and role making.) Succinctly stated, interactional theorists believe that power is the result of action and reaction.[9] In this view, power is a product of the ways people or groups respond to one another. Power is only an issue when its imbalances are accepted by all parties, in particular those over whom it is exercised. Contrary to what we might think, interactional power is *given to* the wielder (i.e., *not taken* by the wielder) by those over whom it is exercised.

Five Types of Interactional Power and Related Behaviors

Let's examine five types of interactional power and their related behaviors in Table 11.1.

Threat power is the ability to intimidate others by convincing them that if thwarted, you have the ability and the will to hurt them or those they love. **Force and threat of force** are obvious examples of behaviors associated with destructive power, but **manipulation** is equally destructive but far more subtle and so deserves attention. Those who manipulate others tend to be cynical, believe that everyone is essentially selfish, and are selfish, too.[10] **Manipulation** is often felt in private meetings, behind-the-scenes telephone calls, and subtle appeals to individuals' self-interest, organizational interests, and private fears. Manipulation has two faces: **Machiavellianism** (named after the medieval writer who first systematically described the behavior) is most often thought of as a manipulative trait of individuals,[11] and **organizational politics** is the way manipulation is manifested in groups, organizations, and communities.[12] While destructive behaviors may seem energizing in the short run, they usually fail in the long term—often resulting in a powerful backlash. You may be tempted to use threat power and destructive behavior irrationally in fits of temper or fall into manipulation to make others do things your way, but they have no place in organizing groups and communities.

Productive Power is based on the ability to make things or provide goods, services, or financial resources of worth to someone.[13] Productive power is closely related to economic power and to the capitalist economic model in which investors provide the financial, material, and human resources needed to make, market, and distribute goods and services. The impact of productive power is as close as your latest newscast, stock market report, and political debate. In the not too distant future as our natural resources become depleted, productive power may be redefined to include the ability to creatively do more with less. **Exchange behavior** uses productive power to enable people to trade goods and services with each other so that all of the trading partners obtain what they need and want. Exchange behavior began eons ago with direct trading arrangements among individuals and tribes but now is usually mediated by a medium of exchange (such as money). Exchange behavior is a vital part of community organizing. It can be as simple as sharing a written or Web-based resource with a colleague or as complex as sharing personnel or facilities. Organizing team members use productive power and

Table 11.1 Power and Related Behaviors

Primary Type of Power	Associated Behavior
Threat	Destructive
Productive	Exchange
Relationship	Integrative
Knowledge	Informative
Soul	Inspirational

exchange behavior when they work hard, share their skills freely with each other, and do what is necessary to get the task done.

Relationship power (i.e., the power of love or respect) is built on the natural bonds that unite people.[14] There are many moving examples of the power of human relationships and mutual commitment. It has often been said that soldiers in battle are willing to die—not for ideas, but for their devotion to their comrades. Positive relationships sustain us when we are discouraged, and they make achievements sweeter. Relationship power is at the heart of effective community organizing. The active component of relationship power is **integrative behavior**, that is, the ability to bring diverse people together. It is based on caring, loyalty, respect, and trust. Threat power or destructive behavior is not often seen within organizations built on integrative behavior, but integrative behavior can ignite destructive behavior in outsiders who feel threatened by organizational unity. The Civil Rights Movement is an example of how violence from outsiders can be aggravated by integrative behaviors. As African Americans became more unified in non-violently working for their rights, the more violent the reprisals from the white power structure became.[15] Unfortunately, integrative behavior can also become destructive if those involved become fanatics and make enemies of all who oppose their ideology. In fact terrorism is, in some ways, the result of integrative behavior gone wrong.[16] Those who use integrative behavior in their organizing efforts are able to step back from their own desires and viewpoints, discern what others are thinking and feeling, and find ways to build on areas of agreement and mitigate areas of conflict. They clearly show their willingness to give and receive support from other people by listening, mediating, and helping people find common ground. They demonstrate openness to receiving help from others. Members of organizations who demonstrate high levels of integrative behavior enjoy being together. They laugh a lot, celebrate joyously, often eat together, and provide everyone with the emotional sustenance that makes hard work worthwhile and builds everyone's self-esteem.

Knowledge power manifests itself as cognitive power, expressive power, emotional intelligence, information power, and connectivity. **Cognitive power** is sheer mental energy—the ability to think clearly, quickly, and accurately and to apply that thinking to important issues. **Expressive power** is the ability to convert information and ideas into easily understood forms through writing, speaking, stories, music, drama, or visual art. **Emotional intelligence** (emotional knowledge power) is the ability to understand and respond appropriately and empathetically to others and to create opportunities to build relationship.[17] **Information power** has two components: **information storage**, which means having needed facts and figures readily available, and **information literacy**—the skills to find, evaluate, analyze, synthesize, and apply data and information. Information literacy is especially important in this technological age. **Connectivity** (or connected knowledge power)[18] is the ability to gather knowledgeable people together often through Web-based means to create ideas and plans together.

Informative behavior is the ability to gather, create, consolidate, and distribute knowledge, ideas, information, facts, and figures in an effective way. Participants in organizing efforts who have knowledge power and can use informative behavior can conduct research and find the information needed by the group, turn raw data into useful information, write or speak clearly to share information with the group and the public, lead the group and help it develop consensus, understand policy creation and the political process, and apply specialized knowledge to issues. Participants can draw upon these and more skills from other participants who may have never dreamed they had such talents.

Soul power (spiritual and moral strength) springs from deep moral conviction and includes the ability to communicate to others the need for social justice, repentance, and change. It has deep roots in many religious traditions including Christianity, Judaism, Buddhism, Islam, and Hinduism; and in the last century, this power was demonstrated in the practice of *ahimsa* (non-violence) by Mahatma Gandhi[19] in India, Martin Luther King Jr.[20] in the United States, and Bishop Desmond Tutu[21] and Nelson Mandela in South Africa.[22] Soul power combines spiritual strength, faith in the ultimate justice and kindness of the universe, determination, and courage practiced with a set of strategies and tactics known as *ahimsa*, that is, non-violence and non-cooperation.

Self-development

Understanding and Mastery: Conscious use of self

Critical Thinking Question: There are five primary types of interactional power and associated behaviors. Rate yourself on each type and give reasons for your ratings. In what ways might your personal power be useful to your community organizing efforts?

Inspirational behavior is based on soul power and involves self-sacrifice, personal risk, and "putting your life where your mouth is." When others see you model inspirational behavior, it motivates them to do the same. Those who demonstrate soul power and inspirational behavior can live with courage and grace in difficult times and sacrifice themselves for others. Inspirational behavior doesn't necessarily include a once-and-for-all sacrifice, imprisonment, social rejection, or even giving up the pleasures of life (although it can mean all of those things). It does mean being willing to (1) ignore your own needs and desires on behalf of the greater good, (2) listen when you are tired, (3) face your fears, (4) rejoice when there seems to be no joy, (5) hope when things seem hopeless, and (6) continue working when it is tempting to give up. It means seeing beyond the practical objectives of your work to the reality that true power exists in the process of living creatively with others.

Assess your comprehension of Interactional Power by completing this quiz.

Interactive Power Transactions

Now that we have defined the kinds of interactive power and some of their related behaviors, let's look at aspects of interactive power as shown in Table 11.2 You can use this table when deciding how to respond to various forms of power and authority.

Human Systems

Understanding and Mastery: Processes to effect social change through advocacy (e.g., community development, community and grassroots organizing, local and global activism)

Critical Thinking Question: Power (as the ability to do what needs to be done) depends on interpersonal and intergroup interactions. Identify instances of the various interactional patterns within your focal community system.

Threat power, productive power, relationship power, knowledge power, and soul power are all present to varying degrees in community organization activities and community organizing leaders and participants. One of the major challenges in community organizing is to find the balance that enhances the quality of life for everyone. It takes a lifetime to understand the forms of power, where they fit into your life and behavior, and how they affect your relationships with other people, organizations, communities, and all of society.

Assess your comprehension of Power Transactions by completing this quiz.

Table 11.2 Power Transactions

Type of Power	Definition	As Used by Opponents	As Used by Organizers
Threat Power	A meaningful threat of severe deprivation if the receiver does not comply.[23]	Community organizing efforts that threaten existing power relationships are sometimes threatened with harassment, arrest, loss of livelihood, and at times even murder and lynching.[24]	The threat of strikes, massive civil disobedience, lawsuits, boycotts, and other activities that can seriously disrupt a target organization's ability to do "business as usual." Coercive tactics can be violent or non-violent so as to disrupt the normal flow of activities and force both the targeted group and the general public to take notice.[25]
Force (type of Threat Power)	Carrying out threats.	Force used against community organizers can include arrest, interrogation, riot control such as tear gas, and even lethal violence.[26]	Force in community organizing and social activism can vary from mildly disruptive actions to terrorism and guerilla warfare.[27]
Manipulation or Machiavellianism (Covert Threat Power)	Manipulation is invisible power or Machiavellianism. It involves getting someone to do what you want without the other person being consciously aware of your efforts.[28]	Powerful people and organizations manipulate community organizers through empty promises, lying, and cooption.[29]	Organizers may use the painful experiences of the poor and disenfranchised for their own fame or gain.[30]
Productive (economic) Power	The ability to make things and provide goods, services, or financial resources that are of worth to someone.	Used to isolate poor communities, deny employment opportunities, deny means of selling and buying necessities, and concentrate wealth in the hands of the few.	Used to creatively "do more with less" and invent sustainable ways of living, especially in localities. Withholding labor power (as in the case of strikes) can lead to increased quality of life for workers and their families.
Relationship Power	The natural loving bonds that unite people.	Can be used manipulatively to divide people by convincing them that some other equally poor group is a threat to their well-being. Racism is a classic example of a perverted exchange power.	Relationship is the basic motivation for most community organizing efforts. It provides the energy for self-sacrifice and mutual strengthening through difficult times.
Knowledge Power	The ability to gather and integrate information and share it with others.	Limit access to knowledge or to the fruits of knowledge such as denying literacy skills to the poor, under-financing schools in peripheral areas, or creating inaccessible jargon.	Open educational resources to all as a "common good," teach the powerless to create their own knowledge, facilitate communication among the disenfranchised, and emphasize the validity of indigenous knowledge.
Soul Power	The ability to influence others through strength of spirit.	Use the power of hatred and evil. The classic example is Adolf Hitler.	Use your own spiritual and moral strength, convictions, and sacrificial love to inspire others to do the same; share the deep abiding belief that good will eventually conquer evil.

Source: Copyright © by Pearson Education, Upper Saddle River, NJ.

Power and Authority

Now let's now turn to the relationship between power and authority. **Authority** is the right to control, demand, or determine what will happen and is directly related to the ability to use power. **Legitimate authority** is granted to the wielder by the receiver who acknowledges the right of the wielder to make a request and to have that request honored. Authority is granted by receivers because they believe that the holder of authority has the right to make requests and to expect compliance.[31] There are four major kinds of legitimate authority:

- **Legal–Rational Authority** is closely associated with political structures and the by-laws of organizations. It is based on laws and regulations that give those in certain positions the right to make requests and to take action.
- **Traditional Authority** is based on time-honored customs and beliefs in the right of certain individuals to make requests and take action on behalf of the community as a whole. For instance, pastors in African-American communities often have traditional authority that helps account for at least some of the authority exercised by the Reverend Martin Luther King in the Civil Rights Movement.
- **Charismatic Authority** is based on the exceptional personality or character (charisma) of the person exercising it.[32]
- **Value-Rational Authority** is the power of values and ideas as expressed by those in leadership. Value-rational authority is usually present as a motivating factor in all kinds of community organizing.[33]

An individual person may have several kinds of authority. For instance, Dr. Martin Luther King had traditional authority as a pastor of the black church. He had charismatic authority through the power of his personality and speaking style, and value-rational authority through the power of his ideas. The stronger the authority base, the more powerful the person.

Influence is a covert from of authority and is the ability to persuade those with legitimate power or authority to act or refrain from acting. Influence often occurs behind the scenes. You need to be concerned about identifying and working with persons who can influence decision makers and also with increasing your own power and influence. Influence in the community setting is often the ability of a power broker to act as gate keeper, a person who operates behind the scenes to give permission or block something from happening. Community influence is often not so much a factor of what you know as who you know. In many tight-knit neighborhoods and small towns, individuals who seem at first glance to have very little position power may actually have enormous influence because of family connections. Factors involved in influence include the **gate keeping role**, for example, the ability of administrative assistants to deny access to decision makers. Other factors that affect influence include centrality in community or organizational networks, time spent in the organization, commitment and interest, willingness to use power, importance of skills or resources, and whether the person is irreplaceable.[34] Influence is not only an individual characteristic but it accrues to organizations. Organizational influence grows as organizational capacities grow, as people learn to trust one another, and as organizations demonstrate cohesiveness and the ability to act effectively. Influence not only follows resources as in traditional theories of power, but resources follow influence as individuals and groups establish internal cohesion and external legitimacy.[35]

Assess your comprehension of the Differences between Power and Authority by completing this quiz.

You may not be aware of your own influence or how you can increase it. For instance, you will find that a reputation for service, kindness, generosity, ability to link people to resources, a willingness to accept help—as well as to give it—and a reputation for personal integrity and reliability are important components of influence. In general, influence is not a given because of your position; rather it must be built and earned.

Wielders of power can choose from either the destructive side of power (threat power, force, and manipulation) or the ethical side of power (legitimate authority and soul power).

How Others Perceive Your Power

It is not only necessary to understand the various forms of power and your ability to use them, but it is necessary to understand how others perceive your power and that of your organizing group members, especially in relationship to their perceptions of their own relative power. **Position Power** is the amount of power assigned to a given position or social status in a particular social interaction. Power is not static. You may have a good deal of power in one social situation and nearly none in another, depending on the perceptions and expectations of those around you.

The power dimensions of your status in any given interaction depend on:

- The value placed on your position(s) by society as a whole. For instance, in U.S. society (and in most community meetings), medical doctors have more power than sanitation workers, although both are necessary for public health.
- The value historically placed upon your status in similar social contexts. For instance, traditionally mothers have had a good deal of power over their children but have had little political power.
- Your **master (main) status** and how others perceive it in a particular setting. Each one of us has a **status set** made up of all the positions we hold. In any setting, it is almost inevitable others will feel that one of the social positions you play is more important than others. This tendency to be labeled or "pigeonholed" is particularly frustrating for members of historically powerless groups (women, young people, people of color, the disabled, the elderly, etc.) because their power is often determined by these **ascribed statuses** (things they cannot change) rather than by **achieved status,** what they know and can contribute or the positions they hold or may have held.
- How you perceive your own power. Your own sense of personal power depends on your **sense of self.** You should strive to be honest and balanced. Others in the community organizing effort, the focal community system, and its surrounding micro- and mezzo-systems may see you as powerful and influential while in your own heart you may feel full of self-doubt; conversely, you may think of yourself as powerful, wise, and influential but others see you quite differently.

Your power will vary a good deal in different contexts. You should neither overestimate your personal power nor sell yourself short. This ability to infuse a sense of effectiveness into your whole life enables you to share your power with others. You should try to help others appreciate their own power and enable them to use it in positive ways. As group members discover and use their own power, they will function well in other circumstances.

Self-development

Understanding and Mastery: Conscious use of self

Critical Thinking Question: Position power (sometimes referred to as "status") is based mostly on others' perceptions of you within a specific social context. Consider the various social contexts in which you frequently find yourself, such as student, worker, family member, volunteer, and community participant. How do others perceive you in each of these settings? What factors influence their perceptions? In what ways are your behaviors influenced by the way you believe others perceive you? What position power do you bring to your chosen community organizing effort? How can you enhance it?

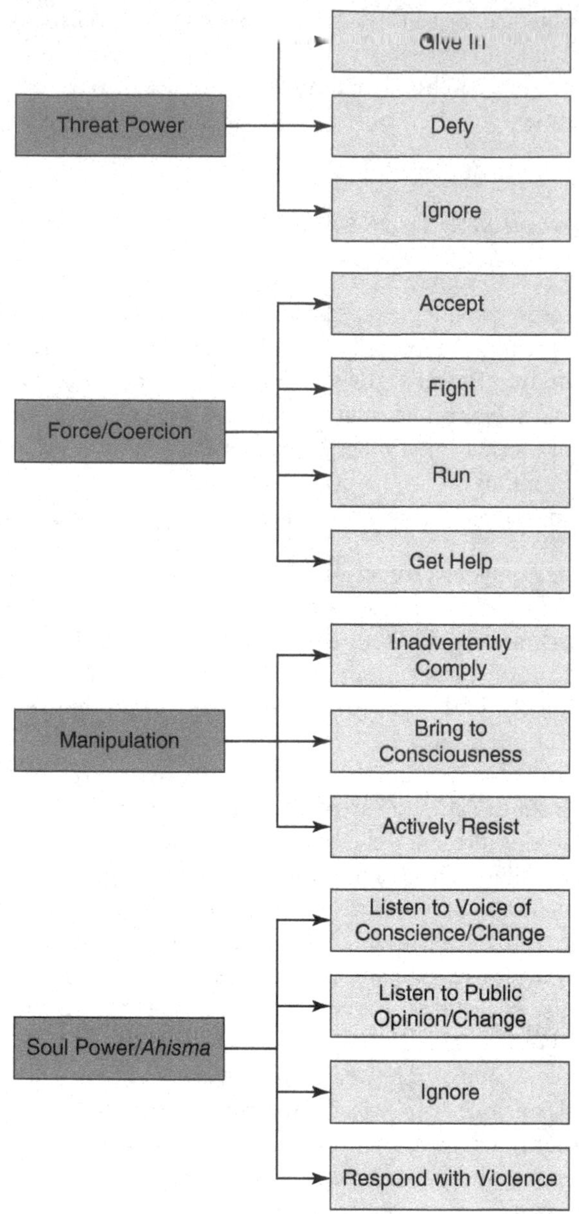

FIGURE 11.2 Choices Available to Receivers
Source: Copyright © by Pearson Education, Upper Saddle River, NJ.

In some ways, power is only as effective as the receiver allows it to be. Figure 11.2 illustrates the various choices that receivers of power have.

Power within the Varieties of Community Organizing

Each of the varieties of community organizing uses power in slightly different ways. Table 11.3 shows typical patterns of power in each type, based on the literature and current cross-case research.

Table 11.3 Power-Related Behaviors and Varieties of Community Organizing

	Threat Power, Destructive Behavior	Productive Power, Exchange Behavior	Relationship Power, Integrative Behavior	Knowledge Power, Informative Behavior	Soul Power, Inspirational Behavior
Place-based	No role	**Major**	**Major**	Moderate	Varying
Entrepreneurial/ Social Innovation	No role	Minor	Moderate	Moderate	**Major**
Advocacy/Social Movements	Moderate	Minor	Minor	Minor	**Major**
Mutual Aid	No role	**Major**	**Major**	Moderate	Minor
Self-help	No role	Moderate	**Major**	Minor	Moderate
Collaboration	Minor	**Major**	Minor	Moderate	Minor

Source: Copyright © by Pearson Education, Upper Saddle River, NJ.

You can use this chart to help determine which power-based tactics are most likely to work under which circumstances.

Empowerment: Increasing the Power of Individuals and Communities

In the mid-1990s, attention moved from the study of power to understanding how powerless individuals, organizations, and community sectors could take control over their own lives and actively influence decision making. The term **empowerment** was coined to describe this process. Although the word empowerment has been overused so it has lost some impact, no other term seems to express so aptly the progression of individuals, organizations, and communities from being controlled by others to affecting their own destinies.

The definition of empowerment used here comes from a consensus of community psychologists about its core meaning. **Empowerment** is "an intentional ongoing process centered in the local community, involving mutual respect, critical reflection, caring, and group participation through which people lacking in an equal share of valued resources gain greater access to and control over those resources . . . or put more simply a process by which people gain control over their lives, democratic participation in the life of their community and a critical understanding of their environment."[36]

Power in community organizing efforts results from constantly changing interactions among individual perceptions, decisions made by the organizing effort, and events in the focal community system and its micro-, mezzo-, and macro-components. To be effective, your leadership team must continually scan itself, the organizing effort, and the focal community—including its micro-, mezzo-, and macro-systems—to discern power relationships. Each of you must examine your own personal power by asking: "What is my relative status in our organization, in the focal community system, and in the micro-, mezzo-, and macro-systems affecting our organization?" "What kinds of power do I have and how effective am I at using them?" "How do I perceive my use of power? Is my perception accurate?" "What can I do to increase my effectiveness?" This self-reflection should be encouraged as an ongoing part of effective community organizing.

Your team should also continuously look its organizational power. You should ask members of the leadership team, participants, and other stakeholders,

- "Are we relatively powerful or relatively powerless?"
- "Where does our power come from?" "How can we increase it?"
- "What is drawing power away from our cause? Is there anything that can be done about it?"

Simultaneously, you should ask about power relationships in the focal community and its micro-, mezzo-, and macro-systems, focusing particular attention on how your organizing effort can enable community members to maximize their individual and shared power to improve the quality of life. Let's examine each of these interactive components in turn.

Maximizing Your Own and Others' Individual Power

Organizing efforts bloom when individual participants become sure of themselves and their ability to persevere and succeed. This **personal empowerment** is a perceptual, cognitive, emotional, behavioral process that results in a strong belief that past efficacy will be linked to future efficacy. In psychological terms, your sense of personal power—as well as your decisions about remaining active in a particular endeavor—is a mental construction built from your **perceived knowledge** and **skill development** (i.e., perceptions that your knowledge and skills have grown), conclusions that your **participatory competencies** (i.e., ability to make valuable contributions) are increasing, **expectations of future contributions** (i.e., your assessments about whether you will be able to physically and mentally maintain or increase your level of effective participation), sense of the organization's level of success, belief in the righteousness of the cause, and your evaluation of the likelihood of future success.[37]

Perceived Knowledge and Skill Development

This is the degree to which members believe that their participation in the organizing effort has increased their overall knowledge and skills. There are two steps your organization should take to foster this belief: you should provide members with many opportunities to build their knowledge and skills and give them constant positive feedback that acknowledges their learning. Your leadership team can enhance members' knowledge and skill development through providing them with time for active reflection on successes and failures; technical information needed to make good decisions; leadership opportunities requiring the use of effective communication, problem solving, and negotiation skills; data and information gathering tasks requiring research skills; and opportunities to reflect on how their worldviews are changing as a result of their organizing experiences (i.e., perspective transformation).[38] You can reinforce their pride and satisfaction by providing them with positive individual feedback, "positive gossip" (i.e., telling others' about their good work so that your praise gets back to them), and publicly celebrating individual contributions. For instance, for many years the Smithville Neighborhood Organization (SNO) was quietly but effectively led by Martha Manning, a neighborhood resident who—in spite of her personal struggle with cancer—gave hours of her own time to ensure that the city government kept its promises to rehabilitate neighborhood homes. Toward the end of her life, other SNO leaders decided to have a Martha Manning Day and awarded her with a plaque for her efforts. They held a celebration that highlighted not only her accomplishments but the work of several other unsung neighborhood members, which, participants say, not only gave Martha well-earned recognition for her life of community service, but also reignited their own commitment to SNO.

Perceived Participatory Competencies

Participants feel competent when their ideas are respected and incorporated into organizational strategies and tactics. Likewise, they experience participatory competence when they are able to speak up in public forums and are given opportunities to share relevant knowledge, to donate resources, and to demonstrate their persuasive abilities both within and outside the organization. You can increase individuals' feelings of competency by such simple things as keeping them informed of meeting times and places, circulating minutes, including them in decision making, listening carefully and respectfully to their ideas, and allowing time for telling personal stories and mutual reflection. Such behaviors communicate trust, respect, and the sense that everyone is needed and appreciated. On the other hand, you can inadvertently push people away by dropping them from your mailing lists, changing meeting times arbitrarily, making decisions behind their backs, publishing inaccurate contact information, interrupting their comments and personal stories, ignoring their attempted input, or putting them down by teasing or sarcasm.

Expectations for Future Individual Contributions

Each of your members must constantly weigh whether the organizing effort is worth their investment of time and effort. The more they feel genuinely needed, appreciated for their unique talents, and that they can count on other members for moral and practical support, the more likely that they will be motivated to stay involved. You should provide one another with mutual emotional support through deep, compassionate listening; thanks; wise coaching; gestures of true welcome; inclusion in events both inside and outside the group; friendship; and respectful mutual engagement. All of these actions communicate that each person is a valued part of a supportive team. As a joint endeavor, it is not just the role of the organizer to keep spirits up—rather, it is the job of all participants whose mutual support is nurtured through these inclusive and heartfelt gestures.

On a practical note, members' continued participation can sometimes be ensured in concrete ways through child or elder care, economic support, temporary or long-term housing, legal aid, cooperative purchasing, and provisions for re-engagement.

Perceptions of Group or Organizational Accomplishments

Members' continued participation is also influenced by their perceptions of group and organizational accomplishments. Their perceptions may have little to do with actual outcomes but rather with the sense that headway is being made toward those desired outcomes. Organizations that start off with bright hopes for immediate results often find themselves caught in bureaucratic red tape and political manipulation that slows their progress. While this is to be expected, it is disconcerting to those who are new to community work and impatient for success.

You must constantly keep group members informed of progress, engage members directly in the work whenever feasible, and reassure everyone that many of the most durable positive changes are those that take the longest to bring to fruition. Let them know that setbacks do not necessarily mean catastrophe or malfeasance.

Failure to communicate with members about such difficulties is especially dangerous in long-range efforts. This is exemplified in the SNO's decades-long cycles of success and failure. SNO was founded twenty years ago by an activist pastor who was well trained in Alinsky-style community advocacy (see Chapter 4 for a description of this variety of organizing). He was initially successful in building an "organization of organizations" and engaged well-connected community members, several of whom lived near the church. After extensive organizing efforts, SNO was able to influence the Industrial City government to sponsor a housing rehabilitation effort for all of Smithville to be done in three stages. Because the six blocks near the pastor's church were most in need of repairs, they were selected for the first round. Round one was completed successfully seventeen years ago, financing was arranged so renters could become home owners, and the area became an island of domesticity in a sea of continuing blight. This initial success led the federal government to allocate additional funds to rehabilitate the rest of the neighborhood with the understanding that the Industrial City government would provide local matching money. It seemed as if Smithville rehabilitation was well on its way until the municipal government changed and the new mayor refused to support the project. In spite of extensive efforts by SNO leadership, the federal money was returned, and no more has been requested or forthcoming. For the last fifteen years, the majority of Smithville has continued to deteriorate.

Although these decisions were made at the mezzo- and macro-levels and were not the fault of anyone on SNO, neighborhood residents blamed its failure on the SNO leadership largely because the leaders neglected to regularly report on their continuing advocacy activities to the rest of the neighborhood. This lack of news made it easy for people who were used to being disappointed to conclude that the SNO leaders had stopped their advocacy once their own homes had been completed. Rumors and resentment abounded on the streets. SNO lost credibility, membership, and effectiveness in a downward spiral that is still very difficult to reverse years later.

Belief in the Value of the Cause

Continuing participation not only depends on perceptions about past and present accomplishments but must include hope for the future and the belief that your mutual effort will prevail because it is good and right. Throughout history, successful groups have been those who are able to relate compelling **narratives** (shared stories) about where they are, have been, and will be in the future because their cause is profoundly just.[39] Successful narratives are tales of bondage, struggle, courage, and eventual triumph and include an emphasis on the righteousness of the cause, the sense that you all are doing what you are meant to do, obedience to some higher power that gives meaning and purpose beyond the struggles of the present moment, and the firm belief in the eventual triumph of good. As successful ventures have done for millennia, your organization's journey narrative should remind everyone of why you each decided to courageously move from your former "bondage" toward a new "promised land." It should enable all of you to reminisce about your adventures, relive good times, shake your heads in amazement over the difficulties you have already overcome, and declare that together you have hope for the future. You should often convey this hopeful saga in varied ways such as songs, dramas, visual art forms, anecdotes, and formal storytelling to engage new members and encourage old ones. As a general rule, the more often you tell the whole story, the more everyone will be reminded of your commitment to one another and to your cause.

Cost–Benefit Analysis: Expectations of Success versus Likelihood of Success

Because most people like to back winners, their expectations for future group or organizational accomplishments are very important and can be very fragile. Members' and outsiders' perceptions of likely future success are greatly influenced by your past organizational track record. Your track record, in turn, is determined by concrete successes, media portrayals, and the degree of positive change experienced. Everyone even remotely connected with your effort continually balances these factors and makes **implicit cost–benefit analyses**, asking whether the results likely to be obtained are worth the investment needed. Such implicit cost–benefit analyses can lead to loss of motivation, anger and violence, or increased motivation.

Loss of motivation or the perception that nothing is happening or ever will happen can lead to discouragement and despair, especially if leaders themselves begin to give up. For example, an attempt to found a teen center in Middle View ended after a few dedicated souls who donated countless hours and hundreds of dollars from their own funds were unable to gain wider support. Their discouragement spread and led to organizational collapse.

A perception that the costs are too high for the results obtained can lead to a kind of implosion as participants become discouraged afraid, or give up. This crushing of the spirit has occurred in many different settings. In 1970, four student protesters were killed by the Ohio National Guard at Kent State University in Ohio. On many campuses, students reacted immediately to these killings with student strikes, but by the following September, most campuses were quiet and even peaceful protests had largely ceased. Except for a few radical members of Students for a Democratic Society (SDS), popular participation in the peace movement of the late 1960s and 1970s essentially died after Kent State, although the impact of the anti-war movement lingered.[40] Likewise, the democracy movement in China was largely crushed after the Tiananmen Square incident in 1989.[41]

Violence is especially likely when promises have been made that have only been partially kept so that community members feel that positive change is stalled or being actively thwarted. Such frustration leads to a loss of faith in non-violent means, which, in turn, can lead to such seemingly irrational violence as riots. This pattern has been repeated in such varied settings as prisons,[42] urban communities,[43] non-violent social movements,[44] and revolutionary social movements.[45]

Increased individual motivation and empowerment occurs when community assets and hopeful signs of change are recognized internally and externally through public celebrations—such as this vivid example from Industrial City (home of the Smithville neighborhood). For years, Industrial City was known as a depressing "rust belt has-been" with little or nothing to be proud of until a coalition of ethnic organizations and service clubs decided to sponsor an annual folk festival. Every Labor Day weekend since the late 1980s, the streets in a neighborhood known for its beautiful Eastern European ethnic churches, labor history, and current diverse population have been blocked off and opened to the whole community. The city transit authority provides special buses, the churches are opened for tours, street vendors are given permits to sell foods and souvenirs from around the world, wandering musicians play, and well-known acts are performed each hour. The folk festival was originally financed by federal funds but is now self-supporting through business sponsorship and modest participant and vendor fees. It involves hundreds of volunteers and draws visitors from miles around. This yearly party has become a tradition and a source of renewed pride for both Industrial City and its target neighborhood, which now sports a year-round labor museum, an ethnic arts center, and many ethnic shops. Many people who began as festival volunteers now actively participate in other worthwhile civic endeavors, and a definite sense of hopefulness pervades the city.

Assess your comprehension of Individual Empowerment by completing this quiz.

Organizational Empowerment

Empowered individuals lead to empowered organizations, which in turn lead to empowered communities. While empowered individuals are certainly required for empowered organizations, there are social processes that can empower or disempower organizations themselves. To be considered empowered, your organizing effort will need to gain a recognized place among the other associations and formal organizations within your focal community system. (Review systems theory and the sociological definitions of various group configurations.)

An empowered organization needs:

- Clear organizational structures that provide many different ways to involve individuals.
- A clear mission and appealing, easily understood outcome statements.
- Many places for participants to plug in and feel needed, wanted, and respected.
- A plan of succession so it is not dependent on just a few people.
- A primary emphasis on local citizens' perceptions of needs and issues.
- A hopeful organizational narrative or story that can be easily understood and embraced by all sorts of people.
- A respected voice in community decision making.
- Access to needed resources.
- A track record of recognized success.
- Independence from outside control.

Among all of these, respect from representatives of other community structures, empowerment of individual members, a hopeful story, and independence from outside control appear to be the most important. Each factor works with the others to strengthen the community organization internally and to build its external credibility and power.[46]

Unfortunately, there are several factors that can weaken or disempower your organization. For starters, loss of mutual trust due to internal conflict over desired outcomes—coupled with hidden agendas—can do great damage. Once destroyed, trust is hard to rebuild. Second, simmering interpersonal or intra-group conflicts can destroy your organizational effectiveness. Often new organizing efforts are composed of individuals who haven't had practice in personal conflict resolution, so their disagreements may dissolve into personal vendettas or grudges that may spill over into group meetings and decision-making forums. Hours of time and emotional energy that could be devoted to the organization's mission may be diverted to infighting.[47] Third, community organizing efforts may be disempowered by **benefactors** (rich, outside volunteers or financial contributors) who intentionally or unintentionally communicate disrespect to community members. The latter issue is raised by theologian Mary Thiessen-Nation who recounts a conversation with one of three women who agreed to participate in a dialogue with her about the nature of inner-city ministry. When the woman heard Thiessen-Nation refer to her work as an outside volunteer as "throwing ropes" to community residents, she asked Thiessen-Nation the uncomfortable question: "Who has the more difficult job? The person who stands at the brink of a well of despair and 'throws a rope' or the person who catches the rope and, although she has no floor to stand on and no handholds to use to climb slippery walls nevertheless hauls herself and her family up to hope?"[48] The answer should be obvious, but too often those of us who are "throwing ropes" have little appreciation for the intelligence, willpower, emotional strength, and deep faith it takes to make a life in spite of nearly impossible odds. Empowering and empowered organizations respect their participants as individuals and the ability of their organizations to bring about positive change.

Human Systems

Understanding and Mastery: Processes to effect social change through advocacy (e.g., community development, community and grassroots organizing, local and global activism)

Critical Thinking Question: Think of several organizations in which you participate regularly. Rate each of them on an "empowerment scale" with "0" being terribly ineffective and "10" being extremely effective. What factors led to your ratings? What does this tell you about the process of creating effective community organizing efforts?

Community Empowerment

Empowered individuals and organizations lead to empowered communities. In many ways, this text is about building empowered focal communities that are characterized by:

- Strong social institutions that are engaged and concerned about the common good, not primarily about organizational survival.
- Citizens with a proactive, "can do" attitude and a history of successful community efforts.
- Individuals who can build bridges among different organizations within the community and with important resources outside of the community.
- Courageous individuals and organizations that encourage hope and joy despite fear and despair.
- Individuals and organizations bound by trust and mutual respect, not necessarily by complete agreement.
- The ability to embrace diverse individuals, groups, and economic classes with an overarching narrative of mutual support and respect.

Human Systems

Understanding and Mastery: Processes to effect social change through advocacy (e.g., community development, community and grassroots organizing, local and global activism)

Critical Thinking Question: The Asset-based approach to communtiy organizing is a very effective way to enable people to experience the power that already exists within themselves and their communities. What steps might be taken to initiate an asset-based approach in your community organizing effort?

- Catalysts or catalytic events and issues that bring people together.
- A reasonably supportive, or at least non-intrusive, broader social context.

Assess your comprehension of Organizational and Community Empowerment by completing this quiz.

Empowering a community is comparable to lighting a fire: (1) you gather the kindling through an assessment of institutional, associational, and individual assets; (2) you bring those assets together through informal networking and through focusing attention on a burning issue or issues; and (3) you continue to feed the fires of mutuality through continued networking efforts, enthusiastic celebration of successes, and mutual sharing of life's journey.

Forces against Community Empowerment

It would be nice if community empowerment were a simple matter of saying and doing the right things, thereby gaining a smooth road to success. Unfortunately, not only are you likely to meet overt opposition to your community, the very term *community empowerment* can be used to hide disempowering practices. Too often structures that claim to "empower" people subtly disable them. Planner Judith Arnstein was among the first to articulate how powerful interest groups manipulate supposed empowering and how seemingly fair and rational planning processes can actually retain and reinforce existing power structures and disempower the very people they are supposed to empower.[49] Arnstein's "ladder of power" gives a somewhat cynical but probably accurate view of how those in power include or exclude community organizing efforts and citizen participation—while giving lip service to empowerment. Table 11.4 illustrates Arnstein's ladder, moving from disempowering processes on the bottom to full empowerment at the top.

Arnstein discerned two categories that give people no control over decisions made on their behalf. **Manipulation** occurs when those in power maneuver people and situations so that the former's desired ends are accomplished before anyone is aware. **Therapy** resembles the mental health treatment model that assumes that those with scientific expertise are better equipped to solve community problems than the people themselves. This occurs when those in power convince the public that the actions that "experts" take on the public's behalf are *really* in the public's best interests and that public input is

Table 11.4 Arnstein's Ladder

Type of Involvement	Level of Citizen Empowerment
Citizen Control	Citizens' power
Delegated Power	Citizens' power
Partnership	Citizens' power
Placation	Tokenism
Consultation	Tokenism
Informing	Tokenism
Therapy	Non-control
Manipulation	Non-control

Source: Copyright © by Pearson Education, Upper Saddle River, NJ.

unneeded and could be harmful. Citizens who disagree are "in denial." At the therapy level, programs and procedures are imposed on the public to convince them to change their beliefs and actions. In both manipulation and therapy, the public is both passive and powerless.

Phase two or tokenism has three categories:

- **Informing** involves calling public meetings, sending press releases to the media, and providing written information on decisions that have already been made by those in power. Informing acknowledges the public's right to know but does not provide for any feedback.
- **Consultation** involves selecting a few representatives from the target population to provide feedback on decisions that have largely been made. Sometimes these community consultants can suggest minor changes, but control of the planning process remains with those already in charge.
- In **placation,** those in charge make a few relatively minor changes to keep protesters quiet but do not really listen to public concerns.

Many community meetings have one of these three agendas, which often fulfill the letter of the citizen participation laws but cynically violate their spirit.

Finally, Arnstein identified three planning processes that truly empower citizens. In **partnerships**, citizens or recognized citizens' groups are given equal voice with other stakeholders—such as business and political interests—but are largely recruited by the power holders and tend to hold their basic values. Partnerships can work if those chosen to participate are indeed truly representative of the community and feel powerful enough to speak up. In **delegated power**, citizens are represented by persons of their own choosing, a process that works well when the delegates are trustworthy. **Citizens' control** is the highest rung and involves putting planning directly in the hands of those affected. Citizens' control is rarely granted by those in power but can be grasped by self-empowered groups, such as those you have learned to build.

Explore the Web to learn more about Arnstein's ladder. What can you do to ensure that participants in your community organizing effort have a real voice in decision making?

It is unlikely that those using Arnstein's lower levels plot to keep the public ignorant of their true intent, although certainly some do put their own personal and organizational needs before the common good. It is more likely that those making decisions simply think of themselves and their fellow "experts" as knowing what is best and proceed accordingly. But your organizing team must be aware that not everything labeled "empowerment" actually accomplishes that goal.

Assess your comprehension of Forces that Disempower Communities by completing this quiz.

Summary

This chapter on power and its uses is divided into two major sections. The first section deals with abstract terms and concepts related to power and its use, and is intended to familiarize you with terms that you will encounter in future reading or when talking with others about the nature of power.

The second section deals with empowerment of individuals, organizations, and whole communities. Community organizations should be both empowering and empowered. Empowering organizations give participants a sense of control over their own destinies. Ideally, experiences in empowering organizations "spill over" into people's daily lives so that they have greater satisfaction, experience a deep sense of security, and no longer feel victimized by fate or other powerful forces. Empowered organizations, in turn, have a voice in the quality of life of constituents and the issues they're interested in. Those with established power take them seriously. Empowered communities and groups with well-supported issues, in turn, have a voice at higher levels of government and policy making—and the whole process builds democracy.

Assess your analysis and evaluation of this chapter's contents by completing the Chapter Review.

CHAPTER 12

Navigating the Political Labyrinth

Suzanne Tucker/Shutterstock

Chapter Outline

You may hate politics and want to avoid involvement with governments and their bureaucracies as much as possible, but unless your organization is very small and completely independent, you will find that a clear understanding of political processes and an ability to live with ambiguity and frustration is an important part of community organizing. This chapter will help you and your organizing team work through political issues affecting your organizing effort and develop some of your own political power along the way.

Community organizing efforts vary greatly in their involvement with formal political structures. Some, such as most self-help groups, are completely independent of government control, intervention, or support and have little or no connection to government or social policy. A few, such as community advocacy groups and social movements, are active players in politics and policy formation. Other varieties fall somewhere in between.

Why We Have Governments

Human beings are a contradictory species. On the one hand we are violent, aggressive, and frequently engage in internal disagreements and external conflicts. On the other hand, we are capable of major feats of cooperative effort and compassion. In a well-functioning society, these two elements are held in tension through a **social contract** (an implied agreement to abide by governing structures so that most of us can live together in peace and prosperity). The United States was and still is an experiment in the development of a dynamically balanced democratic social contract which allows most adults to share in decision making based on a fair balance of rights and privileges. You can see this dynamic balance in the founding documents. The Constitution primarily defines the rights of the powerful while the Bill of Rights and other amendments modify the Constitution to protect the powerless. The executive, legislative, and judicial branches and their various powers were carefully defined so that it is almost impossible for any one person or interest group to control all three at the same time. Moreover, the Constitution defines a federal system of national, state, county, and municipal governments that ensures maximum local input and control while delegating more complex tasks to state and national government.

Explore the United States Government Manual to learn more about the U.S. government. What role, if any, is legislation and regulation likely to play in your community organizing effort?

Assess your comprehension of the Basics of U.S. Government by completing this quiz.

Three Views of the Role of Government

Political decisions are influenced by implicit or explicit ideas about the appropriate role of government in our lives. Historically **residualism** and **institutionalism** have been the two primary abstract views of the appropriate role of government. Those holding a **residual** view believe that the main function of government is to provide safe boundaries in which everyone can act freely with a minimum of interference from law or government regulation. Residualists believe that governments should provide citizens and corporations (which are endowed with the legal characteristics of human beings) with freedom to pursue their private economic goals. They believe that maximum freedom will lead to maximum prosperity for everyone as the success of the rich will eventually "trickle down" to the poor. In the United States, the residual view is usually called **libertarianism, conservatism**, or **"right wing" politics** and is frequently associated with the Republican Party. The residual view of government can be summed up in the phrase: "The government that governs least governs best." Conservatives and libertarians believe that we should all have *freedom to* pursue our individual goals, a value that spurred the original European colonization and western expansion.

The **institutional view** is often associated with the terms **progressivism, liberalism**, or **"left wing" politics** and is usually associated with the Democratic Party. Those holding an institutional view believe that governments have a responsibility to ensure that all of their citizens have the basics such as food, clothing, shelter, safety in emergencies, health care, and educational opportunities. They assert that (1) all people should have a voice in government whether or not they are wealthy; (2) work of all kinds is important no matter what it pays; (3) everyone has equal value in spite of race, gender, ethnicity, religion, gender, sexual preference or physical attributes; and (4) there is a need for laws and regulations to prevent ruthless people and organizations from preying on the weak. Liberals emphasize the responsibility of governments to ensure that their citizens have *freedom from* fear, want, and exploitation and believe that these goals can best accomplished through direct provision of government services and strict regulation of the private sector coordinated by a strong national bureaucracy. They are often accused of over-governing. Both views focus on general abstract principles and macro-systems.

There is an emerging third perspective that emphasizes balance between the two functions of government and adds a dimension of mutual community building. This third viewpoint is coalescing from various directions which emphasize commitment to local engagement, grassroots participation, and participatory democracy. You have been exposed to some of its ideas here through our discussions of systems theory, sustainability, popular education, participatory research, and asset-based community organizing. All of these are united by commitment to **subsidiarity**, the idea that many needs are best addressed locally in the community focal system or its micro-systems by people working together to solve their own problems. In this emerging model, the role of government at all levels is primarily to support such local efforts. It is the government "of the people, by the people and for the people" spoken of by Abraham Lincoln in his Gettysburg address.

Let's look at health care to illustrate this third view. The residual view of health care (which has been the norm in the United States) makes it an individual or family responsibility, largely governed and delivered through private enterprise. On the other hand, the institutional view common in Northern Europe and Canada makes it a human right provided for by government, which largely eliminates the role of the private sector. Both views emphasize curing illness rather than sustaining and maintaining health. The third changes the focus from illness to wellness, opens the doors to alternative treatments, and emphasizes individual, family, and focal community approaches to wellness—while deemphasizing chemically and technologically based treatments that are dependent on an industrial model. Let's look at how this view changes practice using the Smithville neighborhood as an example.

Smithville, like all communities in the United States, has a fragmented health care system that is largely a combination of the residual and institutional views. Under the residual view, medical care is a commodity. Like all commodities, the best medical care is available to those who are able to pay for it. Most of the residents of Smithville are unable to pay. Many go without adequate medical or dental care until they are very ill and then turn to the public hospital emergency room or an under-stocked and under-staffed free medical clinic, a nod to the institutional view. Moreover, most Smithville residents do not have easy access to the elements of a healthy lifestyle. Corner stores do not stock fresh foods, local playgrounds have unsafe equipment and are filled with all kinds of trash, the houses still contain lead paint, and even the soil is contaminated with heavy metals.

If the new paradigm were implemented in Smithville, the current non-system would be replaced with a shared neighborhood emphasis on prevention and mutual responsibility for good health. There would be a multitude of community gardens and access to inexpensive but healthful food, safe playgrounds, indoor exercise and recreation facilities, community sports teams, and culturally diverse medical traditions. Houses would be rehabilitated to increase their safety. Crosswalks would be added on several busy streets. Garbage pickup would be regular to reduce rats, cockroaches, and other disease-carrying vermin. There would be several easily accessible, inexpensive local clinics to provide continuity of care from pre-birth to death. The clinicians would respect natural healers and care givers and would integrate them into their outreach and educational efforts. At the city-wide (mezzo) level, a coordinated network of outpatient resources would provide local clinics with sophisticated diagnostic services, using computer links to experts. Those few people needing to leave the neighborhood for inpatient care would be quickly released and cared for through compassionate and conveniently located follow-up services. As the "Smithville model" became successful, comparable approaches would appear throughout the United States, each tailored to the needs of a specific focal community system.

Some of this vision such as community gardens, improved playgrounds, indoor exercise and recreation, farmers' markets, involvement of alternative care givers and health education could be implemented at the neighborhood level with little or no need for government intervention or funding. Infrastructure improvements such as safe crosswalks, housing inspections, and adequate garbage collection would require municipal involvement. Other components of the vision such as improved clinics and increased means of access to medical treatment would require collaboration with local hospitals, private physicians, and other health care providers supported by regional medical centers. State laws regulating outpatient and inpatient care would need to be developed to financially support true community-based care as well as in-home services. National health care policies would be required to encourage investment in health care alternatives, prevent misuse of funds, and concentrate cost-cutting measures on regulation of large hospitals, pharmaceutical companies, and insurance providers to ensure that no windfall profits are made on human suffering. On the financial side, adequate funds would need to be allocated through the budgeting process to ensure that even low-income areas could receive high-quality care. Other federal laws would be needed requiring that public research dollars be used for investigating and eliminating environmental health hazards, as well as for research on inexpensive, noninvasive treatments. People with expertise in community organizing skills and techniques would be needed at all levels to provide coordinated efforts to make this vision a reality.

Human Systems

Understanding and Mastery: Processes to analyze, interpret, and effect policies and laws at local, state, and national levels

Critical Thinking Question: The principles of subsidiarity imply using appropriate organizing strategies within various systems to bring about desired change. Choose an area of concern within your focal community system and picture desirable outcomes, and then identify what would need to be done at the local, municipal, state, and national levels to make the dream a reality. (Hint: Read the Smithville health care example to get an idea of what might need to be done.)

Those who embrace the residual view of government believe that the "government that governs least governs best" while those with an institutional view believe that government has primary responsibility to ensure that people have the basics needed for a good life. The subsidiarity view asserts that families, private organizations, and various levels of government each have an appropriate role in ensuring that basic needs are met and that the "good life" results from an appropriate balance among them. Think about your goals for your focal community. Will you be more likely to accomplish them by (1) being left alone to work independently (i.e., the residual view), (2) receiving direct help from the government and government agencies (i.e., the institutional view), or (3) some mix of the two (i.e., subsidiarity)? Begin to think about the steps you will take to achieve your desired level of government involvement.

Professional History

Understanding and Mastery: Exposure to a spectrum of political ideologies

Critical Thinking Question: Which of the three primary views of government (1) best expresses your values, (2) is most reflective of the members of your leadership team, (3) represents the general views of those in your focal community, and (4) represents the elected officials and government bureaucrats you will be working with? How will you reconcile differences among these views?

Assess your comprehension of Three Views of Government by completing this quiz.

Political Negotiations

Politicians you encounter will tend to take either the residual or the institutional position (although a few may lean toward the subsidiarity paradigm). You can use your understanding of these views to identify the probable position that a particular politician or group of politicians is likely to take and how you should approach them. For example, Republican officials are likely to have a residual view and are unlikely to support initiatives that require heavy government investment, new laws, bureaucratic structures, strict regulation of private enterprise, or national-level initiatives. However, they may respond well if you emphasize the independence and self-sufficiency of your efforts and cost savings that might be derived. Democrats, on the other hand, tend to take the institutional view and may respond well to appeals based on governmental responsibilities for human needs, projects that will interface with and strengthen existing bureaucracies, and proposals for large initiatives with statewide or national implications. A few progressives may find the locally based participatory action approach appealing. Your own approach should be **pragmatic** (practical) and non-partisan. Your leadership team should carefully define the appropriate role of government based on the issue, your organizational mission, and your desired outcomes. Some issues are best dealt with through independent initiatives in which governments and government representatives have no role. Some do well as private collaborations with little government involvement, while still others may require new or changed laws at the local, county, state, national, or international levels. Many require the enforcement and application of existing policies. Your choice to seek or not to seek government involvement involves balancing freedom and flexibility with the power vested in formal authority. Independent efforts often have freedom of movement and decision making—but little authority. Government action may have authority, but at the expense of flexibility. It is usually best to solve problems through collaboration and a blending of private and public resources, involving formal legislation or government regulation only if necessary.

Six Dimensions of Public Policy

American politics are complicated. Not only do we have a complex federated system of national, state, county, and municipal governments compounded by separate elected bodies (such as local school boards), but each of these often has a legislative, executive, and judicial component. Moreover, policies at various levels frequently contradict one another! It seems crazy but somehow it has worked reasonably well for over two hundred years.

Policies are courses of action. The term *politics* is usually used in reference to the processes governments use to set their courses of action. Here we will look at six levels of policy and their effect on community organizing efforts. The levels are (1) **societal values**, (2) **regime policy**, (3) **sectorial policy**, (4) **jurisdictional policy and laws**, (5) **administrative policy and regulations**, and (6) **delivery-level (street-level) policy and procedures.** The levels interact: each can affect the others and changes in any one can affect the entire policy system. You can help your leadership team analyze the political context when you understand the six levels of policy and how they interact. Let's look at them one at a time.

Level One: Values and Social Policy

All public policies and the laws and regulations that flow from them are based initially in widely held **societal values** (i.e., conscious and unconscious beliefs and assumptions about what is really important in life and what behaviors and norms are foundational to life together). Values are often largely subconscious, but they are the implicit guides to how we live and are the criteria by which we judge others. Many political conflicts are based in a clash between contrasting values held by substantial numbers of people. Therefore, identifying complementary and contrasting social values that impact your community organizing effort is one of the first steps in predicting how your initiative is likely to be received. To understand politics, you must analyze the values and clashes of values involved in living in our society. As a community organizing team, you will first want to ask: "What major social values support our organizing effort?" and then ask "What major social values conflict or compete with ours?" and finally, "What strategies will we use to strengthen our position and encourage people to adopt our values?"

Even seemingly simple projects such as the Middle View runaway prevention program can be plagued with values clashes. As you probably recall from earlier discussions, the runaway project was founded by a group of pastors, educators, and parents who wanted to provide a temporary shelter for young people who were considering running away or who had been thrown out by their parents. The leadership team felt that their community had a responsibility to provide troubled young adults with structure, an opportunity to remain in school, and a path to becoming responsible adults. However, some community members valued the ascendancy of the rights of individuals and families and felt that conflicts between parents and children should remain in the family. Others believed strongly in individual decision making at any age and in the right of young people to run away from home if they chose to do so. Still others felt that young people should be obedient to adult-defined standards for appropriate behavior and should be publicly punished for misbehavior, such as running away. Others felt that caring for runaways was the responsibility of county and state government and *not* a local concern. Figure 12.1 illustrates these conflicts.

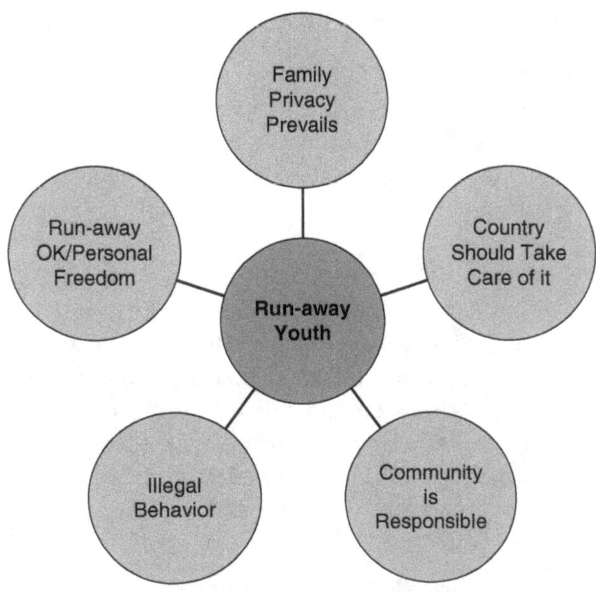

FIGURE 12.1 Values Conflicts in the Middle View Runaway Project

Source: Copyright © by Pearson Education, Upper Saddle River, NJ.

Understanding these values conflicts and especially *working respectfully with those who held them* helped the leadership team to create a program that (1) respected the rights of families, and (2) respected the legal responsibilities of the juvenile courts, while enabling young people to have a stable place to live if family mediation and reunification proved impossible.

Level Two: Regimes and Regime Policies

Once you have identified the various values that are most likely to impact your project, you will need to sort out the various regimes and regime policies that directly affect your work. **Regimes** can best be thought of as "those in charge" and in government are often composed of a symbolic leader such as a president, governor, or mayor and all of those with paid positions who support their views. Every political organization from your local town to the United Nations is run by a regime. Every level of government has a **regime policy**, a broad set of principles applied by governing authorities as their overall approach to governing.

In the United States, there are dozens of regimes and regime policies that often conflict with one another. At the national level, the President and the Executive Branch are the most obvious regime, but each party in both houses of Congress has regime policies coordinated by their leaders, and even the Supreme Court has a sort of regime policy determined by the majority of its members and heavily influenced by the Chief Justice. Likewise, each state government has its regime policies in all three branches of government and so forth down to county, municipal, and school district levels. Think of regimes as a stack of blocks with several different levels as illustrated in Figure 12.2.

In a multi-level system as in the United States, regime policies often conflict. For example, a Republican president and a Democratic governor may have very different views of the appropriate role of the national government, the provision of collective versus private goods, the level and kind of taxation, and a variety of other issues. Regimes can also conflict within the various levels of government. For instance, it is possible for the president and the majority of Congress to be of different parties or for the two houses of Congress to have different party majorities and, of course, the same can be said of state and local level politics. Regime policies may also conflict within a target community or neighborhood. For instance, it is not uncommon for school district policies to conflict with municipal policies or for the policies of nearby municipalities to conflict with one another. Regime policies can even conflict for a single organizing project. For instance,

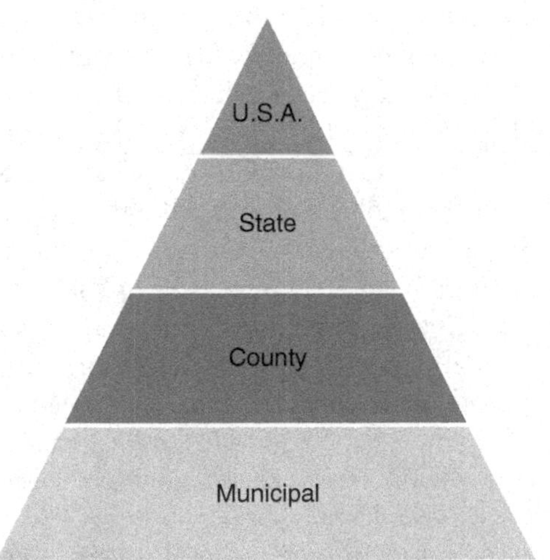

FIGURE 12.2 Regimes in the United States

Source: Copyright © by Pearson Education, Upper Saddle River, NJ.

community organizing work in the Middle View area is often slowed by the need to juggle two county regimes, four town regimes, a consolidated school district regime, and the national park authority.

Three of the many challenging tasks facing you are (1) identifying the regimes most likely to have the greatest impact on your organizing effort, (2) determining how existing regime policies can facilitate or impede concrete action and communication, and (3) determining how the policies of various regimes may contradict one another making it nearly impossible to meet all of their requirements. For example, the runaway prevention program was impacted by:

- a local municipal regime policy that placed the provision of social services outside the realm of municipal responsibility;
- county regime policies that emphasized service delivery through county agencies—with little or no provision for collaboration with independent, private non-profit agencies;
- another county regime policy that emphasized keeping property taxes low by passing costs on to the state; and
- state level regime policies that gave oversight and control of program content, service delivery, health standards, and building safety to a set of fragmented and under-staffed departments with often contradictory expectations and—at the national level—policies that emphasized states' rights, state control, and reduced support of social programs.

Leadership team members were all new to the task of bringing a complex project from dream to reality. They were challenged by the need to identify the regime policies at all levels that impacted or might impact their work; identify the agencies and major contact people involved in enforcing the regime policies; and sort through exactly what each policy meant in concrete terms and figure out how to pay for requirements that all seemed to be geared for large, well-established agencies, all while remaining true to their mission and honoring promises made to community supporters. The task of sorting out regime requirements was doubly challenging because all of the regimes were constantly changing their policies and (true to the rules of systems theory) any changes in the mezzo-system affected the whole focal system (review systems theory in Chapter 2). It was like trying to put a fitted sheet that is slightly too tight on a bed that is slightly too big; some portion or other was always popping up out of control, and then when that was fixed something else would pop up. None of the regimes provided much guidance on how their demands were to be met, nor did they provide financial resources for meeting their demands. Many rules and regulations were written in a "one-size fits all" format aimed at large, financially stable established institutions in urban settings that could not easily be adapted to Middle View's rural context. Perhaps most frustrating of all was the regimes' refusal to help financially. Their representatives agreed that there was indeed a need to prevent young people from running away and for there to be a place for them to sort through their personal and family issues while living and going to school in their own community, but the Town Council said it was not their problem; the County Commissioners through their Department of Human Services said it was not their problem, it was the state's problem; and State representatives said "Oh no, it's a county problem." In the meantime, young people kept running away. Like the potato in the children's game Hot Potato, the innovators felt as if they were being thrown from one regime to another and given no real help anywhere.

An example from Smithville also represents regime clash. For many people the American Dream of individual success and family security is symbolized by home ownership. In Smithville, this dream has been supported at the focal system level by a non-profit agency founded by members of the Smithville Neighborhood Organization (SNO) dedicated to renovating and selling homes within the focal neighborhood. In the late 1990s, these efforts were supported at the mezzo-level by the Industrial City Housing Authority and at the macro-level by the Clinton regime's Department of Housing and Urban Development (HUD). In the 2000s, regimes changed at the Industrial City municipal level and at HUD. Tax money for renovation and new construction dried up. Community Development Block Grant money (money from federal taxes that is given back to states and municipalities for their use) as well as some already allocated housing renovation funds were diverted by the municipal government from low-income housing to other uses. Municipal regime priorities moved from home ownership for the working poor and lower middle class to gentrification for the upper middle class. National funding for housing dried up. As a result of these regime changes, SNO's housing rehabilitation and housing ownership efforts stalled with only one-third of the work accomplished. As a result one part of Smithville looks quite attractive with a substantial number of rehabilitated owner-occupied residences and only a few rundown properties. The rest of Smithville remains occupied by low-income renters or has been abandoned completely. SNO's dream of a thriving neighborhood of proud, working class homeowners has been largely thwarted due to municipal and federal policies beyond SNO's control.

The Middle View and Smithville projects are just two examples of how regime policies affect community organizing efforts, and they demonstrate how important it is to carefully analyze the impact various regimes may have on your work. The following questions may help you sort out regime policies:

- What level of government are we examining?
- What are the regime policies (broad views of the role of government), and are they primarily institutional (supporting the use of government funding and government bureaucracy for the regulation and provision of goods and services) or residual (based on the idea that the government that governs least governs best)?
- Does the regime we are examining emphasize openness, citizen involvement, and making the public aware of available services? Does it make information difficult to find, and are most decisions made by a secret or elite group of insiders?
- What are the regime's priorities? Is it likely that they will emphasize keeping taxes down at the expense of services, or will they make human needs a priority? How is this policy likely to affect our funding resources?
- Are there conflicting regimes at each level of government? For instance, is there a Republican president and a Democratic Congress (or vice versa)? Are the House of Representatives Republican and the Senate Democratic? What are the likely consequences of these splits for our efforts? Likewise, are there divisions at the state, county or municipal regime levels, what are they, and how will they affect our work?

Explore the various regimes in our federal and state system. What U.S. government organizations are most likely to impact your community organizing effort?

The answers to these questions will help you accomplish your mission and outcome goals.

Human Systems

Understanding and Mastery: Organizational structures of communities

Critical Thinking Question: Identify the regimes that most directly affect your community organizing effort. Determine the regime policies that are most likely to affect its success or failure and begin developing strategies for addressing these concerns.

Level Three: Sectorial Policies

Sectorial policies and regime policies are linked. Regime policies define a broad view of the role of government on such general matters as taxation, regulation, and interpretation of the Constitution and are often labeled "liberal," "conservative," or occasionally "utilitarian" (i.e., doing whatever is necessary to make government function well). Sectorial policies that affect particular issues, concerns, and people flow from these general viewpoints. Sectors are broad areas of public life such as health, economic development, education, human services, transportation, housing, food and drug concerns, agriculture, labor, banking, and defense, to name a few. Sectorial policies may be directed toward a particular part of the population or may affect everyone.

Almost all government bureaucracies are organized by social sectors that coincide with significant areas of life. Regime and sectorial policies go together. Regimes not only have a set of principles that provide an overall approach to governing, but these principles lead to their **sectorial policies** (i.e., approaches to particular areas of public life). For instance, at the national level the president's cabinet and various executive departments are divided broadly by social sectors such as health and human services, education, agriculture, commerce, and so forth. State, county, and municipal government departments are also similarly organized by broad social sectors. The national and state political platforms of the two major parties also cover many sectors of life. Figure 12.3 is a representation of how the various sectors fit together in national regimes.

Figure 12.3 illustrates the various social sectors, their size in relation to one another, and areas of overlap. For instance, the commerce and military sectors touch one another in several ways such as government contracts for military expenditures, military demands for industrial goods, and military protection of commercial interests. Health,

FIGURE 12.3 Typical Sector Divisions

Source: Copyright © by Pearson Education, Upper Saddle River, NJ.

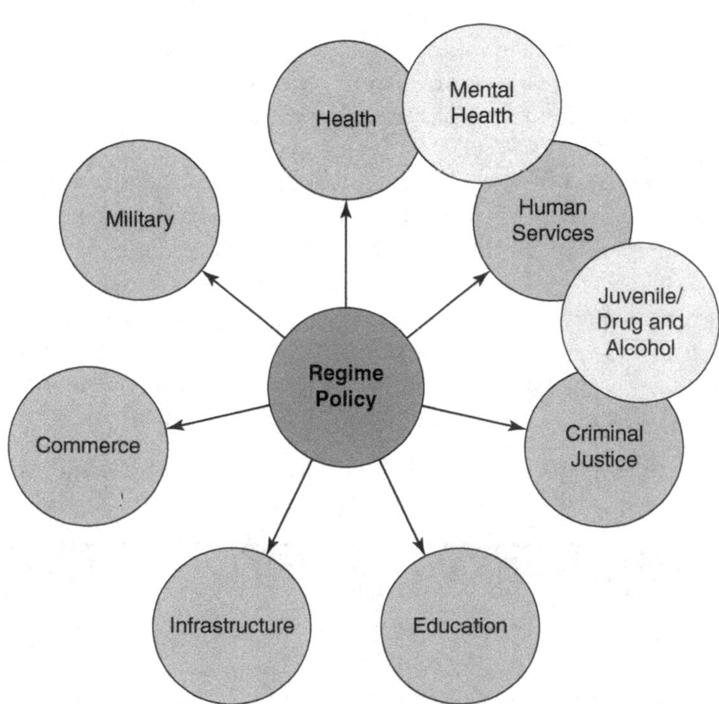

social welfare, and criminal justice touch one another in a cluster of somewhat related services. Moreover, they overlap at various points. For instance, mental health care overlaps both health care and human services, the juvenile justice system overlaps human services and the criminal justice system, drug and alcohol services overlap human services and the criminal justice system, and so forth. Many social innovations and entrepreneurial efforts are impacted by several sectors. For instance, the Middle View Runaway Shelter dealt mostly with the juvenile justice and human services sectors but was also affected by the educational sector because the young people were of school age, the health sector because sanitary conditions had to be maintained in the group home, and even the infrastructure sector which oversaw building code enforcement.

Clashes among sectorial policies are common in all varieties of community organizing, but they are especially troublesome for advocacy groups and social movements that have to decide where, whether, and how to apply social action strategies. Let's use the disabilities movement as an example of an issue that has had to work within several sectors. To ensure access to education, activists worked at the national and state levels to pass the Individuals with Disabilities Education Act (IDEA), which was implemented primarily by state level education departments and at the local school district level through Individualized Educational Plans (IEP). Advocates for the disabled have fought within several levels of the educational sector for access to appropriate educational resources. Almost concurrently, advocates for the physically disabled fought for passage of the Americans with Disabilities Act (ADA). Requirements of the ADA affected accessibility to the buildings, technologies, and services that are part of American society including, but not limited to, government offices, city sidewalks, commercial establishments, employment opportunities, public transportation, health care, housing, parks and recreation, telephone service, and social security disability. Its provisions have benefited old and young alike, as well as such special populations as the developmentally disabled, the mentally challenged, and disabled veterans. In fact, the impact of the ADA is so pervasive across so many government offices that the Obama administration established a national ADA website, which provides an Internet portal to all of them. They are presented here in Table 12.1 to give you an idea of the many sectors of life impacted by disabilities issues.

These are a few of the national offices affected by the ADA. Imagine these multiplied over fifty times (the state level plus the U.S. territories) and thousands of times (the municipal and school district levels). Advocates must use systems thinking and understand the connections among systems to keep the IDEA and ADA effective. For instance, IDEA and ADA must be enforced at the local level, respected by the sectors of society they touch, and applied reliably. IDEA has limited use if there are no places for the disabled to go when they "age out" of public schools. Parking spaces for the handicapped are a cruel joke if non-handicapped people are allowed to use them at will or if curbs are too high to navigate. "Accessible" restaurants can be a source of misery if their restrooms are too small to accommodate wheelchairs. Elevators in multiple-story buildings make them accessible but can be dangerous if there are no alternatives in case of fire. Extensive regulations and enforcement of these laws' provisions can be self-defeating if local stores are forced to close because of costly required changes.

Many seemingly simple solutions require negotiations with many different people, compromise, and creative problem solving. Advocacy efforts require simultaneous multiple approaches and require participants to apply social action strategies where they

Table 12.1 National Level Sectors and Departments Affecting the Disabled (2012)

Sector	Government Department	Acronym
Legal Rights	Department of Justice	DOJ
Employment	Equal Employment Opportunity Commission	EEOC
Public Transportation	Department of Transportation	DOT
Telephone Access	Federal Communications Commission	FCC
Proposed Design Guidelines	United States Access Board	(separate agency)
Labor—Civil Rights Center	Department of Labor	DoL
Education	Department of Education	ED
Health Care	Department of Health and Human Services	HHS
Housing	Department of Housing and Urban Development	HUD
Parks and Recreation	Department of the Interior	DOI

Human Systems

Understanding and Mastery: Organizational structures of communities

Critical Thinking Question: While regimes are the overall governing structures of government, sectors focus on particular needs. Identify relevant sectors and sectoral policies by asking, "What broad areas of society most affect the people and issues we are trying to address? What broad sectors (or divisions) of the various levels of government most affect our work? How will their policies at each level be likely impact our initiative?

feel the most comfortable and where they will do the most good. Therefore, your leadership team may find it helpful to identify the various sectors that impact your effort and to take the time to map the various agencies and organizations involved.

Level Four: Jurisdictional Policies

The term **jurisdiction** connotes the area over which an individual or organization has authority. The term usually has both geographic area and sectorial dimensions. Sorting out the many people and organizations have jurisdiction over all or part of your organizing effort can be very confusing, but some examples might help you figure out how to do it. Let's take transportation as an example, with roads in particular. If you take a look at a typical road map you will notice that different kinds of roads are usually differentiated by size and color. The largest are the "interstates" that are under the jurisdiction of the federal government, followed by state highways, county roads, and then township roads. As you drive from place to place on all these roads, you generally do not notice changes of jurisdiction, but sometimes jurisdictional change is very obvious. For instance, a highway may go from two lanes to four lanes when it crosses a state line, within a matter of a few feet; a country road may go from paved to dirt when it crosses a town border; or a smooth road may become full of potholes or vice versa when you pass a county line. If you investigate a little further, you will find that each of the jurisdictions on each side of such divides maintains its own road crew, heavy equipment, and snowplows; has its own set of laws and ordinances covering road building, repair, and maintenance; and has its own road budget! From time to time you may read about state level initiatives to get all of these local transportation jurisdictions to join forces, maintain shared crews, and buy shared equipment. Such initiatives rarely work because people tend to be jealous of their own power, authority, and independence. Such jurisdictional divisions affect almost every aspect of our lives together.

At the national level, large agencies are often divided into jurisdictions with regions that may encompass several states or parts of states. Regional jurisdictional policies can vary greatly even in the same agency. For instance, one of the reasons that the aftermath of Hurricane Katrina, which struck the Gulf Coast in 2005, was far worse in Louisiana than in Florida was that the regional branch of the Federal Emergency Management Agency (FEMA) with jurisdiction in Florida was better prepared for hurricanes than the one with jurisdiction in Louisiana.[1] The Katrina disaster was not only exacerbated by conflicting policies within FEMA itself, it was worsened by poor coordination of efforts and contradictory regime, sectoral, and jurisdictional policies. Help was greatly delayed because of conflicts among the city, state, and national governments over who had jurisdiction. As a result, effective action was stymied, hundreds of people died, and many others were injured and displaced.[2]

The term *jurisdiction* not only applies to the span of control of a particular person or organization; in politics it also refers to responsibilities for defining, enforcing, and adjudicating regulations related to specific laws and ordinances. While legislative bodies at various levels of government pass laws, these laws are under the jurisdiction of regulatory agencies. In fact, it has become a truism that policy is really made by regulatory agencies. Your community organizing efforts will be required to respond internally to jurisdictional policy expectations, and you will need to shape your own internal policies based on external priorities and constraints. In fact, you will often spend much thought on the impacts of government policies, regulations, and monitoring on strategies, tactics, and desired outcomes of the organizing effort. Most laws are outlines of what the government intends to do, broad guidelines about how it intends it to be done, and general guidelines for enforcing the law including any sanctions that will be imposed for non-compliance. You should make every effort to identify the agencies likely to directly impact your efforts, as well as the direct and indirect roles they play in public policy as it is *really* enacted, not how it is *supposed* to be enacted. You should ask questions such as:

- What government departments and agencies will have jurisdiction (regulatory power) over our initiative?
- Exactly what control will each have?
- Will several different agencies vie for jurisdiction?
- What conflicts are likely to arise at various levels of authority?
- What recourse will we have in solving such conflicts or protesting unfair treatment?

Once again Middle View's runaway prevention project provides a good example. The shelter portion of the program design was impacted by contradictions between local fire department regulations and state-level labor and industry safety regulations. The fire department required that all windows be made of heavy wire-embedded safety glass to prevent explosion during a fire while the Department of Labor and Industry required that these same windows be used for egress by youth living on the second floor. The wire windows were too heavy for adolescent girls to lift, which caused a substantial delay in project implementation until a compromise was reached.

The program was likewise impacted by contradictory jurisdictional demands. For example, the same troubled youth might be subject to different treatment demands

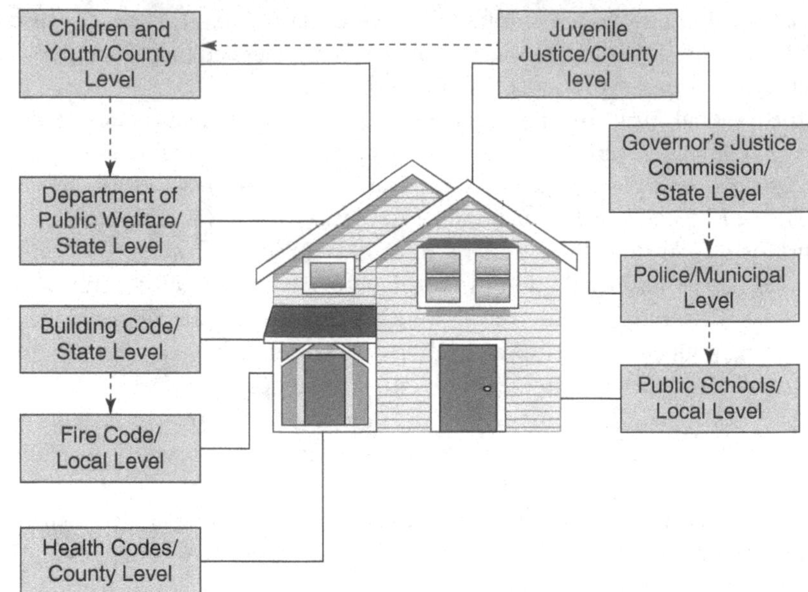

FIGURE 12.4 Jurisdictions Affecting the Middle View Runaway Shelter

Source: Copyright © by Pearson Education, Upper Saddle River, NJ.

depending on whether she or he fell primarily into the mental health system, the drug and alcohol treatment system, or the juvenile justice system. Seventeen-year-olds were required to receive very different treatment under the juvenile justice system than the same person at eighteen under the adult corrections system, regardless of his or her developmental age. An intellectually challenged or mentally ill youth was treated differently by the mental health jurisdiction than by the developmental disability jurisdiction. Figure 12.4 illustrates how these contradictions in jurisdictional policies affected the runaway project. You should map similar contradictions for your own focal project and focal system.

Even simple community events often require permission and cooperation from several different jurisdictions. Imagine that your organizing project has decided to sponsor a community pride day by having a neighborhood clean-up followed by a picnic and street dance in a local park. Identify the government departments that will have jurisdiction over various parts of the event (e.g., trash pick-up and renewal, participant safety, park use) Within these departments, who has the authority to make decisions? Who is responsible for carrying them out? In what ways are they likely to be supportive? Where might they make things difficult? What approaches will ensure maximum cooperation? What tactics will you use should they prove uncooperative?

Human Systems

Understanding and Mastery: Organizational structures of communities

Critical Thinking Question: As a community organizer you will frequently encounter conflicts among jurisdictions. What communication skills will you need in order to reduce these conflicts and obtain your desired outcomes?

Level Five: Organizational Policies

Regime, sectorial, and jurisdictional policies all eventually impact organizational policies. Your organizational policies are created in the context of various jurisdictions and regulatory agencies that may define such things as program design, program delivery, acceptable record keeping including treatment plans and financial records, fiscal year, personnel practices, staffing levels, rules for confidentiality, consumer and personnel safety criteria, reporting procedures, external inspection schedules, and criteria for resolution of consumer complaints. These external rules and regulations, in turn, define the record keeping expectations that you have of paid personnel and even volunteers. It is sad but true in this day and time: "If it isn't written down, it hasn't been done."

Most of your organizational policies and procedures will flow from the expectations of the various agencies that have jurisdiction over your processes and programs. Organizational record keeping almost always causes headaches and complaints, but it can be especially frustrating when different regulatory or funding agencies require different forms and reporting structures (even different fiscal years). For instance, caregivers working in a program for the developmentally disabled located in Smithville were expected to develop two sets of treatment plans; establish measurable objectives; and keep duplicate case notes for each consumer, one for the State Health Department and one for the State Office of Mental Health and Mental Retardation. The State Health Department used a medical model and expected that the treatment plan would emphasize pharmaceutical interventions and physical therapy largely developed by care givers. The Office of Mental Health and Mental Retardation used a cognitive–behavioral approach and expected that consumers or their families would be active participants in the treatment planning process and in their own habilitation efforts. Imagine the confusion when some consumers were funded under Medicaid and supervised by the State Department of Health, others were funded by the Office of Mental Health and Mental Retardation (MH/MR) under the auspices of the State Department of Welfare, and still others received funding from both. Because all had complex records to be filled out daily, many poorly paid direct workers complained that they didn't have time to work with consumers because they were drowned in paperwork. Such confusing and contradictory reporting requirements are difficult to manage even in well-established agencies, so they can cause even more difficulties in new, small agencies where few staff members or volunteers keep organizational records while trying to maximize services. Here are some suggestions for you and your leadership team to help deal with these regulatory realities:

- Be discerning about organizational goals and objectives and do not try to be all things to all people. Regulatory record keeping, financial accounting, and related policies are difficult and time consuming.
- Look carefully at funding opportunities for their costs and benefits. Sometimes the combination of application procedures, record keeping, and reporting take so much time and energy that they are not worth the effort involved.
- Beware of moving too far from your original mission for the sake of funding. Multiple missions often require multiple reporting structures. Chasing after varying funding sources may lead to mission drift and loss of identity.
- Help your direct service staff and volunteers understand that paperwork requirements really aren't designed to make their lives miserable but are necessary to maintain funding, enhance the organization's reputation, and keep everyone in the clear.

Never lose your sense of humor! Bureaucracies and their requirements are inherently frustrating.

Level Six: Street Level Policies

It is ironic but true that what is *supposed* to be done rarely is what *is* done. Street or delivery level policy and procedures are how things are actually done in the real world, but they are rarely written or formal. Street level policies vary widely among similar organizations and even within the same organization and depend on such things as (1) the configuration of the organization; (2) the urgency of the situation; (3) the availability of leaders for consultation; (4) organizational ideology; (5) sectorial values and *mores* (unwritten rules); and (6) the participants' personal values, knowledge, and skills.

Let's now look at each of these influences on street level policies in turn:

- *Configuration of the organization* refers to the strategy being used and the maturity of the organizational structure. Place-based relational initiatives, self-help groups, community advocacy, and social movements are likely to have flexible structures that allow for individuals or small groups to make decisions on their own. Social entrepreneurship and social innovation, mutual economic assistance, and collaborations are likely to be more structured and more dependent on outside funding sources and, therefore, less likely to make room for street level policy making and individual discretion.
- *Urgency of the situation* refers to the importance of timeliness for making a decision. Some decisions are time sensitive and must be made without taking time to consult others.
- *Availability of leaders for consultation:* Some organizations, such as those that are dispersed or that have their resources stretched over a wide area, simply do not have readily available leaders. Decisions must be made by lieutenants in the field.
- *Organizational ideology* refers to the members' views of leadership and authority. For instance, radical groups like Students for a Democratic Society, the Black Panthers, the Student Non-violent Coordinating Committee, and more recently the various Occupy efforts believe that any kind of authoritarian structure is intrinsically wrong. Major decisions are made by assemblies. Any member is empowered to speak for the whole group.[3]
- *Sectorial values and mores:* Some social sectors allow for more street level discretion than others because of the diffuse nature of the work. For instance, police officers may be given discretion because they must make rapid independent decisions. On the other hand, social workers who work in office-based clinical teams are less likely to have discretion and more likely to be urged to seek supervision.
- *Participants' personal values, knowledge, and skills:* Some individuals are more comfortable making street level decisions than others, and some are delegated more responsibility because they have proven trustworthy.

There are two different but equally difficult problems with street level policy creation. On the one hand, some participants may be afraid to act creatively and independently, which may lead to paralysis and missed opportunities. On the other hand, participants may take too much authority, which leads to contradictory messages, uncertainty over tactics, and confusion about who really speaks for the group. While the tendency to circumvent rules and regulations might seem to be best handled by more rules and regulations and clearer bureaucratic lines of control, in fact the more rules (especially contradictory ones) there are, the more attempts to circumvent them, resulting in more chaos.

Human Service Delivery Systems

Understanding and Mastery: Political and ideological aspects of human services

Critical Thinking Question: Examine an existing human services organization with which you are familiar and identify how it is impacted by each of the six levels of policy. What frustrations and contradictions are its leaders facing? How do they cope? What similar frustrations and contradictions is your organizing effort likely to face? What coping strategies will you use?

Assess your comprehension of the Six Levels of Public Policy by completing this quiz.

A Real-World Example

Societal value and regime, sectorial, jurisdictional, organizational, and street level policies are not a hierarchy, but by understanding them and their interactions, you will help your leadership team analyze the political context of your work and how you might increase your chances of success, as seen in the following Smithville example of interaction among various levels of policy.

The Smithville neighborhood is known as a home for prostitutes and their pimps. Historically, based on their social values, people have believed that prostitution is a personal, moral failing of the women involved or that the women are largely victims who are trapped in "the life." Several members of SNO have taken the latter position. They believe that most prostitutes were victims of child sexual abuse and now are victims of their pimps, they do not want to be trapped in prostitution, and they would leave it if they had a way to safely escape. These values have led to a social innovation project—the development of a safe place where prostitutes can get off the streets, rest, take a shower, eat nutritious food, recover their health, and converse with caring people—a place that will meet their basic needs so they have the energy to make an escape plan. Regime policies at the federal, state, and city level all affect this project somewhat negatively because all three governmental levels are pursuing financial austerity—so even if prostitutes were not stigmatized by their profession (which, of course, they are), there is no tax money anywhere for new programs. Moreover, because some of the highest office holders (including the governor, mayor, and at least one judge) are rumored to be "johns," they have no incentive to help the prostitutes because their own involvement might be brought to light. At the sectorial and jurisdictional level, police, laws, jurisdictions, and enforcement patterns negatively affect the project. The police in Industrial City have long followed an unwritten policy of punishing prostitutes and ignoring the pimps (the men who sell the women's services) and the johns (the men who buy their services). Project sponsors and prostitutes alike feel that these unwritten but real sectorial policies put them in danger—from the pimps who may seek to punish them for intervening in their trade and even from some police who may see the safe house as a place to "bust" prostitutes. The SNO leaders who support the project are well aware of all of these political realities so they have created administrative policies that take them into account. The service will be very low key, supported by volunteers and a few churches—there will be no government funds involved; its location will be an "open secret," known mostly by word of mouth among the prostitutes; even the program's name "Molly's Place" has been carefully chosen so that if someone asks where one of the women is going she can say "Molly's place" so that she might be visiting a friend rather than an agency. The major street level policy will be "each one, reach one" with those who have been helped bringing friends and pooling resources. There will be no public advertising.

Those supporting Molly's Place will work together constantly to understand and, in some cases, change policies at each of the six levels. At the societal level they will work to shift the public view of prostitution from moral shortcoming to victimization. At the national and state regime and sectorial levels, they may work to make sure that laws are passed that de-criminalize prostitution, punish those who practice sex trafficking, and make purchasing sexual services a crime. At the local jurisdictional level, they may identify police officers who share their views and seek their help in ensuring that Molly's Place is protected. Finally, at the organizational and street levels, supporters will continue to monitor their own practices to maximize the safety of everyone involved.

Politics often seems like a game with two sides and a bevy of spectators. Each side is motivated by strongly held beliefs and values. Your "side" has two goals: (1) to convince the undecided to support you and (2) to win over as many opponents as you can. It is important for you to understand and respect conflicting values you may encounter and to think about how you will cope with them. "Winning" often depends on how well you understand your opposition, and that means putting yourself in their place. Think about some issues you are likely to face in your organizing effort. Assume that your opponents believe they have very good reasons for their positions. Stand back and consider their values that might contrast, compete, or conflict with yours. Imagine defending their positions. What are their strengths? What are their weaknesses? Are there any components of their positions that can be incorporated into your plans without sacrificing your integrity? What convincing values-based arguments can you develop to support your position? What values-based arguments might you use to dispute their viewpoints? You will find that taking a variety of perspectives and positions will help you negotiate well with others, develop a sense of commonality, and eventually result in a reputation for effectiveness for you and your organization. At first you may find the challenges and contradictions of understanding and coping with the six levels of policy daunting and discouraging, but with practice they became analytical tools that help you and your leadership team understand and work in almost any situation.

Human Service Delivery Systems

Understanding and Mastery: Political and ideological aspects of human services

Critical Thinking Question: In the first section of Chapter 12 we have discussed some of abstract concepts related to policy and policy making. Why were they included? In what ways are these ideas relevant to the practical world of community organizing?

Playing the Political Game

Politics is like a game or perhaps a melee. You may find the main contenders in the arena; an inner core of announcers and die-hard fans; a second tier of concerned but undecided constituents; and the general public (who may pay enough attention to have something to talk about at the office). In the arena metaphor, politics looks something like Figure 12.5.

Imagine yourself in a blimp high above this arena. On the field itself you can see small figures representing different teams. About half of them look like tiny elephants with a few dollar signs and tea pots mixed in (the right-wing team) and about half of them look like little donkeys with some smiley faces and protest signs thrown in (the left-wing team); there are some referees in black-and-white striped shirts (media representatives) as well. Although there are definite goal posts at either end of the field, there seem to be sub-goals in the middle as well. You notice that the field of play is not very well organized. Some of the players are in huddles. Others seem to be running the ball. Still others form defensive lines. Still others are being carried off on stretchers. Your eyes move from the field to the stands. You notice that the first rows of seats are in sections that are roughly divided in half by the left and right wings with the elephants, dollar signs, and tea pots on the right and the donkeys, trees, and protest signs on the left. One thing that strikes you is that the spectators are always moving, changing seats between plays, and that sometimes people from the seats run onto the field and join in the action and vice versa. As you look further

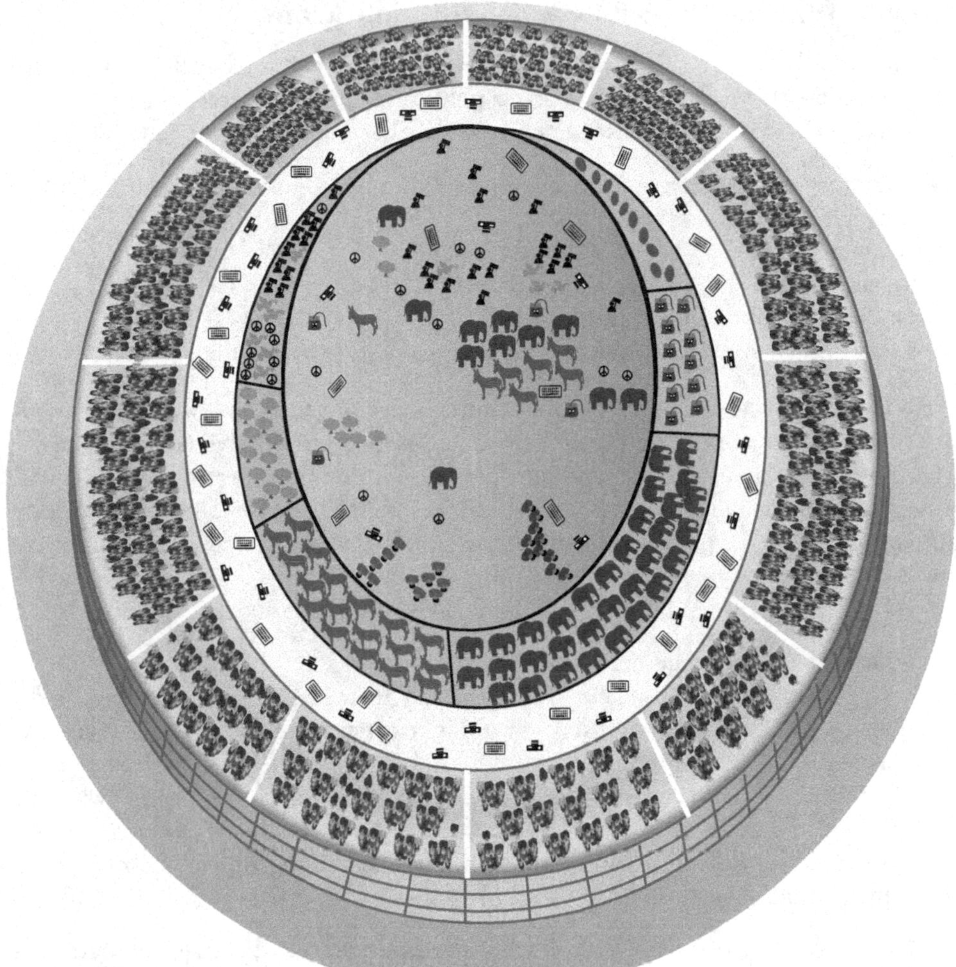

FIGURE 12.5
The Policy Arena
Source: Copyright © by Pearson Education, Upper Saddle River, NJ.

up in the stands you see a section of half-empty seats, occupied at various points with cameras, small computers, newspapers, and so forth. This is the media section with those who report on the action. As your eyes move further from the playing field you notice that there are a few spectators of various ages, colors, and genders who sometimes watch the game but more often talk among themselves, get up to get popcorn, move away from the arena, or leave altogether. Most of the time, they (the general public) do not seem to be paying much attention until a cheer or groan goes up from the inner crowd and causes them to move closer to the field, grab pennants, and put on team apparel. After watching for a while, you decide that although this looks chaotic, it might be challenging and even fun. You ask the pilot to land; you buy a ticket, enter the stadium, and begin to learn to play the "political game."

Human Service Delivery Systems

Understanding and Mastery: Skills to effect and influence social policy

Critical Thinking Question: Where would you place yourself in the political arena? What roles would you need to play to make your community organizing effort a success? What factors enable people to move outside their "comfort zone" as observers of political action become active participants? If you are not now politically active, what would it take for you to become more politically engaged?

How to Play the Political Game with Politicians

Although political teams have several major players, we will look at the two that are most important for community organizing: politicians and bureaucrats.

There seem to be many routes to public office, but common ones include:

- Voluntary participation in political processes through community organizing, advocacy, or appointed office
- Voluntary or paid participation in party politics
- Service on the staff of an elected official
- Life-long interest in politics as a career
- Being drafted by others because of one's connections or leadership potential

Whatever the route to public office, candidates enter the arena with ideas about outcomes of their work and policies they would like to see strengthened or developed. These personal values and ideologies help them develop their personal policies and campaign themes, and often help them determine their choice of political party. Party affiliation, in turn, helps determine the issues they will support and which voters they are likely to attract.

When working with politicians you should ask:

- What types of politicians are we dealing with?
- Are they pragmatic or idealistic? If idealistic, are their personal morals, ethics, and views compatible with our cause, or would it be better to pursue someone else's assistance?
- What other issues do they support, and do these issues coincide or conflict with our interests?
- If they are pragmatic, how can we convince them that supporting our effort will be in their own best interests?"

The answers to these questions will tell you which political officials to approach first for support, which are likely to be neutral, and which are likely to be unhelpful. Remember that trustworthy elected officials want to gain office and stay in office by pleasing as many of their constituents as they can without sacrificing their values or ethical standards.

No matter what their party affiliation, elected officials must eventually answer to the voters. In a geographically based representative democracy such as ours, this means that officials must first and foremost listen to the needs of the residents of their districts before concentrating on other issues. Sometimes these regional needs and priorities remain fairly stable over time. At other times, rapid social change—such as man-made or natural disasters, economic downturns, or rapid changes in population patterns—may necessitate immediate responses. During times of crisis, issues that were not even on the radar may become paramount.

Honest politicians' main goals are to be elected, stay elected to the limits of their legal terms, and, in the interim, serve their constituents as best they can. They do this through external relationships with voters and financial supporters and through internal relationships with colleagues, often balancing time in their geographic districts with time in session. Names for their internal functions vary, but they are similar at all levels of U.S. government and include committee assignments (usually determined by seniority, party affiliation, and personal interests); party caucuses (including expectations that they will, in general, support the "party line"); and ad hoc groups representing internal coalitions of persons with similar interests such as women, ethnic minorities, supporters of balanced budgeting, and so forth. Most elected officials are engaged in several committees, their political party, and one or more informal groups.

Remember that most political work is done ahead of time at the committee level and informally behind the scenes. Often the formal legislative process is rather *pro forma* although it is symbolically important. Voting patterns are particularly important for individual office holders, because they are often used by constituents and interest groups as a sort of litmus test to determine whether the office holder is keeping his or her promises.

The typical elected official spends many hours in various venues using his or her communication skills to hammer out policy agendas, formulate approaches, and negotiate changes. At any level the policy arena is a hectic environment. An elected official can be compared to the chief executive officer of an entrepreneurial organization. It would not be humanly possible to hold most public offices without a staff. Like any entrepreneur, the political official relies heavily on wisely chosen staff members, paid or volunteer, who may have different functions. Some act as case managers who help constituents navigate government structures. They answer questions and generally provide links between the elected official and the people. Other staff members may provide technical planning skills to their employers, constituents, and constituent communities and may procure information on particular issues and initiatives. These technical planners usually do the actual work of formulating policies, writing laws, and negotiating compromises under the authority and guidance of the elected representative. A few staff members are essentially sales managers with the task of presenting the elected official in a positive light, with an eye on the next campaign. You are far more likely to work directly with staff members than elected officials, so get to know staff members, their relative power within their organization, and their personal interests. Staff members are important gate keepers who can open or close the door to opportunities.

Working with elected officials is often difficult. As a neophyte community organizer, you may fail to understand the points of view of the various political officials you encounter. You or your leadership team may mistakenly assume that just because you believe your cause is worthwhile, public officials will automatically leap to help. In truth, public officials are beset by dozens of different worthy causes every day, and it is up to you to convince them why your cause is worthy of their support, how it is politically viable, and how it will increase their **political capital** (standing) with constituents. Remember many worthy causes receive *verbal* support from seemingly friendly political figures, but *concrete* support in the form of legislation, supportive regulations, and especially funding generally depends on your individual and organizational power, including threat power (denying votes or monetary support), exchange power (delivering votes, positive publicity, volunteers, or monetary resources), information power (accurate numbers and moving stories), and soul power (inspiring fervent voter support). Remember power is the currency of politics.

Human Systems

Understanding and Mastery: Processes to effect social change through advocacy (e.g., community development, community and grassroots organizing, local and global activism)

Critical Thinking Question: Non-profit, tax-exempt organizations are not allowed to formally lobby, but chances are you will want to influence government level decision makers in support of your organizing effort. What strategies and tactics can you use?

The whole lobbying industry has grown up around the art and science of influencing elected officials. You will probably lack the time, energy, or funds to compete with professional lobbyists and, in many instances, will be restrained from doing so by federal and state regulations for non-profit organizations. However, there are several inexpensive ways to influence elected officials. Here are a few of them:

Review the MoveOn.org power mapping guide. Consider your organizing efforts. Identify the politicians who will likely have positive or negative effects based on the power map.

- *Get to know your local representatives.* Most politicians genuinely want to hear from their constituents. Visit their offices, attend their public meetings, write them personalized letters, make telephone calls, and send e-mails and even Twitter messages. If you have useful information on a topic, provide it to them. Thank them and their staff members for the help you receive.
- *Let them know that you vote and intend to hold them accountable* and then do it!
- *Get acquainted with the staff member or members assigned to your particular geographic area or area of interest.* Representatives are expected to know about many issues. They divide research tasks among their staff members who tend to rely on experts (like you) for their information. It can help your cause to provide staff members with concise, accurate information in printed or electronic form if possible.
- *Show up at such public events as public hearings, local council meetings, and meet-the-candidate nights that give voters a chance to speak.* Present your viewpoints in reasonable, well-thought-out ways that help you build a reputation for wisdom and common sense—and use strong emotions when clearly needed.
- *Use electronic means of communication and add personalized comments.* Many advocacy groups provide easy ways to send mass mailings to representatives through e-mail, and most now provide space for personalization. Take the time to personalize your letter. Share stories from your experience, backed up by figures to support the extent of the problem, because politicians love personal stories.
- *Use any title you may have, especially if relevant to your cause.* If you have a doctorate, sign as "Dr."; if you are a pastor, sign as "Reverend"; if you have an MSW use that designation; and so on.
- *If you can afford it, make contributions to political candidates whose views you support and find a way to let them know you have contributed.* Candidates' finances are judged by the media in two ways: (1) by the number of dollars raised and (2) by the number of donors. Numbers of donations are often used as gauges of voter support. Because the Supreme Court's Citizens' United ruling—which declared that corporations are fictitious persons with the same rights as individuals to make anonymous political contributions—opened the door to huge political contributions, small donations from real human beings are more important than ever.
- *Assume that elected officials are honest, but be aware that corruption does exist.* Do not participate in corrupt practices.

Assess your comprehension of How to Play the Political Game with Politicians by completing this quiz.

Playing the Policy Game with Bureaucrats

Community organizers frequently breathe a sigh of relief when desired legislation is passed, only to find that the real work is just beginning.

Many good laws and executive orders have been spoiled through poor regulations or inadequate enforcement. Public office holders have mostly indirect roles in policy implementation, although members of **bicameral** (two-part) legislatures—such as the national House of Representatives and Senate—may play a role through conference committees by reconciling different versions of legislation and helping to write the final version of laws. On the executive side, elected administrators (such as mayors, county executives, governors, and the president) have the duty to either sign bills into law or exercise the power of the veto. The judiciary may occasionally be called upon to rule on the constitutionality of a particular piece of legislation, but once a bill becomes law, bureaucratic administrators become the major players. Some bureaucrats are truly dedicated to the common good and will do everything in their power to help community groups. Others enjoy threat power and use it.

While senior agency officials are often political appointees committed to a particular regime and its policies, many mid-level executives are career bureaucrats. Once a law is passed and funds are allocated, government agencies and departments have three primary responsibilities: **rule making**, **rule application**, and **rule adjudication**. Figure 12.6 shows how these functions are related to the basic policy process.

In **rule making**, administrative agencies are charged with taking the often vague wording of enabling legislation and turning it into specific rules and regulations for implementation. In **rule application**, agencies are charged with ensuring that these rules are followed. In **rule adjudication**, agencies (and sometimes the courts) are charged with developing and using a process to ensure that the rule application (enforcement) stage has been conducted fairly. Sometimes, all three functions reside in a single agency or department, but at other times they may be divided. Rule making and rule application are frequently found together, whereas rule adjudication is often separate to ensure lack of bias.

The roles of regulatory agency administrators and your leadership team's role as representatives of community organizing efforts are interactive. Regulations and their enforcement have a great deal to do with how and even whether newly won political gains will be actualized. Typical regulatory processes involve the assignment of a newly passed law or executive order to a designated government agency, along with the legally defined timeline for developing the specific regulations and processes required for implementation. Figure 12.7 illustrates a flow chart of this process.

This flow chart shows the usual progression from passage of a law through the various phases of bureaucratic implementation.

Rule Making Phase

Laws contain broad statements of legislative intent, give timeframes for implementation, and often designate the executive agency that is to ensure implementation. Once the designated agency receives word that the law has been passed, it begins the

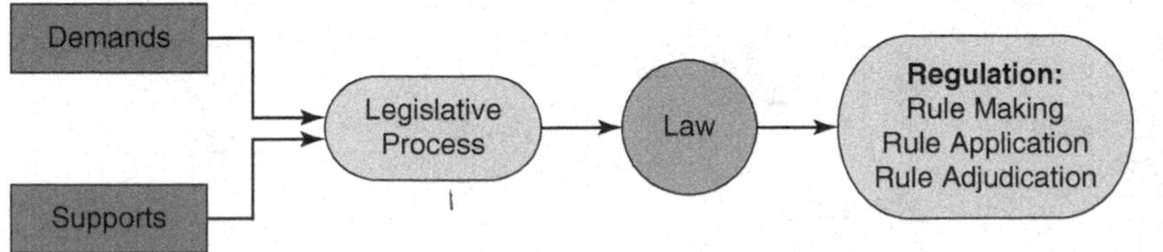

FIGURE 12.6 Role of Regulatory Agencies

Source: Copyright © by Pearson Education, Upper Saddle River, NJ.

implementation process. The top line in the flow chart shows the movement of this **rule making** phase. The designated agency formally or informally collects ideas from various stakeholders regarding their views on implementation, assigns experts to research and review background information, sorts through all of this informal information, and then creates an initial draft of the regulations. This draft is sent out for review, often through a very clearly defined process of public hearings. The agency is required by law to collect all of this public input, sift through it carefully, and publish a final set of regulations. These final regulations generally define the specifics of implementation, how adherence will be measured, who will enforce adherence, and penalties for failure to abide by regulations. These final regulations are sent to the government, non-profit, and profit-making entities that they will affect, ending the rule making phase.

Rule Application Phase

If your organization is going to be affected by the new law and its accompanying regulations, you will either be sent or will need to obtain a set of the finalized regulations. At that point, your leadership team will have to decide how to respond. If the finalized rules do not meet your organizational needs, you may decide to resist them and protest to the regulatory agency, the legislative body, or the courts (the arrow shown going back to the regulatory agency), or you may decide to drop the program altogether. If you do decide to implement the new regulations, you will have to implement a cycle of planning, implementing, managing, keeping good records, and preparing required reports for the regulatory agency.

Rule Adjudication Phase

Primary responsibility for rule adjudication is in the hands of the regulatory agency, which often maintains staff members whose sole responsibility is to ensure that the

FIGURE 12.7 Rule Making, Rule Application, and Rule Adjudication
Source: Copyright © by Pearson Education, Upper Saddle River, NJ.

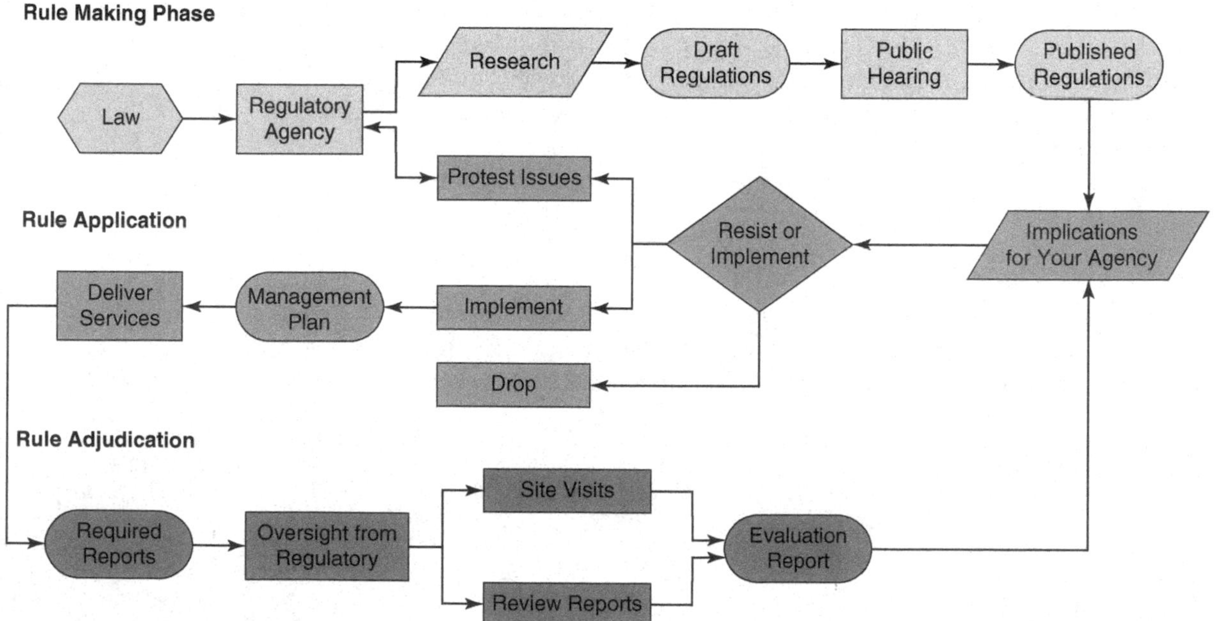

organizations charged with implementing the law carry out their obligations. It is important that you develop smooth working relationships with evaluators and their supervisors, so try to talk with key people about their major expectations and develop your internal policies, procedures, and record keeping in ways that will facilitate the process and communicate your respect for their efforts. Evaluation teams will require you to keep good records, prepare reports in a format they provide, host site visits, allow them to interview staff members at all levels, and often allow them to interview your clients as well. Once the evaluation visit is complete they will take all of this information and write a report on your organization's performance, which will be used to determine such things as renewal of licenses, levels of funding, and the public reputation of your organization—so inspectors have high levels of threat power. Fortunately, many evaluators are dedicated professionals who really want the public to receive excellent services so you can use their reports to improve services or to build a case for increased funding. However, a poor report can be disastrous. You may encounter inspectors or monitors who enjoy their power and generate negative reports that can threaten the existence of your organization. If this happens, most laws have provision for recourse. You can (1) protest to the regulatory agency itself, (2) take your complaints to the next bureaucratic level, (3) organize your supporters to protest your agency's mistreatment, or (4) seek judicial intervention. However, as in most things, the best initial strategy is to negotiate with the regulatory agency, especially because you probably need to work with them in the future.

The truism that "the devil is in the details" is especially valid for the regulatory process. Excellent laws can be destroyed by poorly defined rules and regulations, through poorly designed enforcement, or through unjust adjudication. Your leadership team should insist on having members included in all phases of the regulatory process and should carefully read and be prepared to respond to regulations as they are proposed, finalized, or changed over the years. Table 12.2 shows which issues should be addressed by advocates and administrators at each stage of the regulatory process.

All three stages of the regulatory process can be frustrating because they seem intentionally or unintentionally designed to favor regulatory agencies and large established providers over advocacy groups and community-based organizations. Some common frustrations and their antidotes are included in Table 12.3.

Assess your comprehension of the "Regulatory Game" by completing this quiz.

Politicians at all levels pass laws, but bureaucrats are responsible for carrying them out. Let's look at two examples of working with bureaucracies.

When the folks in Middle View were working on the runaway shelter, the State Department of Labor and Industry had jurisdiction over approval of building renovation plans. Although these plans are usually developed by highly paid architects with longstanding relationships with department officials, the leadership team could only afford an experienced engineer to draw up their plans. The board chairperson took an early morning flight across the state to the capitol where she met with a kindly bureaucrat who understood the community goals and passed the plans. In this instance, relationship power, knowledge power, and a bit of soul power accomplished this community objective.

In contrast, the Industrial City School District (where the Smithville neighborhood is located) wanted to add a cosmetology department to its vocational school but could not get the State Department of Labor and Industry to approve it because free vocational

Table 12.2 Regulatory Tasks for Advocates and Community-based Administrators

	Community Advocates Should	Community Program Managers Should
Rule making	Insist that proposed definitions meet the "spirit of the law." Challenge any barriers to service. Examine proposed levels of bureaucratic management to determine if complexity is likely to hamper implementation. Insist that regulations regarding implementation include a clear voice for advocates and consumers. Insist that financing be used to pay for services for people rather than administrative expenses. . Negotiate a self-regulation process that gives your organization authority to enforce the provisions of the law. Advocate for random independent monitoring.	Insist that eligibility requirements be clear and fair. Demand that requirements for accountability be clear, written in understandable English, and cover a reasonable time period. Insist that all new regulations and regulatory changes include a clear collaborative process among the regulatory agency, the administrative agency, and consumers' representatives. Ask for input into reporting requirements: timelines, form in which data is to be kept, forms, etc. Insist that rules and regulations be humanly possible to follow.
Rule application	Check with providers to determine whether regulations are serving their intended purpose. Insist on adequate resources for implementation. Insist that end users be involved in agency planning and implementation.	Meticulously follow the regulations as you develop your program. Provide high-quality staff training to ensure compliance. Develop internal practices that exceed regulatory expectations.
Rule adjudication	Insist on reviewing monitoring reports and evaluations. Ask that advocates and consumers be included on monitoring teams. Insist on timely monitoring. Insist on sanctions for poor performance of regulatory agency and service agency or agencies. Insist on random monitoring visits. Mediate between regulatory and provider agencies to ensure that services continue as problems are being fixed.	Recruit a staff member who can write reports using language demanded by regulatory agency. Do what you have promised. Keep records in good, consistent order. Teach staff to keep up-to-date, accurate records. Develop a systematic plan for monitoring visits. Insist that adequate notice be given of changes in regulatory expectations. Push for adequate funding to ensure compliance. Have a contingency plan in case of a negative report.

Source: Copyright © by Pearson Education, Upper Saddle River, NJ.

training would compete with local private cosmetology schools. The bureaucrat with the authority to give final approval ignored letter after letter. Even if the agency had denied the application, it would have moved the process along, because there could then have been an appeal. But it was neither approved nor rejected, just tabled. So the school district superintendent and the school solicitor went to the state capital, barged into the

Table 12.3 Frustrations and Antidotes in the Regulatory Process

Frustration	Antidote
Difficulty in finding notices for public hearings and other avenues of input into the rule making process.	Require that all notices be published in commercial newspapers, in free publications, and on the Internet.
Short timelines for rule making impede community people from digesting proposals and preparing responses by deadline.	Require that all laws give adequate time (at least nine months from the date of executive signature) to complete the rule making process.
Public hearings are held at inconvenient times.	Require that all public hearings be held evenings and weekends instead of during the traditional working day.
Public meetings are held in inaccessible places.	Require that hearings be held in locations near those who will receive service. Require that provisions be made for alternative means of input—such as the Internet, telephone, and written—and that the availability of such options be widely advertised in free venues.
Preference given to members of an "in-crowd"—career people who move back and forth between representing government and representing big providers.	Require government employees to wait at least three years before accepting employment in an agency related to their employment. Forbid regimes to appoint regulators who have worked in areas they will be regulating.
Backroom deals	Enforce "sunshine laws" requiring public representation at all major decision-making sessions. Make sure that all stakeholders are aware of negotiation sessions and are encouraged to attend.
Public hearings that result in no changes in proposed regulations	Require published summaries of all public hearings and consolidation of suggestions. Require that suggestions for significant changes be incorporated into final regulations or provide documentation justifying their omission. Allow plenty of time between public hearings and implementation.
No access to results of hearings.	Widely publish hearing results. Freedom of Information.
Frequent regulation changes after initial law is passed.	Require justification for any changes in regulation regardless of regime change.
Little notice of mid-course changes.	Require the same public hearing processes for mid-course regulation change as initial regulation development.
Regulations and procedures not easily accessed, unclear, full of jargon.	Require transparency and openness. Maintain openness even when regimes changes.

Source: Copyright © by Pearson Education, Upper Saddle River, NJ.

bureaucrat's office, and literally sat on his desk the way the bureaucrat had "sat" on their application until he laughingly signed the paper.

There are three morals to these two stories:

1. Many bureaucrats are dedicated to the common good and will try to make rules and regulations livable.
2. Even crusty bureaucrats can be moved— and have a sense of humor.
3. Use whatever works—short of violence.

Understanding and Mastery: Legal/regulatory issues and risk management

Critical Thinking Question: Identify the regulatory agencies that have jurisdiction over your proposed community organizing initiative. Investigate the regulations that will most directly affect your work. Begin considering how you will meet regulatory requirements, and begin developing advocacy strategies you feel may be needed.

Summary

Assess your analysis and evaluation of this chapter's contents by completing the Chapter Review.

Chapter 12 introduced some key concepts of the U.S. political system as they apply to community organizing. You examined six levels of policy formation that must be simultaneously applied at appropriate levels of government. You viewed the political process as a game with multiple players and gained insight into the worldviews of politicians and government bureaucrats. These analytical frameworks, tools, and tips can help you and your leadership team successfully navigate the political labyrinth.

CHAPTER 13

Value Systems and Ethics

Curioso/Shutterstock

Chapter Outline

This chapter is both the most abstract and the most practical chapter in this entire book. **Ethical living** has two dimensions: (1) it is based on an implicit or explicit **value system** (your view of the intent and purpose of life against which you measure your own and others' actions) and (2) how you choose to live your life day by day and moment by moment. In this chapter we will first examine the **quality of life** values that undergird this book and then compare and contrast them with the common **modernist (growth machine)** values that pervade our society. We will then shift to consideration of specific ethical frameworks that support the quality of life value system and will learn how to put them into practice.

Because ethical practice is intimately tied to daily life, it is almost impossible to write completely objectively about it. In fact, those who claim to have an objective ethical framework demonstrate their own rigidity and deny their own humanity. Ethical decisions are made in the rough and tumble of life, not in an ivory tower.

Quality of Life Values

Here are a few of the values and ethical assumptions on which this book is based:

- The current model of unlimited growth that sacrifices the natural world and human well-being cannot be sustained. Quality of Life is more important than increasing life's speed or the number of things one owns.[1]

- There has been a historical bias against people of color and other powerless groups that is implicit in our thinking and laws, which must be redressed.[2]
- All of the earth belongs to all, not just to a privileged minority.[3]
- Everyone has something to contribute. Ways must be found to give everyone a voice.[4]
- Non-violence is always a viable alternative.[5]
- Civil disobedience to immoral laws is acceptable, but one must be willing to accept the consequences.[6]
- Caring for one another is the key to a high quality of life.[7]
- Stand up for justice and fair treatment of everyone.[8]
- Cultural and religious differences are to be understood, respected, and celebrated.[9]
- Everyone should be judged not by physical characteristics or one's circumstances but by the quality of his or her character.[10]
- Creativity, artistic expression, joy, and mutuality are ethical imperatives.[11]
- Community organizing takes courage and determination, often against tremendous odds. Many people find that they are sustained by what they define as spiritual resources.[12]
- Start with community assets, not liabilities.[13]
- Professional ethical codes provide valuable guides for ethical decision making.[14]

Competing Value Systems: Modernism and the Quality of Life

Humanity is engaged in a global battle between **modernism** (the growth machine model of economic well-being that has resulted in 1% of the world's people owning 99% of the world's wealth) and a **quality of life model** that asserts that all the earth belongs to all people. Each of us must choose a side.

Modernism is characterized by the growth of industry, including agri-business, and a belief in the ability of science and technology to solve all human problems. It is also characterized by a belief in the power of science and the scientific method to describe, explain, and eventually control everything in the universe including human behavior.

Practical applications of the social sciences—such as social work, human services, and community organizing—have been deeply influenced by modernism, especially in their desire to be legitimated by cause–effect research and by their search for a universal, overarching meta-narrative explanation of the social world.[15] The impact of modernism can be seen in the techno-centric model of economic development and traditional community planning models of community organizing.[16]

The major problem with modernism is that it has failed. The twentieth century was welcomed by modernists and progressives as likely to herald the end of war, pestilence, hunger, and many other human ills. Instead, the twentieth century was filled with wars, increasing social inequality, and environmental destruction. Technologies such as nuclear energy delivered the horrors of nuclear reactor accidents—rather than unlimited energy—in Chernobyl in the former Soviet Union in 1986 and Fukushima, Japan, in 2011. The so-called green revolution in farming depleted topsoil, created dependence on a limited gene pool, and caused vulnerability to plant and animal diseases of all kinds. Hunger increased. More recently, genetically modified crops lacking the ability to self-germinate led to farmer suicides in India[17] and increasing starvation in Sudan. The increase of greenhouse gases led to global warming and the possibility of massive climate change resulting in droughts, massive flooding, and increased wind storms.[18] Even the wide use of antibiotics led to drug-resistant strains of bacteria. The gap between the world's "haves" and "have nots" has expanded, and new threats such as terrorism, rabid fundamentalism, and factionalism threaten to plunge the world into chaos or totalitarianism. In late 2008, the excesses of modernism (also known as neo-liberalism or neo-conservatism) plunged the entire world into near economic disaster.

In spite of its obvious weaknesses, the modernist paradigm is still alive and well in community development circles, especially in efforts sponsored by all levels of government, powerful international organizations, and most research universities. It has become the foundational value in most economic development efforts. You can find the modernist paradigm present in meetings of local government bodies, Chamber of Commerce discussions, industrial development corporation deliberations, the daily stock market report, and among your friends when they long for new industries to replace old ones in spite of compelling evidence that the paradigm's emphasis on unlimited growth has endangered global ecology and impoverished millions.

On the other hand, the Quality of Life or post-industrial paradigm is a synthesis of the warmth of the communal spirit, the scientific and technological methods of the Industrial Revolution, and the ease of communication of the information age. Creating this post-industrial quality of life world will not be easy. It is predicated on a very different value system than has been the norm since at least the mid-eighteenth century. The premise of this book is that the change to a quality of life paradigm will be accomplished primarily by ordinary but dedicated people who have the courage, convictions, and mutual support to make creative changes in their own communities and, thus, in the world. In Table 13.1 you see a comparison between modernism and the quality of life ethical paradigms.

Professional History

Understanding and Mastery: Exposure to a spectrum of political ideologies

Critical Thinking Question: This section contrasts the modernist and quality of life paradigms. Read the descriptions carefully. Where do you see evidences of the modernist paradigm in your life and in your focal community? Where do you see evidences of a focus on the creation of a high quality life for everyone? How do your daily decisions and actions fit into each paradigm?

Assess your comprehension of the Modernist and Quality of Life Paradigms by completing this quiz.

Ethical Viewpoints

There are several ethical viewpoints that support the quality of life paradigm including the ethics of post-modernism, critical theory, discursive dialogue, power, non-violence, care, joyful sharing, rational choice, cultural humility, religious/spiritual perspectives, and professional ethical standards that come into play in the helping professions, especially social work and human services. Ethics as a branch of philosophy has been explored since ancient times and in many cultures and has taken many different paths. We begin with several recent perspectives: post-modernism, critical theory, discursive ethics, and Foucault's ethics of power.

Post-modernism

Post-modernism is a very complex philosophy based primarily on the idea that social reality is not absolute but has been **constructed** (invented) by human beings and

Table 13.1 Modernism Compared to Quality of Life

Social Sector	Modernism	Quality of Life
Food Production	*Agri-business:* genetic modification, "factory" farms, loss of genetic diversity, corporate ownership of food production, petroleum-based fertilizers	*Locally based:* organic methods, adaptation of proven historic methods, family farms, community gardens, seed banks, genetic diversity
Health Care	*Health Care "Industry":* illness-based emphasis, patented chemicals (pharmacology), costly medical equipment, professional providers supported by costly insurance	*Self-care/Healers:* personal responsibility for wellness, integration of traditional practices from various cultures, emphasis on the interrelationships among energy, chemical balances, cellular functions, organ systems, and the whole person
Economic Well-being	*Globalization:* control by big banks and multi-national corporations; growth machine mentality based on manipulation of monetary system	*Sustainability:* regionalized economics, based on real products and services produced and delivered locally or regionally primarily by micro-businesses (with 1–200 employees)
Education and Learning	*Schooling:* people are "human capital"; education is focused on career; credentials are vital; Western thought and technologies are primary.	*Life-long Learning:* learning is a life-giving activity that occurs in many ways in many places; all the world's knowledge should belong to everyone; all cultural traditions have something to offer
Higher Education	*Business Model:* Income and growth are the main institutional goals; close relationships among government, military, and industry; students are customers whose primary outcome is to become highly skilled workers and managers	*Wisdom Model:* Teaching, service, and adding to cumulative human knowledge (research/writing) are main institutional goals. Professors and students seek the truth in a learning community with a primary outcome of ethical, caring leaders
Community Organizing	*Community Development Model:* Coordinated by experts from the top down; emphasis on economic development that fits into globalization	*Popular Education/Participatory Research:* Controlled by and for members of focal community systems; emphasis on positive relationships, respect, shared wisdom, mutual assistance, and courageous non-violent action when necessary

Source: Copyright © by Pearson Education, Upper Saddle River, NJ.

therefore can be **de-constructed** (taken apart and altered or changed completely). A corollary is that the current construction (fabrication) of social reality grants privileges to white, northern European, heterosexual males that are not available to other people.[19] Post-modernism is a reaction to this dark side of modernism. Like many intellectual movements, post-modernism arose in many countries almost simultaneously, but this perspective is most commonly associated with the French philosopher Jacques Derrida.[20]

Postmodernists view society and social relationships as "texts to be read" rather than as an objective reality to be understood scientifically. For Derrida, life was filled with **aphorias** or puzzles. Life in community is full of ambiguity and choices among competing demands from those he called the "other, others." Each of us face the same choices on a daily, sometimes hourly basis. For instance, you cannot simultaneously spend recreational time with your family and friends, do volunteer work, vacuum the carpet, and study this text. Whatever you choose, someone will be unhappy, and you will feel torn. Since life is full of ambiguous choices, Derrida made clear that decision making requires courage. He urged what he called *differance* or hesitation before acting. Like Soren Kierkegaard[21] and other existentialists, Derrida believed that, after all is said and done, any decision requires a leap into the unknown. He asserted that no matter how one might try to think through all the possibilities the future may bring, there is never any certainty about the results of your actions. All you can do is your best, which is true in community organizing as in the rest of life.

Critical Theory

Critical theory evolved as a way of understanding the mechanisms and de-humanizing aspects of modernism and ways of coping with it. It challenges you to discern the many ways power imbalances lead to injustice and inequality and to stand back from your assumptions about the world and ask whether things as they are things as they have to be.[22] Critical thinkers emphasize that all members of any society (or a focal community system) believe that the way things are is the way things should be. They call this internalized belief **false consciousness**, which makes it very easy for those who are in power to remain in power and is based on the combined forces of hegemony and plutocracy. (**Hegemony** is the control of the many by the few and is a source of false consciousness; **plutocracy** is a similar term that means control of the political process by the wealthy.) These two combined forces create a cultural story that life is about material success through any means possible. This story surrounds us and has become an intrinsic part of the way most of us view the value of life.[23] Although the plutocracy has become symbolized by such institutions as the World Bank, the International Monetary Fund, and Wall Street, the danger of the consumerism or growth model is in the way we have become convinced that the "products and services multinationals offer fulfill genuine needs and are endemic to a happy, fully adult life"[24] or, expressed more colloquially, "The one with the most toys when hedies, wins."

Critical theory is the activist philosophy that supports the popular education and participatory research methods we have discussed. It requires that you (and your leadership team) become conscious of the many ways you and those in your focal community are being exploited, are convinced that there is no hope for change, and believe you are powerless to build a better life, and that you issue a "wake-up call" through a process called **consciousness-raising**, which means to analyze the ways you are being exploited and how you can join together to resist exploitation and build a higher quality of life.[25] As a personal ethical framework, critical theory asks you to constantly look at others' motives and for ways they unconsciously (or consciously) support injustice.[26] Likewise, it demands that you (and

Human Service Delivery Systems

Understanding and Mastery: Economic and social class systems including systemic causes of poverty

Critical Thinking Question: Critical theorists assert that most people believe that the way things *are* is the way things *should be* and are, therefore, living in a dream-like state of false consciousness and oppression. Therefore, the role of the community organizer is to sound a wake-up call, enable people to understand the ways they are oppressed and act together to bring about social justice. Identify areas of false consciousness in your focal community system or elsewhere. What actions might you take to "wake people up" and get them moving?

your leadership team) examine your own motives and behavior to make sure that you are not unconsciously bigoted, that you are not unconsciously supporting the power imbalances inherent in your organizing context, and that your communication practices and organizational structures are designed to empower all of your participants.[27]

Discursive ethics (finding ethical solutions through respectful, rational discussion) is most directly associated with the German philosopher Jurgen Habermas and is the basis of the rational discourse form of communication discussed in Chapter 6. Habermas insists that justice can only be built through the consensus of everyone affected rather than through individual decision making or the decisions of persons in power who act on their behalf.[28] In practice, discursive ethics is based on rational argument or discourse so that, given fair rules of engagement, a group of rational people— each presenting his or her views in a thoughtful, structured way—will eventually agree on an approach that will come close to a **categorical imperative** (an action that if done by everyone would have positive effects).[29]

Successful discursive ethics require what Habermas called a sense of **solidarity** among all participants. This involves concern for everyone involved and for the broader community context in which decisions are made. "Rules of engagement" are also required, which ensure that everyone has an equal chance to speak and be heard.

Discursive ethics are very important in community organizing because they ensure that everyone who is affected by community decisions is involved and respected. However, such ethics are very hard to implement in practice in daily life for a variety of practical and political reasons. For instance, it can be hard to get everyone who should be involved in community decisions together in the same place at the same time. It can be politically difficult to politely ask powerful people to keep quiet and listen, challenging to encourage those who are timid or frightened to speak their minds, and awkward to ask participants to follow rules of discourse if they are used to speaking anytime they please. Yet as an ethical community organizer, you must make sure that all voices are heard and understood by all, a daunting but rewarding task.

Human Systems

Understanding and Mastery: How small groups are utilized, theories of group dynamics, and group facilitation skills

Critical Thinking Question: Discursive ethics is based on the premise that everyone has the right to speak, be heard, and have their good ideas incorporated into community life. Think about some of the meetings you have attended. In what ways were some people "silenced"? What could you have done to make sure that everyone was heard?

Foucault's Ethics of Power

Michel Foucault was a late twentieth century theorist associated with both critical theory and post-modernism who focused on the **nature of power** and the ways in which power is internalized so that we monitor and censor our own thoughts and behaviors almost as if we were constantly being watched.[30] At some time in your organizing efforts, you will be frustrated by lack of participation, and Foucault's work will give insights into why people who have been historically powerless and voiceless are hard to engage in organizing efforts.

Foucault addressed social work and many of the other helping disciplines that seek to manage or discipline human life and conduct, so his thinking is relevant to community organizing. He was very aware of power differences in helping relationships, the danger of the manipulative use of professional skills, and the coercive power of agencies and government regulations.[31] Such power imbalances make honest discursive ethics difficult and belie the modernist view of moral neutrality, whether in individual psychotherapy or community organizing. According to Foucault, ethical action stands at the

nexus (intersection) between care/control and knowledge/power in relationships. Community organizers must examine their own motives and the power imbalances inherent in any organizing context and only then participate in organizing activities, caring for others, and acting responsibly in daily life and decision making.[32]

Community organizing settings are a complex mix of power-laden practices, as illustrated by the following example from a Smithville Neighborhood Organization (SNO) meeting. Imagine that you are a young, poor, white, single woman who has been invited to your first community forum. It is being held in a huge old downtown church where everyone seems to know everyone else. It is a mixed racial group. Most of the people in attendance have clear roles in the process. There are several pastors, some social workers, a few college professors, some professional community organizers, a journalist, and representatives of SNO and other community organizing efforts. You are one of the few people who are just representing themselves as neighborhood residents. Most people sit in small clusters in the pews. You sit alone. The chairperson is a well-respected African-American pastor who speaks from the pulpit and sets ground rules. He encourages everyone to participate but cautions against speaking too long or repeating what others have said. He emphasizes the importance of mutual respect and listening to one another. Clearly he wants the day to go well and for people to feel that their time has been well spent. All of this formality seems a little strange to you since this is your first meeting of this type.

One of the resolutions calls for a prayer walk to be held in the neighborhood. People of all faiths—including Roman Catholics, Jews, Hindus, and Muslims—will be asked to walk together through the neighborhood and pray for justice and peace to prevail. Everyone smiles and nods. Clearly to them this is a "no-brainer," but you have serious doubts. You believe that the only way for people to change is for them to accept the fundamentalist Christian faith you have found for yourself. In fact, you have been walking the streets alone talking personally to prostitutes and other street people and have even had the experience of being mistaken for a prostitute yourself. In spite of your fear, you have begun developing friendships with some of the people you have encountered. In addition to talking with them about Jesus, you have been doing your best to help them in concrete ways. You feel that what is really needed is not a prayer walk but the kind of one-on-one witnessing and serving that you have been doing. When the prayer walk resolution is presented, you dare to get up and speak, awkwardly and a bit belligerently. It is immediately clear that your input as a poor, white fundamentalist Christian is not welcome. The group leader clears his throat rather loudly. There is an intake of breath from some of the other participants. No one actually says anything critical, but the chair moves right along to vote on the resolution almost as if you had said nothing. The resolution passes with only one abstention, yours. You hang around for a few more minutes and then leave. No one seems to notice. The group goes about its business and passes several resolutions on behalf of the community that will be given to various government and private organizations. The meeting ends, and many of the professionals wonder aloud why so few neighborhood people bothered to come out.

Foucault would assert that, although the community forum had advertised itself as a welcoming space where neighborhood people would be free to present their views, your experience shows that only those who were able to meet certain expectations were truly welcome. You felt (probably accurately) that you were under surveillance and that only certain responses were acceptable. You felt unwanted and unneeded and left early. Those who claimed to want input from people who, like you, actually live in the target neighborhood were puzzled because they found themselves talking only to each other!

No one is really to blame in this scenario, but it illustrates Foucault's point that you must be aware of the possibility of power imbalances and the subtle ways that those in power—even in a well-intentioned group—tend to maintain their power.

Foucault challenges us to pay attention to the subtle ways those of us in the helping professions undercut those we claim to empower and asks us to look at our own motivations for engagement in community organizing (and, indeed, in the helping professions generally) and our attitudes toward our clientele. Look deeply into your own beliefs and motivations. Do you see community members as your equals, each with something positive to contribute to the community organizing enterprise? Do you see yourself as having something unique and irreplaceable to offer and implicitly believe that the effort would be helpless without your expertise? What kinds of people do you tend to "write off" as unlikely to make a valuable contribution? How do you differentiate internally between the self-assurance needed to provide leadership and undue pride? What changes are you prepared to make after this introspection?

Self-Development

Understanding and Mastery: Conscious use of self

Critical Thinking Question: What techniques or personal disciplines do you use to make sure that you hold yourself accountable for your moral and ethical behavior?

Assess your comprehension of Recent Ethical Frameworks by completing this quiz.

The Ethics of Non-violence

It is May 1963 in Birmingham, Alabama, in the southern United States. Picture a group of black children as young as eight or nine years old marching, singing, and bravely facing fire hoses, police dogs, and boot-clad, beer-gutted sheriff's deputies in the American South in support of civil rights, and you have a prototype of non-violent resistance.

Non-violence is both a strategy for bringing about social change and an ethical stance. Here non-violence is approached as an ethical model primarily through an examination of the lives and thought of M. K. Gandhi and Martin Luther King Jr.

M. K. Gandhi, called Mahatma or "great soul," was known as the liberator of India who worked tirelessly to end British domination of the sub-continent. Gandhi was known for both an ethical philosophy and for non-violent action. His major ethical principles were as follows:

- ***Ahimsa*** (ahiṃsā) is complete non-violence in thought, word, and deed and was discussed in Chapter 11 as a necessary component of "soul power."
- ***Satyagraha*** (satyāgraha) is respect for the others' points of view and a willingness to take their perspective and search for the "inclusive truth."
- ***Sarvodaya*** (Hindi, no English pronunciation equivalent) means caring for the neediest of the needy and implies service to others beyond self and one's family.
- ***Swadeshi*** (Hindi, no English pronunciation equivalent) describes the ethical responsibility one has for the immediate local environment and community.
- **Simplicity and detachment from material things.** Gandhi believed that ownership of anything more than the bare essentials needed for life is an act of violence, tantamount to stealing.

- **Non-violence is a way of life.** Gandhi was extremely clear that non-violence is a way of life, not simply a strategy used when one lacks resources for violent action.

Although first formulated in the early to mid-twentieth century in India, Gandhi's ethical framework and practical models for non-violent social action are still an important part of social movements and community organizing. They have influenced tactics used by "Occupy Wall Street" and related efforts in 2011, have supported mutual economic aid efforts in locales around the world, and form the basis of large parts of the sustainability movement.[33]

Dr. Martin Luther King Jr., a well-known leader of the American Civil Rights Movement, created his own uniquely American version of non-violence adapted from Gandhi's practices, the social gospel of theologian Reinhold Niebuhr, his own upbringing in the black church, and his own astute mind and heart. Most of the tactics associated with the Civil Rights Movement came from King Jr.'s non-violent ethics, including the Montgomery Bus Boycott, lunch counter sit-ins, peaceful marches, and quiet acceptance of punishment for breaking unjust laws.[34] For both Gandhi and King, non-violence was first and foremost a way of life and secondarily a social action tactic that solidified movement participants, shamed perpetrators, garnered support from on-lookers, and built moral pressure for justice.

Explore Gandhi's non-violent philosophy for a better understanding. In what ways is non-violence a useful ethical tool for social change?

The question of whether non-violence works either as an ethical stance or as a social change strategy is important for community organizers. The answer seems to be both "yes" and "no." Although Gandhi and King both died at the hands of assassins, both would probably say that they died as they had lived: with integrity and a sense of inner peace. Although each had his personal quirks, both lived deeply and richly and left an indelible mark on their families, their countries, and the world—deepening spiritually as they "walked the walk" and "talked the talk." In that profound personal sense, their non-violent ethics were successful. Their impact on the rough-and-tumble world of politics and the depths of human hatred is less clear. India was freed from Great Britain to become the largest democracy in the world, but its history since independence has been marred by internal conflict and ongoing tension with Pakistan: two nations standing with nuclear weapons pointed at each other. The income gap within India is increasing dramatically. Jim Crow laws no longer rule the American South. African Americans sit anywhere they like on public buses, eat at restaurants, and stay at hotels. Many television shows and commercials show an integrated America. Martin Luther King Jr.'s birthday has become a national holiday and a day of community service. His story and that of Rosa Parks (who practiced non-violent resistance which sparked the Montgomery Bus Boycott when she refused to move to the back of the bus) are shared with schoolchildren of all races as examples of wisdom and courage. We have had a mixed racial President who identifies himself as African American. On the other hand, there is growing evidence that racism and classism are largely ignored by the media, public, and decision makers. Violence is rampant from gang warfare in the inner cities to incessant warfare in the Middle East, and many state governments appear to be reinstituting barriers to voting for the poor and minorities. Clearly there is much work still to be done.

Assess your comprehension of the Ethics of Non-Violence by completing this quiz.

An Ethics of Care

In snowy Smithville, a priest lived in a comfortable rectory while homeless men shivered in the cold, so in spite of his housekeeper's grumbling, he opened the house and shared meals and friendship.[35] The priest was operating from an ethics of care.

Love is probably both the most profound and confounding word in the English language. While ethical practices built on love are foundational to most, if not all, of the world's great religions, philosopher Nel Noddings has reconceptualized love and caring for application to education and human services. For Noddings, love or caring is both a virtue and a description of warm reciprocal relationships, a way of being with others based on the primal experience of being cared for and caring in return. While she does not deny that caring exists as a virtue or character trait—and that one can *be* a caring teacher, a caring physician, a caring social worker, or a caring community organizer, her theories are based primarily on caring as a reciprocal relationship.[36] In Noddings' ethical framework, care receivers must perceive that they are the recipients of care and accept it. For instance, she uses the example of a middle school in which the children frequently lament that "nobody cares," but where the teachers are doing their best and feel that they care deeply for their students. Noddings suggests that in such a situation the ethics of care is not working, that a sense of reciprocity is needed for caring to exist. This sense of reciprocity does not necessarily mean that the receivers of care must thank their care givers verbally. The thanks can come with a gentle smile, a touch, excitement generated from learning something new, or the connection felt with others in the completion of a mutually satisfying project.[37] An analogy can be drawn in community organizing. If people on the street feel that nobody cares, something is wrong even if those in charge believe that they care very deeply.

Genuine caring is based on action and reciprocity. Years ago a doctor and his nurse wife moved into the Smithville neighborhood because they felt they were being called to care for the people there. They bought a modest home and set up a medical practice in their living room. They charged only what people could pay and sometimes accepted barter for their services. Their children played with the neighborhood children and attended the local public schools, but they really did not become an accepted part of the community until the doctor himself became ill. Neighbors brought food to the family, provided babysitting so his wife could visit him at the hospital, and prayed for them in their churches. When he recovered, the family found that they had a whole new relationship with their neighbors. Everyone relaxed. Where once they felt lonely and as if they were somehow being held at arms' length, they now felt accepted. They were invited to people's homes for get-togethers, neighbors offered their skills such as car repair or a ride to the store, the doctor was included in neighborhood horseshoe games, and his wife was invited on shopping trips. They were gently teased, greeted with warm smiles, and occasionally patted on the back or shoulder. They belonged within a community of care. As these relationships grew the doctor and his family blossomed, and so did the community as his wife and he were able to make gentle suggestions and informally influence health habits and practices. This kind of reciprocity is the essence of an ethic of care.

A true ethics of care requires reciprocity or mutuality. Think of times in your life when you really knew that someone cared. What was going on? Who was involved? How did you know that you were being cared for? Now think of times when someone let you know that they appreciated your care for them. What did you do that earned their appreciation? Was there reciprocity in the experience? If so, how it show itself? If not, is it possible to have caring without reciprocity? How can you show an ethics of care in your work as a community organizer?

Self-Development

Understanding and Mastery: Conscious use of self

Critical Thinking Question: What actions can you and your leadership team take to make reciprocal caring a natural part of organizational and community life?

The Classical Tradition: Ethical Behavior as a Rational Choice

For millennia, ethics was broadly divided into ethical constructs based on rational choices. Beginning with the ancient Greeks multiple frameworks were developed to enable people to assess the likely consequences of their behavior, cultivate a sense of duty, and live a virtuous life. Here we will explore a few of those frameworks.

Those who use a **utilitarian approach,** focus on consequences and aim for actions that will do the most good with the least harm. John Locke in seventeenth-century England and John Rawls in the twentieth century both applied this utilitarian approach to social justice. John Locke was an English philosopher who invented the idea of the "social contract" in which people agree to abide by decisions based on consensus and a balance of rights and privileges determined by a basic sense of justice (fair play). Locke's ideas were the basis of the U.S. Declaration of Independence and Constitution.[38] Although his theories of land use and property do not leave room for other cultural forms such as those of Native Americans,[39] Locke's idea of the social contract is central to both community organization and social action because it encourages public examination of the unwritten rules of social contracts and allows for protest if those rules are unjust.

John Rawls, a theorist who wrote in the early 1970s, developed his thinking from Locke in the context of **social contract theory**. Social contract theorists believe that government is based on rationality and mutual consent, to which Rawls added the dimension of justice. Rawls' basic contention was that the social contract should be fair to everyone, regardless of race, ethnicity, class, or personal characteristics, but he asserted that this is unlikely to happen in real life because everyone participates in society from a particular social position. Rawls' solution was to recommend that everyone adopt what he called the "veil of ignorance," a stepping back from our own social positions and preconceived notions to design social contracts that maximize liberty and opportunity for all.[40] Rawls' position makes a great deal of rational sense, but it is hard to actualize because people do not really sit down to draw up formal social contracts. Social contracts are implied rather than explicit and are created by ongoing processes of interaction. Participants in social contracting have unequal power, a fact that is nearly impossible to ignore. Finally, although it may be desirable for each of us to put on a veil of ignorance and attempt to view the world from outside ourselves, we are all influenced by unconscious values. This can be seen in the Rawls' own framework that values individual liberty above all, a value that is far from universal. In spite of their weaknesses, though, Rawls' ideas are useful. It is always good to stand back from your own position and interests and to encourage others to do the same as you work together to design actions that will promote positive outcomes for everyone involved.

Philosophers like Immanuel Kant—who operate from an **ethics of duty**—believe that there are moral laws that can be discerned and acted upon through rational decision making.[41] Kant is especially known for his concept of the "categorical imperative," in which you should (1) consider the principles on which you are basing your action and (2) examine them to see if they are self-contradictory or irrational. If they make rational sense, then ask whether you would choose to live in a world where everyone followed your principles. If so, your contemplated action is probably acceptable; if not, you shouldn't do it. In some organizing contexts, the categorical imperative can be challenging, such as when communities organize against pollution and other threats according to the "nimby" (not-in-my-backyard) concept. Kant raises the questions: "If not here, then where?" "If it is bad for our families and us, why is it being done at all?" You have an ethical responsibility to see that those involved in your efforts ask these hard questions.

Those who operate from an **ethics of virtue** aim to be people of good character. They define good character based on an amalgam of religious principles, cultural expectations, family values, and personal reflection. The ethics of virtue originated with the Greek philosophers Plato[42] and Aristotle.[43] Plato felt that the ultimate goal of life was justice. He believed that the human being (soul) was composed of body, mind, and spirit and that the virtuous life was one of balance and control. Physical appetites of all kinds were to be controlled by temperance or moderation in all things. Anger and fear were controlled by courage, while decision making was controlled by wisdom or reason. In proper balance, temperance, courage, and wisdom lead to justice in the individual and in the community. Thus, for Plato, ethical living in society begins with individual self-control. Aristotle, on the other hand, defined the ultimate goal as ***eudaimonia*** or the rational happiness of a balanced life. Aristotle seems to have been more aware of the realities of daily life than Plato. For Aristotle, happiness not only depended on wisdom and virtue but also on life circumstances, health, wealth, and personality. He developed a long list of virtues, but probably his major contribution to ethics was the idea of the **golden mean**. According to Aristotle, there are many virtues, and each is a kind of fulcrum or balance point between two equally unethical actions. For instance, courage is the balance between cowardice and rashness. Generosity is the balance point between stinginess and wastefulness. Justified anger, for the right amount of time for the right reasons, is the balance point between indifference to wrong and uncontrolled rage. The golden mean is not an absolute but depends on the individual, his or her status in life, and the circumstances. For instance, the courage needed to go into battle is different than the courage needed to stand up for your beliefs in a public forum. The courage needed to fight for selfish ends is different from the courage needed to fight for the rights and needs of those who are unable to repay you. The amount of money needed for a rich person to be considered generous is greater than that needed by a poor person. Virtues are the inner characteristics that make it possible for you to serve others fairly and kindly. They are developed through action and reflection on the results of action, as well as through listening to your conscience.

Interpersonal Communication

Understanding and Mastery: Developing and sustaining behaviors that are congruent with the values and ethics of the profession

Critical Thinking Question: Think about what you have learned about the activities required of community organizers. Which of these classic theories speaks to your own values and what you know of the values of your profession? Under what circumstances could each of these views be applied?

Assess your comprehension of Ethics as a Rational Choice by completing this quiz.

An Ethics of Joyful Sharing

One of life's greatest miracles is that there is something rather than nothing. According to the physical principle of entropy, systems tend to move from order to disorder, and so the universe should be a gray haze. Instead, systems often move from simplicity to greater complexity, wounds heal, seeds grow, children are born, and communities flourish. No one knows exactly why this happens, but most of us find this growth very deeply satisfying—especially when we share the experience with others. There are many ways of sharing the life-giving principle. Most are so simple that they are easily overlooked, and many begin in childhood.

Creativity, joy, and sharing life are all important components of ethical practice. At least four components are involved: an intentional focus on the positive, celebration in the midst of despair and external threats, creative sharing as participation in building a high-quality life, and taking care of one another. Through joyful creativity and fun, participants in your organizing efforts will gain a whole new perspective on life and sustain long, tedious, and often frustrating efforts. Celebration not only builds community spirit but can be an effective antidote to destruction and decay.

The **ethic of joyful sharing** is a way of life rather than a formal philosophy. It has many facets, including community kitchens, community playground raisings, installation art, community murals, street dances and block parties, community choirs and bands, community theaters, school sports, and children's recitals. Not only does sharing build the enjoyable side of community life, it engenders cooperation on even more serious activities, such as filling sandbags to prevent floods, participating in volunteer fire departments, and raising money for families devastated by disaster or disease. An ethic of sharing sounds easy, but it involves risk. Not everyone will want to share, and adults, as well as children, will encounter bullies in their lives. In the long run, though, an ongoing ethic of joyful sharing weaves a strong, resilient social fabric that can withstand disaster. We are meant to meet the difficulties of life together with courage and joy. Successful community organizing activities are often built on this ethical foundation.[44]

Practicing Cultural Humility

Cultural humility builds on an earlier idea of **cultural competence**. Cultural competence is the knowledge of how other's cultural heritage may affect their perceptions, responses, and behavior; it is the ability to understand how your own culture affects your values, thoughts, feelings, and behavior and to analyze how cultural perceptions affect interaction and to use this knowledge to act in non-judgmental ways. **Cultural humility** takes this a step further. It is the willingness to listen to and learn from others, the admission that your ways are not necessarily right in all times and all places, and an understanding that simply *knowing about* another culture does not mean that you *understand everything about everyone who shares that culture.* The opposite of cultural humility is cultural arrogance.

The concepts of cultural competence and cultural humility both evolved as a response to the cultural arrogance of the northern European, rationalist, largely white male colonial culture that has dominated the world since at least the Age of Exploration in the late fifteenth century. It should come as no surprise that not everyone shares the self-centered individualism that is a hallmark of the dominant culture. Cultural competency and cultural humility are in essence social movements that oppose the dominant paradigm.

Cultural humility puts respect for individual and cultural differences at the core of effective practice with individuals, families, groups, organizations, and communities. In order to begin practicing cultural humility you should:

- Examine your own cultural history, prejudices, and assumptions without blaming yourself but with a determination to change if necessary.
- Remember that everyone has multiple identities such as race, class, ethnic identity, gender, age, and even size—and everyone prioritizes these identities differently. Be very careful of even unintentional stereotyping.[45]
- Examine and confront your own prejudices, those of people in the target community, and those who are considered adversaries.
- If you are a member of a historically privileged group, be especially conscious of how the privileges you take for granted may be out of reach to others.
- Decide how you will confront prejudice in yourself and in others.
- Act courageously and wisely in response to blatant or implied "-isms" that you encounter.[46]

Client-related Values and Attitudes

Understanding and Mastery: The worth and uniqueness of individuals including: ethnicity, culture, gender, sexual orientation, and other expressions of diversity

Critical Thinking Question: Reflect on your own cultural heritage and how it will impact your work in communities. What might you do to ensure that you constantly practice cultural humility as you participate in community organizing and throughout your life with others?

Doman Lum, an Asian American, wrote an excellent book for everyone who works with members of diverse populations, especially people of color, but that is relevant to lighter skinned, working class people as well.[47] Lum has found that members of a wide range of ethnic groups, philosophies, and religions esteem collective values, family interdependence and obligation, metaphysical harmony in nature or religion, ethnic group identity, and loyalty to family and community above self. Since this is the case you should be aware of (and cultivate) these values within your leadership team, your organization, your focal community system, and yourself. Everyone should:

- Value family unification, parental leadership, respect for the elderly, and collective family decision making.
- Encourage the healthy application of religious and spiritual beliefs and practices which join the individual to collective institutions and forces in the universe, resulting in harmony, unity, and wholeness.
- Seek to use family kinship and community networks as support for persons (and communities) who can benefit from collective helping.
- Value the rediscovery of ethnic language and cultural identity which strengthens individuals' and communities' relationships to their heritage.
- Promote the harmony or sense of congruity and agreement in feelings, actions, ideas, and interest within and between persons. Harmony is essential to the balance of the person in relationship to others, society, the universe, and community life.
- Foster cooperation that brings families and groups together in a common sense of purpose, which may include pooling resources for survival, coping with problem situations, meeting a common crisis, and working with the extended family as part of an ethnic community.
- Acknowledge the reality of historical trauma in the lives of multi-cultural members and strive to understand the impact of such trauma in the present.[48]

Assess your comprehension of Cultural Humility by completing this quiz.

- Be aware of the micro-aggressions which people of color experience daily and be careful with phrases and behaviors that may cause unintentional hurt.[49]

Spirituality, Religious Beliefs, and Practice

In our secular world, many would argue that religious faith is not necessary for effective community organizing. Yet many organizers have found it so helpful that it would be remiss to leave out religious beliefs and practices as a frequently used basis for ethical decision making. At the risk of leaving someone out, here are a few individuals for whom religious faith informed and sustained their organizing practice. Mahatma (the "great soul") Gandhi was a member of the Jain sect of Hinduism who had a great respect for the sanctity of life. Dr. Martin Luther King Jr., an ordained Christian minister who never forgot his roots in the social gospel, began his organizing practice as pastor of Ebenezer Baptist Church in Montgomery Alabama. The Dalai Lama challenges us to develop habits of peace within the context of our own lives and vocations. These habits include movement away from self and toward others, cultivating contentment, being honest and just, acting against injustice, and working together for a better world right where we are. Rabbi Abraham Joshua Heschel, a contemporary of Martin Luther King Jr., was known both for his scholarly focus on the Jewish prophetic vision of social justice and also on his active participation in the Civil Rights Movement. Heschel is known for saying "My legs were praying" during the March on Selma in which he bravely marched at King's side as they faced vicious dogs and riot police. The list goes on: Mother Theresa of Calcutta and her dedication to the dying; Archbishop Oscar Romero, a quiet scholar who became a martyr for the poor of El Salvador; Episcopal Bishop Desmond Tutu of South Africa who—along with Nelson Mandela—was a powerful voice that helped end apartheid and who facilitated reconciliation in that hate-filled country; Ingrid Mattson, a president of the Islamic Society of North America (a diverse body of North American Muslims who stands for orthodox Islamic values and has advocated understanding in spite of the hatred Muslims have faced since 9/11); and dozens of others sustained by faith. Each of these people has shown consistent dedication to others and to a high quality of life for all people, especially the poor and disenfranchised. Some have lived long lives; others were assassinated. Some lived lives of voluntary poverty; others were privileged. Some were tortured; some were honored. Many experienced both disdain and acclaim. They come from different religious traditions and different parts of the world. Together, however, they provide insight into values and spiritual practices that can sustain you over the long haul.

Common spiritual factors among them include:

- Acknowledging that there are many legitimate paths to Truth.
- Embracing a religious tradition and its spiritual disciplines.
- Practicing one or more spiritual disciplines such as prayer, contemplation, meditation, journaling, spiritual reading, or good works.
- Participating in a community of like-minded people.
- Practicing compassion, empathy, and non-violence.
- Being willing to speak the truth in love, no matter what the personal consequences.
- Taking time daily for spiritual reflection.
- Listening to others to discern the inclusive truth when there is controversy.

Self-development

Understanding and Mastery: Clarification of personal and professional values

Critical Thinking Question: Consider the role (or lack of it) that spirituality or religious beliefs and practices play in your life. How will they influence your community organizing practice? How might they affect your work with others of differing beliefs and practices?

The lives of these leaders make it clear that an active spirituality was necessary for them to survive and thrive in the rough-and-tumble world of community organizing.

Professional Ethical Standards and Codes of Ethics

For our purposes, a **profession** is defined as a group of people who share an occupation with a recognized body of scholarly knowledge and sophisticated skills. A **professional association** or **professional organization** is defined as a voluntary group of self-defined professionals which oversees the legitimate practice of the occupation, safeguards the public interest, represents the interest of practitioners, maintains their privileged position, and ensures that regulation remains within the profession, not outside it. Codes of ethics are an intrinsic part of this self-regulatory process.[50]

The functions of professional associations are somewhat self-contradictory. On the one hand, they exist to ensure that services to the public meet high standards of quality and ethical practice so their codes of ethics define acceptable behaviors, provide benchmarks for self-evaluation, and establish a framework for professional behavior and responsibilities. They are a vehicle for professional identity and are a mark of occupational maturity. On the other hand, they protect professional privilege including access to educational programs, licensure, public accountability, and reasonable pay. The privileges of professionalism can be seen everywhere including social work, human services, and community organizing where those who do direct services have the least education, do the hardest hands-on work, are paid the least, and are often part of the target population.[51] As you examine professional ethical standards, keep these tensions and contradictions in mind. When codes of ethics are used in mechanical ways, they can substitute for the hard thinking and intuitive discernment that sensitive life in community demands. However, when combined with reflection—particularly on challenging examples—codes of ethics can help frame daily decision making.

Client-related Values and Attitudes

Understanding and Mastery: Integration of the ethical standards outlined by the National Organization for Human Services and Council for Standards in Human Service Education

Critical Thinking Question: Some people have expressed concern that the code of ethics in its present form may encourage white, middle class privilege and bias and encourage stereotyping of people of color and those of low socio-economic status. What steps will you take to avoid such bias in your community organizing practice?

Community organizing touches many professions including planning, community development, community education, community health care, community psychology, and rural sociology. It is an intrinsic component of macro-level human services and social work. All of these professions adhere broadly to the axiom: "First of all, do no harm." Harm can come in somewhat surprising forms and has broad ethical implications for community organizing. For instance, it may be tempting to seek available grant funding for a time-limited opportunity, but you must ask yourself and potential recipients whether things are likely to be worse once the funding is lost. At other times, it may be tempting to impose strict rules to protect the weak from exploitation, but you must always look for unexpected (*latent* or *dysfunctional*) consequences.

Review the Ethical Standards for Human Services and the National Association of Social Workers Code of Ethics. Consider what you have learned about community organizing thus far. Which of the standards will be most relevant to your community organizing efforts? What do you intend to do to put them into practice?

In addition to the formal values and principles of practice that are intrinsic to both social work and human services, each profession emphasizes the importance of culturally competent practice or the ability of workers to assist persons from a variety of backgrounds and diverse viewpoints. However, you must be careful with these codes, especially when working in diverse communities. Most, if not all, of the values and practice principles in these professional codes are built on the ethical standards of the white, male rationalists of northern Enlightenment Europe. This is especially true of the emphasis on individual self-determination, sometimes without consideration of extended family or community contexts. In fact, the implicit values orientation toward individuality can often be "heard" in the goals set for treatment or even for community organizing. In such an individualistic world, the community becomes a stage for individual actors rather than the web of mutually satisfying relationships that are the basis for a high quality of life for everyone.

Assess your comprehension of the Codes of Ethics of Human Services and Social Work by taking this short quiz.

Summary

In this chapter you had the opportunity to compare and contrast the **modernist paradigm** with the **quality of life paradigm** that is the core value of this text. In addition, you were introduced to several major ethical models and encouraged to use them to guide your practice:

- **Post-modernism** introduced the idea that social reality is constructed through dialogue and consensus. You were encouraged to examine your own assumptions and guide others to do the same.
- **Critical theory** encouraged you to look for ways that you and those you serve have developed a false consciousness that led you to believe that the way life is—with all its injustice—is the way life should be. You were encouraged to think critically about the social world and have the courage to take the actions needed for positive change.
- In **discursive ethics** you learned about the importance of making sure that all participants are able to make themselves heard and were shown a few ways of structuring conversations to enable this to happen.
- **Ethical use of power** encouraged you to critically examine the ways your own attitudes and actions may undercut participants.
- The discussion of **non-violence** centered on the ethical roots for the social movements led by Gandhi and Martin Luther King Jr. and examined non-violence as an ethical stance as well as a social action strategy.
- The **ethics of care** emphasized the importance of warm, loving relationships in community building.
- **Ethical behavior as a rational choice** emphasized the philosophers and philosophies that have traditionally been associated with ethics as an intellectual discipline and the applications of their work to community organizing.
- An **ethic of joyful sharing** introduced the idea that enjoyment of life can be an ethical imperative and that life with others can and should be seen as a creative, rewarding adventure.
- **Cultural humility** provided some concrete suggestions for respecting and celebrating diversity.

- **Religion and spirituality** highlighted some notable people of various cultures and faiths, the religious practices they share, and some of the ways a strong spiritual foundation can sustain engagement in community organizing over the long haul.
- **Professional ethical standards** examined the role such standards play in ethical practice. No attempt was made to cover specific standards because they frequently change and because community organizing touches on many different professions, each of which has its own ethical code.

Assess your analysis and evaluation of the chapter's content by completing the Chapter Review.

As you read this chapter carefully, think about how the ethical concepts affect you and apply them to your community organizing practice. You can be reasonably sure that your decisions—and those of your organizing team—will positively impact the communities you serve and our society.

CHAPTER 14

Community Organizing with Web-based Tools

VLADGRIN/Shutterstock

Chapter Outline

In this chapter, you will examine some of the principles and issues regarding the use of the Internet in community organizing activities.

The Impact of the Internet and Social Networking on Community Organizing

Beginning with its first widespread use in the mid-1990s, the Internet has resulted in many changes in community organizing. Its full impact is yet to be seen, but here are five major changes the internet has brought so far: (1) speed, (2) extent of reach,(3) expansion of means of communication, (4) connectivity, and (5) access to vast quantities of information. Major areas to consider as you incorporate Web-based tools into your organizing efforts are:

- The use of your Web presence.
- Principles of digital storytelling.
- The proper mix of communication tools to keep your constituents involved and to decrease the virtual distance among them.
- The use of Web-based tools in advocacy.
- The role of increased connectivity in the creation of self-organizing, multi-dimensional, blended virtual–real communities.
- Major weaknesses of Web and digitally based organizing efforts and possible threats to its free use.

Broad Impact of the Internet on Community Organizing

There is a debate in the community organizing world about whether the Internet has created a revolution in the way we experience community life—especially in the way we do community organizing—or whether it is simply a set of tools that accelerate existing organizing processes. Certainly, there are things that have not changed. If you are organizing advocacy or social movements, you still need to increase supporters', observers', and adversaries' perceptions of your WUNC (Worthiness, Unity, Numbers, and Commitment). In any kind of organizing, you still have to understand and use the concepts and skills explored in this text including systems thinking, community dynamics, varieties of organizing, the community organizing cycle, engagement of leaders and participants, organizational structures, power, and political realities. You still have to behave ethically. These are basic to community organizing in any time and in any place. On the other hand, the Web makes it possible to

- Do all of these things faster.
- Reach vastly more people.
- Offer a wide variety of communication tools.
- Provide simultaneous global connections that once would have been impossible.
- Allow access to huge quantities of information and opinion.

Assess your comprehension of the Strengths and Weaknesses of Web-Based Tools in Community Organizing by completing this quiz.

Table 14.1 examines the strengths and weaknesses of each of these dimensions.

Table 14.1 Strengths and Weaknesses of Web Use in Community Organizing

Characteristic	Strength	Weakness	Considerations
Speed	Initiate action quickly.	May not give enough thought to actions.	Is this the best move at this time? Is it worthy? Is it ethical?
Reach	Gain access to large numbers of people.	Large numbers of people may be able to reach you, but some of your major constituents may have limited Web access.	Who do we want to reach and why? Are different levels of access needed? In what ways might our adversaries be able to use our technologies to hurt us?
Wide variety of communication tools	Offers many ways to reach supporters. If you miss them through one channel, you will probably reach them through another.	It is hard to manage multiple communication tools and keep them up to date.	How will we manage our communications? What technological and human resources do we need? What technologies are available to our primary constituents?
Connectivity	Provides many opportunities to develop personal and professional relationships with people around the world; aids in building global communities.	Some of these connections can be bogus, misleading, or downright dangerous. There are few cues to discern the difference.	Which of the many opportunities will be the best match for our organizational mission? What criteria will we use for trustworthiness?
Access to information	Affords many opportunities for research and exploration of best practices.	May contain inaccurate, misleading, or malicious information.	What information do we need and why? How are we going to check its accuracy?

Source: Copyright © by Pearson Education, Upper Saddle River, NJ.

Internal Communication Goals and Web-based Tools

In many ways community organizing is about communication. Within your focal community system you must build and maintain your base of support, develop a solid leadership team, and facilitate effective two-way communication between your leadership team and your stakeholders.

Your objective in building an internal communication network and base of support is to ensure that your organizing effort has the ongoing human, financial, and material resources necessary to accomplish its outcome goals in light of your vision, mission, and values. Although the analogy is imperfect, you can learn from the marketing insights of business and industry: **product, promotion, placement/platform**, and **price**. Your **product** is the desired outcome of your organizing effort. The community organizing cycle that you explored in Chapters 5 to 9 is about creating the best **product** possible. You should give some thought to whether and how Web-based communications and services have a role in bringing about your desired outcomes. **Promotion** is about getting people to believe that your organization, the needs you have identified, and your proposed solutions are worth investment of their limited time, money, and personal reputation. For many years, promotion in community organizing was done through conventional means: articles in local newspapers, radio and television coverage, face-to-face community meetings, target mailings to potential supporters, billboards, church bulletins, individual conversations, and flyers distributed throughout the focal community system. These are still good ways to promote your community organizing efforts. The digital world has added others—such as organizational websites, sharing on broad-based social networks like Facebook and Twitter, and "pooled advertising" between organizations with similar missions. However, the digital world has also changed some promotional realities because it has added a whole new dimension of interactivity and receiver choice.[1] Even in the community organizing world, the wide variety of communication channels and opportunities for engagement has exposed people to a constant deluge of similar information. This, in turn, has led to a backlash. Many people now put a premium on privacy and personal control of the messages they acknowledge. They are no longer passive receivers. They appreciate interaction, the ability to have their questions answered in real time or on their schedule, opportunities for engagement, and the option to give feedback even if it is only clicking a button to sign a petition or the chance to answer a quick survey. They enjoy a game-like atmosphere so, for instance, a survey of priorities which allows them to arrange the answers is appealing. Even if it is only for a few seconds, they want their investment of time and energy to matter.[2]

Administration

Understanding and Mastery: Constituency building and other advocacy techniques such as lobbying, grassroots movements, and community development and organizing

Critical Thinking Question: Community organizers use the "P's" of marketing (product, promotion, placement/platform, and price) to develop support for their efforts. Identify the "P's" of your organizing effort. Outline a preliminary marketing campaign. How will you integrate Web-based tools into your effort?

In the initial phases of community organizing, **placement** is about getting the news about your community organizing effort and ways to engage in it out to the people who are most likely to respond positively. In the face-to-face world, placement in the initial phase meant holding meetings or providing services in places and times that were most likely to attract target participants. Placement still means these things. However, the digital world has added new opportunities. Organizational meetings can now be held via real-time collaborative sites that enable participants to communicate simultaneously across many miles, continents, oceans, and time zones.[3] Several sites offer remarkable simultaneous opportunities to communicate via written chat, audio teleconferencing, video linkages, desk-top sharing of websites, online whiteboard spaces for brainstorming, capacities for shared document creation, platforms for visual presentations, and links to videos. They have the capacity to record interactions for future viewing and analysis by participants or those unable to attend in real time. Effective online conferencing is available through open educational resources so it is quite possible to keep costs low and quality high. In general, it is best to find a **platform** (technological support system) that is free, globally accessible, and allows for written chat, oral chat, whiteboard, slide presentations, desktop sharing, and recording. (Note of caution: While video capabilities can add a certain amount of glamour, they are often unnecessary because they can be unreliable and expensive, eat up bandwidth, and do not substantially add to the experience. If you have a choice between video capabilities and reliable simultaneous audio, choose the audio).

In the implementation phase, placement is about connecting those who would benefit from your services to your organization. Here the Web offers **asynchronous** opportunities (available any place at any time) including discussion forums blogs, and wikis, and **synchronous** opportunities (available in real time) such as the meeting areas mentioned above and microblogging applications such as Twitter. You can design such modalities to be accessed by password through your organizational website. Accessibility is the key to online services. Be sure that your service areas are easily available to those with minimum access to technology. One promising avenue for service delivery is the use of cell phones and text messaging because even the poorest of the poor frequently have access to them.[4]

Administration

Understanding and Mastery: Constituency building and other advocacy techniques such as lobbying, grassroots movements, and community development and organizing

Critical Thinking Question: Locate and explore the Web-based tools used by several different charities or advocacy efforts. (Hint: just go to Google and type in the name of the charity.) Note their design and the opportunities they give for interaction and engagement. What aspects of each appeal to you and why? What aspects do you find off-putting? What elements would you probably incorporate into your community organizing efforts?

Price does not really have a direct analogy in community organizing but could refer to the amount of time, energy, and financial resources expended through participation in your organizing effort. You should offer many opportunities for both online as well as face-to-face engagement. For instance, many social movements have online alert systems that apprise people of a need for action and offer the recipient several choices:

- A button to click to send a pre-written message to a target individual or organization
- A space under the pre-written message to include a personalized message along with the pre-written message
- Several places to click and share the message on large social networks, such as Facebook and Twitter
- A place to make a protected financial contribution to the particular action
- Links to video presentations, especially YouTube

Often such alerts give additional options for engagement such as access to telephone numbers of political representatives and bureaucratic decision makers and announcements of social action activities, such as rallies and legislative action days. A few have provision for setting priorities. For instance, some political organizations periodically ask members to prioritize their action agenda or to select which candidates to support through moving and organizing items in a list. These interactive techniques allow the message recipient to consistently feel like a part of the organizing effort.

The Web is especially useful for facilitating distributed leadership and management activities through simple conference calls or the sophisticated conferencing capabilities that were discussed earlier. Before the advent of Web-based technologies, geographically dispersed leaders were forced to spend significant time and money to participate in face-to-face meetings. While there are definite emotional and informational advantages with face-to-face meetings—especially through the sharing and relationship building that goes on during breaks, lunch, and evening relaxation—there are definite disadvantages as well. Face-to-face meetings can reduce productivity because time on the road and recovery from travel take time away from other duties and may sap the energy needed to make good decisions. Online meetings help eliminate such stresses. Experience shows that leadership efforts seem to flourish when both face-to-face and online meetings are used.[5] Face-to-face meetings solidify trust and clarify nuances of meaning. Online meetings or telephone conferences build on that established trust; facilitate mental clarity; and save time, money, and physical energy. Some organizations effectively use blended meetings or conferences, holding small face-to-face gatherings in several locations which are linked to sophisticated distance conferencing technologies, thus simultaneously taking advantage of the strengths of both face-to-face and Net-based communications.

Ongoing communication between leadership and constituents was addressed earlier from the participants' viewpoint. From the leadership viewpoint, Web-based tools can facilitate top-down communication through action alerts, blogs, and newsletters that can be sent directly from the organization to its constituents. Effective communication from leadership to participants depends on timeliness, provision for interaction, and an accurate database of constituents that is constantly updated. It is especially important to keep members apprised of major leadership decisions and to engage participation from those who indicate an interest in some aspect of your work. All of these tasks can be facilitated by a well-designed database management system based on your organization's needs, but database management is both time consuming and jargon filled. Some community organizing movements (and social service agencies) engage students of **community informatics** (an interdisciplinary academic field) in service learning projects that involve the development and management of such databases. You should check with the information technology (IT) department of a local college or university for such assistance.

Assess your comprehension of the Use of Web-Based Tools in Constituency Building by completing this quiz.

Web Presence

Externally, you must make sure that important individuals and organizations within your micro-, mezzo-, and macro-systems understand your outcome goals, support your methods, and are willing to accept the legitimacy of your efforts. Unfortunately, you may also have to defend your effort against attack. Digital tools help enable your organization to meet these communication goals.

Web presence refers to the many ways your organization presents itself publicly in the digital world.[6] Its elements are constantly changing and include your website, any links that your organization has through social networks such as Facebook and Twitter, Web search engines (i.e., Google), as well as Web-based references to your organizing effort from other sources. Of these, your website is crucial because it is often the first glimpse people have of your organization. There are many free or inexpensive services available to help you and your leadership team create an excellent website. But before you can talk intelligently with a Web designer, your leadership team should make some decisions so that your website is

Administration

Understanding and Mastery: Constituency building and other advocacy techniques such as lobbying, grassroots movements, and community development and organizing

Critical Thinking Question: What specific things will you take into account as you build a Web presence for your organization?

- *Readily accessible* to anyone who has Internet access. Beware of "bells and whistles" that exclude potential participants.
- *Simple* and easy to navigate. It should have an internal search capacity that uses terms that are useful to everyone.
- *Clear* so that anyone conducting a search can easily find the legal name of your organization on the homepage and understand your mission and outcomes. Avoid using unique jargon and meaningless acronyms.
- *Easily updated* with as few sections as possible that need regular updating. An infrequently updated website can make your organization look incompetent and may cause searchers to ask if it still exists. But because many community organizing efforts are small and volunteer-based, updating the website tends to become a low priority.
- *Simple and engaging design* attracts viewers. Crowded websites may intrigue Web designers, but they confuse busy searchers and break down easily.
- *Clearly linked to relevant resources* that are periodically checked for their functionality. These resources may include outside links and relevant literature produced by members of your organization. As much as possible, these resources should be available under **Creative Commons** licensing (a way of ensuring that users can freely use materials).
- *Designed with different levels of access.* Carefully assess which information is needed by whom. Your first (public) page should give the facts and inspire interest and support; other public pages should enhance your service mission; and private pages should be designed for enhancing the mission of the organization and conducting the business of the organization and its teams and committees.
- *Equipped with links for memberships and protected donations.* Your website should double as a communication center for your organizing effort and should offer searchers the opportunity to join and support your cause.
- *Clearly dated with attribution for its creation.* This information should be on the bottom of the first page and updated each time changes are made. It gives your site legitimacy and emphasizes the timeliness of the information.
- *Have a clear means of unsubscribing or changing contact information.* People's interests change easily these days. They respect organizations that allow them to easily join and withdraw just as easily.

The leadership team should remember that your website is your space in the virtual world and your organization owns it in much the same way it owns a building or other real property. Since you own it, you have the right and responsibility to care for it so make sure you know what you want it to accomplish and require your Web designer to meet your needs, not vice versa.

Assess your comprehension of Building Your Web-Presence by completing this quiz.

Social Networking

Effective community organizing efforts have effective plans for building participation and engaging their members that blend the best of the old with the tools and techniques of the new to develop **social networks.**[7] The Free Management Library mentioned earlier in this text is a great resource for management information[8] and has many articles on the use of social networking. There is an emerging consensus in these articles that social networking works best when you target existing online communities who may be interested in your organizing effort and find ways to reach them. Lisa Chapman, the library's guru on social networking, has several suggestions that have been adapted here. Your social networking (and other online marketing strategies) should flow consistently from your mission, values, and outcome goals.[9] You should:

- Find and listen to conversations that may already be taking place online about your general area of interest, your efforts so far, your competitors, and your competitors' strategies.
- Find and listen to online expressions of your ideal participants' needs (presumably you have first done this in real time with real people).
- Choose key social media sites that are likely to attract people like those you would like to reach.[10]
- Link the sites you have chosen into your own website.
- Engage in conversations and provide useful information. (Note: Do not be surprised if you do not have many interactive conversations. Many people use social networking sites such as Facebook for information rather than dialogue.)
- Use blogs connected to your website to build a following. Collect useful information on your participants that will provide clues to their interests and their likely level of engagement. Add this information to your databases.
- Use microblogs such as Twitter judiciously.
- Track and monitor your activities and their results.
- Tweak for continuous improvement.
- Systematically repeat these steps.

Chapman also recommends that you find ways to engage your online audience in building your social networking capabilities. The following ideas are adapted from her suggestions:

- Gather a team to strategize social media marketing. For community organizing ventures, this should primarily include key participants on your leadership team, representatives from your focal community, and someone with expertise in social networking or community informatics. (If you don't have such a person on your leadership team, try recruiting a service learning student from a local college or university.)
- Convene this group for a minimum of four hours. Bring the current marketing plan (from the planning and implementation phases of the community organizing cycle). Review its main points. If you do not have a marketing plan or if your marketing plan does not match what you are actually doing or intend to do, go back to the planning and implementation phases of the community organizing cycle and integrate social networking strategies with other approaches. Do not tack social networking onto a dysfunctional existing plan. (A note on process: It is probably better if this first meeting is face to face and rather lengthy to build momentum, develop mutual trust, and build informal working relationships. Make the event as pleasant as possible with good food, comfortable chairs, good lighting, and frequent

breaks. Provide child care if members of the community are involved. Provide travel reimbursement or a small stipend if low-income participants are involved. Later meetings can be held by conference call or in an online communication room like those discussed earlier.)

- Discuss your marketing and advertising goals and how they fit into your organizing mission. Do your current marketing and advertising efforts achieve your goals? If so, challenge the team to set higher goals, and brainstorm ways that social media marketing can be implemented to improve results.
- Identify online communities where your ideal participant congregates or searches. For example, if you are an emerging local organization, log onto your search engine and enter the keywords "(your city) directories" to find local directories in which your organization should be listed.
- Remember that search engines work through key words and phrases typed in by potential users. Make sure that you have searched and decided on specific keywords and keyword phrases that you use consistently in all of your online content that will help potential contacts to find you.
- Make sure your organization is listed in a minimum of two to six online "properties" or sites (all optimized for your keywords) that include *at least* one website, blog, social network site, and directory. The more places you exist online, the greater your chances of being found!
- Brainstorm online campaigns that will help you achieve your goals. Remember, social media are effective *only* if you have an end in mind. Otherwise, they are fun but can be a waste of time and precious resources.
    - Assign specific individuals or teams and time frames for actualizing your plans.
    - Create clear ways for planning participants to communicate between meetings of the whole social networking team.
    - Set a time to re-gather in person, synchronously online, or in a blending of the two to review progress and make needed changes.
    - Have fun and be creative!

Assess your comprehension of Social Networking as an Organizing Tool by completing this quiz.

Using Digital Storytelling

Earlier in this text we discussed the importance of storytelling and narratives as ways of building support for community organizing efforts and increasing participants' identification with your efforts. Try using **digital storytelling**—the use of Web-based tools to create short video-based art forms—that can enhance the ancient art of the storytelling task by enabling creators to combine visual images, music, oral narratives, still photographs, and interactive activities into an aesthetic and compelling whole.[11]

Administration

Understanding and Mastery: Constituency building and other advocacy techniques such as lobbying, grassroots movements, and community development and organizing

Critical Thinking Question: How might digital storytelling and other Web-based tools be used to effectively tell your organization's story to potential supporters?

You will find that digital storytelling can be used in community organizing to

- Use as a marketing tool to tell the story of your organization.
- Make community needs real to potential supporters and to community members.
- Empower individuals by enabling them to reflect on the relationship between their lives and social reality.
- Learn new, relevant skills. When done collaboratively, digital storytelling is a way to build mutual support and trust. Several Web-based organizations that introduce digital storytelling can easily be found through a standard search engine. One that seems very helpful is the Center for Digital Storytelling located in Berkeley, California.[12] Some colleges or universities offer credit-bearing classes in the field.

Explore the Center for Digital Storytelling. Consider the ways digital storytelling might be included in the tools your organizing effort uses to promote its cause.

Horizontal Community Organizing

The Internet has not only expanded the speed of making connections but has also made it possible to gather information quickly and has enabled **horizontal organizing**, in which similar events and projects can be actualized simultaneously while still being tailored to specific communities' needs. One example of horizontal organizing is the Occupy Wall Street movement of 2011 which grew from just a few protesters in New York City to a nationwide movement with "occupations" in dozens of cities in less than two months, mostly through the use of social media such as Facebook and Twitter. The Occupy movement worked on the concept of a **trope**—a stereotypical image, process, or concept passed along through social media—that catches people's imaginations across ethnicities and vocations and becomes part of our common worldview. The Occupy movement used images, such as those of peaceful protesters being pepper sprayed at a University of California campus, and phrases such as "We are the 99%" (that is, those who all together have less of the country's resources than the 1% who are most wealthy), to unite very different people and symbolize many different struggles and fears. From September to November 2011, the Occupy movement spread like a contagion with thousands literally camping out in public parks.

Horizontal Web-based organizing is not so very different from the "radical" days of the late 1960s except that it is much faster. Like the protests of that time, it is an effective means of expressing disillusionment with the current system—but it is unclear whether it is equally effective in supporting positive actions, such as the sustainability movement and rebuilding local economies. While such protests may encourage the change process by exciting and engaging masses of people, the real work of shifting from the current failing growth model to the Quality of Life model will take calm common sense, experimentation, and sharing good ideas in a process that is not as exhilarating as mass protests but is far more important in the long haul.

Human Systems

Understanding and Mastery: An understanding of capacities, limitations, and resiliency of human systems

Critical Thinking Question: Since the so-called Arab Spring in January 2011 and the massive Occupy movement that same year, social movements seem to be emerging ever more rapidly. In what ways did the speed and connectivity of the Internet provide an impetus to their initial success? In what ways might it have contributed to their eventual fragmentation? What does this tell you about the judicious use of Internet tools for community organizing? Have Web-based tools fundamentally changed the nature of community organizing, or have they simply increased its speed?

Connectivism and Community Organizing

Connectivism is a learning theory created primarily by Professor George Siemens of Athabasca University that brings us back to Chapter 2 and its emphasis on the importance of the number and quality of connections among individuals, quasi-groups, associations, and formal organizations as well as adding the dimension of online networking.[13] Siemens' theory is somewhat complex and tied to other complicated theories of learning, but its essence is as follows:

- Learning (and presumably effectiveness in community organizing) depends on the ability to make connections among ideas and people that would not ordinarily be connected.
- The insights gained from these connections can be applied to a wide variety of topics and issues.

Explore Connectivism Slides to learn more about George Siemens' Connectivism theory. How is Connectivism a useful tool to encourage sharing among community organizers around the world?

Connectivity, according to Siemens, is the number, speed, and consistency of connections you or your organization can make and is characterized by multiple relationships and a lack of hierarchy.

The Internet and especially social networking has greatly increased our ability to communicate quickly and easily with people we do not know personally but who share our interests and concerns. Broadly stated, the more connections members of your organization are able to make—combined with careful listening, building on good ideas in your own setting, reflecting on results, and reciprocal sharing with others in your network—the greater the likelihood of wise decision making everywhere. One of your many goals as a locally based community organizer should be to increase the connectivity of your organization through social networking. Conversely, one of your personal goals as someone who is committed to positive engagement of people in improving their quality of life should be to encourage global, non-hierarchical sharing.

The Internet gives you many tools to make connectivity a reality. As in many aspects of community organizing, connectivity starts with a Web search using key words that give you access to organizations and social networking sites relevant to your organizing interests. Spend time investigating these sites, identify links to other sites of interest, jump into ongoing conversations, prioritize those you want to continue to follow, and keep alert for other interesting related links. You should do this as an engaged individual but should also encourage it among your leadership team and key participants. While you should use due diligence to avoid allegiance to spurious efforts, you should be unafraid to participate and contribute ideas and questions. If you intentionally practice connectivism and encourage those involved in your organizing effort to do the same, you will be surprised at the number of ties you have in common with the people you encounter, including those directly relevant to your organizing practice and others that are relevant to your other interests. If you intentionally tie people you know with others who share common interests and concerns, you will be pleasantly surprised at the amount of exchange, knowledge, and even soul power that can be generated—as well as the fun of feeling engaged.

Assess your comprehension of Connectivism by completing this quiz.

Connectivity, Asset-building, and Sustainability

There are a number of Web-based, connected organizations emerging that are based on social networking and that are important supports of sustainability and the asset-based approach. All are versions of the Web-based, connected, horizontal organizing that has become the new norm for community organizing. These organizations are each intentionally designed to facilitate social networking specifically around the topic of sustainability. You will find each to be helpful places to begin your exploration of social networking, particularly for the kind of community organizing advocated here. Each of the websites has its own strengths and weaknesses which give you and your leadership team insights into developing your own Web presence.

Human Systems

Understanding and Mastery: Processes to effect social change through advocacy (e.g., community development, community and grassroots organizing, local and global activism)

Critical Thinking Activity: The Internet has made it possible to build supportive networks for a variety of organizing efforts. Some of these are listed below. Others that are more specific to your organizing mission may have an Internet presence. Identify one or more organizations whose missions support your own. Explore ways they could be helpful to your leadership team.

- *Abundant Community: Awakening the Power of Communities and Neighborhoods.* This is the private website of John McKnight and Peter Block. John McKnight (along with John Kretzman) founded the Asset-based approach to community organizing. This organization simultaneously provides an interactive, constantly updated link to McKnight's and Block's book (also titled *The Abundant Community: Awakening the Power of Families and Neighborhoods*) and a membership-based social network that connects community organizers who use the asset-based approach with one another. Membership is free and entitles you to a bi-weekly online newsletter, access to online and face-to-face workshops, online opportunities to chat with fellow locally based organizers, and access to places for you to post your experiences with community organizing. The website is well designed, easy to navigate, and exudes a warm, welcoming style that embraces the spirit of connectivity. It also provides a multitude of resources from a myriad of sources that include individuals, community outreach efforts, and other community building social networking sites. The site itself would qualify as social entrepreneurship. Its main weakness is its dependence on its creators, without whom it seems that the site would cease to exist. However, the connectivity it has generated among like-minded community organizers would probably remain. Because it has so many opportunities to connect, the Abundant Community site is a good place to plug in to the asset-based approach to community building.
- *The New Economy Working Group.* The New Economy Working Group describes itself as an informal alliance among several core partner organizations, each of which is itself a node in the sustainability and new economics network. According to its website, "NEWGroup functions as an informal alliance of the Institute for Policy Studies (IPS) as an initial policy think tank partner; *YES!* magazine as an initial media partner; the Business Alliance for Local Living Economies (BALLE) (as an initial business network partner); and the Living Economies Forum as an initial system design partner." Each of these alliance member organizations is, in turn, a node in the social network surrounding economic change and what founder economist David Korten calls "the necessary change from Wall Street to Main Street." Its business model is interesting because while it is somewhat dependent on Korten, its structure as an alliance of several organizations is likely to give it stability if there

were a transition in leadership (an important consideration since Korten is of retirement age). The Alliance continues to expand and is a good example of the kind of connectivity it advocates. Its website is a good place to start an exploration of the sustainability network.

- *The Gund Institute for Ecological Economics at the University of Vermont* has developed a collaborative network based on the development of international sustainability indicators. Its website contains many links to the latest work in the field.
- *The New Economics Institute.* The New Economics Institute (formerly the E. F. Schumacher Society) is primarily a collaborative network built on the groundbreaking work of economist E. F. Schumacher, author of *Small is beautiful: Economics as if people mattered*, first published in 1973 and still a classic for the sustainability movement. The network supports a sustainability effort in the Berkshire region of Massachusetts where it coordinates the BerkShares local currency initiative. The Institute has a very professional website, as well as a physical campus, that gives the impression of an established organization that has added a networking component. It adeptly explains the important concepts of alternative economics. Although it is not as warm and user-friendly as the Abundant Community site, its intent is different: it primarily serves to link formal institutions working on sustainability issues.
- *Data Center: Research for Justice.* The Data Center located in Oakland, California (the San Francisco Bay area), has been providing data and guidance to popular education–type organizing efforts for more than 30 years. Although it began as a kind of alternative library where community activists could go to access data and information that was not readily available through conventional libraries, it now uses the connectivity of the Internet to provide activists with access to Web-based resources, offer guidance on participatory community organizing approaches, and link organizing efforts with one another. Their website is a good example of how the Web has transformed the organizing process. It gives an excellent, although somewhat jargon-filled overview of participatory organizing and provides ways your community advocacy or social movement effort can link with other organizations that share similar goals.

Remember that connectivity is essentially a self-directed activity. In addition to creatively and playfully exploring these websites, you will want to enter and explore other social networks related to your own interests and to the focus of your community organizing efforts. Make a note of possible connections and share them with your organizing team, friends, colleagues, and acquaintances on other social networks. The whole process of connectivity works best when everyone is on the lookout for ways to connect with other people and to link them with still other individuals, associations, and organizations of interest. Community organizing has always been about building the world together, and the Web just makes it easier.

Strengths of Using the Web for Community Organizing

The Internet has many positive characteristics that you can use to strengthen your organizing mission. Some of them are as follows:

- *Connectivity.* Your ability to connect with people who have similar interests and concerns now flows at the speed of light.

- *Closeness.* Dr. Michael G. Moore, one of the pioneer theorists in distance education, asserts that learning (and by extension effective community organizing) is the product of a cross among individual freedom, initiative, and a sense of interactional closeness to others from whom one learns.[14] Interactional closeness is emotionally satisfying, personally motivating, and eases loneliness as you establish relationships with likeminded people. The Web and Web-based communities provide interactional closeness across the world at a minimal cost.
- *Free Information.* Almost any information in the world is at your fingertips with just a few key strokes. The Internet research skills covered in Chapter 7 and its related Appendix A provide directions on safely using this time-saving research tool.
- *Scope of audience.* From a social movement point of view, it is possible to reach millions of people quickly with minimum censorship (at least so far).
- *Speed.* Speed can be both an advantage and a threat, but it clearly is an advantage in keeping a movement going. The peace movement and other radical efforts of the late 1960s and early 1970s died in part because the Kent State shootings showed young radicals that marches and demonstrations can have serious consequences. But another factor was that participants in the student strikes and campus unrest returned home from college to summer jobs and were largely separated from one another, except for costly, long-distance telephone calls. There was no Internet, no cell phones, and no unlimited long-distance service. The widespread activism seen in the Occupy movement would have been difficult in 1970.
- *Low cost.* It is possible to set up Internet infrastructures very inexpensively and to run large outreach efforts with minimum numbers of paid staff.
- *Web-based communication can be done outside the mainstream media and around the edges so it is hard to stifle.*
- *Rapid feedback from constituents.* The Internet and related technologies allow organizations to obtain feedback from their members and to decide on goals, strategies, and tactics that are likely to engage them.

Weaknesses, Dangers, and Threats of the Internet or to the Internet

The Internet also has a down side, starting with the fact that it has so much information that is difficult to separate the useful from the inaccurate. Thus, critical thinking skills and shared reasoning are important. Here are some factors to consider when using the Internet:

- The Web is currently free and open, but there are constant direct threats by corporations and government to take it over or shut it down. There are more subtle threats of cooption by global economic interests, increased advertising, and the "industrialization" of sites like Facebook that were once free and fun but are becoming more complex and difficult to use. Even reliable search engines like Google are being redesigned to emphasize commercial sites and commercial interests, so it is harder to locate and network with non-commercial organizations.
- It is hard for small organizations to keep websites current, and loss of currency can quickly lead to a loss of reputation.

- It is often difficult for "ordinary" people to communicate with "techies" (technological experts) because Web-based technologies have a language that is all their own and constantly changing. Your organization will need members who can bridge this communication gap.
- Local groups that serve the poor still find a digital divide: some constituents have access to computers, others lack home telephones or permanent addresses, and still others have cell phones and other electronic devices. But it is very important to include everyone. It is likely that, over time, the use of cell phones and texting may bridge this digital divide. However, formerly free and open sites often close or shift to a commercial model, which leaves networks and organizing activities based on these platforms in the lurch.

On balance you will find that the Web and the interactive possibilities that are often referred to as Web 2.0 make community organizing faster and easier especially for research, internal and external communication, marketing your organization, fund-raising, advocacy, and a myriad of other uses. Your challenge will be to use its many components well to support and strengthen your organizing mission.

Summary

In this chapter, you reviewed the current state of the digital world, applications of Web-based technologies to community organizing, and principles that you and your organizing team can use in your own efforts. The chapter also provided an overview of the dimensions that Web-based technologies add to community organizing and addressed issues related to internal and external communications, social networking, digital storytelling, and connectivity. It concluded with an examination of the strengths and weakness of Web-based technologies in the practice of community organizing.

Assess your analysis and evaluation of this chapter's content by completing the Chapter Review.

CHAPTER 15

Organizations That Support Community Organizing

Michael D Brown/Shutterstock

Chapter Outline

This chapter focuses on infrastructures that currently support community organizing efforts, which are broadly categorized into five major areas. Not incidentally, these infrastructures also provide employment for community organizers. You may find their histories and activities relevant to your own community organizing efforts, and this review may help you in your investigation of other supportive organizations in your focal community system and beyond.

1. **Community and economic development:** Organizations that are maintained and supported by established structures, such as governments and research-based universities.
2. **Social action:** Organizations that have operated largely outside of traditional power structures and support social change.
3. **Popular Education and Participatory Research:** This text is based on an emerging global movement that focuses on the involvement of people themselves.
4. **Intentional faith-based communities:** Organizations based primarily in one of the world's great religious traditions, living communally, sharing possessions, and working toward peace and social justice.
5. **Service organizations:** These organizations exist in almost every community in the United States and in many locations abroad. Most were founded in the early twentieth century and serve a dual purpose: cooperation in projects that benefit local communities, and networking for their members. They are so ubiquitous that it is easy to ignore them, but they do many helpful things, particularly at the local level.

The Community Development Model

The community development model (also referred to in the literature as the economic development model or the locality development model) has historically emphasized the desirability of continual growth, globalization, modernization, and the use of science and technology, as well as the industrial model of production, to improve the material quality of life. It has used a top-down approach in which outside experts enter a focal community system to share their knowledge and technical skills. It is still the major mode of community organizing, although some recent efforts have been made to meld traditional economic development practices with sustainability and participatory approaches.[1] The community development model is supported by a variety of formal institutions that are connected with the established world power structure. This section focuses on those that are related to the United Nations, government structures, and universities.

Economic and community development usually refer to community organizing efforts that focus on improving material well-being through business and industrial development efforts and value chains (links between local producers and global distributors). These efforts are intended to lead to job creation. The economic development model is the main approach used by many of the world's best funded community organizing efforts and probably the largest source of living-wage employment for university-educated planners and organizers. Many organizations and global networks support the community development model, and often projects are the product of collaboration between educational institutions, especially the land grant institutions, and business interests. Here we will critically examine several community and economic development models.

The United Nations: International Economic Development

This text is primarily designed for community organizers who will be working at the local level to improve the quality of life and therefore localities have been the primary focal systems explored. However, localities are embedded in mezzo- and macro-systems must work within them, so you should be conversant with the major international bodies that are responsible for social and economic development. This section provides a brief overview of international economic development and its links to national and, eventually, to local communities.

The United Nations is the primary international organization coordinating global social and economic development, an almost impossible task given the worldwide environmental and financial crises of the last decade. The fifty-four-member **Economic and Social Council** is the UN organ charged with development activities throughout the world. For many years, the Economic and Social Council seems to have been primarily advisory in nature with little real authority, but at the beginning of the millennium it was given broader powers and more authority through the "Millennium Declaration" of the United Nations General Assembly.[2] The Millennium Declaration increased the responsibilities of the Economic and Social Council, outlined specific Millennium Development Goals (MDGs) for the year 2015, and created structures and reporting mechanisms to ensure that progress toward the MDGs was monitored on a regular basis using tested evaluation techniques. An annual ministerial review is conducted to measure progress toward the MDGs, and a high level biannual meeting of a Development Cooperation Forum brings together government and business leaders from the rich countries of the world (often referred to as the North) and the poor countries of the world (often referred to as the South) to create broad agreements on social and economic development issues.[3] The MDGs provide a broad framework for these global efforts; its eight areas and their specific measurable outcomes are as follows:

1. **Eradicate extreme poverty and hunger**
   - Reduce by half the proportion of people living on less than a dollar a day.
   - Achieve full and productive employment and decent work for all, including women and young people.
   - Reduce by half the proportion of people who suffer from hunger.
2. **Achieve universal primary education**
   - Ensure that all boys and girls complete a full course of primary schooling.
3. **Promote gender equity and empower women**
   - Eliminate gender disparity in primary and secondary education preferably by 2005, and at all levels by 2015.
4. **Reduce child mortality**
   - Reduce by two-thirds the mortality rate among children under five.
5. **Improve maternal health**
   - Reduce by three-quarters the maternal mortality ratio.
   - Achieve, by 2015, universal access to reproductive health.
6. **Combat HIV/AIDS, malaria, and other diseases**
   - Halt and begin to reverse the spread of HIV/AIDS.
   - Achieve, by 2010, universal access to treatment for HIV/AIDS for all those who need it.
   - Halt and begin to reverse the incidence of malaria and other major diseases.
7. **Ensure environmental sustainability**
   - Integrate the principles of sustainable development into country policies and programs; reverse loss of environmental resources.
   - Reduce biodiversity loss, achieving, by 2010, a significant reduction in the rate of loss.
   - Reduce by half the proportion of people without sustainable access to safe drinking water and basic sanitation.
   - Achieve significant improvement in the lives of at least 100 million slum dwellers by 2020.
8. **Develop a global partnership for development**
   - Develop further an open trading and financial system that is rule-based, predictable, and non-discriminatory, which includes a commitment to good governance, development, and poverty reduction both nationally and internationally.
   - Address the least developed countries' special needs. This includes tariff- and quota-free access for their exports; enhanced debt relief for heavily indebted poor countries; cancellation of official bilateral debt; and more generous official development assistance for countries committed to poverty reduction.

- Address the special needs of landlocked and small island developing states.
- Deal comprehensively with developing countries' debt problems through national and international measures to make debt sustainable in the long term.
- In cooperation with the developing countries, develop decent and productive work for youth.
- In cooperation with pharmaceutical companies, provide access to affordable essential drugs in developing countries.
- In cooperation with the private sector, make available the benefits of new technologies—especially information and communications technologies.

Although in some instances the 2015 target goal for implementation seems unrealistic, these goals are remarkable because they represent a consensus of the world's leaders, most are measurable, and mechanisms have been set in place to gather the necessary data and do the statistical analysis necessary to measure progress toward results. From a community organizing perspective, it is interesting to note the frequent use of the phrase "in cooperation with, . . ." This phrase is used to indicate that the UN knows that it cannot accomplish these goals alone and that its major role will be to facilitate collaboration and networking among governments and private organizations.

Human Services Delivery Systems

Understanding and Mastery: International and global influences on services delivery

Critical Thinking Question: What role should the UN and its affiliated organizations play in community organizing and community development? What should the UN be doing to support locally based participatory initiatives like the ones discussed here?

The MDGs (the UN loves to use letters for its organizations, meetings, and projects) provide a blueprint for member nations, regions, non-governmental organizations, and the private sector. Their implementation is overseen by the UN Economic and Social Council in cooperation with other international organizations such as the World Bank, the International Monetary Fund (IMF), the Organization for Economic Cooperation and Development (OECD), the World Trade Organization (WTO), and subsidiaries of the World Bank, such as the International Bank for Reconstruction and Development (IBRD), the International Development Association (IDA), and Food and Agriculture Organization (FAO).[4]

Explore the UN Millennium Development Goals to learn more about their goals to end poverty. What is the purpose of such far-reaching international goals? In what ways are they helpful? In what ways might they be discouraging? What relationship (if any) do such international goals have to community organizing at the grassroots level?

The MDGs and their implementation plans, especially those that address economic issues, are hopeful signs that international development may have made a turn toward sustainability and improved quality of life for everyone. However, trends toward globalization and the continuing centralization of wealth in the hands of the few have continued to block achievement of key goals. Decisions made at IMF or World Bank headquarters have repercussions in cities, towns, and villages around the world.

Internationally, the community development model does not work very well for a variety of reasons. Too often the technologies used are appropriate for developed countries but overwhelm the developing world. Often new agricultural innovations have required extensive use of fertilizers, have stripped the land, and have destroyed genetic diversity.[5] Often, well-paid development specialists who do not even speak the native language have been given authority over respected native leaders, which has reproduced a system of colonial subservience and inequality. However, in spite of resistance from a plethora of development specialists with practical, on-the-ground experience, the community development model is still used by international agencies, governments at all levels, and business interests.[6] Its goals are admirable and, in some cases, its methods have led to short-term improvement in living conditions or solutions to particular problems. It is based on the modern or industrial notion that globalization and constantly expanding growth are prerequisites for a high quality of life. It is supported by the hegemony of powerful, like-minded people and organizations throughout the world that largely control the financial and human resources needed for local economic health. There is no escaping its reach or its power. Events since the turn of the millennium have shown that these premises may be fatally flawed, but as yet no comprehensive approaches have replaced them. Therefore, the best local solutions would be to use the resources of the economic hegemony but, as much as possible, retain local control over the economic development.[7]

Assess your comprehension of International Community Development by completing this quiz.

Local Comprehensive Planning

Comprehensive planning and zoning began in the nineteenth century in the United States (although it is now done in Canada and other developed countries) as an established part of municipal government efforts to manage population growth, land use, and economic development. Since its beginning it has been in the hands of established power brokers such as realtors, elected officials, bankers, investors, and industrialists. All of these qualify as a power elite.[8] Comprehensive planning usually operates from the growth machine paradigm in which economic development takes precedence over other issues.[9] Many community organizers are employed by various levels of government or by consulting firms who provide contracting services to government. They usually work with or for departments of community planning or community development and frequently move back and forth between the public and the private sector. These government departments and private organizations provide technical assistance to local, county, and state governments through assistance in the creation of comprehensive plans. Comprehensive planning, in turn, provides a basis for sub-plans for zoning, transportation, infrastructure, parks, and neighborhoods.

Explore the American Planning Association website to learn more about traditional planning and comprehensive planning. How can traditional planning (which is usually done from the top down) be reconciled with participatory planning and organizing, which arises from local community engagement?

Community planning in the United States is most frequently the primary responsibility of **planning commissions** composed of community leaders with knowledge of various aspects of the planning process, who are often representatives of local stakeholders. Commission members are generally appointed by the local government but occasionally are elected directly.[10]

The five major purposes of planning commissions are to (1) establish a planning process, (2) draft a community plan for future private and public development, (3) draft regulations on land use zones and the sub-division of land use into new lots, (4) draft a land use map showing the location, permitted uses, and densities of land uses within the community, and (5) rule on new development proposals according to the community plan, the land use map, and the zoning and subdivision regulations. In most instances, planning commissions act as advisory bodies to elected officials who are responsible for enacting the ordinances and other enabling legislation that put the planning commission's recommendations into effect.[11] Usually the planning commission's work is a team effort between the commissioners who are volunteers and paid staff members or consultants who collect and organize technical data into useful information. Paid staff or consultants may be directly accountable to the planning commission or to the executive branch of local government. Formal planning commission meetings are generally open to the public. Meeting schedules are usually set months in advance, but agenda items may be introduced by support staff, elected officials, the commissioners, or by the general public. In a typical process, professional staff members prepare an agenda and summaries of topics to be discussed in consultation with the commission chairperson. These are made available to commissioners for review before the formal meeting. In reality, though, most planning commission work is actually done between formal meetings behind the scenes through informal meetings, closed committee sessions, and telephone calls. Often the formal meetings are rather *pro forma* as many of the critical decisions will have already been agreed upon ahead of time.

Planning commissions wield a good deal of power in local governments and greatly impact the future of geographic communities of all kinds including neighborhoods, cities, villages, and towns or townships. Members of geographically based organizing efforts should become familiar with the planning commission process, understand the composition of their local planning commission, and seek to influence commission decision making directly through securing appointment or indirectly through the development of positive working relationships with commissioners and planning staff. Planning meetings are often lengthy, boring, full of jargon, and puzzling to the ordinary citizen, but they are very important because comprehensive planning and zoning make a great deal of difference in land use and what can and cannot be done in local neighborhoods. If you are actively engaged in planning processes, you are likely to have a voice in what happens within your focal community system. If you do not pay attention to the process, you will find that important decisions are made for you, often by those who do not have your best interests at heart.

Human Service Delivery Systems

Understanding and Mastery: Economic and social class systems including systemic causes of poverty

Critical Thinking Question: Traditional comprehensive planning processes often seem to support those who are already well-off and have sometimes devastated poor communities. What can you as a community organizer do to make sure that any comprehensive planning that affects your focal community provides for adequate community input?

Community Development Corporations

While planning commissions are intrinsic parts of local governments, Community Development Corporations (CDCs) are quasi-governmental bodies. Although legally organized as private, non-profit corporations, they typically work very closely with local governments and planning commissions. Development corporations and governments make good partners because each enjoys certain legal rights not available to the other.

CDCs emerged during the federal government's War on Poverty in the 1960s. At that time the industrial paradigm was at its apex. The basic assumption of CDCs was (and is) that a high quality of community life depends on a strong industrial base. Some of the assumptions of CDCs are local control of the development process, a holistic approach to quality of life issues, and a focus on business and economic development. In almost all cases, business and economic development is given priority over the other two.[12]

CDCs were originally intended to give a voice to the poor as well as to more established members of the community, but over the years most have formed and maintained strong connections to government, business, and banking while their connection to the needs of the general public has been allowed to atrophy. Today many CDCs think of the public as a potential labor force and the natural environment as a source of raw materials for economic development. However, some CDCs take a more sustainable approach and look at community development in more than simply economic terms.

CDCs have been wielding increasing power over the last few decades as direct government intervention has decreased. As non-profit organizations, CDCs have more flexibility than either government or the profit-making sector. For instance, CDCs can broker funding packages that include government grants, foundation or other private non-profit funding, and private investment to fund economic packages that would not otherwise be possible. Well-organized CDCs not only serve a useful role as financial brokers but can also hold developers and other special interest groups accountable to a holistic view of community needs. The challenge is to assure that CDCs truly represent everyone, including those who are not part of any elite.

If your focal community does not already have a CDC, you may want to start one. Local community development efforts, at least in the United States and Canada, often begin with the municipal government, organizations such as a CDC or Chamber of Commerce, or a combination of community leaders who have identified a local need and have decided to meet that need through a formal planning and implementation process. Often CDCs are generated as a result of legally required comprehensive planning, but they can be initiated by local demand. There are three primary ways to approach community development projects: do the necessary research and planning yourselves, use government or university resources, or hire a private consulting firm.[13] Each of these has strengths and weaknesses as is shown in Table 15.1.

There is no right answer for every community or for every project, but there are some intuitive guidelines that help. In general, it is wise to hire a trustworthy, knowledgeable consultant when

- The project is complex.
- Many agencies and regulations are involved.
- The project is important to the long-term welfare of the community.
- Time is of the essence.
- Similar projects have been successfully implemented in other communities.

On the other hand, local efforts or local efforts augmented with assistance from government, university, or community college resources are usually in order if

- The project is relatively simple.
- Few outside agencies and regulations are involved.
- The project affects only a small sector of the community.
- There is no real hurry for implementation.
- The need or probable solution is unique to the target locale.

The local community should do as much internally as it can to save taxpayers money in the long run and develop local capacity. The program truly belongs to the community when it is not dependent on outside funding or technical resources. Although community-controlled initiatives take longer, they last.

Assess your comprehension of Local Comprehensive Planning by completing this quiz.

Land Grant Universities: Cooperative Extension

In the mid-nineteenth century, the Morrill Act created land grant universities for every U.S. state with the goal of ensuring an educated rural populace.[14] Shortly thereafter,

Cooperative Extension Divisions were created to bring university research to rural communities. In fact, Cooperative Extension is the oldest link between rural communities and the land-grant colleges, and this model has been copied all around the world, leading to a large, rather loosely structured cooperative effort among governments, public universities, agri-business, and rural communities that has both positive and negative aspects.[15] Almost every county in the United States has a Cooperative Extension office. Some offices are very helpful and engaged in participatory community organizing processes while others are supportive of powerful local, national, and international

Table 15.1 Processes for Planning and Implementing Community Projects

	Pros	Cons	Keys to Decision Making
Do it yourselves	Saves money. Gives people experience. Tailored to your own community needs.	Takes time. Limits networking and connections. May lack credibility either from outside funding sources or from the community.	Planning and implementing even a simple project takes time, energy, and expertise. Does the community have these?
Use public or quasi-public resources	Tax dollars are already paying for these services. Connections have already been made. Credibility has already been built. Established awareness of benchmarks and model programs that may be useful. Awareness of regulations affecting projects. Because consultants are usually "insiders," they may be able to work around unreasonable regulations. Consulting firms' staff members, including professional planners and support personnel, are usually friendly, knowledgeable, and willing to help with your questions	It is often hard to find the right one(s); they are often buried on websites, etc. Often stretched too thin to provide in-depth assistance. Often change configurations as funding and regimes shift. Staff turnover makes it hard to work with the same person. Takes a lot of time and phone calls. Regulations may make it difficult to get needed help. Because services are free, there is no real accountability.	These resources can be very helpful but rarely can they coordinate a project. They seem to work best when someone locally can dedicate a substantial amount of time to overseeing the work and collating the data. Beware of depending too much on these resources because they are usually stretched too thin. Control of the project and its momentum must remain local.
Hire paid consultant	Has expertise in field. Has connections to resources. Provides staff to do the work. Has incentive to do well. Offers presentation and writing skills. Usually will be quicker than either of the above alternatives. More credibility than local work.	Costs money that may be needed elsewhere. Depends a great deal on integrity of firm. Danger of getting "boiler plate." Danger of not getting community buy-in. Elitist; often does not involve all sectors of the community. May not develop community capacity to do similar projects.	Mostly a cost–benefit balance. Do the benefits of saving time and having established expertise outweigh the costs of hiring a consultant?

interests. A knowledge of the history and struggles within Cooperative Extension coupled with direct contacts with extension personnel in your area will enable your organizing team to decide what role if any Cooperative Extension will play.

Historically, Cooperative Extension has played two major organizing roles: techno-centric organizing and educational organizing.[16] Initially, **techno-centric organizing** was innovative in that research in farm and home economics at the state university was shared with poor, undereducated farm families. The dissemination of research findings helped increase food production and benefited both the farmers and the nation.[17] The goal of **educational organizing** was to support techno-centric organizing and also to use participatory, community-based methods to ensure that farmers and farm communities had a voice in economic development. Although the two missions were intended to be complementary, at times they have been contradictory. Techno-centric organizing has tended to support existing power structures and agri-business, while educational organizing has tended to support the interests of small farmers and local communities.[18] Each worked well when they functioned in balance.

However, over the last quarter century the role of the land grant universities and the Cooperative Extension in rural community economic development has become more and more complicated. On the one hand, many local extension agents and other staff members are quite active in their communities and often are community leaders in their own right. They donate their organizing skills and provide important links to the land grant university. At the international level, Cooperative Extension professionals from such institutions as Cornell University have assisted in the development of mutual aid organizations for the poor in developing nations around the world and have been leaders in the worldwide sustainability movement. However, there is some question about whether university researchers, agri-business, and community political and economic leaders may be engaged in a quest for short-range profits that may, in the end, be destructive to communities, ordinary citizens, and the natural environment.[19] The problem is that the university research that was originally funded by state and national government is now funded primarily by huge industrial firms producing fertilizer, farm equipment, pesticides, and hybrid genetically modified seeds.[20] Therefore, some people are concerned that the techno-centric approach to Cooperative Extension has become a taxpayer-supported marketing tool for agri-business. Research at the university's experimental farms produces new products for their industrial funders. Cooperative Extension experts are then sent to rural areas to disseminate the latest research findings and encourage farmers to try the new products. **Early adopters** (those that try the new technologies first) are given assistance in purchasing and applying the new products or techniques. Often these new products or processes result in increased production, at least in the short run. When others within the community see that production has increased, they adopt the new product or process. Soon, everyone in the community is using the product to remain competitive, providing supporting industries with a new set of customers.[21]

The tight collaboration between land grant universities, Cooperative Extension, and agri-business have raised concerns about

- Loss of effective traditional farming methods
- Unnecessary debt for technical innovations
- Increased dependence on chemical fertilizer, with the associated loss of natural means of soil replenishment (such as crop rotation)

- Use of genetically modified seeds that are infertile, which then guarantee dependence on seed companies
- Application of pesticides that have decimated helpful, as well as harmful, insects
- Reliance on mechanized equipment that has compacted and ruined the soil
- Industrialized production of living organisms such as poultry, hogs, cattle, bees, and frogs, leading to the spread of disease and massive die-offs in both domesticated and wild varieties
- Sale of highly hybridized seeds that have led to the loss of genetic variability, which make food crops vulnerable to being wiped out by disease and pestilence.
- The spread of harmful chemicals within the food chain.
- The overuse of antibiotics and growth hormones in meat production.
- The unknown effects of genetic modification on food crops.

Human Service Delivery Systems

Understanding and Mastery: Economic and social class systems including systemic causes of poverty

Critical Thinking Question: Loss of direct government funding for agricultural research has compelled many university based researchers as well as Cooperative Extension professionals to seek financing from large multi-national food companies. What are the ethical implications of these financially driven decisions? What can local people do to "take back" the original vision of the Cooperative Extension movement?

This industrialization of farming and the rise of agribusiness appear to have led to the demise of family farms and may eventually allow agribusiness to monopolize the food industry the way that that oil companies have monopolized the energy industry, so the ethics of the first goal of educational organizing (i.e., sharing new technologies) have come into question.[22]

Attention to community engagement in local decision making (the second goal of educational organizing in Cooperative Extension) has had its ups and downs. The greatest problems have been a lack of community awareness of extension community development services, coupled with the overemphasis on the techno-centric aspects of extension work. However, in the early years of the twenty-first century, there has been a rebirth of interest in educational organizing and local community input as an important component of Cooperative Extension practice. Since February 2002, the National Association of Community Development Extension Professionals has represented extension professionals with an interest in community development. The organization sponsors an annual conference, newsletters, and forums for its members.[23] Hopefully, this rebirth of interest in the educational role of Cooperative Extension will provide a much needed balance to the techno-centric, agri-business–driven model.

Assess your comprehension of Cooperative Extension in Community Development by completing this quiz.

Community organizers tend to hold conflicting views of Cooperative Extension and the relationship between research universities and local communities. Visit the website of your local Cooperative Extension office or visit its offices in person. In what ways does your local office show a commitment to sustainable, locally based agriculture and community self-determination? In what ways does it seem to be a mouthpiece of agri-business? What role, if any, do you see Cooperative Extension playing in your community organizing activities?

The Social Action Model

While the community development model is based primarily on the consensus view of society and is organized primarily by those in power, the social action model is based on the belief that the poor must work together to build an effective power base and must insist on having a voice in their own lives. There are two primary social action models that have been used in the United States since the 1930s. The first emphasizes the importance of organizing organizations within neighborhoods. The second solicits individual memberships. Both use a combination of mildly coercive tactics and negotiation with powerful interests.

We will look first at the organization-based "Alinsky model." Saul Alinsky, who has been named the father of the "organization of organizations" model, was a radical organizer dedicated to enabling "have nots" to gain power.[24] In the late 1930s, Alinsky became a participant observer researching the causes of juvenile delinquency in the tough "Back of the Yards" neighborhood in Chicago. At the time, the Back of the Yards was a vast, mostly white slum located near the Union Stockyards, one of the largest industrial complexes in America at the time. Through his participation in neighborhood life, Alinsky realized that many "deviant activities" were actually a logical result of stressful social conditions. He began to feel that only widespread participation in the democratic process would prevent violent revolution or fascism, and thus conceived of an organization of organizations that would unite various interest groups on behalf of the entire neighborhood's needs. This was particularly difficult because the Back of the Yards was characterized by conflict among a wide variety of Southern European and Eastern European ethnic groups. The neighborhood also had a well-established German population and a very strong Irish presence. Alinsky was able to engage the help of the powerful Roman Catholic Church to enable the warring groups to understand their common interests and common enemies. On July 14, 1939, he convened the first Back-of-the-Yards Council meeting, which was the first time a whole community had been organized in the United States, and possibly in the world.

In the 1950s and early 1960s, Alinsky shifted his work from the predominately white Back of the Yards area to the predominately African-American Woodlawn area, where he co-founded The Woodlawn Organization (TWO). TWO managed to force the first Mayor Richard J. Daley's regime to provide basic services, such as garbage collection and police protection.

Alinsky was known for his unique confrontational strategies. For instance, he once encouraged African-American leaders in Rochester, New York, to literally "raise a stink" by holding a bean supper before attending the opulent symphony with its snobbish, affluent white audience. The "stink" was to be a protest against poverty and discrimination at a time when Rochester was known for its wealth, sophistication, and wide gap between rich whites and poor African Americans. There is no indication that his suggestion was taken seriously, but it is indicative of his creative tactics.[25]

Alinsky's reputation grew as he consolidated his understanding of community organization and developed systematic strategies and tactics. He was encouraged to systematize his training approach and broaden his outreach by CIO President John L. Lewis. This led to the founding of the Industrial Areas Foundation (IAF) that trains radical community organizers mostly through coalitions of churches and other religious organizations.[26]

The Gamaliel Foundation, where President Obama was trained in community organizing, is similar to the IAF in that it also is composed of regional affiliates, mostly coalitions of religious organizations. Many of these affiliates focus on what might be called mid-range issues rather than strictly neighborhood concerns. Gamaliel follows the Alinsky model in its development of organizations mostly in urban areas. These neighborhood groups primarily develop petitions and proposals that are presented to municipal decision makers through formal political processes and community meetings.[27] PICO, the National Network—Unlocking the Power of People,[28] is a similar faith-based organization that uses an Alinsky-type approach to organize mostly faith-based organizations to represent the broad needs of local communities.[29]

Review the Industrial Areas Foundation, PICO National Network, and Gamaliel Foundation websites that present the Alinsky model. Locate branches near you. Consider what ideas or organizing skills could contribute to your organizing efforts.

The Alinsky approach has both strengths and weaknesses. The organization-of-organizations model works very well in large neighborhoods, such as the Back of the Yards or Woodlawn, where there are many well-organized groups. It is less effective in smaller neighborhoods and transitional areas where few such groups exist. Those seem to benefit more from the asset-based approach described in Chapter 7, the development of block club–type organizations, or from a combination of approaches. While there is some indication that the Alinsky/Gamaliel/PICO approach can net short-term gains for local neighborhoods, it seems to fail to build the infrastructure necessary to sustain grassroots initiatives.

Until 2009, when it fell apart from internal malfeasance and external scandal, the Association of Community Organizations for Reform Now (ACORN) was the largest social action organization of the poor in the United States. While the IAF, Gamaliel, and PICO are examples of organizations of organizations, ACORN was based on individual memberships solicited by paid organizers who made door-to-door visits in poor communities. ACORN's political actions were then initiated and supported by its local members with extensive input from ACORN staff who were supported by the portion of the local dues paid to the national organization.[30]

ACORN began as an offshoot of the National Welfare Rights Organization (NWRO) founded by George Wiley in the 1960s. Although NWRO had support among welfare recipients, it was always a marginalized organization of a marginalized constituency. By 1966 it became clear to Wiley that a broader base of support was needed, so he sent a young organizer named Wade Rathke to Little Rock, Arkansas.[31] In 1966, Arkansas was deeply divided racially, fundamentally conservative, and run by a wealthy political elite. Rathke faced the difficult task of convincing low and moderate income white Southerners (most of whom had never organized anything more radical than a church social) that political organization could bring about positive change and, moreover, that they shared more in common with their poor black neighbors than with the elite white upper class. Rathke accomplished this task through carefully chosen political issues that resonated across racial and class lines. In Little Rock, for instance, the issues were free school lunches, unemployed workers' concerns, Vietnam veterans' rights, and hospital emergency room care. Small successes in these areas led to growing support for ACORN's efforts. Over the years, ACORN grew in the south and in rural communities. Sometimes, as in the case of Little Rock, ACORN organizers targeted a particular town or issue. Often, they were approached by natural community leaders for help. The basic social action strategy, using established political means to bring about change, remained the same throughout ACORN's history as was the policy of choosing issues that unified rather than divided the poor. Local or focused ACORN groups set local agendas and selected volunteer leaders guided by modestly paid organizers from the national organization. ACORN organizers were supposed to act only as consultants to these local constituencies.

By 2009, ACORN had 350,000 member families in 850 chapters in over 100 cities in the United States, Argentina, Peru, Mexico, the Dominican Republic, and Canada—but the roots of its destruction were at hand. In 2008, Wade Rathke's brother Dale was found to have embezzled nearly one million dollars from the organization, a major betrayal that led to the dismissal of both brothers.[32] Then in late 2009, ACORN became the center of an attack from conservative Republicans who conducted a sting operation at one of ACORN's Baltimore offices. In a "doctored" video, ACORN employees were shown allegedly assisting a purported prostitute and her pimp in developing a prostitution ring involving underage illegal immigrant girls. Although the tape was later proved to be a fabrication, the prostitution scandal resulted in a bill specifically denying any federal funding to ACORN, in clear violation of the First Amendment of the Constitution, which forbids legislation singling out a single individual or organization for special legislation. Although the law has since been declared unconstitutional and ACORN has been cleared of all accusations of voter registration fraud, the damage was done. ACORN was disbanded as a national organization in 2010. The fall of the Rathke brothers and its tragic effect on ACORN act as a warning against personal greed and dishonesty, but the ACORN story is also a cautionary tale about the dangers of confronting powerful interests as there is compelling evidence that the real motivation for defunding ACORN was its success in registering millions of poor people in the 2008 presidential election and the likelihood that it would be able to reach many poor people for the U.S. Census in 2010, thus demonstrating the extent of poverty in the United States.[33] Greed and selfishness coupled with lack of oversight and accountability have led many originally fine people (and their organizations) to disaster, and powerful interests can be dangerous adversaries, but ACORN's use of individual, rather than organization, memberships as well as its use of confrontational tactics is intriguing despite its tragic end.

Client-related Values and Attitudes

Understanding and Mastery: Integration of the ethical standards outlined by the National Organization for Human Services and Council for Standards in Human Service Education

Critical Thinking Question: Imagine that you were a national board member at the time the financial scandal broke; what ethical issues would you have faced? How would you have responded? What could have been done to prevent the malfeasance in the first place? What, if anything, could have been done to rebuild the organization's credibility and the credibility of secular social action organizing generally?

Assess your comprehension of the Strengths and Weaknesses of Organizations that Support Social Action by completing this quiz.

Supports for Participatory Research and Popular Education

Participatory research and popular Education have been important themes within this text. Although they have their roots in the work of critical adult educators such as Myles Horton and Paulo Freire in the mid-twentieth century, their legacy has continued into the twenty-first century in many of the organizations and social networks that you read about in Chapter 14. Here we will look at some individuals and institutions who initiated these practices and their descendants today.

Facilitating Popular Education: The Highlander Approach

Often community organizers need a time and place to reflect on their work and share ideas with others. Highlander Research and Education Center (formerly the Highlander Folk School) has been such a major resource in Appalachia, especially for poor residents. Highlander began with labor organizing, moved to civil rights, and now concentrates on land preservation and immigration issues.[34] Highlander celebrated its seventy-fifth anniversary in 2007, a testimony to its perseverance and dedication.

The heart of the Highlander method has been workshops where representatives of organizations that are dealing with major social issues come together to focus on an issue, learn to listen to others, and build solutions together. Highlander staff members do not do community organizing themselves. Highlander provides the space, and participants themselves do the work. As Myles Horton said of Highlander's work with the labor and civil rights movements:

> The Highlander workshop is part of a continuum of identifying a problem and finding other people who are trying to deal with it. The people who come to the workshops have a lot of knowledge that they don't know they have. Highlander gives them a *chance* to explore what they know and what some people we bring in as resources can share with them. Then they go back home and test what they learn in action. If they have learned anything useful, they can teach others because it is now part of their knowledge and not something merely handed to them. ...[35]

The equality and wisdom of all participants is assumed at Highlander. Likewise community participants are discouraged from leaning too much on the Highlander staff or resource persons. As Horton explained:

> I think of a workshop as a circle of learners. "Circle" is not an accidental term, for there is no head of the table... The job of the staff members is to create a relaxed atmosphere in which the participants feel free to share their experiences. Then they are encouraged to analyze, learn from, and build on these experiences. Like other participants in the workshops, staff members are expected to share experiences that relate to the discussions and sources of information and alternative suggestions. They have to provide more information (in preparation for the session) than they will be able to work into the thinking process of the group and often they must discard prepared suggestions that become inappropriate to the turn a workshop has taken... Each session had to take its own form and develop according to the students' needs.[36]

Students at Highlander learn to live what they are learning through the workshops and the living arrangements where people of all races and classes live under the same roof and share meals, bathrooms, and fun. For many this is transformative. After her first visit to Highlander, Rosa Parks said that Highlander was the first place in her adult life that she had ever encountered a true sense of peace and unity among people of different races. She was very reluctant to leave and often credited her time at Highlander as a source of courage and strength for her later work.[37] Highlander still offers excellent training for community organizers. Here are some Highlander-based principles assembled by adult educator Jane Vella[38] that you can apply to community organizing:

1. Needs assessment must be done with the learners, not for the learners. If learners' needs do not match facilitators' expectations, the facilitators should adapt the learning experience to fit them.
2. The environment should be safe so everyone can feel they can be heard without reprisal or ridicule.
3. There should be time "around the edges" to build friendships and have fun.

4. Learners should participate in workshop design—for instance, early in the labor movement groups kept notebooks on what worked and what did not work which they passed on to subsequent workshop leaders, creating a "labor movement curriculum" created completely by participants.
5. The emphasis should be on praxis or action, reflection, more action, and more reflection in a spiraling process. Participants are welcome to talk with Highlander staff about their experiences and are encouraged to keep in touch with one another, a practice that has been greatly enhanced by the Internet.
6. Respect for learners is one of Highlander's main principles that Horton learned early in his career through speaking with parents of children attending summer Bible school in rural Ozone, Tennessee. The Ozone experiences were very significant in Horton's life. Many times during his long life he found himself asking, "Would this 'play' in Ozone?" If the answer was "no," then he didn't proceed.[39]
7. Highlander's whole educational program is built around having a safe place to explore ideas, express even negative feelings, and then take action.[40] Horton and the other staff members allow group members to work through storm periods themselves. Both individuals and groups become stronger for it.
8. Highlander workshops always generated ideas and strategies that participants could take back to their sponsoring organizations, adapt to their local situations, and use immediately.
9. Highlander staff members are facilitators and resource persons, not information givers, which sometimes angers people who want "expert answers" rather than the responsibility of deciding for themselves. At one point in the union-organizing days Horton's life was threatened by a frustrated union officer because he refused to tell others what to do[41])—exhibiting true commitment to learner self-direction!
10. Horton believed that learning is circular—we all teach and learn from one another in a circle of equals.
11. Highlander staff believe that workshops are incomplete without engagement back at home after the workshops are over.
12. At Highlander each workshop is designed in light of the participants' needs, outside resources are provided when information or expertise is needed, but the final accountability occurs when participants apply what they have learned in their own communities to problems that they have identified.

The Vella principles, especially as they are used at Highlander provide an excellent guide for community organizers and/or grassroots groups to use in designing learning and research events. A primary role of community organizing should be popular education, enabling people to have the knowledge and skills needed to organize themselves. To learn more about the ongoing work of Highlander go to the website for the Highlander Research Center.[42]

Literacy for Social Justice: Paulo Freire

Thomas Jefferson believed that only a literate people can succeed at democracy. Over many years, slave owners, tyrants, and oppressors have been able to succeed in maintaining the *status quo* by keeping the powerless from reading and writing.[43] Literacy that facilitates communication about key issues and encourages *problem posing* (problem analysis) is a powerful tool for social justice. Paulo Freire was something of a guru for adult educators and social workers who are interested in empowerment through literacy.[44] His techniques for combining adult literacy initiatives with consciousness raising and action have been widely emulated throughout the world. Freire's intent was primarily transformative learning. His goal was to enable Brazilian peasants not only to learn to read and write but to understand their world and the ways that they were oppressed and to begin to work together toward change. For instance, Brazilian cities, like many in the developing world, consist of a core of prosperity surrounded by a ring of crowded, miserable shantytowns, called *favillas* in Portuguese. Freire brought pictures of life in the *favilla* to his literacy classes and asked, "What is this?" When someone inevitably answered "It's the *favilla.*" Freire led learners in a discussion of what life is like in the slum, a process he called **problem posing**. He then wrote the word *favilla* on a blackboard and encouraged learners to generate a list of words describing the *favilla* using its own syllables. For instance *favilla* is composed of the syllables "fa" and "villa." They generated other words with the syllable "fa" and then "villa" and so on with other syllables from the new words. At the end of these literacy sessions the adult students had generated a long list of vocabulary words that pointed to their real-life experiences and, not incidentally, they had had the opportunity to share their life experiences. This was very freeing for the peasants, who not only learned to read and link written symbols to real-life people, things, and experiences but also learned to think about the ways they were being mistreated. These discussions, in turn, led to plans for action and demands for social change. Freire's tactics were so successful in beginning to change the balance of power in Brazil that they were eventually repressed by military dictatorship. Freire was arrested and kept in a cage-like metal box for several days in the sun. Freire, toward the end of his life, was able to resume his work, which has been emulated around the world. Although Freire died in 1997, popular educators and participatory researchers throughout the world still make use of his methods and have adapted them to many settings. To learn more about how Freire's work has been continued by others since his death, go to the Freire Project on the Web.[45]

Use of the Theater and Other Arts

Imagine yourself in the downtown area of a major city. Suddenly there is a commotion: a man grabs a woman by her hair, drags her to the middle of the street, and begins to beat her. All activity on the street comes to a halt. Before anyone can call the police, though, an authoritative person shouts "Stop the action!" and proceeds to engage you and other bystanders in a discussion of domestic violence, public responsibility and other topics. You have just experienced a bit of street theater designed for consciousness raising. You are in a mall. Suddenly someone bursts into song, followed by others in groups of twos and threes until eventually a whole chorus is singing loudly and joyfully. Everyone is smiling and enjoying the show. You have just experienced a bit of community building (and probably will find yourself on YouTube). You are an illiterate woman in the Kingdom of Lesotho (a landlocked country surrounded by South Africa). Your village has been decimated by AIDS, but no one talks about it because it carries a great stigma. A group of dramatists come and talk with you and your friends about how AIDS has changed your lives and helps you and your friends put together several small but powerful skits based on your experiences. These skits dramatize things like your husbands' refusal to wear condoms when they return from working in South Africa, struggles you have talking with other women about your worries, being unable to get the medicines you need, and the sadness you feel when your husbands are forced to leave to work in South Africa. The skits have colorful costumes and some singing. They are designed to open up discussions and reveal secrets that everyone shares but few talk about. They are performed outside in the common area, and time is given for discussion. You and your fellow actors make sure that the dialogue continues afterward. You find ways to support one another and begin to work toward solving some of your common problems.[46] All of these are examples of the use of theater in community organizing.

Participatory researchers and popular educators often use drama as a way of developing dialogue. The original use of what became known as the Theatre of the Oppressed began serendipitously when its founder Augusto Boals developed an improvisational production around the topic of domestic violence. An audience member took exception to the way the "wife-beating" actor was behaving, jumped on stage, and began beating the hapless man with a broom! Thus began the tradition of encouraging audience members to actively participate in such improvisations.[47] Unlike traditional theater, Theatre of the Oppressed is not value-neutral. It is intended to provide participants with a relatively safe place to create a drama that expresses their personal experiences, reflect upon the implications of the drama, and then decide how to respond in real life.[48] Variations of Boal's methods have been used in a wide variety of situations.

While Boal always used his methods and techniques as a consciousness-raising tool and a non-violent tactic against oppression, similar techniques have been used for anthropological research,[49] to open discussions of emotional topics such as the experience of struggling with metastatic cancer,[50] to facilitate feminist conversation,[51] and for economic development under the guise of "Theatre for Development."[52] For an example of an organization that encourages the use of theater in community advocacy, go to the website of Theatre of the Oppressed.

While theater is probably the art form most widely used in participatory research and popular education, other arts such as dance, music, and visual arts (for example, the creation of community murals and installation art)[53] can be used as well. All participatory art forms are rich in symbolic and ontological meaning and generally build trust among participants.

Internet-based Organizations

The Internet has spawned a new generation of organizations that support popular education and participatory research in the broadest sense. Several were listed in Chapter 14 and need not be repeated here. Others include MoveOn.org, which has a political component, a civic action component, and a petitioning component; Change.org, where dozens of ordinary people have started petitions that have influenced decision makers in business and government to make changes large and small; and the various branches of the Occupy movement, which has evolved from a specific cause (Occupy Wall Street) into multiple organizing efforts, including #occupytogether, a loose network of social action and popular education style organizers who help one another on particular issues. These organizations change rapidly in true kaleidoscopic fashion but can provide you with resources and ideas.

Taken together, all of these organizations and movements from the venerable Highlander to the newest Internet efforts offer support for the type of popular education and participatory research paradigm that has been a major emphasis of this text.

Volunteer Efforts and Movements

The Corporation for National and Community Service and Points of Light Foundation

Both the Corporation for National and Community Service and the Points of Light Foundation have been partnering for many years to encourage the private sector to assume its fair share of public service through volunteer efforts. The Corporation for National and Community Service is an umbrella organization founded in 1993 that encompasses several major volunteer programs including Americorps, Senior Corps, Learn and Serve America, the Nonprofit Capacity Building Fund, the Social Innovation Fund, and the Volunteer Generation Fund. It also leads in coordinating yearly events such as the Martin Luther King Jr. Day of Service each January, the yearly National Conference on Volunteering and Service, and rapid response to disaster relief. It is primarily funded by the federal government. In addition to its national programs, the corporation has state offices and programs. It is a huge organization, and its site is somewhat difficult to navigate, but once you connect with the right people it can be helpful in finding "people power" for your programs.[54] Americorps, in particular, has had a very good track record providing positions, health insurance, and college accounts for thousands of people, as well as accomplishing hundreds of worthwhile community projects.

Administration

Understanding and Mastery: Recruiting and managing volunteers

Critical Thinking Question: What volunteer resources exist at the micro-, focal-, mezzo-, and macro-levels that might provide time, financial assistance, or technical aid to your community organizing effort? What procedures will you put in place to recruit and manage them?

The Points of Light Institute was originally founded by President George H. W. Bush to encourage private voluntarism. It has developed a history of collaboration among major industries, powerful politicians in both parties, leading clergy, large nonprofit organizations, and the Corporation for National and Community Service, which is a major sponsor of the National Conference on Volunteering and Service.[55] Some locally initiated projects have had good success attaining help from the Corporation for National and Community Service and the Points of Light Foundation where others seem to have trouble making the necessary connections. As in most things, the success in using these resources depends largely on your ability to make connections with the right person at the right time. Americorps and other volunteer programs can be quite helpful in filling around the edges, to accomplish short-term goals, and to work with one-time projects. Once an organization is able to establish a relationship with an Americorps or Senior Corps group, the relationship is likely to continue—but the initial connections are hard to achieve.

Service Learning

Historically, institutions of higher education have a three-part mission: teaching, research, and community service. Within the past twenty years or so, many have combined the three into a movement called **service learning**, in which students and faculty are encouraged to engage with their local communities in a variety of service efforts,[56] with many high schools and even elementary schools following suit. At the college level, students at the State University of New York/Empire State College do service learning projects in their own focal communities around the world and, in 2010, the college won an award from the Obama administration for these efforts. The work of the ABCD Institute at Northwestern University —with its asset-based approach to community development—has already been discussed at length in Chapters 7 and 14. These are just two of many examples of partnerships between communities and higher education. You should investigate resources at your local community college, college, or university as you develop your community projects. Even elementary and high schools are developing service learning projects that incorporate academic skills into solving real world problems. Many local schools have such projects, and they are especially common in Catholic education. Service learning projects that directly impact the lives of children are particularly appealing at the K–12 level. Ideal projects involve those with concrete results, such as building a playground and utilizing skills such as planning, measuring, and cooperative hands-on work. If you have such a project, talk with local school officials about ways to involve teachers and students and to assist them with the development of both academic and community organizing objectives.

Explore more about service learning as an educational component. Explore your local education community to determine if they offer service learning opportunities. How could your organization be connected to their efforts?

Assess your comprehension of the Role of Organized Volunteerism in Community Building by completing this quiz.

Faith-based Communities Working For and Modeling Social Change

Many community organizers become involved because of their religious faith, especially the call to love one's neighbor as oneself. The following four examples are some of the many communities around the world that support organizing efforts by living and working together with each other and the people they serve. These examples were chosen because of their diversity, the author's familiarity with them, and because they have not been discussed elsewhere in the book. There are many others that are equally as worthy.

Hospitality and Radical Politics: The Catholic Worker Movement

Organizations that support altruistic grassroots community organizing come in many shapes and sizes and have many motivations. Some, like the Catholic Worker Movement, are loosely organized and depend entirely on faith. The Catholic Worker Movement was founded in the 1930s by Dorothy Day, a Catholic writer and social reformer[57] and Peter Maurin, a "street philosopher" and poet whom Day often credited as the real inspiration for the effort.[58] The Catholic Worker Movement began as a response to the suffering of unemployed workers who were often Catholic immigrants from Eastern or Southern Europe.[59] Through the years, the movement has had its ups and downs. During the Great Depression of the 1930s, the Catholic Worker houses and its newspaper, *The Catholic Worker*, provided important material and political support for the unemployed. During the McCarthy anti-communist witch hunts in the early 1950s, the organization came under close scrutiny and criticism but survived. Even after the death of its founders, it has continued to serve quietly and without political ties. Catholic Worker Houses of Hospitality provide direct assistance to the unemployed with food, shelter, and clothing. The movement gives a voice to the working poor through its newspaper and a website, which is updated daily.[60]

The Catholic Worker Movement has never sought nonprofit status for fund-raising; it has preferred to remain autonomous and self-supporting. It has no boards of directors, no sponsors, no system of governance, no paychecks, and no pension plans. Since the death of founder Dorothy Day in 1980, there has been no central leader. Throughout its existence, the Catholic Worker Movement has maintained houses and communities in both urban and rural areas. Anyone who agrees to live in a peaceful community of mutual care and respect can stay for a day, a week, or a lifetime. Over 200 Catholic Worker communities existed at this writing in 2012, mostly in the United States.

Explore the Web to learn more about the Catholic Worker Movement. What is the role of historic social action movements such as the Catholic Worker Movement in community organizing today?

The Catholic Worker Movement not only provides hospitality, asylum, and the necessities of life to those who seek assistance but also shows characteristics of a social movement. Many of its volunteers have been jailed for non-violent protests against racism, unfair labor practices, social injustice, and war. Catholic Worker communities serve as a haven for those who embrace such philosophies. The *Catholic Worker* newspaper has been a radical voice for the rights of labor and the disenfranchised since it was founded in 1933. The paper was first sold at a Communist Party May Day rally in Union Square, New York City, for a penny a copy. The price and the message still remain the same in 2013.

Institute for Cultural Affairs[61]

The Institute of Cultural Affairs began life as the Ecumenical Institute: Chicago as a result of a meeting of the World Council of Churches in Evanston, Illinois, in 1954, which directed the establishment of two lay education centers or ecumenical institutes, one in Europe and the other in the United States. The Ecumenical Institute: Evanston was directed by German theologian Dr. Walter Leibrecht, who returned to Germany in 1962 and was followed by Dr. Joseph Mathews, who at the time was living at the Faith and Life Community at Perkins Theological Seminary with his wife, children, and seven other families. Their intentional community was modeled on the early church practice of sharing all resources, so they all moved to Evanston and lived on a single salary.[62]

The early 1960s was a time of upheaval in U.S. cities, and the group soon realized that they could not accomplish urban renewal from comfortable Evanston. They decided to move the institute to an abandoned Brethren seminary in the heart of Chicago's West Side ghetto. In the early years, the institute was completely self-supporting. The initial group of families became the Order Ecumenical, an intentional community based loosely on historic religious orders in which members shared all of their family income and, in turn, were allotted "stipends" for personal expenses based on individual and family needs. The average stipend was $100 per couple, per week, with additional compensation for children. Food costs, utilities, rent, health insurance, and some transportation costs were borne through the organization. Everyone had assigned tasks. About half were required to hold paid secular positions; the others were assigned internally to various institute projects and programs, including child care.

During the early Chicago years, the Institute had three missions: It (1) provided lay education in modern theology, (2) experimented with life as an intentional religious community (the Order Ecumenical), and (3) developed models of community organization and renewal, beginning in the old seminary's immediate neighborhood. A popular sociological theory in the late 1950s defined cities in terms of four concentric circles, spreading from the "first city" (the core of economic prosperity) through the poorest "second city" areas and the working class "third city" to the prosperous white "fourth city" suburbs. Ecumenical Institute staff proclaimed themselves to be the "Fifth City" of well-educated, white pioneers returning to work with local residents to renew a blighted area. A section of the West Side of Chicago around Ecumenical Institute headquarters was designated as "Fifth City." The intent was for community organizing to take place that would "meet all the needs of all the people in a delimited geographic area" through identifying potential local community leaders and enabling them to overcome their crippling "victim image" by creating and revitalizing needed social structures. Fifth City did indeed become a model. Its preschool was one of the prototypes for Head Start. Its community organizing methods became a guide for the Community Action Agencies and Economic Opportunity Councils of Lyndon Johnson's War on Poverty. In retrospect, participants (including this author)[63] were idealistic, naïve, and unintentionally patronizing. But our African-American neighbors appreciated our efforts in spite of our obvious ignorance, and so the Institute grounds were one of just a few white-owned structures to escape destruction in the Chicago riots of 1967 that followed the death of Martin Luther King Jr.

In the decades after its founding, the Fifth City experiment became a prototype for community organizing around the world. In 1973, Chicago headquarters were moved from Fifth City to the Near North Side when Kemper Insurance donated its former headquarters to the Institute. Work in Fifth City was turned over to the neighborhood. At that time, a decision was made to separate Institute functions. The Order Ecumenical remained the main staffing body, the community organizing arm became the Institute of Cultural Affairs (ICA), and the religious education mission to local churches and laypeople dwindled as the ICA, especially its founder Joseph Mathews, became disillusioned with local churches as vehicles for community change.

In 1988, the financial realities of educating children and preparing for retirement caught up with Institute staff (the average "order stipend" was $100 per week) so the Order Ecumenical was disbanded in favor of a more traditional non-profit structure. Each international affiliate became an independent non-profit organization.[64]

Three groups of people have been affected by the Institute and its work:

1. The full-time staff that lived communally as families sharing responsibility for self-support, child rearing, and the work of the Institute were the most profoundly affected. Many now live more conventionally but in close contact with one another and are still involved in the mission of the Institute.
2. The many volunteer staff members who, like this author, spent part of their lives at the Institute and have gone on to apply its principles to a myriad of community organizing efforts.
3. The many community members throughout the world who have been trained in Institute models and methods and who have applied them in a wide variety of settings. As of 2013, the Institute of Cultural Affairs in the United States is still headquartered in the former Kemper Insurance Building on Chicago's Near North Side, participates in local organizing in Chicago, and has become part of the sustainability and service learning movements.[65]

Explore the Web to learn more about the Institute of Cultural Affairs: International and Institute of Cultural Affairs: USA. Why do volunteer organizations like the ICA often evolve into traditional bureaucracies? Is this trend inevitable? In what ways is this trend positive? How might it be negative?

Koinonia Farm

While the Catholic Worker Movement and the Institute of Cultural Affairs focused first primarily on urban needs, in its early days Koinonia Farm focused on the needs of mostly black sharecroppers and tenant farmers in rural Georgia.[66] Koinonia Farm was settled in 1945 by two couples, Clarence and Florence Jordan and Martin and Mabel England. Clarence Jordan[67] had an undergraduate degree in agriculture with a love of the land and a vision of teaching scientific agriculture to his neighbors. Both men were Southern Baptist Church pastors and professors of theology. Clarence Jordan was a New Testament scholar with a vision of providing advanced biblical education to nearby black Baptist preachers.[68] In addition to their desire to teach and preach, the community founders had a radical vision of life where people of all ages, races, and abilities shared life in common and supported themselves through the pecan crops they produced. Soon other people joined them at the farm as guests, interns, residents, and workers. Both black and white workers were paid equally, and everyone ate at the common table, shared the common areas and rest rooms, and attended Bible studies and youth camps. This was not socially acceptable in Georgia in the 1950s and 1960s. Koinonia Farm was repeatedly fire-bombed, its products were boycotted, participants were threatened, and it became impossible to insure their property, but they prevailed, as did the Civil Rights Movement. In the late 1960s, things began to settle down in Sumter County where Koinonia is located. There were only two families left on the farm, including the Jordans, and Clarence had settled down to write his *Cotton Patch Version of the Gospels and Acts*. The Jordans wondered whether Koinonia Farm had served its purpose when an old friend, Millard Fuller, wrote a note asking "What have you got up your sleeve?" That simple note led to the founding of the project which became Habitat for Humanity. Although Clarence Jordan did not live to see the first house completed (he died writing a sermon just before the first house was dedicated in 1969), Habitat and its many affiliates— including the more recently chartered Fuller Center for Housing (re-inaugurated at Koinonia as a Christian ministry in 2005)— have collaborated with poor families all around the world to provide decent, affordable housing one family at a time.[69] In recent years, Koinonia Farm moved from being an intentional religious community to a more traditional nonprofit format, but a new group of members has once again created a shared lifestyle similar to that of the early Christian church. (A simplified shared lifestyle can be emotionally and spiritually sustaining in the difficult work of community organizing, but it can be frustrating when someone steals your soda out of the fridge or leaves the kitchen a mess!)

Explore Koinonia Community to learn more. What is the historic and contemporary significance of Christian communities like Koinonia in improving life for all?

Shinnyo-en Buddhist Community

The Shinnyo-en Foundation and the Shinnyo-en Buddhist denomination was a sponsor of the 2010 National Conference on Volunteering and Service in New York City, a joint conference among the private Points of Light Foundation and the Corporation for National and Community Service, an impressive event held both in real time and online.[70] Shinnyo-en Buddhism was founded in Japan in 1936 and emphasizes peace, cooperation, and philanthropy. Its practical and symbolic projects span the world and reach out to Buddhists and non-Buddhists alike.[71] In some places, Shinnyo-en operates like a typical religious denomination where members live in their own homes, go to a central place for worship, and share in community service projects. In other locations, members live together in monastic-style communities. Practical projects include a group that regularly cleans up the local railroad station in the early morning, performing the dirtiest and lowliest tasks. Other projects include disaster relief from earthquake and tidal tsunami damage in Hindu, Muslim, and Buddhist areas. In fact, their strategy is always to ask community elders what is most needed after a disaster. When the Muslim elders in an earthquake-stricken Pakistani village said that the people longed to have their mosque restored, Shinnyo-en provided the money and laborers for the project. This practical yet symbolic service makes them admirable.[72] The Shinnyo-en community is particularly active in Hawaii, a state which seems like paradise but actually has a diverse, sometimes divided multicultural population that includes Native Hawaiians, mostly Buddhist Japanese and Chinese farm workers, and a variety of white transplants from the U.S. mainland.[73] In honor of unity in diversity, Shinnyo-en sponsors a yearly lantern floating event on Memorial Day with hundreds of quiet flames floating in tiny boats on a peaceful bay to commemorate lost loved ones of all races and faiths. The Nā Lei Aloha Foundation, which sponsors the lantern event, supports other events throughout the year to celebrate the multicultural heritage of the islands and unity within diversity.[74]

Explore Shinnyo-en Buddhist to learn more. What is the role of non-Western, faith-based organizations in community organizing?

To Heal, Repair, and Transform the World: A Jewish Community[75]

Dating back to the times of the Hebrew prophets, Judaism has upheld a tradition that each person has the responsibility to repair the world. This responsibility is called ***tikkun*** and is represented by the Network of Spiritual Progressives, a mostly Jewish social networking-based organization (such as those described in Chapter 14). While the Network of Spiritual Progressives primarily addresses national and international social justice issues, they are also an online community that supports people of all faiths who work locally and globally on peace and justice issues. Their website not only provides insights into some spiritual aspects of community organizing but is also an excellent example of using Web technologies in service of social justice.

Explore Network of Spiritual Progressives to learn more. What has been the historic role of Judaism in improving community life for all?

There are dozens of other religious communities large and small—in the real, virtual, and blended worlds—that could have been included in this section, such as ashrams in India based on Gandhian principles, Islamic community centers, and various ecumenical endeavors. But the religious communities described here provide good examples of diversity in their approaches to supporting community organizing efforts. Each effort is characterized by a single-minded commitment to justice and mercy, to working at the grassroots level, and to assisting the poor and disenfranchised. Participants often have sacrificed financial gain, have forgone professional acclaim, and have sometimes faced physical danger to ensure that justice will prevail. Life within these communities is often intense, energizing, and deeply spiritual but rarely materially enriching.

Assess your comprehension of the Role of Faith-based Organizations in Community Organizing by completing this quiz.

Service Organizations

Service clubs were originally intended for networking; many worthwhile service organizations are the backbone of many practical community organizing events and ongoing projects. **Lions International** is a prototypical example of an effective service organization composed of a network of local clubs.[76] The Lions are best known for their dedication to providing services to the blind, the sight impaired, and the hearing impaired. However, in Middle View, they also built and now fund the local food pantry, provide Christmas toys, and invest sweat equity into one of Paul Newman's camps for children with life-threatening illnesses. **Rotary International**,[77] whose membership is composed of an individual from each of the main professions in a community, is known for its good works. Its founding concept holds that such a structure leads to the cross-fertilization of ideas, and its ongoing goal is the eradication of polio worldwide. **Kiwanis International**[78] concentrates on the needs of children. All three of these major service clubs were originally all-male but began including both genders during the 1970s.

Community projects worldwide have originated through networking among service club members locally, regionally, nationally, and internationally. Service clubs can be a world of their own with local, regional, state, national, and international affiliations. Unfortunately, all seem to be suffering decline as their existing membership grows older, although all emphasize youth through the Lions' Leo Clubs, the Kiwanis' Key Clubs, and the Rotary's international exchange program, respectively. Recent changes in membership rules allowing for affiliation without required attendance at weekly or monthly meetings may lead to an upturn in membership so they can continue their vital role in community life. You will find that their networks can be very helpful in gaining financial and moral support for local programs. They are certainly worth investigating and maybe even joining.

Human Systems

Understanding and Mastery: Organizational structures of communities

Critical Thinking Question: Identify the service organizations in a geographic focal community. Investigate ways they might be helpful in your community organizing efforts.

In African-American communities, the service club niche is often filled by the Improved Benevolent Protective Order of Elks of the World,[79] the Prince Hall Masons,[80] and the "Divine 9" black sororities. These sororities are a unique institution, founded in the early twentieth century in historically black colleges. Like all sororities, they enable college women to make friends and form lifelong bonds but, unlike most white sororities, they have gone far beyond coordinating college social life and have supported many causes within black communities throughout the United States.[81]

Assess your comprehension of the Role of Service Clubs in Community Organizing by completing this quiz.

Summary

Assess your analysis and evaluation of this chapter's content by completing the Chapter Review.

While this chapter was not intended to be all-inclusive, it does give you a brief historical review of community development, social action, volunteer support initiatives, religious communities, and service organizations that will give you a sense of the kinds of organizations and resources that strongly support community organizing.

APPENDIX A

Details of Participatory Research Strategies

This appendix is designed to help you work step by step through several of the major social science research techniques and analytical frameworks. This appendix, together with its accompanying assignments, will give you practice in using these research skills.

How to Do Reliable, Valid Web Research

Often the first step in systematic community organizing research is to explore reliable Internet sites for information on your focal system. To evaluate the validity of such information, you should review and apply information literacy criteria, such as that provided by the State University of New York/Empire State College Commons.

You should critically evaluate all Internet sites for:

- *Accuracy*: You can judge the accuracy of the information by assessing the reputation of the sponsoring organization and the intent of the site. For instance, government sites (.gov), colleges and universities (.edu), and well-known non-profit organizations (.org) likely strive for accuracy because their reputations depend on the validity of their claims.
- *Credibility of the author(s)*: On a reputable site, you will find the name of an author or authors, the department responsible for the site, and contact information if you have questions. You can use your general search engine or an academic search engine to learn more about the author's experience, areas of expertise, reputation in the field, and probable biases.
- *Bias*: Unfortunately, many websites are ideologically skewed. Learn to look for words and phrases that overstate a particular case, appeal to emotions, are not supported by credible sources, or are funded by individuals or organizations with a clear prejudice or self-interest. You may find it helpful to explore such sites to understand various viewpoints, but be sure to sift carefully to differentiate fact from fiction.
- *Currency*: How recent is the information? Newer is often, but not necessarily, better. Newer sites are usually preferable in fields which change rapidly, such as politics, medicine, psychology, the natural sciences, economics, the Internet, and funding opportunities Accuracy and credibility are more important than currency if you are exploring areas such as history, examples of model programs, or classics in a field.
- *Accessibility*: Accessibility is determined by the ease of connecting to a website and whether a site is open to the public or charges a fee. In general, there are enough free sites available that it's unnecessary to use paid sites. Be wary of commercial sites that offer some information for free but promise more for a fee or that require credit card information before providing access Avoid sites that charge for doing Web research because many use freely available information that you could access yourself.

Unless your community organization is extremely wealthy or you have very little time, it's usually better to do your own research—not only because you will save money but because the research process itself will help you perceive creative connections as you collect and analyze information.

- *Intent of sponsoring organization*: There is a trend toward dual sponsorship of websites that pairs non-profit organizations, self-help groups, and other social action initiatives with for-profit organizations. While dual sponsorship benefits the altruistic organization financially, it can also lead to co-option, such as when a medical self-help or support group implicitly encourages use of a pharmaceutical company's products. Such sites are increasingly common and search engines tend to promote them because they appear at the top of any search list.
- *Comparability or generalizability*: Comparability or generalizability is how closely a site compares to your organization's interests, mission, outcome goals, target population, and location. Usually, the more comparable the site, the more useful it will be. For example, while a youth center in a rural community will have some things in common with a youth center in an urban area, it will also have significant differences. Be prepared to analyze programmatic similarities and differences, take some good ideas, and leave the rest.
- *Useful links*: Helpful websites provide useful links to other resources. You will find it helpful to think of a Web search as a stroll through a fascinating forest with many by-ways. Follow you intuition and resolve to enjoy yourself by following any link that intrigues you or seems likely to add to your store of knowledge.
- *Uniqueness:* Once you have studied comparable organizations—but before you make final implementation plans—look for unique approaches to your focal issue. Unique approaches to old problems can spark creative thinking and enable innovative solutions.

Mining Data Online

Create a systematic Web-search strategy that provides structure but also allows for flexibility and serendipity. Use Google or other reliable search engines. Identify various search terms that might apply. If you have difficulty locating the information on the first try, use different combinations of search terms. Pay attention to recurring words, phrases, or acronyms as you explore your area of interest because specific areas may develop their own terms or jargon which you can use as key words for additional searches.

You can use flow charts, such as the one in Figure A.1, to map the steps you plan to take.

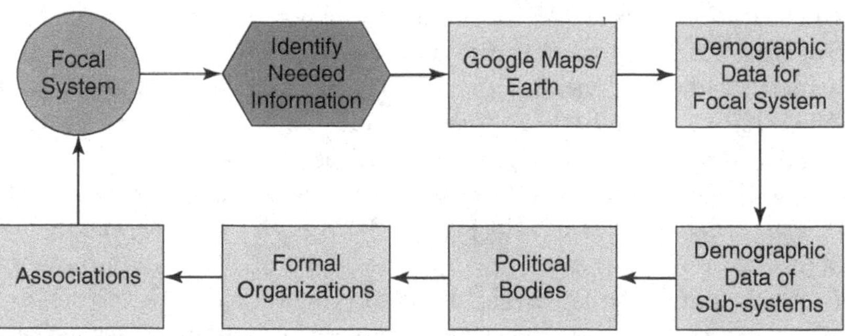

FIGURE A.1 Exploring the Geographic Community Systems
Uncovering the needs of a specific focal system and understanding how it functions require researching its demographics, sub-systems, and constituents (such as local government, organizations, and associations).

Gathering Data for Geographically-based Organizing

If you are focusing on a geographic community, some of your key research questions will be, "How many people are we talking about?" "What are their ages?" "What is their ethnic origin?" "How much money do they make?" "What are their living conditions?" Geographic community organizing often begins with gathering these kinds of **demographic data** about the focal community system, its micro-systems, and its mezzo-systems—often including its municipality, county, region of the state, and state as a whole. The U.S. Census is your primary tool for such searches, although learning how to use it requires time, a high tolerance for frustration, and a sense of humor. The U.S. Census (http://www.census.gov/) has a very valuable site for learning about your focal community, micro-, and mezzo-systems because it has vast information broken down in multiple ways. Go to the site and practice using the tools to find the ones you feel are most useful. As of July 2012, the simplest way to use the Census is to (1) go to the main site and click "American Fact Finder" in the list at the bottom of the page or Google "American Fact Finder" and (2) click the tab titled "Using Fact Finder" and follow its instructions for using the search options. The site will provide a prioritized list of the census tables that are most likely to contain the information you need.

However, remember that because the Census depends on the willingness and availability of people to reply to its questions, it is very accurate for stable, mostly middle or upper income areas like Middle View. It is notoriously inaccurate for places, like Smithville, that have large numbers of legal and illegal aliens, non-English speakers, and people who are homeless or who move frequently. Moreover, because the U.S. Census is only updated every ten years (at the turn of each decade), it becomes *less* reliable as the decade progresses. As you reach the end of a decade, you will need to compare census data with observational data, especially in geographic areas experiencing rapid demographic change. In spite of its weaknesses, most planning efforts depend heavily on U.S. Census data. Unfortunately, the Census has recently been under attack by congressional cost cutters so some of its services, such as the Fact Finder, may be cut. Check on their availability, and if you need help, ask a librarian or a representative from your municipal or county planning department with experience in locating and accessing data.

Gathering Data on Specific Issues

If you are focusing specific issues or concerns in a geographic focal system or a community of interest, you need to develop strategies for learning as much as you can about the numbers of people affected, policies and programs already are in place, initiatives that have been suggested, and likely future directions. Developing this knowledge base should begin with collecting information and then comparing and consolidating data from many different online sources.

Government sites are excellent for getting an overview of existing programs, policies, and new initiatives at the international, national, state, regional, and local levels. The best place to start is the USA.gov initiative, a portal that makes all kinds of national, state, and local government agency sites quickly and easily available. Once you understand its design, it will help answer many different questions without searching multiple sites and using multiple search terms.

All U.S. states and territories have websites that are accessible from the USA.gov site, or you can go directly to your state's site using your search engine to find the main site. State sites are particularly useful if you are interested in state-level services provided for a particular group of people, such as the developmentally disabled, or by a particular government agency. State sites and their sub-categories vary in quality and in ease of navigation; plan to spend an hour exploring the site to get your bearings.

As of 2013, the USA.gov site enables you to find local government sites in two or three easy steps, or you can use your search engine to locate sites directly. As with the state sites, local government sites vary greatly in their design, ease of use, and quality of information. After exploring relevant websites, visit your local government offices in person and attend a council meeting or other decision-making event. If you can't make a live event, read meeting minutes—which are usually posted on local websites—or watch the event on public access television.

The CIA World Factbook is well-designed, updated weekly, and very useful if you want to work outside the United States. It offers gives a quick overview of the geography, people and society, government, economy, transportation, military capabilities, and transnational issues affecting hundreds of nations and political entities around the world and provides links to other sources of information, such as biographies of world leaders and a link to an electronic reading room to access materials under the Freedom of Information Act.

While government sites are good sources of information about focal community strengths, areas of concern, and government services, they may present a one-sided (and largely positive) view. Therefore, you should explore the websites of other organizations, associations, and individuals to understand your focal system and/or focal issues from a variety of perspectives. In geographic communities, this process often starts with a visit to the municipal website. For example, if you wanted to learn more about Middle View, you might use a search engine like Google to find sites like "Town of Middle View," "Village of Middle View," "Middle View Chamber of Commerce," and "Middle View Consolidated Schools." Often such sites mention other sites or have subsections to explore. A typical town site contains minutes of council meetings and links to county resources, such as internal departments like planning, parks, streets and roads, and so forth. It may also cover such outside resources as the local historical society, churches, and service clubs. Each of these sites provides other links, which often include visuals, podcasts, and videos. As you view these websites, analyze (1) their content, (2) the emotional message they convey, and (3) the motives of their sponsors. You can quickly develop a solid base for understanding your focal system after an hour or two of such visual exploration, coupled with a systematic summary of what you learn, your personal experience, and group reflection. If you are employing designated learners, instruct each member of the learning team to conduct a specific Web search and then have the learning team organize their findings to share with other participants. If you find an interesting organization, call and ask questions.

While data gathering and consolidation of information is especially important at the beginning of a participatory research process, it should continue throughout the community organizing cycle. Your ongoing goal should be to create a thorough kaleidoscopic picture of your focal system with special emphasis on its assets and interconnections.

Surveys

While Chapter 7 covered the basics of survey research, this section is intended to answer your specific questions and concerns.

While community groups and other private organizations can conduct survey and other social science research without permission, it must be noted that any research done under the auspices of a college or university that involves human subjects and which will be made public must first have its entire research plan approved by that school's Institutional Review Board (IRB). If you intend for your community organizing research—including surveys, interviews, observations, focus groups, and other sources—to be included in an academic paper such as a thesis or professional publication, you will need permission from your school's IRB before beginning. Talk with your professor about what this entails for your institution and determine how and whether your student project must be reviewed.

Surveys are probably the most commonly used quantitative research tools used in community research, with the possible exception of publicly available data. If you decide to do a survey, you should ask the following analytical questions:

- *What questions do we need to answer that can only be answered through a survey?* These questions usually have to do with the nature of the needs of your focal community. A survey can be especially useful if members of your core group only represent a small segment of the focal community and you sense that you may be missing important viewpoints.
- *How shall we design the questions?* Surveys are commonly written using multiple choice formats or rating scales because these can be fairly easily calculated. However, they may not be valid because (1) respondents may differ in their interpretation of the questions, (2) it is difficult to cover all of the nuances of a topic in the multiple choice format, and (3) people differ in their approaches to rating scales (that is, some people almost never make highly positive choices, others consistently give low ratings, and many tend to choose the middle ground). Because of these validity issues, multiple choice and rating scales are often combined with a few open-ended questions to clarify respondents' viewpoints. Several online services can be used to design surveys, and some offer free trials of short surveys but charge for longer or multiple ones. Google the keywords—survey designers—to access such sites.
- *How shall we word the questions?* Because you want useful information, you must take care that the survey questions do not lead respondents to a particular answer. In general, if you are asking about whether a new service is needed, it is best to avoid questions that ask whether the respondent agrees or disagrees. For instance, in recent work on a teen center, teens were asked to rate their level of agreement on this statement: "Our area needs a teen center." Almost 100% agreed with that statement. The same teens were asked to rate the statement, "I would definitely come to a local teen center," the numbers dropped to 60%. When they were asked to rate the statement, "I would definitely help in the creation of such a center," the numbers dropped still further, and when they were to include their names, telephone numbers, and e-mails if they were interested in helping us, the response rate was negligible. It became clear that there was not enough interest or momentum to follow through with the project.
- *How can we reach those who know the extent and importance of the need we have identified?* A survey of those likely to be affected may give you an idea of the extent of a need and its importance. Sometimes a need is rare but intense, as is the case with life-threatening disease. At other times a need may be common but not perceived as very important by those affected. A well-designed survey can help you determine which is true.
- *Whom should we ask?* That is, how should we choose the sample. Unless the issue affects an extremely small number of people, you will usually only be able to survey a small **sample** (portion) of the **total population** (everyone who could possibly be affected). If you want to have an idea of what all members of the general population think, it is best to choose a **random sample** (or portion of the population in which each person in the target population has an equal opportunity to be chosen). If you need wisdom from specific people, it is best to use some sort of **selective sampling**. Often, **snowball sampling** (in which you begin with a few key people and then ask them to suggest others who should be surveyed until you keep getting the same names) is particularly helpful in

community settings because it not only provides you with needed data but also with the names of key people and an idea of their connections with one another.

- *How shall we distribute the survey?* There are various ways to reach people through surveys: mailing them, printing them in a newspaper or other publication, offering them on the Internet, leaving them in various public locations, passing them out on the street or door to door, paying an organization to distribute and collect them, or any and all of the above. Consider such factors as cost, timely return of the information, likelihood of return, and likelihood that the replies will provide a valid measurement of community sentiment.
- *How can we be sure to reach our main target group?* Finding creative ways to reach end users can be particularly difficult for organizers in economically poor communities because residents often do not buy newspapers, respond to mail surveys, belong to Internet advocacy groups, have easily accessible telephone numbers, or respond to door-to-door surveys, especially in dangerous neighborhoods. In such cases, in addition to these traditional means, ask for the help of recognized community leaders to distribute and collect surveys in places where people gather—such as churches and other places of worship, convenience stores, beauty parlors, laundries, and bars or restaurants. Some target groups—such as school children and health care and social service recipients—can be particularly hard to reach because they are protected by privacy laws and institutional policies. In such cases, you will have to work closely with organizational leaders, such as school administrators, to gain permission to survey or interview members of your target population.
- *How will we ensure confidentiality?* Social science research ethics requires that the confidentiality of human subjects be maintained so you will have to provide methods for sending, receiving, tabulating, organizing, and interpreting survey responses so that they cannot be traced back to individual respondents—while still preventing duplication. Not only does clearly guaranteeing confidentiality ensure protection of human subjects, but it also makes practical sense as respondents are more likely to reply honestly if they know their privacy is protected.
- *How much will this cost? How much can we afford to spend?* Even when surveys are done by volunteers, they take time and energy, which equates to money. Explore various means of delivery that maximize your ability to reach your target group and minimize costs. This can be done by limiting the number of questions, limiting the sample size, simplifying data analysis, using students engaged in service learning projects, using free Internet services, and so forth.
- *How can we maximize the rate of return?*
  - Make the survey interesting, short, and easy to complete, with an element of fun.
  - Use multiple modes of delivery to reach the largest possible number of people in the target group.
  - Provide a stamped, self-addressed envelope for mailed surveys or a small monetary reward or prize, or a chance to win a raffle prize, for everyone who returns the survey. (As long as there is a way to guard against duplication, the more ways of distributing and collecting surveys the better.)
- *How do we choose what kind of survey to use?* Web-based surveys are a good choice if your target group has easy Internet access. Several Internet companies, such as Survey Monkey, offer free online services to easily develop surveys, deliver them directly to your mailing list, and enable respondents to answer online as part of their daily e-mails.

Web-based surveys should almost always be supplemented with mail surveys, house-to-house distribution, telephone surveys, and distribution at community gathering places to reach those who do not have Internet access or e-mail addresses.

Tips for Effective Qualitative Research

Quantitative research such as we have been discussing from government sources often provides rather cold facts and figures that become more outdated as the end of the decade approaches. In contrast, observation of formal meetings, informal discussions, chance encounters, watching and listening to others' interactions, and being aware of the environment are all components of qualitative research that enrich your understanding of the focal system and its related micro-, mezzo-, overlapping-, and macro-systems.

The observational process mentioned in Chapter 7, which uses the acronym EDIT, begins with simply **experiencing** the system by being curious and open to what is happening, while being careful not to jump to conclusions too soon. It moves to a written **description** of what has been observed and is often organized by answers to a series of questions. **Interpretation** occurs only after (1) the description has been carefully prepared and shared, (2) there has been time to reflect on it, (3) your observations have been compared with the other data you have collected, and (4) everyone has had a chance to explore alternative interpretations. The final step, **transfer**, occurs when your team develops hypotheses about the meaning of the observations in light of the total system and develops your next steps accordingly. Interpretation and transfer should occur only after you are that you have thoroughly described what has really occurred.

The foci of observational research in community organizing are the environmental context and the interactional context. Table A.1 shows their components.

Table A.1 Observational Research Contexts

Environmental Context	Interactional Context
Natural environment	Informal interactions
Built environment	Formal interactions

The **environmental context** is divided into the natural environment and the built environment, while the interactional context is divided into informal and formal interactions. The **natural environment** refers to aspects of the world—such as air quality, watersheds (rivers, lakes, streams, etc.), green areas, topography (mountains, hills, valleys, flatlands, and other features)—that may be affected by or affect human activity but are not dependent on it. The **built environment** refers to material things that human beings create, including houses, factories, schools, churches, stores, roads, bridges, fences, and infrastructures, such as water pipes and electric lines. Together, the natural and the built worlds comprise the environmental context of the community where the "action" takes place.

Informal interactions and formal interactions add the human dimension to communities. Interactions are determined by norms or the unwritten rules of social life. **Informal interaction** refers to the everyday encounters of people as they go about living together. Observation of these interactions gives you a sense of what it "feels like" to be part of a focal neighborhood or community system, or smaller micro-system, like a school or church. You encountered many of these interactions in Chapter 1 when you explored Middle View and Smithville on foot and by car. **Formal interaction** refers to more patterned ways of behaving, such as planning meetings, community hearings, and scheduled appointments. The town meeting in Middle View was an example of such a formal interaction.

Observation should be intentional and ongoing. Many qualitative researchers recommend that you keep a research journal handy and that you record your observations during or as soon after the event as possible. The writings in the journal should be reviewed from time to time, used for reflection on the focal system, and periodically synthesized into tentative conclusions.

Interviewing

Interviewing in a variety of forms is probably the most robust qualitative technique. **Informal interviews** are the most fun and involve chatting with anyone and everyone who may have relevant knowledge or insights. Informal interviews resemble everyday give and take, but you gently guide the conversation to evoke stories, history, opinions, and what might even be thought of as gossip to clarify the dynamics of the focal community system. Community elders and children are especially important sources because both groups like to tell their stories. Elders can be especially helpful in enabling an understanding of history and family ties.

Semi-structured interviews are more formal. You use a relatively short, broad list of questions that can be answered in no particular order. You may take notes that are organized and transcribed later, or you may use a tape recorder (with the permission of the subject) to capture what is said for later transcription. It is good ethical protocol to share the transcribed version with the subject for editing, so that the information is accurate from his or her perspective.

Formal interviews are completely structured, have a particular order of presentation, and contain questions which must be asked in precise ways. At their extreme, they become oral surveys rather than qualitative instruments. Many of the considerations mentioned for surveys apply to semi-structured and formal interviews as well. All three kinds of interviews are useful in participatory research, but informal and semi-structured interviews are likely to add the newest data and surprising insights and enable you to cement friendly relationships with those you interview and to share some of your thoughts with them.

Focus groups are a specialized form of interviewing, originally used in business to develop marketing strategies. In research based on focus groups, you invite a small number of people to come together to examine an issue and use your group process skills to enable them to share their ideas about the focal community system or on an issue of mutual concern. Focus groups have many of the advantages of informal and semi-structured interviewing, can save time because it is possible to interview several people simultaneously, can spark connected learning processes, and generate new ideas that might not occur to individuals. Like all small groups, they suffer from the danger of being dominated by a few vocal individuals or persons who are perceived as having more power than others, so your facilitator role is extremely important.

You can use **narrative inquiry** (gathering people's stories) for **data gathering** (collecting specific facts, figures, and perceptions) and **consolidation of information** (putting the pieces together in ways that make sense to the designated learners, the organizing team, and external audiences). Narrative inquiry (storytelling) simply involves asking the subjects to "Tell me about. . . ." Typical stories revolve around family histories, neighborhood events, and important turning points. Narratives (stories) often have characters, a basic plot, one or several key events or turning points, and an interpretation (or interpretations) which may be spoken or unspoken. If you choose to use narrative inquiry and storytelling, you should be a good listener and know how to use nods, affirmative sounds, and open-ended questions to encourage the storyteller to elaborate. Data from narratives need not be in written form. Fascinating ways of gathering narrative information include audio and video taping of oral histories, especially when children and young adults interview community elders.[1]

Storytelling in groups can be especially enjoyable and enlightening as different people add their own perspectives to the main story. A Native American custom called the "talking stick" can be used effectively in group-based narrative research. Group members sit in a circle and pass around a stick or other symbolic object, taking turns as they do so to tell their personal stories or speak about a matter to be decided. The others quietly listen and take their turns at telling their own related stories. This technique is particularly powerful when you are dealing with emotionally charged topics, where it becomes a tool for both data collection and trust building.[2]

Narratives are an effective alternative to dry facts, figures, and tables as a way of consolidating and sharing your research. You or your designated learners pull together all the information you have gathered into a **journey narrative** that relates participants' experiences and their meaning. Journey narratives are especially helpful when you want readers to imagine themselves sharing the experiences of members of the focal community system.

Use of Drama, Dance, Music, and the Visual Arts for Gathering Data

Some people think and learn best using visual, aural, and kinesthetic means of expression. Use of the arts and shared reflection with participants and audience members can help you reach levels of understanding that may not be possible using only written or verbal techniques.[3] The following are some examples of how these techniques are used.

Imagine yourself in the heart of the Smithville neighborhood. Suddenly there is a commotion: a man grabs a woman by her hair, drags her to the middle of the street, and begins to beat her. All activity on the street comes to a halt. Before anyone can call the police, an authoritative person shouts, "Stop the action!" and proceeds to engage you and other by-standers in a discussion of domestic violence, public responsibility, and other topics. This method is intentionally intrusive, since it is primarily used for consciousness-raising and to incite action, but the contiguous discussions can give you important clues about how ordinary people approach volatile issues.

Again, imagine. You are in a mall near Middle View. Suddenly someone bursts into song, followed by others in groups of twos and threes until eventually a whole chorus is singing loudly and joyfully. Everyone is smiling and enjoying the show. Afterward, someone approaches you for your reflections on the event. You have just experienced a bit of community building called a flash mob (and probably will find yourself on YouTube) and have participated in a bit of participatory research.

Now let's take a trip literally around the world. You are an illiterate woman in the Kingdom of Lesotho (a landlocked country surrounded by South Africa). Your village has been decimated by AIDS, but no one talks about it because AIDS carries a great stigma due to its association with sexual promiscuity. A group of dramatists comes and talks with you and your friends about how AIDS has changed your lives. These organizers help you and your friends put together several small but powerful skits based on your experiences, which dramatize common themes, such as your husbands' refusal to wear condoms when they return from working in South Africa, struggles you have talking with other women about your worries, being unable to get the medicines you need, and the sadness you feel when your husbands are forced to leave to work in South Africa. The skits have colorful costumes and some singing. They are designed to open up discussions and enable women to reveal secrets that they share in common but few have been able to talk about. These skits are performed outside in the common area, and after the production you and your fellow actors talk with audience members about the experience and encourage them to reflect with you on its meaning. Your participatory research group feels an ethical responsibility to those who have taken the risk of talking about a forbidden subject, so you make sure that the dialogue continues after the production. You find ways to help the village women support one another and begin to work toward solving some of their common problems.[4] All of these are examples illustrate the use of theater in community organizing.

Although theater is probably the art form most widely used in participatory research and popular education, other arts such as dance, music, and visual arts—such as the creation of community murals and **installation art** (large, interactive, often short-term art forms usually constructed in cities that allow people to interact with one another and with the art)—can be used as well. For instance, a series of building-sized murals in Middle View that depict the new tourist train line, as well as local scenic spots, have engaged youth in their creation, sparked conversation among viewers, built community ties, and provided relational organizers with information about peoples' feelings about their community. Meanwhile in Smithville, one cold January was made cheerful by installation art when a micro-community of artists, activists, and youth turned the interior of an abandoned building into the facsimile of a community park. People were free to enter and do park-like things: sit on green grass, watch the fountains, push children on swings, even make out if they liked. The creators took videos of the event and talked with the participants about their perceptions of the neighborhood and hopes for its future. The participants not only enjoyed themselves, but their behaviors and comments provided the community team with insights about what people need and want from their green spaces.

All participatory art forms are rich in symbolic and **ontological** (emotionally and spiritually deep) meaning[5] and generally build trust among participants. The insights gained from participatory theater, visual art, and music can be used along with information gathered from quantitative techniques, like surveys, as well as the qualitative techniques to create a complete and valid picture of the realities of members of kaleidoscopic communities.

Analytic Frameworks

This section of Chapter 7 explored various frameworks for analyzing community issues, including the Asset-based approach, the problem-centered approach, Gap analysis, and sustainability indicators.

Asset-based community organizing is explained in detail in Chapter 7, so it is not addressed here. You can explore further at the Asset-based Community Development (ABCD) Institute at Northwestern University or at AbundantCommunity.com.

The Problem-centered Approach

Chapter 7 provides a list of questions that should be used by those taking a problem-centered approach. That list is expanded here.

- What are the important aspects of the problem? Who does it affect? How many people are involved? If there are victims of injustice, how seriously are they hurt? How do the victims themselves (or their families) view the problem? How does it feel to be a victim of these conditions? If the problem were solved, how would the world be better for the victims? How would it be better for all of us?
- What outcomes do you *really* want? Is your solution a process or an outcome? For some reason, many leadership teams wrestle with the differences between outcomes and processes. For example, those involved in the creation of the runaway shelter in Middle View thought they wanted to create a shelter, when they actually wanted to enable teens remain in their own community while dealing with adolescent issues. The community went to a great deal of unnecessary expense and effort to rehabilitate a house when the same objectives could have been met with just an office. Fortunately, many times process solutions will lead to desirable outcomes, but often they are not the best way, the least expensive, or the most empowering to the target group. Thus, it is better to resist "jumping to solutions."

- Who are the important players or stakeholders? Which individuals, groups, and organizations are involved? What are their perspectives on the problem? Which are likely to support change efforts and why? Which are likely to oppose change and why? Which important potential stakeholders may not yet be aware that a problem exists?
- Who are the potential audiences for the information gathered and the proposals generated from it? How can the information and ideas best be presented to these individuals and groups?
- What are the pay-offs for various players? Which groups or interest groups are benefiting *because* the problem exists? What are the direct benefits? What are the indirect benefits?
- Who has the power in the situation, and what is its nature? Who has the power to oppose your goals? What is the source and level of their power? What power is present in the organizing effort, and how can it be strengthened? What groups and organizations might be potential allies? What is their power base?
- What other social problems may be taking precedence over this issue? How can you move it closer to the top? In other words, what are the politics involved?

The development of systematic answers to these and other questions will help you develop approaches that acknowledge conflicting views and interests but still make consensus building possible.

Gap Analysis

Gap Analysis was covered briefly in Chapter 7, but its somewhat complex process is expanded here. The development of systematic answers to these and other questions your group may generate will help you develop approaches that acknowledge conflicting views and interests but still make consensus building possible. Figure A.2 shows the first phase of the Gap Analysis process.

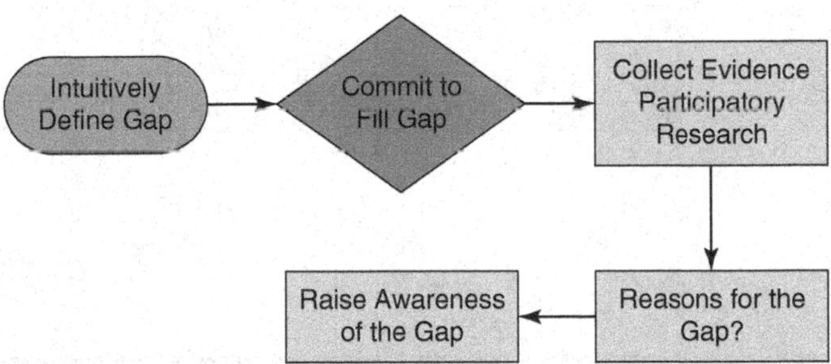

FIGURE A.2 The Gap Analysis Process: Phase I—Identifying the Gap

- **Phase 1: Identifying the Gap**

  Step 1: Identifying the gap intuitively. The process of identifying a gap begins when an individual or small group notices that something is wrong that needs fixing, that something is missing that would make life better, or that the quality of life would be improved if something new were added.

  Step 2: Committing to filling the gap. Once the gap is identified, the individual or small group must make a commitment to filling it. At this point, idle conversations and dreaming begin to be separated from the hard work of creating change.

Step 3: Collecting evidence about the "size and shape" of the gap. At this point, it is often necessary to use both quantitative and qualitative research techniques to determine if the gap really exists, how many people are affected, and a variety of details about its exact nature. Quantitative or numerical data often takes the form of surveys or census information, while qualitative research often takes the form of formal and informal interviews, group discussions, participant observation, and searching through written documents (e.g., newspaper articles, meeting minutes, advertising flyers, meeting agendas). This phase also includes putting the data into a form that can be used in decision making. The Internet research processes described earlier can also be useful in this phase.

Step 4: Figuring out reasons for the gap: analyzing information. Many of the steps for conducting such an analysis were described in Chapter 7 in the section on participatory research.

Step 5: Raising consciousness about the gap. Before a gap can be bridged, it is usually necessary to develop fairly broad-based support for the effort. This can often be done best just by sharing concerns with friends, colleagues, and those who are most likely to be concerned with the issue. This consciousness raising should be a two-way street: it is important to not only share concerns but to use conversations with others to continue to clarify the nature of the gap—especially in the earliest phases of gap analysis. Serious conversations can lead to new ideas that can be included in and can strengthen the eventual solution, as well as build important relationships and trust.

- **Phase 2: Magnifying the Gap to See it within the Big Picture** Figure A.3 shows the second phase of the Gap Analysis process.

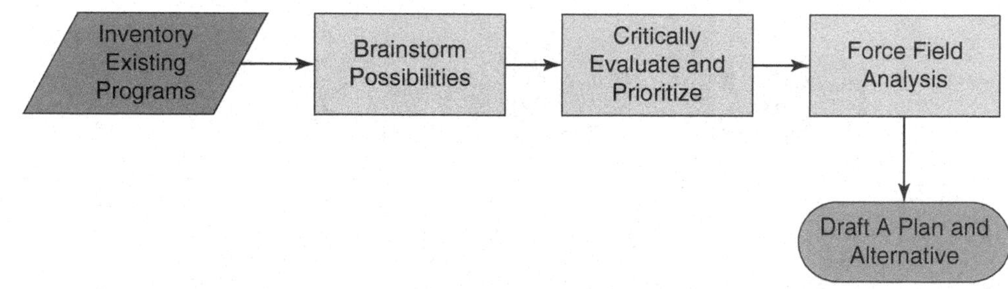

FIGURE A.3 Magnifying the Gap

Step 1: Inventorying other programs. Don't be redundant! It is important to determine which services are available in your own community that might be making similar efforts to meet the identified need. It is also interesting and important to identify other programs in other communities (or even other parts of the world) that have successfully met similar needs.

Step 2: Brainstorming ideas. In the brainstorming phase, you should explore as many ideas for meeting the gap as possible. The chief rule of brainstorming is that "anything goes." All ideas are accepted without criticism.

Step 3: Critically evaluating suggestions and ranking them. The switch from brainstorming to critical evaluation requires a change from easygoing, "right-brained" creativity to hard-nosed decision making. So try to schedule a break of minutes or even days between the two stages. At the critical thinking stage, the group should develop some criteria for evaluating the brainstorm suggestions, such as the likelihood of the plan to meet the identified needs, its costs, its acceptability to funders and decision makers, the time and human resource investment needed, the interest and excitement it generates, and so on. The goal at this phase is to come up with one or two broad strategies that evoke some excitement and probable commitment.

Step 4: **Doing a force field analysis.** In the force field analysis phase, you take a hard look at the factors favoring the project and those opposing the project. This involves not only listing items in each column but also giving each a value (or valence) to clarify the reality of the situation. A SWOT (unknowns) analysis approaches the same task by identifying the strengths, weaknesses, opportunities, and threats inherent in the situation. It helps to add a category called "unknowns" to identify areas in which additional information is needed to make a good decision. Both techniques help ensure that plans are realistic and avoid surprises.

Step 5: **Drafting a plan and an alternative.** Once all of this analytical work is done, it is time to draft a plan and a backup plan as well.

- **Phase 3: Micro-scoping (Breaking Your Work into Specific Actions)** Figure A.4 shows the third phase of the Gap Analysis process.

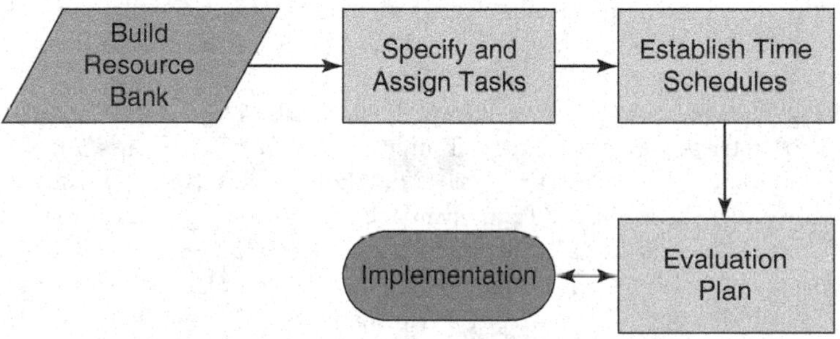

FIGURE A.4 Micro-scoping (Action Steps)

Here are the steps used in the micro-scoping phase.

Step 1: **Building a resource bank.** This is very much like the asset-based approach discussed earlier. In this phase, list all the human, financial, and material resources you have available for the project and include details such as addresses, telephone numbers, e-mails, times available, specific resources, and links to others involved in the project,.

Step 2: **Specifying and assigning tasks to be done.** At this point, the group links their human resources with specific tasks to be done. This can be very difficult in volunteer groups as it requires discerning the amount and type of involvement each person wants, as well as such intangibles as their reliability. Because most community projects depend heavily on goodwill and cooperation, this phase takes excellent communication skills and considerable diplomacy.

Step 3: Establishing time schedules. Time schedules are related to assignments. It is often challenging to schedule the various tasks so that each is completed in a way that supports the others. In community groups, it is important to give plenty of time for completing tasks because (1) they are typically volunteer efforts that must be sandwiched in and around other duties and life events, and (2) they almost always take longer than expected. It is important just to keep working toward goals without becoming discouraged.

Step 4: Evaluating the plan and following up. There are two kinds of evaluation used in community projects. Formative evaluation is done as you work on the project and is used to make minor course changes and improvements. Summative evaluation occurs at the end of the project (or at a reasonable stopping point, such as an annual review) and summarizes accomplishments. Both are important.

This appendix was intended to guide you on the use of social science research techniques and frameworks in participatory action research. I hope you will find it useful.

Notes

1. Rappaport, J. (1995). Empowerment meets narrative: Listening to stories and creating settings. *Journal of Community Psychology, 23*(5): 795–807; Richie, D. (2003). *Doing oral history: A practical guide* (2nd ed.). Oxford, UK: Oxford University Press. Technology is changing rapidly and will soon make this edition outdated, but it gives key tools and concepts; Janesick, V. J. (2010). *Oral history for the qualitative researcher: Choreographing the story.* New York City, NY: Guilford Press.
2. Fujioka, K. (1998). The talking stick: An American Indian tradition in the ESL classroom. *The Internet TESL Journal, 4*(9). Retrieved August 11, 2011, from http://iteslj.org/Techniques/Fujioka-TalkingStick.html; "Talking stick" experience. (1994). Five University Adult Education Retreat, Cornell, Rutgers, Columbia, Indiana University of Pennsylvania, and Pennsylvania State University graduate programs, Ithaca, NY.
3. Boal, A. (1990). "The cop in the head: Three hypotheses" *TDR, 34*(3): 35–42; Boal, A. (1993). *Theater of the oppressed.* (McBride,C.A & M.L, Trans.). New York City, NY: Theater Communications Group. Castaneda, Q. (2006). The invisible theater of ethnography: Performative principles of fieldwork. *Anthropological Quarterly, 79*(1): 47–76; Gray, R., Sinding, C., Ivanoffski, V., Fitch, M., Hampton, A., Greenburg, M., & Gray, R. (2000). The use of research based theater in a project related to metastatic breast cancer. *Health Expectations, 2*(2); Prentki, T. (1998). Must the show go on? The case for theater for development" *Development in Practice, 8*(4): 419–429.
4. Winner, L. and students. (2008). "Stigma, denial and HIV/AIDS, Lesotho presentation." Presented at Theater for Development, Student Academic Conference, SUNY Empire State College, NY.
5. Castaneda, Q. (2006). The invisible theater of ethnography: Performative principles of fieldwork. *Anthropological Quarterly, 79*(1): 47–76.

APPENDIX B

Expanded Coverage of Budgeting and Fund-raising

This appendix is intended to provide additional details on budgeting and financing for members of leadership teams who are charged with the financial aspects of the organizing effort.[1]

Yearly Operating Budgets

All well-functioning organizations have yearly operating budgets that can be designed in various ways, but the two most common are (1) budgeting by a central authority (or top-down budgeting) and (2) participatory budgets that build on the knowledge and skills of those who are actually doing the work, in consultation with those they serve. Because maximizing constituent involvement is a goal of participatory organizing, this section will help your leadership team manage a participatory (bottom-up) budgeting process. A participatory budgeting process begins with the teams or task forces charged with particular activities and programs as follows:

1. Managers (or management teams) at the activity and program levels are asked to prepare their annual budget requests based on broad guidelines from the leadership team.
2. Within these broad parameters, program or activity level budgeting teams develop budget projections based on their mission, probable growth, expected expenses, and an allowance for contingencies. These budgets include projections of **sunk costs** (the costs of personnel, rent, utilities, etc.) that remain constant and **variable expenses** that depend on numbers of people served, or cost, and number of programs offered.
3. These activity or program budgets are then presented and defended at the unit level where they may be renegotiated. In complex organizations, these unit budgets may then be presented and negotiated at a third (division) level and then are sent on to the leadership level where they receive a final polish and are approved. Although there may be internal conflicts throughout the process and the final product may not be perfect, this bottom-up process honors the participatory ideal and respects input from grassroots participants. Figure B.1 depicts this upward information flow.

Figure B.1 can be applied to the Smithville Neighborhood Organization (SNO) that you have been examining. SNO is a good example of participatory budgeting or distributed budgeting because it is primarily an organization of organizations that supports many far-flung efforts, including the community gardens, the farmers' market, a collaborative effort for nurturing micro-business ventures, several block clubs, and some housing initiatives. In addition, SNO leads its own local organizing, advocacy efforts at the municipal and state levels, and connections with similar neighborhood organizations in Industrial

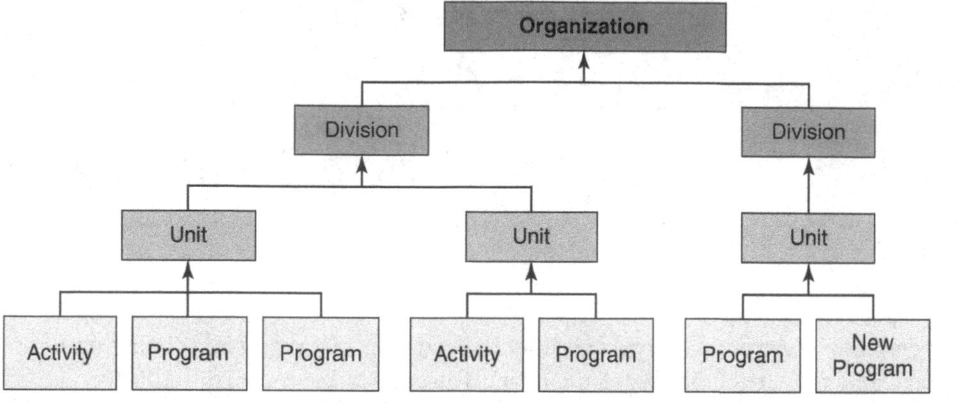

FIGURE B.1
Upward Flow of Budgeting

City and throughout the world. The SNO leadership team (i.e., board of directors) has decided to divide these activities into three coordinating units:

1. Unit One covers all of its food and economic security programs, such as the community gardens, the farmers' markets, family nutrition, mutual economic aid, and micro-businesses.
2. Unit Two covers block clubs and housing issues. These two service units are combined into a single division that is incorporated as a 501c-3 organization (see Chapter 10).
3. Unit Three focuses on advocacy issues at the municipal, county, and state levels; connections to national and international efforts; and the administrative structures of SNO itself. Because it is sometimes involved in political action, SNO's advocacy and administration efforts are a separate division incorporated as a 527 organization so they can legally lobby. So even though SNO operates as a single organization, the two divisions have separate budgets and funding streams to avoid legal problems.

Figure B.1 shows how budgeting works in a participatory budgeting process like SNO's. First, communication among various levels must be organized and managed, so SNO's leadership team has designated a small budget team headed by a volunteer who is skilled in financial management. The budget team's responsibility is to ensure that the budget process moves smoothly in a timely and professional manner.

Their concrete tasks are as follows:

- Create a budget development calendar and ensure that deadlines are met, as well as ensuring that deadlines set by government funding sources are met.
- Transparently communicate budgeting policies and procedures to all volunteers and paid staff members, as well as to residents of the Smithville neighborhood.
- Establish the format for draft budgets.
- Share information from the organizational level with the staff of the various activities and programs staff and their budgeting teams. This information includes income and expense forecasts based on reviews of external economic and competitive trends, and—when applicable—probable government funding levels.

- Develop a process to help the program and activity budget teams make income and expense forecasts based on reviews of external economic and competitive trends and/or probable government funding levels as applicable.
- Directly collaborate with the program and activity budget teams in setting expense and income targets in line with strategic plans for programs or units.
- Evaluate draft program and activity budgets for accuracy, reasonableness, applicable guidelines, and anticipated resources.
- Discuss draft budgets from the various programs and activities with the leadership team (i.e., board of directors) as needed.
- Write up all recommendations for reducing, increasing, or reallocating requested resources.
- Prepare the budget document and help present it to the board of directors for approval and to the yearly neighborhood assembly for openness.
- Implement financial monitoring, preparation and analysis of budgeted-versus-actual income and expense reports for management, board, regulatory, or public use. Oversee any corrections needed.

Let's follow SNO's 2012 budget cycle. SNO has a Finance Committee, headed by Certified Public Accountant Ravi Gupta (a community volunteer who is a member of the SNO Board of Directors). In June, 2011, the Finance Committee met to set broad parameters and a timeline for the 2012 budgeting process. Since SNO uses the **calendar year** (January 1 to December 31) as its **fiscal year** (financial year), Mr. Gupta sent the following letter on July 1 to the committee chairpersons of each of its three units. His letter said:

> Greetings friends and colleagues: It is that time of year again. SNO has had a successful 2011 and we are looking forward to more success in 2012, but in order to plan for our expenditures and revenue needs we need to have a budget request from your unit by September 30. We ask that you appoint a team comprised of your most active volunteers to work with you in your budget effort. Here is a template for you to use in your planning effort. We anticipate that the revenues will remain flat or grow slightly over the course of the year. Please estimate your financial requirements and complete a budget narrative that explains your priorities for the year. If you plan new programs or initiatives, please show new sources of revenue and/or where reductions will be made in existing programs. I will be available to answer any questions and assist you in any way possible.

This letter went by e-mail and U.S. mail to three key volunteers: Maria Fernandez, chairperson of the Food Security and Micro-business Initiatives Committee; Harold Stone, chairperson of the Housing Program and the Block Club Committee; and Nakeisha Williams, chairperson of the Advocacy Committee. Copies also went to two part-time staff members, Reverend William Watson, Coordinator of Direct Services (an Americorps worker), and Manuel Perez, Coordinator of Community Organizing and Advocacy. The committee chairpersons and the two paid staff members met to discuss the budgeting process. It was agreed that Maria and Harold would each develop a budgeting task force that would involve six to eight of their most reliable volunteers. Nakeisha did the same. It was further agreed that the paid staff would provide administrative support but would not manage the process, which would be completed by the community volunteers.

Maria's task force decided that in 2012 they wanted to develop two new community gardens and continue an ongoing one; provide $1,000 in start-up loans to four new micro-enterprises; and hold a two-week summer camp for neighborhood children which would include lunch for fifty children and five adult volunteers, Monday to Friday, for seven weeks. Since this was a large increase over 2011, they decided to combine their expenditure budget with a revenue budget to ensure the broader SNO organization that they were planning responsibly. The Food Security and Micro-enterprises Annual Expenditure Budget from Maria's team was as follows:

SNO Food Security and Micro-Enterprises Budget—Fiscal 2012

ITEM	COSTS	IN-KIND CONTRIBUTIONS	INCOME	SNO EXPENSES
¼ time coordinator + benefits	**$8,400**	------------		$8,400
4 micro-enterprise grants	**$4,000**		$1,500 repayment of loans	$2,500
2 new community gardens (building elevated beds, hauling top soil and fertilizer, basic gardening tools, seeds, fencing)	**$5,000**	$4,000 donations of materials;	$400 grant American Community Gardens $100 lot rental fees	$500
1 continuing garden (renew fertilizer, seeds, repair beds)	**$500**	$450 donation of in-kind goods	$50 lot rental fees	$0
6-week "summer feeding" program—rent for church hall & kitchen 6 weeks @ $25 week	**$9,300**	$9,150 In kind kitchen rent, professional volunteers (2 teachers @ $100 day × 5 × 6 = ($6,000); 4 aides at $50 day × 5 × 6 = ($3,000) Food costs borne by Industrial City Schools.		$150
Total	**$27,200**	$13, 600	$2,050	$11,550

Budget Narrative: The mission of the SNO Food Security and Micro-Enterprise Committee is to enable the residents of the Smithville neighborhood to improve their health and family financial stability through coordinated efforts in food security, micro-enterprise, and youth nutrition. In 2012, we propose to offer three programs that will require support from the broader SNO: 4 loans @ $1,000 each for microenterprises, 2 new and 1 ongoing community gardens @ $500, and a six week summer feeding program and day camp @ $150. These SNO sponsored programs along with other activities related to the food and economic security program will be coordinated by a ¼ time facilitator from SNO @ $8,400. These SNO outlays will be matched by in-kind and direct donations as follows:

- **Micro-enterprises:** $1500 repayment of outstanding loans that will be put into the revolving loan fund.
- **Community Gardens:** So far we have commitments from several farm and garden stores for the garden supplies, top soil and fertilizer (manure) from two local farmers delivered by volunteer truck owners, a $400 grant from the American Community Gardening Association, and lot rental for 30 garden plots @ $5 each.

- **Summer Feeding Program and Day Camp:** The summer feeding program and day camp is a collaborative effort among the Industrial City School District, Smithville United Church, the Youth Collaborative Board, and SNO. The school district will provide breakfasts and lunches for families with children for six weeks, Monday to Friday. Their portion of the program will include funds for a site supervisor and two aides. These costs are not included here because the program is not directly supervised by SNO (the Smithville site is only one of five programs within Industrial City and budget figures are not available). The Smithville United Church has agreed to provide their building and grounds for the program but have asked that we provide a $150 rental fee to help off-set building costs that they estimate at $300 for the summer program. The educational/nutritional portion of the program will be handled by the Industrial City Youth Collaborative Board, a consortium of twelve youth-serving agencies. These agencies have agreed to work in pairs with each pair of agencies providing in kind staff and supplies for one week of programming. SNO is the lead agency for the summer project.
- **Food Pantries:** SNO coordinates the four food pantries in the Smithville Neighborhood under the auspices of the Industrial City Ministerial Collaborative. They handle all budgeting for these projects.

The Housing and Block Club and Advocacy Committees completed their budgets following the format used by Maria and forwarded them to the Finance Committee by the September 30 deadline. The Finance Committee reviewed their requests, asked some questions of the chairpersons, and combined the three program budgets and agency administrative costs into an expenditure budget as follows:

Smithville Community Organization: Expenditure Budget 2012

Personnel Costs	
• Direct Services Coordinator (½ time salary and benefits)	$16,800
• Advocacy Coordinator (½ time salary and benefits)	$16,800
Total Personnel (includes 40% for full benefits)	**$33,600**
Non-personnel Costs	
• Office Supplies	$500
• Printing	$500
• Multi-county Community Conference (2 attending)	$1,500
Total Non-personnel Costs	**$2,000**
Program Costs	
• Community Gardens and Micro-enterprises	$3,100
• Housing and Block Clubs	$5,600
• Advocacy	$2,800
Total Program Costs	**$11,500**
Equipment	
• Computer	$1,500
Total Equipment	**$1,500**
SNO Budget Total	**$48,600**

Budget Narrative: This budget is based on our best estimates of agency costs for 2012. Because SNO is a dual agency with separate nonprofit and advocacy components, we recommend that the two operations be kept completely separate in order to avoid any appearance of mixing funds. Each component will be managed by a ½ time community organizing professional who will be responsible for organizing and clerical activities. Non-personnel costs for the overall SNO effort include office supplies, printing, and two registrations, and housing and travel for the Multi County Community Conference. This Conference is an event we have found to be very important for networking and advocacy. The direct service program division will consist of both a food security and micro-enterprise unit and a housing and block club unit. The advocacy unit will consist of organizing efforts at the municipal, state, and national levels as determined by the Smithville Neighborhood Organization's Annual Assembly. Office space, telephones, Internet connections, and other utilities have been donated by the Smithville Community Church. We are requesting $1,500 for the purchase of a new computer as our current model was purchased in 2003 and does not contain enough memory.

Simultaneously, the Finance Committee created the following revenue budget for SNO.

SNO Annual Revenue Budget 2012

Americorps Worker (501-C3 coordination)	**$16,400**
Membership Income:	**$10,200**
• Individual Memberships: 1,500 individual/family memberships @ $5	$7,500
• Non-profit Memberships: 50 non-profit memberships @ $25	$1,250
• Business Memberships: 18 memberships (1–5 employees) @ $25	$450
• 10 memberships (6–25 employees) @ $50	$500;
• 5 memberships (26+ employees) @ $100	$500
Foundation Income:	**$12,000**
Hepplewhite Foundation:	$10,000
Industrial City Foundation:	$2,000
Donations:	**$10,000**
Total Projected Revenues:	**48,600**

The annual expenditure budget, each of the program budgets, and the revenue budget were presented to the SNO Board of Directors by the Finance Committee chairperson. The board asked each of the three program committee chairpersons to meet with them to discuss their budget requirements. The Finance Committee chairperson was asked to explain administrative costs and the revenue budget. After some debate over whether the budget was realistic and whether a new computer was really needed, the SNO Board of Directors approved the expenditure budget on December 1, 2011. Once the budget was finalized, it was shared as openly as possible with all of those it affected—especially the program and activity management teams that comprise the **budget centers** which are charged with actual day-by-day management of SNO programs and activities. The SNO budgeting team made sure that the program and activity leaders received the budget information needed to manage their work well. They provided each activity or program budgeting team with the approved budget and an idea of whether there would be any opportunities for flexibility. Figure B.2 follows the budget path back to the program level.

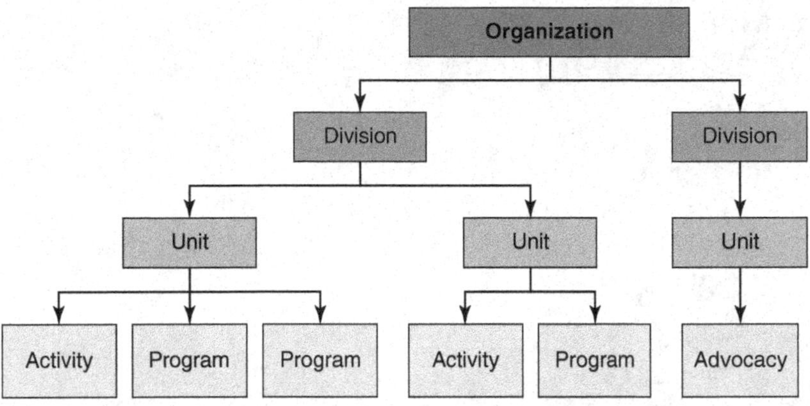

FIGURE B.2
Approved Budget

Once the program or activity budgeting teams received their probable budgets from SNO, the respective teams took responsibility for managing their own budgets. The teams

- Informed volunteers about any operational or budgetary changes, discussed the impact that these additions or cuts would have, and gave them the opportunity to work with the program or activity budget team on ways to cope.
- Planned and executed marketing and funding campaigns. For instance, because it is not a 501c-3 organization, the advocacy unit must be mostly self-supporting. They developed coordinated efforts to recruit members at all levels and decided to conduct several fund-raising events in case of a shortfall in memberships. Because the food, micro-enterprise, housing, and block club efforts fall under the 501c-3 designation, the teams developed task forces to work on continuation of the two foundation grants already secured for 2012 and a major funding campaign for tax-deductible donations. (Funds received were managed by the Finance Committee, especially Mr. Gupta, a Certified Public Accountant.)
- Reviewed regular financial reports, monitored income and expenses, and made adjustments as necessary.
- Helped the larger SNO budgeting committee develop and implement corrective action plans.
- Communicated emerging financial issues to the SNO budgeting and leadership team for renegotiation, as necessary.
- Made changes in expenditures if directed to do so by the SNO leadership team.

Monthly financial reports can be quite sophisticated, making use of tools such as Microsoft Excel, or they can be very simple. Here is a simple one for a single month of the Food Security and Micro-enterprise component of SNO.

January Financial Report Food Security and Micro-Enterprise Beginning Balance, 1-01-12: $1,250			
Date	**Item**	**Income**	**Expenditure**
1-10-12	Donation from XYZ church	$120	
1-12-12	Stamps to contact contributors: 100 @ $0.50 = $50		$50
1-14-12	Food for MLK Day party		$90
1-14-12	Decorations for MLK Day party		$50
1-16-12	Cash donation to MLK Day party	$100	
1-20-12	Refrigerator repairs for Food Pantry		$40
1-25 -12	Donation to Food Pantries	$50	
1-30-12 Repayment on micro-loan 1	Repayment on micro-loan 1	$25	
1-30-12 Repayment on micro-loan 2	Repayment on micro-loan 2	$25	
Totals		$320 Income	($230) Expenses

Net: $90
January 31: Balance: $1,340

Of course, even this budget could be more sophisticated depending on your needs. For instance, you might want to add a column for in-kind donations based on contributions of volunteer time and goods, but this will give you an idea of the basic content of a monthly budget statement.

In SNO, there is mutual trust and an emphasis on grassroots control, so most budget decisions are delegated to the program and activity teams. Upward reporting and downward permission giving is kept to a minimum as is consistent with participatory principles.

SNO leaders have found that different stakeholders vary in their relative importance, but, in general, it is important to involve core volunteers, members of the target community, and representatives of potential funding organizations. The most workable yearly budgets have been those that have had the most people systematically involved in their creation and that have had the most agreement among all stakeholders. Unfortunately, they were also the most time consuming, so it is best to strive for a balance between stakeholder involvement and timeliness. It is likely that your organizing effort will benefit from SNO's example.

Ongoing Budget Cycles

Budgeting in the early, growing years of any organization is difficult because you lack a track record. You may find that you overestimated some expenses, underestimated others, and have had some unexpected costs. But once you have some experience, the past can guide the future. After your first operational year, the budgeting team will have access to more solid information on which to base its initial budget parameters. Figure B.3 shows some sources of this information:

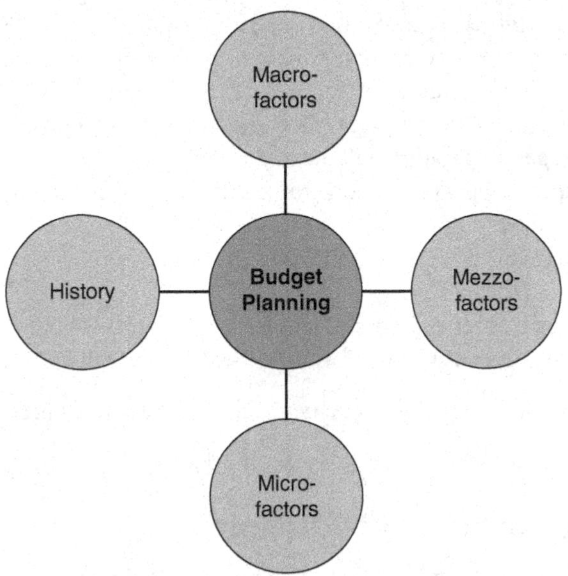

FIGURE B.3
Sources of Information for Budget Planning

History refers to the past track record of the whole organization and each of its parts. In many cases, past history is the best indicator of future revenues and expenses. **Macro-factors** refer to information and rumors from the broader economic and social environment. For instance, many SNO activities were adversely affected by the Great Recession of 2008. Funding sources dried up as the needs of neighborhood residents increased, and these macro-factors affected both program development and funding. **Mezzo-factors** refer to changes closer to your focal community. For instance, in 2009, SNO's housing and block club budget was adversely affected when the city administration decided to withdraw its support from housing rehabilitation and homeownership programs in Smithville, but it was positively affected by the municipal administration's decision to invest money in streets, storm drains, and other infrastructure improvements. **Micro-factors** refer to financial opportunities and threats at the program and activity levels. For example, SNO's food initiative was positively affected by downstate farmers' donations of excess fruits and vegetables that made it unnecessary for the neighborhood food pantries to purchase these products. The money budgeted for these purchases was re-allocated to other food and economic self-help efforts. On the other hand, rent became a problem for the summer feeding and day-camp program when the governing board of the host church decided that it needed to charge some rent to defray utilities costs. These and similar issues were considered by the SNO committee chairpersons as they prepared their annual budgets.

General Budgeting Tips

The following are tips that will help facilitate budgeting:

- Elicit feedback through as many channels as possible, including e-mail, individual discussions, and focus groups.

- Revise outcome goals and performance measures based on feedback. (Note: This does not mean reinventing the whole enterprise but only clarifying these important measures prior to engagement in the process so that everyone is in agreement.)
- Circulate revisions to stakeholders, making clear that this is indeed a "final call" for changes and a clear timeline for when budget preparation will begin and end.
- Develop a formal agreed-upon budget plan among team members. (This step will take the most time.)
- Create a polished format suitable for presentation.
- Share the plan with final decision makers as defined by the organizational structure.
- Obtain approval, recorded in written form.
- Distribute a budget information package which includes organizational goals and anticipated funding levels to all those who are responsible for components of the overall initiative.

The budget creation process and budget management should be as transparent as possible to everyone concerned.

Zero-based Budgeting (An Alternative Approach)

Zero-based budgeting (ZBB) was discussed briefly in Chapter 10. It is a process that can be used when your organization needs fresh thinking. Specific questions you should address in ZBB include:

- Should a given program, activity, or position be continued, or would other activities be more important or appropriate?
- If the program, activity, or position is justified, should it continue operating in the same manner, or should it be modified?
- If modified, how will it be modified, when, and by whom?
- How much should the organization spend on the program, activity, or position being studied?

The best way to answer these questions in a participatory organization is through a systematic process that starts with the units (micro-systems) of your organization and works upward to your leadership team. Participants in every unit (micro-system) should be asked to develop a process that will engage as many of their own stakeholders as possible in identifying its major intents or outcomes. The process should describe its overall mission, its desired outcomes, exactly what it does, who does it, when it is done, and how much it costs. Then, the process should honestly answer questions such as, "Is this really the best and most cost-effective way to do things? If so, how much will it cost in the coming year, and how can we gather the resources and support needed to continue? If not, what other activities might work as well or better at a lower or equal cost?" The answers to these questions then become part of the participatory budgeting process.

Exploring and answering these questions can lead decision makers to abandon the specific unit, program, or activity. Other options may be thought to be more effective. You may decide to change, strengthen, simplify, redirect, reorganize, outsource, or otherwise change the existing effort, or make no change.

Zero-based budgeting can be a good choice when an organization has been running for a while and is operating on assumptions that are no longer valid. However, it can be very difficult and painful because often jobs and long cherished practices are at stake. If you decide to implement ZBB, remember:

- ZBB must have dependable, detailed-cost information available from the accounting system (which is not always possible).
- ZBB often feels very threatening because it involves evaluating, making comparisons, and deciding on desired changes about activities that may have involved a great deal of personal cognitive and emotional investment.
- ZBB requires fairly detailed planning.

You will find that the choice of budgeting strategy depends on the organization, its stage of development, and the type of organization. Most new participatory organizations benefit from a participatory budgeting strategy, while community collaborations may benefit from a top-down approach. Distributed organizations may benefit from a participatory approach that is delegated to teams at the various units or sites. Zero-based budgeting may be helpful for organizations that have existed for a while and may be flagging in their effectiveness.

Capital Budgets

While yearly budgets are designed to guide your day-to-day spending, **capital budgets** are for major projects and come in two forms, **capital improvement projects** (used to buy, construct, or extensively renovate physical facilities) and **capital equipment projects** (used to acquire expensive equipment for long-term use). They are often associated with capital campaigns designed to raise designated funds.

For an example of a capital campaign budget, we move from Smithville to Middle View, where the Middle View Teen Connection has decided to raise money to purchase and renovate a small office building owned by the village. The capital budget and its related revenue budget are as follows:

Middle View Teen Connection Capital Needs	
Building Purchase Price	$120,000
Snack Bar Equipment	$50,000
Interior Renovations	$30,000
Total Capital Needs	$200,000

Middle View Teen Connection Capital Campaign Revenue Goals	
Snodgrass Foundation Grant	**$100,000**
Major Donors ($1,000 or more)	$75,000
Family and Individual Donors	**$25,000**

These budgets are very simple, but they illustrate some common strategies for capital campaigns. Capital campaigns are always for one-time, major purchases that are likely to catch the attention of donors. Most capital campaigns provide for three gift categories: large grants, especially from private foundations; major gifts from wealthy donors; and smaller gifts from the general public or those who will benefit. Of these, the vast majority of the funds raised come from foundations or other corporate contributors and wealthy, but the funds raised from the board of directors, active volunteers, and general public are often used to assure the larger donors that the capital investment will be used and appreciated by its target community. Capital campaigns are usually the responsibility of a team or task force that divides itself into smaller sub-teams, each of which is charged with one of the donor categories. While some wealthy nonprofits are able to hire consulting firms to handle their capital campaigns, it is likely that your community organizing effort will plan and manage its own effort. Several useful books are cited below.[2]

Cash Flow Budgets

Cash flow budgets give your financial managers and the leadership team the information needed to cope with financial ups and downs. Cash flow, as the name implies, is the amount of actual cash coming into your organization from all of its revenue streams and the money going out of your organization to pay your bills. You have probably experienced cash flow issues in your own household over the course of a year. For example, you may have a monthly household income that is stable over the course of a year, but your expenses may vary considerably from month to month. If you live in the north, you may face a combination of holiday bills and high heating costs in January so your cash flow slows to a trickle. But in June, you may have a high amount of available cash because of an income tax refund and lower summer heating bills. Conversely, you may run a seasonal business with high income during some months and lower income at others which means you have to save during more prosperous times so that you can meet your fixed expenses during leaner times. If you are wise, you will make a family budget plan that allows for these predictable differences in income and expenditures. The same basic principles apply to community organizations. For instance, SNO relies on membership drives for a portion of its income and holds them twice a year in January and June. Inevitably the January revenue is smaller, mainly because the households and small businesses SNO relies on for support are cash strapped in January. The June campaign is often more successful because people are feeling more prosperous, are out and about, and are more likely to take an interest in their neighborhood. SNO is also affected by grant dispersals from its major funding sources. A few years ago, one of its primary foundation supporters was caught in the Bernie Madoff investment fraud and so for several months was only able to provide SNO with half of its expected disbursements. The foundation eventually recovered some of its funding and was able to meet its obligations, but in the meantime, SNO and other grant recipients suffered. You can plan for predictable variations like the annual membership fluctuations. It is much harder to plan for emergencies such as the Madoff crisis. A cash flow budget is an attempt to map the timing of expected highs and lows as well as providing a plan for coping with them. The idea is to time maximum expenditures with maximum income and to plan for ways to cover lean times.[3]

Cash flow issues are particularly difficult in organizations depending heavily on public grants because of the uncertainty of the public budgeting process and public allocations. For instance, because program authorization and funding approval are separate legislative processes, your advocacy program or social movement may have fought hard at the state or national levels for authorization of a new program, only to find that no implementation money is provided in the budget. Or there may be a shortfall in tax revenues during the fiscal year, making third and fourth quarter allocations smaller than anticipated. Or there may be an emergency at the national, state, county, or municipal level requiring reallocation of funds at all levels. Or projected numbers of clientele may fall short so that allocations that are dependent on numbers of clients served may be cut back for the following quarter. All of these can cause major headaches for budget managers.

Let's go back to SNO for an example of cash flow budgeting and follow the 2011 budget patterns in preparation for 2012 cash flow planning. The 2012 SNO expenditure budget totaled $48,600. Fixed monthly expenses were $2,800 for salaries and benefits and $42 for supplies or a total of $2,842 per month. The organization plans to receive $12,000 in foundation grant funding divided by quarters and to raise $20,200 in membership and donations across the year with principal campaigns in January and June. Here is a breakdown of expenses and income:

SNO 2012 Cash Flow Budget			
Month	**Expenses**	**Income**	**Balance**
January	$2,842	Major foundation income $3,000 + memberships and donations (winter campaign) $6,734 + monthly Americorps payment $1,421 = $11,155	$8,313
February	$2,842	Americorps payment $1,421	$6,892
March	$2,842	Americorps payment $1,421	$5,471
April	$2, 842 + Conference fees $1,500 = $4,342	Foundation income $3,000; Americorps payment $1,421 = $4,421	$5,550
May	$2,842 + $500 prep for June campaign + $1,000 micro-loan + $500 garden expense = $4,842	Americorps payment $1,421	$2,129
June	$2,842 + $500 block party = $3,342	Americorps payment $1,421	$208
July	$2,842 + $500 block party + $1,000 micro-loan = $4,342	Foundation income $3,000; Americorps payment $1,421; Summer campaign $13,468 = $17,889	$13,755
August	$2,842 + 2 block parties $1,000 + micro-loan $1,000 + church rent $150 = $4,992	Americorps payment $1,421	$10,184
September	$2,842 + 2 block parties $1,000 + 1 micro-loan $1,000 = $4,842	Americorps payment $1,421	$6,763
October	$2,842	Foundation income $3,000; Americorps payment $1,421 = $4,421	$7,142
November	$2,842	Americorps payment $1,421	$6,721
December	$2,842 + January campaign $500 + advocacy campaign $2,000 + Block Club holiday expenses $500 = $5842	Americorps payment $1,421	$2,300

The cash flow budget shows that SNO managed its cash flow fairly well during 2011 with a noticeable surge in expenses starting in April and continuing into June when the annual organizing conference, expenses for the June fund-raising campaign, expenses for the community gardens, and some micro-enterprise expenses coincided. It was decided that although the 2012 budget would parallel the 2011 budget in some respects, the May outlay for a micro-enterprise loan would be delayed until July after receipt of the grant payments. This, of course, is a very simple version of a cash flow budget. In real life budget adjustments would occur every month as income decreased or increased, but this gives you an idea of how income and expenses may flow across the course of a year.

Contingency Management and Coping with Funding Emergencies

Contingency management is related to cash flow budgeting because it provides a process you can use to help your organization weather both cash flow slowdowns and major disasters. The following is a guide to contingency planning and coping with funding emergencies.

PHASE ONE: BEFORE THE STORM—PREPARATION The best preparation is prevention. If at all possible, you should develop redundant funding streams, especially from unrestricted funding sources that can be moved from one budget category to another. So, for instance, if a contract falls through, money can be moved to that program temporarily so that staffing can be maintained and clients can continue to be served.

You should develop a contingency fund or funds in the budget preparation phase that can be used in time of need. The ideal contingency fund contains enough money to maintain your operation for two pay periods or in the case of volunteer efforts for two or three months. Components of a contingency fund may include savings accounts or investments (based on IRS regulations), unrestricted endowments that can be used in the short term for general operating costs, and money brought forward from past years. Contingency funds are for the unexpected. They should *never* be used to fund expenses that should have been anticipated. Agencies that have used contingency funds for ongoing expenses have been censured by the IRS and have sometimes lost their non-profit standing, and the officials responsible have occasionally been fired.

Many well-established non-profits develop working relationships with banks and other financial institutions ahead of a budget crisis so that a line of credit is immediately available for cash flow problems. Large organizations such as Community Action Agencies that are heavily grant dependent often find themselves taking this route. One selling point of the for-benefit or private form of altruism is that, as private entities, for-benefit organizations are more attractive to financial institutions than are typical non-profit organizations. Newer initiatives do not usually have an established line of credit, but even mutual aid–based organizations can develop a small contingency fund for emergencies and develop ways of sharing resources and supporting one another through difficult times. They may develop contingency plans for sharing housing expenses, food, transportation, and child care until funding levels improve.

PHASE TWO: AS THE STORM NEARS—BATTENING THE HATCHES Budgeting crises often hit rather quickly, but there may be a few days or weeks in which to prepare. The best approach when facing an impending major budget crisis is to develop an ad hoc crisis team to examine the situation and make recommendations to the leadership team. The ad hoc team should be appointed by the leadership team and should have authority to gather any information needed for good decision making. It should use principles of healthy teamwork and equality. The team leader should have authority to direct the communication process and should be encouraged to use democratic (that is, turn taking) or nominal group (such as going around the circle to get everyone's opinion) methods to ensure that no single person dominates. Membership on the ad hoc team should be between four and seven people. Because time is of the essence, the team should be empowered to make recommendations even if every member cannot be present for every meeting. The facilitator should take responsibility for keeping all members "up to speed," and decision making should be by consensus as much as possible.

Team membership should include respected representatives of all stakeholders who will be affected by the budget crisis, including direct service personnel, beneficiaries, and members of the public. The inclusion of people who are "on the firing line" can do a great deal to ensure that high-quality services are maintained. The composition of the team may vary but might include (1) the chief executive officer or chief financial officer or designee, (2) board members or other decision makers representing the budget and funding committees, (3) program manager(s) of the endangered program, (4) direct service staff known to be respected among their colleagues, and occasionally (5) clients or family representatives.

The team mission should be to make concrete recommendations for ways to meet the fiscal crisis in a timely manner. The secondary mission is to build solidarity and trust among team participants which they, in turn, communicate to others in the organization. As a result, everyone is ready to face a "common enemy" and in-fighting is minimized.

The facilitator (team leader) should ensure that timely written recommendations of the ad hoc committee are presented to all committee participants who have decision-making authority. Once the necessary approvals are granted, the leadership team should outline the plan to all stakeholders through written memos and formal meetings. The goal of this phase is to quell rumors and to gain support for recommended strategies.

Of course, some emergencies come quickly and do not allow for the creation of such a crisis team. In those instances, the members of the leadership team must be prepared to act, much as a sea captain acts in the midst of a storm. Such authoritarian leadership should not be exercised lightly but may be necessary.

PHASE THREE: RIDING OUT THE STORM One key to riding out a financial storm is to enable all stakeholders including board, administration, service staff, clients, and the community to maintain trust and mutual support. Continuous uninterrupted service to those being served should be a priority, as should the maintenance of staff morale. Everyone's morale can be maintained by keeping lines of communication open. This prevents rumors from running rampant and the potential disruption of the daily flow of service due to endless gossip sessions. Open communication may also prevent vital staff members from "jumping ship," leaving the organization adrift without its most creative talent.

Managers in the midst of financial crisis tend to use various means to cut costs, usually by laying off staff. While this is easy and tempting, it is also very demotivating not only for those who are eliminated but for those who remain. Too often, cost-cutting managers eliminate direct service personnel. Not only does this decrease the quality of services, but it may result in limited savings because direct care provider salaries are relatively low when compared to managers'. Moreover, elimination of direct care providers may be frightening to clients and their families since clients lose the very people with whom they have developed caring relationships. For these reasons, cost-cutting managers should consider eliminating administrative or support positions or cutting their own salaries before eliminating direct service providers.

It may be that the best managers negotiate across-the-board salary cuts with the highest paid people, taking the cuts in proportionate dollar amounts. This willingness to sacrifice on the part of administrators sends a clear message to direct service workers, making them much more willing to work extra hours if necessary to maintain high-quality services. On the other hand, cutting direct service providers while maintaining a top-heavy administration is extremely demotivating and usually hurts services.

A second key to riding out a financial storm is to make the friends and potential friends of the organization aware of its needs. Friends of the organization include persons or organizations that have provided substantial funding in the past, as well as clients and their families. This inner circle of supporters may be most likely to provide immediate assistance. The second group that should be informed of a financial crisis is comprised of elected officials who can often unblock problems such as stalled allocations, unreasonable regulations, or refusal of the executive branch to sign off on funding. Local, regional, and even national media are also part of this second circle. The media are often looking for human interest stories. Funding cuts to needed services, especially those delivered to persons who are considered worthy—such as children, the disabled, and the elderly—are often considered news. Positive media attention can bring in donations and other direct support, as well as putting pressure on reticent funding sources to provide promised support. The general public is the third circle of support, although they are the hardest to reach. Friends of the organization should be encouraged to tell of its need through word of mouth. Rapidly organized fund-raising events, such as concerts, can also be useful for both raising needed money and garnering general awareness of the cause and its struggles.

Such "rallying of the troops" is important for all organizations facing financial crisis. It can work very well for organizations serving clients who appeal to the public because of their vulnerability (for example, young children), but it can be much harder for organizations serving stigmatized individuals, such released prisoners, drug addicts, the mentally ill, or social action groups that are considered troublemakers.

However, even the most desperate financial storms can usually be ridden out with minimum damage if teamwork and hope are maintained. Stakeholders at all levels—but especially upper management—should be encouraged to voluntarily make reasonable cuts in purchases, maintenance, staff training, travel, and other expenses and to look for ways to cut costs. Even if the savings attained are minimal, the message of fiscal responsibility and shared sacrifice will be appreciated.

PHASE FOUR: RECOVERY After every storm a new day eventually dawns. If the other three phases have been successfully managed, the recovery phase can be reasonably painless. The recovery phase involves taking inventory of the situation, doing triage, and bringing services back up to maximum levels smoothly. Once the organization is on a reasonably even keel, a systematic effort should be made to obtain feedback on how well (or poorly) the situation was handled. Information gathering techniques at this phase may include confidential surveys of stakeholders, focus groups, personal interviews with key players, and systematic observation. The goal of information gathering should be to present a clear picture of what happened, why it happened, what was done about it, and whether the response was excellent, adequate, or in need of improvement. This information should, in turn, be used in a new preparation phase so that the organization is ready for the next inevitable crisis.

Contingency planning and the development of contingency funding should be an ongoing process. As the organization builds its reputation for good service and acquires contingency funding, fiscal crises should decrease. As in most ventures, the first few years are usually the hardest.

Income Budgeting and Funding Strategies

The best way to avoid or at least mitigate funding emergencies is to have funding from a variety of resources so that you are not too dependent on a single source of income. Funding is a constant concern, especially for new initiatives, so income budgeting and fund-raising is a continuous process. It is likely that you will find yourselves frequently revising your income budget(s) depending on the availability (or loss) of income sources.

Income budgeting can be tricky. You will often be tempted to seek funding just because it is available, but be sure that funding source requirements match your desired outcomes, support your mission, do not come with too many "strings" attached, and are not more trouble administratively than they are worth. Your goal should always be organizational stability even if that means somewhat limited growth.

One of the many myths of our society is that money is everything. Many times community organizers and grassroots community leaders say, "If only we could just get a grant somewhere, we could do Y" or "Our first task is to raise money." Community organizing efforts actually often work in the opposite direction. Some success breeds more success. Once you begin to demonstrate that you have identified a need and are meeting it even on a limited budget, more substantial funding often follows. Many, if not most, successful initiatives begin with almost nothing but a dream and WUNC (worthiness, unity, numbers, and commitment).

Although you will soon learn the meaning of the phrase "pinching every penny twice," astute resource development will enable your effort to survive and thrive. Thus, this section concentrates on funding and presents various funding strategies. Remember it is usually best to mix sources of income so that your venture is not too dependent on any particular source.

Government Grants

Grants are often a useful way to obtain start-up funding for a new initiative. There are literally thousands of grants available for a multitude of purposes, many of which are coordinated through a collaborative effort headed by the federal Department of Health and Human Services. See Grants.gov at http://www.grants.gov/ to start your Web search. Eligibility for funding of different kinds flows directly from your organization's tax status and mission. Innovative nonprofit 501c-3 corporations are given priority for government grants. In fact, eligibility for grants is the reason many organizations take the time and trouble to apply for the non-profit designation. However, do *not* make the mistake of believing that government grants are the answer to funding problems. Most government grants are actually intended to be field experiments or demonstration projects and are not intended for long-term funding. Because they are experiments, they are likely to be designed to test certain hypotheses and have strict parameters and extensive record keeping requirements which take time and energy away from your mission. Recipients often find that after a few years with a promising beginning, they are left without continuing funding.

Grants can help demonstrate that your service is needed and buy time until a major funding stream can be located, but they are not reliable in the long run. Although many government grants are intended to help underserved areas and underserved populations, they are often only intended to provide **seed money** (that is, start-up funds). All too soon you will be expected to provide local funding. Many grants fund for three years in decreasing percentages: first year the grant will cover 90% of the costs while your organization will be expected to bear 10%, the second year grant will cover half of the costs while you will be expected to bear the other half, the third year the grant will pay 10% of the costs, and then you will be expected to be on your own. Time moves very quickly, and because many community organizing efforts are located in poor communities, it is often impossible to develop a local funding base in just three years. Without enough local funding, an excellent program may die. If people have come to count on its services, the death of a grant-funded program can be worse for its clients than never having had it at all.

Only apply for grants that match your mission, values, desired outcomes, and implementation plans. Agencies which chase a different grant every time their former grant runs out often find that they have drifted from their original mission and no longer have an identity. This **mission drift** can alienate donors, staff, and volunteers.

Moreover, some grants are literally more trouble than they are worth. Because public agencies often use grantees as demonstration projects to test treatment approaches, their tightly defined target audience, outcomes, and recommended processes may or may not fit directly into your mission. They can be overly restrictive, have fiscal years or payment outlay schedules that conflict with your cash flow needs, insist upon quantitative outcomes measures that are inappropriate or impossible to compile, or depend upon service models that are known to be ineffective. It can be very frustrating to turn away needy people or reject worthy activities because they conflict with strict grant criteria. But violating grant restrictions can lead to serious legal trouble.

Your leadership and budgeting team should examine **requests for proposals** (RFPs—documents that grant-making agencies provide to interested providers) carefully to ensure that they fit well into the mission of the organization, do not require unreasonable restrictions or extensive reporting requirements, do not take resources away from your primary mission, and are compatible with other funding sources. Grants can be helpful if you use them carefully as a part of an overall funding mix and as a way to fill in service gaps, not as an ongoing source of operating funds.

Government Contracts

Government contracts can often become a major source of long-term funding. County and state governments, in particular, have chosen to rely less on directly providing services and more on contracting with private non-profit and for-benefit agencies. Contracts are important sources of funding for the core administrative functions and may become your major source of long-term financing because many government grants fund only direct services, often for a limited period, and many foundation grants fund primarily capital projects. For instance, the Middle View runaway prevention program began with a small amount of local funding from donors and the Middle View United Fund, then moved to a year of grant-based funding, but has operated for almost forty years on contracts with the county and state governments. For many social innovations, attaining such long-term government contracts makes sense. If you choose to pursue long-term government contracts, your leadership and funding teams will need to understand how these contracts are negotiated and maintained. You will need to be politically astute and maintain communication with key decision makers because competition among agencies can be intense, especially in lean times and where established agencies already have a "lock" on available contracts.

Block Grant Allocations

The block grant process was initiated in 1974 under President Gerald Ford and has been part of the federal system in various forms ever since. It is an attempt to redistribute federal tax income by recognizing that states and local governments may have a better idea of where federal money should be spent than national-level decision makers would. Block grant rules change frequently and are too complicated to discuss in detail, but the enabling legislation typically sets broad parameters for its uses, and then local governments are charged with specific distribution plans. Some municipalities use their block grants for the same services year after year, while others are more willing to use a zero based budgeting process in which those receiving block grant funds must justify their requests each year and new organizations are reviewed on equal footing with more established ones. However, block grant funding generally follows precedent. It is possible for new organizations to use mildly coercive social action tactics to be considered for block grant funding, but politicians are frequently reluctant to offend their established political supporters or disrupt established services by funding new efforts.

Foundation Grants

There are many foundations throughout the country that provide funding for a multitude of services.[4] Foundation grants have many of the same problems as public grants, but generally they have the advantage of additional flexibility and some informality. For example, it is generally possible to more easily negotiate line item budget changes with a foundation board than to change a public grant. Foundations, in general, do not like to fund operating budgets. However, foundation grants can be very useful for brick-and-mortar projects or as the core of a broader capital campaign. Community foundations—which are supported by many small bequests—can be particularly helpful to small community-based projects, especially if your group clearly identifies its target system. For example, the Middle View runaway prevention project benefited from a bequest that specifically targeted Middle View and enabled it to complete major renovations, including an expensive new roof.

Foundations often fund collaborations among large, established organizations such as universities, medical centers, economic development corporations, and governments, but many have no provision for ensuring that place-based relational organizing efforts or community advocacy groups are included. This tendency of foundations to overlook small community-based organizations almost caused major problems for Smithville and the SNO. Smithville is bordered by the campus of XYZ State University. Several years ago, three forces came together within the university's walls: the university's administration became concerned about (1) the proximity of deteriorating buildings, (2) the introduction of crime, and (3) increasing incidence of drug abuse on its pristine campus. The state university's development office became aware of the potential for lucrative government grants for projects that address the needs of inner-city communities, and several professors saw the potential for community-based service learning experiences. With encouragement from the administration and professors, the development office contacted a local foundation, developed a proposal, and received substantial funding to develop a coalition charged with improving the quality of life in Smithville. University representatives recruited several large non-profit agencies, government organizations, and a few of the larger employers in and around Smithville to send representatives to serve on the coalition's decision-making body. At first no one thought of including the SNO, because none of the coalition members lived in Smithville and most thought of the area as hopelessly blighted. Fortunately, the XYZ staff coordinator of the foundation grant was well aware of the SNO, lived in the neighborhood, and respected many of the natural community leaders. The coordinator made sure that several SNO representatives were included on the XYZ coalition and that their voices were heard at coalition meetings. To their credit, the other coalition members listened. The result was an initiative that benefited everyone. Foundation money was used wisely and the university–neighborhood bond was strengthened.

Benefactors

Many community organizing efforts (as well as established institutions) spend much time cultivating **benefactors** (moneyed individuals) for major financial support. The term *benefactor* is most commonly associated with advocacy and social movements and connotes a person or social institution that is committed to a social justice issue but is not directly affected by it. Benefactors play very useful roles, providing direct funding, legitimacy and protection through their reputation and connections, and links to their wealthy friends and colleagues. Your leadership team may decide to make identifying and cultivating such benefactors a priority. However, remember that the common saying "money talks loudly" can be true of benefactors. Many expect that their financial contributions will give them a greater say than others in the mission, objectives, strategies, and tactics of your organization. Although benefactors have a right to be thanked and have the same right as everyone else to have their ideas and concerns heard, their contributions and powerful connections do not give them the right to explicitly or implicitly demand obedience. Your focal community's needs and your organizational mission should remain your top priorities no matter what your benefactors may want.

Dues and Memberships

You may want to offer memberships to people who support your mission. Memberships may simply be a type of donation, or they may have benefits, such as reduced admission to special events or access to publications. Memberships can be especially helpful to organizations that serve a relatively well-off population or are focused on issues that may be unpopular with the general public. The advantage of memberships is that they may generally be used for any legitimate purpose within the by-laws of the organization.

"In Kind" Contributions

Many grants require a "local match" to prove that there is substantial commitment to a project. Sometimes this local match is in the form of cash, but often it is in the form of "in-kind" contributions, especially in communities and among target populations where cash is limited and time is readily available. An in-kind contribution is the donation of goods or services based on their fair market value. Volunteers are an excellent source of in-kind contributions, but their services must be counted according to their market value. For instance, if a therapist volunteers to counsel families, his counseling services may be worth $50 to $100 per hour based on the fair market rate in your area. If the same therapist volunteers to paint the agency kitchen or design pamphlets, his services would only be worth minimum wage, unless he is a painting contractor or marketing specialist as well as a therapist. If you choose to include in-kind services in your budget, you must develop clear ways of accounting for them. This takes time and effort but can be very worthwhile not only for matching other sources of funding but for demonstrating the depth of volunteer commitment.

Per Diem Funding

Many institutions, group homes, and day programs rely on *per diem* **funding** (funding by the day). This is particularly common with agencies that work with court placement, such as family services and juvenile probation, as well as such services as day care and elder care, and is often based on the level and number of services needed by a particular person. It is important to set the *per diem* costs high enough to meet your expenses because fixed expenses remain stable despite variations in program census. However, it is also important to keep fees low enough to remain competitive. It is also important to develop positive relationships with potential referral resources. *Per diems* can be a major source of income but can be somewhat unreliable because they depend totally on referrals. For the Middle View runaway prevention project that you have been following, *per diem* is only the second major source of funding (after a consistent state contract for services) because it is somewhat unreliable.

Fees for Service

Many social entrepreneurships and social innovations rely on fees for service for at least part of their budget. Fee for service funding can be obtained directly from clients, their families, or from third parties, such as insurance companies or the government. Most human service organizations with fee-for-service arrangements operate on a **sliding fee scale** based on consumer income. As with *per diem* funding, it is important to develop a fee schedule that will support the agency without overcharging. Many altruistic efforts, especially those that provide services to the very poor, are reluctant to collect fees, but ironically—because of an innate suspicion of "getting something for nothing"—people often respond better to services that require some payment than those that are completely free. Payment does not always have to be in currency; it can be in volunteer time committed by recipients as in the very successful model used by Habitat for Humanity.

Fund-raising

Chances are you will decide to begin raising funds as soon as you decide to move from talk to action.[5] Fund-raising can be especially important for new organizations. It gives seed money for initial activities and demonstrates broad-based community support. Demonstrable community support, in turn, opens outside funding streams and may also even help with other issues such as government regulation and political resistance.

Fund-raising efforts come in a variety of forms. Some successful organizations develop **auxiliaries**, **foundations**, or **advisory groups** to coordinate fund-raising activities. These collective volunteers function as liaisons between the organization and the broader community and raise needed funds. Often such organizations serve as a social outlet for their members who provide the extra energy needed for major fund-raising special events, such as golf outings, banquets, bazaars, carnivals, concerts, and casino nights, to name a few. For instance, the Town of Middle View—like many rural areas—has a very active volunteer fire department. Its auxiliary holds weekly chicken-and-biscuit dinners, semi-annual craft fairs, and periodic car washes and other events throughout the year. Over the years, these activities have raised thousands of dollars for needed equipment while serving the community as opportunities to gather to enjoy a good meal and good company. If you are choosing an event, be very careful to accurately estimate expenses beforehand. Remember: your goal is to *increase* net revenues.

Other fund-raising tactics include direct mail or e-mail solicitation, door-to-door campaigns, annual campaigns, and capital campaigns. Your fund-raising team should develop a systematic marketing plan that strives to "cast a wide net" that includes all of your various constituencies: staff, board members, benefactors, client families, and former clients. Make donating as easy as possible through as many means as possible. For example, most people find it easier to donate online through their credit or debit card accounts rather than to mail in payments; setting up such payment options is worth the effort. Your website should provide an easy, protected way for people to donate throughout the year, as well as alerting constituents to opportunities to support particular projects or special needs of the organization.

You may wish to contact some potential major donors individually. Sometimes your board members may have social or business contacts who can be approached for major gifts. Anyone who establishes a record of giving, no matter how small, should be thanked, acknowledged, and kept informed of further developments in the work of your organization. Any fund-raising should be done tastefully and with attention to issues such as confidentiality. Selling your donor list to another agency is ethically questionable. If you decide to do so, you should make your donors aware of your practice and give them the opportunity to opt out. The Free Nonprofit Management Library at http://managementhelp.org/ offers many suggestions for marketing campaigns.

Partnering with Businesses

At times it may be beneficial to solicit or accept support from a business entity in exchange for free advertising and goodwill. For instance, Smithville's largest hospital in Industrial City gave a grant to the community garden and was rewarded with a large visible "thank you" sign on the site at a busy urban intersection. In Middle View, the local pizza shops, grocery stores, and other food stores often donate food for fund-raising dinners. Other business owners buy advertising space in concert and theater programs and the high school yearbook. This form of fund-raising appears to be more and more common. For instance, the fight against breast cancer has benefited from association with different products (aimed mostly at women) which advertise that part of every purchase goes to the cause. The best partnerships seem to be based on mutual benefit; businesses benefit from goodwill and sometimes free advertising while the non-profits benefit from financing. As in other situations, you must beware of co-option. For example, it seems that at least some health-related, self-help, and research efforts may have been at least partially co-opted by the pharmaceutical companies that provide much of their funding.

More on Accurate Accounting

You now know how to use participatory methods to build budgets; and you have a yearly expenditure budget balanced by a revenue budget. You have some idea of your likely cash flow, a contingency plan for emergencies, and ongoing strategies for diversified funding. Now let's take another look at accounting issues. Budgeting and accurate accounting go hand in hand. Contributors and especially grant funders often require complex accounting practices. This section is intended to expand your thinking on this topic:

- Accurate, honest, clear accounting practices that scrupulously follow reporting guidelines required by funding agencies, the IRS, and programmatic regulatory agencies are absolutely crucial to financial management in non-profit and for-benefit organizations. In many instances, agency managers are publicly accused of fraud and face ruined careers when they are simply the victims of poor accounting procedures in which funds were moved from one useful category or account to another without proper authorization. Improper budget management can lead to serious trouble even if no malfeasance was intended. Altruistic intentions never excuse poor budget practices.
- Accounts must be set up in light of the fiscal year of each funding source, and clear tracking must be available so that the status of each of the separate accounts is clearly visible in the main accounting record. A very basic rule for accounting is that all income and all expenditures must be clearly tracked as required by the funding agencies and in the agency's master accounts. Note that each funding source or grant program may have different reporting requirements and different fiscal years. For instance:
  - Many state and local governments operate on a fiscal year of July 1 to June 30.
  - The federal government's fiscal year is from November 1 to October 31.
  - Many foundations and other organizations operate on the calendar year, January 1 to December 31.
  - Good accounting practice requires that there be little possibility or temptation to misuse funds.
  - At a minimum, this means that every check must have at least two signatures.
  - There should be clear separation of accounting functions. For instance, the person requisitioning supplies and the person authorizing purchases should be different people. In small organizations where it is not possible to have two positions, the two functions should be clearly differentiated in the job description, and clear, written procedures should be in place.
  - Cash should be used as little as possible. If cash is used, receipts should be given and accounted for.
  - Receipts should be used scrupulously for in-kind contributions of services or goods. In-kind services should be accounted for according to the work performed, not the credentials of the donor. Contributions of goods should likewise be evaluated at or even below their fair market value. For instance, a rusty automobile that needs extensive repairs should not be appraised as a new car! All of these points may seem to be just good common sense, but poor accounting for even a few dollars can cause multiple repercussions.

Every 501c-3 organization is expected to file Form 990 with the IRS yearly while other tax-exempt organizations have their own filing requirements. Form 990 provides extensive information on the organization's services, management practices, the ratio of money spent for service provision to administrative costs, and so forth. It is important to keep accurate data for this important form in case of an audit. In addition to its obvious interest to the IRS, Form 990 is used by so called watch-dog groups to track and rate the efficiency of use of charitable funds. Such groups publish information on non-profit organizations on the Internet. Donors frequently make decisions based on these ratings, so it is best to be very aware of the organization's cost–benefit ratio and keep costs down and direct benefits up.

Notes

1. Scot, L. (2010). *The simplified guide to not-for-profit accounting formation and reporting.* Hoboken, NJ:Wiley; Dropkin, M., Halpin, J., & LaTouche, B. (2007). *The budget building book for nonprofits: A step-by-step guide for managers and boards* (2nd ed.). San Francisco, CA: Jossey-Bass.
2. Grover, S. (2006). *Capital* campaigns*: A guide for board members and others who aren't professional fundraisers but who will be the heroes who create a better community.* Bloomington, IN: iUniverse Inc.; Kihlstedt, A. (2009). *Capital campaigns: Strategies that work* (3rd ed.). Burlington, MA: Jones and Bartlett Publishers; Bray, I. (2010). *Effective fundraising for nonprofits: Real-world strategies that work.* Berkley, CA: NoLo.
3. Dropkin, M., Halpin, & LaTouche (2007).
4. Korten, A. (2009). Change philanthropy: Candid stories of foundations maximizing results through social justice. Kim Kline's Fund Raising Series. San Francisco, CA: Jossey-Bass; Fleishman, J. (2009). The foundation: A great American secret—How private wealth is changing the world. New York City, NY: Public Affairs; The Foundation Center. (n.d.). Retrieved October 31, 2012, from http://foundationcenter.org—the major resource for foundation funding in the U.S.
5. Helwig, R., & Sandlin, E. (2010). 199 fun and effective fundraising events for nonprofit organizations. Ocala, FL: Atlantic Publishing Company.

Notes for Chapter 2

1. D. Hyman, J. McKnight and F. Higdon. (2001). *Doing Democracy: Conflict and Consensus Strategies for Citizens, Organizations, and Communities*. Ann Arbor Michigan, XanEdu.
2. Liddle, K. "Commerce, connections, and community: The case of feminist bookstore customers." Paper presented at the Annual Meeting of the Society for the Study of Social Problems. Montreal, Quebec, Canada: August 2006.

Notes for Chapter 3

1. Piaget, J. *The Equilibration of Cognitive Structures*. Chicago, IL: University of Chicago Press: 1985. Note on terms: **Assimilation** is the slow, consistent process of adding new information to old. It is the way most learning occurs, including our understanding of community life. **Accommodation**, on the other hand, involves a significant shift in the way we view the world and usually occurs through the disruption of our daily patterns. Accommodation requires stretching our mental categories to make room for new ideas, experiences, and feelings. **Equilibration** is Piaget's term for the master learning process, encompassing both assimilation and accommodation—a dynamic process of constantly constructing and reconstructing cognitive structures, for example, our understanding of community dynamics.
2. Anderson, John R. *Cognitive Psychology and Its Implications*. 7th ed. Worth Publishers: 2009 Note: Such experiences can be direct or indirect. While direct personal experiences are probably the most powerful building blocks of schemata, they are also affected by imagined experiences and vicarious experiences through stories, reading, movies, and other media. For instance, many of our stereotypes of community life in rural areas, suburbs, and inner cities are greatly influenced by movies and television.
3. Block, Peter and John McKnight. "Abundant Community: Awakening the Power of Communities and Neighborhoods." January 1, 2001. http://www.abundantcommunity.com/forms/pages/page/home.html (accessed August 14, 2011); McKnight, John and Peter Block. *The Abundant Community: Awakening the Power of Families and Neighborhoods*. American Planning Association and BK Publishers, 2010; Kretzman, John and John McKnight. *Building Communities from the Inside Out: A Path toward Finding and Mobilizing a Community's Assets*. ACTA Publications, 1993.
4. Thiessen-Nation, M. *Realizing Hope in the Midst of Despair: Narratives of an Urban Mission Community*. Fuller Theological Seminary, Doctoral Thesis in Intercultural Studies.
5. Lamont, M. and V. Molnar. "The Study of Boundaries in the Social Sciences." *Annual Review of Sociology*. Vol. 28(1) (2002): 167–195.
6. Ashmore, R. D., K. Deux, and T. McLaughlin-Volpe. "An Organizing Framework for Collective Identity: Articulation and Significance of Multidimensionality" *Psychological Bulletin*. Vol. 130(1) (2004): 18–114.
7. Ibid.
8. Ibid.
9. Warner, R., M. Hornsey, and J. Jetten. "Why Minority Groups Resent Imposters." *European Journal of Social Psychology* Vol. 37(1) (2007): 1–17 .
10. Ashmore, Deux, and McLaughlin-Volpe; Gecas, V. and M. Schwalbe. "Beyond the Looking Glass Self: Social Structure and Efficacy Based Self-esteem." *Social Science Quarterly*. Vol. 46(2) (1983): 77–88; Gecas, V. "The Self-concept." *Annual Review of Sociology*. Vol. 8 (1982): 1–33.
11. Brubaker, R. and F. Cooper. "Beyond Identity." *Theory and Society*. Vol. 29(1) (2000): 1–47 (Note: Group or community identity is based on what the famous German sociologist Max Weber called *zusammengehorigkeitsgeful*, a feeling of "belonging together" that includes commonality and connectedness through the sharing of particular meaningful events and compelling narratives or stories).
12. Jenkins, 1996, quoted in Lamont, M. and Virag Molnar. "The Study of Boundaries in the Social Sciences." *Annual Review of Sociology*. Vol. 28(1) (2002): 167–195.
13. Brewer, M. and W. Gardner. "Who Is This 'We'? Levels of Collective Identity and Self-representation." *Journal of Personality and Social Psychology*. Vol. 71(1) (1996): 83–93.
14. Lamont and Molnar, 2002.
15. Cooley, C. H. *Human Nature and the Social Order*. New York: Charles Scribner's Sons, 1902; revised ed., 1922.
16. Mead, G. H. *Mind, Self, and Society*. Ed. by Charles W. Morris. Chicago, IL: University of Chicago Press, 1934. Note: Mead did not write any books of his own; his student Charles W. Morris collected and edited his papers and published them as this book through the press of the University of Chicago, where Mead taught for many years.

17. Blumer, H. *Symbolic Interactionism: Perspective and Method.* New Jersey: Prentice-Hall, 1969.
18. Cooley, C. H. "The Looking Glass Self." In *Human Nature and the Social Order.* New York: Scribners, 1902 (available online in the public domain). Scheff, T. J. "Looking Glass Self: Goffman as Symbolic Interactionist." *Symbolic Interaction* Vol. 28(2) (2005): 145–166.
19. Goffman, E. *The Presentation of Self in Everyday Life.* Edinburgh, UK: University of Edinburgh Social Sciences Research Centre. Anchor Books edition, 1959.
20. Granovetter, M. "The Strength of Weak Ties." *American Journal of Sociology.* Vol. 78(6) (May, 1973): 1360–1380; Granovetter, M. "The Strength of Weak Ties: A Network Theory Revisited." *Sociological Theory.* (1983): 201–233.

Notes for Chapter 4

1. McKnight, J. (1995). *Toward a grounded substantive theory of the control of learning in altruistic grassroots initiatives.* Ann Arbor, MI: UMI #9531987, and ongoing unpublished research.
2. Noddings, N. (2003). *Caring: A feminine approach to ethics and moral education* (2nd ed.). Berkley, CA: University of California Press; Noddings, N. (2002). *Starting at home: Caring and social policy.* University of California Press. Berkley, CA.
3. Mizrahi, Terry. (n.d.). Educational center for community organizing. Hunter College. Retrieved May 4, 2010, from http://www.hunter.cuny.edu/socwork/ecco/; Joseph, B., Lob, S., McLaughlin, P., Mizrahi, T., Peterson, J., Richie, B., Rosenthal, B., & Sugarman, F. (n.d.) Women Organizers' Project: Hunter College. Retrieved May 4, 2010, from http://www.hunter.cuny.edu/socwork/ecco/
4. McKnight, J. (1995). *Toward a grounded substantive theory of the control of learning in altruistic grassroots initiatives.* Ann Arbor, MI: UMI #9531987, and ongoing unpublished research.
5. Martin, R. & Osberg, S. (2007). Social entrepreneurship: The case for definition. *Stanford Social Innovation Review* (Spring).Vol. 11 p. 28–39. The author is aware that the term *social entrepreneurship* is now frequently used to indicate a mixed organizational form that combines the business goal of profit making with the altruistic goal of making a positive difference in society. Here the term is used in the sense that it is used in the business world, for an enterprise that is the "brain child" of a single individual or partnership who provide its driving force.
6. Roberts, D. & Woods, C. (2005). Changing the world on a shoestring: The concept of social entrepreneurship. *University of Maryland Business Review, 7*(1), 45–51.
7. Thompson, J. L. (2002). The world of the social entrepreneur. *The International Journal of Public Sector Management, 15*(4/5), 412.
8. Santora, J. & Sarros, J. (1995). Mortality and leadership succession: A case study. *Leadership and Organization Development Journal,* 16(7), 29–32; Stevens, S. K. (1999). "Tricky transitions: Healthy boards help founding entrepreneurs with succession." *Grantmakers in the Arts Newsletter,*10, 9–10.
9. McNamara, C. (2007). Founders' syndrome: How corporations suffer and can recover. Free Management Library. Retrieved July 15, 2010, from http://www.managementhelp.org/misc/founders.htm
10. McKnight, J. (1995). *Toward a grounded substantive theory of the control of learning in altruistic grassroots initiatives.* Ann Arbor, MI: UMI #9531987.
11. Ibid.
12. Kristof, N. & WuDunn, S. (2010). *Half the sky: Turning oppression into opportunity for women worldwide.* New York: Vintage Books; Yunus, M. (2007). *Creating a world without poverty: Social business and the future of capitalism.* New York: Public Affairs; Schumacher, E. F. (1973). *Small is beautiful: Economics as if people mattered.* New York: Harper Row; Crowley, E., Baas, S., Termine, P. & Dionne, G. (2005). Organizations of the poor: Conditions for success. *Proceedings of Cornell/SEWA/ETP/WIEGO International Conference on Membership Based Organizations of the Poor: Theory, Experience, and Policy,* Amedabad, India, 23–25; Korten, D. (2010). *Agenda for a new economy: From phantom wealth to real wealth.* San Francisco, CA: Barrett-Kohler Publishers.
13. Williams, C. (1996). Local purchasing schemes and rural development: An evaluation of local exchange and trading systems (LETS). *Journal of Rural Studies, 12*(3), 231–244.
14. Time Banks USA. (n.d.). Time banks. Retrieved July 29, 2010, from http://www.timebanks.org/
15. Tiso, P. (n.d.). BerkShares: Local currency for the Berkshire region. Retrieved February 21, 2011, from http://www.berkshares.org/index.htm; North, P. (2007). *Money and liberation: The micropolitics of alternative currency movements.* Minneapolis,MN:University of Minnesota Press; North, P. (2010). *Local money: How to make it happen in your community.* Cambridge,UK: Green Books.
16. Chen, Jhabala, Kandur, & Richards. (2005). Membership organizations of the poor: Concepts, experience, and policy. *Proceedings of Cornell/SEWA/ETP/WIEGO International Conference on Membership Based Organizations of the Poor: Theory, Experience, and Policy.* Ahmedabad, India, 23–25.

17. Koshal, R. & Koshal, M. (1973). Gandhian economic philosophy. *American Journal of Economics and Sociology, 22*(2)191–2210; Gandhi, M. (2008). *Mahatma Gandhi: The essential writings.* Judith M. Brown (Ed.). New York: Oxford University Press.
18. Kristof, N. & WuDunn, S. (2010). *Half the sky: Turning oppression into opportunity for women worldwide.* New York: Vintage Books; USAID Women in Development. (n.d.). Gender and economic value chains: Two case studies from the GATE Project. Retrieved July 30, 2010, from http://www.fsnnetwork.org/sites/default/gender_agriculture_value_chain_guide.pdf
19. Maton, K. (2000). Mutual aid and *self-help. In Encyclopedia of Psychology*, Vol. 5. Kazdin, A. (Ed.). New York, Oxfprd University Press, 369–373.
20. Humphreys, K. (1997). Individual and social benefits of mutual aid self-help groups. *Social Policy, 27*(3), 12–19.
21. The Arc. (n.d.). History of Arc. Retrieved August 5, 2010, from http://www.thearc.org/page.aspx?pid=270
22. Wituk, S., Shepherd, M., Warren, M. & Meissen, G. (2002). Factors contributing to the survival of *self-help groups. American Journal of Community Psychology, 30*(3), 349–367.
23. Josefsson, U. (2005). Coping with illness online: The case of patients' online communities. *Information Society, 21*(2); Leibert, T., Smith-Adcock, S. & Munson, J. (2003). Exploring how on-line self-help groups compare to face-to-face groups. *Journal of Technology in Counseling, 1*(5). Retrieved August 4, 2010, fromhttp://jtc.columbusstate.edu/Vol5_1/Leibert.htm Levine, Joanne. (2005). An exploration of female social work students' participation in on-line and face-to-face self-help groups. *Groupwork, 13*(2) 61–79.
24. Madara, E. (n.d.). How to develop or find an online support group or web-site. American Self-help Support Clearing House, Self-help Group Sourcebook Online. Retrieved August 4, 2010, from http://www.mentalhelp.net/selfhelp/selfhelp.php?id=863
25. Tilly, C. & Wood, L. J. (2009). *Social movements: 1768–2008* (2nd ed.). Boulder, CO. ParadigmLondon,UK.
26. Atlas, J. (2010). *Seeds of change: The story of America's most controversial organizing group.* Nashville, TN: Vanderbilt University Press, pp. 223–224; Swarts, H. (2008). *Organizing urban America: Secular and faith-based movements.* Minneapolis: University of Minnesota Press; McKnight, J. (1995). Toward a *grounded substantive theory of the control of learning in altruistic grassroots initiatives.* Ann Arbor, MI: UMI #9531987.
27. Alinsky, S. (1989). *Rules for radicals: A pragmatic primer for realistic radicals.* New York: Vintage Press. (Original work published 1971).
28. Swarts, H. (2008). *Organizing urban America: Secular and faith-based movements.* Minneapolis: University of Minnesota Press.
29. Atlas, J. (2010). *Seeds of change: The story of America's most controversial organizing group.* Nashville, TN: Vanderbilt University Press.
30. Ibid.
31. Ibid.
32. Ibid.
33. Lustgarten, A. (2012). *Hydrofracked? One man's mystery leads to a backlash against natural gas drilling* (Amazon Kindle ed.). Propublica Investigative Journalism; Wilber, T. (2012). *Under the surface: Fracking, fortunes, and the fate of the Marcellus shale.* Ithaca, NY: Cornell University Press.
34. Hamel, S. (2011). *Gas drilling and the fracking of a marriage. Seattle, WA*: Coffeetown Press.
35. Venkatesh, S. (2000). *American project: The rise and fall of a modern ghetto.* Cambridge, MA: Harvard University Press; Venkatesh, S. (2000). *American project: The rise and fall of a modern ghetto.* Cambridge, MA: Harvard University Press.
36. Erikson, E. (1994). *Gandhi's truth: On the origins of militant non-violence.* New York: W.W. Norton (Original work published 1969); Branch, T. (1999). *Pillar of fire: America in the King years 1964–65.* New York: Simon and Schuster; Haley, A. (1965). *The autobiography of Malcolm X (as told to Alex Haley).* New York: Ballantine Books. Mandela, N. (1995). *Long walk to freedom.* New York, NY: Little Brown; Jones. (n.d.). The autobiography of Mother Jones. Retrieved August 27, 2010, from http://www.angelfire.com/nj3/RonMBaseman/mojones.htm (Original work published 1925 by Charles Kerr and available from Amazon.com)
37. Tilly, C. & Wood, L. J. (2009). *Social movements: 1768–2008* (2nd ed.). Paradigm. London, UK.
38. Aberle, D. (1966). A classification of social movements." In *The peyote religion among the Navajo.* Norman OK: University of Oklahoma Press.

39. Gandhi, M. K. (2008). *Mahatma Gandhi: The essential writings.* Judith Brown (Ed.). New York: Oxford University Press; King, M. L. (1990). *A testament of hope: The essential writings and speeches of Martin Luther King, Jr.* New York: Harper One; Mandela, N. (1995). *Long walk to freedom.* Boston: Little Brown; Tutu, D. (2005). *God has a dream: A vision of hope for our time.*New York, NY: Image.
40. Larana, E., Johnson, H. & Gusfield, J. (Eds.). (1994). *New social movements: From ideology to identity.* Philadelphia: Temple University Press.
41. Freire, P. (1980). *Pedagogy of the oppressed.* New York: Continuum; Brookfield, S. (2005). *The power of critical thinking: Liberating adult learning and teaching.* San Francisco: Jossey-Bass.
42. Tilly, C. & Wood, L. J. (2009). *Social movements: 1768–2008* (2nd ed.). Paradigm London, UK.
43. Huxham, C. (2003). "Theorizing collaborative practice." *Public Management Review, 5*(3)401–423.
44. Bacheldor, L. (2007). *Developing tools for measuring collaborative effectiveness: Two case studies.* Unpublished master's thesis, SUNY/Empire State College, Saratoga Springs, NY.
45. White, J. & Wechlage, G. C. (1995). Community collaboration: If it's such a good idea, why is it so hard to do? *Educational Evaluation and Policy Analysis, 17*(123–38); Johnson, Winstrow, Schultz, & Hardy. (2003). Interagency and inter-professional collaboration in community care: The interdependence of structures and values. *Journal of Interprofessional Care, 17*(1); Chavis, D. M. (2001). The paradoxes and promises of community collaborations. *American Journal of Community Psychology, 29*(2), 309–320.
46. Bacheldor, L. (2007). *Developing tools for measuring collaborative effectiveness: Two case studies.* Unpublished master's thesis, SUNY/Empire State College, Saratoga Springs, NY.
47. Hibert, P. & Huxham, C. (2005). A little about the mystery: Process learning as collaboration evolves. *European Management Review, 2*(1), 59–69.

Notes for Chapter 5

1. Hyman, D., McKnight, J. & Higdon, F. (2001). *Doing democracy: Conflict and consensus strategies for citizens, communities, and organizations* (3rd ed.). XanEdu. Ann Arbor, MI.
2. Ibid.
3. Naughton, D. & Shied, F. (2012). Darkness visible: A critical, communicative, reflective, transformative, timely inquiry into the coming to be of adult education in the early 21st century. Symposium presented at the 53rd Adult Education Research Conference, State University of New York, Empire State College, Saratoga Springs, NY, June.
4. Senge, P. (2006). *The fifth dimension: The art and practice of the learning organization* (rev. ed.). Crown Business: New York, NY; Deming, E. (2000). *Out of the crisis.* Cambridge, MA: MIT Press; Walton, M. (1988). *The Deming management method.* Perigee Books: New York, NY.
5. Jones, D. (n.d.). *Understanding the form, function and logic of clandestine cellular networks: The first step in counternetwork operations.* Monograph. Ft. Levenworth, KS: School of Advanced Military Studies.
6. Birden, S. (2012). Confronting the post-modern malaise: Embracing education as "rhizome." Presented at the 53rd Adult Education Research Conference, State University of New York, Empire State College, Saratoga Springs, NY, June; Siemens, G. (2005). Connectivism: A learning theory for the digital Age." January 5. Retrieved July 13, 2011, from http://www.itdl.org/journal/jan_05/article01.htm
7. Adapted from Hyman, D., McKnight, J., & Higdon, F. (2001). *Doing democracy: Conflict and consensus strategies for citizens, communities, and organizations* (3rd ed.). XanEdu. Ann Arbor, MI.
8. Rogers, C. (1951). *Client centered therapy: Its current practice, implications, and theory.* New York: Constable; Maslow, A. H. (1954). *Motivation and personality.* New York: Harper and Row.

Notes for Chapter 6

1. Tuckman, B. (1965). Developmental sequence in small groups. *Psychological Bulletin, 63*(6), 384–399; Tuckman, B. W., & Jensen, M. A. C. (1977). Stages of small group development revisited. *Group and Organizational Studies, 2*, 419–427.
2. The most helpful ground rules I have ever heard were set by Jean Fei, a community activist in the Saratoga Springs, Albany, New York area. She talked about the "stepping forward–stepping back" model and urged those of us who generally were quiet and reluctant to speak to take the risk of stepping forward and those of us who generally were used to being outspoken to step back and listen. I found that just being conscious of my tendency to speak too much in groups, and listen too little, helped me understand what others were saying. I found that those who spoke more than they usually would have had many good things to say. Bringing such communication patterns to consciousness feels a bit awkward in a meeting context, but it pays big dividends.
3. Corey, M. S., Corey, C. & Corey, G. (2008). *Groups: Process and practice* (8th ed). Belmont, CA. Brooks-Cole.
4. Ibid.
5. Ibid.
6. Ibid.
7. Ibid.
8. Senge, P. (2006). *The fifth discipline: The art and practice of the learning organization* (rev. ed.). New York, NY. Crown Business.
9. Brinkerhoff, D. B., & White, L. (1991). *Sociology.* St. Paul, MN: West Publishing, p. 119.
10. Dickinson, J. A. (1989). *Experiential social learning and management for transformation: A case study of a community development project in Lima, Peru* (Vols. 1 &. 2). Unpublished doctoral dissertation, Michigan State University.
11. Kolb, D. (1984). *Experiential learning: Experience as the source of learning and development.* Englewood Cliffs, NJ: Prentice-Hall.
12. McKnight, J. (1995). *Toward a grounded, substantive theory of the control of learning in altruistic grassroots initiatives.* Unpublished doctoral dissertation, UMI Dissertation Services #9531987.
13. Brinkerhoff & White (1991), pp. 114–117.
14. Maxwell, J. (2009). *Teamwork 101: What every leader needs to know.* Thomas Nelson. New York, NY.
15. Bacheldor, L. (2007). Tools for measuring the effectiveness of community collaborations. Presented at the Conference of the Society for the Study of Social Problems, New York, August 10.
16. Belenky, M., Clinchy, B., Goldberger, N., & Tarule, J. (1986). *Women's ways of knowing: The development of mind, self, and voice.* New York: Basic Books.
17. Brinkerhoff & White (1991), pp. 114–117.
18. Whyte, W. F. (1984). *Learning from the field.* Beverly Hills, CA: Sage.
19. Curtis, S. (2003). Lies, damned lies, and organizational politics. *Industrial and Commercial Training,* 35(6/7), 293–297; Paal, T. & Bereczkei, T. (2007). Adult theory of mind, cooperation, Machiavellianism: The effect of mind reading on social relations. *Personality and Individual Differences, 43*(3), 541–551; Wilson, D. S. (1996). Machiavellianism: A synthesis of the evolutionary and psychological literatures. *Psychological Bulletin, 119*(2), 285–299.
20. Yalom, J. D. with Leszcz, M. (2005). *The theory and practice of group psychotherapy* (5th ed.). New York: Basic Books.

Notes for Chapter 7

1. McKnight, J. S. (1995). *Toward a grounded substantive theory of the control of learning in altruistic grassroots initiatives.* Unpublished doctoral dissertation, Pennsylvania State University, UMI #9531987.
2. Belenky, M., Clinchy, B., Goldberger, N., and Tarule, J. (1986). *Women's ways of knowing: The development of mind, self, and voice.* New York: Basic Books.
3. Park, P. (1999). People knowledge and change in participatory research. *Management Learning, 30*(2), 141–157; Horton, M., with Kohl, J., & Kohl, H. (1989). *The long haul: An autobiography.* New York: Teachers' College, Columbia University; Horton, M., & Freire, P. (1990). *We make the road by walking: Conversations on education and social change.* Philadelphia: Temple University Press; Freire, P. (1980). *Pedagogy of the oppressed.* New York: Continuum; Hayward, C., Simpson, L., & L. Ward. (2004). Still left out in the cold: Problematizing participatory research and development. *Sociologia Ruralis, 44*(1), 95–108; Mayoux, L., & Chambers, R. (2005). Revising the paradigm: Quantification, participatory methods, and pro-poor impact assessment. *Journal of International Development, 17*(2), 271–298; Pain, R., & Frances, P. (2003). Reflections on participatory research. *Area, 35*(1), 46–54.
4. McKnight, J. S. (1995).
5. Block, P., & McKnight, J. (2011). Abundant community: Awakening the power of communities and neighborhoods. January 1. Retrieved August 14, 2011, from http://www.abundantcommunity.com/forms/pages/page/home.html; McKnight, J., & Block, P. (2010). *The abundant community: Awakening the power of families and neighborhoods.* American Planning Association and BK Publishers, San Francisco, CA; Kretzman, J., & McKnight, J. (1993). *Building communities from the inside out: A path toward finding and mobilizing a community's assets.* ACTA Publications, Chicago, IL. Please note: John McKnight is not related to Joyce McKnight, the author of this text.
6. Hyman, D., McKnight, J., & Higdon, F. (2001). *Doing democracy: Conflict and consensus strategies for citizens, organizations, and communities* (3rd ed.). XanEdu Original Works. Ann Arbor, MI.
7. Mandell, B., & Schram, B. (2011). *An introduction to human service policy and practice* (8th ed.). Pearson, Upper Saddle River, NJ.
8. Sustainable Pittsburgh, Executive Director. (2001). Developing sustainability indicators. Presented at regional meeting of community organizers. The organization still existed as of August 2011: Sustainable Pittsburgh. (2009). Sustainable Pittsburgh: Our region, our resources, our future. Retrieved August 14, 2011, from http://www.sustainablepittsburgh.org/ (ongoing updates); Partnership for Sustainable Communities: An Interagency Partnership HUD, DOT and EPA. (n.d.). About us. Retrieved August 15, 2011, from http://www.sustainablecommunities.gov/aboutUs.html#2 (continuous updates).
9. Sustainable Pittsburgh, Executive Director. (2001). Developing sustainability indicators. Presented at regional meeting of community organizers.

Notes for Chapter 8

1. Tilly, C. & Wood, L. (2009). *Social movements: 1768–2008* (2nd ed). Paradigm, Boulder, CO.
2. Rothman, J., Erlich, J. L. & Tropman, J. (Eds.). (2001). *Strategies for community intervention* (6th ed.). Ithaca, NY: F.E. Peacock; Zander, A. (2001). Pressuring methods used by groups. In Rothman, Erlich, & Tropman (Eds.) (2001). 177–199
3. U.S. Department of Housing and Urban Development. (n.d.) Community Development Block Grant Program. Retrieved September 29, 2012, from http://portal.hud.gov/hudportal/HUD?src=/program_offices/comm_planning/communitydevelopment/programs
4. Freire, P. (1980). *Pedagogy of the oppressed.* New York: Continuum.
5. Horton, M. & Freire, P. (1990). *We make the road by walking: Conversations on education and social change.* Philadelphia: Temple University Press.
6. Freire (1980).

Notes for Chapter 9

1. Hyman, D., McKnight, J. & Higdon, F. (2001). *Doing democracy: Conflict and consensus strategies for clients, organizations and communities*. Ann Arbor, MI. XanEdu.
2. Rogers, C. (2003). *Client centered therapy: Its current practice, implications, and theory.* London, UK: Constable. (Original work published 1951).
3. Maslow, A. (1970). *Motivation and personality* (2nd ed). New York: Harper. (Original work published 1954)
4. Freire, P. (1980). *Pedagogy of the oppressed.* New York: Continuum.
5. Deming, W. D. (2000). *Out of the crisis.* Cambridge, MA: MIT Press; Senge, P. (2006). *The fifth discipline: The art and practice of the learning organization.* New York, NY. Crown Business; Senge, P. (1994). *The fifth discipline fieldbook: Strategies and tools for building a learning organization.* New York, NY. Crown Business.
6. Donaldson, L. (2001). *The contingency theory of organizations: Foundations of organizational science.* Thousand Oaks, CA. Sage; Burns, T., & Stalker, G. M. (1994). *The management of innovation*, Oxford, UK: Oxford University Press.
7. Quinn, R. E., Faerman, S., Thompson, M. P., McGrath, M., & St. Clair, L. (2010). *Becoming a master manager: A competing values framework.* New York: Wiley.
8. Deming (2000), Juran, J. M. (1992). *Juran on quality by design: The new steps for planning quality into goods and services.* New York: Free Press; Juran, J. M. (2003). *Architect of quality.* New York: McGraw-Hill.
9. Vella, J. (1994). *Learning to listen, learning to teach: The power of dialogue in educating adults.* San Francisco: Jossey-Bass.

Notes for Chapter 10

1. The following are some websites to guide your understanding of NGOs. All were retrieved on October 8, 2012, from Duke University Libraries Non Governmental Organization (NGO) Guide, http://guides.library.duke.edu/ngo_guide. School of Development Studies, Trinity College, Dublin. (n.d.). The role of NGO's. http://www.tcd.ie/Economics/Development_Studies/link.php?id=95; The NGO Café. (n.d.). http://www.gdrc.org/ngo/ncafe-ph.html.
   Drucker, P. (1993). *Managing for results.* New York, NY Collins. (Original work published 1964)
   Goldmark, A. (2011). "The benefit corporation: Can business be about more than profit?" *Good Business*, July 1. Retrieved August 25, 2011, from http://www.good.is/post/the-national-march-of-the-benefit-corporation-continues-now-protecting-ben-and-jerry-s-backyard-from-future-sellouts/
2. B Corporation. (2011). Using the power of business to solve social and environmental problems. January 1. Retrieved August 25, 2011, from http://www.bcorporation.net/
3. IRS. (n.d.). Types of tax deductible organizations. Retrieved May 11, 2013, from http://www.irs.gov/Charities-&-Non-Profits/Types-of-Tax-Exempt-Organizations
4. Grant Space: A Service of the Foundation Center. (n.d.). What is a foundation? Retrieved May 11, 2013, from http://www.grantspace.org/Tools/Knowledge-Base/Funding-Resources/Foundations/What-is-a-foundation
5. Eikenberry, A. (2006). Research notes: Growing grassroots philanthropy. *Non-profit and Voluntary Sector Quarterly, 25* (January 1), 517–532; Giving Circles Network. (n.d.). Retrieved May 11, 2013, from http://www.givingcircles.org/.

Notes for Chapter 11

1. This discussion of power as an attribute and power as a process comes from the following primary sources: Hyman, D., McKnight, J., & Higdon, F. (2001). *Doing democracy: Conflict and consensus strategies for citizens, organizations, and communities.* Ann Arbor, MI: XanEdu; Turner, J. C. (2005). Explaining the nature of power: A three process theory. *European Journal of Social Psychology, 35*(1), 1–22; Boulding, K. (1989). *Three faces of power.* Thousand Oaks, CA. Sage; Cleaver, E. (1970). *Soul on ice.* Miller Place, NY: Laurel; Fanon, F. (1965). *The wretched of the earth.* New York, NY: Grove Press; Mills, C. W. (1956). *The power elite.* London: Oxford University Press; Roberts, N. (2004). "Fanon, Sartre, violence and freedom." *Sartre Studies International, 10*(2)139–160 ; Lukes, S. (Ed.). (1986). *Power: Readings in social and political theory, no. 4.* New York: NYU Press (contains several classic essays on the nature of power); Lukes, S. (2004). *Power: A radical view* (2nd ed.). Basingstoke, New England Palgrave MacMillan.
2. Mills, C. W. (1956). *The Power Elite.* New York, NY: Oxford University Press.
3. Hyman, McKnight, & Higdon (2001); Mills, C. W. (1956).
4. Karl, B. (1997). Philanthropy and the maintenance of democratic elites. *Minerva: A Review of Science, Learning and Policy, 35*(3) (Fall), 207–220; Mill, J. S. (1869). On liberty. Retrieved July 6, 2011, from http://www.bartleby.com/130/; Hollinger, R. (1996). *The dark side of liberalism: Elitism versus democracy.* West Port, CT, Praeger; Boyle, M. E., & Silver, I. (2005). Poverty, partnerships, and privilege: Elite institutions and community empowerment. *City and Community, 4*(3), 233–253; Zinn, H. (2010). *A people's history of the United States.* New York, NY, Harper Perennial Modern Classics.
5. Hyman, McKnight, & Higdon (2001); Provan, K., Veazie, M. A., Staten, L. K., & Teufel-Stone, N. (2005). The use of network analysis to strengthen community partnerships." *Public Administration Review, 65*(5), 603–613; Warren, M. (1998). Community building and political power. *American Behavioral Scientist, 42*(1), 78–92; Keller, S. (1991). *Beyond the ruling class: Strategic elites in modern society.* Piscataway, NJ: Transaction Publishers; Dahl, R. (1972). *Polyarchy: Participation and opposition.* New Haven, CT: Yale University Press.
6. Warren, M. (1998). Community building and political power. *American Behavioral Scientist, 42*(1), 78–92; Dahl, R. A. (1961). *Who governs? Democracy and power in an American city.* New Haven, CT: Yale University Press; Dahl, R. (1972). *Polyarchy: Participation and opposition.* New Haven, CT: Yale University Press (a classic).
7. Keller, S. (1991). Beyond the ruling class: Strategic elites in modern society. Piscataway, NJ, Transaction Publishers.
8. McFarland, A. (2004). *Neopluralism: The evolution of political process theory.* Lawrence, KS: University Press of Kansas; Dahl (1961); Dahl, R. A. (1958). A critique of the ruling elite model. *The American Political Science Review, 52*(2), 463–496.
9. Blumer, H. (1969). *Symbolic interactionism.* Englewood Cliffs, NJ: Prentice Hall; Mead, G. H. (1934). *Mind, self, and society.* Chicago: University of Chicago Press (available online in the public domain); Mead, G. H. (1913). The social self. *Journal of Philosophy, Psychology, and Scientific Methods, 10,* 374–380 (available online in the public domain).
10. Rauthman, J. F. & Will, T. (2011). Proposing a multidimensional Machiavellianism conceptualization. *Social Behavior and Personality, 39*(3), 391–404; Jones, D. N., & Paulhus, D. L. (2009). Machiavellianism. In M. R. Leary & R. H. Doyle (Eds.). *Handbook of individual differences in social behavior.* New York: Guilford, pp. 93–108; Wilson, D. S., Near, D. C., & Miller, R. R. (1996). Machiavellianism: A synthesis of the evolutionary and psychological literatures. *Psychological Bulletin, 119*(2), 285–299; Paal, T., & Bereczker, T. (2007). Adult theory of mind, cooperation, Machiavellianism: The effect of mind reading on social relations. *Personality and Individual Differences, 43*(3), 351–364; Parlarles-Quenza, C. (2006). Astuteness, trust, social intelligence. *Journal for the Theory of Social Behaviour, 36*(1), 39–56.
11. Machiavelli, N. (1515). *The prince.* Marriott English translation (1908). Retrieved October 17, 2012, from http://www.constitution.org/mac/prince00.htm (in the public domain).

12. Curtis, S. (2003). Lies, damned lies, and organizational politics. *Industrial and Commercial Training, 35*(6/7), 293–297.
13. Hyman, McKnight, & Higdon (2001); Marx, K. (1967) *Capital (Das Kapital).* New York: International Publishers. (Original work published 1867); Smith, A. (1776). *An inquiry into the nature and causes of the wealth of nations.* Retrieved October 17, 2012, from http://www.econlib.org/library/Smith/smWN.html (in the public domain).
14. Boulding, K. (1989). *Three faces of power.* Thousand Oaks, CA: Sage Publications; Hyman, McKnight, & Higdon (2001).
15. Branch, T. (1989*). Parting the waters: America in the King years 1954–1963.* New York: Simon-Schuster; Branch, T. (1999). *Pillar of fire: America in the King years 1963–1965.* New York: Simon-Schuster; Branch, T. (2007). *At Canann's edge: America in the King years: 1965–1968.* New York: Simon-Schuster; King, M. (1986). *The essential writings of Martin Luther King, Jr.* (James M. Washington, Ed.). New York, NY: Harper-Collins.
16. Munzim, Z. (2001). Islamic mobilization, social movement theory, and the Egyptian Moslem Brotherhood. *The Sociological Quarterly, 42*(4), 487–510; Wiktororwitz, Q. (2002). Killing in the name of Islam: Al Qaeda's justification for September 11. *Middle East Policy, 10*(2), 76–92; Chaliand, G. (Ed.), and Blin, A. (2007). *The history of terrorism: From antiquity to al Qaeda.* Berkley, CA: University of California Press.
17. Goleman, D. (2006). *Emotional intelligence: Why it can matter more than IQ* (10th anniv. ed.). Ealing, England Bantam.
18. Siemens, G. (2004). Connectivism: A learning theory for the digital age. Retrieved July 28, 2011, from http://www.elearnspace.org/Articles/connectivism.htm.
19. The following are some major Gandhian resources: Gandhi, M. K. (2008). *Mahatma Gandhi: The essential writings.* (Judith M. Brown, Ed.). New York: Oxford University Press; Gandhi, M. K. (1922). *Freedom's battle: Being a comprehensive collection of writings and speeches on the present situation.* Rockville, MD: Wildside Press; Gandhi, M. K. (2008). *Non-violent resistance (satyagraha).* Mineola, NY: Dover Publications. (Original work published 1961); Gandhi Research Foundation. (2011). Gandhi's philosophy. January 1. Retrieved July 12, 2011, from http://www.mkgandhi.org/philosophy/main.htm. Many of Gandhi's major ideas are available for free online in e-book format.
20. Branch (2006); Branch (1998); Branch (1989); King (1986).
21. Battle, M. J. and Tutu, D. (1997). *Reconciliation: The Ubuntu theology of Desmond Tutu.* Cleveland, OH: Pilgrim Press; Tutu, D. (2000). *No future without forgiveness.* Colorado Springs, CO: Image Books; Allen, J. (2006). *Rabble-rouser for peace: The authorized biography of Desmond Tutu.* Washington D.C. Free Press; Tutu, D. (2005). *God has a dream: A vision of hope for our time.* Colorado Springs,CO: Image.
22. Mandela, N. (1995). *Long walk to freedom: The autobiography of Nelson Mandela.* New York, NY: Back Bay Books; Mandela, N. (2010). *Conversations with myself* (with a forward by Barack Obama). New York, NY: Farrar, Straus and Giroux.
23. Readings on threat power: Boulding, K. (1989); Fanon, F. (1965). *The wretched of the earth.* New York, NY: Grove Press; Hyman, McKnight, & Higdon (2001); Munzim, Z. (2001). Islamic mobilization, social movement theory, and the Egyptian Moslem Brotherhood. *The Sociological Quarterly, 42*(4); Roberts, N. (2004). Fanon, Sartre, violence and freedom. *Sartre Studies International, 10*(2), 139–160; Wiktororwitz, Q. (2002). Killing in the name of Islam: Al Qaeda's justification for September 11. *Middle East Policy, 10*(2), 76–92; Cleaver, E. (1970). *Soul on ice.* Miller Place, NY: Laurel.
24. Gaventa, J. (1982). *Power and powerlessness: Quiescence and rebellion in an Appalachian valley.* Champaign, IL: University of Illinois Press; Mandela (1995); Gandhi (1922); Gandhi, M. K. (2008). *Mahatma Gandhi: The essential writings.* (Judith M. Brown, Ed.). New York: Oxford University Press (especially writings on the Salt March); Levinson, C. (2012). *We've got a job: The 1963 Birmingham Children's March.* Atlanta, GA: Peachtree Publishers.
25. Zander, A. (2001). Pressuring methods used by groups. In Rothman, J., Erlich, J. L. & Tropman, J. E. (Eds.), *Strategies of community intervention* (6th ed.). Itasca, IL: F. E. Peacock.
26. Zander (2001) (talks in part about the relative efficacy of force and violence); Polk, W. (2008). *Violent politics: A history of insurgency, terrorism, and guerilla war from the American Revolution to Iraq.* New York, NY: Harper Perennial; Gareau, F. (2010). *State terrorism and the United States: From counterinsurgency to the war on terrorism.* Atlanta, GA: Clarity Press (this presents a somewhat different perspective on terrorism,

violence, and force and asks us to reflect on whether an established government—a state—can engage in terrorist-like actions and, if so, what this means for the legitimacy of power).

27. Zander (2001); Polk (2008); Fanon (1965); Munzim (2001); Roberts (2004); Cleaver (1970).
28. Machiavellianism is a personality trait and a behavior. Those with Machiavellian traits are able to understand others' motivations but instead of working with them toward common goals use them to gain their own ends. The following references provide insight into this phenomenon. Rauthman, J. F. & Will, T. (2011). Proposing a multidimensional Machiavellianism conceptualization. *Social Behavior and Personality, 39*(3), 391–404; Jones, D. N., & Paulhus, D. L. (2009). Machiavellianism. In M. R. Leary & R. H. Doyle (Eds.), *Handbook of individual differences in social behavior.* New York: Guilford, pp. 93–108; Wilson, D. S., Near, D. C., & Miller, R. R. (1996). Machiavellianism: A synthesis of the evolutionary and psychological literatures. *Psychological Bulletin, 119*(2), 285–299; Paal, T., & Bereczker, T. (2007). Adult theory of mind, cooperation, Machiavellianism: The effect of mind reading on social relations. *Personality and Individual Differences, 43*(3), 351–364.
29. Robson, T. (2001). The co-option of radicalism: Conflict, community and civil society community action and social change in a post-colonial context. *Critical Sociology, 27*(2), 221–245.
30. A very disappointing example of this was the cynical actions of Wade Rathke, the founder of ACORN, and his brother that eventually were the real cause of the demise of the organization. The story is recorded in Atlas, J. (2010). *Seeds of change: The story of ACORN, America's most controversial organizing group*. Nashville,TN: Vanderbilt University Press
31. Hyman, McKnight, & Higdon (2001), p. 131; Turner, J. C. (2005). Explaining the nature of power: A three process theory. *European Journal of Social Psychology, 35*(1), 1–22.
32. Conger, J., & Kunungo, R. (1998). *Charismatic leadership in organizations.* Thousand Oaks, CA: Sage.
33. Hyman, McKnight, & Higdon (2001), p. 31; Bass, B. and Riggio, E. (2005). *Transformational leadership* (2nd ed.). Mahwah, NJ: Lawrence Erlbaum Associates.
34. Pfeffer, J. (1993). *Managing with power: Politics and influence in organizations.* Cambridge, MA: Harvard Business Press.
35. Turner (2005).
36. *Empowerment* is a term often associated with the field of community psychology. I found the 1995 special edition of the *Journal of Community Psychology, 23*(5), particularly interesting; many of its articles are cited here. Buckwalter, P. (2003). Building power. Finding and developing leaders in Arizona congregations. *Social Policy, 33*(3), 2–9; Fawcett, S. B., Paine-Anderson, A., Francisco, V. T., & Shultz, J. A. (1995). Using empowerment theory in collaborative partnerships for community development. *Journal of Community Psychology, 23*(5) (special issue on empowerment); Hatzidmitriadou, E. (2002). Political ideology, helping mechanisms, and empowerment of mental health/self-help groups. *Journal of Community Applied Social Psychology, 12*, 271–285; Kroeker, C. J. (1995). Individual, organizational, and societal empowerment: A study of a Nicaraguan agricultural cooperative. *Journal of Community Psychology, 23*(5), 749–764 (special issue on empowerment); Maton, K. I., & Salem, D. (1995). Organizational characteristics of empowering community settings: A multiple case approach. *Journal of Community Psychology, 23*(5), 631–656 (special issue on empowerment); McMillan, B., Florin, P., Stevenson, J., Kerman, B., & Mitchell, R. E. (1995). Empowerment *praxis* in community coalitions. *Journal of Community Psychology, 23*(5), 699–727 (special issue on empowerment); Perkins, D. D., & Zimmerman, M. A. (1995). Empowerment theory, research, and application. *Journal of Community Psychology, 23*(5), 569–579 (special issue on empowerment); Rappaport, J. (1995). Empowerment meets narrative: Listening to stories and creating settings. *Journal of Community Psychology, 23*(5), 795–807 (special issue on empowerment); Rappaport, J. (2000). Community narratives: Tales of terror and joy. *American Journal of Community Psychology, 28*(1), 1–24; Rich, R. C., Edelstein, M., Hallman, W. K., & Wandersman, A. H. (1995). Citizen participation and empowerment: The case of local environmental hazards. *Journal of Community Psychology, 23*(5), 657–676 (special issue on empowerment); Speer, P. W., & Hughey, J. (1995). Community organizing: An ecological route to empowerment and power. *Journal of Community Psychology, 23*(5), 729–748 (special issue on empowerment); Theissen-Nation, M. (2004). *Realizing hope in the midst of despair: Narratives of an urban mission community.* Unpublished doctoral dissertation in intercultural studies, Fuller Theological Seminary; Tritter, Q., & McCullum, A. (2006). The snakes and ladders of empowerment: Moving beyond Arnstein. *Health Policy, 76*(2), 156–168; Warren, M. (1998). Community building and political power. *American Behavioral Scientist, 42*(1), 78–92; Zimmerman, M. A.

(2000). Empowerment theory: Psychological, organizational, and community levels of analysis. In Rappaport, J. & Seidman, E., *Handbook of community psychology*. New York, NY: Springer.

37. McMillan, Florin, Stevenson, Kerman, & Mitchell (1995).
38. Kroeker (1995); Rappaport (1995); Rappaport (2000).
39. It would be impossible to compile a comprehensive list of all of the journey narratives that have enabled social movements and community organizing efforts to succeed, but there are a few that are prominently mentioned in the literature. One of the most important is the Hebrew Exodus from Egypt to Israel at the time of Moses, which has not only spoken to the Jewish people but to the early New England colonists, African-American slaves, and the civil rights movement. The Hebrew Exodus is mentioned prominently in Exodus, Numbers, and Deuteronomy in the Hebrew Bible and the epistle to Hebrews in the Christian New Testament; see also Heschel, A. (1996). *Moral grandeur and spiritual audacity: Essays edited by Susanna Heschel.* New York: Farrar, Straus and Giroux (see especially the sections on the Hebrew prophets); DuBois, W. E. B. (2011). *The souls of black folk.* New York, NY, Trebba Books. (Original work published 1903); Bremer, F. J. (1995). *The Puritan experiment: New England society from Bradford to Edwards.* Lebanon, NH: UPNE; Gamble, R. M. (2012). *In search of a city on a hill: The making and the unmaking of an American myth London, England* Continuum (Chapter 1 on the original Puritans); Franklin, V. P. (1995). *Living our stories, telling our truths: Autobiography and the making of African American intellectual tradition.* New York, NY Oxford University Press; King, M. L. (1986). *A testament of hope: The essential writings and speeches of Martin Luther King, Jr.* (James M. Washington, Ed.) New York: HarperCollins.
40. Wells, T. (2005). *The war within: America's battle over Vietnam*. New York, NY: Backinprint.com.
41. Zhao, D. (2004). *The power of Tiananmen: State–society relations and the 1989 Beijing student movement. Chicago*: University of Chicago Press.
42. Useem, B., & Kimball, P.(1991) *State of siege: US prison riots: 1971–1986.* New York, NY: Oxford University Press.
43. Mumford, K. (2008). *Newark: A history of race, rights, and riots in America (American history and culture).* New York: NYU Press.
44. Branch (2006); Cleaver (1970); Douglass, J. (2012). *Gandhi and the unspeakable: His final experiment with truth.* Maryknoll, NY: Orbis Books; Haley, A. (1965). *The autobiography of Malcolm X (as told to Alex Haley).* New York: Ballantine Books.
45. Munzim, Z. (2001); Wiktororwitz, Q. (2002); Fanon (1965); Roberts (2004).
46. McMillan, Florin, Stevenson, Kerman, & Mitchell (1995).
47. Kroeker (1995); McKnight, J. S. (1995). *Toward a grounded, substantive theory of the control of learning in altruistic grassroots initiatives.* Unpublished doctoral dissertation, Pennsylvania State University, UMI #9531987.
48. Theissen-Nation, M. (2004). *Realizing hope in the midst of despair: Narratives of an urban mission community.* Unpublished doctoral dissertation in intercultural studies, Fuller Theological Seminary.
49. Arnstein, S. (1969). A ladder of community participation. *American Institute of Planning Journal, 35*, 216–224.

Notes for Chapter 12

1. Freudenburg, W. R., Gramling, R. B., Laska, S. & Erikson, K. (2009). *Catastrophe in the Making: The Engineering of Katrina and the Disasters of Tomorrow*. Washington, DC: Island Press
2. Freudenburg, Gramling, Laska, & Erikson (2009). Wailoo, K., O'Neill, K., Dowd, J., & Anglin, R. (Eds.). (2010). *Katrina's Imprint: Race and Vulnerability in America*. Rutgers Studies on Race and Ethnicity. New Brunswick, NJ: Rutgers University Press.
3. Fitzgerald, K. J. & Rogers, D. M. (2000). Radical social movement organizations: a theoretical model. *Sociological Quarterly, 41*(4573-592); Cleaver, E. (1970). *Soul on ice*. Miller Place, NY: Laurel; Williams, Y. (2008). Some abstract thing called "freedom": Civil rights, black power, and the legacy of the Black Panther Party. *OAH Magazine of History, 22*(316-21); Pekar, H., Buhle, P., & Dumm, G. (2009). *Students for a Democratic Society: A Graphic History*. Hill and Wang New York City, NY (a really intriguing graphic history of the SDS that gives the "flavor" of the movement and its street level decision making).

Notes for Chapter 13

1. Hyman, D. (1994). Toward a quality-of-life paradigm for sustainable communities. In D. McSwan & M. McShane (Eds.), *Issues affecting rural communities*. Townsville, Queensland, AU: Rural Education Research and Development Centre, James Cook University; Hyman, D. (1997). Toward a quality-of-life paradigm for sustainable communities, ED 390 621. Reproduced in *ERIC Clearinghouse on rural education and small schools*, September; Hyman, D., Shingler, J., & Gamm, L. (1995). Paradigm gridlock and the two faces of technology." In L. J. Beaulieu & D. Mulkey (Eds.), *Investing in people: The human capital needs of rural America*. Boulder, CO: Westview Press, Ch. 4; Daley, H., & Farley, J. (2010). *Ecological economics: Principles and applications* (2nd ed.). Washington, DC: Island Press; Kate, R. W. (2011). What kind of a science is sustainability science? *PNAS, 108*(49). Retrieved October 26, 2012, from http://www.uvm.edu/~gundiee/pdfs/Kates.pdf; Bettencourt, L. M. A., & J. Kaur. (2011). Evolution and structure of sustainability science. *PNAS, 108*(49). http://www.uvm.edu/~gundiee/pdfs/Bettencourt.pdf; Korten, D. (2010). *Agenda for a new economy: From phantom wealth to real wealth—a declaration of independence from Wall Street*. San Francisco: Berett-Koehler Publishers.
2. Delgado, R., & Stefancic, J. (Eds.). (2000). *Critical race theory: The cutting edge*. Philadelphia: Temple University Press; Schumacher, E. F. (2000). *Small is beautiful: Economics as if people mattered* (25th anniv. ed.).Vancouver, BC: Hartley and Marks. (Original work published 1965); Brookfield, S. (2005). *The power of critical theory: Liberating adult learning and teaching*. San Francisco: Jossey-Bass; Zinn, H. (2010). *A people's history of the* United States. New York City, NY: Harper Perennial Modern Classics; King, M. L. (1986). *A testament of hope: The essential writings and speeches of Martin Luther King, Jr.* (J. M. Washington, Ed.). New York City, NY: Harper-Collins.
3. Gandhi, M. K. (2008). *Mahatma Gandhi: The essential writings*. (J. M. Brown, (Ed.). New York: Oxford University Press; Zinn, H. (2010).
4. Freire, P. (1996). *Pedagogy of the oppressed* (2nd ed.). New York City, NY: Penguin. (Original work published 1968); Horton, P., Friere, M., & Freire, P. (1990). *We make the road by walking: Conversations on education and social change*. Philadelphia: Temple University Press; Horton, M., with Kohl, J., & Kohl, H. (1989). *The long haul: An autobiography*. New York: Teachers' College Columbia University; Vella, J. (1997). *Learning to listen—learning to teach: The power of dialogue in educating adults*. San Francisco: Jossey Bass; Brookfield, S. (1987). *Developing critical thinkers: Challenging adults to explore alternative ways of thinking and acting*. San Francisco: Jossey-Bass.
5. Gandhi (2008); King (1986).
6. Gandhi (2008); King (1986); Zinn (2010); National Association of Social Workers. (1996). Code of ethics of the National Association of Social Workers. Retrieved October 26, 2012, from http://www.socialworkers.org/pubs/code/default.asp; National Organization for Human Service Professionals. (1996). Ethical standards for human service professionals. Retrieved October 26, 2012, from http://www.nationalhumanservices.org/ethical-standards-for-hs-professionals.
7. Noddings, N. (2003). *Caring: A feminine approach to ethics and moral education* (2nd ed.). Berkley, CA: University of California Press; Noddings, N. (2002). *Starting at home: Caring and social policy*. Berkley, CA: University of California Press; Gilligan, C. (1982). *In a different voice: Psychological theory and women's development*. Cambridge, MA. Harvard University Press.
8. Katz, M. S., Noddings, N. & Strike, K. A. (1999). Justice and caring: The search for common ground in education. New York City, NY: Teachers' College Press; Kohlberg, L. (1981). The philosophy of moral development: Moral stages and the idea of justice. Essays on moral development, Vol. 1. New York City, NY: Harper and Row; Kohlberg, L. (1984). The psychology of moral development: The nature and validity of moral stages. Essays on moral development, Vol. 2. New York City, NY: Harper-Collins College Division; Reimer, J., Paolitto, D. P. & Hersh, R. H. (1990). Promoting moral growth from Piaget to Kohlberg (2nd ed.). Long Grove, IL: Waveland Press, Inc.

9. Lum, D. (2004). *Social work practice and people of color*. Belmont, CA: Brooks-Cole.http://www.amazon.com/Psychology-Moral-Development-Nature-Validity/dp/0060647612/ref=ntt_at_ep_dpi_2
10. King, M. L. (1963). "I have a dream." Speech delivered on August 28 on the steps of the Lincoln Memorial, Washington, D.C. In King (1986), p. 217.
11. Borwick, D. (2012). *Building communities, not audiences: The future of the arts in the United States.* Winston-Salem NC: Arts, Engaged; Walker-Kuhne, D. (2005). *Invitation to the party: Building bridges to the arts, culture, and community.* New York City, NY: Theatre Communications Group; Schwarzman, M. (auth.), & K. Knight (illus.) (2005). *Guide to community-based arts*. Oakland, CA: New Village Press.
12. Frankl, V. (2006). *Man's search for meaning*. Boston, MA: Beacon. (Original work in English published 1959); King (1986); Gandhi (2008); Mandela, N. (2002). *Long walk to freedom*. London, UK: Orbit and Abacus; Tutu, D., & Tutu, M. (2010). *Made for goodness, and why this makes all the difference*. New York City, NY: HarperOne; Tutu, D. (2000). *No future without forgiveness*. New York City, NY: Image; Tutu, D. (2005). *God has a dream: A vision of hope for our time*. New York City, NY: Image; Obama, B. (2006). *The audacity of hope: Thoughts on reclaiming the American Dream*. New York City, NY: Three Rivers Press.
13. Block, P. & McKnight, J. (2011). Abundant community: Awakening the power of communities and neighborhoods. January 1, 2011. Retrieved August 14, 2011, from http://www.abundantcommunity.com/forms/pages/page/home.html; McKnight, J. & Block, P. (2010). *The abundant community: Awakening the power of families and neighborhoods*. San Francisco, CA: American Planning Association and BK Publishers; Kretzman, J., & McKnight, J. (1993). *Building communities from the inside out: A path toward finding and mobilizing a community's assets*. Chicago, IL: ACTA Publications; Putnam, R., & Feldstein, L. (2004). *Better together: Restoring American community*. Simon and Schuster.
14. National Association of Social Workers. (1996). Code of ethics of the National Association of Social Workers. Retrieved October 26, 2012, from http://www.socialworkers.org/pubs/code/default.asp; National Organization for Human Service Professionals. (1996). Ethical standards for human service professionals. Retrieved October 26, 2012, from http://www.nationalhumanservices.org/ethical-standards-for-hs-professionals.
15. Hugman, R. (2003). Reconsidering post-modernism. *British Journal of Social Work, 33*, 1025–1041.
16. Brookfield, S. (2005). *The power of critical theory: Liberating adult learning and teaching*. San Francisco: Jossey-Bass; McKnight, J. S. (1995). Toward a grounded substantive theory of the control of learning in altruistic grassroots initiatives. Unpublished doctoral dissertation, Pennsylvania State University, UMI #9531987; Hyman, D., McKnight, J & Higdon, F. (2001). *Doing democracy: Conflict and consensus strategies for citizens, organizations and communities*. Ann Arbor, MI: XanEdu.
17. Malone, A. (2008). The GM genocide: Thousands of Indian farmers are committing suicide after using genetically modified crops. Mail Online. Retrieved August 16, 2011, from http://www.dailymail.co.uk/news/article-1082559/The-GM-genocide-Thousands-Indian-farmers-committing-suicide-using-genetically-modified-crops.html.
18. Gore, A. (2006). *Earth in the balance: Ecology and the human spirit*. Emmaus, PA: Rodale Books; Gore, A. (2006). *An inconvenient truth: the planetary emergency of global warming and what we can do about it*. Emmaus, PA: Rodale Books.
19. Delgado & Stefancic (Eds.). (2000). *Critical race theory: The cutting edge*.
20. Peters, B. (2012). *Derrida: A biography*. Cambridge, UK: Polity.
21. Kierkegaard, S. (2000). *The essential Kierkegaard.* (Hong, H. V. & Hong, E. H., Eds.). Princeton, NJ: Princeton University Press.
22. Brookfield (2005), p. 3.
23. Brookfield (2005); Gramsci, A. (1957). *The modern prince and other writings*. New York: International Publishers. Cited in Brookfield, S. (2005). *The power of critical theory: Liberating adult learning and teaching*. San Francisco: Jossey-Bass; Gramsci, A. (1988). *The Antonio Gramsci reader* (D. Forgacs, Ed.). New York: New York University Press. Cited in Brookfield, S. (2005). *The power of critical theory: Liberating adult learning and teaching*. San Francisco: Jossey-Bass.
24. Brookfield (2005), p. 45.
25. Brookfield (2005); Freire (1980); Gandhi (2008); Marx, K. (1973). *Capital: A critical analysis of capitalist production. Vol.1* (S. Moore & E. Aveling, Trans.). New York: International. (Original work published 1867); Steinbeck, J., with Henning, C. [his wife who did most of the writing]. (2006). *The grapes of wrath*. New York

City, NY: Penguin Classics. (Original work published 1939); Zinn, H. (2010). *A people's history of the United States*. New York City, NY: Harper Perennial Modern Classics; Zinn, H. & Arnove, A. *Voices of "a people's history of the United States"* (2nd ed.). New York: Seven Story Press.

26. Delgado & Stefancic (2000) (all of the pieces in this work ask us to examine legal and social premises carefully to perceive clear or latent injustice); Freire (1980); Gandhi (2008); Brookfield (2005).
27. Brookfield (2005).
28. Habermas, J. (1985). *The theory of communicative action: Vol. 1. Reason and the rationalization of society* (T. McCarthy, Trans.). Boston, MA: Beacon Press; Habermas, J. (1985). *The theory of communicative action: Vol. II. Lifeworld and system: A critique of functionalist reason* (T. McCarthy, Trans.). Boston, MA: Beacon Press.
29. Habermas (2001).
30. Brookfield (2005); Foucault, M. (1980). *Power/knowledge: Selected interviews and other writings, 1972–77*. New York: Pantheon Books. Cited in Brookfield, S. (2005).
31. Hugman, R. (2003). Reconsidering post-modernism. *British Journal of Social Work, 33*, 1025–1041.
32. Hugman (2003), p. 1028.
33. Gandhi, M. K. (2008). *Mahatma Gandhi: The essential writings* (J. M. Brown, Ed.). New York: Oxford University Press; Gandhi, M. K. (2008). *Non-violent resistance (satayagraha)*. Mineola, NY: Dover Publications. (Original work published 1961); Gugel, G. (2011). D@dalos: Gandhi, the 1930 Salt March. D@dalos: UNESCO education server for democracy, peace, and human rights education. Accessed August 17, 2011. http://www.dadalos.org/int/Vorbilder/vorbilder/gandhi/salzmarsch.htm. This was translated from an original German article: Gugel, G. (1996). *Wir werden nicht weichen. Erfahrungen mit Gewaltfreiheit. Eine praxisorientierte Einführung*. Tubingen, Germany: Verein für Friedenspädagogik. e.V.; Waltz, T., & Richie, H. (2000). Gandhian principles in social work practice: Ethics revisited. *Social Work, 45*(), 213–222; Erikson, E. (1993). *Gandhi's truth: On the origins of militant non-violence*. New York City, NY: W.W. Norton and Company. (Original work published 1969); Gandhi, M. K. (2011). *An autobiography: The story of my experiments with truth*. CreateSpace Independent Publishing Platform (Original work published 1929); Gandhi, M. K. (2007). *Gandhi on nonviolence*. (T. Merton, Ed.). New York City, NY: New Directions; Douglass, J. W. (2012). *Gandhi and the unspeakable: His final experiment with truth*. Maryknoll, NY: Orbis.
34. King, M. L. (1986). *A testament of hope: The essential writings and speeches of Martin Luther King, Jr.* (J. M. Washington, Ed.). New York City, NY: Harper-Collins; Branch, T. (1988). *Parting the waters: America in the King years 1954–1963*. New York: Simon and Schuster: pp. 82–85; Branch, T. (1999). *Pillar of fire: America in the King years: 1963–1965*. New York: Simon and Schuster; Branch, T. (2006). *At Canaan's edge: America in the King years 1965–68*. New York: Simon and Schuster; Niebuhr, R. 1932). *Moral man and immoral society*. New York: Charles Scribner's Sons.
35. McKnight, J. S. (1995). *Toward a grounded substantive theory of the control of learning in altruistic grassroots initiatives*. Unpublished doctoral dissertation, Pennsylvania State University, UMI #9531987.
36. Noddings, N. (2003). *Caring: A feminine approach to ethics and moral education* (2nd ed.). Berkley, CA: University of California Press; Noddings, N. (2002). *Starting at home: Caring and social policy*. Berkley, CA: University of California Press; Katz, M. S., Noddings, N & Strike, K. A. (1999). *Justice and caring: The search for common ground in education*. New York City, NY: Teachers' College Press.
37. Noddings (2003).
38. Uzgalis, W. (2010). John Locke. In E. N. Zalta (Ed.), The Stanford encyclopedia of philosophy (Winter 2010 Ed.). Retrieved August 18, 2011, from http://plato.stanford.edu/archives/win2010/entries/locke/; Locke, J. (1690). *Two treatises of government*. Retrieved August 18, 2011, from http://oregonstate.edu/instruct/phl302/texts/locke/locke2/locke2nd-a.html.
39. Williams, R. (2000). Documents of barbarism: The contemporary legacy of European racism and colonialism in the narrative traditions of federal Indian law. In Delgado & Stefancic (Eds.). *Critical race theory: The cutting edge*. Philadelphia: Temple University Press.
40. Rawls, J. (2005). *A theory of justice*. Cambridge, MA: Belknap Press of Harvard University Press.

41. Kant, I. (1996). *The metaphysics of morals* (M. J. McGregor, Trans.). Cambridge Texts on the History of Philosophy. Cambridge, UK: Cambridge University Press. (Original work published 1797); Kant, I. (1998). *Groundwork on the metaphysics of morals* (M. J. McGregor, Trans.). Cambridge, UK: Cambridge University Press.
42. Irwin, T. (1995). *Plato's ethics.* Oxford, UK: Oxford University Press; Rist, J. (2012). *Plato's moral realism: The discovery of the presuppositions of ethics.* Washington, DC: The Catholic University of America Press.
43. Aristotle. (1999). *Aristotle: Nicomachean Ethics* (T. Irwin, Trans.). Hackett Publishing Company.
44. Borwick (2012); Walker-Kuhne (2005); Schwarzman, M. (auth.) & Knight, K. (illus.) (2005); Block & McKnight (2011); McKnight, J., & Block, P. (2010); Kretzman, J., & McKnight, J. (1993). *Building communities from the inside out: A path toward finding and mobilizing a community's assets.* Chicago, IL: ACTA Publications.
45. Allport, G. (1979). *The nature of prejudice* (25th Anniv. Ed.). New York: Basic Books. (Original work published 1954). The classic work on the psychology of prejudice.
46. Lum, D. (2004). *Social work practice and people of color.* Belmont, CA: Brooks-Cole.
47. Ibid.
48. Duran, E. (2006). *Healing the soul wound: Counseling with American Indians and other native peoples.* New York: Teacher's College Press.
49. Delgado, R. (2000). Words that wound: A tort action for racial insults, epithets, and name calling. In Delgado, R. & Stefancic, J. (Eds.), *Critical race theory: The cutting edge.* Philadelphia: Temple University Press; Davis, P. (2000). Law as micro-aggression. In Delgado, R. & Stefancic, J. (eds.), *Critical race theory: The cutting edge.* Philadelphia: Temple University Press. The following articles are all from Delgado, R. & Stefancic, J. (Eds.). (2000). *Critical race theory: The cutting edge.* Philadelphia: Temple University Press. In various ways they all make points about the dangers of stereotyping. Armour, J. Race *ipsa loquitur*: Of reasonable racists, intelligent Bayesians, and involuntary negrophobes. pp. 180–193; Espinoza, L. & Harris, A. Embracing the tar-baby: LatCrit theory and the sticky mess of race. pp. 440–447; Marable, M. Beyond racial identity politics: Towards a liberation theory for multicultural democracy. pp. 448–454; Yamamoto, E. Rethinking alliances: Agency, responsibility, and interracial justice. pp. 455–463; Grillo, T. & Wildman, S. M. Obscuring the importance of race: the implications of making comparisons between racism and sexism (or other isms). p. 62.
50. Kultgen, J. (1988). *Ethics and professionalism*. Phillidelphia,PA: University of Pennsylvania Press; National Association of Social Workers. (1996). Code of ethics of the National Association of Social Workers. Retrieved October 26, 2012, from http://www.socialworkers.org/pubs/code/default.asp; National Organization for Human Service Professionals. (1996). Ethical standards for human service professionals. Retrieved October 26, 2012, from http://www.nationalhumanservices.org/ethical-standards-for-hs-professionals.
51. Ife, J. (2008). *Human rights and social work: Toward a rights based practice.* Cambridge, UK: Cambridge University Press.

Notes for Chapter 14

1. Forh, M., Forlano, L., Satchell, C., & Gibbs, M. (2011). *From social butterfly to engaged citizen: Urban informatics, social media, ubiquitous computing, and mobile technology to support citizen engagement.* Cambridge, MA: MIT Press.
2. Mathos, M. & Norman, C. (2012). *101 Social media tactics for nonprofits: A field guide.* Oxford, UK. Wiley; Rainie, L., & Wellman, B. (2012). *Networked: The new social operating system.* Cambridge, MA: MIT Press; Mansfield, H. (2011). *Social media for the social good: A how to guide for non-profits:* New York City, NY: McGraw-Hill. This printed resource gives good general advice on the use of the Web and is updated by its author regularly on her blog, www.nonprofitorgsblog.org, retrieved October 29, 2012.
3. Anderson, L., & Anderson, T. (2010). *Online conferences: Professional development for a networked era.* Charlotte, NC: Information Age Publishing.
4. Forh, Forlano, Satchell, & Gibbs (2011).
5. Senior author Joyce McKnight is an Associate Professor at SUNY Empire State College's Center for Distance Learning and has had extensive experience with face-to-face, online, and blended conferences. These comments are based on her direct experiences and those of her colleagues.
6. Mansfield (2011); Mathos, M., & Norman, C. (2012). *101 social media tactics for nonprofits: A field guide.* Oxford, UK: Wiley; Rainie, L., & Wellman, B. (2012). *Networked: The new social operating system.* Cambridge, MA: MIT Press; Safko, L. (2012). *The social media bible: Tactics, tools, and strategies for business success* (3rd ed.).Oxford, UK: Wiley.
7. Kraut, R., & Resnick, P. (2012). *Building successful online communities: Evidence based social design.* Cambridge, MA: MIT Press.
8. Free Management Library. Retrieved October 31, 2012, from http://managementhelp.org/.
9. Chapman, L. All about social networking. Free Management Library. Retrieved October 31, 2012, from http://managementhelp.org/socialnetworking/index.htm.
10. List of social networking sites. Wikipedia. Retrieved October 31, 2012, from http://en.wikipedia.org/wiki/List_of_social_networking_websites. This site is updated periodically and excludes dating sites.
11. Google for nonprofits. Retrieved October 31, 2012, from www.google.com/nonprofits/. This site includes suggestions for using YouTube—Google has opened many of its business-based tools for use by nonprofit organization. It provides free seminars and a variety of other services. The seminars are readily available online; the other services require membership (unfortunately, you have to have 501C-3 status; see Chapter 10), YouTube for nonprofits, http://www.youtube.com/nonprofits?info_lang=au, is related to Google for nonprofits (because Google owns YouTube). It has many resources available but, again, only for 501C-3 organizations.
12. The Center for Digital Story Telling. http://www.storycenter.org/. This site is sponsored by YouTube and gives assistance to people and communities who want to tell their stories.
13. Siemens, G. (2006). *Knowing knowledge.* Lulu.com; Bonk, C. (2011). *The world is open: How web technology is revolutionizing education.* Hoboken, NJ: Jossey-Bass.
14. Moore, M. G. (1990). Distance education theory. *The American Journal of Distance Education,* 5(3), 1–6.

Notes for Chapter 15

1. Todaro, M., & Smith, S. (2011). *Economic development* (11th Ed.). The Pearson Series in Economics. Upper Saddle River, NJ: Prentice-Hall.
2. Office of the United Nations High Commissioner for Human Rights. (2000). United Nations millennium declaration. September 8. Retrieved August 28, 2011, from http://www.un.org/ddocuments/ga/docs/55/a5536.pdf.
3. ECOSOC United Nations Economic and Social Council. (2010). Development cooperation forum. February 23. Retrieved August 28, 2011, from http://www.un.org/en/ecosoc/newfunct/develop.shtml.
4. Like the United Nations itself, many of the various banking institutions were set up at the end of World War II to assist nations with reconstruction and later with building the developing world. Since they were begun there have been arguments about whether they really benefit the poor countries and the poorer people or whether they are simply a way for rich countries and rich industries to exploit the poor. The following books have different perspectives on the matter: Vreeland, J. (2007).*Global institutions: The politics of conditional lending*. London, UK: Routledge; Woods, N. (2007). *The globalizers: The IMF, the World Bank and their borrowers*. Ithaca, NY: Cornell University Press; Peet, P. (2007). *Unholy trinity: The IMF, World Bank and WTO* (2nd ed.) London, UK: Zed Press.
5. Klinkenborg, V. (2009). Why I still oppose genetically modified crops. *New York Times Opinion*. September 17. Retrieved November 27, 2011, from http://e360.yale.edu/content/feature.msp?id=2191; Malone, A. (2008). "The GM genocide: Thousands of Indian farmers are committing suicide after using genetically modified crops." MailOnline. November 2. Retrieved November 27, 2011, from http://www.dailymail.co.uk/news/article-1082559/The-GM-genocide-Thousands-Indian-farmers-committing-suicide-using-genetically-modified-crops.html.
6. Korten, D. (2009). *Agenda for a new economy: From phantom wealth to real wealth—a declaration of independence from Wall Street*. San Francisco: Berrett-Kohler Publishers; Wolff, R. (2009). *Capitalism hits the fan: The global economic meltdown and what to do about it*. Ithaca, NY: Olive Branch Press; Schumacher, E. F. (2000). *Small is beautiful: Economics as if people mattered* (25th anniv. ed.). Dublin, Ireland: Hartley and Marks Publishers.
7. Korten (2009).
8. C. W. Mills. (2000). *The power elite*. Oxford, UK: Oxford University Press. (Original work published 1956).
9. Kelly, E. (2009). *Community planning: An introduction to the comprehensive plan* (2nd ed.). Washington, DC: Island Press.
10. Daniels, Keller, & Lapping. (1995). *The small town planning handbook*. Washington, DC: Planners Press, p. 9.
11. Hyman, D., McKnight, J., & Higdon, F. (2001). *Doing democracy: Conflict and consensus strategies for citizens, organizations, and communities*. Ann Arbor, MI: XanEdu, p. 207.
12. Hyman, D., McKnight, J., & Higdon, F. (2001), p. 209.
13. Ontario Ministry of Agriculture, Food and Rural Affairs. (2011). How to choose a consultant: A resource for your community or organization. April 7. Retrieved August 29, 2011, from http://www.omafra.gov.on.ca/english/rural/facts/98-053.htm.
14. Morrill Act. (1862). Chap. CXXX.—An act donating public lands to the several states and territories which may provide colleges for the benefit of agriculture and mechanic arts. 100 Documents that Shaped America. January 1, 2011. Retrieved August 29, 2011, from http://www.ourdocuments.gov/doc.php?flash=true&doc=33&page=transcript.
15. Rasmussen, W. (2002). *Taking the university to the people: Seventy-five years of Cooperative Extension*. Lafayette, IN: Purdue University Press.
16. Peters, S. (2002). Rousing the people on the land: The roots of the educational organizing tradition in extension work. *Journal of Extension, 40*(3) (June); Peters, S. J. (2002). Citizens developing a voice at the table: A story of educational organizing in contemporary extension work. *Journal of Cooperative Extension, 40*(4) (August).

17. Scheuring, A. F. (n. d.). A sustaining comradeship: The story of University of California Cooperative Extension, 1913–1988. Cooperative Extension. Retrieved June 3, 2013, from http://ucanr.edu/sites/Toolkit/files/164825.pdf; Rasmussen, W. (2002). *Taking the university to the people: Seventy-five years of Cooperative Extension.* Lafayette, IN: Purdue University Press.
18. Peters (2002, June); Peters (2002, August).
19. Schurman, R. & Dennis, D. T. K. (2003). *Engineering trouble: Biotechnology and its discontents.* Berkley, CA: University of California Press; Douthwaite, R. (1995). *Strengthening local economics for security in an unstable world.* Feasta: The Foundation for the Economics of Sustainability, Short Circuit on the Web. Retrieved August 29, 2011, from http://www.feasta.org/documents/shortcircuit/index.html?sc6/c6.html.
20. The genetic modification of seeds is a major controversy. On the one hand Cooperative Extension representatives and others involved in traditional development efforts argue that they produce drought-resistant crops and are necessary to end world hunger. On the other hand, others argue that these sterile seeds make small subsistence farmers dependent on large companies for seed, do not improve yields over time, and may destroy genetic diversity, making food crops very vulnerable to pests and disease. The following present both sides of the issue: *Pinstrup-Andersen, P., & Schioler,* E. (2001). *Seeds of contention: World hunger and the contention over GM crops: International Food Policy Institute.* Washington, D. C.: International Food Policy Research Institute; Schurman, R., & Munro, W. (2010). *Fighting for the future of food: Activists versus agribusiness in the struggle over biotechnology.* University of Minnesota Press.
21. Peters (2002, June); Peters (2002, August).
22. Schurman & Munro (2010).
23. National Association of Community Development Extension Professionals. (2011). NACDEP vision. January 1. Retrieved August 29, 2011, from http://nacdep.net/vision.php. Ayers, J., Barefield, A., Beaulieu, B., Clark, D., Daniels, S., French, C., Howe, R., Leuci, M., & Sense, D. (2005). Foundations of practice. Retrieved June 3, 2013, from http://srdc.msstate.edu/fop/brochures/fop.pdf. This article is about the community organizing role of Cooperative Extension.
24. Von Hoffman, N. (2010). *Radical: A portrait of Saul Alinsky.* New York City, NY: Nation Books.
25. Alinsky, S. (1989). *Rules for radicals: A pragmatic primer for realistic radicals.* New York City, NY: Vintage. (Original work published 1971); Alinsky, S. (1989). *Reveille for radicals.* New York City, NY: Vintage (Original work published 1946; updated 1969).
26. Industrial Areas Foundation. Retrieved November 27, 2011, from http://www.industrialareasfoundation.org/.
27. Swarts, H. (2008). *Organizing urban America: Secular and faith-based movements.* Minneapolis: University of Minnesota Press; Gamaliel Foundation. Retrieved November 27, 2011, from http://www.gamaliel.org/.
28. PICO National Network. Retrieved November 27, 2011, from http://www.piconetwork.org/.
29. Swarts (2008).
30. Swarts (2008); Atlas, J. (2010). *Seeds of change: The story of ACORN, America's most controversial organizing group.* Nashville, TN: Vanderbilt University Press.
31. Atlas (2010).
32. Atlas (2010).
33. Atlas (2010).
34. Highlander Research and Education Center. (n. d.). Retrieved September 27, 2013, from http://highlandercenter.org/ retrieved 09-27-13.
35. Horton, M., with Kohl, J., & Kohl, H. (1989) *The long haul: An autobiography.* New York City, NY: Teacher's College, Columbia University.
36. Horton, M. (1989), p. 148.
37. Parks, R., quoted in Horton, M. (1989), p. 150.
38. Vella, J. (1994). *Learning to listen, learning to teach: The power of dialogue in educating adults.* San Francisco, CA: Jossey Bass.
39. Horton, M. (1989), p. 23.
40. Horton, M. (1989); Horton, M. & Freire, P. (1990). *We make the road by walking: Conversations on education and social change.* Philadelphia, PA: Temple University Press.
41. Horton, M. & Freire, P. (1990).

42. Highlander Research and Education Center. (n. d.). Retrieved September 27, 2013, from http://highlandercenter.org/.
43. Zinn, H. (2010). *A people's history of the United States.* New York City, NY: Perennial Modern Classics.
44. Freire, P. (1980). *Pedagogy of the oppressed.* New York City, NY: Continuum; Horton, M. & Freire, P. (1990).
45. The Freire Project: Critical Cultural, Community, Youth, and Media Activism. (n. d.). Retrieved September 27, 2013 from http://www.freireproject.org/.
46. Winner, L., & Students. (2008) "Stigma, denial, and HIV/AIDS." Lesotho Presentation at the 2008 Student Academic Conference, SUNY/Empire State College.
47. Boal, A. (1993). *Theatre of the oppressed* (Trans. McBride). New York City, NY: Theatre Communications Group.
48. Ibid.
49. Castaneda, Q. (2006). "The invisible theater of ethnography: Performative principles of fieldwork." *Anthropological Quarterly, 79*(1): 75–104.
50. Gray, R., Sinding, C., Ivanoffski, V., Fitch, M., Hampton, A., Greenburg, M., & Gray, R. (2000). "The use of research based theatre in a project related to metastatic breast cancer." *Health Expectations, 2*(2): 137–144.
51. Butterick, S., & Selman, J. (2003). "Deep listening in a feminist popular theatre project: Upsetting the position of audience in participatory education." *Adult Education Quarterly, 54*(1): 7–22.
52. Prentki, T. (1998). "Must the show go on? The case for theatre development." *Development in Practice, 8*(4): 419–429.
53. Bishop, C. (2011). *Installation art.* Mustang, OK: Tate Publishing.
54. Points of Light Institute. (n. d.). Retrieved September 29, 2013, from http://www.pointsoflight.org/.
55. Ibid.
56. Jacoby, B., et al. (2003). *Building partnerships for service learning.* Oxford, OH: Jossey-Bass.
57. Day, D. (1996). *The long loneliness: The autobiography of the legendary Catholic social activist.* San Francisco, CA: HarperOne. (Original work published 1952.)
58. Day, D., & Sicius, F. (2004). *Peter Maurin: Apostle to the world.* Maryknoll, NY: Orbis Books.
59. Zwick, M., & Zwick, L. (2005). *The Catholic Worker Movement: Intellectual and spiritual origins.* Mahwah, NJ: Paulist Press; Ellsberg, R. (2005). *Dorothy Day selected writings: By little and by little.* Maryknoll, NY: Orbis; Day, D. (1997). *Loaves and fishes: The inspiring story of the Catholic Worker Movement.* Maryknoll, NY: Orbis.
60. Catholic Worker Movement. (n. d.). "Celebrating 80 years: 1933 to 2013." Retrieved August 29, 2011, from http://www.catholicworker.org/. Updated frequently.
61. Institute for Cultural Affairs: USA. (n. d.) Retrieved November 1, 2012, from http://www.ica-usa.org/. Updated frequently.
62. Umpleby, S. & Oyler, A. (n. d.). A global strategy for human development: The work of the Institute of Cultural Affairs." Institute for Cultural Affairs: International. Retrieved November 2, 2012, from http://www.ica-international.org/history_2.htm.
63. The author and her husband were members of the Order Ecumenical from 1970 to 1973 and remained actively involved until the mid-1980s. The early chronology is taken from her direct experiences. The later chronology is taken from the Institute for Cultural Affairs websites.
64. Institute for Cultural Affairs: International. (n. d.). Retrieved November 1, 2012, from http://www.ica-international.org.
65. Institute for Cultural Affairs: USA. (n. d.). Retrieved November 1, 2012, from http://www.ica-usa.org/. Updated frequently
66. K'Meyer, T. (1997). *Interracialism and Christian community in the postwar South: The story of Koinonia Farm.* Charlottesville, VA: University of Virginia Press.
67. Barnette, H. (1992). *Clarence Jordan: Turning dreams into deeds.* Macon, GA: Smyth & Helwys Publishing.
68. Koinonia Partners. (2011). A brief history: Koinonia Farms—an introductory history. January 1. Retrieved August 30, 2011, from http://www.koinoniapartners.org/History/brief.html; Koinonia Partners. (1995). *Koinonia remembered.* Retrieved August 30, 2011, from http://www.koinoniapartners.org/History/remembered/index.html. Also available in hard copy; Hollyday, J. (2009). *Clarence Jordan: Essential writings modern spiritual writings series.* Maryknoll, NY: Orbis Books.

69. Youngs, B. (2007). *The house that love built: The story of Linda and Millard Fuller, founders of Habitat for Humanity and the Fuller Center for Housing.* Charlottesville, VA: Hampton Roads Publishing Co.
70. Corporation for National and Community Service. (2010). National Conference on Volunteering and Service: Conference histories. Retrieved November 1, 2012, from http://www.nationalservice.gov/newsroom/press-releases/2010/
71. Shinnyo-en Buddhist Community. (n. d.). Retrieved November 1, 2012, from http://www.shinnyoen.org/.
72. Shinnyo-en Buddhist Community. (n. d.). Philanthropic activities of Shinnyo-en Buddhist Community. Retrieved November 1, 2012, from http://www.shinnyoen.org/philanthropic-activities.html.
73. Merry, S. (1999). *Colonizing Hawaii'.* Princeton, NJ: Princeton University Press; Sila, N. (2004). *Aloha betrayed: Native Hawaiian resistance to American colonialism.* Durham, NC: Duke University Press, a John Hope Franklin Center book; Okamura, J. Y. (2008). *Ethnicity and inequality in Hawai'i: Asian American history and culture.* Philadelphia, PA: Temple University Press; Rohrer, J. (2010). *Haoles in Hawai'i: Race and ethnicity in Hawai'i.* Honolulu, HI: University of Hawaii Press.
74. Nā Lei Aloha Foundation. (n. d.). Retrieved November 27, 2011, from http://www.naleialoha.org/.
75. Tikkun Magazine. (n. d.). Retrieved November 1, 2012, from http://www.tikkun.org/nextgen/.
76. Lions Clubs International. (n. d.). Retrieved November 27, 2011, from http://www.lionsclubs.org/EN/index.php.
77. Rotary International/Rotary Foundation. (n. d.). Retrieved November 27, 2011, from http://www.rotary.org/en/Members/Pages/ridefault.aspx.
78. Kiwanis International. (n. d.). Retrieved November 27, 2011, from http://sites.kiwanis.org/kiwanis/en/home.aspx.
79. Improved Benevolent and Protective Order of Elks of the World. (n. d.). Retrieved November 1, 2012, from ibpoew.org.
80. Prince Hall Freemasonry. (n. d.). Retrieved November 1, 2012, from http://fosterglenn.tripod.com/prince_hall_freemasonry.htm; Walkes, J. A. (1994). *Black square and compass: 200 Years of Prince Hall Freemasonry.* Richmond, VA: Macoy Pub & Masonic Supply Co; Buta, J. (2011). *Black freemasons in white America.* Seattle, WA: Amazon Digital Services.
81. Ross, L. (2001). The Divine Nine: The history of African American fraternities and sororities. New York City, NY: Kensington; Brown, T., Parks, G., & Phillips, C. (Eds.). (2010). *African American fraternities and sororities: The legacy and the vision.* Lexington, KY: University Press of Kentucky.

Index

Information in tables is denoted with a "t" after the page number. Information in figures is denoted with an "f" after the page number

D

E

F

G

H

I

J

K

L

M

N

O

P

Q

R

S

T

U

V

W

Y

Z